AF778720

The Unity of the Capitalist Economy and State

Historical Materialism Book Series

The Historical Materialism Book Series is a major publishing initiative of the radical left. The capitalist crisis of the twenty-first century has been met by a resurgence of interest in critical Marxist theory. At the same time, the publishing institutions committed to Marxism have contracted markedly since the high point of the 1970s. The Historical Materialism Book Series is dedicated to addressing this situation by making available important works of Marxist theory. The aim of the series is to publish important theoretical contributions as the basis for vigorous intellectual debate and exchange on the left.

The peer-reviewed series publishes original monographs, translated texts, and reprints of classics across the bounds of academic disciplinary agendas and across the divisions of the left. The series is particularly concerned to encourage the internationalization of Marxist debate and aims to translate significant studies from beyond the English-speaking world.

For a full list of titles in the Historical Materialism Book Series available in paperback from Haymarket Books, visit:
https://www.haymarketbooks.org/series_collections/1-historical-materialism

The Unity of the Capitalist Economy and State

A Systematic-Dialectical Exposition of the Capitalist System

Geert Reuten

Haymarket Books
Chicago, IL

First published in 2018 by Brill Academic Publishers, The Netherlands

Published in paperback in 2020 by
Haymarket Books
P.O. Box 180165
Chicago, IL 60618
773-583-7884
www.haymarketbooks.org

ISBN: 978-1-64259-373-0

Distributed to the trade in the US through Consortium Book Sales and Distribution (www.cbsd.com) and internationally through Ingram Publisher Services International (www.ingramcontent.com).

This book was published with the generous support of Lannan Foundation and Wallace Action Fund.

Cover design by Jamie Kerry and Ragina Johnson.

Printed in the United States.

10 9 8 7 6 5 4 3 2 1

Library of Congress Cataloging-in-Publication data is available.

Contents

Systematic-dialectical exposition by chapter

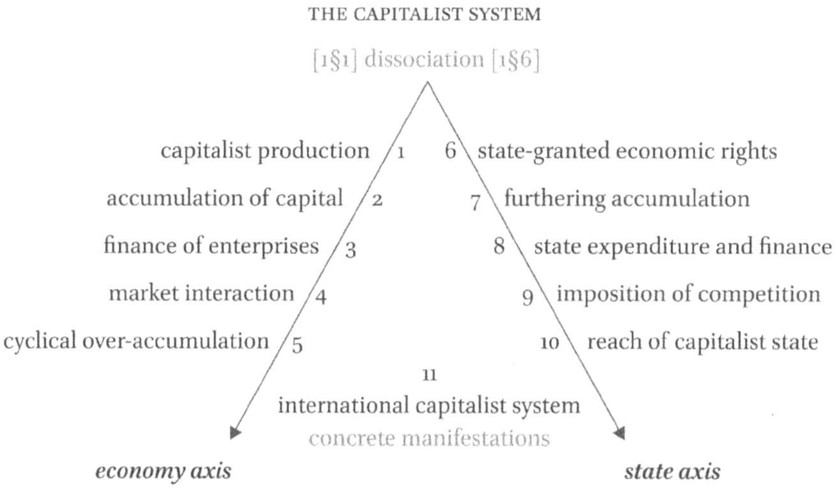

Chapters 1–5 set out an increasingly concrete exposition of the capitalist economy: first its conditions of existence and next its manifestations. The same applies to Chapters 6–10 for the capitalist state.

The reader may wish to read the book in this order. However, Chapter 6 equally provides the grounds of Chapter 1. As does Chapter 7 for Chapter 2, and so forth. The book has been written in such a way that the reader might also read the book in this zigzag order [1;6], [2;7] and so on. This is further amplified on in the General Introduction.

The systematic core of the text makes up about half of the book. The rest consists of 'explications', 'amplifications' and 'addenda' of/on the core text, variously serving the less advanced and the advanced reader in a field – these can be read according to the reader's requirements, or skipped without losing the main thread of the core text.

Preface

This book provides a systematic outline of the constellation and functioning of the capitalist system. It is an exposition of the relations, institutions and processes that are necessary for the continued existence of the capitalist system – that is, the capitalist economy as interconnected with the capitalist state.

In its systematic character, the book is inspired by Marx's incomplete synthetic outline of the capitalist system in his Capital – incomplete because that work did not reach the capitalist state. The latter is dealt with in Part Two of the current book. Part One, on the capitalist economy, is the result of a critical appraisal of current orthodox and heterodox economics, and of the systematic problems and gaps of Capital – the latter especially in hindsight of the development of the contemporary monetary and financial institutions.

Without underestimating the merits of analyses of partial components of the capitalist system (such as those regarding the labour market, infrastructure or monetary policy), the writing of this book derives from the insight that comprehension of the capitalist system is (also) gained from a full synthetic outline of the system by interconnecting all of its main components. Such a synthetic approach also sheds light on the components that are often obscured by a partial analysis.

The book is addressed to scholars who share this insight, or are at least curious about it. More specifically, it is written for scholars and advanced students in the social sciences (political economy, economics, political science, social geography, sociology, and the philosophy of these sciences).

Geert Reuten
June 2018

General introduction

Contents

A Aim and outline of the book

General aim and outline

Much of the conventional research in economics focuses on partial aspects of society, such as its labour market or financial markets – often also in abstraction from the state and its policies. The aim of this book is to systematically identify the interconnections and manifestations of the full range of those economic and political relations, institutions and processes that are necessary for the continued existence of the capitalist system – that is, the capitalist economy together with the capitalist state. In doing so, the reader will be equipped with an outline of the constitution and functioning of the capitalist system.

Any science, and any scientific project, begins with certain presumed facts and questions. I will briefly outline some of my questions. To some extent this is of limited relevance, because the results of scientific investigation often have repercussions and implications that go beyond their initial remit. Within capitalist society we observe social divisions along the lines of:

- rich – poor
- powerful – powerless
- employed – unemployed
- satisfactory work – unsatisfactory work.

These evoke three questions. First, why are these divisions apparently enduring characteristics of the capitalist system? Are they conditions for the continued existence of the capitalist system? Second, if so, how do these relate to other conditions that are required for the continued existence of the system? Third, how does the actual institutionalisation of these conditions determine the actual functioning of the system such that it reproduces these divisions? In brief the challenge is to comprehend the capitalist system. Conscious change within and beyond the capitalist system requires its comprehension – in this I am an ardent pupil of Marx.

To answer these questions, we need to investigate the interconnection between a wide range of elements that constitute that system. The method that I adopt in this book, 'systematic dialectics' (see section C), is well suited to the comprehension of complex systems composed of many interdependent constituent parts.

Part One of the book presents the 'capitalist economy', and Part Two the 'capitalist state'. Part Three considers the international constellation of capitalist economies and states. Each of the subsequent chapters of Part One has its counterpart in each of the subsequent chapters of Part Two.

The starting point of the book: dissociation

As we will see below in the methodological section C, the starting point of the book (the first section of Chapter 1) has a special status. It sets out an encompassing concept of the capitalist system which essentially characterises its problematic. This is the institutional separation, unique to capitalism, between households and enterprises, which I will refer to as '*dissociation*'. In itself this separation is not controversial, and in fact many mainstream approaches to capitalism start with this separation. The difference here is that I immediately pack into it specifically capitalist property relations: enterprises claim ownership of much of the earth, and they claim ownership of the means of production other than the earth.

The rest of Chapter 1, and indeed the entire book, sets out how this separation is bridged within capitalism, and how the ways of bridging it often create new problems that require new solutions.

Chapter outlines

As indicated, ***Part One*** (Chapters 1–5) is an exposition of the capitalist economy.

Chapter 1 starts with the 'dissociation' just mentioned, before establishing how trade – in terms of the 'monetary-value dimension' – constitutes the elementary 'bridge' of the separation. This engenders the commodification of goods; along with it the property of enterprises takes the monetary form of the property of capital. Foremost, however, it engenders the capitalist 'commodification of labour-capacity'. The existence of a generalised labour market distinguishes capitalism from previous modes of production. The subsequent focus of the chapter is on the capitalist production process. 'Full-fledged capitalism' is not only predicated on the trade of commodities and labour-capacity in terms of the 'monetary-value dimension'. We will see how the monetary-value dimension pervades the activity of production itself – which again distinguishes capitalism from all historically prior modes of production – and how the enlargement of capital via the production of surplus-value (or profit) becomes the motivating force of capitalist production.[1] We will see why and how labour is the only source of profit. (This thesis is not new – we find it, for example, in Adam Smith's (1776) analysis of the capitalist system). We will also discover why enterprises can nevertheless appropriate these profits, and how

1 There is a distinction between 'surplus-value' and profit that will be neglected in this outline. In brief the production of surplus-value includes the production of any interest equivalent.

capitalist production takes the – simultaneously abstract and concrete – form of the production of capital by labour.

Chapter 2 starts by outlining that the logic of the one-dimensional production of profit for the sake of production of capital is 'more of the same'. This is reached by the continuous investment of profit and so the continuous accumulation of capital, its corollary being economic growth. There are two main conditions for the generalised accumulation of capital: first, a continuous expansion of profit and hence an expansion of *labour-capacity*; second, a continuous expansion of the quantity-flow of *money*. Money is created by banks – and given that this chapter abstracts from a Central Bank, which is introduced in Chapter 7 – money is inevitably created by commercial banks (as is in fact also the case when there is a central bank). We will see how the tuning of the continuous creation of money by banks and of the continuous (re)creation of labour-capacity in the household sphere, is essential to the system. By then we will have revealed that money and labour are not only necessary to the accumulation of capital; they are also central vulnerabilities of the capitalist economy. The creation of, and markets for, money and labour-capacity are unlike the production of commodities in enterprises and their markets. Regarding labour we will see, for some perhaps paradoxically, that continuous accumulation of capital requires continuous unemployment.

We will further note that the continuous accumulation of capital is enhanced by the tendency to the incorporation of enterprises. This entails a layered form of the enterprises' ownership and its management.

Chapter 3 will demonstrate that an initial financing of enterprises by banks is a necessary condition for the accumulation of capital. Banking finance is a pre-condition for any other form of finance. Only after the initial financing by banks of the investment and production by enterprises can other financiers take the place of banking finance. Thus 'investment' must precede 'saving', saving being a 'result' of investment in the first place. Once such savings result, other forms of finance out of these savings may ex-post act as a substitute for the initial banking finance. Hence these other forms of finance inevitably 'derive' from banking finance. (This opposes mainstream economic theory, which views the causality as flowing the other way – savings are seen to lead to investment. This leaves unexplained how and why the quantity flow of money would grow). Finally, Chapter 3 shows how macroeconomic expenditure conditions the validation of production, and hence the continuous accumulation of capital.

This completes the necessary 'economic' (or economy-immanent) 'conditions of existence' of the capitalist economy. The following two chapters present its implications and manifestations in the market interaction between enterprises (Chapter 4) and in the cyclical over-accumulation and destruction of capital (Chapter 5).

Chapter 4 is an exposition of the main forms of market interaction between enterprises: namely those of competition, cartel formation, oligopolisation and monopolisation. (The introduction of these phenomena only at this stage of the exposition is indicative of how this book's approach diverges from that of mainstream economics. The latter would usually start with the idea of competition). We will see how the technique of production, as well as the degree of technical change and innovation, affects the form of market interaction. It will also be shown that for sectors dominated by competitive interaction, much of the dynamic between sectors of production (capital flowing from one sector to another) is predicated on a tendency towards equalisation of average rates of profit between sectors. However, it will also be shown that within such sectors the rates of profit tend to be stratified.

Chapter 5, the final chapter of Part One, outlines the cyclical movement of the accumulation of capital (the business cycle). It will be shown how this results from capital's tendency to over-accumulation, which accompanies a decline in the rate of profit (in the upturn). This over-accumulation is redressed (in the crisis and downturn) by a partial annihilation of the capital accumulated along with lay-offs of labour; through this activity, the rate of profit is restored. The bulk of the misery caused by this recurrent process is heaped upon those expelled into unemployment. However, the same recurrent process of over-investment and annihilation of productive capacity damages the climate and destroys applied natural resources.

The exposition in this chapter synthesises the earlier exposition (including many of the thorough aspects that the outline above has not touched upon). Along the way – because actual economic reality is inevitably always in some phase of this cyclical movement (one phase of the business cycle) – the exposition in this chapter sets out the concrete mode of existence of the earlier exposition (Chapters 1–4).

So far, this book apparently covers much of the material dealt with by mainstream economics, and indeed all of the main economic concepts will be surveyed. However, the book is significantly different in respect of both its content and its methodology. Because of the specific interconnection posited between concepts, the latter will 'shift' for the reader educated in mainstream economics, giving way to a different view of the science of economics.

Until this point, the methodological strategy of the book is to detect to what extent it is possible to present the capitalist economy in abstraction from a 'state'. While this might appear somewhat strange to social scientists, economists will be aware that this is how most mainstream economics textbooks begin and end. Through Chapters 1–5, the need to regulate economic institutions and processes is often apparent. In these chapters this need is often dealt with (implicitly or explicitly) via modes of self-regulation, thus drawing out the limits of such self-regulation. However, by the end of Chapter 5, the need to present the 'state' is unavoidable.

Part Two (Chapters 6–10) makes explicit what has thus far remained implicit: namely the necessity of a state and the necessity of economic policy for a capitalist economy. Here the aim of the presentation is analogous to the earlier aim: to identify what relations, institutions and processes are necessary for the continued existence of the capitalist system – only now with regard to the state. The reference is to 'the state' as an institutional continuity, rather than to governments that come and go.[2]

Chapter 6 sets out why the capitalist system inevitably requires a capitalist state. Its starting point is again the 'dissociation' described in Chapter 1. That is, the encompassing concept of the capitalist system, which essentially characterises its problematic. Whereas Chapters 1–3 set out its 'economic' conditions of existence, we now move on to the politico-juridical conditions of existence. The exposition in Chapter 1 (and all of Part One) was implicitly based on the economic actors' *claims* of being entitled to act as set out. The core of these are, firstly, the enterprises' claims of entitlement to the private property of much of the earth; secondly, their claims of entitlement to private property in means of production other than for production by the claimant; thirdly, their claims of entitlement to employ labour as combined with the appropriation of the surplus-value (profit) produced by that labour. The state as an extraordinary institution *grants* these claims in the form of legal rights. Because and to the extent that the state grants *these* rights in particular, it is identified as a 'capitalist state', which constitutes a unity with the capitalist economy. The state's legal formulation of these granted rights, as well as their maintenance, requires structures of law that are often inherently conflictual in a variety of ways. These are presented in Chapter 6.

Chapter 7 first sets out how these structures of law require taxation, which inevitably overrides economic actors' property claims – thus the state's defence of such claims inevitably requires some degree of neglect of these property claims. This is followed by an outline of the 'action radius of the state', which determines what it can do, given the constraint of feasible taxation. The latter is determined by the prevailing vigour of the accumulation of capital. To the

2 In addition: the term 'state' is used in reference to a 'central state'. Some central states result from a union or federation of (what I call) 'subordinate states' in terms of full jurisdiction.

extent that this vigour is not sufficient for the state's necessary action radius, it must improve that vigour and thus further the conditions for capital accumulation and economic growth.

The main body of this chapter consists of the exposition of these conditions: regulation of monetary and financial institutions; regulation of the labour market as well as public education; and the state's engagement in infrastructural requirements. This chapter also sets out why social security transfers are inevitable for the legitimation of the capitalist state, and hence for the capitalist system.

Chapter 8 provides an exposition of the state's activities (as presented in Chapters 6 and 7) in terms of the monetary expenditure of the state and their finance. Analogous to the exposition in Chapter 3, it is shown how the state's macroeconomic expenditure conditions production and the validation of production, and hence the continuous accumulation of capital. One of the main areas of focus is on the various forms of taxation – where these are levied (enterprises, capital owners, labour) – and their associated tax rates, as well as their effects on the net profits of enterprises and on the distribution of income and wealth more generally.

Analogous to the exposition of the first three chapters of Part One for the economy-immanent 'conditions of existence' of capitalist production, Chapter 8 completes the exposition of the state's legislative, regulative and taxation frameworks that are necessary 'conditions for the existence' of the capitalist economy and for the state itself – and so for the capitalist system. The following two chapters present the state's 'manifestation' in its imposition of competition (Chapter 9), and in its general reach on the capitalist economy (Chapter 10).

Chapter 9 presents the state's concrete manifestation in its imposing a framework of constraints on the modes of market interaction of enterprises and banks, and of constraints on the outcomes of such interaction. The first constraint is a general one: in the form of 'competition policy', the state imposes on enterprises and banks *its* view about 'proper' competitive interaction. The second constraint regards the competitive constellation that would result in (potential) generalised price deflation and stagnation, whence the state adopts a monetary policy engendering 'creeping inflation'. The third constraint relates to a phenomenon that was only thrown into relief with the emergence of the 2007/08 financial crisis, that is, entities, especially banks, that have grown 'too big to fail', as a result of which the state is enforced to impose (highly conflicting) limits on the functioning of such entities.

Chapter 10 sets out three main manifestations of the reach of the state – implied by the exposition in Chapters 6–9. First, whereas capital accumulation is necessarily manifest in cyclical movements (Chapter 5), the degree of state expenditure affects the degree of the amplitude of these cycles (structurally increased expenditure moderates the amplitudes). Secondly, it will be shown that the dynamics of the capitalist economy, together with the necessary regulation by the state (Chapter 7), inevitably result in not only an increasing quantity of regulation, but also an increasing complexity of regulation. Thirdly, it will be outlined why increasing social security transfers (increasing as a percentage of GDP) are inevitable.

The chapter concludes that even if the two main problems of 'too big to fail' banks and environmental damage could be resolved (again by complex regulation), both the continuously increasing social security transfers and the continuously increasing quantity and complexity of regulation are inevitable and impossible for the capitalist system.

Part Three (*Chapter 11*) presents the international mode of existence of the capitalist system. As with Chapters 4–5 and 9–10, this chapter does not set out the capitalist system's conditions of existence, but rather its manifestations. It focuses on the two main forms of international economic relations: namely international trade and the international migration of capital as manifest in the international migration of production. International trade is not fundamentally different from intra-nation regional specialisation and trade. However, the effects of international migration of production are potentially far-reaching (when I finished the typescript for this book, the scale of this migration was yet modest). To the extent that this migration is left uninhibited, it evokes the mutually reinforcing combination of a gradual movement towards international convergence of average wage structures on the one hand, and a gradual movement towards internationally similar structures of regulation on the other. The chapter sets out a variety of conflicting interests that are associated with these movements.

B Intellectual inheritance

As the book covers a wide range of subjects, it is not feasible to review all of the existing literature on each of those subjects. Instead, references are mainly restricted to tributes and acknowledgements. Therefore, a few words on the intellectual inheritance on which I build are also appropriate. Like most current economists I was educated in neoclassical theory. Dissatisfied, I became acquainted with Marx's and marxian political economy of capitalism, and later Post-Keynesian and Institutionalist theory. Thus, after my initial orthodox background, I became what is now called a heterodox economist, and it is generally heterodox theory that I build on, although that is probably too broad a label.

Marx (1818–83) and to a lesser extent Hegel (1770–1831) have been my primary sparring partners, with whom there is a continuous dialogue of ideas. There is a great advantage in having studied one or, for that matter, two great thinkers closely. Often the study of such great thinkers begins with a certain respect for their aims, but once one is able to critically reflect on the theoretical content (different for each) – to see each author's limitations and shortcomings, and yet still learn from them – one's relationship to such thinkers matures.

Hegel and Marx also produced the chief paradigmatic examples of a social-scientific systematic dialectic, that is, the method that is adopted in this book (see section C). Although the systematic-dialectical method used here sometimes deviates significantly from that of Hegel and Marx, I nevertheless proceed in their scientific tradition and am greatly indebted to these authors.

In this tradition, I am also indebted to some living authors. First of all Michael Williams with whom I wrote my first comprehensive systematic-dialectical work: *Value-form and the State; the tendencies of accumulation and the determination of economics policy in capitalist society* (1989). Although the content of the current work often substantively deviates from our joint work, it is unsurprising that the methodology and systematic structure of the two works share much in common. In hindsight, I think that this joint work was a great methodological achievement as, to my knowledge, this was the first comprehensive systematic-dialectical work in political economy written since Marx's *Capital*.[3] In the period since the late 1980s, quite a few authors have written on the method of systematic dialectics.

Further, I am also much indebted to the members of the International Symposium on Marxian Theory (ISMT).[4] This small group of philosophers and political economists has met for a summer week every year from 1991 to 2014, for a thorough discussion of each other's work on the writings of Marx and develop-

3 In 1984 Michael Eldred published a systematic-dialectical account of economic competition and the capitalist state. A wider project of his, together with Kleiber, Hanlon and Roth, unfortunately stagnated after their 1982–85 articles on value-form theory.

4 This group has generally consisted of eight to ten members: Christopher Arthur, Martha Campbell, Fred Moseley, Patrick Murray, Geert Reuten, Tony Smith (all 1991–current), Guglielmo Carchedi (1991–93), Paul Mattick Jr. (1991–2000), Riccardo Bellofiore (1996–current), Nicola Taylor (2001–03), Roberto Fineschi (2004–current), Andrew Brown (2006–current) and Guido Starosta (2009–current). Between 1993 and 2015, nine books have been published following ISMT conferences (with several translations in Chinese, Italian and Spanish).

ments thereof, with a focus on his method especially in relation to its (variously judged) roots in Hegel. The present book has benefited greatly from these discussions.

As an inheritance in another sense, I have been helped (particularly in Part Two) by the intellectual and political experience of having served for the Socialist Party in the Senate of the Parliament of the Netherlands from 2007–15. I especially learned and experienced, first, how the (that) state's view of 'the general interest' – often implicitly – is identified with the 'unquestionable' existence of the capitalist system (Chapter 6); second, how feasible tax rates are a perennial concern for the (non-)doing of the state (Chapter 7); third, to what extent the state and the capitalist system tremble when the banking constellation trembles (Chapters 7 and 9); fourth, how the state tries to avoid conflict by delegating the most conflicting issues to semi- or quasi-independent institutions of the state (Chapters 7–9 *passim*); and fifth, why legislation and other regulation inevitably increases in size, and especially why it becomes more complicated and complex (Chapter 10). Generally the second part of the book has benefited significantly from debates with three different ministers of finance, three different secretaries of state for taxation, and spokespersons for finance and economic affairs during those eight years.

C Systematic dialectics: methodological introduction

Through the experience of teaching the material of this book, I have learned that it is not very instructive to begin with a comprehensive methodological account. Nevertheless, it is helpful for the reader to at least have an outline of the method in mind while absorbing the content of the book. In terms of the methodology, I therefore proceed in three stages. Firstly, in this General Introduction I present a number of general notions concerning the method of systematic dialectics. Secondly, details of the method are introduced, as the content requires, at several points throughout the chapters. Thus, I expand on the methodological notion of 'tendency' when I introduce tendencies for the first time. A general methodological appendix, at the end of the book, is the third, most comprehensive treatment and presents an interconnected outline of systematic dialectics. For most readers, it is probably best to read the appendix last. However, for readers who prefer to have expanded methodological information earlier on, I refer below to sections of the appendix as A§1, A§2, and so on.

Although this General Introduction outlines the systematic-dialectical method – and hence will use some dialectical jargon – in the chapters to come

I have tried to reduce such jargon to a minimum. For Chapters 1 and 6, however, a somewhat heavier load is unavoidable.

A Glossary of field-specific terms (regarding the method as well as the content) is included at the end of the book.

C§1 *Limitations of mainstream methods*

The systematic-dialectical method that I adopt in this book is appropriate to the theorisation of a system or a structured totality. It is especially an adequate scientific method for the *synthesis* of knowledge about a social system (this is the subject of the following sections). However, one must have good reasons to deviate from the common or established research methods, so it will be useful to first sketch out the limitations of mainstream methods.

Much of the mainstream science proudly casts its endeavours in terms of 'analysis', whereas systematic dialectics proceeds by way of 'synthesis'. The following brief descriptions of these terms will suffice for now. *Analysis*: to scrutinise by way of the division of wholes into their elements, or the deconstruction of initial knowledge. *Synthesis*: to connect, assemble, or unite knowledge; the combination of often diverse concepts into a whole by indicating their interconnections.

Current mainstream methods are generally founded on the philosophical tradition of *positivism*. Their aim is to describe and explain the outward appearances of the institutions of the status quo. Whereas in economics the professed method is generally an empiricist positivism, the practice is usually a rationalistic positivism, or more precisely, an axiomatic positivism for which axiomatic mathematics is the prototype.[5]

The modern positivist tradition may be traced back to the early seventeenth-century writings of Francis Bacon and René Descartes. Central to this is the latter's *subject–object dualism*, or the division between thought and being ('cogito ergo sum'; 'je pense donc je suis'). This division gave rise to the two main methodological-philosophical frames of rationalism and empiricism. (For the object–subject dualism I also use the modern pair of *entity* and *discourse*).

These two frames – rationalism and empiricism – stood in a dualist opposition (separation) to one another. Phenomena were variously reduced to one or the other pole (reductionism). In mainstream economics we see this exemplified in:

---

5 Empiricism understands sensual experience to be the source of knowledge. Rationalism stresses the role of reason in understanding phenomena. Axiomatic positivism is examined further in Reuten 1996, esp. pp. 40–1.

- *axiomatic analytical* approaches (as in the models of much of microeconomics);
- *empirical analytical* approaches (as in the models of much of macroeconomics, and especially those applied by National Research Bureaus and Central Banks).

From my perspective, the first major limitation of these models is that notions of structure and system are alien to them, or simply ignored. Usually these models proceed and expand from partial problems (this is not problematic when the aim is the solution of a partial problem from some specified perspective).[6] The difficulty of restricting oneself to partial terrains is 'solved' by the use of various assumptions, notably *ceteris paribus* conditions, about 'the rest of the world'. Students of these models (should) know how crucial these assumptions are, casting the problem at hand in terms of caricatures (think of the stylised 'rational behaviour' approaches in economics), and also how these assumptions often lead to caricatures of the rest of the world.

This first limitation is related to two others. The second limitation is that models are in fact complex sets of *definitions*.[7] This is indeed useful for *analysis* and for tackling partial problems. However, setting out fixed definitions inhibits *conceptual development*, thus impeding broad scientific development to which conceptual change is central.

These two limitations are *epistemological* in kind. The third limitation concerns the particular road taken by mainstream economics (i.e. neoclassical economics), which tends to cast these models in terms of individual behaviour. This is called 'methodological individualism'. Rigorous methodological individualists deny the existence of 'social structures' and 'social forces' – this leaves references to 'market forces', 'market structures' or indeed the 'capitalist system' (commonplace terms within orthodox economics) rather unintelligible. For those that do not deny the existence of structures, methodological indi-

6 A simple example of positing a problem as a partial one can be seen in the reduction of unemployment to characteristics of individuals (sometimes this might be part of a specific problem), rather than, for example, linking unemployment to the command of one section of society over the means of production (vested in enterprises), the incentive structure of that layer, and so on. An endeavour that links problems such as that of unemployment with other problems, and with general structures, posits 'interconnection'. Anticipating a point to be introduced later, it may be added that such a (common) reduction of problems to the characteristics of individuals apparently absolves the researcher of taking into account interconnected structures. Note that I am not arguing that all problems can be cast in terms of interconnected structures, nor that all problems necessarily should be understood or solved in those terms.

7 Hausman 1992, pp. 75–82.

vidualism operates as a self-imposed restriction – it is not at all clear how we can ascend from individual behaviour to these structures (at least not in a theoretically informed way).

More far-reaching than 'methodological individualism' on its own is its combination with the idea of 'ontological individualism'. That is, the idea that (in the event that structures are 'assumed' to exist at all) social structures are seen to be entirely *determined* by individual behaviour, instead of the other way around ('ontological structuralism'), or instead by some interdependent or dialectical interconnection between individuals and social structures.[8]

These limitations are not sufficient reasons for not taking mainstream science seriously, or to entirely ignore its results; the point is rather that any method is limited by its self-imposed or internal constraints, and those limitations must be clearly understood and kept in mind when looking at the results. The systematic-dialectical method goes quite some way in tackling these problems. Generally it is possible to incorporate the accomplishments of mainstream methodologies into the dialectical method, but movement in the opposite direction is not so straightforward. (A§3 sets out how systematic dialectics makes use of mainstream accomplishments).

C§2 *'System'*

So far I have referred to the capitalist 'system'. Is capitalism actually a system, that is, a self-reproducing integrated whole consisting of interdependent constituent parts? If we are not content to settle for journalism and history telling – without doubt both meritorious activities – then *for science and scientific explanation to be an intelligible activity* it must be presumed that the constellation we study is *both systematic and, in principle, comprehensible.*[9] Thus some structured totality will be presumed.

'Systematic dialectics' refers to the method of a dialectical investigation and exposition of such a system.

C§3 *Presumptions and pre-positions (contrary to assumptions)*

Systematic dialectics eschews assumptions. However, the exposition in this book adopts three 'presumptions'. Firstly, a *culturally determined language* (in

8 On the latter see especially Hollis 1994; cf. Reuten 2003c, ch. 10.

9 In this book the term 'constellation' has the following meanings: interconnected organisational units and/or interconnected processes and/or structures (often called configurations). The term may also refer to what in ordinary language is called a 'subsystem' (such as the 'banking system'). Most often the term is used when, for methodological and sometimes stylistic reasons, I want to avoid the term 'system'.

our case, specifically, 'English'). Along with this goes an *episteme*.[10] We can, in degree, be conscious of this, but no scientific endeavour can escape this broad presumption. (It is sometimes believed that mathematics escapes it. However, mathematics requires at least 'initial translations' from cultural language into mathematics). Secondly, it is presumed that the object of investigation exists. That is, capitalist social formations and especially capitalist economies and states. Empirically these are exemplified in, at least, OECD countries (see C§4, subsection 'empirical domain'). Thirdly, it is presumed that this object of investigation is systematic (C§2 above). This is, as indicated, a precondition for any scientific study of an object of investigation beyond mere description.

Next to these three presumptions I will adopt 'pre-positions' in Chapters 1–3 and 6–8. I adopt these merely because all the constituent elements of a 'system' cannot be presented at the same time. I use the term 'pre-position' (instead of 'assumption') so as to indicate that these have a temporary status. (In modelling approaches many 'assumptions' have a permanent status). Thus in the course of the dialectical exposition, I will introduce entities that at the stage of their introduction are not (fully) 'grounded'. (For example, when I introduce 'money' in Chapter 1, the creation of money by banks, which is only introduced in Chapter 2, is pre-posited). A major difference between systematic-dialectical pre-positions and the assumptions of a standard model building approach is that systematic-dialectical pre-positions must *always* be grounded within the exposition – a systematic-dialectical exposition is never complete until all determinations relevant for the object realm have been determined *endogenously*, that is, when no pre-positions (or assumptions) are required, and all earlier (temporary) pre-positions have in fact been eliminated. In the main systematic text of this book I will never use assumptions (in an Explication I may sometimes use an assumption, merely to simplify an example).

When in a modelling approach some assumption is dropped, earlier statements (based on the dropped assumption) may no longer hold. This is different for pre-positions. All the statements formulated at each level (e.g. at the expositional level of Chapter 1 or 2) are claimed to be true, and still held to be true when we have reached Chapter 5 or 11.

10 Foucault (in *The Order of Things*) uses the term *épistème* to refer to the 'unconscious' mental arrangements that underpin the production and the *possibility* of the production of scientific knowledge over an extended time period (think of the Middle Ages versus 'modernity'). An *épistème* is far more comprehensive and inescapable than Kuhn's notion of paradigm.

All the foregoing remarks about pre-positions concern the object realm we study here. Although capitalism cannot exist in a void, it is hardly opportune to begin this book by offering a dialectical exposition of natural scientific entities (if I could).

C§4 *Systematic-dialectical exposition* [*A§10-A§14*]

Systematic dialectics examines the constellation of a particular socio-economic system, such as capitalism – not its historical emergence (see also the Appendix on historical dialectics). Systematic dialectics (SD) is comparable to other scientific methods insofar as it seeks to reliably know what can be known. However, SD differs from *most* other approaches in its claim that the key to the reliability of such knowledge lies in the *interconnection* of all relevant knowledge about some object totality. SD is sceptical of any partial knowledge, including model building, although it does not dismiss this knowledge *a priori* (C§1) [A§3, A§8]. However, wider perspectives can show the limits, or the falsity, of partial knowledge.

A second major distinction between SD and *all* other approaches is the method through which the interconnection of the relevant knowledge is gained. Using the metaphor of a pyramid, as shown in *Figure 1*, will help in outlining the method.

FIGURE 1 *Systematic-dialectical exposition*

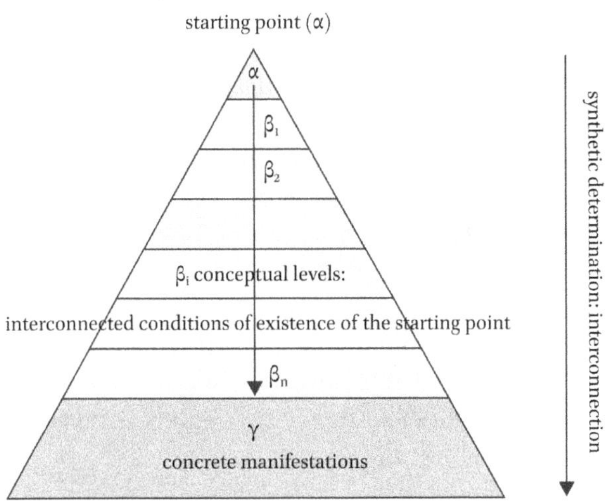

In seeking to grasp a systematic object totality (capitalism), the beginning requires a concept that captures the essence of the entire system. This starting point is denoted in the figure by 'α'. (Cf. 'commodification' for Marx's *Capital*, and 'dissociation' in the current book). We will see in Chapter 1 that, once posited, such an encompassing starting point may seem obvious – as it should. However, I know form Marx's intellectual struggles, and those of myself, that the intellectual process of *getting to* an appropriate starting point is far from simple.

The next layers, denoted by β1 … βn, set out the interconnected conditions of existence of the starting point. These layers are called 'moments'. More specifically, beginning with the starting point, a SD exposition must pose the *proximate* condition of existence of a moment, that is, the *immediate* requirements necessary for the existence of that moment. To the extent that this grounding moment cannot exist in isolation (that is, to the extent that it is yet non-endogenous), that moment requires *new* proximate grounding moments. For example, the first necessary moments to bridge 'dissociation' are money and the commodification of goods, labour-capacity, and the production process (Chapter 1). Money is conditioned by the existence of banks (Chapter 2). Much of the SD investigation consists in determining the proximate order of these. (In this case: rather than introducing banks immediately after the introduction of money, to 'pre-posit' these and to postpone their introduction).[11]

The connection of two or more moments has a synthetic character, and the more we move down the pyramid, the greater the synthesis obtained. Because necessary conditions of existence – and again their necessary conditions of existence – are a leading methodological principle, we in fact get to the exposition of the *interconnected* totality of the capitalist system. For the same reason it is essential to abstain from assumptions because these would open the way for gaps.

For this General Introduction I need not say much about the final layer of the pyramid: concrete manifestations (γ). This can be postponed until the relevant chapters. Here I merely mention that manifestations pertain to *implications* of the previous exposition, culminating in a synthesis of the (or several) threads of the previous exposition.

Along the process of the exposition (from starting point to manifestations), we each time extend our comprehension of the capitalist system. In the end, this will be appropriate to fully comprehend its essential working as appearing in empirical reality.

11 Readers familiar with Marx's *Capital* will recall that he introduces money in Chapter 1 of the first volume, only systematically dealing with banks in Chapter 22 of the third volume.

Figure 2 shows this process in terms of each chapter throughout the book (the chapter numbers are placed inside the pyramid of this figure).

FIGURE 1

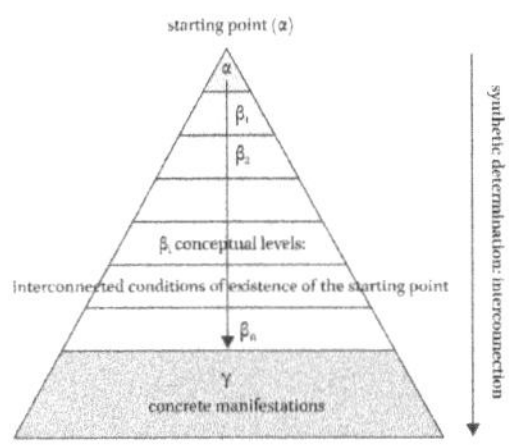

FIGURE 2 *Systematic-dialectical exposition by chapter*

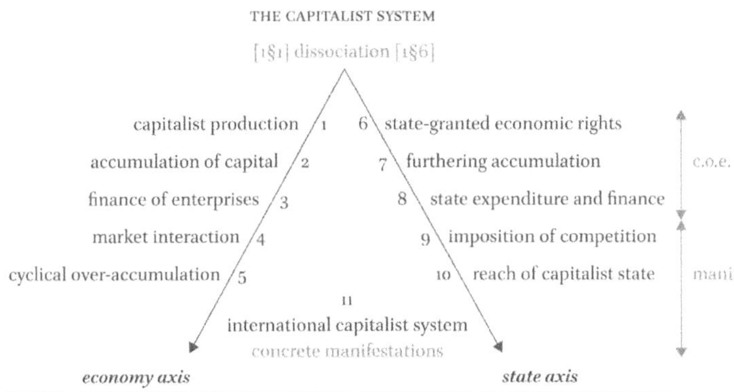

Note: 'c.o.e.' abbreviates conditions of existence and 'manif.' manifestations.

Two reading strategies

Refer to *Figure* 2. The reader can read the book in its chapter order (1–11). In this order it is perhaps easiest to digest. However, the text has been written in such a way that the reader might also opt for a zigzag reading, that is, in the chapter order 1, 6, 2, 7, and so on. From the point of view of the method, the exposition in Chapter 1 is proximately grounded in Chapter 6 as much as in Chapter 2, and so forth.

The empirical domain of the book

Full-fledged capitalism emerges when not merely trade but also – predicated on a labour market – the production process is dominated by the monetary dimension and profit. This started in Britain and France around 1800. When capitalist *production* is dominant in a country I typify it as 'capitalist' (when the context requires it, I use the term 'full-fledged capitalist').

In 1961 the then capitalist advanced countries organised, loosely, in the OECD (Organisation for Economic Development and Co-operation). At the time the OECD had 20 member countries; as of 2016 it has 35.[12] When I use the term

12 1961: Austria, Belgium, Canada, Denmark, France, Germany, Greece, Iceland, Ireland, Italy, Luxembourg, Netherlands, Norway, Portugal, Spain, Sweden, Switzerland, Turkey, United Kingdom, United States of America (20).
1964: Japan. Around 1970: Australia, Finland, New Zealand (24).
1994–96: Czech Republic, Hungary, South Korea, Mexico, Poland (29).

'capitalist system' I have the institutional economic and state structure of these countries in mind, as well as that of all other countries with a similar structure, independently of their level of development in terms of GDP per capita and state expenditure. This then is the empirical domain of this book (i.e. the starting and endpoint of Figure 2).

In various chapters of Part Two I will refer to the averages of empirical data of a selection of these countries. For Part One – the outline of the capitalist economy as if there were no capitalist state – there are no clear empirical data, as a capitalist economy can have no existence without a capitalist state.[13]

C§5 *Systematic order versus historical order*

The actual history of humankind has determined the constellation of the current capitalist system through the decline of previous modes of production (such as feudalism) to its current form. However, the historical emergence (and the order thereof) of a particular entity, institution or process might bear no relation to its 'systematic importance'. For example, the fact that commodity markets developed before labour markets does not imply that a commodity market is more important than a labour market in terms of the functioning of the capitalist system – both are absolutely necessary. The fact that forms of commodity money (such as gold) evolved long before 'bank account money' does not imply at all that a systematic treatment of money should start with commodity money, or even refer to it. The systematic *order* in this book bears no relation to historical order. (History, to be sure, is very important. However, systematic dialectics is no historical science. And, for that matter, a historical dialectical approach – such as that of Hegel or Marx – has little to do with their or my systematic dialectics).[14]

2010: Chile, Estonia, Israel, Slovak Republic, Slovenia (34).
2016: Latvia (35).

13 Rigorously, the exposition of Part One pre-posits that of Part Two whence I could present empirical data in Part One. I refrain from doing so as this would require continuous elaborations.

14 Both Hegel and Marx devised a historical dialectic – that is, for the study of history – as well as a systematic dialectic – that is, for the study of one phase, one particular system, in history. These dialectics are very different. Because their historical dialectic is *relatively* easy to explain, popular accounts of dialectics most often limit themselves to the historical dialectic and neglect the systematic dialectic. Marx, for example, was engaged in a historical dialectic until about the age of 30 (in 1848, the year in which *The Communist Manifesto* was published). For the rest of his life he was engaged with the systematic dialectic of the capitalist system. (See Reuten 2003a). For a succinct comparison between historical dialectics and systematic dialectics see Murray 2003, pp. 150–8.

However, a distinction will be made between *trans-historical necessities* (universal) and *system necessities* (general). One trans-historical necessity is, for example, that we need food and shelter in order to survive. While all trans-historical necessities are also system necessities, it is not necessarily the case that all system necessities are also trans-historical necessities. Money, for example, is a necessity for the capitalist system, but money is not a trans-historical necessity. In order to maintain this crucial distinction, when the term 'necessity' is used it always refers to 'system necessities', whereas the term 'trans-historical necessities' appears in full.

C§6 *Immanent critique*

Through the method of systematic dialectics emerges another methodological principle that stems from Marx, that of 'immanent critique'. Immanent critique (in brief critique) is distinguished from 'external criticism' (in brief criticism). Criticism adopts a normative *external* criterion (be it ethical, aesthetic or methodological) to evaluate society or social productions as artistic and scientific endeavours. The method of *critique* evaluates society and social productions on the basis of the norms and standards of the object of inquiry itself.[15]

Thus this book aims to present the capitalist system in terms of its own logic, norms and standards. In this sense, it is presented *from within itself*. However, this does not imply the absence of any evaluation or assessment. Firstly, presenting the capitalist system in terms of its own norms and standards does not imply that the depiction of those norms and standards and of their results (for example, profit-driven lay-offs of workers) must be presented 'in rosy colours'. Secondly, when the capitalist system's norms and standards are taken to their internal logical conclusions, we can detect possible inconsistencies and contradictions – as when capitalist business lauds 'market competition' while at the same time seeking to eliminate competitors and secure a monopoly position. Immanent critique makes such inconsistencies explicit.

D A note on mathematics and the readership

This book is written for scholars and advanced students in the social sciences (political economy, economics, political science, social geography, sociology and the philosophy of these sciences). In order to be understandable to people

15 This is briefly expanded upon in Reuten 2003a, pp. 152–3.

of various backgrounds, I have minimised the use of mathematics. Formulas are generally merely used as shorthand (such as A+B = C). I also use simple ratios (X = Y/Z). I have evaded calculus and instead limit the representation of quantitative change to simple notation such as x↓ (decrease), x↑ (increase) or x′↑ (growth of x increases). When I introduce a functional relationship (X depends on Y) I start by Y→X.

E Format of the book and internal references

Systematic dialectics requires a systematic format. The two main parts of the book set out the two broad 'parallel' axes of economy and state (Figure 2). These parts are then structured into three levels, which also relate to distinct conceptual levels or stages: Chapters, Divisions and Sections.

- The parts are divided into ***Chapters*** (all chapters are consecutively numbered 1 through 11).
- These chapters are further divided into ***Divisions***.
  - Divisions are the main structure for the various conceptual levels.
  - In internal cross-references Chapter 1, Division 1 is abbreviated as **1D1** and so on.
- Divisions are divided into ***Sections*** (these are consecutively numbered within each chapter).
  - The Sections are the main text, and only Sections contain the *systematic argument* (these texts have been shaded).
  - In internal cross-references Chapter 1, Section 1 (§1) is abbreviated as **1§1**.

  In order to keep the systematic argument of the sections concise, the main sections text is usually followed by explanatory or expanding texts that may be read according to need. There are three types of the latter:
  - ***Explications*** serve to clarify the main section for diversified readerships. These expand on the systematic argument, most often with minimal jargon and a looser style. Sometimes these will also set out some analysis, in the case that received mainstream views are inappropriate. Explications may also refer to later sections and chapters. When required these explanations also expand on the dialectical method (this should be clear from the brief title of the Explication). In principle, Explications can be skipped if the main text is sufficiently clear or uncontroversial to the reader.
  - ***Amplifications***. These expand on the main section, though in the form of an aside. The reader can skip these without losing the thread of the systematic argument.

- *Addenda* go into details of the argument or locate the argument in the literature. Addenda are for specialists and may be skipped by the non-specialist.
- Explications, Amplifications and Addenda are consecutively numbered by section as a, b, c, etc. An internal cross-reference to Chapter 1, Section 1 (§1), Explication (a) will read **1§1-a** – the same system applies to Amplifications and Addenda.

In most chapters the systematic argument of the main sections makes up about 50% of the total text, the other 50% being Explications, Amplifications and Addenda.

Appendix. A note on historical dialectics: 'historical materialism'

Systematic dialectics is the dialectical method pertaining to the study of a particular socio-economic system, such as capitalism. This should be clearly distinguished from historical dialectics, whose aim is to comprehend the driving forces of historical development and the transitions between those systems. Thus whereas a historical dialectic considers the *diachronic* development between socio-economic systems, systematic dialectics considers one particular socio-economic system *synchronically*.[16]

Students are most often introduced to dialectics by way of the historical dialectics of Hegel and Marx. Whatever their merits in this field, a focus on this aspect of their work does not do justice to their main dialectical work. Hegel, having been engaged most of his lifetime with systematic dialectics, delivered towards the end of his life five series of lectures on a historical dialectic. He did not publish this material; rather his students posthumously published notes from these lectures.[17] Marx, on the other hand, began his scientific work with the development of a historical dialectic, but he published few of those works.

Together with Engels, Marx was the originator of a dialectical materialist conception of history (often called 'historical materialism', although the label is not Marx's). The following is a brief summary.[18]

Analytically and institutionally, any society can be seen as a number of domains – political and legal, cultural (including education), and economic. For Marx, the economic domain takes a central place – production is central,

16 Murray 2003, p. 156. Murray's article concisely sets out the distinction between the two dialectics – see especially pp. 150–8.

17 Hegel 1984 [1837].

18 Most of the following paragraphs have been taken from Reuten 2003a, p. 152.

but has a dialectical interaction with all the other domains. It does not assume a fully deterministic or mono-causal role, as is sometimes asserted (such an interpretation was particularly prevalent in the first half of the twentieth century).[19] More precisely, the relationship between the 'productive forces' and the social 'relations of production' play the central role in the development of a society at large (a whole 'social formation', such as a feudal or a capitalist society).[20] That is to say, what happens in the 'superstructure' – the juridico-political and cultural domains – is largely conditioned by the economic 'base'. When at a certain stage the relations of production become fetters for the productive forces, an era of social revolution leads to the transformation of society such that the forms of (social) property relations are re-shaped to suit the newly developed (or more accurately, 'developing') character of the forces of production. This schema is especially significant for comprehending *changes* between structures, particularly the dynamics of uneven development. 'Grand' history can be seen in terms of revolutionary transitions – 'restructuring' of social relations into forms that 'fit' the forces of production more closely.

Marx developed these ideas between the ages of 25 and 30, and they can be clearly discerned in *The Communist Manifesto* of 1848. From that year on, Marx undertook investigations in political economy, culminating in his magnum opus *Capital*, which can be seen as a systematic-dialectical exposition of the economic base of capitalism. Further, even if there are a few, mostly speculative, references to transitional elements within capitalism, transition is not the focus of that work.

Acknowledgements

Many people have in some form or another contributed to the emergence of this book. Under the heading 'intellectual inheritance' I already mentioned Michael Williams, my co-author of an earlier systematic-dialectical endeavour, and the ISMT members Christopher Arthur, Riccardo Bellofiore, Andrew Brown, Martha Campbell, Guglielmo Carchedi, Roberto Fineschi, Paul Mattick

19 For a critical appraisal from within that period see Jakubowski 1976 [1936].

20 The *'productive forces'* are the unity (combination) of labour and the means of production as including technology (which, in turn, includes organisational forms) as understood in grand, epochal terms. The *'relations of production'* are the material relations formed between people in the process of social production, exchange, and distribution of material wealth, including relations between the social class that does the actual work, and the class that has the power to live off the surplus produced by the former, usually through possession of the means of production that the exploited class works upon.

Jr., Fred Moseley, Patrick Murray, Tony Smith, Guido Starosta and Nicola Taylor. Amongst the latter special thanks go to Riccardo Bellofiore who introduced me to 'monetary circuit theory' and to Christopher Arthur, Patrick Murray and Tony Smith who incessantly sharpened my take on our longstanding shared interest in systematic dialectics in combination with value-form theory.

I would like to express my further gratitude to the following individuals who commented at various stages on draft chapters of the book: Dirk Damsma, Riccardo Bellofiore, Herman van Gunsteren, Murat Kotan, Peter Thomas, Tony Smith, Boe Thio, Jan Toporowski and Wijnand van der Woude. Included here are also the students of my course in Political Economy at the University of Amsterdam on whom I tried out early drafts.

All or most of the penultimate version of the book was commented on by Christopher Arthur, Dirk Damsma, Tony Smith and Boe Thio, for which I am immensely grateful. Tony Smith sent me 30 pages of important comments and he saved me from a major mistake in the composition of Chapter 11. I have been fortunate enough to engage in many hours of discussion with Boe Thio who saved me from making a considerable error in my exposition of production in the final part of Chapter 1. I am also grateful for the refereeing comments that I received via the publisher.

Without the input and assistance of these people, this book would not be what it is.

The above regards the academic content of the book. English not being my native language, I am very grateful to Simon Mussell for polishing my English. For the material production and publication of the book I thank Danny Hayward (manager of the Historical Materialism book series) as well as the Brill staff members Jennifer Obdam and Debbie de Wit, the latter especially for her great help in adapting the usual Brill typography to accommodate the special formatting requirements of the book. Finally, I thank the (for me) anonymous production workers of Brill in materialising the book.

PART 1

The capitalist economy

CHAPTER 1

The capitalist mode of production

The capitalist economy in general: the production of monetary value and the enterprises' appropriation of surplus-value

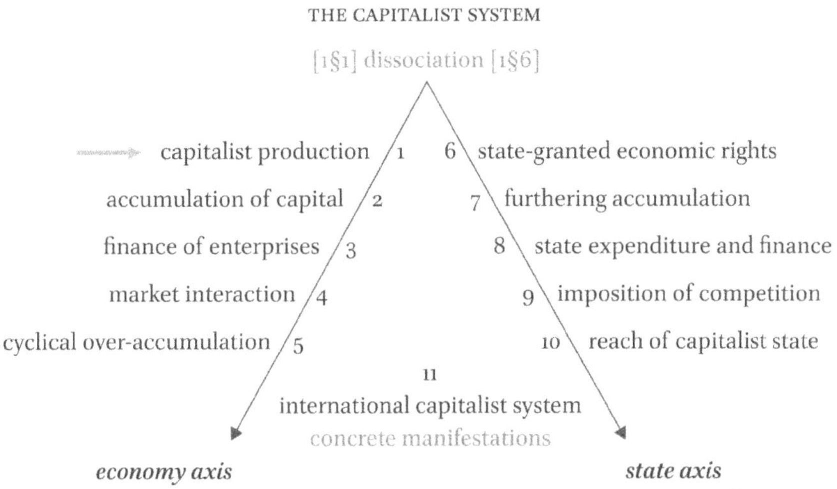

Contents

© GEERT REUTEN, 2019 | DOI:10.1163/9789004392809_003

Introduction

As indicated in the General Introduction, this book aims to set out the capitalist system. Because a social system is inherently a series of *interconnected* institutions, relations and processes, it is not obvious at the outset of the investigation what should be the appropriate starting point of its exposition. The idea of a systematic-dialectical methodology is that one can best present a system in a layered movement that begins with general-abstract concepts of the (putative) system, gradually developing these into more concrete complex ones.[1] At the same time, the starting general-abstract concepts should capture key characteristics of the system as a whole. In the systematic-dialectical methodology adopted in this book, the exposition also moves from absolutely necessary elements of the system to proximate necessities.

Given that I will be setting out a system, the status of the starting point in Division 1 is a relative matter. Chapter 1 in its entirety may be considered as the starting point. Given that production is absolutely indispensable for the material survival of any society, and considering that the historically specific form of production is a chief determinant of the totality, the exposition in this chapter starts with the specific capitalist form of production. This exposition is reached in the chapter's final Division 5, where we will see that capitalist production essentially takes on the form of 'production of capital'. The earlier divisions provide the arguments as to why it takes on this form.

Apart from some preparatory ideas that are introduced in a Division numbered '0' (on 'sociation'), the formal starting point of this chapter is Division 1 (on 'dissociation'), which establishes that a key characteristic of the capitalist system is its structural-institutional *separation* between households and privately owned enterprises.

All of Chapter 1, and indeed the entire book, sets out how this separation is bridged within capitalism, and how the ways of bridging it often create new problems along the way. The first and major institution for resolving the separation is the market, a key element of which, as we will see, is that it homogenises heterogeneous products as one-dimensional monetary value (Division 2). The commodification that accompanies this process applies not only to nonhuman entities ('goods'), but also to the capacity to labour (Division 3). It is this two-fold trading – of commodities and of the capacity to labour – that

1 'Putative': although I will not repeat this term, the eventual proof that a 'system' is being presented is only delivered when all of the system has been presented – i.e. at the end of the book.

SCHEME 1.1 *The capitalist mode of production (outline Chapter 1)*

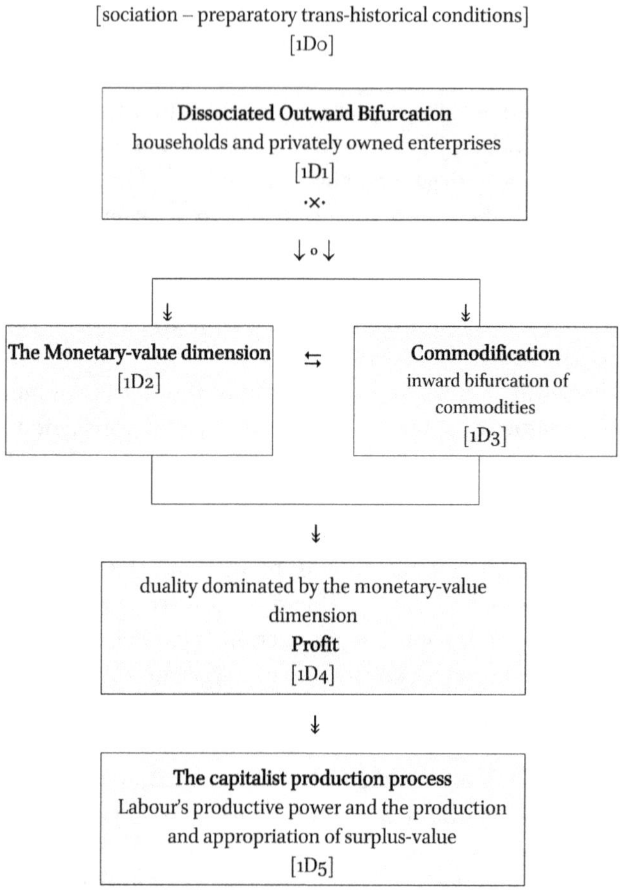

Legend
(the further meaning of the signs is explained throughout the chapter)

·×· continuity impediment
↓∘↓ sublated in (partially resolved in) *
⤈ grounded in (conditioned by)
⇆ dialectical mutuality **

* If at all, a full resolution is reached only at the book's end of the exposition.
** Dialectical mutuality: moments (here divisions) that presuppose each other.

determines the particular capitalist drive for profit (Division 4), but foremost the profit-driven production process (Division 5). See *Scheme 1.1* for the outline.

The starting point of this chapter will not prove to be difficult. Nevertheless, the first chapter will be the most demanding one for the reader. First of all it will be seen in Divisions 2–3 that although (or rather 'because') 'market trade in terms of monetary value' is an everyday phenomenon, adequately comprehending it is far from easy. Second, these same divisions, which are already difficult *qua* content, also constitute the reader's first significant acquaintance with the systematic-dialectical method adopted in this book.

Recall from the General Introduction that the text's systematic argument is offered in its *main sections* (shaded). The main text is usually followed by one or more 'Explications' that may be read according to need. Next to these there are 'Amplifications' and 'Addenda' that go into further detail or locate the argument within the wider literature. These are *not* part of the systematic argument and, in principle, the reader may forgo them if the main text is deemed sufficiently clear or uncontroversial.

For an explanation of field-specific and uncommon terms, the reader can refer to the Glossary at the end of the book.

Division 0. Sociation – preparatory trans-historical notions

This Division sets out very general and abstract *necessary* socio-economic requirements that must be fulfilled for any imaginable society to be a potentially continuous constellation – be it a society organised along familial, communal, feudal, capitalist, socialist, cooperative or any other lines. These requirements are also what all imaginable societies have in common. It is possible to imagine a society in which the birth rate falls to zero, but such a society would no longer be continuous, and as such it does not fit the category of potentially continuous societies.

1§0 *Sociation: abstract conditions for social continuity*

'Sociation' refers to the abstract minimum conditions that any imaginable society must meet in order for it to be a 'potentially continuous' social whole. Thus these conditions are trans-historical in that they apply to any concrete historical society.

Any such constellation requires social-human activities of *creation, use and care of entities*.[2] The entities necessarily include food, shelter and clothing. The

2 Throughout this book the term 'entity' will be used in reference to 'a something' that has not yet been (fully) identified conceptually.

potential continuity of the constellation requires that these activities include the *procreation and socialisation of children*.[3]

The creation of the entities entails a *transformation of physical inputs into qualitatively divergent physical outputs*. This transformation requires some combination of four elements:

- nature;
- human activity itself (the act of the transformative creation); this is predicated on the heritage of social knowledge, both formal and informal (tacit);
- cultivated nature;
- previously created entities as instruments.

All these conditions are abstract on two counts. First, in that these are formulated in terms of *general concepts* (trans-historically abstract). Second, in that these conditions do not set out the *social relations* through which these conditions are actualised (these are unique to a historically specific society).

1§0-a Explication. Sociation as a general and abstract trans-historical concept

Sociation refers to an abstract socio-economic totality. It merely posits the abstract concept of a system without showing *how* it is a system, that is, a potentially continuous social whole. What is more, the purpose of the concept of sociation is merely to refer to the historical phenomenon of systemic economies – or, in the terminology of Marx and Engels, 'modes of production'.[4] For example, 'communal', 'patriarchal', 'feudal' or 'capitalist' economies. The concept of sociation is *trans-historical* to the extent that it may be a preliminary entry point to the exposition of *any* systemic economy.

Herewith it should also be emphasised that the subject matter of the rest of this book – the capitalist system – is a historically specific, and therefore potentially finite, system. Early communal societies came to an end, systems of slavery came to an end, and feudalism is now, in the early twenty-first century, coming to an end throughout the world. It would be surprising if capitalism – in some form – were to last forever. Nevertheless, much as a naïve university student may believe that today's knowledge will also be that of tomorrow, so naïve social actors may also believe that social history ends with capitalism. This could come to pass, but historically there are more reasons to believe that it will not.

---

3 Socialisation: the acquirement of language, skills, knowledge and norms.

4 *The German Ideology*, 1976 [1932[1], 1965/66[2]] {ms.1845/46}.

Some elements of capitalism emerged many centuries ago in one antediluvian shape or another. Key to capitalism as a system, however, is capitalist *production*, as combining monetary profit criteria for production and wage-labour as an input to production, which requires the existence of a labour market (systematically outlined in the current chapter). Capitalist production only gradually emerged from the end of the eighteenth century in England, Scotland and France, and at that time it existed alongside feudal production, which dominated in most countries of the North-West of the globe throughout the nineteenth century. However, in respect of Britain, the year 1846 (which saw the repeal of the 1815 Corn Laws) may be used as benchmark for the economic and political dominance of the capitalist over the feudal mode of production.

As indicated in the General Introduction, this book is not concerned with historical transitions. The empirical reference for the object of inquiry, and hence for Division 1 and the rest of the book, is roughly the type of economies as organised presently in the OECD, and more precisely those current OECD countries for which we have a reasonable amount of averages data from 1870 onwards.

Division 1. Dissociation – outward bifurcation into households and privately owned enterprises

Capitalist dissociation is conceptualised by four sets of 'bifurcations' (separations), each presented in this chapter. The first section presents the most encompassing one from which, as we will see, the other bifurcations derive as their conditions of existence.

1§1 *Dissociated outward bifurcation into households and privately owned enterprises*

1 *Outward bifurcation into households and privately owned enterprises*
In capitalist society the 'activities' that are required for any sociation (1§0) are generally institutionally separated, or *outwardly bifurcated, into 'households' and 'privately owned enterprises'*. In addition, these households and enterprises are generally non-self-sufficient and mutually dependent, whilst the enterprises between them are also dependent on one another.

2 *Particular forms of activities along with the outward bifurcation*

Along with this bifurcation, the 'activities' take on *particular forms* – forms that are specific to the historically specific capitalist system.

The creation of entities (1§0) takes on the form of *production* at the site of enterprises. Regarding its requirements, the act of transformative creation of entities (1§0) takes on the form of '*labour*' as the distinctive activity of production. Of the other requirements, cultivated nature (1§0) takes on the form of the *privately appropriated earth* whereas previously created instruments (1§0) take on the form of *privately appropriated means of production* – each appropriated by enterprises. Only free nature, that is, the part of nature that is not privately appropriated, does not take on a particular form (in the end, free nature is nature that cannot (yet) be appropriated – such as, hitherto, the sun, rain and wind).

The form of labour as the distinctive activity of production implies for workers that 'non-labour' takes the form of *revitalisation and recreation* at the site of households. (Revitalisation includes not only passive rest, but also various non-occupational individual or communal activities.)

Apart from formal education, all the other sociation requirements are located in households, where they take the forms of consumption or of housework, whilst the procreation of children has not generally taken on a capitalist form.

These forms are summarised in *Table 1.2*.

3 *Particularly capitalist outward bifurcation*

In capitalist society another major feature of the outward bifurcation is that in general enterprises are not owned by the labourers who carry out the production. Hence capitalist society is characterised by an extended outward bifurcation into the *owners of private enterprises* on the one hand, and the – generally non-overlapping – *labourers carrying out the production* on the other. Hence this outward bifurcation – rather than being an already far-reaching matter of 'mere' forms and locus of activities (*Table 1.2*) – is characterised by particular private property *relations*.

Along with these private property relations, the enterprise appropriates the product produced by labour – in whatever way, for what, and to what extent, labour receives a 'compensation' for its production.

4 *'Dissociated outward bifurcation' – reflection and preview*

The starting point of the exposition so far (1§1 above) reveals nothing spectacular, because it merely sets out condensed-abstractly how the capitalist economy

[*continued*]

TABLE 1.2 *Particular forms of activity pertaining to the outwardly bifurcated capitalist economy – specific to its mode of production*

Trans-historical sociation (1§0) *General concepts*	**Dissociated outward bifurcation into households and privately owned enterprises (1§1)** ***Particular forms*** **pertaining to the capitalist economy**	
	Site of privately owned enterprises	**Site of households**
1. creation of entities (transformation)	form of production (here and below, for 'form of ...' read: 'takes on form of ...')	
requiring:		
• nature	(free nature: no particular form)*	(free nature: no particular form)
• act of transformative creation	form of labour	form of non-labour: forms of revitalisation and recreation†
• cultivated nature	form of privately appropriated nature	
• previously created instruments	form of privately appropriated means of production	
2. use of entities		form of consumption
3. care of entities		form of housework
4. procreation of children		procreation (no particular form)‡
5. socialisation of children	form of apprenticeship, or form of production (formal education)††	form of housework (early education)‡‡

* Now mainly restricted to elements such as the sun, rain and wind.

† Much of the recreation increasingly takes on the form of commodified consumption – row 2. (The term commodification is systematically introduced in 1D2.)

‡ When this book was completed, the procreation of children had not generally taken on a particularly capitalist form (even if various forms of commodification were emerging).

†† Part One yet abstracts from the State, hence also from state-provided education. Next to the form of apprenticeship, any other formal education then takes on the form of producing this education.

‡‡ Much of the early education increasingly takes on the form of production (row 1) and consumption (row 2) – e.g. 'day care'.

Later on the terms of 'increasingly' (under † and ‡‡) will be conceptualised as 'tendencies'.

1§1 *Continued*

appears in empirical reality. However, the starting point does not reveal *how* it can have 'existence in' concretely interconnected relations between these households and enterprises. (For example, via what relations does labour get from households to enterprises, via what relations is production carried out, and via what relations does the product of enterprises reach households?) Given that a form of material 'production' (generally: transformative activity) is indispensable for the survival of any society, the capitalist outward bifurcation into households and privately owned enterprises appears as dissociated and hence highly problematic.

This constellation is posited as dissociated, even if we know that in reality the bifurcated poles are in some way bridged. The object of the exposition in this book is to comprehend both the range of this dissociation and the extent of its actual resolution.

Therefore, the remainder of this chapter presents the first and elementary stages of the *conditions of existence* of the starting point outlined above. To this end, it presents the first stages of the capitalist economy's way of 'sublating' the outward bifurcation (that is, stages of partially resolving the bifurcation without the bifurcation itself being undone – see Explication 1§1-a).

Pending the complete exposition of these conditions of existence, the entirety of the outward bifurcation presented above – including its forms and property relations – is referred to as 'dissociated outward bifurcation'. Pending the complete exposition, this bifurcation is as yet an 'impediment' to the continuity of the capitalist economy.

1§1-a Explication. The terms 'sublation' and 'grounding'

The term 'sublation' refers to the (initially) partial resolution of a major impediment, without that impediment itself being undone. In this book this is the impediment posed by dissociated outward bifurcation. These partial resolutions, though increasingly less partial, are presented in the rest of this chapter, and the several stages of this book in its entirety. A full resolution is only reached, if at all, at the end of the exposition. The term sublation is mainly used in Chapters 1 and 6. For the rest (and already in these chapters) I simply use the term 'grounding' (a series of grounding throughout the book), that is, the grounding of the outward bifurcation posited at the starting point (1§1). Grounding is the same as the determination of a (partial) condition of existence of the outward bifurcation.

1§1-b Explication. Logical systematic exposition

Systematic dialectics investigates systemic constellations, in our case that of capitalism. It does not investigate transitions towards that constellation from a previous one (as in a historical dialectic). Therefore the bifurcation and dissociation posited in 1§1 should be understood as logical, not historical. (A similar remark applies to *all* the sections to follow in this book.) This bifurcation is posited as the general-abstract reference to the current capitalist system, and its economy in particular.

1§1-c Explication. 'Dissociated outward bifurcation' and the initial reference to the capitalist totality

Although dissociation refers to the capitalist totality, it is no more than an initial reference. As we will see, it is *the mode of resolving* (*i.e. sublating*) *this bifurcation*, and the contrarieties deriving from it, which *characterises the capitalist system.*

The outward bifurcation as posited in 1§1 is both simple and complex. It is simple insofar as we all know that there is this institutional separation between households and enterprises (this is also the first lesson of mainstream microeconomics). It is complex, as we will see, because the ways of resolving this separation are far from evident. Even if we 'know' the constellation in terms of this separation, it cannot exist without *a mode* of sublating that bifurcation. Hence, posited as such, that is, without any connections between the bifurcated poles, it is an impossible constellation because it (still) lacks the conditions for its existence, the grounds for its existence.

We will see that each effort at sublation (at least until we reach the end of the exposition) poses new problems, thus revealing this sublation as being yet insufficient and so requiring further sublation. Hence, each time the exposition of the system is *driven forward by the 'insufficiency'* of the moment or moments posited at the earlier level of the exposition. (See 1§1-d for the term 'moment'.)

1§1-d Explication. The meaning of 'moment'

Consider *Scheme 1.1*. Each division of the current chapter and of later chapters is indicated as a 'moment' (sometimes the term also applies to the separate sections of a division). A 'moment' is a more or less cohesive institutional make-up (at a more concrete plane one may think, for example, of 'the labour market' or 'banking'), or a more or less cohesive set of entities, that can be analysed by itself (sometimes like a model) but that nevertheless derives its full meaning from its interconnection with other moments, and ultimately from its interconnectedness within the whole exposition. Thus moments derive their full meaning through synthesis.[5]

In respect of the current chapter, for example, the moment of outward bifurcation (1D1) is first sublated in the moments of monetary value and commodification (1D2–1D4). Their insufficiency prompts the introduction of the moment of capitalist production (1D5) into the exposition.

---

5 See also Reuten and Williams 1989, p. 22, where this is framed rather more dialectically.

1§1-e Amplification. The term 'general' in 1§1: the general and predominant character of the capitalist dissociation

I always adopt the term 'generally' to refer beyond contingencies that are compatible with capitalism, whilst, if those current contingencies were to be generalised, there would no longer be capitalism. (Take two simple examples: contingently a pair of people may not be able to have children; however, if this were generalised, then humanity would come to an end. Similarly – in reference to the end of this chapter – contingently capitalist enterprises may not make profits, but if this were generalised, then capitalism would come to an end.)

The capitalist economy is characterised by the outward bifurcation between households and privately owned enterprises. In 1§1 I used the term 'generally' on a number of occasions in reference to the outward bifurcation between households and privately owned enterprises that characterises capitalism. However, this does not exclude the fact that, contingently, there are households to which the separation does not apply – even if the non-dependence on other units (i.e. enterprises) is rare within full-fledged capitalism. Similarly, regarding the property relations it is far less rare, though again contingent, that – now within the outward household–enterprise bifurcation – one or more members of a household run a business (in economics this is often called 'independent' or 'self-employment') without employing labour.

In this book I refrain from characterising the type of economy that would exist if there were a market economy with generalised self-employment or generalised workers' cooperatives or a combination of the two (Smith 2017, ch. 12, is very thought-provoking on this).

1§1-f Amplification. The terms private ownership and possession

The full meaning of 'private ownership' will only become explicit in Chapter 6 (that chapter introduces the state's granting of 'legal property right', which is a major condition for the dissociation). In Part One (still abstracting from the State), 'possession' (actual physical control of an entity) and 'ownership' are used in a broad sense. In this usage, the term ownership in particular bears no explicit or implicit reference to 'title to legal right' and thus a possible legally recognized ownership.

1§1-g Addendum. Separation, dissociation, labour: references

The separation of the units of production from the units of consumption is also stressed by Weber (1968 [1920], p. 21): 'The modern rational organization of the capitalist enterprise would not have been possible without … the separation of business from the household, which completely dominates modern economic life …'. The insight of the separation of 'activity' into productive and consumption activity derives from Himmelweit (1984). The term 'dissociation' is also used by De Vroey (1981, p. 176) Eldred, Hanlon, Kleiber and Roth (1984, p. 354), Reuten (1988), Reuten and Williams (1989) and Smith (2017).

1§1-h Addendum. Marx's starting point in *Capital*

In *Capital* Marx's starting point is 'the commodity' (Volume I, Chapter 1). On the one hand, this refers to everyday perception. ('The wealth of those societies in which the capitalist mode of production prevails, presents itself as "an immense accumulation of commodities"' – the opening of Marx's *Capital*). On the other hand, the commodity is the initial abstract resolution of the dissociation problematic – as we will see in 1§4–1§7. Thus, in a way, Marx starts with the 'abstract perception' of the initial resolution. If so conceived, Marx's starting point may not be fundamentally different from the current one.

1§1-i Addendum. Dissociation: no 'falling apart' vis-à-vis sociation

This book adopts a development from a Hegelian-Marxian *systematic* dialectic. Both Hegel and Marx *also* adopted a *historical* dialectic (General Introduction, Appendix).[6] From a Hegelian historical dialectic point of view it might be tempting to conceive the 'dissociation' in terms of a 'falling apart' vis-à-vis 'sociation' (see Plant 1977, on 'falling apart' and reconciliation). For the current systematic dialectic, however, 'sociation' is not an ideal but rather an *abstract* concept, of *general requirements*, without the *social relations* through which these conditions are actualised. Hence 'dissociation' cannot be a falling apart relative to 'sociation'. The dissociated outward bifurcation just aims to refer to the totality of the capitalist system.

1§1-j Addendum. 'Contradiction' – dissociation as a contradictory constellation

In the main text I have avoided – and will avoid henceforth – the dialectical term 'contradiction' mainly because expounding it would require a disproportionate amount of space relative to the insight that it might provide. For the purposes of this book I can do with the term 'continuity impediment'. Here I nevertheless provide a brief inkling. The dissociated bifurcation as posited in 1§1, that is, without particular interconnections between households and privately owned enterprises, it is apparently impossible, it can have no existence, it is in itself contradictory. Hence, posited as such, it is a *contra-*

6 See also Murray 2003.

dictory constellation because it (still) lacks the conditions for its existence, the grounds for its existence. Thus a contradictory entity or a contradictory constellation is one that cannot exist in the absence of particular conditions or grounds. In systematic-dialectical works these are most often referred to as sublations, which each time reveal new defects that require further sublation (see Inwood 1992, pp. 63–5, 283–5 and 115–16, for a brief expounding of the terms of 'contradiction', 'sublation' and 'ground' in reference to Hegel's works).

Division 2. The monetary-value dimension

This division presents the first moment of the particular way in which the capitalist economy resolves the dissociated outward bifurcation.

1§2 *The trade relation*

The continuity impediment of the dissociated outward bifurcation (1§1) is apparently resolved in trade relations. Trade potentially connects households and enterprises.

In the current division, trade is considered from the perspective of enterprises. It is pre-posited that enterprises dispose of labour-capacity (presented in Division 3). The production *process* is also pre-posited (presented in Division 5). Hence the current division considers trade in terms of the inputs and the outputs of production.

1§2-a Explication. Abstract trade

The idea that dissociated outward bifurcation (1§1) – in whatever particular type of conceptualisation – requires some form of trade is nothing new. It has been a key issue in political economy and economics from Adam Smith's (1776) 'invisible hand' to the Arrow and Debreu's (1954) 'general equilibrium theory'.

However, the trade relation posited in 1§2 is utterly abstract: especially the form of the trade relation has not been determined. The trade relation is merely the first condition of existence of this dissociation. However, this cannot be turned around: trade does not necessarily imply capitalist relations. Generally, trade in the abstract is *compatible* with a multitude of trade criteria, including, e.g., quid pro quo labour time, and reciprocal need.

1§2-b Explication. Note on the following sections (1§3–1§5)
The following three sections posit 'value', 'money' and the 'commodity'. Classical Political Economy (Smith, Ricardo, Mill), as well as Marx, start their treatment of value by observing that in practice we have the duality of 'use-value' (usefulness) and 'exchange-value' (the latter is what they call, in brief, 'value'). Instead of just observing this, the following three sections ground this duality. While these sections might prove difficult, the reader is advised to keep in mind that this duality is just grounded. It must be grounded because this duality is crucial to the capitalist system, and decisive for much of what follows in the chapters to come.

1§3 *The value dimension: abstract general one-dimensional value*

The outward bifurcation (1§1) not only requires the trade relation (1§2), but also determines the latter's character, that is, the capitalist social form, the social dimension, of the trade relation.

Physical inputs to processes of production qualitatively diverge from the physical outputs. The dissociated outward bifurcation (1§1) entails that the physical product of enterprises is generally not destined for its producers. If enterprises and households were *not* bifurcated, then the physical divergence might generally be the aim (food, shelter, clothing, etc.). However, when an *enterprise* produces, e.g., laces only, then the use of laces by the producers is not the immanent aim. The dissociated outward bifurcation entails that the *driving force* of enterprises must be an aim other than the physical entity produced – an aim external to the physical product.

Hence the processes of production and trade necessarily require inputs and outputs to be *reduced to a homogeneous common denominator*. Therefore the capitalist social form of the trade relation is necessarily one of absorption into and reduction to a common denominator. *One-dimensional abstract value* is the *sui generis* of this homogeneous common denominator. Value must be constituted as general value as opposed to the particularity and specific usefulness, or specific multifaceted characteristics, of the physical input and output. Thus abstract generality, one-dimensional general value, absorbs concrete specificity. In other words, the particular products of particular labour necessarily have to take on the *general form of value*; without them being validated as such, they are socially non-existent.[7] As such, value as social form is the necessary dimension of the entities produced by labour in a dissociated mode of production.

7 At this point 'validation' just refers to 'valid'. From 1§4 onwards it will, more specifically, mean the turning of outputs into money.

Henceforth the term 'value' is used as shorthand for 'abstract general, one-dimensional, value'.

1§3-a Explication. Value as social dimension

In everyday language 'value' often has a multifaceted meaning.[8] Within the economic domain it has one-dimensional meaning. One-dimensional value is tied to specific social constellations, thus it is a historically specific social concept. As a social dimension 'value' is not an a priori (in Kant's sense) natural-physical dimension nor is it universal (space and continuity), although value is a category as abstract as space and continuity. Note that at the current level of the exposition (1§3), the concept of value is near to empty. Concepts such as measure of value will be introduced in the next section. The point is that the positing of any form or dimension (in this case that of value) should precede that of its measure(s) and standard measure(s).

1§3-b Amplification. Specific usefulness

The main text states: 'Value must be constituted as general value as opposed to the particularity and specific usefulness, or specific characteristics, of the physical input and output'. Up to this point in the text it may have seemed that 'one-dimensional abstract value' might include the Marginalist and Neoclassical concept of 'utility'. However, that concept is meant to capture subjective 'use-value', which is the opposite of the concept of value at hand. The latter connects rather with the Classical concept of 'exchange-value' – one that these economists indeed opposed to 'value in use'. (Cf. Smith 1776, Book I, Ch. 4, section 13). This issue will be further articulated in sections 1§4 and 1§5.

1§3-c Addendum. Value and measure of value in marxian theory

Within the marxian tradition to this day, there has been quite an important penchant for turning 'immediately' from the concept of value to a, or 'the', measure of value, and to take the two as *identical*. Labour-time is often supposed to perform this two-in-one job (in fact this error of moving too fast stems from Ricardo 1981 [1817^1; 1821^3]). More details are set out in Reuten (1999a).

8 When the Dutch poet Lucebert wrote: 'Alles van waarde is weerloos' (everything of value is defenceless – in *'De zeer oude zingt'*, published 1974), he obviously did not refer to stocks or similar financial assets. The nineteenth-century philosopher Rudolf Lotze imported the 'economic' concept of value from political economy into philosophy (Stirk 2000, p. 160; Nauta 1980 [1971], p. 104). From there the term was imported into sociology where it is key to the conceptualisation of social formations.

Note: The reader may be warned that the next two main sections (1§4 and 1§5) are more demanding than any other in this chapter and, indeed, in the entire book.

1§4 *The monetary-value dimension – market trans-abstraction and the requirement of money as the union of measure and medium of value*

The interplay of the trade relation (1§2) and the reduction to a common denominator, i.e. the absorption into abstract general, one-dimensional, value (1§3) is constituted in the market.

1 *Actual market trade: commensuration as abstraction in practice*

Prior to the trade act in the market, the buyers assess the heterogeneous useful characteristics of the entities brought to market, whilst the sellers sing their praises (and perhaps try to hide an evil trait). In the end, however, upon the actual market trade, heterogeneous entities are made commensurate in terms of something that is no part whatsoever of their concrete physical bodily form or concrete constitution. We have a *trans-abstraction in practice:* the alien dimension of 'value' is ascribed to the entity, or rather it is vested in the entity.[9]

2 *Money as measure of value*

So far (1§3) the conceptual focus on value has been qualitative, dimensional. Market trade of entities, however, takes place in specific quantities of the quality posited. This necessarily requires measurement and a measure for the quality of value. The value trans-abstraction at the market operates through *money*. Put more strongly, money is a necessary condition of existence of one-dimensional value. The *first requirement* for something to be money is that it can be a *measure of value*.

3 *Money as medium of value*

Nevertheless, the measurement in terms of money (perhaps in a value-assaying procedure between seller and buyer establishing that some price is appropriate) does not determine the value quantity of the entity. Value, a fortiori value quantity, does not exist without actual market trade, and money as actual *medium* of quantity of value. With the actual market trade the value assaying procedure, the measurement, is no longer without commitment. Thus actual market trade is the value *salto*, the value leap – the telling (*hic est*) is not enough:

9 The term 'trans-abstraction' is expanded upon in 1§4-b. In brief: a trans-abstraction in practice is not an abstraction of the mind that sorts or grasps sensuous phenomena, but rather the result of action, i.e. of social intercourse.

hic saltus.[10] Hence the *second requirement* for something to be money is that it is a quantitative *medium of value*.[11]

4 *Money as unity of measure and medium of value*

Because, and to the extent that, (some) money acts as medium of value in market trade, and so proves and reproves itself, it can be an effective measure of value.[12] *Thus money is the necessary unity of measure and medium of one-dimensional value.*

5 *Standard measure of money*

So far the matter of *standard measure* has not been alluded to. In comparison with the issues presented so far, it is secondary and uncomplicated. Suffice it to posit that generalised market trade requires a standard or convertible standards of money (e.g. dollar, yuan or euro). Then, in terms of some standard measure (e.g. €), entities are grasped in terms of a number (e.g. €12) that we call *price*. Thus the price of an entity is its monetary value as expressed in a particular standard.

6 *Money: no inherent content, no inherent value*

Unlike the entities that money measures, money has *no inherent content* – neither bullion, nor paper, nor electronic pulses; even if some particular shape of money may be more adequate than another (amplified in 2D4). Consequently, money has *no inherent value*. Money is inherently merely a quantifier of one-dimensional value.[13]

---

10 *Salto* (jump) refers to Marx's phrase about the crucial 'jump' in exchange of the commodity into money (*Capital I*, Ch. 3, Section 2-a); the *hic est* (this is; 'this is my body') refers to the consecration in the Catholic Mass (a much neglected metaphor used by Marx in a similar context – see Reuten 1993, p. 97); the *hic saltus* (thou should jump here) refers to Hegel's phrase in the Preface to his *Philosophy of Right* (1967 [1821[1]]) in reference to a boastful person who is invited to demonstrate his tricks here and now.

11 This is notably different from the misleading neoclassical notion of money as 'medium of *exchange*' (see 1§4-c).

12 To the extent that money proves to be an effective medium of value in market trade, it is reinforced as an effective measure. The two are mutually reinforcing.

13 Money measures and mediates value but it has no value in itself. This applies for capitalist money (as further grounded in 2D4). (For the time being, the following may perhaps help. A metre-stick measures length and has itself relevant length. However, an electronic scale or a spring may measure weight without them having the relevant weight.)

7 *Value and the Monetary-Value Dimension*
Because value is a super-sensuous dimension and, as such, utterly abstract – that is, abstract in practice – and because it is in daily practice known *only* through the money medium, it is in daily practice identified with 'value as measured by money'. That is, *value* is in mundane practice *identified with 'monetary value' as a hypostatic union of dimension and medium.*[14] Even further, in mundane practice money may not be perceived as 'medium' but, hypostatically, as being value itself.

Nevertheless, even in that perception value and money are not seen to be identical (as in 'value ≡ money'). Something may be ascribed 'monetary value' without being money. Indeed this is what happens outside the market when some monetary value is ascribed to entities (for example, a building, a machine or a pen). Again, as with abstract value, this monetary value is super-sensuous in that it is no sensuous characteristic of the entity (amplified in 1§10). This conception in practice is captured by the term *Monetary-Value Dimension* (MVD).

1§4-a Explication. Pre-posited money creation
The main text posits the abstract concept of money – that is sufficient for the rest of this chapter. It pre-posits the actual creation of money by banks, which is presented in Chapter 2 (2D4).

1§4-b Explication. Abstraction and 'trans-abstraction in practice'
Generally an *abstraction* is considered to be a mental act. There are at least four types of mental abstraction, of which the first three have overlapping aspects. The first posits abstract *generality* as opposed to concrete specificity (this is the common usage of the term in this book – see the Glossary for further explanation). In the second type, various elements of reality are (temporarily) *neglected* so as to focus on one or several elements that are thought to be key to a certain realm of reality, or perhaps all of reality. In the third type, the same aim of focusing is reached by way of the *reduction* of the various elements of reality to known common elements or categories. In the fourth one, we have a *reduction* to hitherto unknown common elements or categories. Although processes of abstraction are engrained in our common language, they are part and parcel of the sciences in particular.

14 The term 'hypostatic' is a metaphorical reference to Christianity for which God is much too abstract, so that a human being, Christ, mediates between God and (other) human beings. Nevertheless the human being Christ acquires divinity. This double identity is called hypostasis. By analogy value is too abstract, and as such it must be mediated by money; even further: in everyday practice money and value are often seen as identical.

However, there are also abstractions that do not (primarily) evolve as mental acts but rather in the practice of life – and especially in economic life. The exemplary case is the actual reduction of entities at the market to a monetary denominator. I call these *abstractions in practice* (cf. Reuten and Williams 1989, pp. 62–4). (In fact one reason why economics, in comparison with other social sciences, has a much easier job in quantifying elements of its domain is that the domain itself produces key abstractions as well as key measures for them – compare, for example, 'power' in political science for which the scientist has to devise measures.)

The main text of 1§4 states: 'upon the actual market trade, heterogeneous entities are made commensurate in terms of something that is no part whatsoever of their concrete physical bodily form or concrete constitution ... the alien dimension of "value" is ascribed to the entity, or rather it is vested in the entity'. If the dimension of value, like perhaps that of mass, were one physical aspect of the entity, then we would have an '*actual* abstraction in practice' – which already would be remarkable enough. However, it has been emphasised that value is in fact a dimension *alien* to the entity. Thus the abstraction that is performed in the market is in fact super-sensuous, or transcendental – whence I adopt the term *trans-abstraction*. In the market, at the point of trade, sensuousness is installed by the money mediator. But beyond the point of trade this sensuousness vanishes into super-sensuous monetary value.

As we will see in Division 5 and in Chapters 2–3, the sensuousness of the money mediator does not absolve us from the concept of value: most of the time, especially during production, and always when non-money assets are at stake, economic entities are supposed to 'have' value – that is, super-sensuous monetary value – in the absence of the money mediator's act. When money comes in – in acts of trade – money makes us at least nearly touch on value, much like in various religions wherein the prophets allow believers to feel closer to God.

We need an uncommon language (trans-abstraction in practice) because we are dealing with – as far as I can see – the most complicated part of the capitalist economy and of all of the sciences of political economy and economics.

1§4-c Explication. The misleading notion of money as 'medium of exchange'

The reader may have noticed that from 1§2 onwards I have used the term 'trade', not 'exchange'. The latter has often (also) a connotation of barter. Indeed many discourses of the capitalist economy start with notions of barter (and some remain somewhat enmeshed in it). The main text (1§4) introduced the concept of money as 'medium of value' ($C_i \leftrightarrow M$, where C_i indicates commodity i, M money and ↔ transfer). Herewith I distance myself from the orthodox economic concept of money as 'medium of exchange' (which would be $C_i \to M \to C_j$, where C_j indicates commodity j). The latter term carries implicit or explicit notions of barter exchange ($C_i \leftrightarrow C_j$), with just the non-coincidence of wants evaded.[15] In that orthodox view money is of subordinate importance: money as medium of exchange is merely more efficient. However, no systematic barter exists in capitalism. Market trade always takes the form of $C_i \leftrightarrow M$; so money is a medium of value and never a medium of exchange.[16] The watershed between the two concepts (medium of value and medium of exchange) is the value-dimension (i.e. the value-form). The orthodox terminology implicitly neglects that there might be a dimensional problematic at all.

1§4-d Addendum. The term 'actual'

Throughout this book I use the term 'actual' not in Hegel's sense, but rather in reference to existence.

Division 3. Commodification – the inward bifurcation of commodities

As indicated, Divisions 2 and 3 are posited at the same level of the exposition and presuppose each other (dialectical mutuality).

Note: From the next section onwards, the sections will often start with a brief summary statement that is indented.

1§5 *Commodification of goods through their market transformation*

> Trade (1§2) concretised as actual market trade in terms of money – the unity of measure and medium of one-dimensional value (1§3–1§4) – potentially constitutes the inputs and outputs of enterprises (1§1) as a determinate magnitude of one-dimensional monetary value (1§4).

15 The *motive* for a bicycle producer might perhaps be the purchase of a car or perhaps to make a saving. None of these motives makes money a medium of exchange.

16 A term that is at least on the edge of being problematic is that of 'medium of circulation', one that was unfortunately also used in Reuten and Williams 1989 (for which I take responsibility). It may be noted at this point that for Marx (1867, Ch. 3) money's two main 'functions' are that of 'measure of value' and 'medium of circulation' (alongside means of hoarding and means of payment). Medium of value versus medium of circulation is not just a terminological difference; the former posits a concretisation of value that is (at least) less obvious for the latter.

The actual market trade operates through the discrete money medium as quantitative medium *of* value. Money is the quantifier *through which value appears*, and is perceived *as reflected* onto entities. Through the money medium the trans-abstraction of value at the market concretely appears as a reflected *transformation* of entities – henceforth the 'market transformation of entities'.[17] Hence the entities appear in a dual guise, an inwardly bifurcated guise: that of their physical shape and that of reflected value. This *inward bifurcation* constitutes entities as *commodities*. Thus commodities have a dual character: their physical make-up and their value reflected through money. This transformation and hence this duality applies to goods, including good-like services (services that for their production require material inputs).

1§5-a Explication. The market and monetary value as 'too normal' phenomena

The main text of 1§3–1§5 is key to this book. Implicitly it aims to answer the question 'what is value?'. Note first that an answer along the lines of 'costs' is circular insofar as costs, presumably, are in the same dimension. If costs were in a different dimension – as in classical labour theories of value – we would run into a regress because we would still have to make a jump, a transformation, from, say, labour-time to value. (In some varieties of marxian theory – but not in Marx's – the problem is polished away by just reducing value to labour-time – I briefly return to this in 1§5-d and e). If the answer were given in terms of heterogeneous 'preferences' (as in neoclassical theory), equally we would encounter a regress to the extent that preferences have to be transformed into the value dimension.

It is not obvious that entities acquire a social dimension that is alien to their physical make-up. At the same time the problem of comprehending market trade in terms of value, and of responding to the question of 'what is value', is so complicated because we are hindered by the fact that it is overwhelmingly part of our everyday experience and so it seems 'too' familiar. Each day the sun rises in the morning and sets in the evening. Why think about it? Well, we know that this rising and setting is a false appearance, even if we ignore this in our language and experience. You buy a loaf of bread in the morning and a beer in the evening by tossing some coins on the counter or inserting a smart card in a slot. It happens every day. Why ruminate on this further?

17 This complex 'reflected transformation' is to be distinguished from the so far relatively simple 'transformative creation of physical entities' (in capitalism taking the form of production) – as alluded to in 1§1.

The point is that the forces engendered by the monetary-value dimension overwhelmingly determine our lives. At the same time these are not inevitable facts of nature, but rather the result of our own political-economic doing.[18]

1§5-b Addendum. Inwardly bifurcated commodities: notes on the history of economic theory

I have dedicated quite a lot of space (1§2–1§5) to the task of positing the inward bifurcation of commodities. Classical political economists (CPE) such as Adam Smith (1776, Book I, Ch. 4, section 13) and David Ricardo (1981 [1817¹], Ch. 1, section 1), without much ado, simply mention the duality (internal bifurcation) as a fact of life, merely to delineate that political economy is about 'value in exchange' rather than 'value in use'. Thus although these economists are aware of the two aspects of the commodity, they do not problematise it and reduce their discourse de facto to exchange-value (in short, also for them, 'value').

Neoclassical economists neglect the issue by reducing value to use-value (utility). As a consequence they are forced to treat money as some strange appendix to the science of economics: prices are utility determined (or preference determined) *barter* 'prices' (in fact barter ratios). Then, via the 'good' that happens to be a handy medium of barter exchange, i.e. 'money', the general price level is determined by a Quantity Theory of Money. Apart from the determination of the price level, money does not matter.[19|20]

Although Keynes (1936) – as well as current post-keynesian economics – is a leading critic of the neglect of money in neoclassical economics, his point of application is not – what we now call – microeconomic issues and the market as such, but rather the macroeconomic aspects of money. When dealing with these in Chapters 2–3, I will return to Keynes.

---

18 More specifically, our own political-economic doing in the sense that Marx expressed it: 'Men make their own history, but they do not make it just as they please; they do not make it under circumstances chosen by themselves, but under circumstances directly encountered, given and transmitted from the past. The tradition of all the dead generations weighs like a nightmare on the brain of the living' (Marx 1979 [1852¹], p. 115).

19 It is rather impractical to deliver a university diploma in economics stamped with the message that money does not matter; so economics departments deliver an appendix course on 'money, credit and banking' setting out some nasty details of the matter – the main economics courses can do without this. (In a critical essay, Frank Hahn (1981), a prominent proponent of General Equilibrium Theory, set out the limitations of (this) neoclassical economics.)

20 Twisting the matter Milton Friedman (e.g. 1959 or 1968) argued that 'money matters' because it determines the price level.

What Marx calls the two-fold character of the commodity is key to his *Critique of Political Economy* [1859] as well as to the first 100 pages or so of the first Part (Chs. 1–3) of *Capital*, Volume I [1867^1] where he uses the terms 'double character', 'two-fold character' and 'duality' of the commodity as synonyms. Marx's way of proceeding is somewhat different from the one presented above. He starts from the commodity and commodity trade (exchange) and derives the commodity's duality from it, before expanding on value and finally arriving at monetary value. Above I started with the dissociated outward bifurcation (which remains implicit at Marx's starting point), then introduced the trade relation, value and monetary value and finally arrived at the commodity and its duality that I posited as an inward bifurcation (1§5). (Bifurcation is a translation of the German 'Entzweiung').[21]

1§5-c Addendum. Marx on money as the measure of value

Because Marx's *Capital* – as much as the current book – adopts the method of systematic-dialectical *immanent critique*, it is not surprising that when discussing the concept of value in the first chapter of that book, he starts off from the received view of his day. Namely that of Classical Political Economy, which posits – in several varieties – a 'labour theory of value' (in brief: labour is the source of value – see e.g. Reuten 1999a and 2018a). He assumes that the reader is familiar with this (at the time) mainstream view. However, a present-day reader might believe that Marx, in setting out how labour is the source of value – without, however, calling his own theory a 'labour theory of value' – is describing something new (in fact this problem has played a role even throughout the twentieth century).[22] Such a focus completely misses the really innovative message of the text, namely that it is *not labour but rather money that constitutes the dominant measure of value*, the measure and the criterion for what is (not) produced.

Classical Political Economy posits that labour is the source of profit (Marx agrees with this, as do I, as is set out in Division 5). However, the defect of CPE is that it simultaneously takes 'labour' (in different varieties for different authors) to be the *measure* of value. In Reuten (1999a) I set out the similar confusion within some strands of current marxian economics. In Reuten (2005) I show how this confusion is also related to an inappropriate reading of the first three

21 In *Capital* Marx does not use the term 'Entzweiung' (literally 'splitting in two'). However, it is a term that Hegel (sparingly) used – see Benhabib 1986, p. 23 and Inwood 1992, p. 36.

22 For Marx, labour is the source of value; however, he is far from proposing that 'labour *is* value' (which was Ricardo's view).

chapters of *Capital* (where the term 'abstract labour' in the first two sections of chapter 1 is a placeholder for money, prior to the introduction of money).

1§5-d Addendum. Value-form theory: from value-form to monetary-value dimension

Since 1988 I have been a fierce proponent of 'value-form' theory. Nevertheless, to this point I have abstained from using the term 'value-form'. This is an issue of how to phrase the matter, rather than making any fundamental changes to the content. Value-form theorists, including myself, took on Marx's term of value-form (*Capital I*, Ch. 1) in their breaking away from value-theoretical 'labour embodied' interpretations of Marx's work (appraised in e.g. Reuten 1993 and 2004a) as well as from analogous currents within contemporary marxian theory (appraised in e.g. Reuten and Williams 1989; Reuten 1988 and 1995). This is clear for the theoretical experts. The expert knows that the term 'value-form' – in one of its main focuses – is used to emphasise that 'value' is not a naturalistic concept, but rather one that is always specific to and 'determinate' (Murray 1988) for particular social formations (such as capitalism); furthermore, for capitalism value's main determinate form is *monetary*. However, the term 'value-form' by itself leaves the latter unspecified. In short, I have mainly substituted the term 'monetary-value dimension' for 'capitalist value-form', even if the connotations of the two terms are somewhat different.

1§6 *Commodification of labour-capacity and commodified consumption*

As labour is required for production (1§1), it now becomes manifest that – with the trade relation, the monetary-value dimension and the commodification presented so far (1§2–1§5) – the existence of enterprises generally requires them to *purchase the capacity to labour* during production, in which sense they are *employers of labour*.

Correspondingly, to the extent that labourers lack means of production, their existence compels them to sell their labour-capacity, to be employed for part of the day (thus their existence is grounded in that sale). Depending on their skills, they are not forced to sell their labour-capacity to a particular enterprise; however, they are *forced to sell* it to some enterprise. Thus the dissociated outward bifurcation requires that labour-capacity is traded on a market.

Because in capitalism the capacity to labour is not traded in its entirety (as is the case in systems of slavery), but rather for a stipulated amount of time, its trade occurs in terms of hiring and renting out (i.e. time-constrained buying and selling).

As with the outputs of production and the other inputs to production, the capacity to labour is assessed at the market such that heterogeneous capacities are made commensurate in terms of one-dimensional monetary value – a dimension alien to the physical capacity to labour (cf. 1§4). Thus we have a commodification of labour-capacity – it is traded on a market like a commodity. Similarly, it is through the money medium that the trans-abstraction of value concretely appears as reflected market transformation of labour-capacity (cf. 1§5). Hence the latter appears in the *inwardly bifurcated guise of 'capacity' and 'monetary value'*, which constitutes it as 'commodified' (cf. 1§5). More specifically, the commodified labour-capacity is bifurcated into 'capacity rented out for a certain amount of time' and 'rent in monetary value for a certain amount of time', the name for the latter being the 'wage for a certain amount of time' or, in short, the '*wage rate*'.

Along with this commodification and the wage income deriving from it, the households' acquirement of production outputs of enterprises takes the form of commodified 'consumption'.

1§6-a Explication. The 'too common' market for labour-capacity

Without the 'mirror' of other, different, societies it is notoriously difficult to analyse the most common aspects of one's own society. The market for labour-capacity (usually called the 'labour market') is a case in point. Our psychological need for concordance forbids us to even remotely compare the trading of labour-capacity with the trading of slaves. These are not the same; nevertheless, if we consider the matter in terms of selling and renting labour-capacity, this trading is something of a remnant of slavery trading. That is, with the qualification that labourers are free to choose an owner (of means of production) – they are, generally, not free to not choose an owner.[23] It may well be that the people of a few generations hence will look back on this in horror, just as we look back in horror at slavery.

1§6-b Explication. Contingency of 'self-employment'

The main text states: 'the existence of enterprises generally requires them to purchase the capacity to labour during production, in which sense they are employers of labour'. The term 'generally' implicitly refers to the *contingency* of small enterprises that do not hire any labour-capacity. Contingently a layer of self-employed labour is compatible with capitalism, which is conditioned

23 Again, as in the main text, this is predicated on the lack of means of production as including the capacity for borrowing these. (Hence the 'not being free' is a general statement; it does not rule out that some may be able to gather the means for being self-employed or to start up an enterprise; however the 'not being free' in this respect is a systemic statement; a society in which everyone were self-employed is definitely not capitalist.)

on these labourers having ownership of their means of production. As indicated in 1§1-e, in this book I refrain from characterising the type of economy we would have if this were no longer a mere compatible contingency, and instead pure self-employment had become generalised.

1§6-c Explication. 'Labour-capacity' versus 'labour'

I follow the marxian tradition which – contrary to mainstream economics – makes a strict distinction between the concepts of 'labour-capacity' and 'labour'. It is the labour-capacity, or labour potential, that is traded at the market. In contradistinction, the activity of 'labour' (some manifestation of the capacity) ensues in production at some pace and intensity (expanded on in 1§14 and 2§2). Note that Marx considered the distinction as one of his main conceptual advances. The reason is that it articulates his particular exposition of the interconnection of the capitalist production process and the labour market, which is vital to his main work *Capital*.

1§6-d Addendum. The terms 'labour-capacity' and 'labour power'

Within the marxian tradition the common term for 'capacity to labour' is 'labour power'. The latter is a translation of the German 'Arbeitskraft' that Marx uses in his mature work. Capacity to labour is rather equivalent to 'Arbeitsvermögen', the term that Marx adopts in his early work and his drafts for *Capital* (until about 1865). One reason for adopting the term 'capacity to labour' is that, in my view, the term more appropriately covers the concept (i.e. of *potential* activity). Another reason is that I will introduce later on (1§14) the term 'productive power of labour' (a refinement of labour productivity) and I would not want to have this term confused with 'labour power'.

1§7 *Inward bifurcation of commodities: the commodification of inputs and outputs 'in total'*

The capitalist commodity-form of entities – resulting from their reflected market transformation through the money medium – reveals the commodities' duality in their inward bifurcation into 'use-value' (usability) and 'monetary value'. With the exposition so far (esp. 1§5–1§6) the near total commodification of the inputs and outputs of enterprises has been presented. I say 'near' because free nature (1§1) does not take on the form of monetary value, and hence does not appear as input costs for enterprises. (Later on it will be made explicit that this can be seen as a curse rather than a blessing.)

Herewith, the exposition has reached the point where elements for a potential solution to the 'dissociated outward bifurcation' appear (1§1). However, whereas the dualities posited may seem surmountable (if not straightforwardly so) for households, dual measures deliver no determinate criterion for the production within enterprises – so far the trade of specific inputs and outputs. Hence the exposition must be expanded (1D4 below).

Division 4. Profit – duality dominated by the monetary-value dimension

1§8 ***Profit as the monistic driving force of enterprises***

The dissociated outward bifurcation entails that the physical product of enterprises is generally not destined for its producers; hence the *driving force* of enterprises must be an aim external to its physical product (1§3). With market trade, both the inputs and outputs of enterprises are constituted as dual entities: inwardly bifurcated commodities that are qualitatively homogeneous in terms of monetary value (1§4, 1§7).

The non-physical external driving force of enterprises engenders monetary value as the dominant moment of the duality. Hence the external driving force of enterprises is a positive quantitative difference between the monetary value of the commodity inputs and the commodity outputs. This difference is called profit, which is – within the duality – the dominating monistic driving force of enterprises.

Whereas incidental profit can be explained on the basis of market trade (selling a commodity at a higher price than that for which it was bought), general, or macroeconomic, profit cannot be explained on the basis of the trade of goods in the form of commodities, since trade-gains would be cancelled out by trade-losses.

Thus, although we can comprehend the significance of the drive for profit, profit itself cannot be explained at the level of the moment of market trade (1D2–1D3). Hence the exposition is still enmeshed in an 'impediment' to the continuity of the capitalist economy (cf. 1D1), whence it must expand to a new moment, which is production (1D5 below).

1§8-a Explication. Dominance of one-dimensional profit

So far the exposition has moved from outward institutional duality (outward bifurcation) to inward duality (commodification of entities). Each of the dualities is engrained in everyday capitalist life (as to the second: 'beautiful furniture you have, must be expensive'). Even if one-dimensional monetary profit drives enterprises, this is the dominant pole of the commodification. Dominance implies that the moment that is dominated (usability and physical and mental capacities) remains a moment albeit one shaped by the dominant moment.

1§8-b Explication. Profit, trade and general equilibrium theory
The argument that within a (national) economy, trade surpluses and deficits cancel each other out – and hence that a macroeconomic surplus (i.e. macroeconomic profit) cannot be explained by pure trade (1§8) – is analogous to the cancelling out of international trade surpluses and deficits.

In neoclassical General Equilibrium Theory, 'net profits' (profits after interest payment) reduce to zero due to competition. This seems to absolve that theory from the explanation of the net profits (see also Naples and Aslanbeigui 1996). However, it does not relieve the theory of the task of explaining 'gross profits' (profits before interest payment). This fails to set out if and how general equilibrium, or anything even close to it, could be a feasible capitalist constellation, because zero profits, in each of these definitions, would presumably paralyse investment. (It is quite another issue that apart from periods of severe recession, macroeconomic profits are robustly positive.)

Division 5. The capitalist production process

Labour's productive power and the appropriation of surplus-value

In this division the exposition moves from the market and the commodification of the inputs and outputs of production (1D2–1D4), to the *production process* of the outputs of enterprises – part of these serving again as inputs for other production processes.

Subdivision 5A. The general form of the capitalist production process: duality of the production process and dominance of the monetary valorisation process

1§9 ***The production process as technical process***

In the exposition of abstract sociation, I used the phrase the *creation* of entities (1§0), which, with the outward bifurcation concomitant on dissociation, was particularised as *production* (1§1). Along with this, the *activity* of creation of entities (1§0) was particularised as *labour* (1§1).

Like the activity of creation, the capitalist *production process* in its *technical* aspect is in essence a metabolism of human beings – more particularly 'labour' – with nature. The 'gift' of freely available nature is worked up by labour into means of production as products, and these together are worked up by labour into final products to be consumed.

With privately owned enterprises, means of production are privately owned (1§1). Then we may distinguish between the (still) *freely available nature*, such as sunshine, and *appropriated nature*, such as the majority of land. Appropriated nature is subsumed under the category of 'means of production' because it is traded like commodities, and functions like commodified means of production. Thus physical *production* entails *some combination of*:

• Freely available nature	worked up by	labour →	• Means of Production or • Final Product
• Freely av. nature and means of production	worked up by	labour →	• Means of Production or • Final Product

The working up by labour of nature, or of nature and means of production, is called the physical *production process*, or the technical production process A *technique* of production refers to a qualitatively and quantitatively specific combination of nature, means of production and labour alongside a qualitatively specific labour process.

1§10 *The production process as monetary valorisation process: 'ideal pre-commensuration' and the inward bifurcation of the production process*

Through the money medium in the market, the trans-abstraction of value concretely appears as the reflected transformation of entities into dual commodities (1§7).

Because trade in the market is not accidental but systematic, the abstraction of the equation of a product to some definite amount of money can be anticipated *prior* to market trade. Before the actual market trade, stocks ideally represent an amount of monetary value. The same applies for the commodities that are in the process of production, i.e. for the inputs that are being worked up by labour. Thus the actual commensuration in the market (1§5) is anticipated by an *ideal pre-commensuration*, and the transformation in the market is anticipated by an ideal transformation.

Or, to put it in slightly different terms: Only by way of the actual trade in the market do commodities show their actual value in terms of money (in that split second, so to speak). At all other times, commodities and commodities in process of production merely have an expected, or anticipated, value (i.e. value in the minds of the owners of the enterprises and the management), that is, 'ideal value'.[24]

---

24 Here and in the following section, 'management' is referred to in passing. It will be systematically introduced in Chapter 2. At the current stage of the exposition, the owners of enterprises can also be considered as the management.

Hence the multifaceted physical technical labour process is *inwardly bifurcated* into the *technical labour process* and the one-dimensional ideal monetary-value-producing process, or, in short, the ideal *valorisation process*, the production of ideal value.

Given the value of the material inputs (means of production), this ideal valorisation process thus regards the production of new, additional value, commonly called 'value-added' (expanded in 1§12).

(Generally, 'valorisation' is the production of monetary value; its production is actually validated when the output is sold on the market – 'validation' being the turning of the output into money.[25] Having made explicit, first, that valorisation always refers to monetary valorisation, and second, that during production valorisation is always 'ideal' valorisation, the remainder of this chapter uses the shorthand 'valorisation' or 'valorisation process', unless the adjectives monetary and/or ideal require emphasis.)

1§10-a Addendum. Ideal pre-commensuration

The concept of ideal pre-commensuration of production was first outlined in Reuten (1988, pp. 53–5) and Reuten and Williams (1989, pp. 66–8). This concept is of great importance for the appraisal of the capitalist production processes, because it is denied that the latter are pure technical processes of 'neutral progress'.[26] A notion of putative neutrality applies to all of mainstream economics. Viewing ideal pre-commensuration in terms of inward bifurcation – one of the major themes of the present book – makes this even more explicit.

Positively, pre-commensuration is key to the intervention in one variety of marxian theory, i.e. one that casts the production process in physical 'labour embodied' or similar terms (see Reuten 1993). Pre-commensuration clears the way for the analysis and synthesis of production in terms of monetary value.

---

25 Addendum 1§12-b offers a brief comparison of Marx's and my delineations of the term 'valorisation'.

26 When Arthur (2001, p. 22) uses the term ideal pre-commensuration, he focuses on an aspect that is alien to my meaning of the term. He writes: 'Of course it is convenient for capital if the concrete forms of labour are simple enough to make an ideal 'pre-commensuration' of the labour time determining the value it hopes to realise on the market'. This is not the point of 1§10 above, where the pre-commensuration is in terms of the monetary value realised on the market; the (non-)complexity of the physical production does not affect this.

1§11 *Dominance of the monetary valorisation process over the technical process: the inwarded drive for profit*

The production process as yet being bracketed (abstracted from), profit has so far been posited as the (within the commodity duality, dominant) monistic external driving force of enterprises, aiming at a positive quantitative difference between the monetary value of the commodity inputs and the commodity outputs (1§8).

With the inward bifurcation of the production process into technical labour process and valorisation process (1§10), the external driving force of profit (1§8) is homogeneously connected to the process of production. More precisely, the connection lies in the production process being *dominated* by one of its two bifurcated poles, that is, the *valorisation process*.[27] Thus through the monistic driving force, the dual production process is dominated by the production of ideal monetary value. Herewith the profit as external driving force (1§8) is ideally *inwarded* within the enterprise as unit of production. In other words, the external profit drive in terms of inputs and outputs (1§8) transforms into an inwarded driving force of production: the *production of ideal profit*.[28]

The inwarded drive for profit, a surplus of one-dimensional monetary value, is essential to the capitalist system. However much the market trans-abstraction (1D2, 1§4) and the market transformation and inward bifurcation of the commodity (1D3) are constituent for the inward bifurcation of capitalist production (1§10), it is the latter bifurcation together with the inwarded drive for profit that is pivotal to the capitalist system. The trans-abstraction in the market reflects on ready entities. However, *the inward bifurcation of production, together with the inwarded drive, is much more far-reaching*, to the extent that valorisation-driven production affects the human creation of entities, that is, their material make-up, their material constitution; in this way the technical labour process (1§9) is *instrumental* to the valorisation process.

Thus it is not the case that merely a 'pre-given', neutral, technical labour process is denominated in terms of ideal monetary value; rather the technical process is *devised and managed as a valorisation process* and *so affects the technical process*. Thus with the inwarded driving force, the commodity that was presented in 1D3 is 'not innocent', so to speak. Rather, the output of enterprises that was presented as *actually* trans-abstracted and transformed on the market

27 Valorisation is the generation of monetary value (cf. 1§10).

28 It is *ideal* because prior to the actual sale of commodities, we have no more than an expected value as including an expected profit (cf. 1§10).

(the value leap referred to in 1§4) – as indeed it is – is *preceded by* the capitalist *profit-driven production* as production of commodities, that is, production of ideal commodities ('ideal' before the actual leap).

Hence the necessary requirement for the production of multifaceted entities (1§0) is *overarched* by the driving force of production for one-dimensional monetary value: profit. Therefore, first, that which can be perceived – in production plants or on retail shelves – is pre-selected on the basis of the profit criterion; entities that cannot be produced profitably are simply not on offer. Second, the quality of the entities (in terms of nutrition, health, durability, environmental symbiosis) is subordinate to the quantity of one-dimensional profit.

1§11-a Explication. Potential threat of inward bifurcation of production

The main section just presented is one core of this chapter. In brief: the combination of the inward bifurcation of the commodity with the pre-commensuration means that the (now 'merely') external profit drive, in terms of inputs and outputs, transforms into an inwarded production drive, whereby production itself is affected by the monetary-value dimension.

This poses a *potential* threat to a continuous social whole (the subordination of quality in terms of nutrition, health, durability and environmental symbiosis referred to). Because it is 'merely' a *potential* threat, I methodologically absolve myself from providing a solution to it at the current level of the exposition. What is more, the (potential) problem cannot be resolved at the level of the capitalist economy pure (i.e. Part One of this book). I will return to this issue when the exposition can deal with it, that is, when the state has been introduced in Part Two (see Chapter 6).

1§11-b Explication. Linear exposition along with reinforcing simultaneity of moments

The exposition in the text of a book is inevitably linear (see the middle column of *Scheme 1.3*). In fact we have a reinforcing simultaneity of the moments as in a circuit (the dotted lines in that scheme). Similar schemes can be made for other parts of the exposition.

SCHEME 1.3 *Linear exposition along with reinforcing simultaneity of moments: 1D3–1D5A (1§5–1§11)*

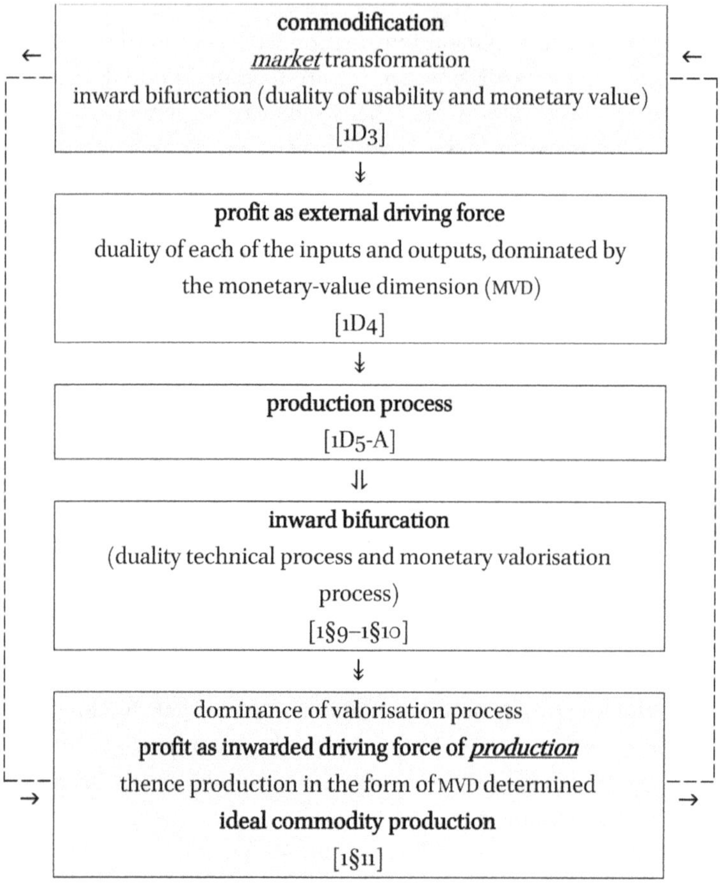

Legend
↡ grounded in (conditioned by)
⇊ implicit herein
← → reinforcing simultaneity

Subdivision 5B. Measures and determinations: surplus-value, capital as time-grasping investment, and the production of capital

1§12 *The articulation of value-added and surplus-value (integral profit)*

The result of the enterprises' valorisation (1§10) is the *value-added* in enterprises, which is the sum of all the income categories generated in enterprises. In brief, these income categories are the sum of *wages* and *surplus-value*.

So far the term 'profit' (1§8) has yet to be delineated – it was used in a rather general everyday sense of the term. This is a matter of exposition, simply because all the relevant interconnected concepts cannot be introduced at the same time. The term 'surplus-value' is the genus term for the two sub-categories of *profit* (retained and distributed) and *interest*. The latter applies to the extent that enterprises use external finance. This sub-division of surplus-value is systematically introduced in Chapters 2–3.

Next to wages the remainder of the current chapter focuses on the production of *surplus-value* because surplus-value is independent of the contingent ways in which particular enterprises finance the production.

Throughout this book the term surplus-value will be used interchangeably with the term 'integral profit' (with exactly the same meaning). The reason is simply that I need the concept of the 'rate of integral profit' (introduced in the next section), whereas for theory-historical reasons the term 'rate of surplus-value' would be confusing.[29]

Returning to the first sentence above, the *result* of the enterprises' valorisation is the *value-added* in enterprises. The latter is the starting point for what follows in this division. Thus we have:

Surplus-value ⋖ = *Value-added – wages*

(where the sign ⋖ denotes right to left hand determination).[30]

In this chapter the level of the wages is pre-posited (presented in Chapter 2). Hence given the wages level, the level of the surplus-value is determined by the value-added, that is, the valorisation. Thus, for now, the main question is the explanation of value-added (presented in 1§14), which we arrive at after the introduction of the concept of capital (1§13).

1§12-a Amplification. The concept of surplus-value and the SNA concept of 'operating surplus'

The current *System of National Accounts* 2008 (UN 2009) adopts the macroeconomic surplus concept of 'operating surplus'. The SNA starting point is output minus intermediates (purchases and sales between enterprises) and minus wages. That starting point for the operating surplus (OS) would be equival-

---

29 I would have preferred to evade the term integral profit. However, the term 'rate of surplus-value' has ineradicably been coined by Marx as a measure for the capital–labour distribution of income (more precisely, the rate of exploitation).

30 In common macroeconomic terms (SNA) the domestic value-added is defined as Y = operating surplus + wages. See 1§12-a on the distinction between operating surplus and surplus-value. Definition (=) is not the same as order of determination, for which I adopt the sign ⋖ =.

ent to our concept of surplus-value. However, the SNA also adopts a number of arbitrary imputations, which cause the two concepts to deviate (expanded in 8§6-d).

1§12-b Addendum. The term 'valorisation' in comparison with Marx's use of the term

In 1§10 I introduced the term 'valorisation'. Now that the term 'surplus-value' has been introduced (1§12), I can properly comment on my usage of the term 'valorisation'. In *Das Kapital I*, Marx makes a distinction between the *Wertbildungsprozeß* (which refers to the production/creation/generation of value) and the *Verwertungsprozeß* (which refers to the production/creation/generation of surplus-value). For the latter Marx also uses the term *Bildung von Mehrwert*.[31] The term *Verwertung* is now commonly translated by 'valorisation' (following Fowkes; see the previous footnote).

For the purposes of the current chapter I use the single term 'valorisation' for value creation (that is, the production of 'value-added'), making clear when I specifically refer to surplus-value. My main reason for this usage is methodological: in capitalism the production of surplus-value is a necessary moment; capitalist value-production is *generally* value-production as including the production of surplus-value (only contingently may this not be the case).[32] From this point of view, Marx's two terms coincide (or rather the one is sublated into the other).

1§13 ***Capital and time – the rate of integral profit and standard time***

Both the inputs and outputs of enterprises are constituted as dual entities: inwardly bifurcated commodities that are qualitatively homogeneous in terms of monetary value (1§4, 1§7). The enterprises' driving force of profit, aiming at a positive quantitative difference between the monetary value of the commodity inputs and the commodity outputs (1§8), is constituted as an inwarded production of ideal profit (1§11) further specified as integral profit, or surplus-value (1§12).

31 Marx's German terms are somewhat idiosyncratic and for each of these terms there is no simple English translation. Here are some page references. Marx, *Das Kapital I* (1962 [1867^1; 1890^4]), p. 171 and p. 209; Fowkes translations: Marx, *Capital I* (1976 [1867^1; 1890^4]), p. 259 and p. 302.

32 Marx in fact introduces the capitalist necessity of surplus-value via its contingent negation.

1 Capital and time

On the basis of divisions 1D2–1D5A we can now identify the enterprises' inputs to production under their common empirical names of 'investment' and 'capital'. One aspect of active 'capital' is the *monetary value* of the enterprises' investment in physical inputs for production – inputs that themselves are constituted as dimensionally dual inputs. However, the developed concept of capital also incorporates 'time', that is, the duration of the production process and so the duration of investments. Thus capitalist production entails not 'merely' its grasping of 'usability' under the dominating monetary value-form; it also entails its grasping of time under 'production time'. Efficient process management in terms of valorisation (as quantity of value) is twinned with efficient process management in terms of production time, as distinct from any other time. (When a feudal farmer, after much hard work, takes the corn harvest to the miller during a quiet three-hour horse and carriage ride, this activity is not obviously perceived as work rather than rest.) In the economics discourse 'efficiency' is often something of a catch-all term. Unless otherwise stated I use the term to mean 'profit-geared efficiency'.

2 Contingent time span of physical-technical production processes

Given this production process efficiency in its twinned aspects (quantity of monetary value and duration), production is nevertheless chained to the moment of a *physical-technical* production process and its duration. In particular, surplus-value is gained on the investment of inputs for the specific technical length of time of various particular 'singular production processes' (of wheat, computers, pens, etc., taking a number of months, weeks or less than an hour, as the case may be). That is, surplus-value seems chained to the contingent pace of physical-technical production, even if this is subsumed under valorisation. In principle this 'singular-process-integral-profit' (spp) can be calculated per the amount of 'singular-process-inputs' (spi) at some rate – that is, (spp)/(spi).[33] However, the different duration of the singular processes in different branches of production (or perhaps also within the same branch) means that (spp)/(spi) is insufficient as a measure for the comparison of achievements between enterprises. Thus this measure provides no criterion for *what* physical commodities are most profitable to produce.

---

33 This is how Marx initiates his exposition of the production of surplus-value in *Capital I*, getting to turnover times of capital in the second part of *Capital II*. What I present in the next subsection (3) is what Marx, *qua field* of exposition, presents in the second part of *Capital III*.

3 *Capital and surplus-value as constituted relative to standard time*

The total 'active capital' (K) consists of, first, the enterprise's investment in inputs for production and, second, the running valorisation – the latter being co-materialised in the ideal monetary value of half products and not yet validated output stocks. This capital can, in principle, be measured at each point in time, as reported on an enterprise's balance sheet (see explication 1§13-a). The latter is captured in the notion of 'active capital' adopted henceforth, which, to be sure, is a sum of one-dimensional monetary value. So as to overcome the insufficiency alluded to under point 2, the duration of capital investment – instead of measuring it relative to the rhythm of physical production – is established relative to a conventional standard time: the calendar year (from now on indicated by subscript t).

Then the standardised *total* integral profit (pi, Π_t) is the summation over a year of the integral profits gained in each singular production process during the year.

Along with it, the integral-profit-driven production is purified in the measure of the *integral-profit-rate of capital* as unchained from the rhythm of physical production. This is the rate of the integral profit gained during the year, and measured at the end of the year, over the capital invested at the beginning of the year (omega, ω):

$$\omega_t = \Pi_t / K_{t'} \qquad (1.1)$$

(where the subscript t indicates the end of year t, and t′ indicates the beginning of year t). Note that Π_t is a flow and $K_{t'}$ a stock.

Thus capital and the production of integral profit (i.e. surplus-value) is constituted as unity of investment, valorisation and standard time. The rate of integral profit per standard time (ω_t) is the purified criterion for what, and how, physical commodities are most profitably produced. Ultimately each of the particular commodity that is produced, and how it is produced, is merely instrumental for the generation of the thus measured optimal rate of integral profit.

1§13-a Explication. Active capital: simplified balance sheet of enterprises

Whereas capital has the monetary-value dimension, it is *not* money. Most of the time, i.e. during production, it exists in a state of ideal value (cf. 1§10). This is revealed on the enterprises' balance sheet (*Figure 1.4*), which in fact expresses the 'state' of capital at the point in time of the report.[34]

---

34 This value ideality of capital poses a major problem for enterprises, statistical bureaus, the science of economics, and the business press. The values stated are book values. This

FIGURE 1.4 *Simplified balance sheet of an enterprise (per some specific date)*

Assets (active side)		**Liabilities (passive side)**	
Plant and fixed equipment	....	Capital‡	....
Raw materials and current equipment ('floating' means of production)	....		
Production in process	....		
Ready product	....		
Bank account (+/–)†	....		
Total active capital	K	Total passive capital	K

† Introduced in Chapter 2. (In fact this entry is no active capital; generally it cancels out when bank loans are taken into account, also introduced in that chapter).

‡ This entry abstracts from the way of finance – introduced in Chapter 3. (Provisionally the entry may be conceived of as one in which all finance is internal finance, as might contingently be the case).

1§13-b Explication. Equalities and equality signs in this book

An equality is always an equality in terms of a particular dimension and standard (this applies for any applied mathematics generally). Let euro (€) be the monetary standard. Then the monetary-value dimension in terms of € may be denoted as **mv€**. Precision requires that we always write, for example:

$M =_{mv€} C$

i.e. M is equal to C 'in the monetary-value dimension with the standard measure of €' (see Ellis 1968, p. 25). Henceforth in this book, and unless otherwise indicated, the symbols of > of = and of < always mean, respectively, 'greater in mv€', 'equal in mv€', and 'less in mv€' (or any other monetary standard).

1§14 *Appropriation of the productive power of labour*

The generalised explanation of (integral) profit requires the movement from the market to production (1§8). Regarding production as a physical-technical process, labour works up freely available nature as well appropriated means of production – the latter including appropriated nature (1§9). The next sections show how production itself takes on the monet-

issue will be a major theme throughout Part One of this book, and especially in Chapter 3. This will also be crucial in further, more concrete, determinations of the relation between Finance Capital and Production Capital (Ch. 3) and of economic crises (Ch. 5).

ary value-form and how the technical process is dominated by the valorisation process and the profit drive (1§10–1§11), 'the rate of integral profit over capital invested' being the quantitative criterion for the achievement (1§13).

On this basis I now return to the question of the explanation of valorisation, that is, the explanation of value-added and the surplus-value accruing to enterprises (1§12). In short, this section provides the *grounding* of the existence of value-added and of surplus-value. I note that until subsection 7, the equations in this section are microeconomic (referring to an average enterprise).

1 Costs of production and output

Production is the transformation of inputs into outputs. The capitalist production process is accounted in terms of monetary value quantities and quantities of labour. I consider first the following main input and output quantities and quantitative relations. (Note that this subsection is somewhat tedious on account of the introduction of a number of new symbols).

- L_t denotes the average number of workers employed during the year (in terms of the going full-time equivalent). The labour process, and hence L_t, is considered as a whole and includes the work around purchases and sales.
- L_t is hired against a wage rate w. Hence wL_t is the wages sum.
- K_t denotes the yearly average amount of capital in terms of monetary value, measured as the assets of the enterprise's balance sheet (see 1§13-a, *Figure 1.4*). The assets include the fixed means of production, the floating means of production (as including input stocks – raw materials) and output stocks.[35] In this chapter I pre-posit the existing amount of capital as previously accumulated and invested in production. (This pre-position will be grounded in 3D4.) K_t is the amount of capital that can, on average, be operated by labour at each point of labour-time during the year.
- δK_t is the value of the fixed assets *used up* during the year. These are expressed as a fraction (δ, e.g. ⅕) of the total assets K. Fixed assets are those that last for more than one year. (Usually these used up assets are also replaced during the year.)[36]
- μK_t denotes the value of the floating means of production used up during a year. These are expressed as a coefficient (μ) of the total assets K. Floating means of production last less than one year, and these are purchased during

35 In the literature, the floating means of production (including input stocks) and the output stocks are also called 'working assets' or 'current assets'.

36 Replacement, non-replacement and depreciation are expanded on in Chapters 4 and 5.

the year. However, a part of these also appears on the balance sheet as stocks (used and replaced) as a continuous investment. (Therefore, and unlike δ, μ is usually not a fraction of K. However, μ is like δ a 'technical coefficient', their sizes being determined by the technique adopted.) Macroeconomically μK is also denoted as the 'intermediate inputs'.[37]

- δK_t and μK_t are more precisely to be measured as coefficients of the beginning of the year total assets $K_{t'}$. In what follows I neglect this, as it would make the notation of the equations below cumbersome.
- Π_t (pi) denotes the surplus-value produced during the year.
- X_t denotes the year's output of production.
- Except the stock of K_t (or $K_{t'}$) all these variables above (including δK_t and μK_t) are flows.

Taking these together we have:

$$X_t \triangleleft = [(\delta + \mu)K + wL + \Pi]_t \qquad (1.2)$$

(Where the sign $\triangleleft$ denotes that the determination is from the right hand side to the left hand side.)

This (1.2) is a costs and revenue equation, *after* production has taken place. The question is how the surplus-value (Π) emerges. Before we have this result (1.2), in the early mornings so to speak, there is the enterprise that has yet to open its gates, at value 'K'. At the gate of the enterprise we merely have the *labour-capacity* L. When the gate opens, and the production process begins, this labour-capacity is exerted as actual *labour*, which I denote as L^{α}, as further explained below.

2 *Means of production in the form of capital*

Production considered purely technically is the working up of nature and means of production by labour (1§9). Although freely available nature contributes to production, it has no price; it is freely available to all enterprises and therefore does not enter production prices, hence it is neglected in capitalist practice: it has no monetary value.[38] Considering nature, it is only *appropriated* nature that, commodity-like, is traded and so has a price. Because for enterprises the distinction between appropriated nature and produced means of production is immaterial, I subsume the former under the latter.

---

37 The latter is the term usually adopted in macroeconomic accounts (cf. UN 2009, SNA 2008).

38 Perhaps the policy of the state might somehow enforce enterprises to mimic a price for the use of non-appropriated nature. However, the state has not yet been introduced into the exposition (see Part Two).

Means of production derive their value from the process of production in which they were produced.[39] They provide no value-added; rather they represent previous value-added, namely from the valorisation processes in which they have been produced previously.[40] At the current level of the exposition, the input prices of means of production are taken as given (amplified in 4D2 and 4D3).

3 *Labour-capacity*

In contradistinction to means of production, 'labour' is not produced in the past, as it is the activity of production itself. If anything, it is labour-capacity that is "produced" previously. But the key point is that whilst labour-capacity is grasped by the monetary-value dimension (the wage), it is not 'produced' within the capitalist sphere of production as a commodity. Rather, it is *created* within the sphere of households (1§1). The price of labour-capacity (i.e. the wage) does not represent previous value-added and it has nothing to do with the 'price of production' of labour-capacity.[41] At the current level of the exposition, I take the wage, the price of labour-capacity, as given (its determinants are amplified in 2D2).

4 *Production: exertion of labour*

In terms of valorisation (the production of value) the main distinction between means of production (K) and labour-capacity (L) is that the former is inherently a ***static*** element in the production process in which it functions, whereas labour-capacity in operation, i.e. labour (L^{α}), is the ***active*** element. Means of production can merely be operated or not be operated. Within the agreed amount of labour-time, labour-capacity operates means of production, and so exerts labour at some productive power (α), including a component of the intensity of labour. At zero intensity (in effect a strike) there is no production of value. Hence only labour potentially generates value-added.

---

39 Quite another matter is that the property of, or the command over, any (temporarily) absolutely scarce element of production can always give rise to rent. I return to rent in Chapter 3 (Appendix 3c).

40 Nevertheless, it is the *current ideal value* of means of production (as related to the current cost price of similar means of production) that is in all or in part transmitted in the current production process (cf. 4§7).

41 Labour-capacity is *created* in the private sphere of the household; what is involved is the activity of procreation – it is not produced with a view to sale. It is created within the household sphere, and used (exerted labour) in enterprises; (final) commodities are produced within enterprises and used within households. The fact that skilled labour-capacity may have a higher price than the non-skilled is besides the main point that children are not produced for sale and hence do not have an actual price of production.

Take the case of a (nowadays apparently fascinating) ready-made robot as means of production, and imagine that it requires hardly any operation by labour. That robot (as with any other means of production, as indicated under 2) derives its value from the process of production in which it was produced. Assuming for the sake of simplicity that the robot would require no current inputs at all, then the output value of the robot (X^R) reduces to its purchase costs, whence there is no value-added. If the robot is not ready-made (and so requires adaptation within the current process of production), then the current operation by labour comes in again.[42] (With some amendments about current costs, in respect of *value* there is no fundamental difference between robots and the early nineteenth-century use in production of horses – with apologies to the horses – and indeed between robots and any other means of production.)

Fascinating, generally, is not so much the actual use of 'K' in current production, but rather the previous production of new means of production and hence the human creation of new technology and new technical applications of it – which are creations by labour.

5 *Production: components of the productive power of labour*

I just mentioned the productive power of labour and the intensity of labour. I make a distinction between the actual labour as exerted at some technique-associated productive power ($\acute{\alpha}$), and the actual labour as exerted at some intensity of labour ($\ddot{\iota}$, iota). As such we have $\alpha = (\acute{\alpha})*(\ddot{\iota})$ and

$$L^{\alpha} = L^{\acute{\alpha}\ddot{\iota}} \qquad (1.3)^{43}$$

Note that α, $\acute{\alpha}$ and $\ddot{\iota}$ are exponents (not indices). Thus α is, *qua* content and mathematically, the power to which L is raised.[44]

6 *Technique of production, the 'productive power of labour', the 'unit monetary value of labour' and the rate of integral profit*

A technique of production refers to a qualitatively and quantitatively specific combination of nature, means of production and labour together with a qual-

---

42 The same applies if the sales and transport of the robot output are themselves not robotised – that would again involve a production process.

43 This concerns what Marx, in *Capital I*, chapter 1, calls 'concrete labour' (1976 [1867[1], 1890[4]], p. 128).

44 Mathematically this implies decreasing returns to scale. The economic rationale is that given a technique of production and the associated α and $\acute{\alpha}$, there are increasingly limits to the potential intensity of labour: at some point the intensity of labour cannot be increased any further.

itatively specific labour process, resulting in an output (1§9). For different commodities this physical output is no more than an intuitive notion because these cannot reasonably be added up (1D2–1D3 and 1§10).

At the start of the production process 'K' is the value of the production plant and equipment when workers have just entered the premises' gates, without yet having worked. Even if the production process is dominated by monetary value and valorisation (1§11), it necessarily also remains a physical-technical process. In the actual production process, labour physically works up the plant and equipment to something qualitatively different (the physical output). This qualitative transformation is one aspect of labour's power. The other aspect is the quantitative valorising transformation. Alpha (α) is the 'parameter' of transformation: the productive power of labour in both these respects.

On the basis of the previous argument (points 2–5), equation 1.2 can now be concretised into:

$$X_t \triangleleft = [(\delta + \mu)K + mL^{\alpha}]_t \quad (1.4)$$

where mL^{α} has the dimension of homogeneous monetary value.[45] I call mL^{α} the *actual monetary value of labour*, with 'm' being the *actual unit monetary value of labour*. (Practically 'm' measures the validation, the sale, of the net product of labour).[46] Note that mL^{α} includes the equivalent of the wages component wL.

Thus given K and the implied (potential) technique of production, with the technical coefficients δ and μ, the net value-added (mL^{α}) is determined by the productive power of labour (α) as resulting in the actual monetary value produced by labour. So we have for 'surplus-value' or 'integral profit' (pi, Π):

$$\Pi_t \triangleleft = mL^{\alpha}_t - wL_t \quad (1.5)$$

Whereas K, the means of production that have been purchased, constrains *possible production*, the power of labour (α) determines how much output is actually produced. This is *the* big leap in a capitalist economy. The implication is that labour – more specifically, the actual productive power of labour – is the unique source of valorisation. Nevertheless this productive power is always based on the actual technique of production. Technology and its application in specific techniques is inevitably the result of social labour. (Choices of particular techniques are driven by competitive forces, amplified in Chapter 4.) Further, the productive power of labour usually diverges between sectors of

---

45 This is analogous to what Marx calls 'abstract labour' (in the same reference as in the one but last note).

46 If this is helpful for the reader: at this point 'm' can be considered as the realised price of the net product of labour. I return to this in more detail in Chapter 3 (3§10).

production as well as within sectors of production, along with differing techniques of production.[47]

Finally on this point, using equations 1.1 and 1.5, we have for the rate of integral profit (1§13):

$$\omega_t = \Pi_t \,/\, K_{t'} = [(mL^{\alpha})_t - (wL)_t] \,/\, K_{t'} \qquad (1.6)$$

Thus given K, L and the technique, the rate of integral profit (ω) varies with the wage rate (w) and the productive power of labour (α).

7 *The production of capital*

Neglecting for now any distribution of surplus-value (and hence consumption out of surplus-value by capital owners – presented in Chapter 3), it follows from the exposition above that capitalist production, as dominated by valorisation, results in essence in a growth of capital (amplified in 2D1):

$$K_{t'} + \Pi_t = \blacktriangleright K_t \text{ or}$$

$$K_{t'} + \Delta K_{t'} = \blacktriangleright K_t$$

Because it is labour that produces the surplus-value (Π) and hence any growth of capital, *labour essentially produces capital* – the owners of capital claiming the entitlement to its appropriation (amplified in 6D1).

8 *Measures of value-added*

We had, for what I now explicitly call *gross* production:

$$X_t \blacktriangleleft = [(\delta + \mu)K + wL + \Pi]_t \qquad (1.2)$$

and next:

$$X_t \blacktriangleleft = [(\delta + \mu)K + mL^{\alpha}]_t \qquad (1.4)$$

For gross value-added, Y^G (macroeconomically, GDP) we have:[48]

$$Y^G{}_t \blacktriangleleft = [\delta K + mL^{\alpha}]_t \qquad (1.7)$$

For *net* value-added (macroeconomically, NDP):

$$Y_t \blacktriangleleft = [mL^{\alpha}]_t \qquad (1.8)$$

---

47 Because α in L^{α} is a technique-associated power (in its component of $\acute{\alpha}$), α varies between sectors of production (expanded in 2§2). In Chapter 4 (4§4) we will see that α usually also differs within sectors of production, though within smaller margins.

48 In a macroeconomic account, all microeconomic enterprises are by convention taken to be integrated into one single enterprise. This implies (assuming a self-sufficient macroeconomic constellation) that the intermediate deliveries between enterprises cancel out. (*One* reason for this convention is that the thus measured 'output' is independent of the actual degree of enterprises' merging.) In terms of the equations above, this especially implies $\mu = 0$. (Note that for current economies μK often amounts to roughly the sum of the GDP thus the sum of the microeconomic production being very roughly twice the sum of the macroeconomic production.)

Note that the previous equations can be applied both macroeconomically and microeconomically (for individual enterprises or for sectors of production) – for the latter, as indicated, both α and m may diverge within and between sectors of production.

1§14-a Explication. Market- and production-related concepts of labour

A strict distinction has been made between 'labour-capacity' and 'labour' (see 1§6, 1§6-c, 1§6-d and 1§14). *Table 1.5* summarises this in comparison with orthodox economics and marxian political economy (MPE).

TABLE 1.5 *Summary of the distinction between market- and production-related concepts of labour*

	Orthodox economics	Conventional marxian PE	This chapter
• distinction market- and production-related concepts of labour	no	yes	yes
• market concept of labour	labour (L)	labour-power (L)	labour-capacity (L)
• market value of labour(-...)	wL	wL	wL
• production concept of labour	labour (L) (= market concept)	labour (L) = labour-power exerted as labour	labour (L^{α}) = labour-capacity exerted as labour, at a certain production power (α)
• surplus (VA = value-added) (SV = surplus-value)	OS = VA – wL†	SV = mL – wL ‡ (mL = value-added)	SV = mL^{α} – wL‡ (mL^{α} = value-added)

† OS = operating surplus. It is explained by the so-called 'productivity of capital' or by 'waiting with consumption', sometimes in combination with managerial labour as a separate labour category. (See also Naples and Aslanbeigui 1996).

‡ See also 1§14-c.

1§14-b Addendum. Smith, Marshall and Keynes on labour and profits

To conceive of only labour as potentially creative of value-added (1§14) has nothing to do with the question of whether or not profits are necessary within the capitalist system. For Adam Smith (1776), for example, profits are necessary. At the same time he leaves no doubt that labour is the source of value-added and hence of profit:

> 'Thus, the labour of a manufacturer adds, generally, to the value of the materials which he works upon, that of his own maintenance, and of his master's profit. ... Though the manufacturer has his wages advanced to

> him by his master, he, in reality, costs him no expense, the value of those wages being generally restored, together with a profit, in the improved value of the subject upon which his labour is bestowed'.
>
> SMITH 1776[49]

However, for Marshall – one of the founders of neoclassical economics – as well as many neoclassical economists after him, capital is asserted to be productive, though not on capital immanent grounds, but rather because without its (presumed) productivity there would be no 'justification' (!) for profit:

> 'It is not true that the spinning of yarn in a factory, after allowance has been made for the wear-and-tear of the machinery, is the product of the labour of the operatives. It is the product of their labour, together with that of the employer and subordinate managers, and of the capital employed; and that capital itself is the product of labour and waiting: and therefore the spinning is the product of labour of many kinds and of waiting. If we *admit* that it is the product of labour alone, and not of labour and waiting, we can no doubt be compelled by inexorable logic to admit that there is no *justification* for Interest, the reward of waiting; for the conclusion is implied in the premiss'.
>
> MARSHALL 1972 [1890[1]], p. 587; emphasis added

The point to be stressed is not so much the odd concept of waiting which is somehow physically productive, but that 'justification' should be the reason for providing the argument.

Here follow two excerpts from what Keynes (1936) has to say on the issue:

> 'It is much preferable to speak of capital as having a yield over the course of its life in excess of its original cost, than as being *productive*. For the only reason why an asset offers a prospect of yielding during its life services having an aggregate value greater than its initial supply price is because it is *scarce*; and it is kept scarce because of the competition of the rate of interest on money. If capital becomes less scarce, the excess yield will diminish, without its having become less productive – at least in the physical sense.
>
> I sympathise, therefore, with the pre-classical doctrine [i.e. prior to Marshall *c.s.*, i.e. what is now called classical political economy] that everything is *produced* by *labour*, aided by what used to be called art and is now called technique, by natural resources which are free or cost a rent according to their scarcity or abundance, and by the results of past labour, embodied in assets, which also command a price according to

49 Smith 1776, Book II, Ch. 3, section 1; see also e.g. Book I, Ch. 8, sections 7–8.

> their scarcity or abundance. It is preferable to regard labour, including, of course, the personal services of the entrepreneur and his assistants, as the sole factor of production, operating in a given environment of technique, natural resources, capital equipment and effective demand'.
>
> KEYNES 1936, pp. 213–14
>
> 'Interest to-day rewards no genuine sacrifice … The owner of capital can obtain interest because capital is scarce. But … there are no intrinsic reasons for the scarcity of capital'.
>
> KEYNES 1936, p. 376

In Chapter 3 we will see why there is no intrinsic reason for a scarcity of capital.

1§14-c Addendum. Comparison of the main text with conventional marxian theory

I begin with a brief reference to Marx's *Capital I*, Chapter 1. If we could abstract from the duality of capitalist commodity production (in fact we cannot), L^{α} could be viewed as a vector of 'concrete labour' in the process of producing heterogeneous goods (useful entities). Given the actual duality, Marx's concept of what he calls 'abstract labour' is commodity-*value* producing labour (one pole of the duality).[50] My mL^{α} is analogous to the latter, after Marx's introduction of money as the actual measure of value (*Capital I*, Chapter 3). I note three issues. First, the dimension of mL^{α} is monetary. Second, after Marx has introduced the measure of money, his term 'abstract labour' disappears in *Capital*. Third, in *Capital I*, Parts One to Three, Marx considers averages (the average enterprise and average capital and labour); therefore here my α is not prominent (Marx considers here 'socially average' – also called 'socially necessary' – labour-time).[51] See Reuten 2017 about Marx's dynamic exposition in this respect in Part Four and after.

I now compare the exposition in 1§14 with conventional marxian theory, focusing on three main issues.

(*1*) *Labour as the unique source of valorisation* (*1§14, heading* 6). I argued why labour is the unique source of valorisation. In conventional marxian theory, labour has also been put forward as the unique element of the process of value creation. However, this has most often been argued for on the basis of some 'labour-embodied' theory of value. The argument in 1§14 posits the uniqueness of labour without any recourse to labour-embodied. (Indeed, the argument that only labour potentially creates value-added should in no way be read to

50 Marx 1976 [1867¹, 1890⁴], p. 128.

51 Ibid., p. 129.

imply that value-added is in some way proportional to labour-time as a labour-embodied theory of value would have it. The key point is that α is a variable at both the microeconomic and the macroeconomic level; and that α usually diverges between and within sectors of production.) The uniqueness of labour as presented in 1§14 is no reason for calling that a 'labour theory of value'. Rather, I have presented a *monetary theory of value* (1D2). However, it is correct to characterise the exposition of 1§14 as a *labour theory of surplus-value (integral profit)* – further amplified in the next chapters. Note that within the framework of a 'labour-embodied theory of value' my term 'value of labour' belongs to the negative heuristic (in the sense of Lakatos 1970).

(2) *The price of labour-capacity (1§14, heading 3).* The thesis that the price of the capacity to labour (i.e. the wage) has nothing to do with the 'price of production' of labour-capacity, and that these terms are indeed incompatible, appears very un-marxian.[52] The determination of the wage is amplified in 2D2.

(3) *The productive power of labour (L^α) and the 'unit monetary value of labour' (m), in the context of net value-added (1§14, heading 8).* Recall the equation for net value-added:

$$Y_t \lessdot = [mL^\alpha]_t \qquad (1.8)$$

This is a development and re-conceptualisation of an equation presented in a path-breaking work by Aglietta (1979 [1976], pp. 43–4). He writes (in a different notation for Y and L):

$$m = Y/L \qquad (1.8A)$$

calling m 'the monetary expression of the working hour'. He next emphasises that this equation is not a definition, but rather '*the monetary constraint*' for the realisation of value (i.e. the sale of commodities). I agree with his view about m, and will return to this in Chapter 3 (3D5). However, after Aglietta, equation 1.8A became fashionable among a strand in marxian political economy (e.g. via the works of Lipietz 1985 and Foley 1986),[53] and 'm' came to be called the 'monetary expression of labour-time' (MELT), *with the constraint aspect moving to the background*, though maintaining equation (1.8A) in varying notations.

Here I merely stress the fundamental difference between these equations in the terms L versus L^α. This is not about a simple mathematical point of the difference between the two equations being that the second (i.e. MELT) has α=1. Instead, all the MELT conceptualisations neglect the varying productive power of labour between sectors of production (and often there is a homogeneous

52 Marx at least seems to have had in mind something like a price of production of labour-capacity, as he conceives the wage related to the 'reproduction of labour-power' ('labour power', i.e. in our terminology, the capacity to labour).

53 See also Foley 2005.

labour and a labour-embodied notion behind this – e.g. Moseley 2005, esp. p. 3). Thus this concerns not a simplification (α=1), but rather a non-distinction.[54] Even further, as far as I know, this distinction has never been made within marxian political economy, or in mainstream economics.[55]

Anticipating Chapter 4 I mention that sector-wise relatively high K/L ratios are usually associated with relatively high productive powers of labour ($\alpha > 1$) and vice versa ($\alpha < 1$). In fact an expected rise in the productive power of labour is a *condition* for the introduction of K/L rising techniques (addendum 4§4-d).

1§14-d Addendum. Capitalist production of babies and labour-capacity – speculative remarks

Aldous Huxley's story in *Brave New World* is nowadays less of a fiction than it was at the time of its writing (1932). It is technically possible to produce babies in a capitalist production process and also to raise these to fit labour-capacity. The question is whether and when this could be profitable (and legally permitted). If this would be the case, then a self-contained circuit would be constructed in which it costs (aggregated) less than one hour of labour to produce the capacity for one hour of labour. As a result, labour-capacity would become an intermediate output and input, and the value of labour would reduce to zero. Hence with such an annexation of the 'creation'/'production' of labour-capacity, the source of value-added would disappear. Along with it, capitalism would disappear (cf. Reuten and Williams 1989, p. 90).

Subdivision 5C. Grounding (sublation) of the dissociated outward bifurcation

1§15 *The capitalist mode of production as solution to the dissociative 'provision of the material elements for survival' by enterprises*

Given that a form of material 'production' (generally: transformative activity) is indispensable for the survival of any society, the capitalist outward bifurcation into households and privately owned enterprises

54 This has nothing to do with the MELT being applied either micro- or macroeconomically. Reconsider the following equation, now interpreted as macroeconomic (but for what follows, the microeconomic case is no different):

$$\Pi_t \lessdot = mL^{\alpha}{}_t - wL_t \qquad (1.5)$$

For the sake of argument, assume m, L and w to be constant, with α being normalised to α=1 (which is implicitly the case for the MELT approach). In this case a rise in Π (integral profit) could not be explained because an increasing intensity of labour ($\ddot{\iota}$) or a technique-associated rise in the productive power of labour ($\acute{\alpha}$) escapes from view.

55 However, it is very interesting that Marx, in a neglected chapter of *Capital I* (in Part Four, chapter 10 of the German edition, chapter 12 in the English edition), first makes the dis-

> **appears as dissociative and hence utmost problematical** (1D1). ***The enterprises' dissociative production*** appears as resolved (sublated) in the grounds (conditions of existence) of the monetary-value dimension, commodification and the dominance of the enterprises' profit drive (1D2–1D4).

However, the enterprises' profit – more precisely surplus-value (1§12) – must be produced. One main condition for the production of surplus-value is that the 'physical-technical labour process' is grasped as a 'valorisation process' and be dominated by the latter in face of the production of surplus-value (1§9–1§11). Along with it, 'capital' is constituted as the monetary value-form of the enterprises' investment in the inwardly bifurcated inputs for production, and as twinned with the grasping of time under production time. Posited relative to standard time the 'rate of integral profit on capital' is the purified criterion for the successful production of surplus-value (1§13). The so far final condition (ground) for the production of surplus-value is the enterprises' absorption of the productive power of labour as taking on the form of valorisation – the production of the value-added. Given the wages, labour so produces the surplus-value and hence essentially produces capital (1§14).

Herewith the enterprises' dissociative production appears as resolved (sublated) in labour's production of surplus-value, which, along with the enterprises appropriating the surplus-value, satisfies the enterprises' driving force.

Although some major problems for the reproduction of the capitalist bifurcated economy now seem resolved, we will see in the following chapters that the resolution reached so far requires further conditions to be met.

1§15-a Addendum. General comparison of Chapter 1 with Marx's *Capital*

In terms of the *systematic* of Marx's *Capital*, this chapter covers the *fields* of, roughly, Parts One and Two of each of the three volumes of *Capital* (together about 675 pages).[56] Thus although we have in each case a movement from the abstract-general to the concrete-specific, the order is nevertheless different. Theoretically this chapter adopts a value-form approach emphasising the 'monetary-value dimension' taken on by entities within the capitalist system. Next to a particular bifurcation dialectic, the chapter presents theoretical progress on six issues.

---

tinction, but later (in Part Five of the book) provides an averages account in which the distinction is levelled out (discussed in Reuten 2017 and 2018).

56 Volume I, Chapters 1–6 (Chapters 1–4 in the German edition); Volume II, Chapters 1–17; Volume III, Chapters 1–12.

(1) A development of the 'monetary value-form' theoretic approach for all of the fields mentioned (building on my earlier work when I used the brief term 'value-form' with the same meaning – cf. 1§5-d).
(2) A refinement of the interconnection of value and money (1D2).
(3) The concept of ideal pre-commensuration and its effect on production (1§10) – building on my earlier work.
(4) A re-conceptualisation of 'capital' as ideal monetary value, constituted relative to standard time, from the first introduction of 'capital' onwards (1§13). (This conceptualisation is only remotely connected to Marx's and marxian ideas of the circuit of a 'singular process' capital (1§13, point 2) – which does not imply that the latter can be dispensed with in other contexts).
(5) A particular exposition of labour as the unique source of surplus-value, in connection with the 'productive power of labour' (1§14).
(6) Points (1), (4) and (5) together imply that there is no general rate of profit related 'transformation problem', because my point of departure is 'full capital' rather than Marx's 'singular process' capital (which, in my view, is an embryonic conception of capital).[57] In his exposition Marx postpones the concept of the rate of profit until *Capital III*, Part One. In my view, because the rate of integral profit (ω_t) is essential at an abstract-general level (one that abstractly captures the totality of the capitalist economy), it must be presented early on.

These are also major interventions in much current marxian theory. (In order to keep this book within a reasonable length, I have refrained from extensive references to the current literature. Whilst it is straightforward enough to insert brief critical references when needed, it would take much more space to do justice to the authors.)

Summary and conclusions

This chapter presents a first and abstract-general exposition of the capitalist economy, focusing on its mode of production. The starting point is its appearance in empirical reality of the outward bifurcation – the institutional separation – between, on the one hand, households that are the site of consumption and of the pro-creation of labour-capacity and, on the other hand, privately owned enterprises in which the production is carried out. This constellation is

57 Its problems are most transparent in Marx's draft text for *Capital*, Volume II, Part Two, on the 'Turnover of Capital'.

posited as dissociative even if we know that in reality the bifurcated poles are in some way bridged. The object of the exposition is to comprehend the range of this dissociation and the extent of its actual resolution. (Division 1.)

The poles of the outward bifurcation are apparently bridged via the trade relation. However, the inherently multifaceted dimensions of goods and capacities require commensuration in terms of a common denominator. The latter derives from the everyday market 'trans-abstraction' that ascribes to goods and capacities the super-sensuous dimension of 'value' as mediated by money – money, which itself has no inherent content or value. Entities are made commensurate in terms of this super-sensuous dimension that we 'know' only through money as its quantifier, a quantifier whose guise is insignificant. The market interaction so constitutes goods and capacities as commodities, that is, as dual (or inwardly bifurcated) entities – duality along the multifaceted dimensions of usability, on the one hand, and the mono-dimension of monetary value, on the other.

The monetary-value dimension and the commodification of goods and labour-capacity determine the market-interconnection of the poles, the enterprises being driven by monetary profit. The market-interconnection engenders 'merely' the duality of things and capacities. (Divisions 2–4.)

This 'mere' duality becomes serious when the production in enterprises is considered in face of the mono-drive of monetary profit. The latter then is concretely dominant in respect of what is (not) produced and how it is (not) produced. It affects what counts and what does not count. Astonishingly the super-sensuousness of the monetary value of things and capacities affects their sensuous being and coming into being. As such sensuous physical-technical production becomes a mere instrument for valorisation – the production of monetary value, or value-added. So much for the general form of the capitalist production process. (Subdivision 5A.)

However, this general form lacks a criterion for determining what instrumental guise – namely what physical commodity and what physical technique – is most efficacious for profit.

This requires: first, a common measure for the amount of investments, which is 'capital'; secondly, the grasping of time of investment as 'production time'; and thirdly, a measure for the duration of capital investment in terms of a standard time, which is the calendar year. The profit – more precisely the surplus-value – gained during a year, over a year's capital investment, that is, the 'rate of integral profit', delivers the criterion. (Metaphorically: the end 'omega'.)[58]

58 Apocalypse 21:6. https://www.tldm.org/bible/new testament/apoc.htm.

Given the enterprises' profit drive, the production must encompass the equivalent of the value-added component of profit. Even if the general form of the capitalist production process is dominated by monetary value and valorisation, it necessarily also remains a physical-technical process, hence it remains a dual process. Within this duality the main distinction between means of production and *labour-capacity* (L) is that the former are inherently *static* elements, whereas labour-capacity in operation, that is *labour* (L^{α}), is the *active* element. Means of production can merely be operated or not be operated. Labour-capacity operates means of production, and so exerts labour at the level of some productive power (α), including a component of the intensity of labour. At zero intensity (in effect a strike) there is no production, either physical or through valorisation. Hence, along with its physical production, labour creates the (yet ideal) value and so also the surplus-value (integral profit). Thus alpha (α) is the 'parameter' of the productive transformation: the productive power of labour in both these aspects. (Metaphorically: the beginning 'alpha'.)[59]

Whereas capital constrains the *possible production*, the power of labour (α) determines how much output is actually produced. The implication is that labour – more specifically, the actual productive power of labour – is the unique source of valorisation. Nevertheless this productive power is always based on an actual technique of production. Technology and its application in specific techniques is inevitably the result of social labour.

Labour being the creator of value-added, it is merely 'compensated' by the wage, the enterprise appropriating the surplus-value, that is, the difference between value-added and the wage. Surplus-value is generally the source of the growth of capital. Because labour is the unique source of valorisation and hence of surplus-value, labour essentially produces the equivalent of its own wage as well as that of the growth of capital. Hence labour essentially produces capital.[60] (Subdivision 5B.)

Herewith, in sum, the enterprises' dissociative production appears as resolved (sublated) in labour's production of surplus-value, which thereby – with the enterprises appropriating the surplus-value – satisfies the enterprises' driving force. Although some major problems for the reproduction of the capitalist bifurcated economy now seem resolved, we will see in the coming chapters that the resolution reached so far requires further conditions to be met. (Subdivision 5C.)

59 Apocalypse 21:6.

60 Thus the labour comprehending the process might claim to be the source of 'Alpha and Omega, the beginning and the end' (Apocalypse 21:6).

List of figures chapter 1

CHAPTER 2

Accumulation of capital

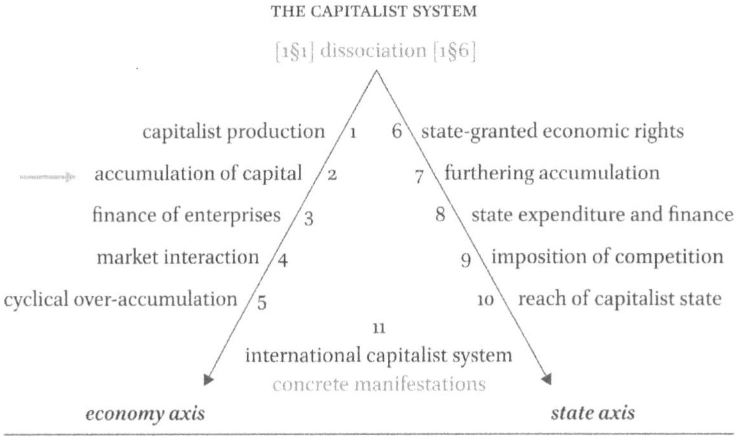

Contents

Introduction

Division 1 of this chapter sets out how the profit-driven production of enterprises – presented in Chapter 1 – necessarily gives rise to the accumulation of capital, that is, the expansion of capital. Generally a macroeconomic growth of the economy is produced alongside this. The next divisions of this chapter present three main conditions of existence of the accumulation of capital.

The first condition is the expansion of labour-capacity (Division 2). This expansion is embedded in a fairly complex constellation of determining factors. Each one of those factors has, by itself, received abundant attention in the economic literature. The feature of their exposition in this chapter is their interconnection. This centres, on the one hand, on the growth of the labour population, the rate of unemployment and the wage rate, and, on the other, on labour's compliance during the production process, which together determine surplus-value, the accumulation of capital and employment.

More specifically, the adjacent Division 3 presents the management of labour's compliance during production.

The second condition for the accumulation of capital is the expansion of money (Division 4). Concretising the concept of money from Chapter 1 into bank-issued money, it will be shown how the creation of money by commercial banks accommodates the accumulation of capital.

The adjacent Division 5 indicates how the former condition is predicated on an institutional separation between enterprises and banks.

The third condition, the corporate form of the enterprise, grounds the continuity and the possible scale of the accumulation of capital (Division 6).

The final Division 7 puts the corporate form of the enterprise in the perspective of the bifurcation starting point of Chapter 1, and elaborates on the character of the private ownership of enterprises.

Scheme 2.1 outlines the systematic moments of this chapter.

At the expositional level posited thus far (Chapter 1), 'capital in general' was considered. That is, individual capital in the perspective of the whole (total capital), or, the enterprise in macroeconomic perspective. In the current chapter, this perspective will be continued. It may be repeated that, as before, the exposition moves from general-abstract to gradually more specific-concrete concepts. Thus, for example, whereas the concept of money as bank-issued money that will be presented in this chapter is fairly concrete, it still lacks concrete connection with finance (Chapter 3). Note also that the exposition continues to present institutions and processes that are necessary rather than contingent to the capitalist system.

SCHEME 2.1 *Systematic of the Accumulation of Capital (Outline Chapter 2)*

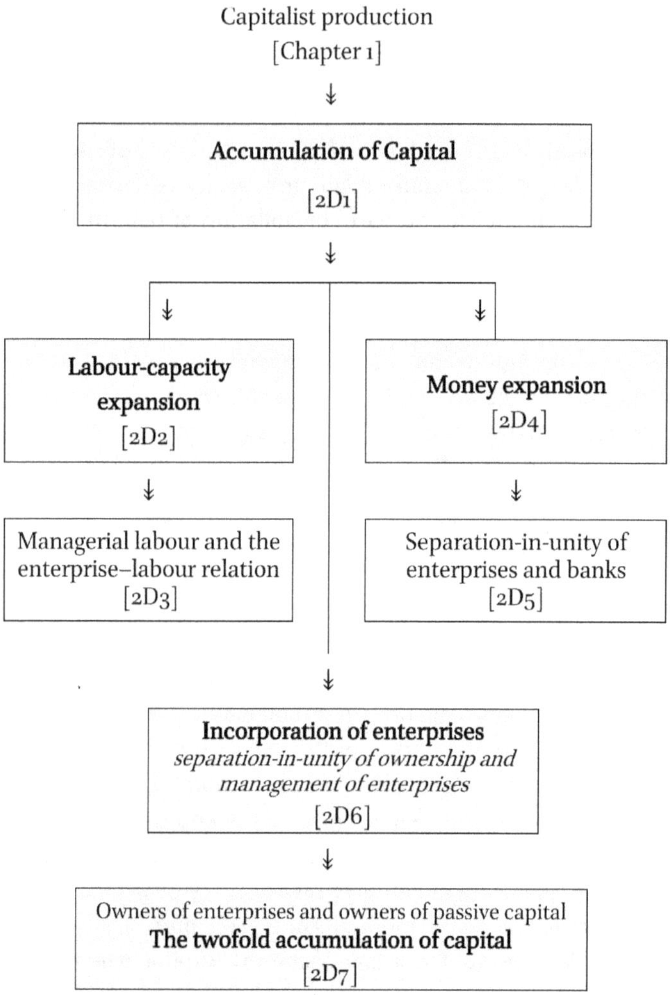

Legend
⸸ grounded in (conditioned by)

Division 1. Accumulation of capital

2§1 *Profit augmentation*

We have seen that capitalist production is driven by one-dimensional monetary profit – rather than by the multifaceted usability of goods or the realisation of human capabilities (1§11). The rationale of this mono-dimensional driving force is more of the same: profit augmentation.

2§1-a Explication. Drive for 'surplus-value' and drive for 'profit'

Recall from 1§12 the distinction between profit and surplus-value (or integral profit), the latter being independent of the way enterprises are financed. Finance is only introduced in Chapter 3. Assuming for now a constant degree of external finance, the terms 'drive for profit' and 'drive for surplus-value' can be used interchangeably.

2§2 *Management of the productive power of labour*

> It was shown that labour – more specifically the actual productive power of labour – is the unique source of value-added, and hence also of surplus-value and of profit. The productive power of labour covers two components: the intensity of labour and the 'technique-associated productive power of labour' (1§14).

Profit could in principle be augmented by an increasing intensity of labour, or by a productive power of labour increasing technical change.

1 *Management of the intensity of labour*

Given a technique of production, a major part of the management of the production process is that of managing the *degree of intensity of labour*.[1] This is predicated on the skills of the labour-capacity hired as inputs on the one hand, and the management of the specific development of these skills within the production process on the other. The management of the degree of intensity of labour is connected to the organisational routines associated with a particular technique. Even so, there are physical limits to the intensity of labour, whence profit augmentation (2§1) seems limited.

---

1 Recall from 1§14, equation 1.3 the denotation of the productive power of labour by L^{α}, with $\alpha = \acute{\alpha} * \ddot{\iota}$. Here $\acute{\alpha}$ denotes a technique component and $\ddot{\iota}$ an intensity component. Note that L refers to specifically skilled labour-capacity.

2 *Management of technological and technical change*

Given these physical limits, another major part of the management of the production process regards the choice of a technique and its specific adaptation to the process at hand. The introduction of a new technique of production may enhance the 'technique-associated productive power of labour'. Along with this enhanced productive power, a new process technique may both itself reduce unit costs and create the possibility for new organisational routines to increase the intensity of labour, and thence further decrease unit costs. With its introduction the (potential) profits tend to increase for the initiating enterprises.[2]

Part of a given total amount of capital invested tends to be invested in the 'research and development' for profit-increasing new techniques of production – that is, in valoro-technology (see 2§2-c for the latter term). Labour's production of knowledge leading to inventions then also takes on the monetary-value form. This leads to the development of particular technology and the search for particular techniques that are expected to increase profits.

2§2-a Explication. Management

The section above introduces management regarding the productive power of labour. Management in general will be systematically introduced in 2D3.

2§2-b Explication. Limits to intensity of labour, and trade-off between intensity and capacity utilisation

Regarding the increase in the intensity of labour, not only are there physiological limits; there are psychological, social and moral limits, too. With a decrease in the length of the working day there are enhanced possibilities for an increase in intensity of labour per hour. There is therefore a trade-off – depending on the technique of production – between the intensive use of labour and the degree of utilisation of capacity of means of production.

2§2-c Explication. Valoro-technology and valoro-technique

The concepts of 'technology' and 'technological change' (knowledge) and 'technique' and 'technical change' (application) are broadly analogous to the 'Schumpeterian' concepts of 'invention' and 'innovation' respectively (cf. Freeman 1974, p. 7). In order to emphasise that the capitalist form of technology and the form of techniques of production are non-neutral, but rather *valorisation driven* (1§11), it would be preferable to use the terms *valoro-technology*

2 That this applies to the 'initiating' enterprises is amplified in 4§6 and 4§12 on stratification of enterprises.

and *valoro-techniques*. Having emphasised this, I henceforth most often refrain from explicitly adopting this terminology.

2§2-d Addendum. Marx on the productive power and intensity of labour

Marx was the first political economist to undertake an extensive analysis of the capitalist process of production. Almost half of the first volume of *Capital* deals with this analysis in terms of the production of absolute and relative surplus-value (Parts 3–5).[3] Particularly in Chapter 12 (Chapter 10 of the German edition) he presents the productive power of labour and in Chapter 15 (Chapter 13 of the German edition) he presents the intensity of labour. Twentieth-century standard interpretations of Marx's *Capital* have largely neglected how his exposition inevitably distances itself from (Ricardian) labour-embodied concepts of value (this is expanded upon in Reuten 2017).

2§3 *Accumulation of capital*

So far, profit augmentation (2§1) is limited by the given amount of capital and the prevailing limits of the productive power of labour (2§2).

1 Augmentation of profit via investment of profit, hence capital accumulation

Profit is further enlarged via its investment as capital, whence capital is accumulated. The logic of the inward driving force of capital is the continuously expanding valorisation of capital via its accumulation. This was briefly anticipated at the end of 1§14 when it was mentioned that labour essentially produces capital, which means that surplus-value is accumulated.

Even if the mono-dimensional profit drive would seem to engender that all surplus-value be invested (then $\Delta K = \Pi$), this vies with the consumptive spending out of surplus-value. At the current expositional level I simply posit some, largely contingent, ratio of accumulation out of surplus-value (å):

$$\Delta K = \text{å}\Pi \qquad [0 < \text{å} < 1] \quad (2.1)$$

Thus labour produces capital (ΔK) plus the equivalent of the consumption out of surplus-value: $(1- \text{å})\Pi$.

3 Increasing 'absolute surplus-value' refers to lengthening of the working day at a given wage per day; increasing 'relative surplus-value' refers to cheapening of the wage bundle at a given real-wage. Thus these are, in effect, two mechanisms via which the real-wage per hour, i.e. the wage rate, may decrease, thereby increasing the surplus-value per hour. In the relative surplus-value case, real-wages might increase along with increasing surplus-value (cf. Reuten 2004a).

2 *Conditions for generalised accumulation of capital*

Generalised accumulation of capital generates macroeconomic growth. However, because the latter is no motive for enterprises, I start from the generalised accumulation of capital and so get to macroeconomic effects.

There are two main conditions for generalised accumulation of capital.[4] First, a continuous expansion of surplus-value and hence an expansion of *labour-capacity* (Division 2). Second, a continuous expansion of the quantity-flow of *money* (Division 4).[5] These thus ground the accumulation of capital.

A third ground, the corporate form of the enterprise, contributes to the *continuous* accumulation of capital (Division 6).

2§3-a Explication: Investment and consumptive spending out of profits – forward reference

At the current level of the exposition, a (largely contingent) ratio of accumulation out of profits (å) is posited. Some determinants are presented in 3§10.

Division 2. Expansion of labour-capacity

This division presents the required expansion of labour-capacity via a series of interconnections. The starting point in 2§4 of some rate of growth of capital accumulation will be shown to be a result in 2§6.

2§4 *Accumulation of capital – the required labour-capacity and the wage rate*

Given the technique component ($\acute{\alpha}$) of the productive power of labour (α), the micro- and macroeconomic accumulation of capital (ΔK) necessarily requires:

- An expansion of *labour-capacity* (ΔL) – as created within households. This requirement is modified by:
- An increase in the intensity component of the *productive power of labour* ($\Delta\ddot{\imath}$) – as managed within enterprises (2§2).

This section expands on the first aspect; the second aspect is presented in 2§5.

---

4 That is, yet abstracting from the state (Part Two).

5 It might be considered that, analytically, we could have a generalised price deflation, which would not require an expansion of the quantity-flow of money. However, it will be shown in Chapter 4 that, apart from brief intervals, the capitalist system cannot survive with generalised price deflation.

Henceforth the underlining of variables refers to their rate of growth.[6] Henceforth also – → (or ← –) stands for 'negatively related effect' and +→ (or ←+) stands for positively related effect.

1 *The required labour-capacity*

The growth rate in labour-capacity required ($\underline{L}$) is first determined by the growth rate of capital accumulation ($\underline{K}$) and by the valoro-technical capital to labour ratio ($K/L = \tau$) – see the left hand side of *Figure* 2.2. Thus:

$$\underline{L} = (1/\tau)\,\underline{K} \qquad \text{[requirement]} \quad (2.2)$$

[*continued*]

FIGURE 2.2 *Interconnection of the rate of capital accumulation and the growth rate of labour-capacity input*

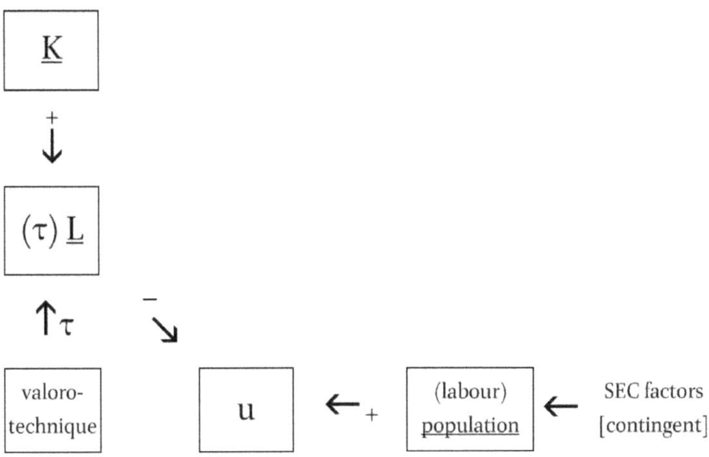

Legend

The meaning of the arrow between, for example, $\underline{L}$ and u is that $\underline{L}$ affects u (in this case negatively).

+→	positively related effect	–→	negatively related effect
$\underline{K}$	growth of capital (%)	τ	capital-labour ratio
$\underline{L}$	growth of employment (%)		
u	rate of unemployment (%): reserve of labour-capacity	SEC	socio-economic and socio-cultural factors (contingent)

6 Thus $\underline{x}_t - (x_{t-1} - x_t) / (x_{t-1})$. Note that in the main text, unless otherwise indicated, time sub scripts t are implicit (thus for x read x_t).

2§4 *Continued*

Whereas labour-capacity is an input for the enterprises, and whereas it is traded commodity-like on a market (1D3) it is not produced as a commodity but rather 'created' in the sphere of households (cf. 1§14, point 3). Children, generally, are not created and reared with a view to sale. (Nevertheless a particular education may be instrumental to the 'saleability' of labour-capacity on the market).[7]

Generally the input of labour-capacity is fed from the reserve of labour-capacity, i.e. the unemployed (U), with the latter being fed by the growth of the labour population (see the bottom of *Figure 2.2*). Thus the rate of unemployment (u) increases with the growth of the labour population, and decreases with the growth of employment:[8]

$$\tau\underline{L} - \rightarrow \mathbf{u} \leftarrow + \text{labour population} \qquad (2.3')$$

Or, for the same, algebraic:

$$u = f_1(\tau\underline{L}) + f_2(\underline{pop}) \qquad [f_1' < 0; f_2' > 0] \quad (2.3)$$

Population and labour population growth is determined by apparently contingent socio-economic and socio-cultural factors. It is a problem for capitalist enterprises that the reserve of labour is rather indeterminate and thus hard to control.[9]

The interconnections presented in *Figure 2.4* summarise how employers (and many economists with them) like to see the matter: the growth of capital positively affects employment, and so decreases unemployment (that is, when τ is fixed). Then any remaining unemployment results from ('their') labour population growth. This reasoning is correct. However, we will see in 2§6 that this is only half of the story.

2 *Labour-capacity and the wage rate*

Whereas for straight commodities a demand-induced price increase evokes an increase in their production, demand-induced wage increases do not evoke an increasing 'production' of children. In this respect the 'labour market' – inasmuch as the 'money market' – is very different from ordinary commodity markets (Explication 2§4-a).

At the current level of the exposition, it suffices to establish that to the extent that population growth results in a continuous or recurrent reserve of labour, there is a continuous or recurrent downward pressure on wages, and

---

7 Public education is presented in Chapter 7.

8 The rate of unemployment (u) is defined as u = (N – L)/N, where N is the labour population, i.e. the potential labour-capacity in contradistinction to the employed labour-capacity (L).

9 See Chapter 7, esp. 7D3.

vice versa. Thus, more specifically (see equations 2.4), changes in the rate of unemployment (Δu) are the major determinant of changes in the wage rate (Δw). However, a secondary determinant of wage rate changes is a change in the rate of growth of employment of labour-capacity ($\Delta \underline{L}$). (Amplification 2§4-b.)

$$\Delta u \; -\!\!\rightarrow \Delta w \leftarrow\!\!+ \; \Delta \underline{L} \qquad (2.4')$$

Or, for the same, algebraic:

$$\Delta w = f_1(\Delta u) + f_2(\Delta \underline{L}) \qquad [f_1' < 0;\ f_2' > 0;\ f_1 \text{ dominates}] \quad (2.4)$$

Because the rate of growth of employment of labour-capacity also affects changes in the rate of unemployment, there is also a second order effect of the former on the wage rate. (See *Figure 2.3*).

FIGURE 2.3 *General determinants of changes in the wage rate*

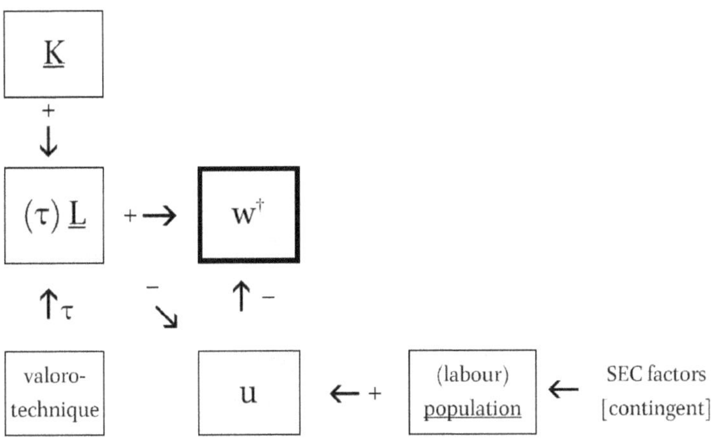

† The unemployment effect on wages tends to dominate the employment effect.

Legend

+→	positively related effect	−→	negatively related effect
$\underline{K}$	growth of capital (%)	τ	Capital-Labour ratio
$\underline{L}$	growth of employment (%)	w	wage rate
u	rate of unemployment (%): reserve of labour-capacity	SEC	socio-economic and socio-cultural factors (contingent)

2§4-a Explication. Peculiarities of the money and labour markets as compared with straight commodity markets

Money and labour-capacity are similar in that it is merely their demand, not their supply, which mimics commodity markets. As to their supply they are similar in that they are not 'produced', but rather created (in the sense of

1§1 – the processes of creation are dissimilar). For the money market this non-production and creation is amplified in 2D4.

2§4-b Amplification. The effect of changes in (un)employment on the wage rate (equation 2.4)

The insight of the effect of changes in *employment* on the wage rate can be traced back to Smith (1776) and is also emphasised by Marx (1976 [1867], pp. 763 and 772). (Cf. Reuten 2004b, p. 285). Briefly, the *unemployment* effect stems from unemployed workers bidding down wages; the *employment* effect stems from enterprises' bidding up wages when employment accelerates and when various types of labour become scarce. The combination of the two may account for wage increases even when there is unemployment.

2§4-c Addendum. Subsistence wages and population growth

Recall that the exposition is about full capitalism in general, which for quite a few countries dates back to the nineteenth century. Generally, demand-induced wage increases do not evoke an increasing 'production' of children. Nevertheless, in the limit case of an around subsistence wage, wages do have an *indirect* effect on population growth and the supply of labour-capacity.[10] In this limit case we have, in brief, the following long-run cyclical development. A prevailing labour abundance drives wages down to below the subsistence level. Population growth then decreases, not so much because of birth rates, but rather because starvation (and especially child starvation) increases. This decrease would generate a labour shortage in relation to the rate of accumulation, whence wages increase again (above subsistence level), giving rise to population growth (less starvation) and labour abundance. And so on.[11] Along this path, the rate of accumulation may accelerate up when wages decrease, and down when wages increase.

10 Compare the 'laws of population growth' as theorised by classical political economy. Whilst Malthus's account is best known, there are many forerunners (see Schumpeter 1972 [1954], pp. 250–8). Note that the reasoning in the remainder of this Addendum applies to a constellation in the absence of any (perhaps state-instituted) welfare provisions. For its manifestation the reader might think of nineteenth-century Europe or much of Africa at the turn of the twenty-first century.

11 Thus the main 'mechanism' lies in rates of starvation rather than birth rates. For the reader trained in neoclassical economics, who is perplexed by this 'picture', they may contemplate that in the traditional exposition of the labour market (think of the cross diagram) there are no guarantees whatsoever that the equilibrium wage is one above the subsistence level.

2§5 *The rate of surplus-value: wages and the productive power of labour*

Recall from 1§14 the formulas for production (X), for the amount of surplus-value (Π), and for the rate of integral profit (ω):

$$X_t \sphericalangle = [(\delta + \mu)K + mL^{\alpha}]_t \qquad (1.4)$$

$$\Pi_t = mL^{\alpha}{}_t - wL_t \qquad (1.5)$$

$$\omega_t = \Pi_t \,/\, K_{t'} = [(mL^{\alpha})_t - (wL)_t] \,/\, K_{t'} \qquad (1.6)$$

I now merely introduce a new definition: the 'rate of surplus-value' (e), which is a measure for the capital-labour distribution of income, that is, the capital share (Π) over the labour share (wL)[12]

$$e_t = \Pi_t \,/\, wL_t = (mL^{\alpha}{}_t - wL_t)/(wL_t) \qquad \text{[definition]} \quad (2.5)$$

A positive rate of surplus-value (e > 0) is a condition for a positive rate of integral profit of capital (omega, ω). Substituting 2.5 into 1.6 we get:[13]

$$\omega_t = \frac{e_t}{K_{t'} \,/\, wL_t} \qquad \text{[implication]} \quad (2.6)$$

A positive rate of surplus-value is conditioned by a range of *combinations* of some wage rate (w) along with some exerted power of labour in production (α).

$$w\uparrow \dashrightarrow e \leftarrow + \alpha\uparrow \qquad (2.7')$$

Or, for the same, algebraic:

$$e_t = f_1(w)_t + f_2(\alpha)_t \qquad [f_1' < 0;\ f_2' > 0] \quad (2.7)$$

The condition allows for the mutual variation of both factors. However, for any given valoro-technique (2§3) the range of the variability of the productive power of labour is limited, to the extent that the intensity of labour ($L^{\ddot{\iota}}$) is limited (2§2). Thus:

$$(\ddot{\iota})_t = (|\ddot{\iota}|)_t \qquad (2.8)$$

Because $\alpha = \acute{\alpha} * \ddot{\iota}$ (equation 1.3), we also have

$$(\alpha)_t = (|\alpha|)_t \qquad \text{[implication]} \quad (2.9)$$

Whereas the valoro-technique conditions the productive power of labour, the intensity component is co-determined by the labourer's degree of *compliance* with the conditions of the production process. Compliance is a complex factor that is itself determined by both micro factors (such as the local management of the production process and the rate of unemployment within a sector) and macro factors (such as the general rate of unemployment and the general enterprise-labour relations) that are themselves intricate. A 'high' rate of unemployment tends to go along with compliance (fear of being sacked: being

---

12 The rate of surplus-value is the core concept in Marx's *Capital*, Volume I, Parts 3–6 (about 430 pages).

13 The systemic necessity is for positive rate of surplus value (which does not exclude 'maximum' profits as in neoclassical theory – cf. Alchian 1950).

substituted by another worker). Further there is a positive relation between compliance and changes in the wage rate. Within limits wage increases then positively affect the intensity component of the power of labour (and vice versa).[14] Thus as to the rate of surplus-value there is a trade-off between what is reached in wage bargaining and in production (see *Figure 2.4*).

FIGURE 2.4 *Determinants of the rate of surplus-value*

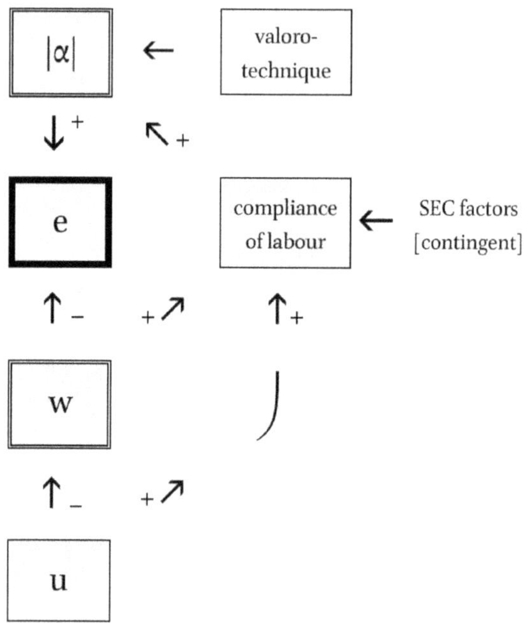

Legend

+→	positively related effect	−→	negatively related effect
|α|	limited productive power of labour	e	rate of surplus-value [e = Π/wL]
SEC	socio-economic and socio-cultural factors (contingent)	u	rate of unemployment (%): reserve of labour-capacity
w	wage rate		

14 In 'New Keynesian' economics a similar thesis is proposed in the 'efficiency wage theory' (see e.g. Snowdon and Vane 2002a, pp. 200–1).

2§6 *Interconnection of capital accumulation, labour-capacity and the rate of unemployment*

Along with the amount of labour employed, the resulting rate of surplus-value (e) determines profits ($\Pi = ewL$), which, together with any given ratio of accumulation out of surplus-value (å, eqn. 2.1, 2§3), determines the degree of capital accumulation (ΔK):

$$\Delta K = \mathring{a}ewL \qquad \text{[implication]} \quad (2.10)$$

Then the growth in employment of labour-capacity ($\underline{L}$) moves along with the rate of capital accumulation ($\underline{K} = \Delta K/K$) and the technically determined capital-labour ratio:

$$\underline{L} = (1/\tau)\underline{K} \qquad (2.2)$$

And so forth – see *Figure 2.5*. Note that this outline is based on a prevailing state of techniques and K/L ratio, and hence τ is not a constant (2§2).[15]

Thus 'e', the rate of surplus-value, determines the degree of the employment of labour.[16] Reasoned purely from the side of the enterprises' employment of labour, the following simple 'equilibrating' mechanism prevails:

- an *increasing* rate of accumulation of capital ($\Delta\underline{K}$) gives rise to an increasing wage rate – equations 2.2 and 2.4 – (the latter is moderated or annihilated by unemployment, in which case the accumulation may further accelerate; however, at some point an increasing rate of accumulation will lower unemployment to a level where it no longer moderates or annihilates an increase in the wage rate);
- if the increasing wage rate does not, or can no longer, go along with an increasing power of labour in production (the physically and/or mentally limited intensity component of α), the rate of surplus-value (e) is tempered and so the rate of accumulation of capital (equations 2.5 and 2.6);
- a stagnating or decreasing rate of accumulation presses down wages and pushes up the rate of surplus-value whence the rate of accumulation may again take off.

Labour feeds the process of the expansion of capital inwardly (e) and at distance outwardly (population growth). However, the conditions are set by the implications of the inward bifurcation of the capitalist production process.

[*continued*]

---

15 Amplified in 4§4 and 4D2–4D3.

16 From the perspective of labour as a whole, it is rather perverse that employment depends on exploitation and that wage rate increases may effectuate stagnating or decreasing employment.

FIGURE 2.5 *Interconnection of the unemployment rate, productive power of labour and rate of capital accumulation (integration Figures 2.2–2.4)*

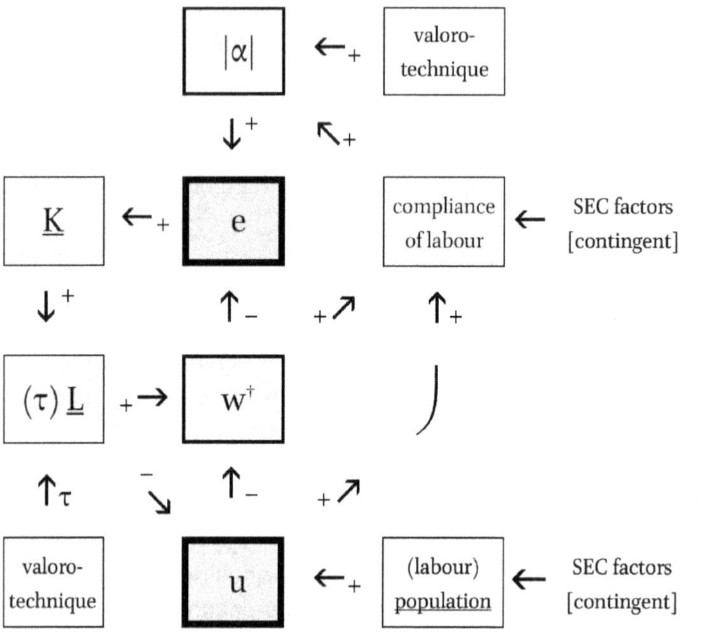

† The unemployment effect on wages tends to dominate the employment effect.

Legend

+→	positively related effect	–→	negatively related effect
K	growth of capital (%)	τ	capital-labour ratio
L	growth of employment (%)	w	wage rate
|α|	limited productive power of labour	e	rate of surplus-value [e = Π/wL]
u	rate of unemployment (%): reserve of labour-capacity	SEC	socio-economic and socio-cultural factors (contingent)

2§6 *continued*

Although labour is the active generative power of the process, it is bound to passively follow the track set by the conditions (as long as the conditions are accepted).

Ultimately this track is determined by the enterprises' (rather than labour's) private property of the means of production (1§1). Reconsidering the employment and unemployment 'benevolent' Figure 2.2, and comparing it with Figure 2.5, further reflection reveals that, within capitalist relations, the rate of unemployment is in fact a key factor. At zero unemployment, wages rise and (given the limited intensity of labour) the production of surplus-value dampens. Thus, in brief, capitalist production and the accumulation of capital require unemployment.

2§6-a Amplification. The world behind the unemployment figures
We are accustomed to read the regularly published rates of unemployment (4%, 11% or whatever) as an inevitable fact of life. Behind it is not only loss of income and the humiliating redundancy of the former (or new) workers concerned, but also the effects on their children (my mother/father is redundant) that are carried with them well beyond the dreadful times.

Division 3. Managerial labour and the enterprise-labour relation

So far, the main part of the exposition explicitly presented two categories of actors: labourers and enterprises. This brief division (one section) introduces the category of managerial labour.

2§7 ***Managerial labour and the enterprise-labour relation***

The production of surplus-value (1§14) is in many respects the 'Achilles heel' of the system, one that must be overcome by making labour comply during production with the monetary-value dimension and the requirements of profit-making (2D2).

1 *Managerial labour or 'management'*

Only in very small enterprises is the owner of the enterprise able to be the sole manager. Generally the ownership of the enterprise (owner or owners) is dependent on managerial labour to carry out managerial work. Whatever the particular institutional form of the enterprise (expanded on in 2D6), it must be managed so as to make labour comply with the objectives of the enterprise. Ultimately the upshot of this management is the welcoming of labour that does comply, and the sacking of labour that does not comply. However, because there may be subtle modes of non-compliance, there must be subtle methods of securing compliance, that is, ways of reaching what is called 'good labour relations'.

This management is itself labour, and so is carried out by managerial labour. Its function entails that it must be *elevated beyond*, and considered to be superior to, '*ordinary labour*' (much like an ordinary person being raised to the peerage). The requirement for such elevation is that the managerial labourer – now 'manager' – has *internalised the norms* of the enterprise. In brief these concern the optimal production of surplus-value, with a view to an optimal rate of integral profit and accumulation of capital. (See 2§7-b on the terms of internalisation versus compliance).

Consequent on the elevation, this 'labour', rather than being 'waged', is nominated to be 'salaried' (non-mundane) and is often held out the prospect of sharing in the profit of the enterprise.[17]

2 *Labour, managerial labour and wage differentials*

'Management' in the previous subsection referred especially to the top executive management (and ultimately its 'chiefs') as the executive officer(s) of capital.

However, this does not exclude that the middle and lower management, or even the ordinary labour, may have internalised the norms of the enterprise rather than merely complying with these.

Ultimately the most important function of the top management is to secure the compliance of labour by raising the degree of voluntary rather than involuntary conformism of its labour. There are several ways of 'human resources management' contributing to this. However, it is consistent with the monetary-value dimension to achieve this predominantly through the wage rate. Given the perception that an overall increase in the wages sum generally impedes profits, the compliance of the majority of labour is achieved via wage rate differentials between labour, and the perspective (or dream) of the lower echelons of upward movement on the wages ladder. Along with it go the status and influence associated with an upward movement. All this requires the (self-)perception that the lower rated work is important though inferior. Such a self-perception is required for the lower echelons so that they can reconcile themselves to their position.

Thus for a given wages sum of each enterprise, the top management must seek a wages ladder (including their own wages) that optimises the overall compliance (see also 2§7-c on ideology).

3 *The enterprise-labour relation*

In sum, the top-management manages what I henceforth will briefly call the 'enterprise-labour relation'. This is the employment relation through which

---

17 'Labour' in the first part of this sentence is in inverted comma's because from the self-perspective of these managers they 'work' without being sociologically a labourer or a worker.

labour, as determined by its 'productive power', produces the value-added and hence also the surplus-value, the latter being appropriated by the enterprise (1§14–1§15). In its quantitative aspect (the rate of surplus-value) this relation is constrained by, first, the technique of production, second, the rate of unemployment (2§6), and third (in face of that rate), the management of the compliance of labour during production, as assisted by the managerial device of a wages ladder that optimises this compliance.

2§7-a Explication. 'Actors'

I use the term 'actor' or 'social actor' in a very general sense of 'activity'. An actor may be an individual (that is, an individual in a particular role, for example that of labourer, entrepreneur, manager) *or* a (corporate) 'person' in the legal sense, hence also an institution such as an enterprise, *or* the agent of a particular institution (e.g. enterprise).

2§7-b Explication. Compliance with and internalisation of norms

Whereas ordinary labour must be incited to comply with the norms of the enterprise, the requirement for the management is that it has internalised the norms of the enterprise. Christian Bay expounds the social-psychological concepts of compliance and internalisation as follows:

> '*Compliance* refers to obedience or conformity without a conviction that this behavior is desirable in itself. (…) *Internalization* … means a readiness to conform to norms that have become integrated in the individual's self or in his cognitive outlook. (…) Internalization can insure conformity throughout the lives of the individuals affected. Moreover, … internalization, unlike coerced compliance, tend[s] to produce a "responsible" kind of conformity. The voluntary conformist differs from the involuntary one in that he is motivated and flexible enough to add elements of rationality or efficiency in promoting the norms or purposes for which he has been recruited.'
>
> BAY 1979 [1958], pp. 252, 317–18

I merely record that the attitudes contributing to this internalisation are often imparted in the mainstream business and economics schools that educate prospective managers.[18]

18 The 'principal-agent' literature in economics in general lacks any notion of internalisation on the part of the agent. Hence its primary focus on 'monitoring' and on individual financial rewards.

2§7-c Amplification. The (self-)perception of the inferiority or superiority of one type of labour versus the other

Heilbroner (1986 [1985], p. 107) conceives of 'ideologies' as 'systems of thought and belief by which dominant classes explain *to themselves* how their social system operates and what principles it exemplifies. Ideological systems therefore exist not as fictions but as "truth" – and not only evidential truths but as moral truths.'

For wage differences this would relate to the belief of the top management that their own labour is superior to that of the middle management and so forth for 'ordinary' labour, and hence that the executive management deserves a superior wage, and so forth the inferior labour deserving inferior wages. In the self-perception of groups of labour these differentials then work in the opposite direction: because of the superior/inferior wage, the work must be superior/inferior. This is how ideologies as systems of belief have real effect.

Regarding changes in the distribution of labour income over time (for example in terms of deciles), it would be hard to defend that a further skewing of the distribution towards the top decile(s) would hence mean that the work of the top has become more superior.

All this (2§7) implies that whereas 'labour' is a homogeneous economic category, it is not sociologically homogeneous. Even further, the sociological heterogeneity is a requirement for the reproduction of the capitalist system.[19]

Division 4. Money expansion

The first condition of existence of the accumulation of capital (2D1) is the expansion of labour-capacity and its productive power at a wage rate enabling an average positive rate of profit (2D2). Its second condition – presented in the current division – is the expansion in some way of the quantity-flow of money accommodating the accumulation of capital. The division starts with a concretisation of the Chapter 1 concept of money into bank-created money (2§8); it then moves to inter-bank relations (2§9); and finally connects money creation to the accumulation of capital (2§10).

19 I am grateful to Susan Himmelweit for a thought-provoking discussion that convinced me that this is a necessity rather than a contingency.

2§8 *Money concretised as bank-issued money: money creation by banks*

We have seen that 'value' is the abstract-general one-dimensionality that absorbs and reduces the heterogeneous qualities of entities as their common denominator in the market (1§3). Money is the mundane mediator and measure of value. It has no *inherent* content and it has no *inherent* value. It is 'merely' the quantifier through which value appears (1§4).

When in this chapter (and the following chapters of Part One) I refer to 'banks', these are commercial banks, without reference to a Central Bank or to the state. Thus money creation (presented below) refers purely to the money creation by commercial banks (i.e. profit-seeking entities). Such a presentation is adequate, because in actual practice – even when the state and a Central Bank have been introduced in Chapter 7 – it is primarily the commercial banks (henceforth 'banks') that carry out the money creation. This section introduces money creation from the perspective of one single independent bank. The next section introduces the constellation of several banks.

Whereas all economic actors are, or can be, clients of a bank, in this division – in view of the accumulation of capital – the focus is on the enterprises' clientele.

1 Money creation

Consistent with the concepts of money (1§4), capital (1§13–1§14) and the accumulation of capital (2§3) developed thus far, money concretely exists as *bank-issued money*. Thus bank-issued money is the *concrete* medium through which value appears, and is perceived as reflected onto entities (1§4).

A bank issues money that it *creates 'ex nihilo'* (out of nothing). The basis for that creation is a *reciprocal credit* relationship between the bank and a client. On the basis of some collateral, the client borrows a sum of money from the bank (booked as an entry on the asset side of the bank's balance sheet; an obligation by the client to the bank). At the same time the bank creates this sum of money '*ex nihilo*' and credits the client's account for it (booked as an equivalent entry on the liabilities side of the bank's balance sheet; an obligation by the bank to the client). See *Figure 2.6*. So initially at least, the bank immediately borrows back the sum of money that it lent out. Initially, that is, before the client makes payments from its account to other accounts – when it pays into other accounts, the latter account holders lend in that money to the bank. (See Explication 2§8-a).

[*continued*]

FIGURE 2.6 *'Ex nihilo' money creation by commercial banks on the basis of a reciprocal credit relationship*

new loan to client by bank	⟶	*ex nihilo* money creation by bank
[= client's issue of an obligation]†		[= crediting of client's account]‡
[= asset of bank]		[= liability of bank]

† Collateral based, as specified by contract.

‡ Alternatively: banknotes newly issued by the bank at hand (alternatively: cheques instead of banknotes)

2§8 *continued*

Alternatively, instead of paying the sum of money into the client's account, the bank may issue its banknotes to the client (equally an obligation by the bank that appears on the liabilities side of its balance sheet).[20]

As indicated, the bank creates money on the basis of some collateral, i.e. the pawning, mortgaging or cession of some *security title*: that in some property or an expected future income stream. An interest – or a commission – is charged as price for this service.[21] For the bank the latter is the driving motive for the money creation.

The bank (implicitly) promises that the money that it lends is a *trustworthy medium of value*, accepted (at least) by the other clients of the bank.[22] The client promises that it will return the borrowed money in due time as stipulated by contract, along with an agreed interest. Thus the client (implicitly) promises that the activity for which the sum of money is going to be used will be successful enough to repay the loan, thus that the activity is also trustworthy.

To the extent that the client must offer a security title, whereas the bank provides no guarantees about its money being trustworthy – other than the bank's good name – the reciprocal credit relationship is uneven.

20 These would indeed be banknotes issued by this bank. If the bank is called 'Emicon Bank', then the bank issues Emicon notes – somewhat similar to Emicon cheques. There is no reason to have more or less trust in the bank's account than in the bank's notes or cheques.

21 The concept of interest is systematically introduced in Chapter 3 (3§4–3§5). For the current expositional level, the concept of 'commission' is sufficient. When in this chapter I use the term 'interest' this may be substituted for the term 'commission'.

22 Throughout this chapter I use the term 'trustworthy' instead of 'fiduciary' or 'fiducial' in order to evade the perhaps different connotations of the latter terms in various monetary and financial discourses.

2 *Bank account money*

Regarding money creation there is no fundamental difference between 'bank-issued money notes' and 'bank account money' (or 'bookkeeping money'), the latter being transferred by signature or electronically.[23] There is a tendency for bank-issued money notes to develop into bank account money. This tendency is predicated on, first, cost efficiency. For each of the bank and the enterprises (as well as other agents), the holding of physical money incurs 'carrying costs'.[24] Secondly, the created bank account money stays with the bank so that, on average at least, its lending power increases. Its profit tends to increase at the same time.

Because there is no fundamental difference between the two forms of money, and because of the tendency referred to, I henceforth restrict myself to presenting bank account money.[25]

The implication and condition of full 'bank account money' is that all actors hold bank accounts; in particular it implies that the wage bill is paid into the bank accounts of labourers and that (most) household transactions are carried out via bank accounts. Loans from banks to households are only dealt with in Chapter 3 (these are important though contingent and are therefore dealt with in its Appendix 3B).

It is important to the exposition (and the comprehension of money) that the section above presents money as created by a commercial bank without it being predicated on the existence of a Central Bank. (The latter is introduced only in the next section; though prior to the introduction of the state in Part Two, a Central Bank will be called a 'Clearing Bank').

2§8-a Explication. Money creation by a bank

Sheet 2.7a displays the simplified (end of year) balance sheet of a bank. The amount ƒB on the assets side is the sum of the money created by this bank on the basis of 'securities backed loans', the equivalent is the current accounts on the liabilities side. The bank's own capital ƒA is invested in property such as the bank's buildings and other material assets. (Systematically the bank's capital ƒA is pre-posited. This pre-position is grounded in 3D4).

---

23 Although other authors may use the term 'money of account' in other senses, the term 'bank account money' is henceforth used in the sense of 'current account' money, that is, 'book entries' with banks.

24 The term 'carrying costs' stems from Keynes (1936), I presume. When he uses the term in reference to money, he refers to money of account and its low or negligible carrying costs (Keynes 1936, p. 227).

25 To be sure: the bank notes issued by the Emicon bank that someone holds represent a credit *to* the Emicon bank. Notes issued by a Central Bank (introduced only in Chapter 7) represent a credit *to* the Central Bank – moreover, a zero interest credit.

SHEET 2.7A *Simplified balance sheet of a bank*

Assets		Liabilities	
property	ƒA	capital	ƒA
securities backed loans	ƒB	current accounts	ƒB
(at some average interest rate of b%)		(or alternatively: 'banknotes issued')	

Sheet 2.7b displays the balance alteration upon the creation of new money for client X against a securities backed loan.

SHEET 2.7B *Additional money creation: alteration of bank's balance sheet*

securities backed loan to client X (at 4%)	ƒ100	current account client X (= borrowed from X)	ƒ100

Sheet 2.7b reveals a 'lengthening' of the bank's balance, i.e. a growth of the bank's activity. When clients cancel loans we see the reverse. *Sheet 2.7c* displays the alteration upon the payment of a sum of ƒ80 from client X to client Z.

SHEET 2.7C *Transfer of money between bank's clients: alteration of bank's balance sheet*

securities backed loan to client X (at 4%)	ƒ100	current account client X (= borrowed from X)	ƒ20
		current account client Z (= borrowed from Z)	ƒ80

2§8-b Amplification. Historical forms of bank issued money

The main text of 2§8 immediately presents the contemporary dominant form of money (entries in bank accounts). Most economics textbooks from around the year 2015 still present 'modern' money (1973 and after) by way of historical narratives in terms of commodity money (e.g. gold) and next so-called 'high powered money' as issued by Central Banks.

Several concrete forms of money (including commodity money or commodity-based money) are compatible with the necessary requirements of money set out in the previous chapter (1§4). However, to the extent that the concept of capital is associated with unrelenting accumulation of capital, some forms of money will be more appropriate than others and the former will tend to drive out the latter.

First. A pure gold-commodity-money configuration, for example, may be compatible with capitalism only as long as the rate of accumulation of capital in the physical gold sector can keep pace with the general rate of accumulation of capital; it would further require comparable rates of productivity increase since with productivity in the gold sector lagging behind, the economy would run into a constellation of general price deflation and potential depression.

Second. Regarding the potential for accumulation of capital, there is an important difference between the cases of, first, the storing of commodities as securities *at the bank* (as with pure commodity money), and second, the mere pledging of the *title* to commodities. In the first case the commodities are retreated from circulation, thus throughout a twofold accumulation is required, not only that in production capital but also that in, say, precious metals or other commodity stocks. Obviously this hampers the potential speed of the accumulation of capital since the precious metals securities (in this case) are mere hoards. In the second case the securitised commodities (plant, equipment, etc.) can function in production as it is merely their title that is pledged.

2§8-c Addendum. A Monetary Circuit approach

The exposition of money in the current division is different from that of mainstream economics, and especially that of the mainstream textbook economics. In its formal aspect (cf. the bank balance sheets in this and a number of Explications to come) the current exposition has roots in the Post-Keynesian and especially the Monetary Circuit approaches to money. (References are provided in Addendum 3§2-d).

Around 2015, and as against the mainstream economics textbook approaches to 'money', the notion that money is endogenous and that it is predominantly created by commercial banks, is gaining momentum amongst researchers associated with central banks and the IMF. See especially Bindseil and König (2013) and Jakab and Kumhof (2015) and the references they provide. These authors work, respectively, at the European Central Bank, the German Institute for Economic Research, the IMF, and the Bank of England.

2§9 *Domain extension and inter-bank clearing: inter-bank trust and the Clearing Bank*

1 Interconnection between banks

To the extent that banks operate independently of each other, I refer to that constellation as a 'fragmented banking system'. (This is what was implicitly presented in the previous section).[26] Such a constellation limits the market domain for enterprises (the 'extent of the market') to the domain over which that money is an effective medium of value.

In order *to extend the operation of the money* they issue, independently operating banks must seek agreement between them to accept each other's money, at some exchange rate (conversion rate), for the settlement of their clients' debts. This implies that there may be *debt relations between banks* – serviced at some rate of interest agreed upon. Thus *banks must trust each other* – at least temporarily. A transfer of money between bank clients, e.g. from bank A to bank B, implies that the 'receiving' bank B must provide credit to the transferring bank A. Bank B might be in the position to clear with bank A,[27] otherwise the credit would have to be sustained against an interest. (Explication 2§9-c, Sheets 2.8).

2 *Interconnections between banks as mediated by a Clearing Bank*

Alternatively banks may clear via a (dominant) bank in which they place 'high trust'. The latter bank then operates as a *Clearing Bank* (ClB), against an interest or commission. Then this ClB may impose its own *standard of money* on the banks for which it clears. To the extent that the other banks adopt this standard, their domain of operation is extended. Should one bank (e.g. A) remain in debt with the ClB, and so via the ClB with other banks, then the ClB will request interest as well as *securities* (collateral) from the bank in debt – part of the interest that the ClB charges may be distributed to the creditor banks.[28] (Explication 2§9-c, Sheets 2.9.)

This way the ClB will also set a *standard for securities* and impose *liability rules* (see 2§9-b). In fact this is one of the main necessary conditions for the

---

26 Historically all regional banking systems started off from a high degree of fragmentation. This is immaterial to the systematic exposition, even if on *this* matter the historical and the systematic accounts run somewhat parallel.

27 That is, in case of an equivalent counter transfer from B to A, the debt-credit relationships cancel out.

28 Note that when particular banks place high trust in each other, they may evade the ClB's interest margin by borrowing and lending directly to each other.

money domain extension. Once some ClB is dominant, a self-reinforcing process compels banks to operate under the umbrella of this ClB, first because this extends the domain for their clients, and second (and relatedly), because other banks may refuse to deal with banks that adopt different standards.

Note that because the state and especially its monetary framework has not yet been introduced, the ClB has no legal powers. It is merely a dominant commercial bank.

3 *Money creation*

Whereas the ClB can impose a standard for securities and impose liability rules, it has, in comparison with the other banks, no specific powers regarding money creation. It creates money for its own clients, inasmuch as the other banks do for their clients. However, if it were to abstain from competition with the other banks, it might abstain from relations with non-bank actors, and so abstain from regular money creation.[29] As such it would be a pure clearing bank (so earning profits purely from the clearing).

2§9-a Explication. Systematic exposition – no historical narrative

I emphasise once more that all of the exposition – including that of money – is not a historical narrative, but a purely systematic exposition. It is the latter's logic of grounding the moments that were presented earlier on that determines the next step. Nevertheless it may at times be the case that the systematic exposition happens to parallel an apparent 'logical' history. Thus even if historically we may have seen, for example, a development from fragmented banking to a clustering of banks around a dominant bank that operates as a Clearing Bank, this is accidental to the systematic exposition. In other words, I am just *gradually* setting out the *systematic* logic of the current capitalist banking structure (2D4 as continued in Chapter 3), albeit with the state and its Central Bank abstracted from it (Chapter 7).

In fact the current division sets out (the limits of) the conditions of existence of a banking constellation under the umbrella of a completely independent 'Central Bank' – at the current level of abstraction (all of Part One), this is what is called a 'Clearing Bank'.

---

29 It might then still engage in money creation via the purchase of financial paper on the open market (usually with the purpose of selling it later, so undoing the money creation). Thus by 'regular' money creation I refer to the continuous process of money creation – at the current stage of the exposition especially for enterprises.

2§9-b Explication. Standard for securities and liability rules

The Clearing Bank (in Chapter 7 the Central Bank) sets rules for the banks operating under its umbrella. Standards for security pertain to the banks' assets, especially the composition of types of assets and their degree of risk. These may also determine the degree of enforced loans of banks with the ClB. The more general 'liability rules' relate to the liabilities side of the banks' balance sheet. These may include conditions on the banks' degree of solvency, specific (other) ratios of the composition of the liabilities, and on the assets-liabilities maturity matches.

2§9-c Explication. Clearing via the Clearing Bank

The clearing between banks themselves, or clearing via a Clearing Bank (ClB), is illustrated in the following sets of balance sheet alterations. It is assumed that the banks clear, apart from one sum, which is a payment (of ƒ80) by a client X of Bank A to a client Z of Bank B.

Sheets 2.8 are about clearing between banks (florin, ƒ, is the standard of money)[30]

Sheet 2.8a records an initial creation of money: a reciprocal credit (2§8-b).

SHEET 2.8A *Alteration Balance Sheet Bank A: money creation*

Assets			Liabilities
securities backed loan to client X (at 4%)	ƒ100	current account client X (= borrowed from X)	ƒ100

SHEET 2.8B *Alteration Balance Sheet Bank A: transfer of ƒ80 from X with Bank A, to Z with Bank B*

sec. backed loan to X	ƒ100	current account client X	ƒ20
		borrowed from Bank B (at 3%)	ƒ80

30 To simplify the presentation it is assumed that banks A and B have already adopted the standard of money of the Clearing Bank.

SHEET 2.8C *Alteration Balance Sheet Bank B: transfer of f80 from X with Bank A to Z with Bank B*

loan to Bank A (at 3%)	f80	current account client Z	f80

Sheets 2.8b and 2.8c: On the transfer of money from bank A to bank B, the receiving bank (B) must provide an equivalent loan to the money transferring bank (A). Bank B will only be happy to *receive* this money, and hence to provide a loan to A, *if it has confidence in A*. (In the absence of clearing via a clearing bank, possible non-confidence is the root of a potential paralysing of the payment system).

Sheets 2.9 show the clearing via the Clearing Bank (ClB). Starting from *Sheet 2.8a*, banks A and B may, instead of a direct clearing between them, clear via a ClB.

SHEET 2.9A *Alteration Balance Sheet ClB: clearing and inter-bank credit*

Assets			**Liabilities**
loan to bank A (at 3.5%) (securities backed)†	f80	borrowed from Bank B (at 2.5%)	f80

SHEET 2.9B *Alteration Balance Sheet Bank A: clearing and inter-bank credit*

sec. backed loan to X (4%)	f100	current account client X	f20
		borrowed from ClB (3.5%)	f80

SHEET 2.9C *Alteration Balance Sheet Bank B: clearing and inter-bank credit*

loan to ClB (at 2.5%)	f80	current account client Z	f80

† If bank A cannot provide securities we see the simple basis of a potential banking crisis (expanded on in 2§10 and 2§10-b).

2§9-d Amplification. Enforced borrowing by banks from the ClB

Anticipating any non-clearing (or for other policy reasons) the dominant Clearing Bank may compel the banks that operate under its umbrella to (continuously) borrow an amount of money *from* the ClB. Recall the simplified full balance sheet 2.7a from 2§8-b for a single bank (now called bank A).

SHEET 2.7A *Simplified balance sheet Bank A*

Assets			Liabilities
property	ƒA	capital	ƒA
securities backed loans (at some average interest rate of b%)	ƒB	current accounts	ƒB

Suppose the compelled borrowing, against a security title, amounts to a sum ƒC. This sum appears on the liabilities side of *Sheet 2.10a* as a debt to the ClB (the sum C_2), and equally at the assets side of the ClB in *Sheet 2.10b* (the sum C_3). C_1=C_2=C_3=C_4.

SHEET 2.10A *Simplified Balance Sheet Bank A: enforced borrowing from ClB*

Assets			Liabilities
property	ƒA	capital	ƒA
loan to ClB (at c%)	ƒC_1	debt to ClB (at c+%)	ƒC_2
securities backed loans (at avg. interest rate of b%)	ƒB	current accounts	ƒB

Next the ClB lends out this sum to bank A: it credits the account of A for the sum C_4 (which appears at B's assets side as C_1).

SHEET 2.10B *Alteration Balance Sheet ClB: enforced borrowing from ClB*

securities backed loan to bank A (at c+%)	ƒC_3	account bank A (at c%) (borrowed from A)	ƒC_4

For odd historical reasons (in the old days banks might predominantly buy ClB Notes from the ClB – in which case we have the entry ClB Notes), mainstream economists often call the sum C_1 'high-powered' money and in my view erroneously so. (It is not money, and even these mainstream economists would not call C_1 'money in circulation'). Nevertheless we do have a reciprocal credit relationship.

2§9-e Explication. The Clearing Bank as foreshadowing the 'Central Bank', and the predominant money creation by commercial banks

The Clearing Bank as introduced in 2§9 foreshadows the Central Bank. The Clearing Bank, and its 'standard of money' and 'liability rules', has been presented in complete abstraction from 'the state'. Therefore there has been no mention of concepts such as 'legally enforced currency' and 'legal tender'.

Even if in actuality the Central Bank has most often been granted by the state the monopoly to issue 'legal tender money notes', it has (like the ClB) no monopoly to create money. In fact commercial banks – as licensed to be a bank – predominantly issue the money, i.e. current account money. (This last notion is what B.J. Moore in 1988 called 'horizontalism', as opposed to 'verticalism', which is the idea that Central Banks generate or control the money supply).

Bindseil and König (2013)[31] argue that even if economics textbooks such as those of Ball, Mankiw, or Mishkin[32] still explain the money supply by means of the multiplier process and proceed under the assumption that the central bank controls the supply of money, 'central bankers have by now largely buried [this] "verticalism", at least when it comes to monetary policy implementation – that is, the choice and technique to achieve the operational target of monetary policy. And even though the textbook and academic mainstream view on the money supply still largely maintains that the central bank can control it, the real-world developments in monetary policy practice have paved the way for an understanding of monetary policy as interest rate policies that must necessarily sooner or later result in the horizontalist view of Moore' (Bindseil and König 2013, pp. 385–6).

31 The first author works at the European Central Bank, the second at the German Institute for Economic Research.

32 They refer to L. Ball's *Money, Banking and Financial Markets* (2010), G. Mankiw's *Macroeconomics* (2003), and F. Mishkin's *Economics of Money, Banking and Financial Markets* (2009).

2§10 *The private pre-validation of production by banks*

This section connects money-creation for enterprises (2§8) explicitly to the accumulation of capital.

1 Pre-validation of production by banks

Whereas bank-issued account money originates in a *private* reciprocal credit relationship between bank and client (2§8), it subsequently acquires a *social* character by 'circulating' in the bookkeeping of banks (2§9).[33]

Any money that circulates as transfers *to* enterprises – to accounts with the same bank or any other – is money that *has* validated, or is in the process of validating, *previous production*.[34] On the other hand, money newly created in a reciprocal relation between bank and enterprise is an *anticipation of production and realisation* in the future. This way the current circuit of money is 'opened' and expanded. In other words, the bank that creates this new money on the basis of a loan performs a *private pre-validation* of production, which is socially validated when the anticipated production is sold – the loan can then be cancelled. Such a pre-validation is a necessary condition for the ongoing overall accumulation of capital. Along with the growth in the accumulation of capital (and macroeconomic growth generally), the amount of the pre-validating money creation grows.

2 The monetary condition of social validation: extended expansion and re-creation of money

In pre-validating the future production of an enterprise via money creation, the bank anticipates the success of the borrowing enterprise, expecting that the pre-validation will be followed by production and actual social validation (i.e. sale) of commodities. Then the money would return to the enterprise's account, whereupon the loan, including the interest agreed upon, could be cancelled.

Thus the sum of money to be returned to the bank must be larger than the pre-validating loan. The condition is that the pre-validation of one enterprise (anticipating its expansion), is socially confirmed at some stage by the expansion of *other* enterprises – normally requiring money creation and pre-validation for other enterprises.

33 I hesitantly adopt the term 'circulation' as it is rather anachronistic. Surely in the eighteenth, nineteenth and much of the twentieth century, 'circulation of money' used to refer to the circulation of currency from hand to hand. Now it 'circulates' from account to account.

34 Validation: the turning of outputs into money, i.e. sale of commodities (1§10).

Thus, generally, *expansion can only be validated by expansion.* Only then is the initially created new money a successful lever to the accumulation of capital. And so too for the validation of the expansion validating the initial expansion.

In any case (and at a constant average velocity of circulation, that is, a constant average rate of transfer of money from one account to the other), accumulation of capital requires a concomitant expansion of the pre-validation by banks, that is, a concomitant rate of re-creation of money.

3 *Over-optimism, over-crediting and vulnerabilities of a multi-bank constellation*

Most of the time, a multi-bank constellation under the umbrella of a Clearing Bank adequately accommodates the accumulation of capital – that is, in normal times and even in normal recessions. However, such a constellation is also vulnerable to the failure of banks, which reduces or even paralyses the accumulation of capital.

An enterprise's getting into debt with a bank goes along with a degree of the enterprise's optimism about the future – sometimes over-optimism. The same holds for the bank, although the bank hedges against possible failure of the enterprise's investment project by requiring securities. However, because money creation is profitable for banks, these may also be over-optimistic and require securities that are on the edge of covering possible losses. Competition between banks may further provoke this. Generally this is a matter of risk taking and risk premiums as calculated in the interest rate charged – losses against one client may be made good with profits from other clients. However, as Keynes (1936, 1937) emphasised, next to statistically calculable risk, non-calculable *uncertainty* is inherent to a capitalist economy.

Over-optimism and banks' over-crediting comprise a multi-bank constellation (2§9) vulnerable to failure of a bank, and even for failures on a large scale, leading to a crisis of the banking system (Explication 2§10-b).

It was indicated in 2§9 that the ClB's *standard for securities* and *liability rules* (2§9-b) are one of the main necessary conditions for a multi-bank constellation. It is a major problem for a capitalist economy that whereas tight rules are necessary, these also put restrictions on the granting of the demand for money by enterprises (and social actors generally) and hence on the rate of accumulation of capital. (Expanded in 7D2 and 9D2).

2§10-a Explication. Expansion validated by expansion

Because banks – and banks only – create money, it is impossible for them to receive back more money (interest) than they created. Therefore the validation of the expansion of one enterprise necessarily requires the expansion of other enterprises. Thus the pre-validation of the others provides the monetary equivalent for the realisation of the surplus-value of the one, including the interest to be paid to the bank (expanded in 3D1). This is the answer to the long-standing dubious question of 'where the money comes from' so as to realise surplus-value (cf. Marx in *Capital II*, pp. 641 and 676).[35] The required expanding expansion is also one of the main reasons why it is very difficult for a capitalist economy to cope with decreasing growth, and especially with a negative rate of growth (amplified in Chapter 5).

2§10-b Explication. Impossibility of bankruptcy of the banking system, along with the vulnerability of individual banks to failure and the paralysation of the banking system

- *No exit from the banking system – impossibility of bankruptcy of the banking system*

Section 2§8 started off from one single *independent* bank, without any relations with other banks. Conceptually it is essential to see that such a bank cannot go bankrupt, at least not as a result of its pure banking business.[36] There cannot be such a thing as withdrawing money from that bank. Clients can undertake only two kinds of action. First, they can take loans (against interest) and cancel loans. Second, they can transfer money to other clients of the bank (or receive money from them). That is all.

A similar notion applies for the *constellation* of a multitude of interrelated banks (2§9): that constellation *as a whole* cannot go bankrupt. Clients of one bank can become a client of another bank (by transferring money to that other bank). However, there can be no such thing as withdrawing money from the banking system. (In actual practice this is no different for holders of US dollars, euros or yuans – the only one additional action is that they might try to exchange between these. Escaping from the whole of the banking system is impossible).

- *Failure of individual banks within a constellation of interrelated banks*

For various reasons that do not matter for now, the security and liability rules set by the ClB (2§9) may not be appropriately tight or appropriately enforced. Alongside this, when individual banks behave too optimistically in their credit provision (and thus money creation), their bad loans may build up to the point of insolvency. In this case the ClB (which via its rules or its non-enforcing of the

35 A question taken up by Rosa Luxemburg 1963 [1913], ch. 8, esp. p. 146 ff.; see also Pastrello 2013.

36 Cf. Bellofiore and Realfonzo 2003, p. 200.

rules is a party concerned in the insolvency!) has two options at its discretion. (Recall from 2§9-c, Sheets 2.9, that clearing entails interbank loans).

First, the ClB can stop clearing for this bank, which soon implies the bankruptcy of said bank. The other banks no longer want to receive money from this bank (that is, they no longer accept transfers from the clients of the bank in trouble – recall 2§9-c, Sheets 2.8) meaning that the bad bank's current account holders are stuck – they cannot escape and ultimately lose their money up to the level of the bank's insolvency.

Second, it can keep on clearing against bad securities – hoping that the bank in trouble will improve its degree of solvency (perhaps forcing it to take measures to reach that end). However, if and when it becomes known to the public that the bank at hand is a 'bad bank', its account holders will try to transfer their money to accounts with other banks en masse, which the latter will not accept. This second case then reduces to the first one.

A crisis of the total banking system develops to the extent that more banks, and big ones, run into an insolvent position. As long as this is not publicly known, the ClB could in principle keep on clearing for the lot against bad securities. However, when it becomes publicly known, account holders will try to flee to 'good' banks, which (as indicated before) the latter will not accept. Quite apart from the losses of the individual account holders, the capacity of the remaining banking system to accommodate the accumulation of capital is reduced with the reduction in the number of banks (at least for a considerable period of time).

The ClB's security and liability rules, and their upholding, are therefore essential to the banking system. Would lack of either of those nevertheless result in the beginning of a banking crisis, then the latter can only be prevented if the ClB (or at a later stage of the exposition, the Central Bank) would have sufficient means, first, to pre-empt the flight of clients of the bad banks, by vast loans to the bad banks, or to other banks that are willing to take over the bad banks, and secondly, such that its trustworthiness remains intact. (The latter relates to the amount of dubiously backed loans as assets, which in the end might need to be written down, and along with it the ClB's capital).[37]

The failure of one or perhaps a few small banks will usually have no significant impact on the economy. *Graph 2.11* provides information on the frequency of banking crises (more broadly financial crises) resulting in a recession. This figure is based on data collected by Jorda, Schularick and Taylor (2012) from 14

37 We will see later (7D2) that for this reason it is hard for a Central Bank to be 'independent' of the state.

OECD countries over the period 1870–2008.[38] Of the total number of the recessions/crises in this period, 22% were of financial origin. The figure shows the average number of financially originated recessions per country per decade.

GRAPH 2.11 *Average number of recessions associated with financial crises, per decade and per country 1870–2008, for a sample of 14 current OECD countries*[39]

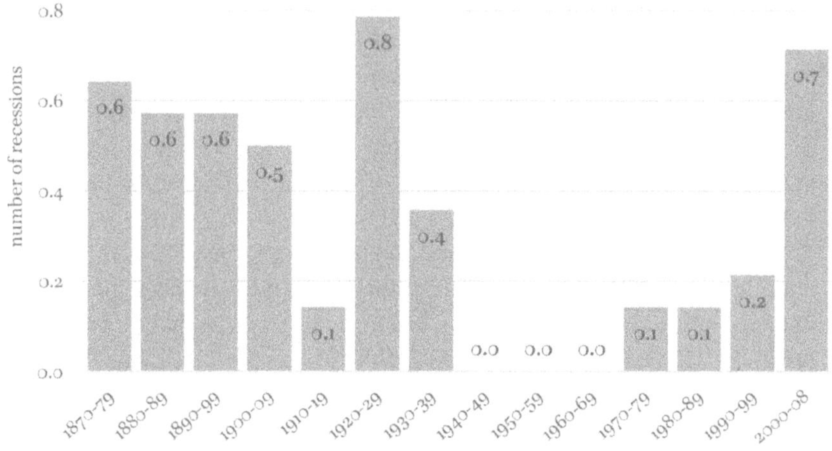

DATA SOURCE: calculated from Jorda, Schularick and Taylor (2012), Table 1

2§10-c Explication. Money at the current level of the exposition

With the current concretisation of money (2§8–2§10), the requirement of the expansion of the quantity-flow of money in connection with the accumulation of capital (2§3) has been grounded in the 'fairly' concrete *actual* existence of money.

However, at this level of the exposition, abstraction is yet made from two main subjects. First, the state and its Central Bank (Chapter 7) – as we will see, this abstraction is only moderately important in normal times, though it is important in times of severe financial crisis. Second, banks in their role as financiers of enterprises (Chapter 3), which is vital. So far, banks have mainly been presented in their role of creating money, which is a general condition for the accumulation of capital.

In fact the current division presented (the limits of) the conditions of existence of a banking constellation under the umbrella of a completely independ-

38 Australia, Canada, Denmark, France, Germany, Italy, Japan, Netherlands, Norway, Spain, Sweden, Switzerland, UK and USA.

39 See the previous footnote.

ent 'Central Bank' – at the current level of abstraction (all of Part One), I have used the term 'Clearing Bank'.

2§10-d Addendum. References

The terminology in 2§10 of 'anticipation', 'private pre-validation' and 'social validation' originates from De Brunhoff (1978 [1976], p. 46); see also Aglietta (1979 [1976], pp. 332–5). Much of the exposition of money at a similar expositional level in Reuten and Williams (1989) drew on these two authors as well as De Vroey (1984). However, the exposition of the creation of money in the current division deviates from these authors (that is, the current division posits money creation as completely disconnected from any remnants of commodity to commodity exchange, commodity money, and so-called 'high-powered' money). This exposition is rather in line with the Monetary Circuit theory (amplified in addendum 3§2-e).

Division 5. Separation-in-unity of enterprises and banks

2§11 ***Separation-in-unity of enterprises and banks***

We have seen how the creation of money by banks is one of the two major conditions of existence of the accumulation of capital (2D4). The early starting point was the capitalist economy's outward bifurcation into households and privately owned enterprises (1D1). Banks entered the exposition at the point required (2D4), though without amplification on their identity.

The necessary condition of existence of banks is the *separation between banks and enterprises*. (The latter can now more specifically be called 'production enterprises', and when henceforth I use the term 'enterprise', the term can be replaced by 'production enterprise'). The separation is necessary to the extent that bank-issued money must be generally accepted as money. Were this separation not the case, we would have the unresolved fragmentation of 'trade' at the level of 1§2, i.e. prior to the exposition of money as the unity of measure and medium of value. Further, the separation is enforced by the operation of banks under the umbrella of a rules-setting Clearing Bank (2§9).

Nevertheless, banks, as much as enterprises, are driven by profit-making in monetary terms and by expanded profit-making through the accumulation of capital. In this respect there is *no difference* between enterprises and banks. Further, each of the enterprises and banks have no existence independently from each other. In these respects, they constitute a 'unity'. There is a 'mere' functional 'difference in unity'. Commodities (as always this includes commodified services) are produced within enterprises, and money is created within banks. However, *for banks* this activity is *dealing in money* as if it were a commodity like any other, and in this sense we have, *for banks*, a *commodification of money*.[40]

This complexity – of necessary difference and separation versus non-difference and identity – between enterprises and banks, is captured by positing it as a *separation-in-unity*. This necessary separation-in-unity is a concrete institutional reflection of the abstract 'inward bifurcation of the commodity' (1§5).

Thus we have the seeming paradox that banks are driven by profit-making in terms of money, the entity that, concretely, they themselves create. Rather, they create money for others (other enterprises, generally other actors) but calculate their own degree of success in the same monetary terms.

2§11-a Explication. The distinction between 'separation-in-unity' and 'outward bifurcation'

Both 'outward bifurcations' and 'separations-in-unity' relate to major institutional separation. In this book the only outward bifurcation is that between households and privately owned enterprises (1§1). Outwardly bifurcated entities are generally each *driven by different objectives*. In contradistinction, the different institutional entities of a 'separation-in-unity' (s-i-u) are (*ultimately*) *each driven by the same objective*. Next to the current s-i-u (2D5) one more follows in 2D7 of this chapter. Three further s-i-u's are presented in Chapters 6–7.

2§11-b Explication. Similarity and difference between enterprises and banks

The main text posits that banks, as much as enterprises, are driven by profit-making in monetary terms and by expanded profit-making through the accumulation of capital, concluding that – in this respect – there is no difference between enterprises and banks. Nevertheless it is also the case that banks, in their role of *money creation and lending*, do not produce surplus-value, but rather share in the surplus-value produced in enterprises (amplified in Chapter 3). Even so, the degree of banks' success, as well as that of enterprises, is measured by the rate of profit on their capital (1§13 – amplified in Chapter 3).

40 It is important to keep the terminology subtle here. This 'commodification of money' has nothing to do with the historical phenomenon of 'commodity money'.

Division 6. Incorporation of enterprises

Labour-capacity expansion (2D2) and money expansion (2D4) are the proximate conditions of the accumulation of capital (2D1). The continuity and scale of the latter is further grounded in the corporate enterprise, as presented in the final two divisions of this chapter (see *Scheme 2.1*).

So far, the main part of the exposition explicitly presented four categories of actors: labour; managerial labour; enterprises; and banks (the latter two so far coinciding with their owners). This division introduces two further categories of actors: shareholders and the administrative management of the enterprise.

2§12 *The tendency for enterprises to take the corporate form*

The expansion of labour-capacity and money (2D2 and 2D4) are necessary conditions for the accumulation of capital. The incorporation of enterprises grounds the continuity and the possible scale of the accumulation of capital. Whereas small enterprises can come and go as non-incorporated firms, there is a strong drive to incorporation and generally a necessary one for medium- to large-sized enterprises, which is reinforced over time (diachronically). The non-absolute character of the corporate form (especially for small enterprises) is captured by the concept of 'tendency' (see Explication 2§12-a).

There is a tendency for enterprises to take the corporate form for five reasons. First, regarding the continuity of a single enterprise, the corporate form potentially overcomes problems of succession (the shares rather than the enterprise are passed on to the inheritors). Second, the corporate enterprise allows for the *limitation* of risk and uncertainty (that is, to the value of the share). Third, the corporate form allows for the *spread* of risk and uncertainty over many corporations – many owners spreading their capital over many corporations.[41] Fourth, the corporate form overcomes limits associated with the required scale of enterprises (either technically or competitively). A fifth main drive to incorporation pertains to the expansion of the finance of the enterprise (presented in 3§5.)

A similar tendency to incorporation applies to banks.

The corporate form of enterprises entails a particular separation of its ownership, the ownership being a layered one. Whereas the *shareholders* are the owners of the enterprise, *the enterprise* as corporate body is the owner of the

41 In the latter respect there is a disparity between these capital owners and labour: labourers cannot spread the risk and uncertainty for unemployment over many enterprises (If the employer does not insist on a full-time engagement, they can sometimes spread the risk over some but not many enterprises).

'active capital' (the assets).[42] The management of the latter ownership is delegated to administrators (see 2§13). Further, the shareholder is not responsible for the practices of the enterprise (the enterprise is).[43] The shareholder is merely financially liable, and limited to the extent of the nominal value of the shares brought in.[44]

The executive management of the corporate enterprise, as set out in 2§13, also applies to banks.

2§12-a Explication. Tendencies

A tendency should be distinguished from an empirical 'trend'. A tendency is a process working in a certain direction, such that an entity takes a certain form or quantitative expression. A tendency is always predicated on certain forces or compulsions. Therefore an alternative formulation is: A tendency is the generation of a particular form of an entity or the particular quantitative expression of an entity, this generation being predicated on certain forces or compulsions. (In the current case of the tendency for enterprises to take the corporate form, the tendency is predicated on the five forces indicated in 2§12).

In general, tendencies may be *counteracted* by other tendencies, or by other, lower level complexities. A tendency is a determinant whose *actualisation* might not always predominate in any individual case (for example, enterprises that do not take the corporate form because of their financial structure or for taxation reasons). However, to have the status of a tendency (in this book), it must apply to a significant number of cases such that, when abstracting from counteracting tendencies, it has a *predominant character for the totality*. (See also the General Appendix, A§14).

The 'tendency for enterprises to take the corporate form' is predicated on the forces associated with the growth of the average capital of enterprises.

2§12-b Explication. Enterprise: form of 'firm', form of 'corporation'

With the introduction of the corporation it is now explicit that enterprises operate either as 'firms' (non-incorporated enterprises) or as a 'corporation' (incorporated enterprises). In 6§10 these are posited as legal forms of the enterprise.

42 The specific powers of the shareholders are defined in the corporation's charter.

43 Responsibility rests with the enterprise and its administrator(s). However, with the possible exception of criminal matters (cf. criminal law as introduced in Ch. 6), the administrator is not financially liable.

44 For non-corporate forms of the enterprise, the owner(s) is (or are) fully liable – extended to their wealth in person.

2§13 *The executive management of the corporate enterprise*

The executive management is the administrator and representative of the enterprise as corporate body. The main requirement for these officers is that they have *internalised the norms* of the enterprise (2§7). Briefly, these relate to the optimal production of surplus-value, with a view to an optimal rate of integral profit and accumulation of capital.

Regarding especially the accumulation of capital, the effectiveness of the management's internalisation of the enterprise's norms may contingently be more encompassing than the shareholders' norms of the enterprise, as revealed in (contingent) conflicts over the degree of retaining profits (2§14-a).

Whereas the executive management is formally employed by the enterprise, these managers perceive themselves as employers. This reveals their internalisation of the norms of the enterprise as corporate body. Effectively this management is no longer 'managerial labour' (2§7), but rather the *executive officer of active capital*, and hence of the enterprise-labour relation (2§7 for the latter).

Although the above pertains to the top executive management (which tends to be larger to the extent that the enterprise is larger), I reiterate what was mentioned in 2§7 about the middle and lower management, which may, qua aspiration, feel itself attached to the top management rather than to ordinary labour. (From the perspective of the enterprise side of the enterprise-labour relation, this is quite an achievement).

2§13-a Amplification. Conflicts between management and shareholders over information and distribution of profits

In the relation between the corporate management and shareholders there is ample scope for contingent conflicts of interest. In this amplification I mention the two major themes of such conflict: information and distribution of profits.

Information. For shareholders the selection of shareholding in one or another enterprise is a matter of perception of diverging risk and uncertainty and expected concomitant returns (systematically introduced in 2§15). Shareholders therefore usually have an interest in obtaining optimal information about the enterprises and accordingly in binding the management to rules for transparent and consistent annual reports and accounts, as uniformly applicable between enterprises. The management, on the other hand, will usually be reluctant to provide transparency for reasons of competitive strategy. There seems to be no ready solution to this conflict.

Distribution of profits. The distribution of the profits of the enterprise (profits meaning surplus-value after payment of interest) centres on two aspects.

Firstly, the decision as to what share of profits is retained or distributed. Generally the logic of the enterprise is that profit is accumulated, and hence that it – microeconomically – be retained and invested (2D1). The management's internalisation of the norms of the enterprise would then normally imply a moderate distribution of profits, along with a substantial accumulation of capital. Given this logic it is not obvious why shareholders would want profits to be distributed beyond some threshold. Retained profits would normally result in an increase in both the equity and share prices – which an individual shareholder might wish to sell.

Secondly, given agreement on the share of profits retained, there is a potential source of conflict over the question of *if*, and if so to what degree, the management should be rewarded in terms of shares in the enterprise – be it via donation out of a share buyback or out of new shares. (I present the matter in this analytical order. In practice this may have been decided upon the appointment of the management). The reasoning on the part of existing shareholders is apparently straightforward: when the management has a stake in shareholding it will look after itself, hence after 'us' (assuming guarantees that the management cannot sell in the short-run). However, the assumption behind this shareholders' view, rightly or wrongly, is that quite a lot of shareholders do not have much confidence in the average manager's internalisation of the norms of the enterprise. The same applies for the case when the management's salary is linked to the enterprise's results (bonuses).

2§14 *Separation-in-unity of the shareholders and the executive management of the incorporated enterprise*

The corporate enterprise entails a layered separation of its ownership (2§12). In addition, there is a separation between, on the one hand, the ownership and management of the corporation's 'active capital', and, on the other, the ownership of the enterprise in the form of the shareholding 'passive capital' (2§12–2§13).

Even if and when the corporate enterprise's layered ownership separation may contingently result in conflicts between the shareholders and the executive management (2§13-a), the two constitute a *separation-in-unity*. The unity pertains to the aims of the enterprise, that is, the objective of the 'enterprise-labour relation' (2§7). That is, they unite (in brief) in the perceived requirement for the extraction of surplus-value from labour, and ultimately also in its accumulation within the enterprise.

Division 7. The twofold accumulation of capital

Owners of enterprises and owners of passive capital; the enterprise-labour relation as reflected in the capital-labour relation

The previous division focused on the ownership-management relation of the corporate enterprise. The current division (one section) focuses exclusively on ownership relations, particularly in face of the starting point's 'privately owned enterprises' (1D1). It considers the form and character of 'privately owned enterprises' in relation to the form of the 'ownership of passive capital'.

2§15 *Twofold accumulation of capital – enterprises and owners of passive capital*

The exposition's starting point is the bifurcation between households and privately owned enterprises (1§1). We have seen that enterprises are driven by the production of surplus-value and the accumulation of capital, conceived as the 'active capital', that is, the capital assets of the enterprise (1§13). We have a parallel accumulation for the 'passive capital', that is, the enterprise's liabilities (recall the enterprise's balance sheet of Figure 1.4 in 1§13-a).

1 The detached form of capital ownership together with the owner's mere instrumental ownership of enterprises

Regarding the ownership of 'passive capital', the exposition at this point is restricted to passive capital as the enterprise's 'own-capital' (in cases of non-incorporated enterprises) or as 'equity' (in cases of incorporated enterprises – equity being the sum of the nominal value of the shares and the reserves of the enterprise).[45]

The private ownership of the non-incorporated enterprise (the firm), together with the owner's 'own-capital', can be characterised as an 'involved ownership'. With the moment of the corporate enterprise (2D6) and especially the shareholder's objective to limit and to spread its risk and uncertainty (2§12), a new form of passive capital has been introduced. We now have a *detached* form of passive capital ownership – detached from the management and the direct production of capital. This implies that the ownership of the enterprise, or of a particular enterprise, is not the capital owner's object, but rather an *instrument* for its capital ownership in general. Thus whereas for an enterprise, the particular commodity produced is merely instrumental for the generation of

45 Other forms of ownership of passive capital are presented in 3§5.

surplus-value (1§13), the particular corporate enterprise now appears as instrumental for the passive capital owner – switching the passive capital to another enterprise if this seems advantageous. Hence the already abstract drive for mono-dimensional surplus-value and accumulation of active capital (for any enterprise) is, for the corporate enterprises, concretely paralleled by a detached abstract drive for accumulation of mono-dimensional passive capital. Nevertheless, the corporate capital owner cannot simply escape from an enterprise: it has to find another capital owner willing to substitute, at some price, its shareholding.

Table 2.12 summarises these distinctions. Thus in reference to the exposition's starting point (private property of enterprises), the exposition has now reached two forms of private property of enterprises (non-incorporated or incorporated), each with a different character (involved or detached), and in addition, two forms of passive capital ownership (own-capital or equity).

TABLE 2.12 *Forms of the ownership of enterprises and forms of ownership of passive capital*

Form of ownership enterprise	Character	Form of passive capital ownership†
non-incorporated enterprises (sole owner or partnership)‡	involved ownership	(share of) the own-capital of enterprises
incorporated enterprises (limited liability shares)	detached instrumental ownership	share of the equity of enterprises

† Other forms of capital ownership are presented in Chapter 3.
‡ One or more partners can have a limited liability, though not all.

2 *Twofold accumulation of capital*

As indicated, the ownership of the incorporated enterprise is instrumental and rather formal for the passive capital owner, whereas for a non-incorporated enterprise (a firm) the ownership of the enterprise is an involved one.[46] Sooner or later there are nevertheless limits to this involvement, that is, when the owner considers selling the enterprise (perhaps at the owner's retirement age) – so being 'in process of detachment'. Even without that possible prospect, the owner is evidently conscious of the amount of 'own-capital'.

46 This is different when a sole owner of a firm (or a partnership) opts for conversion into a corporation, without aiming for a major spread of risk.

Even if for any *individual* enterprise the active capital is simply equal to, as well as inherently inseparable from, the passive capital (assets = liabilities), the detached form of capital ownership makes the *accumulation of passive capital* into a separate motive, whence accumulation of capital (2D1) now appears as a disunited *twofold accumulation of capital*. Nevertheless, even if the passive capital ownership is such a detached one, active capital and the growth of active capital is produced in enterprises and in enterprises only. Passive capital is only its reflection. Thus *some* enterprise is the necessary instrument for the detached capital ownership.[47]

3 *The capital-labour relation*

Alongside the twofold accumulation of capital, the concrete 'enterprise-labour relation' (2§7) is reflected in an actually abstract 'capital-labour' relation. This is the indirect exploitative relation between the passive capital ownership and labour. As passive capital grows on the basis of the enterprise's appropriation, and next the distribution, of surplus-value, passive capital owners are involved in the exploitative relation (including those that have never seen 'their enterprise vehicle' from the inside).

2§15-a Amplification. The categories of capital owners, managers and labour, in terms of their relative size and income shares: USA 1918–2012 (Mohun 2016)

At the current level of the exposition, 'passive capital ownership' is an as yet incomplete category (of the components lacking, loan capital is the most important one – this is presented in 3§5). Nevertheless, I already provide at this point some quantitative empirical information about the categories of passive capital owners, managers and labour. In an important and novel paper, Mohun (2016) has estimated the development of these three main classes in the USA from 1918–2012. He adopts the following definitions – as operationalised in his paper, that is, given the available data. (1) 'Subordinate workers' are managed without managing themselves. 'Managers' do manage other workers, though they are themselves also managed by other managers – and ultimately by the capital owners.[48] (2) 'Capitalists' have sufficient non-labour income meaning that they are not forced to engage in an employment contract (although typically they do engage in such employment); managers do not have enough non-labour income to meet that threshold. (3) Labour income is composed of

---

47 This indeed relates to 'capital' ownership. Later on in the exposition, we will see that there are other forms of 'monetary wealth' to which this necessity may not apply.

48 Note that this managerial class is thus much wider than merely CEOs.

wages, salaries and pensions. The latter, when employment-related, is in fact a postponed wages component (cf. Chapter 3, Appendix 3A-2). *Table 2.13* summarises these definitions.

TABLE 2.13 *Economic characteristics of the three main classes*

	Non-labour income (from asset ownership = all income except wages, salaries and pensions)	**labour income (wages, salaries and pensions)**	**management position**
capitalists	sufficient	not required	†
managers	not sufficient	yes	manage and being managed
subordinate workers	not sufficient	yes	being managed

† When capitalists are engaged in an employment contract this will typically be in a management function.

Mohun bases the threshold for capitalists' 'sufficient' non-labour income on the average of various measures, including the mean labour income and the maximum labour income, and also including weights for the number of persons dependent on one income. In effect the threshold for the year 2012, for example, is set at about $56,000 for a single person tax unit (Mohun 2016, pp. 345–8), which was about two times the average working class labour income (ibid., p. 353).

Graph 2.14 shows some of Mohun's main findings (he himself produces more detailed graphs). The first graph shows the development of the classes mentioned in terms of their numbers, and the second one in terms of income shares. See Mohun (2016) for comments on the development of the class composition and the income shares throughout the period shown in these graphs. He concludes that the 'inequality of income in class terms is currently [i.e. in 2012] greater than at any other time since 1918' (ibid., p. 359).

Summary and conclusions

The rationale of the enterprises' driving force of mono-dimensional profit (Chapter 1) is more of the same: profit augmentation. Such augmentation could in principle be reached by continuously increasing the productive power of

GRAPH 2.14 *Main classes in terms of number of tax units and in terms of income shares – USA 1918–2012. Lefts panel: main classes in terms of number of tax units (% of total); right panel: income share of classes (area chart) and income ratio of capitalist class to subordinated working class and to managerial class (column graph)*

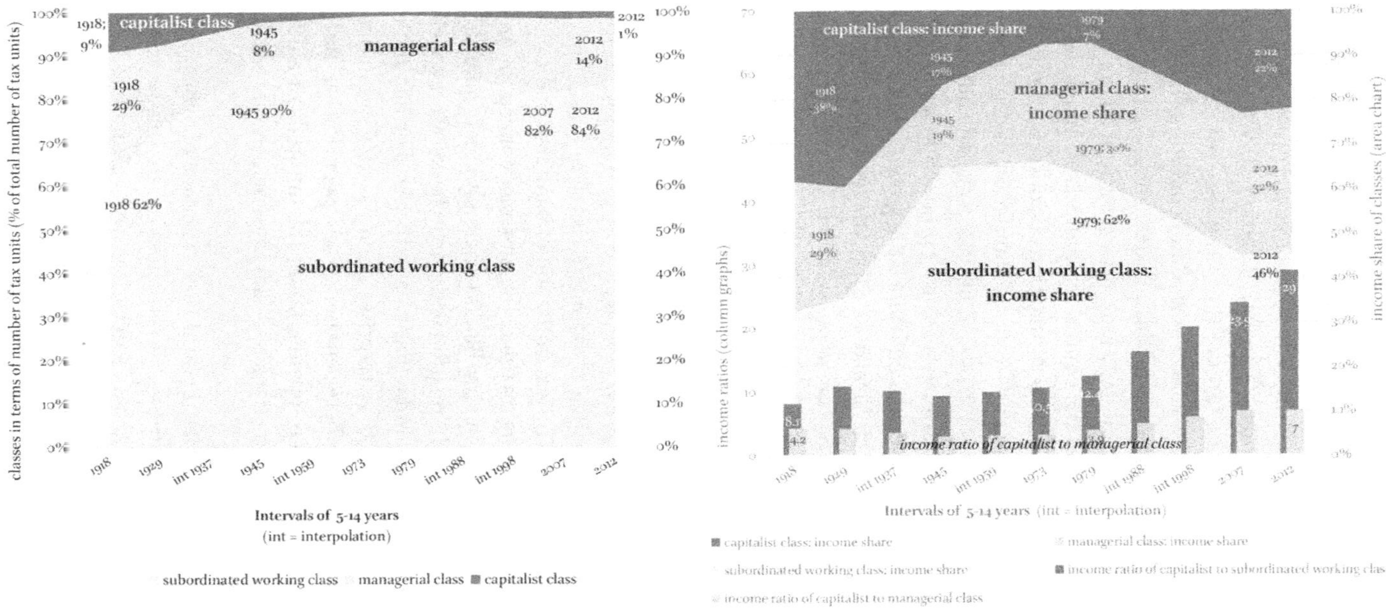

DATA SOURCE: Mohun 2016, Table 1. The years 1918, 1929, 1945 1973, 1979 and 2007 are approximately USA peak years of the cycle (that is, the non-interpolated years except the year 2012).

labour, but such increase is nevertheless limited. Profit is further enlarged via its investment as capital, whence capital is accumulated. (Division 1).

There are two major necessary conditions of existence for this accumulation. First, an accommodating expansion of labour-capacity (Division 2), and second, an accommodating expansion of money (Division 4). A third condition, namely the corporate form of the enterprise, contributes to continuous accumulation of capital, without being a hard condition (Division 6).

The first condition. At a given technically determined capital-labour ratio, the accumulation of capital generally requires a growth in labour population. The latter, however, is beyond the control of enterprises. At a given growth in the labour population, the rate of accumulation of capital is ultimately determined by the rate of unemployment – thus accumulation of capital requires unemployment. Unemployment presses the average wage rate down, and presses up 'the degree of compliance of labour during production', each positively affecting the surplus-value produced and hence the growth of capital. (Division 2.)

Given the labour-capacity available, the management of the enterprise manages what I call the '*enterprise-labour relation*'. This is the employment relation at the point of production through which surplus-value is extracted from labour, as constrained by: first, the technique of production; second, the rate of unemployment; and third (in face of that rate), the management of the compliance of labour during production, as assisted by the managerial device of a wages ladder that optimises this compliance. This requires the workers' (self-)perception that the lower rated work is important though inferior, so that they can be reconciled to their position. (Division 3.)

The second condition. The accumulation of capital's condition of an expansion of money is – building on the earlier abstract concept of money of 1D2 – grounded in bank-issued money. Banks concretely create quantities of money, based on a reciprocal credit relation with their clients. More specifically, banks 'pre-validate' the future production of enterprises. Further, the expansion of the domain of operation of enterprises requires cooperation between banks, resulting in debt relations between them. The insecurities of the latter are mitigated when banks agree to operate under the umbrella of a dominant bank that functions as a Clearing Bank and that imposes security and liability rules. (Division 4.)

The subsequent necessary condition of existence of banks is the *separation* between banks and enterprises. Nevertheless the two also constitute a 'unity', because banks, just as much as enterprises, are driven by profit-making, and because both enterprises and banks have no existence independent of each other. Hence banks and enterprises constitute a *separation-in-unity*. (Division 5.)

The third condition. Small enterprises can come and go as non-incorporated firms. However, the continuity of the accumulation of capital by medium- and large-scale enterprises generally requires their incorporation. Incorporation is driven by the threats surrounding succession, by the limitation and spread of risk and uncertainty, and by limits in respect of the scale of enterprises. The corporate form of the enterprise entails a layered form of its ownership, with the shareholders being the owners of the enterprise, and the enterprise as corporate body being the owner of the 'active capital', which is administered by the executive management of the corporation. Although this particular governance separation may contingently result in conflicts between the two layers, these nevertheless constitute a separation-in-unity. (Division 6.)

The last division of the chapter puts the corporate enterprise in the perspective of the exposition's starting point of privately owned enterprises (1D1). Along with the shareholder's objective to limit and spread its risk and uncertainty, we have a *detached* form of passive capital ownership. The ownership of a particular enterprise is not the capital owner's object, but rather an *instrument* for its passive capital ownership in general – a detachment that, sooner or later, also applies to the non-incorporated enterprise. Although for an *individual* enterprise the 'active capital' (assets) and the 'passive capital' (liabilities) are inherently *inseparable*, the detached form of passive capital ownership turns the *accumulation of passive capital* into a separate motive, whereby the accumulation of capital (2D1) now appears as a disunited *twofold accumulation of capital*. Nevertheless, *some* enterprise must be the necessary instrument for the detached capital ownership. In this way the concrete, directly exploitative 'enterprise-labour relation' is reflected in the actually abstract indirect exploitative relation between the passive capital owner and labour, that is, the actually abstract 'capital-labour' relation. (Division 7.)

List of figures chapter 2

CHAPTER 3

Finance of enterprises

The macroeconomic pre-validation and validation of production

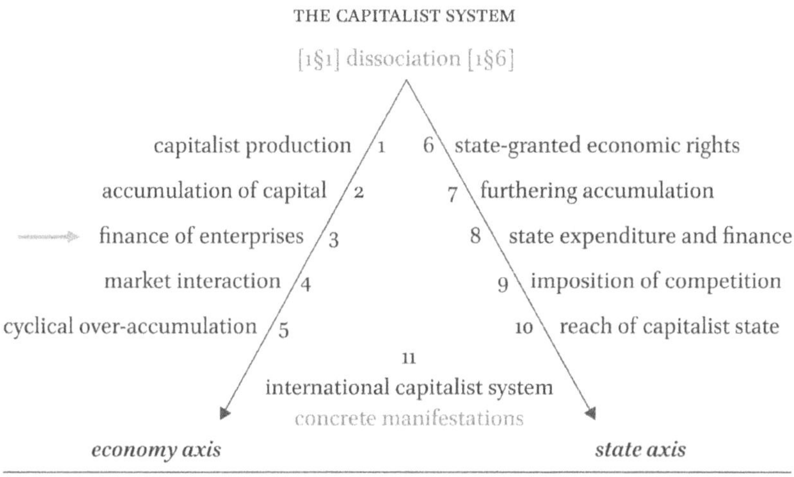

Contents

DOI:10.1163/9789004392809_005

Introduction

This chapter grounds the production and accumulation of capital in the financing of enterprises by banks. It was shown that money creation by banks is a necessary condition of existence for the accumulation of capital (2D4). In the way this grounding moment of money creation was presented – that is, starting from the concept of *money* – it has been implicit that banks in fact *finance* enterprises. In making this explicit in the current chapter (Division 2) we will see not only that the finance by banks is a continuous necessity for the accumulation of capital, but also that it is unlike any other type of finance. In the course of Division 3 it will be shown how other types of finance, once bank finance has done its work, may substitute for the finance provided by banks.

At that stage of the exposition, a grounding of the starting point's preposition (1§1) of 'capital accumulated' can be provided (Division 4).

It will be seen in this chapter that a systematic exposition of finance is inevitably connected to key macroeconomic questions and theorems. Next to the concept of finance, the key concepts are investment and saving. Based on a 'monetary circuit approach' – as opposed to the traditional quantity of money (or money fund) approach – it will be shown: (1) that saving is no precondition for *investment*;[1] (2) that – given the existence of saving – there is no macroeconomic investment 'out of saving'; (3) that there may be merely an 'ex post' *portfolio* investment out of savings; (4) that the latter is always preceded by banks' financing of the enterprises' *investment*; a finance on the basis of an ex nihilo creation of money (Divisions 2 and 5).

Even if saving is no precondition for investment and the accumulation of capital, saving is nevertheless ubiquitous. Its negative effect on the realisation of surplus-value – and hence on the accumulation of capital – is presented in Division 5 in terms of macroeconomic effective demand; here I build on insights from Kalecki.

Beside the chapter's main focus of the finance of enterprises, Appendix B outlines lending by banks to labour and to capital owners. Appendix A outlines two contingencies of the finance-capital market regarding the scope of pension funds and the secondary trade in financial paper. Appendix C briefly expands on the treatment of rent in this book.

Scheme 3.1 outlines the systematic of the chapter.

1 When I use the term 'investment' I *always* mean 'direct' or 'real' investment (mainly in means of production) as opposed to 'portfolio investment'.

SCHEME 3.1 *Systematic of the finance of enterprises (outline Chapter 3)*

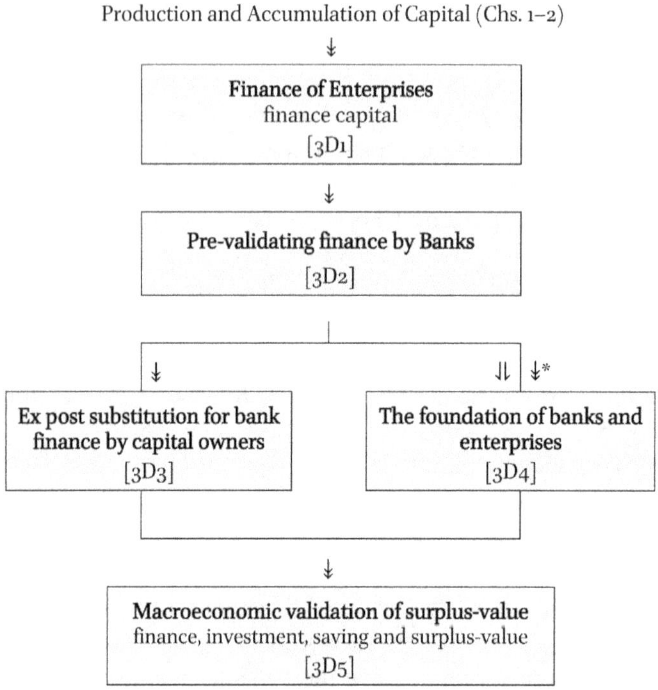

Appendix 3A: Contingent intertemporal and re-substitution financial trade
Appendix 3B: Contingent lending by banks to labour and capital owners
Appendix 3C: Rent as a contingent share in the production enterprises' surplus-value

Legend

↡ grounded in (conditioned by)
⇃↾ bottom moment derives from top moment

* The moment 3D4 derives from 3D2. Along with it, it is a major ground of the starting point (1D1).

Division 1. Finance of enterprises and finance capital

3§1 *Finance of enterprises, passive finance capital and the distribution of surplus-value to financiers*

1 *Finance and the distribution of surplus-value*

In the last division of Chapter 2 (2D7), I started distinguishing between 'active capital' (the capital assets of the enterprise) and 'passive capital'. From now on, the latter will more specifically be called 'passive finance capital' – the main subject of the current chapter. Active capital is always financed by some form of 'passive finance capital'.

Within the latter category a distinction is made between the *external* form of finance capital (provided by external financiers), and the remaining *internal* form of finance capital, which is the 'own capital' (firm) or the 'equity' (corporation) of the enterprises' owners.

Within the form of *external* finance capital, a distinction is made between external finance by banks and other external finance (finance by capital owners) – see *Figure 3.2a*. At the top of this figure (column four) we have banks – we will see in 3D2 that *any* finance (including internal finance) necessarily starts with bank finance.

Figure 3.2b shows where, and in what form, surplus-value (stemming from the enterprises' production, associated with active capital) is distributed. In the form of interest it is distributed to banks and to capital owners (amplified in 3§4–3§5). The remaining part is *internal profit* (in common parlance, 'profit').[2] One part of the latter is distributed to capital owners in the form of a 'dividend', whilst the remaining part of 'retained profit' is added to the enterprise's 'own capital' (for firms) or 'equity' (corporations).

2 *Banks and 'banking entities'*

In order to keep the exposition in this chapter as simple as possible, banks are conceptualised purely as creators of money and as financiers. Any labour that this might require is outsourced to a separate 'production branch' of the banking entity, which I subsume under the enterprises sector. This means that the (pure) banks are not producers. Empirically 'banking entities' are engaged in gigantic bookkeeping services (account management), credit evaluations and

[*continued*]

2 Marx and much of marxian political economy use the term 'profit of enterprise'. This term does not fit the conceptualisation in this book as 'surplus-value' is the 'integral profit' of the enterprise. The concept of 'internal profit' will be expanded on in 5§1.

FIGURE 3.2A *Active capital and forms of passive finance capital*

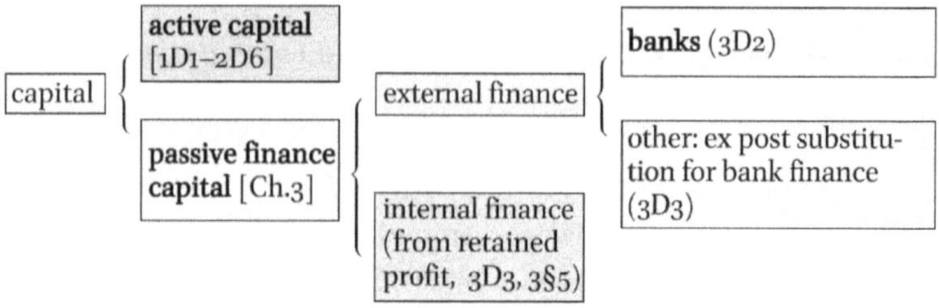

FIGURE 3.2B *The distribution of surplus-value to passive finance capital*†

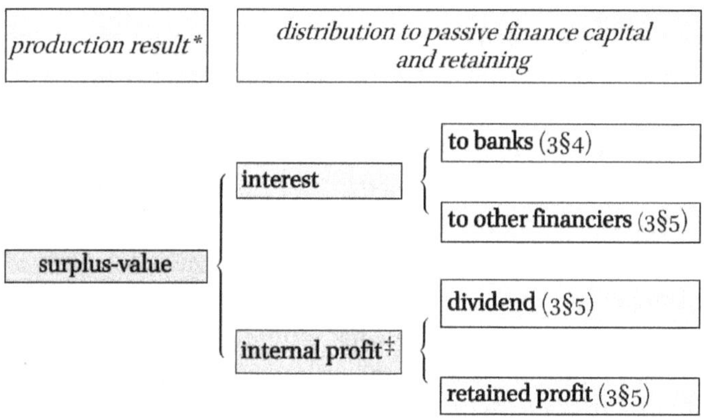

† Prior to introduction of the state.
* More precisely the result of production and its validation (explained in 3§10).
‡ Includes rent (see Appendix 3C).

3§1 *Continued*

various advisory services. These are equally allotted to the banking entity's 'production branch'.

Banks receive (net) interest from enterprises. Part of this interest is added to the bank's own capital (own capital or equity). The remaining part of the interest is distributed to the banking entity's 'production branch', which may itself also have commission income for its various activities.

As indicated, this chapter (its main text) deals with the finance of enterprises. Banks are also engaged in money creation and the finance of other actors. This is briefly dealt with in Appendix 3B (and regarding the state in Chapter 8).

3§1-a Explication. The balance sheet of enterprises

Sheet 3.3 shows the equivalent of Figure 3.2a in the form of the balance sheet of enterprises.

SHEET 3.3 *Balance sheet of enterprises*†

Assets [active capital]		**Liabilities [passive finance capital]**	
• plant and equipment • raw materials etc. • work in progress • commodities produced • current account with banks		*External finance capital* • Loans from banks • Loans from non-bank financiers (bonds) *Internal finance capital*	a b
value equivalent of a + b	K		K=FC

† This sheet relates to enterprises that produce commodities, rather than enterprises engaged in their distribution (mainly transport and retail) or various services, for which the assets side would have a modified form. Commercial claims and commercial debts have been omitted (and are neglected in this chapter).

Division 2. Pre-validating finance by banks

3§2 *The monetary circuit of pre-validating finance by banks (PVF): the pure case of non-saving*

In a capitalist economy, the creation of money coincides with the act of lending by banks (2§8). Put more strongly, net lending by banks *is* money creation. It was shown that the expanded creation of money by banks is necessary for the accumulation of capital (2§10).

1 *Accumulation of capital necessarily initiated by banks' pre-validating finance*

Expanded money creation is now further concretised as the banks' *finance* of enterprises (the current division). In a capitalist economy, any macroeconomic accumulation of capital, and hence any economic growth, must be not only accommodated but also necessarily *initiated* with money creation by banks. More precisely, with the provision of money-creating loans to enterprises, banks provide a flow of *pre-validating finance* of production (cf. 2§10 on pre-validation). Banks thus provide enterprises with passive *finance capital.*

The pre-validating money creation by banks is required for the finance of investment in means of production. On top of that, there is a systemic continuous necessity for the creation of money to finance the payment of wages.[3] (Cf. the 'monetary circuit approach' – Addendum 3§2-e).

The required pre-validating money creation by banks is the common theme throughout this chapter. The current section presents this for the analytical case – the 'pure case' – in which economic actors do not save. As we will see, this pure case sheds an important light on the functioning of a capitalist economy. We will see this especially in the next section (3§3) when we consider the actually common situation in which many actors do save.

Banks are not usually interested in the enterprises' intended destination of a 'pre-validating finance' of production (PVF) as long as enterprises can provide sufficient securities to the bank. However, for *analytical* reasons the exposition in the current and the following division specifies the intended destination of the bank credit (PVF), thus revealing analytical circuits of credit flows.

The current section presents the pre-validation in three stages (subsections 2–4). Subsection 5 draws some conclusions.

2 *PVF for wages payment and for purchase of means of production: three macroeconomic categories (capital owners yet implicit)*

For the credit flows presented in *Circuit 3.4* three macroeconomic categories are distinguished: banks; the integrated set of enterprises; and labour. In pre-validating production (2§10), banks create account money for the set of enterprises.

Regarding the pre-validating finance (PVF) that enterprises destine for wages payments, the money created is transferred to the accounts of the labourers hired. Were all of this money transferred to labour or be spent with enterprises – that is, if there were no saving – then the money returns to the enterprises' accounts, so that the loan for the PVF with the bank can be fully redeemed (see the left stream in *Circuit 3.4*). The influx of money (start stream 1) is so compensated by a full efflux.

[continued]

3 This is even so when wages are paid at the end of the production period. Wages cannot be paid out of sales without a prior influx of money for those sales. They could only be paid out of sales if there were a sufficient influx stemming from money creation for the payment of means of production (cf. Explication 3§2-b).

CIRCUIT 3.4 *Macroeconomic pre-validating finance (PVF) by banks for wages payment and for purchase of means of production (MP) and their full redemption in case of full expenditure of the wage (capital owners being implicit)*

Imaginary 'circulation' within bank accounts

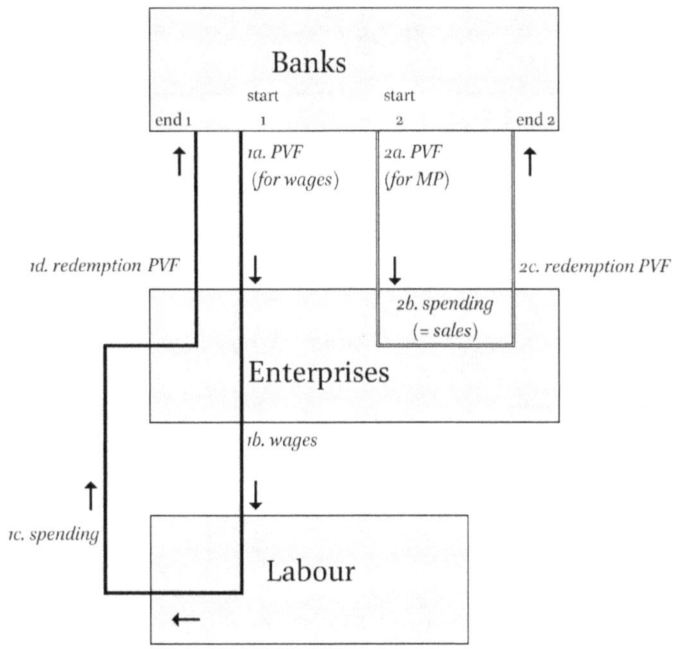

Note: *Circuit 3.4* is a picture of the money 'circulation' within bank accounts (the banks' bookkeeping), that is, first, the money creation (1a) followed by the transfers (1b–1d), and second, the money creation (2) followed by (internal) transfers (2b–2c) between enterprises.

3§2 *Continued*

Regarding the PVF that enterprises destine for the purchase of means of production (the right stream in *Circuit 3.4*), purchases and sales occur as equivalents within the macroeconomic set of enterprises, whence macroeconomically the PVF gets fully redeemed. (That is, provided the pre-validation of production indeed gets validated, or, in other words, when the planned validation of production would get realised – see Division 4).[4]

[continued]

4 See 2§10 under heading 3 for the case when enterprises make losses (expanded in Chapter 5).

CIRCUIT 3.5 *Pre-validating finance* (PVF) *by banks for the purchase of means of production (MP), and its full redemption in case of full expenditure of the wage; two macroeconomic enterprises' sectors (capital owners being implicit)*

Imaginary 'circulation' within bank accounts

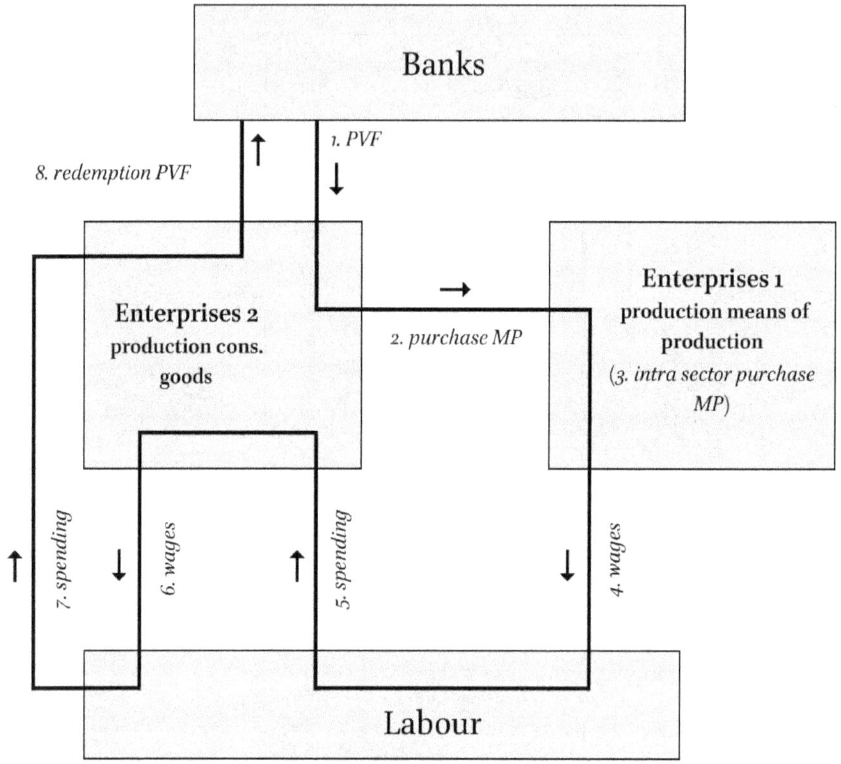

Note: For simplicity the PVF is reduced to one 'shot' (to Enterprises 2). Depending on the rate of depreciation of MP, the initial PVF may be redeemed within one period (rate 1 – this is what the picture shows) – or within several periods (rate <1); in the latter case the initial PVF may be equivalent to redemptions by other enterprises within the period. (For example, Enterprises 1 may immediately redeem a previous loan, in which case a stream 3 would go up to the banks, so postponing the streams 4–8).

3§2 *Continued*

3 PVF *for purchase of means of production along with wages payment: four macroeconomic categories (capital owners yet implicit)*

Circuit 3.5 presents the matter distinguishing two macroeconomic enterprises' sectors (those producing means of production and those producing consumer goods). Here the PVF combines purchases of means of production and wages payments. (All these are analytically reduced to 'one shot' of PVF – in practice there are numerous shots).

Note that both circuits 3.4. and 3.5 merely show how the production is *financed* by banks (and so far only by banks). These circuits do not show any surplus-value result along the production processes (1D5, specifically 1§14). (Explication 3§2-b shows the connection).

4 PVF *for wages payment, purchase of means of production and payment of dividends*

Circuit 3.6 reintegrates the macroeconomic enterprises sector (as in *Circuit 3.4*). Now, however, capital owners and their consumption are made explicit. Part of the surplus-value is distributed to capital owners in the form of dividends. Henceforth the term 'dividends' will include the 'quasi dividends' that flow from non-incorporated enterprises to their owners. At this point of the exposition it is analytically assumed that capital owners collect dividends of no more than their consumption (as is actually most often the case for non-incorporated enterprises).[5] In the next section (3§3) this assumption will be dropped.

Enterprises tend to maximally accumulate surplus-value as active capital, and to minimise on bank-credits, including for any transfers to capital owners (at some agreed point in time). To the extent that capital owners spend dividends for their consumption, this consumption validates production (amplified in 3D5). The payment of dividends therefore tends to be financed via a pre-validating bank finance, one that macroeconomically is redeemed to the extent that capital owners spend (in this section fully).[6] This is shown in the outer right flow of *Circuit 3.6*. I repeat that the PVFs shown analytically pertain to their destination, and that banks are not usually interested in the destination so long as enterprises provide sufficient securities to the bank.

5 For incorporated enterprises retained profits are reflected in the value of shares.

6 It could perhaps be argued that these dividends or interest payments might be settled out of monetary inflows to enterprises from sales. It might, but that would merely mean that the redemption of PVFs for wages and/or means of production would be postponed. It is insightful, and analytically pure, to separate these flows.

Alternatively the payment of dividends might be settled out of monetary inflows to enterprises from sales. That would merely mean that the redemption of PVFs for wages and/or means of production would be postponed. In whatever way enterprises actually settle the payment of dividends, it is analytically insightful to separate these flows. (The same holds for interest payments to capital owners, which will be systematically introduced only in 3§5).

CIRCUIT 3.6 *Pre-validating finance for wages, means of production and dividends; no saving by labour and by capital owners*

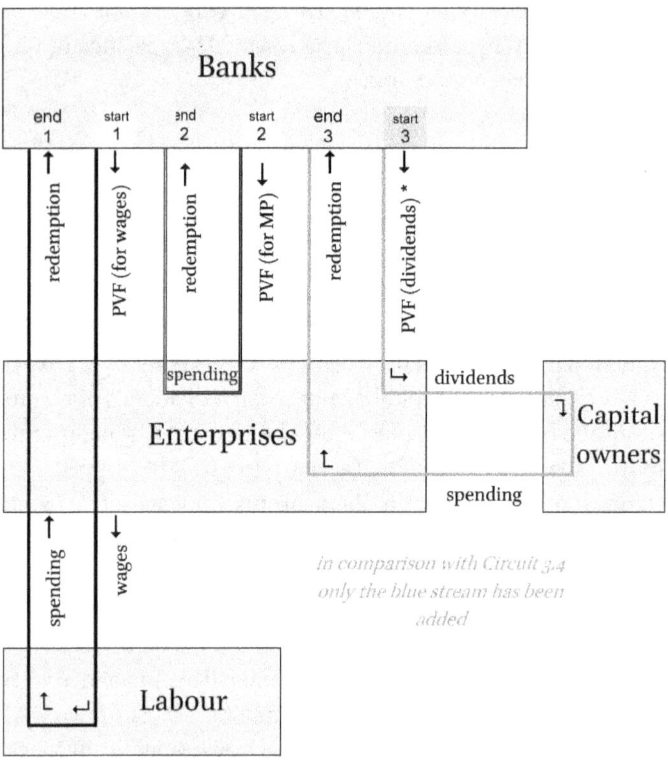

* The same applies for interest to capital owners (implicit until 3§5).

5 *PVF: saving not a precondition for investment*

So far this section has shown that savings are no condition for investment because in the 'pure case' presented above none of the actors saves. This is economically of utmost importance (expanded in 3§2-c).

In the three PVF circuits presented above, the influx of money is compensated by a full efflux. Upon economic growth, this is followed by an increasing PVF and along with it an increased re-influx and re-efflux of money (thus in non-recession periods, the macroeconomic PVF increases over time).

Savings are not necessary for the existence of the capitalist economy, but rather contingent (introduced in 3§3). The interest that banks charge is presented in 3§4.

3§2-a Explication. Macroeconomic varieties

Generally a macroeconomic approach provides particular insights that cannot be derived from a microeconomic approach, and vice versa. This explication briefly expands on some main macroeconomic varieties. (1) A *one-enterprise-sector macroeconomic* approach implies that all intermediate sales between enterprises are treated as being cancelled out (*Circuits 3.4 and 3.6*). In effect it implies a constellation 'as if' all enterprises are integrated into one enterprise. (2) The monetary circuit theory that I build on in this chapter insists that *banks as creators of money* should be treated as a separate macroeconomic category (cf. Addendum 3§2-e). (3) A *two-enterprise-sector macroeconomic* approach (*Circuit 3.5*) distinguishes between enterprises producing investment goods and those producing consumer goods. In effect this implies a constellation 'as if' all enterprises were treated as being integrated into two such distinguished enterprises.

These distinctions apply before and after the state and foreign relations are taken into account.

3§2-b Explication. Pre-validating finance and realisation of surplus-value – an illustration by way of a two-enterprises-sector model

This Explication is for those readers who might wonder how the constellation of pre-validating finance, as set out in 3§2, could accommodate the realisation of surplus-value for enterprises. This can be illustrated by way of a simple two-enterprises-sector model.[7] We have two sectors of production: *Sector 1* produces means of production (MP); *Sector 2* produces consumer goods (CG). Assume that: (1) all surplus-value (integral profit) is accumulated as capital (in the form of MP) – thus capital owners do not consume (or they also have a job as a worker); (2) there are no savings out of wages; and (3) all means of production are fully used up within the production period. The simple numerical example below (*Figure 3.7*) is in e.g. billions of some monetary standard ¤ and depicts an equilibrium case: the output of Sector 2 (CG) of ¤200 just equals the wages sum

7 This type of model derives from Marx's *Capital*, Volume II, Part Three (see Reuten 1998 for an appreciation).

of the two sectors together (¤200); the output of Sector 1 (MP) just equals the replacement of the means of production of the two sectors together (¤160) plus their surplus-value (¤40) as accumulated into additional means of production.

FIGURE 3.7 *Numerical example of a simple two-enterprises-sector model (in monetary standard ¤)*

	current input costs		value-added				output	
1. MP sector	80	+	100	+	20	=	200	(1)
2. CG sector	80	+	100	+	20	=	200	(2)
macro total	*160*	+	*200*	+	*40*	=	*400*	

(1) Sales: $(80_{\text{replacement-1}} + 20_{\text{investment-1}}) + (80_{\text{replacement-2}} + 20_{\text{investment-2}}) = 200$
(2) Sales: $100_{\text{consumption-Labourers-1}} + 100_{\text{consumption-Labourers-2}} = 200$

Then the question is how this constellation is accommodated in terms of pre-validating finance by banks. Normally this would go in several 'shots' of finance to each of the sectors. In order to keep this illustration as simple as possible, I assume just one PVF shot of ¤100 from the banks to the CG-producing enterprises. This caricatures the extent of the money-creating PVF, which is normally a fraction thereof. The earlier *Circuit 3.5* can now be reinterpreted in these terms (thus each stream in this circuit, 1, 2, etc., represents a value ¤100).

- Each sector started production (stylised) with a current flow stock in MP of ¤80. We are at the (stylised) end of the production period; the MP input has been used up. Each sector has ended up with an output of ¤200. Wages have not been paid yet. No one has money means to buy.
- The bank pre-validates Sector 2's ¤100 purchase of MP for the next period (streams 1 and 2 in *Circuit 3.5*). Sector 2 has now ¤100 MP on stock for the next period of production.
- With the ¤100 received, Sector 1 enterprises internally spend for ¤100 on MP whence they equally have ¤100 MP on stock for the next period (stream 3). This ¤100 is also a sales revenue for Sector 1, upon which they pay wages (stream 4), etc.
- Finally (stream 8) Sector 2 cancels the PVF with the bank.[8]

8 In order to keep the example concise, I have neglected interest. The simplest way to include

Generally, if workers spend all their wages, then: (1) the total surplus-value (integral profits) of enterprises would be just equal to the total investment of enterprises (investment → realisation of surplus-value);[9] (2) enterprises would merely require shots of credit from banks (in the example simply reduced to one shot), credit that would be cancelled by the spending on investment and consumption.

For completeness I must here briefly anticipate 3D5 (readers who find this anticipation too difficult may return to it later). The surplus-value (SV in the third column) is not a saving; rather this surplus-value only exists as such when it *has been* expended in the form of additional means of production (i.e. as investment expenditure). The banks provide the financial means for this expenditure, and these same means and expenditure realise the surplus-value. Thus there is (so to speak) no 'intermediating act' of saving by enterprises. Rather, I repeat, there is merely an investment expenditure by enterprises as accommodated by the banks. (To further complicate the matter, we will see in 3D5 that orthodox mainstream economics *defines* this investment expenditure as a saving (!), which is analytically not very helpful – thus it defines an expenditure as a saving).

3§2-c Explication. The redundancy of saving as a precondition for investment

Section 3§2 has been called 'the pure case' of finance by banks. It is also a transparent case and so one that we will regularly return to in this chapter. In terms of the necessary requirements for the reproduction of the capitalist economy, the stage of exposition that we now reach is pretty near to complete for those requirements. It is just that we still lack the concept of saving (and saving, as we will see in the sections to follow, introduces a vast set of complications). However, in principle, the capitalist economy could do without saving. This is in effect what 3§2 shows. For some readers educated in neoclassical economics, this must come as a surprise, because that strand strongly holds that savings are a blessing and that these are a precondition for investment.[10]

---

interest to banks (a deduction from surplus-value) is via the introduction of a sub-sector of sector 1: banks spend the interest on means of production.

9 This is Kalecki's insight: 'labour spends what it earns' (¤200) and 'capital earns (¤160+¤40) what it spends' (that is, given the production of surplus-value). See e.g. Kalecki 1942 (amplified in 3§10-a).

10 This idea in fact stems from classical political economy, and it is widespread – also beyond strict economics. In his influential *The Protestant Ethic and the Spirit of Capitalism* (1968 [1904[1]]) Max Weber argued that the Protestant (esp. Calvinistic) inclination to thrift contributed to the rise of capitalism. On the other hand, within economics there has always

The theoretical details of this can only be set out in 3D3 (after savings have been introduced in 3§3).

Keynes (1936) largely ignored production and rather challenged the 'received' (classical and neoclassical) view as one in which money plays no determining role (if there were any use of money at all, this would be a 'veil' over the real economy, one that must be revealed). He showed that the erroneous idea that saving enables investment is based on the false thesis that a capitalist economy can be modelled along the lines of a barter economy instead of a monetary economy. Although my line of argument in the sections to follow will be somewhat different from that of Keynes, I most often agree with him on this matter.

3§2-d Amplification. Point in time of wages payment and the implicit credit provided by labour

The point of time at which wages are paid (end of the day, week, month, etc.) is contingent. The longer the time span, the more it is labour that provides (implicitly) a credit to the enterprises. This is in the enterprises' interest because as such they require less capital. However, given that benefit, enterprises are faced with the question as to whether to finance wages payments out of a capital fund or rather on the basis of a credit line with banks. The longer the time span between wages payments, the more the opening credit lines will scale down the capital requirements. This implies that, next to any other requirement for pre-validating finance by banks, the pre-validation for wages payments will tend to be permanent. See *Figure 3.8*, which shows, schematically, the development of credit lines for end of the month wage payments.

Just to get a feel for the numbers involved, consider that around 2010 the average labour income share in the EU and the USA was just under 60% of GDP. Hence, neglecting holidays and end of year allowances, about 5% of GDP must be paid each month from the accounts of enterprises to those of labour.

In the 'pure case' of 3§2 the influx of money to pay wages is compensated by a full efflux of money upon the full expenditure of the wages. More precisely 'full expenditure' is time dependent. Even if the wages are paid at the end of the day, they are not fully spent at the end of the day but within some lapse of time.

---

been a side stream of heretics in this respect from Bernard de Mandeville's *Fable of the Bees* (1714) onwards that is still vivid in current discussions about Keynes's (1936) 'paradox of thrift'.

FIGURE 3.8 *Bank-provided* PVF *for wages payment: full redemption*

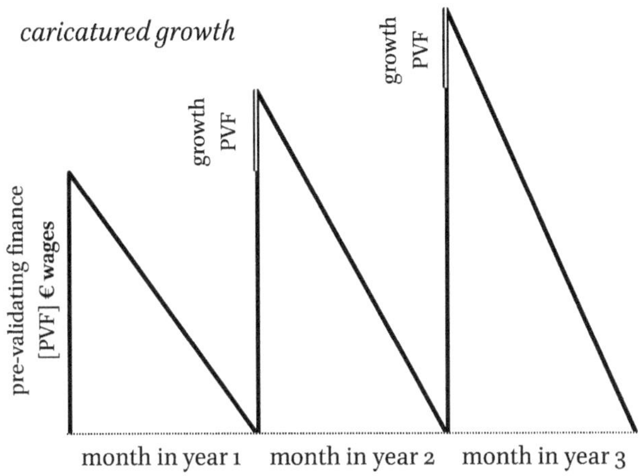

diagonal: decreasing account balance of labourers due to spending out of wages (€); reverse of enterprises' accounts

3§2-e Addendum. The Monetary Circuit Theory

Much of the current division has commonalities with the theory of the Monetary Circuit that evolved from about 1980 in France and Italy, though it has important forerunners before 1950 (including Schumpeter – see Bellofiore 1992). For overviews and further references see Graziani (1989, 2003) and the introductions and contributions in Deleplace and Nell (eds) (1996), Rochon and Rossi (eds) (2003), Fontana and Realfonzo (eds) (2005), Arestis and Sayer (eds) (2006), and Argitis, Evans, Michell and Toporowski (2014, sections 8 and 10).

Among the contributors to this literature that have sought to integrate Monetary Circuit theory into the marxian paradigm as a 'monetary theory of production', I mention (non-exhaustively) Bellofiore (1989, 2004, 2005a, 2005b), Bellofiore, Forges Davanzati and Realfonzo (2000), Bellofiore and Realfonzo (1997, 2003), and Forges Davanzati (2011).

Both the post-Keynesian and the Monetary Circuit approaches agree that money is essentially created ex nihilo and that normally it is endogenously created by commercial banks (as opposed to the view that an 'exogenous' supply of money by the central bank determines the money in circulation, as neoclassicals and also 'new Keynesians' would have it).[11] They also agree that banks should *not* be seen as financial intermediaries that channel savings to investment (again, contrary to the neoclassical and 'new Keynesian' views that do see banks as intermediaries in this respect); instead, and as Keynes emphasised, investment gives rise to saving. (See Rochon and Rossi 2003 for a comparison).

11 The Central Bank will be systematically introduced in 7D2.

However, and in reference to *Circuits* 3.4–3.5 above, post-Keynesians tend to start off with money-creating lending for investment (or also consumption); Circuitists, on the other hand, insist that, for reasons of transparent theory, one should start with money-creating lending for wage payments.[12] For the latter this would also fit a pure macroeconomic approach. I agree with these Circuitist considerations. However, the two approaches are not inconsistent; rather it is a question of whether one *starts* with a macroeconomic one-enterprises-sector or with a macroeconomic two-enterprises-sector model. In each case the key point is rather that the theorisation of the capitalist monetary economy, and a macroeconomic account of it, inevitably requires the distinction between enterprises and banks as creators of money (cf. Graziani 1989; cf. 2D5 on the separation-in-unity of enterprises and banks), and that the accumulation of capital inevitably requires the money-creating pre-validation by banks (2§10).

3§3 *Saving by capital owners and labour: triadic debt-credit relationships*

Bank loans to enterprises pre-validate the latter's production. With the bank account money created, enterprises settle money transfers between them and transfer money to labour and capital owners. It was shown in 3§2 that if all of the money transferred to labour and capital owners were spent with enterprises – that is, in the event that there would be no savings – then the money returns to the enterprises' accounts, so that the PVF loan with the bank can be fully redeemed. Thus, in principle, capitalist production and its validation could proceed and grow without any saving.

Saving is contingent. However, it is rather that 'saving' or 'non-saving' is contingent: one of the two must necessarily be the case. Thus the two being methodologically on a par, saving and the degree of saving is nevertheless contingent.[13]

When there are these savings, this has important necessary consequences. The money transferred to labour and capital owners that is saved does not return to enterprises' accounts, and thus cannot be used to cancel their bank credit, and so ends up as a saving of account money. This results in *triadic*

---

12 See Gnos 2003 for a comparison and for an atttempt to accommodate the post-Keynesian concerns within a Circuitist framework; cf. Rossi 2003 and Seccareccia 2003.

13 Positing these as contingent by no means denies that for individual actors within a capitalist economy, it may make sense to save for precautionary reasons.

debt-credit relationships: banks are in debt to these actors for this saving of accountmoney, the latter sum being just equivalent to the remaining debt of enterprises to banks. (See *Circuit 3.9*: in comparison with *Circuit 3.6* only the items in blue have been added).

[*continued*]

CIRCUIT 3.9 *Pre-validating finance for wages, means of production and dividends; saving by labour and by capital owners*

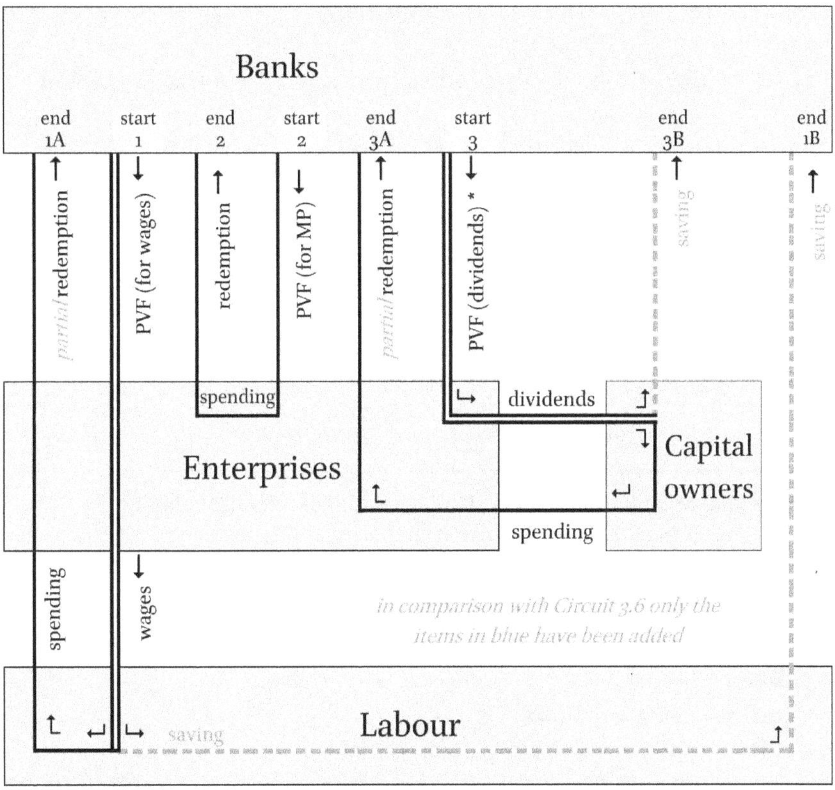

* The same applies for interest to capital owners (implicit until 3§5).

Note 1. The 'only' difference between this circuit and *Circuit 3.6* consists in the savings by labour and capital owners (the dotted lines with ends 1B and 3B), and as a result the mere partial redemptions of the PVF (ends 1A and 3A).

Note 2. The dotted lines are in fact not transfers: after the payment of wages and dividends, the relevant savings remain on the accounts of labourers and capital owners. (Only in the historically relevant case of banknote circulation might these be transfers: a deposit at the bank).

3§3 *Continued*

From the perspective of enterprises then, savings are in fact a nuisance. The upshot is that the banks are (continue to be) the enterprises' financiers for the amounts saved. Given these savings, enterprises as a whole are inevitably in debt.

For enterprises the PVF from banks is an *ex ante finance*, the finance precedes (the expansion of) investment and production. This is a finance created ex nihilo. For banks, however, the expansion of their own finance (their liabilities) is an *ex post finance* through the savings.

3§3-a Explication. The non-necessity of saving for the investment by enterprises

It was emphasised in 3§3 that saving is a nuisance for enterprises. Even if saving is ubiquitous in a capitalist economy (and even if for individual actors it can be rational for precautionary reasons), savings are not necessary for enterprises, and enterprises would be better off without savings because their loans with banks could be non-problematically redeemed.

For banks, however, savings are no nuisance at all, as lending is their main business.

SHEET 3.10A *Integrated balance sheet of enterprises*

Assets [active capital]		Liabilities [passive finance capital]	
• plant and equipment • raw materials etc. • work in progress • commodities produced • current account with banks		*External finance capital* • loans from banks • ~~loans from non-bank financiers (bonds)~~† *Internal finance capital*	 a b
value equivalent of a + b	K		K=FC

† Introduced in 3§6

3§3-b Explication. Ex ante finance of enterprises by banks, and enforced ex post finance of banks by labour and capital owners – the balance sheets of enterprises and banks

I expand on 3§1-a. Recall that the 'assets side' of the balance sheet of enterprises measures the active capital (K). The 'liabilities side' indicates how the enterprise is financed through 'finance capital' (FC). See *Sheet 3.10a*.

For the aggregate of enterprises, the expansion of the liabilities side is an *ex ante finance* of the expansion of the assets side: the finance precedes new investment in the assets. The expansion of the liabilities originates exclusively from a PVF – finance created by the banks ex nihilo. (It will be shown in 3§6 that this also applies, or has applied, for the internal finance capital of the enterprise; all of the latter stem from PVFs).

SHEET 3.10B *Integrated balance sheet of banks*

Assets [financial]*		**Liabilities [finance]***	
~~Assets bank: non-financial (leased)~~**		Own capital banks	e
Assets bank: financial	d	~~Borrowed from non-bank financiers~~† ~~(bank bonds, time accounts)~~	
		Current accounts [CA]: borrowings	g
• Loans to enterprises	(d)	• Current accounts: enterprises (borrowed)	
• ~~Loans to non-enterprises~~†		• Current accounts: labour (borrowed)	
		• Current accounts: capital owners (borrowed)	
		• ~~Current accounts: other (borrowed)~~†	
• ~~Loans to other banks~~‡		• ~~Borrowed from other banks~~‡	
Balance Sheet Total	[a =] d = e + g	Balance Sheet Total	e + g = d

* Only in *this* balance sheet (with these items crossed out) do all of the banks' activities serve as Finance Capital for enterprises.
** Leased from the banking entities' production branch (3§1, heading 2).
† Presented in Appendix 3B.
‡ Because the balance sheets of banks have been integrated, these items cancel out.

Regarding the banks' balance sheet, however (see *Sheet 3.10b*), the expansion of their own finance (liabilities) is an *ex post finance* through the savings, which are generated only *after* the PVF has been provided. Hence banks do not finance enterprises (or other actors) out of a pre-existing 'loanable fund of savings'. The neglect of this distinction between ex ante and ex post finance in the conventional macroeconomics that neglects banks is a source of enormous confusion (amplified in 3§6-d).

Savings, if any, are no precondition for any of the finances (enterprises, banks). We sufficiently saw this for the 'pure' constellation of 3§2. Again – for the case of saving – the finance of enterprises being an ex ante one, this finance does not originate with savings: it originates with the bank's PVF, which itself is financed ex post.

Moreover, in the aggregate the latter is an *enforced finance*. Capital owners or labourers that save might switch from one bank to another, but they cannot escape from financing the lot. The only freedom within this enforcement is that of the degree of liquidity: current accounts, time accounts, etc. (In the day of the fading away of the notes of the Clearing/Central Bank, people may still take illusionary comfort in the possibility of hoarding heaps of CB-notes, through which – in fact – they finance the CB).[14]

In this perspective, consider *Sheet 3.11*, which casts the money streams of *Circuit 3.9* regarding labour in terms of alterations of the banks' balance sheet (a similar sheet might be made for capital owners).

SHEET 3.11 *Alteration of banks' balance sheet: case of saving by labour*

1. money-creating loans to Enterprises for wages payment:

loans to Enterprises (PVF)	$ x	current accounts Enterprises	$ x

2. payment of wages:

loans to Enterprises (PVF)	$ x	current accounts Enterprises	o
		current accounts Labour	$ x

3. spending of $(x-s) (hence a saving of $ s):

loans to Enterprises (PVF)	$ x	current accounts Enterprises	$ (x-s)
		current accounts Labour	$ s

4. Enterprises cancel part of their loans:

loans to Enterprises (RPVF*) [x-(x-s)]	$ s	current accounts Enterprises	o
		current accounts Labour	$ s

* RPVF: Remaining PFV

14 The commercial bank books at the assets side 'holding of CB-notes' and at its liabilities side 'borrowed from the CB'. The CB books at the assets side 'loans to banks' and at its liabilities side 'banknotes issued', which is how it finances the loan to the commercial bank. When (or if) a worker or capital owner collects CB-notes from the commercial bank (for which its current account is debited), they become the anonymous holder of CB debt ('banknotes issued') and so become a financier of the CB.

In the last row of *Sheet 3.11* we have the equivalent of labour's enforced ex post finance *of banks*.

Because of the saving out of wages ($s), the initial loans to enterprises cannot be fully cancelled, whence *the bank* keeps on financing them for the amount $s, which is the equivalent of the bank's debt to labour. Note that *ex post* it seems as if enterprises are indirectly financed out of savings (as if we had bank intermediation of 'loanable funds'). However, this is a false appearance. From the start the *enterprises'* investment was financed by ex nihilo created money, and the non-redeemed part is still being financed by ex nihilo created money. Saving does not give rise to investment; rather the investment – as accommodated by ex nihilo created money – gave rise to income out of which saving took place (cf. Keynes 1936).

Considering the *banks'* balance sheet, the enterprises at first financed the bank(!) through their current account: see *Sheet 3.11* entry 1 (liabilities side). In the end (entry 4), labour substitutes for the enterprises. The enterprises' finance of the banks (entry 1) had nothing to do with any saving.

3§4 *The payment of interest by enterprises to banks*

Recall the distinction between on the one hand 'banks' as purely creators of money and as financiers, and on the other hand the banking entities' 'production branch' that is subsumed under the enterprises sector (3§1, heading 2).

In the form of the interest that enterprises have to pay to banks, the banks receive a share in the surplus-value produced in enterprises. Because pure banks only engage in money-creating finance, it does not matter how individual enterprises settle the way of *payment* of the interest (as long as they pay the interest on the date due). They might pay the interest out of their monetary inflow from sales, or alternatively they might use their credit line with banks, which means that they take an additional loan – as always this just requires that they can offer the bank sufficient securities. When the latter is satisfied, banks do not care about the destination of a loan, and on the other hand they do not care from what fund the enterprise pays the interest.

Considering this macroeconomically, two points are at issue.

First, especially from *Circuit 3.5* (and from that circuit in combination with *Figure 3.7*) it can be seen that one or several 'shots' of pre-validating finance can generate a numerically much larger income stream (in terms of e.g. net production) – PVFS indeed flow through the economy. (This point is blurred in macroeconomic circuits with only one enterprises sector: the other circuits presented so far).

Second, because banks, and banks alone, create money, it is impossible for them to receive back more money (PVF plus interest) than they created (PVF).

This simple fact also contains the solution: macroeconomically, banks create the money for their own interest receipts. This reveals the essence of banking. Banks earn on loans, including on loans to pay interest. The only one requirement is that loans are security backed.

Further, banks earn their profit from net interest (gross interest after deduction of costs for the bank). If, for the sake of simplicity, we assume the cost to be zero, all of the interest streams *to* the bank are profits of the bank. If all profits are retained, this interest is added to the own capital of the bank. Banks' financial assets are a form of financial *paper*. Their financial liabilities are also a form of financial paper (electronic paper for accounts), and especially also the own capital of the bank. All these are ultimately *creations* of the bank (in reciprocal credit relationships – 2§8).

CIRCUIT 3.12 *Banking entities as financier ('banks') and as employer ('active branch') (note: this circuit relates to Amplification 3§4-a)*

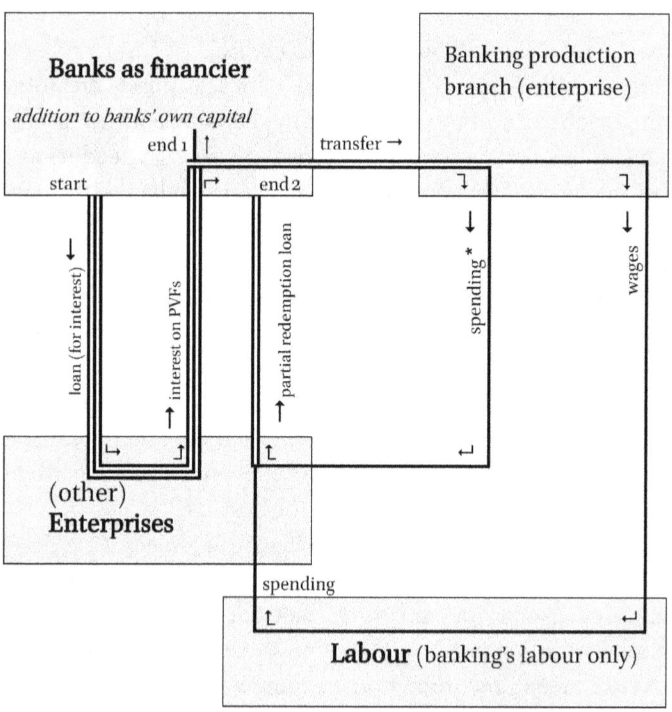

* Spending: including material investment of the banking enterprise branch.

3§4-a Amplification. 'Banking entities' and payment of interest from enterprises to banks

So far 'banks' are conceptualised purely as creators of money and as financiers. Any other activities of the 'banking entities' are allotted to their 'production branch' that is subsumed under the category of enterprises (3§1, heading 2). Henceforth I will continue to do this. However, for one time the 'production activity branch' of 'banking entities' is made explicit. See *Circuit 3.12*. The banks as financier internally transfer part of their interest receipts to their 'production branch' (costs of leasing and outsourcing). From it, the latter spend with enterprises and also pay wages (for simplicity all these wages are spent). The streams on the left hand side ('start') represent a loan from banks to enterprises (one that enterprises intend to use for the payment of interest, but that for banks is just a security backed loan like any other loan – see the main text of 3§4).

Division 3. Ex post substitution for the pre-validating finance by banks

The grounding of the accumulation of capital in the expansion of bank-created money (2D4) was further grounded and so concretised in the finance of enterprises by banks (3D2). The current division sets out how any limits to the grounds of 3D2 are overcome or at least moderated (see 3§6). Preliminary concepts for 3§6 are presented in 3§5.

3§5 *Capital owners as financiers: dividend bearing and interest bearing finance capital*

Chapter 2 (2D6 and 2D7) introduced the category of 'owners of passive capital'. These are the 'internal financiers' of enterprises (3§1, Figure 3.2a), as further explained below.

Until this stage of the exposition, banks are the sole *external* financiers of enterprises. The degree of their accommodation of the accumulation of capital via the PVF also operates as a constraint on the unlimited expansion of capital. One consideration for the banks' accommodation is the quantity and quality of the securities that the enterprise can deliver for the PVF. Another consideration, in terms of the liabilities of the enterprise, is the enterprise's degree of 'solvency', that is, the ratio of internal over total finance capital (see balance sheet 3.10a in 3§3-b). This implies that the expansion of capital is constrained by the growth of the internal (own) finance capital of the enterprise and hence by the retained profits (3§1, Figure 3.2b).[15] Any non-retained profit is distrib-

15 At this point retained profits are solely the surplus-value that is not distributed to banks

uted to the shareholders in the form of dividends. In principle the internal capital of enterprises can so be extended via the issuing of new shares, paid out of dividends from any enterprise. As such we have '*dividend bearing finance capital*'.

Further, via the distribution of profits to shareholders in the form of dividends, their wealth grows. In principle they can further limit and spread their risk and uncertainty (cf. 2§12) by, instead of sharing, *lending* finance capital to enterprises, perhaps in the form of bonds or direct placements.[16|17] Like the banks' PVF, this is '*interest bearing finance capital*'.

3§5-a Amplification. The level of the rate of interest

Regarding the *demand* for loans by enterprises, interest is the price for being able to command finance capital for the generation of surplus-value (cf. Robinson 1953, p. 87). As to the *supply* of loans *other* than loans provided by banks, the level of the rate of interest is usually considered to be a matter either of 'time preference' (in which case interest might also be negative – as Robinson 1953 has argued),[18] or of 'the price for waiting with consumption' (Marshall's 1972 [1890] version of Senior's 'abstinence' from consumption) – a rather ideological concept, which was one of the chief targets of Keynes's (1936) critique of the received view of his day.[19] Instead, Keynes posited interest as 'the reward for parting with liquidity for a specific period' (1936, p. 167).[20] For the supply side I consider the latter to be the best conceptualisation available. In 3§5 I generalised this as the limiting and spreading of risk and uncertainty.

---

in the form of interest, and the part that is not distributed to the owners of the enterprise in the form of (quasi) dividends.

16 The risk and uncertainty is further spread to the extent that the interest rate is fixed, and the payment of interest is prioritised before the payment of dividend.

17 Systematically the category of 'capital owners' – as separate from the owners of enterprises – was introduced with the introduction of the corporate enterprise. Historically the category of lending by capital owners emerged before the emergence of the corporate enterprise.

18 For example, one might wish to command over sums of money at some retirement age, even if the net interest over the period leading up to that time is negative.

19 The disputed idea is that savings are seen to be evoked by interest. Instead, actors save because they want to save (for old age or some expense or precaution). This can be seen especially in times of deep recession when, for (middle) layers that can afford it, savings go up for reasons of precaution even when the interest goes down.

20 Relatedly, apart from any other actors, banks may offer such rewards for tempting actors to keep their account money with their particular bank. (If savings are kept with another bank, then the investment-loan providing bank is, for the amount saved, in debt to another bank, not to the saver – cf. 2§12).

3§6 *Pre-validating finance by banks as ex post substituted for by non-banking finance capital (the RPVF)*

Banks necessarily provide credit to enterprises, which is a flow of pre-validating finance (PVF). This flow returns to the banks on aggregate full spending, thereby cancelling the pre-validating credit (3§2). However, any non-spending of income interferes with this, and it implies that the bank is (continues to be) the enterprises' financier for this amount not spent (3§3).

The non-redeemed part of the PVF, which equals the saving by labour and capital owners, is called the *remaining pre-validating finance* (RPVF). Hence banks provide, in effect, next to a money-creating flow of finance (PVF), a non-money-creating stock of finance (RPVF) – the latter being based on previous money creation, and now equally being based on the triadic debt-credit relationship between the bank, the saver of money and the enterprise (cf. 3§3).[21]

At the same time, the non-spenders are *potential ex post financiers*. To the extent that the latter explicitly enter into a (additional) finance relation with the enterprises – thus substituting for the bank RPVF – they become *actual ex post financiers, or owners of* (additional) *finance capital*.[22] (See *Circuit 3.13*).

Even stronger, on average, non-bank financiers can be no more than *ex post* financiers. They do *not* finance the process of the macro *accumulation* of capital and so macroeconomic growth – this is what the banks do. They can, on average, merely finance *already accumulated* capital, that is, ex post, after the deed of accumulation.[23] Through the necessary creation of money, banks are *always* the origin of finance capital. There is no ex ante finance beyond the revolving pre-validating finance by banks (PVF). *Because any new investment is so accommodated, any existing investment has been so accommodated.*[24] (See also 3§7, which expands on banks as the providers of the finance capital for the founders of an enterprise).

A corollary is that actors do not become owners of finance capital by a mere saving of money. In the latter case the bank is the owner of finance capital, whereas these savers are holders, claimants, of account money.

[*continued*]

21 In comparison with 3§3, I now have introduced the terms of 'flow' and 'stock'. Although these terms are correct, it should be kept in mind that the time-weighted-average of a flow has a stock character.

22 The precise form of the ex post finance is not important in this context. These can be loans (bonds or direct placements), or the enterprise may also issue additional shares.

23 The qualification 'on average' is expanded upon in explication 3§6-d.

24 That is, systematically at least: the mechanism for any remnants of banknote circulation may be different, although the principle is the same.

CIRCUIT 3.13 *Ex post substitution by capital owners for 'Remaining Pre-validating Finance'*

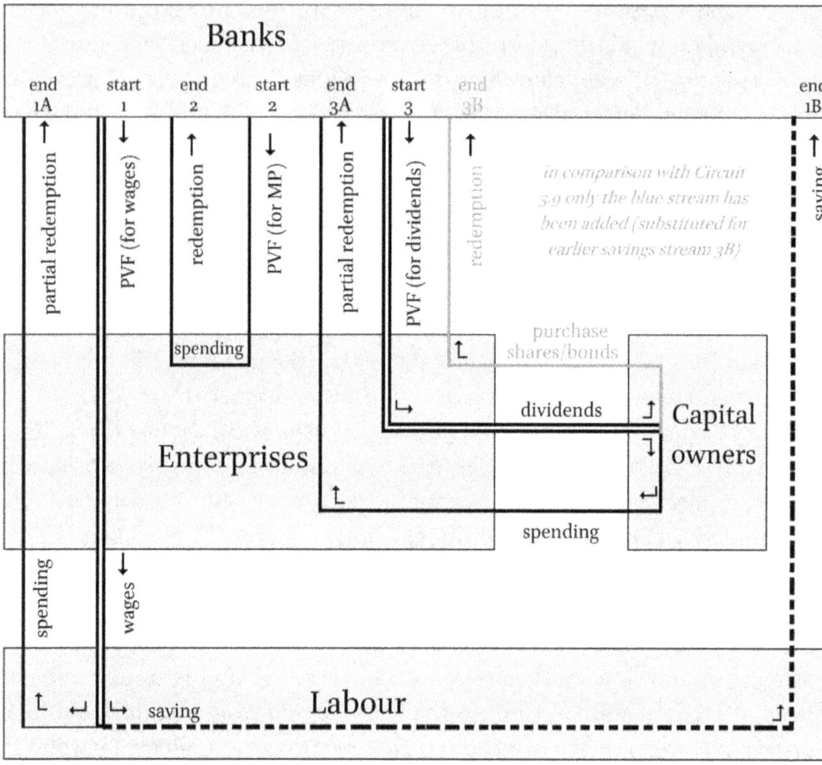

Note 1. To keep this circuit transparent, it is assumed that all savings of capital owners from *Circuit 3.9* are used to purchase shares or bonds. The latter are *newly* issued shares and bonds (the so-called primary market).

Note 2. Stream 3: a similar stream applies for the payment of interest to capital owners.

Note 3. In principle workers might also purchase bonds or shares, in which case, for that part, the categories of labour and capital owner would overlap.

3§6 *Continued*

However, there is a *tendency to incite the capital owners engaged in saving, to substitute,* in part, *for the bank-provided finance capital.* Yet, I repeat, this can only be a *substitution ex post,* that is, a substitution after the necessary initial provision of finance capital (PVF) by the bank (amplified in 3§6-d).[25] This tendency is driven by:

25 These other actors are the money savers themselves, or institutions channelling these sav-

- first, the degree of actual indebtedness of banks along with the savings-engendered indebtedness of enterprises (cf. Sheet 3.10b in 3§3-b);[26]
- second, the banks seeking to limit the saving- and RPVF-engendered risk and uncertainty (so requiring from enterprises a finance buffer, in the form of the latter's internal capital and non-bank external capital);
- third, the enterprises seeking finance at a price lower than that required by banks.

In conclusion: *A 'loanable fund' of current and past saving is no precondition for investment* (amplified in 3§6-d). *Ex post* substitution for the bank's RPVF by capital owners contributes to the banks' ongoing accommodation of the accumulation of capital via their PVF.

Finally, it should be remarked that there is no implication of the previous exposition that there should be a macroeconomic equality of investment and the PVF.[27] Rather, investment must take off with 'shots' of pre-validating finance by banks. (The PVF circulates – see Circuit 3.5).

3§6-a Addendum. 'Banks are not intermediaries of loanable funds'

When I wrote the first drafts of the current chapter, it was a heresy to consider banks as the initiating financiers of the accumulation of capital (see also Addendum 3§2-e on monetary circuit theory). However, in a 2015 paper, entitled 'Banks are not Intermediaries of Loanable Funds – and Why This Matters', Jakab and Kumhof, members of the research departments of the IMF and the Bank of England, distance themselves from the orthodox economics notion of loanable finds (Jakab and Kumhof 2015). To get the main thrust of this 57-page paper, the reader might turn to its summary (ibid., pp. i–iii).[28] In the context of 3§6 the latter's key sentence is: 'Saving does not finance investment, financing does' (ibid., p. ii).

ings (institutional portfolio investors, such as pension funds – cf. Appendix 3A, section 3A-1). Recall that the term 'actor' or 'social actor' is used in a general sense (2§14-a).

26 Cf. 2§10 (heading 3) on crediting rules set by the ClB. At this point of the exposition, banks lend to enterprises only (lending to other actors is introduced in Appendix 3B).

27 First, the PVF serves various purposes (including wage payments); second, the degree of actual circulation of the PVF through the economy is dependent on the degree of savings along that process.

28 Available at: http://z822j1x8tde3wuovlgo7ue15.wpengine.netdna-cdn.com/wp-content/uploads/2015/02/wp529.pdf.

3§6-b Explication. The connection between the PVF and the RPVF

New (additional) inputs of production are financed through money-creating PVFs (keeping in mind the last sentence of 3§6). This relates to labour's wages (that are continuously an additional input) and the *growth* of means of production (intermediate inputs and investment).

In the absence of any saving we 'merely' have a growing PVF flow along with the rate of economic growth (this is serviced out of enterprises' interest payments to banks).

With any *saving*, we have this growing PVF flow, *as well as* a RPVF stock. In case there is no ex post substitution for the RPVF, we have a continuous growth of the RPVF stock (saving period (t) = Δ RPFV period (t) – with the symbol Δ for 'change').[29] This ΔRPFV is a liability (to banks) on the enterprises' balance sheet (equivalent to a change of the banks' financial assets at their balance sheet) and for which enterprises pay interest to the banks.

The banks finance the ΔRPVF *ex post* by the current accounts of labour (saving from wages) and of capital owners (saving from dividends and interest). This saving by labour and capital owners pertains to money created by the bank via the PVF.

Finally, especially capital owners and rich wage earners may in part substitute for the ΔRPVF through the purchase of newly issued shares or bonds from enterprises.[30]

3§6-c Amplification. Shorthand summary of the required type of finance

Figure 3.14 summarises the types of finance that are required at each conceptual stage in 3§2–3§3 and 3§6. Recall that PVF is an abbreviation for pre-validating finance by banks, and RPVF is an abbreviation for any remaining PVF (i.e. the non-redeemed part of the PVF upon saving by labour and capital owners).

29 Thus whereas generally the macroeconomic PVF < investment (the last sentence of 3§6), macroeconomic saving = Δ RPFV (prior to substitution for it).

30 Some of this substitution takes place via savings channelling institutions such as pension funds (Appendix 3A, sections 3A-1 and 3A-2).

FIGURE 3.14 *Forms of finance capital along with (non-)saving and (non-)substitution for bank* RPVF

<table>
<tr><th colspan="2">Flows of finance capital
during period t [from (t') to (t'')]</th><th colspan="3">Stocks of finance capital
at the beginning of period t</th></tr>
<tr><td colspan="5">1. Absence of saving (3§2; Circuits 3.4, 3.5 and 3.6)</td></tr>
<tr><td colspan="2">PVF(t) [short-term bank loan]</td><td colspan="3">no other external FC</td></tr>
<tr><td colspan="2">PVF(t'') redeemed [Δ RPVF(t'') = 0]</td><td colspan="3"></td></tr>
<tr><td colspan="5">2. Saving, no substitution for RPVF (3§3; Circuit 3.9)</td></tr>
<tr><td colspan="2">PVF(t)</td><td colspan="3">other bank-loans =
Σ RPVF(t-1) ... RPVF(t-n)</td></tr>
<tr><td>γPVF(t'') redeemed
[redeemed fraction γ]</td><td>Δ RPVF(t'') > 0
[= (1-γ)PVF(t)]</td><td colspan="3"></td></tr>
<tr><td colspan="5">3. Saving, with substitution for RPVF (3§6; Circuit 3.13)</td></tr>
<tr><td colspan="2">identical to the previous block</td><td colspan="3">quantity identical to the previous block</td></tr>
<tr><td colspan="2">PVF(t)</td><td>other bank loans</td><td>shares</td><td>non-bank loans</td></tr>
<tr><td>γPVF(t'') redeemed
[redeemed fraction γ]</td><td>Δ RPVF(t'') > 0
[= (1-γ)PVF(t)]</td><td colspan="3">together equal to
Σ RPVF(t-1) ... RPVF(t-n)</td></tr>
</table>

3§6-d Amplification. Ex post substitution for bank-provided finance capital and *deferred substitution* (the illusion of loanable funds of savings)

Throughout 3D2 and 3D3 I have distanced myself from a 'loanable funds' approach to finance, investment and accumulation of capital. (I repeat that by 'investment' I *always* mean what is often called 'direct investment' – as opposed to 'portfolio investment'). Thus I distance myself from the classical and neoclassical view, which holds that *generally* in a developed capitalist system, the accumulation of capital and any *new* investment is financed out of a pre-existing money fund of savings, that is, of current and previous savings (a loanable fund).[31] This explication is about the qualification 'generally'. We will see that new investment may at times be financed out of a fund, but that this cannot be on average the case. Consider rows 1 and 4 of *Sheet 3.15*.

SHEET 3.15 *Alteration of banks' balance sheet (savings case) with various forms of substitution (sheet continued in the text below)*

money-creating loans to Enterprises for dividends payment:

1 loans to Enterprises (PVF)	$ x	current accounts Enterprises	$ x

payment of dividends:

2 loans to Enterprises (PVF)	$ x	current accounts Enterprises	0
		current accounts Capital Owners	$ x

spending of $(x-s) (hence a saving of $ s):

3 loans to Enterprises (PVF)	$ x	current accounts Enterprises	$ (x-s)
		current accounts Capital Owners	$ s

Enterprises cancel part of their loans

4 loans to Enterprises (RPVF[*]) [x-(x-s)]	$ s	current accounts Enterprises	0
		current accounts Capital Owners (RCB[‡])	$ s

* RPVF: Remaining PFV
‡ RCB: Remaining credit balance flow

The initial loan was called the PVF (pre-validating finance). The current account balances (the right hand side of row 4) are called the RCBF (remaining credit balance flow – remaining from the dividends transfer). I call the remaining part of the PVF (the left hand side of row 4) the RPVF. These are analytical names.

31 Note that I distance myself from any bank intermediated 'loanable funds' notion, including those versions in which banks combine ex nihilo credit with loanable funds intermediation.

Enterprises may sell bonds for $s to capital owners. If enterprises use the money thus collected (the RCBF) to cancel the RPVF, i.e. the final part of their dividends PVF loan with the bank, we have the analytically transparent case of ***ex post substitution** for the remaining bank-provided finance* (RPVF).

5a	loans to E [RPVF(t)]	$ s	CA E (due to sale bond) CA CO (due to purchase bond)	$ s $0
5b	loans to E [RPVF(t)] (cancelled)	$0	CA E (cancelling RPVF(t))	$0

* CA: Current accounts; E: Enterprises; CO: capital owners; (t) is a time indicator (some year)

All credits and debts with the bank for dividend payments have been cleared (awaiting a new sequence). The finance substitution relates to investment (a quantity larger than the dividend sum) that has taken place already: the assets side (active capital) of the enterprises balance sheet grew, and equally so the liabilities side (finance capital), initially through the banks' finance that is now in part substituted for (the saved dividends).

However, enterprises may not want to sell bonds now (perhaps because of their long-term commitments), or they may not manage to sell bonds (because of the liquidity preference of current account holders). Note that the bank must allow this situation to persist. Thus rows 5 are crossed out.

We now turn to the next period (t+1), row 6, which starts with the end result of row 4. In this case we do seem to have a loanable fund (the RCB of row 4).

START OF PERIOD (t+1), = row 4

6	loans to E [**RPVF(t)**]	$ s	CA E 0 CA CO [**RCB(t)**]	 $ s

In this period (t+1) (or later), the RCB of capital owners might be used for a *deferred substitution* for the bank loan (the RPVF from period t). This would be equivalent to row 5.

However, it might instead be used to finance a *new* investment. The latter case is to be conceived as a *substitution for a pre-validating finance* [PVF(t+1)] that would 'normally' have been taken on by the bank (see row 7a below).

	[*following on from row 6*]			
7a	loans to E [**RPVF(t)**] (not cancelled)	$ s	CA E (sale bond for new investment t+1) CA CO (due to purchase bond)	$ s 0
7b	(previous) loans to E [**RPVF(t)**] (new) loans to E [**PVF(t+1)**] (x′= x plus the 'normal' rate of growth)	$ s $ x′-s	CA E (due to sale bond t+1) CA E (new PVF, analogous to row 1)	$ s $ x′-s
7	*7b in sum (analogous to row 1):* *loans to Enterprises*	*$ x′*	*CA Enterprises*	*$ x′*

In effect the sum of money $s from (t) – row 6 – remained 'in circulation'. In (t+1), therefore, the 'normal' influx of money can be reduced from $x′ to $x′-s (row 7b), in sum resulting in a circulation of $x′ as in row 7 (where x′ = x plus the 'normal' rate of growth).

In the situation exemplified in rows 6 and 7 the bank, in effect, 'allows' for the (temporary) existence of a loanable fund ($s) by not forcing enterprises to fully redeem the initial loan (PVF(t)).

Note that the enterprises' expiration of previous non-bank loans (such as bonds) provides no net loanable fund: if the loan is not renewed (reissue of bonds), banks will have to provide a loan for the redemption.

I conclude that *on average investment is not financed out of loanable funds* of savings and that the specific case of such finance is *in effect a* ***deferred substitution*** for the bank's pre-validating finance as *fully* accommodated by ex nihilo created bank account money. Thus generally, and on average, investment is (either directly or indirectly) *necessarily accommodated by a pre-validating finance by banks* (PVF). Without it, savings and hence also the specific case of a 'loanable credit balance' (RCB) could not have existed. The latter is just the remnant of a prior PVF.

3§6-e Addendum. Minsky on the substitution of bank loans for other loans

Enterprises may prefer other financiers to banks insofar as the latter's charges are higher. Conversely, the reason for (non-banking) 'potential financiers' to become 'actual financiers' is that enterprises may provide them with a higher yield (interest, dividend) than the interest that the bank might pay them. The drawback is a decrease in (the degree of) liquidity. Minsky (2004 [1954], p. 233) apparently used the term substitution from the perspective of the financier (portfolio investor), linking it to Keynes's (1936) liquidity preference theory: 'the liquidity preference relation, which is shorthand for the substitution relation between money and other assets [e.g. bonds that "other financiers" buy from enterprises], becomes the appropriate tool to use in the analysis of the behavior of the monetary system' (quoted by Toporowski 2006, p. 13).

Division 4. The foundation of banks and enterprises

Grounding of the starting point's capital accumulated

The systematic entry point to the exposition of the capitalist system (1§1) is the outward bifurcation between households and privately owned means of production. For a systematic-dialectical exposition, it is irrelevant how the capitalist system came into being historically (even if the latter is intriguing), as the purpose is to exhibit the requirements and functioning of the existing system.

Nevertheless it seems broadly within the remit of a systematic-dialectical account of capitalism to set out how enterprises and banks *come* into being *within* capitalism. Building on the previous divisions of this chapter, the current brief division (one section) sets out an elementary outline of this. The focus is on the foundation of banks. However, because enterprises and banks mutually presuppose one another, and constitute a separation-in-unity (2§11), the following section starts with a brief look at the foundation of enterprises.

3§7 *The foundation of banks and enterprises*

It was shown that banks provide enterprises with a pre-validating finance of production and so with finance capital (3§1–3§2). This leaves unanswered the question of where banks get their founding capital from.

1 The foundation of enterprises

The initial production and accumulation of capital of a new enterprise ('within capitalism') is in effect generated by labour's production of surplus-value (1D5), with the pre-validating finance by banks as a condition (see heading 2).

The transparent constellation for the foundation of enterprises is one of an absence of savings (3§2), as well as an absence of 'hard' collateral to be offered to a bank. Hence the bank is merely confronted with a 'business plan' together with the novice enterprise's promise that it will pay back the loan with an interest, and that, in the meantime, it offers the collateral of future purchases (means of production) and future profits.[32] With merely a 'business plan' the bank takes relatively more risk than in the case of 'hard' collateral – against it the bank will require a relatively higher rate of interest.

2 *The foundation of banks*

New banks may originate as offshoots from existing banks or enterprises. However, that position about foundation is regressive, so we need to abstract from existing banks and enterprises. Abstracting from those, the foundation of a bank originates with *a loan from that new bank to the founders of that bank.*[33] This loan is a pre-validating finance (PVF), which is in principle no different from the banking of currently existing banks. From that loan, the founders finance the own finance capital of the bank. The loan is redeemed from the bank's future distributed profits. The result is the particular type of liability that the own finance capital of any existing bank is, namely a liability to itself. (Explication 3§7-a provides the details).

This initiating process of the foundation of a bank is in principle no different from the *extension* of the own finance capital of an *existing bank* via the issue of new shares. This proceeds by a transfer of current account money (of the new shareholder) to the bank's liabilities entry of 'own capital' (equity). However, current account money is always the result of a money-creating loan by the bank. Hence, *the extra own capital comes (or has come) indirectly into being by way of money creation* by the bank at hand, or another one. (Explication 3§7-a).

This is all there is to it, so setting up a bank appears to be rather simple (though further reflection on this reveals the very essence of what banking is). Nevertheless, the problem – as with the establishing of a new enterprise – is 'getting clients'. That is, clients on top of the founders of the bank. (Founders acting as clients is not an illusionary matter, because in the actual history of capitalism, some banks – especially cooperative ones – have functioned as founders' banks). This 'clients problem' is a matter of the domain of a single bank (2§8).

---

32 Note that this also happens in current practice, even if exceptionally. Note also that a bank that itself is new (heading 2) has no option but to choose between such business plans.

33 Quite apart from my concern to present the systematic foundation of banks, Lavoie correctly states the following in respect of the own capital of a bank in general: 'The own capital of the bank constitutes a liability to itself. It represents the funds which the firm [the bank] owes to its owners. In general, the own funds play a role similar to deposits [current accounts] that would be in the hands of the owners. … The own funds are an accounting entry, but in contrast to deposits [current accounts] they cannot be drawn on by the owners' (2003, p. 512).

Once there are extended domains, a 'new' bank will have to cope with the rules set by a Clearing Bank (2§9). However, this is not the point of the current section. Division 2D4 was entered by a mere reference to the actual existence of banks. The brief outline above concerns the systematic coming into being of that existence.

3§7-a Explication: The systematic foundation of banks in terms of their balance sheets

We start with the *extension* of the own finance capital of an existing bank (*Sheet 3.16*). This sheet shows alterations of the bank's balance sheet (a simplified full balance sheet was presented in 3§3-b, Sheet 3.9b).

SHEET 3.16 *Extension of the own capital of a bank: alterations of the bank's balance sheet (Bank Z)*

Assets			Liabilities
1. Existing loans to enterprises (non-substituted part) of bank Z			
loans to enterprises (RPVF)	€ x	current accounts non-enterpr. (non-bank)	€ x
2a. Case of own capital extension of bank Z by clients of bank Z			
loans to enterprises (RPVF)	€ x	current accounts non-enterpr. (non-bank)	€ – x
		own finance capital bank Z (shares)	€ x
2b. Case of own finance capital extension of bank Z by clients of other banks (the money receiving bank always provides a loan to the money transferring bank – 2§9-b)			
loans to other banks	€ x	own finance capital bank Z	€ x
3a. Sum of 1 and 2a			
loans to enterprises (RPVF)	€ x	own finance capital bank Z	€ x
3b. Sum of 1 and 2b			
loans to enterprises (RPVF)	€ x	current accounts non-enterpr. (non-bank)	€ x
loans to other banks	€ x	own finance capital bank Z	€ x

Concerning either the extension or the foundation of the 'own capital' of banks, that term should be taken in two senses: ownership and creation. *Sheet 3.17* shows the bookkeeping act for the foundation of a bank (starting from scratch).

SHEET 3.17 *Foundation of a bank in terms of its balance sheet*

Assets		Liabilities	
1. money-creating loans to bank founders			
loans to bank founders (PVF)	€ x	current accounts bank founders	€ x
2. paying in of the own capital			
loans to bank founders (PVF)	€ x	current accounts bank founders own capital (shares)	0 € x

The collateral for the loans might be based on a variety of possessions. However, in the 'pure' case it is merely based on the bank's claim on the founders' future income stream from the bank capital, i.e. the distributed profits. Further, as the founders are the owners of the bank, the future net value of the bank may be offered as collateral.

Next, in the course of time, the loans to bank founders are redeemed out of the bank profits distributed to the holders of the own capital (shareholders).

Thus the main difference between the extension (*Sheet 3.16*) and the foundation (*Sheet 3.17*) is the degree of collateral.

3§7-b Explication. Grounding of the starting point

With the previous section (3§7) the starting point's pre-position of capital accumulated (1§1) has been grounded (hence it is no longer a pre-position). With it, all the previous 'economic' pre-positions have been grounded. However, the state (Part Two) is still pre-posited.

3§7-c Addendum. Marx on the historically initial accumulation of capital

At the end of *Capital*, Volume I, Marx has a famous and interesting chapter on what he calls the initial accumulation of capital.[34] It describes the historical transition from feudalism to capitalism. Hence it describes where the initial capitalists got their 'capital' from. Even if such a history is important, it does not quite square with a pure systematic-dialectical account of capitalism. Systematically such a history is a *deus ex machina*, the point being the problematic phrase above: 'where did the initial capitalists get their *capital* from'. This is not so much a problem in terms of 'physical' entities; though it is a problem in terms of the inward bifurcation of commodities (their physical and monetary dimensions) and next the concept of capital itself. At some point, apparently, non-capital turns into capital. Historically this must be true. Nevertheless, if we were to rely on a historical procedure, this would question the appropriateness of the *systematic* starting point (this applies for Marx's *Capital* and for the current book's 1§1).

Division 5. Validation of macroeconomic surplus-value by macroeconomic expenditure

Finance, investment, saving and surplus-value

Building on the connection between finance, expenditure and saving (3§3 of 3D2 and 3§6 of 3D2), the current division expands on the macroeconomic interconnections regarding finance, investment, saving and surplus-value. Its last section 3§10 (which bears the same title as the full division) is the key one. It grounds the production of surplus-value (1D5) in macroeconomic expenditure. The earlier sections (3§8 and 3§9) present some preliminaries to it.

3§8 *Investment versus finance*

- *Primary and secondary substitution: primary and secondary financial markets*

The ex post substitution for the pre-validating finance by banks (3D3, 3§6) pertains to the so-called 'primary market': the issuance of new shares or new bonds or new direct placements of loans. Again, the purchase of this primary financial paper is necessarily based on a prior money creation by banks; the purchase always involves the transfer of money from one bank account (the substitu-

34 Chapter 24 of the German edition, Part Eight of the English edition (English translation of the title amended).

ent's) to another (the enterprise's). Appendix 3A (section 3A-3) expands on some contingencies of the *secondary* financial market: the trade in existing financial paper, or the re-substitution for the banks' PVF.

- *Investment as against finance: enterprises as against financiers*

The distinction between the purchasing *investment* in means of production by enterprises and the purchase of financial paper by financiers (primary or secondary) is economically crucial. When before and henceforth I use(d) the term 'investment', this always means *investment in means of production*. For the purchase of financial paper I will avoid using the term 'portfolio investment' and 'portfolio investor'; instead I will use the terms '*finance*' – be it primary or secondary finance – and '*financier*'.

Macroeconomically *investment is independent of saving* (3§2, 3§6, expanded in 3§9). However, *non-bank finance* (the purchase of financial paper) *is dependent on saving*: 'a' prior saving is a condition for it.[35]

3§8-a Amplification. 'Real investment' versus 'portfolio investment'

In English we have 'real investment' versus 'portfolio investment'.[36] Economists and the business press often abbreviate these (one of these) in 'investment', which gives rise to an enormous confusion (even in the mind of the author – one can see this even in the work of a usually careful writer and thinker such as Keynes). The term 'finance' is unambiguous.

3§9 *Investment and saving: the macroeconomic inequality of investment and saving (I≠S)*

Orthodox economics posits the macroeconomic equality of investment and saving, holding that saving is a precondition for investment. Keynes, Kalecki and post-Keynesian economics hold that saving results from investment, positing nevertheless the ex post macroeconomic equality of investment (I) and saving (S). As far as I know, all economic theory posits the macroeconomic equality of investment and saving (I=S) in one of these variants. The exposition in this section explicitly departs from these views. In fact this was implicit in the exposition from 3§2 onwards.

35 Appendix 3B (sections 3B-4 and 3B–4b) shows that in fact merely 'some' saving is a major condition for it.

36 In many other languages, the terms have different roots. For example, German has *investieren* (verb), *Investition* or *Investierung* (noun) for 'direct' investment and *anlegen* (verb), *Anlage* (noun) for the portfolio meaning. Dutch has, respectively, *investeren* and *beleggen*. French has *investissement* and *placement*.

The previous divisions regularly used the terms expenditure, saving and investment. As the state (Part Two) and international relations (Part Three) are so far abstracted from (bracketed), there are only two forms of expenditure: private consumption and private investment. Given the bifurcation between households and enterprises (1D1), only households consume and only enterprises invest. These are addressed in turn.

1 Consumption expenditure by households

Only households consume.[37] Alternatively they may in part abstain from expenditure and hence save part of their income. For their savings there are only two possibilities: keeping it in a bank account or purchasing financial paper.[38]

2 Investment expenditure by enterprises

Only enterprises invest. This is the enterprises' form of expenditure. As it is an expenditure, it is not a saving. However, (remotely) similar to households that may in part abstain from spending, enterprises might occasionally do some saving: exceptionally for reasons of pure liquidity preference; or for strategic reasons, whereby they purchase financial paper (perhaps in face of conglomeration).

3 The non-connection between investment and saving

It was shown in Chapter 1 (1D5) that labour, and labour alone, is the source of surplus-value. Apart from the specific argumentation in that chapter, the general thrust of this idea is no different from that of Adam Smith (1776). This is about *production*.

However, Smith also argued that because 'the masters' (capitalists) do the *saving*, and *because* in his view saving is a precondition for production ('advances'), there must be profits for the 'masters'.[39] This is about the *distribution* of production's value-added.

---

37 This includes durable consumer goods, which again includes (e.g.) owner-occupied dwellings. (See Appendix 3C-1, under point 6).

38 Recall from 2§8 the positing of unique bank account money. In the case of circulating remnants of bank notes (as is still the case today), the third possibility is to substitute account money in ClB-notes (which is in fact to purchase current zero-interest paper ('currency') from the ClB via an ordinary bank).

39 Smith: '*The value which the workmen add* to the materials, therefore, *resolves itself in* this case into two parts, of which the one pays *their wages*, the other *the profits* of their employer upon the whole stock of materials and wages which he advanced. He could have no interest to employ them, unless he expected from the sale of their work something

From Smith onwards, this idea about saving took root in all mainstream economic theory: saving is a justification for private profits including interest (cf. the Marshall citation in 1§14-b). (Marx would not agree with this, but he nevertheless somewhat uncritically took on board Smith's notion of 'advances' by the capitalist – as do many marxian political economists today).

In fact the mainstream macroeconomic notion of I=S (in both of its variants) can only be defended by way of an utterly strange *definition*, which functions as an *assumption*. This is to *define* the (PVF accommodated) expenditure of investment as saving(!), thereby defining an expenditure as a non-expenditure. More specifically, the investment *expenditure* equivalent of retained profits is *defined* as a saving.[40] This is categorially odd, though ideologically it does the job of providing the alleged justification mentioned.

It was already explicit that the exposition in this chapter is not based on a macroeconomic *ex ante* equality of investment and saving (this was explicit from 3§2, and the critique of the notion of saved loanable funds – 3§3-b, 3§6, 3§6-a, 3§6-d). It is now also explicit that the exposition is neither based on a macroeconomic *ex post* equality of saving and investment. Thus, in general, macroeconomically I ≠ S, and more specifically I > S.

3§9-a Amplification. Keynes's incomplete break from orthodox theory

Next to Kalecki, Keynes argued – against the orthodoxy of his day (which persists to this day) – that instead of saving giving rise to investment, investment gives rise to saving.[41] The greatness of Keynes is that he integrated macro and monetary theory. Neo-Keynesians (in contradistinction to post-Keynesians) soon disintegrated the matter. Nevertheless, Keynes postulated the *ex post* equality of the two (I→S, I=S ex post). Keynes's break from prior economic theory in this respect (I and S) is important. Nevertheless it is not a full break. In hindsight Keynes allowed the ex ante equality to sneak back in via the (erroneous) argument that in equilibrium the ex ante and ex post distinc-

more than what was sufficient to replace his stock to him; …' (1776, Book I, Ch. 6, para. 5, emphasis added). On saving specifically: 'As *the capital of an individual can be increased only by what he saves from his annual revenue* or his annual gains, *so the capital of a society*, which is the same with that of all the individuals who compose it, *can be increased only in the same manner*. *Parsimony, and not industry, is the immediate cause of the increase of capital.* Industry, indeed, provides the subject which parsimony accumulates. … Parsimony, by increasing the fund which is destined for the maintenance of productive hands, tends to increase the number of those hands whose labour adds to the value of the subject upon which it is bestowed.' (Book II, Ch. 3, paras 15–17, emphasis added).

40 In 3§10 this assumption will be criticised from a different perspective.

41 Bellofiore and Realfonzo (2003) argue how Marx is a precursor of this view.

tion does not matter. Next the whole ideology of loanable funds and of parsimony can be smuggled back in.

The strange definition/assumption of the (ex post) investment expenditure equivalent of retained profits as a saving is not only dominant in economic theory; it is also the national accounts practice.

Without, apparently, explicitly questioning the standard I=S notion, Jakab and Kumhof (2015, p. 4, fn. 6) keenly remark: 'in a closed economy, *macroeconomic* (national accounts) saving is equal to investment by accounting definition rather than as a result of equilibrium, and the quantity of that saving is unrelated to the overall quantity of financing'.

Simply as a definition (in effect that of 'saving = non-consumption') the ex post equality of investment and saving does not do much analytical harm – and in what follows in this book nothing hinges on their equality or non-equality. The mainstream notion is indeed 'merely' an ideological matter about the 'justification by definition' of profits and interest by parsimony, and often also a 'justification by definition' of a skewed distribution of income.

3§10 *Validation of macroeconomic surplus-value by macroeconomic expenditure*

In the exposition of the finance of enterprises, the focus in Divisions 2–3 was on the *pre-validation* of production by banks. This final section focuses on the macroeconomic *validation* (realisation) of production, and especially of surplus-value. It explicitly connects the exposition of Chapter 1 to macroeconomic implications of the exposition in Chapters 2–3 so far. After an introductory subsection, the exposition focuses on the interconnection of the three sequential processes of *production* (subsection 2), of the macroeconomic *validation of production and of surplus-value* in particular (subsection 3), and of the *distribution of surplus-value* (subsection 4).

1 The previous exposition

This subsection sums up the relevant stages of the exposition so far.

A. In Chapter 1 (1D5), production in general was presented, and hence the production of surplus-value in general.[42]

B. In Chapter 2, enterprises and banks were distinguished. Even so the two were presented as a separation-in-unity (2D5).

42 The macroeconomic concept of surplus-value is in principle no different from the concept of 'operating surplus' as adopted in the current *System of National Accounts*. However, I refrain from using the latter concept in order to evade the specific imputations that go along with the *SNA*'s concept of the operating surplus – see 3§10-b.

C. In 3§1 the production activities of banking entities (as against the bank's financing activities) were subsumed under the enterprises – thus 'banks' as money-creating financiers do not produce, produce no value-added, and thus no surplus-value. The same section outlined the interest flow from enterprises to banks and other financiers as a share in the surplus-value of enterprises.

On this basis the remainder of this section presents a pure macroeconomic account.

2 *Macroeconomic production*

In 1D5 it was pre-posited that capitalist production requires pre-validating finance by banks (PVF) as treated in 3D2–3D3. The exposition in 1D5 (1§14, heading 6) set out how the production of capital is generated by labour's production of surplus-value.

$X_t \lessdot = [(\delta + \mu)K + mL^{\alpha}]_t$ [micro account] (1.4)

For a macro account the μK cancels out as intermediate deliveries; thus macroeconomically μ=0. When considering net production (as in NDP) instead of gross production (as in GDP) δK is abstracted from. Thus we have for net production (Y):

$Y \lessdot = mL^{\alpha}_t$ [micro and macro account] (1.8)

$\Pi_t \lessdot = mL^{\alpha}_t - wL_t$ [idem] (1.5)

In 1§14 it was indicated that mL^{α} is the *actual* monetary value of labour, with 'm' being the *actual* unit monetary value of labour, and that 'm' measures the validation, the sale, of the product of labour. (Recall that 'w' is the wage rate and that $\lessdot$ indicates right hand side to left hand side determination.)

The wages sum (W) is defined as

$W_t = wL_t$ [idem] (3.1)

It is now made explicit that the constellation presented in 1D5 is such that the validation of production as planned by enterprises on average squares with the actually validated production. However, in the current section we allow for a deviation between the production as planned by enterprises, and the actual validation of production (the adaptation taking time).[43] Therefore the equations for production (X), value-added (Y for net production) and surplus-value (Π) presented in 1§14 are now rewritten in terms of planned production vari-

43 The previous sentence (about 1D5) means that sector deviations (or deviations within sectors) roughly cancel out. The last sentence allows for divergences. These divergences must be moderate in order to prevent that (from one period to the other) the economy spirals into overheating, prompting the next recession. This implies that we are in something of a steady-state phase of the business cycle (amplified in Chapter 5). Even so, the equations presented in the remainder of this section do apply in each phase of the business cycle.

ables (superscript p). Especially relevant is the possible deviation between the planned unit monetary value of labour, 'm^p', and the actual unit 'm'.

We so have (time subscripts (t) are omitted):

$X^p \sphericalangle = (\delta + \mu)K + m^p L^\alpha$ [macro account for μ=0] (3.2; cf. 1.4)

$Y^p \sphericalangle = m^p L^\alpha$ [micro and macro account] (3.3; cf. 1.8)

$\Pi^p \sphericalangle = m^p L^\alpha - W$ [idem] (3.4; cf. 1.5)

All variables (above and below) without the superscript p denote actually *validated* variables.

Macroeconomically a deviation between the planned validation of production and the actual validation is determined by macroeconomic expenditure deviating from the planned one.[44] Section 3§3 introduced the 'savings' aspect of this expenditure on which I now expand.

3 *Validation of macroeconomic production by expenditure*

In this subsection the main focus will be on the macroeconomic categories of investment (I) and consumption (C). As for production, the validation of production by expenditure requires accommodation by the PVF provided by banks. Most of this accommodation coincides with the PVF of production. The PVF for investment results in investment expenditure, and the PVF for wages results in consumption expenditure by wage earners. However, the PVF for the payment of dividend and interest to capital owners occurs after production (*Circuit 3.9* in 3§3), and so does not coincide with the PVF of production. (See heading 4 on the distribution of surplus-value Π).

Regarding the economic domain treated, it is noted that at the current stage of the exposition (with the state bracketed), macroeconomic income (Y) consists merely of the two categories of surplus-value realised (Π) and of wages paid by enterprises (W):

$Y = \Pi + W$ [macroeconomic domain] (3.5)

$\Pi = Y - W$ (3.5′)

Similarly for the current domain, macroeconomic net expenditure (E) consists merely of the net investment by enterprises (I) and consumption by households (C).

$E = I + C$ [macroeconomic domain] (3.6)

Equations (3.5) and (3.6) do not represent a 'determination' but rather the formal definition of the domain at this stage.

---

44 In what economists call 'equilibrium', the planned unit m^p is equal to the actual unit m, whence $m^p L^\alpha = mL^\alpha$. Usually there is some degree of disequilibrium whereby we have some degree of deviation between the two, the deviation being adapted for by changes in investment and production in the next period of production.

Given production (X^P and Y^P), *the validation of production results in income* as determined by expenditures (also called 'effective demand'):

$$Y \lessdot = E \qquad (3.7)$$

$$Y \lessdot = I + C \qquad \text{[implication]} \quad (3.7')$$

The investment expenditure (I), i.e. the purchases of means of production, is the investment concomitant of the current production X^P (3.2). At this stage its determinants are merely provisionally made explicit, without further amplifying on these (expanded in Chapter 5).

$$I_t \lessdot = f(\omega_{t-1}; X^d_t; PVF_t) \qquad (3.8)$$

Thus current investment (and current investment expenditure) is determined by the rate of integral profit realised in the previous year (ω_{t-1}) and the desired current production (X^d_t), as conditioned by the current pre-validating finance by banks (PVF_t). Generally investment applies, on the one hand, to a possible gap between the planned unit monetary value of labour, m^P, and the actual unit 'm' (as indicated above), and, on the other hand, to enterprises' expectations about the future (Keynes called such informed guesses 'animal spirits').

For consumption a distinction is made between consumption by capital owners (Ck) and by wage earners (Cw):

$$C = Ck + Cw \qquad \text{[definition]} \quad (3.9)$$

On average the consumption by capital owners (Ck) autonomously depends on their standard of living. That is, it is independent of the ebb and flow of the level of the surplus-value distributed (expanded in Chapter 5). However, the consumption by wage earners is dependent on the wages (W), and the degree of consumption out of wages is dependent on the level of wages and changes thereof (expanded in Chapter 5). Given the payment of wages out of the PVF, we have (substituting 3.9 and 3.7′ in 3.5′) for the surplus-value realised (Π):

$$\Pi \lessdot = I + Ck + (Cw - W) \qquad \text{[implication]} \quad (3.10)$$

Thus the validation of surplus-value is determined by, on the one hand, the investment expenditure of enterprises (I) and the consumption expenditure of capital owners (Ck), and, on the other hand, the consumption expenditure by labour (Cw) minus wages (W).[45] Note that the validation of surplus-value is thus determined by three distinct categories of actors: enterprises (I); capital owners (Ck); and wage earners (Cw–W). It is emphasised that – as before – the determination in (3.10) runs from the right hand side to the left hand side. None of the right hand side *current* expenditure factors is determined by *current* surplus-value (Π); it is indeed the other way around. Restricting to investment:

45 This insight is inspired by Kalecki – see 3§10-a.

the act of investment expenditure by enterprises (via the banks' PVF) determines the validation of surplus-value of other enterprises. Even so, the validation of surplus-value in the current period (year) may affect the plans for production and investment in the next period.

The saving out of wages (Sw) is by definition equal to wages (W) minus consumption out of wages (Cw).

$$Sw = W - Cw \qquad \text{[definition]} \quad (3.11)$$

Substituting 3.11 into 3.10 we have

$$\Pi \Lsh = I + Ck - Sw \qquad (3.12)$$

Thus the validation of surplus-value (Π) is positively determined by the expenditures of enterprises (I) and capital owners (Ck) and negatively by labour's saving. In terms of validation of surplus-value, this affirms what was presented in 3D2 and 3D3 in terms of finance. That is, rather than being a macroeconomic benevolence, saving burdens enterprises. *Saving hampers the validation of surplus-value (integral profit), the accumulation of capital and economic growth.* (Nevertheless, as indicated before, saving may make sense for individual actors).

4 *Distribution of surplus-value*

The distinction between the three sequential processes of *production*, *validation* and *distribution* of surplus-value is essential to the exposition of the capitalist economy. These processes are distinct, though interconnected. Production of output, and hence of surplus-value, inevitably precedes the validation of output and surplus-value. Similarly, the validation of surplus-value inevitably precedes the distribution of surplus-value. Therefore, there is no investment *out of* surplus-value (integral profit), as much of orthodox economics would have it. (Investments are not 'advances' by enterprises or capitalists or 'masters', as mainstream economics since Adam Smith has proposed; rather, banks 'advance' PVFs).

Only after the validation of the surplus-value produced can it be distributed, namely in the three forms of:

- interest to banks (from which banks' finance capital is fed);
- dividends and interest to capital owners;[46]

---

46 Immediately after equation 3.9 above it was stated: 'The consumption by capital owners (Ck) autonomously depends on their standard of living. That is, it is independent of the ebb and flow of level of the surplus-value distributed'. Even so, with part of the validated surplus-value being variously distributed throughout the year to capital owners, some variable ex post saving from distributed surplus-value results (expanded in Chapter 5).

- retained profits, as already embodied in the capital assets during the pre-validated process of production via investment purchases (on the enterprises' balance sheet this appears as addition to its equity).[47]

Thus these are the three *ex post* shares in surplus-value.[48] In hindsight *Figure 3.2b*, from which we started in 3§1, is to be interpreted in this way.

5 *Concluding summary*

We have three distinct, though interconnected, sequential processes: (1) production of surplus-value; (2) validation of surplus-value; and (3) distribution of surplus-value. The production of surplus-value (1D5) and the accumulation of capital (Ch. 2) are grounded in the pre-validating finance by banks (3D2–3D3). The redemption of this finance, as well as the validation of surplus-value, is conditioned on the macroeconomic expenditure. There is no investment *out of* surplus-value distributed (including the retained part). Rather, surplus-value is a *result* of the first two processes. The first process establishes (for all enterprises) any additional investment via the banks' PVF. The second process validates the production of investment goods via their sale (for producers of investment goods), and it validates the production of consumer goods via their sale (for producers of consumer goods).

3§10-a Addendum. Michał Kalecki

Recall equation (3.9): $\Pi \lessdot = I + Ck + (Cw–W)$. Equations (3.9) and (3.12) are inspired by Kalecki (1935; 1942) – who, working in the marxian discourse, was a contemporary and precursor of Keynes. Kalecki's view is aptly summarised in Kaldor's (1955/56, p. 85) well-known paraphrase of Kalecki: 'capitalists earn what they spend, and workers spend what they earn' – that is, pending the distinction between enterprises and capital owners, and pending saving by workers.[49] In the article from 1942 he remarks that capitalists 'may decide to consume and to invest more in a certain short period than in the preceding period, but they cannot decide to earn more. It is therefore their investment

47 In the penultimate sentence above, it was stated that there is no investment *out of* surplus-value. However, ex post we have an equivalent of investment in retained profits, that is, for that part of the investment for which PVF loans have been redeemed.

48 These are the three shares in surplus-value with the state bracketed. In Chapter 8 we will see that taxes constitute a fourth share in surplus-value.

49 In *Capital II* Marx wrote: 'In relation to the capitalist class as a whole ... the proposition that it must itself cast into circulation the money needed to realize its surplus-value ... is not only far from paradoxical, it is in fact a necessary condition of the overall mechanism' (Marx 1885^1, 1893^2; Fernbach translation p. 497).

and consumption decisions which determine profits, and not the other way round' (Kalecki 1942, p. 259).

For an overview and appreciation of Kalecki's work, see, for example, López and Assous (2010), Toporowski (2013), and various essays in Bellofiore, Karwowski and Toporowski (eds) (2013, 2014) and in Toporowski and Mamica (eds) (2015).

3§10-b Addendum. Surplus-value and the Operating Surplus (SNA) – a preliminary note

The *System of National Accounts 2008* (UN 2009) adopts the macroeconomic surplus concept of '*operating surplus*'. Its starting point is output minus intermediates (purchases and sales between enterprises) and minus wages. Taking this for all enterprises together (production and financial enterprises) that starting point for the operating surplus (OS) would be equivalent to our concept of surplus-value. However, the *SNA* also adopts a number of arbitrary imputations, which mean that the two concepts deviate. I mention the two most important ones. First, imputations regarding the interest margin of banks (via which value-added is imputed to banks), and second, the imputation of rental income regarding owner-occupied dwellings. (I expand on this and related matters in Appendix 3C, section 3C-1 under point 6, and in 8§6-d).

Summary and conclusions

The first section of this chapter provided guidance for the reader, distinguishing between 'active capital' (enterprises' assets) and 'passive capital' (the finance of the assets). Along with it surplus-value (the result of production) is qua distribution decomposed into 'internal profit' (the sum of dividends and retained profit) and 'interest' (as distributed to banks and other financiers) (3D1).[50]

In the type of macroeconomics developed in this chapter – as inspired by the Monetary Circuit theory – the distinction between enterprises and banks is essential. Bank-provided pre-validating finance (PVF) for enterprises is not only unconditionally necessary to the capitalist system; it is also fundamentally different from any other type of finance. One fundamental feature is that this PVF is a pure ex nihilo accounting money operation, and another is that it requires no saving, neither prior to nor after the investment that it accommodates. Generally saving is *not* necessary to the capitalist system (3D2).

50 See the summary in Figures 3.2a and 3.2b.

Nevertheless, savings are ubiquitous and their existence necessarily gives rise to forms of finance other than the PVF. From a systematic point of view, all other types of finance are derived from the bank-provided PVF. All these other types are 'ex post' types of finance, that is, these serve to finance already *accumulated* capital, or ready investments on the basis of the PVF. Therefore, generally, saving does not precede investment; investment is not financed 'out of' saving. Only the bank-provided PVF finances the *accumulation* of capital. Other types of finance may, ex post, substitute for a non-redeemed part of the PVF, the non-redemption being caused by savings (3D3).

Whereas macroeconomic investment is independent of saving, the purchase of financial paper (often misleadingly called portfolio 'investment' rather than finance) is not independent of saving. Not only is there no macroeconomic *ex ante* equality of saving and investment; there is also no macroeconomic *ex post* equality of saving and investment (the positing of such an equality in most of economics is a categorial mistake, confusing expenditure and saving) (3D5).

The sequential character of the interconnected processes of pre-validation, production, validation and distribution of output and surplus-value is essential to a capitalist economy. Production and the pre-validating finance of production precede sales and so the validation of surplus-value. The degree of redemption of this pre-validating finance, as well as the validation of surplus-value (integral profit), is conditioned on macroeconomic effective demand. In line with a Kalecki type of approach, it was posited that – at the stage of exposition of Chapter 3 (with the state and international relations bracketed) – the macroeconomic validation of the surplus-value produced is determined by investment (+), the consumption by capital owners (+), and the saving by labour (−). The distribution of surplus-value (to banks, capital owners and as retained profits) inevitably follows after the validation, whence there is no investment out of a pre-existing surplus-value. In this way the investment-saving matter is connected to the investment-surplus-value matter (3D5).

The brief 3D4 on the foundation of banks is simple and may not warrant summarising. However, it deserves mention in terms of 'conclusions'. That division grounds the starting point's capital accumulated (1§1). At that point of the exposition (3D4), all prior pre-positions regarding the capitalist *economy* appear to have been grounded within the exposition (3§7-b). However, regarding the capitalist system as a whole, the capitalist state is still being pre-posited (exhibited in Part Two).

Appendix 3A. Two contingencies of the finance-capital market: intertemporal trade and re-substitution trade

The main text of Chapter 3 presented the necessities of the finance of enterprises in face of the reproduction of the capitalist system. The contingencies of this finance are ubiquitous and this book generally does not treat outright contingent constellations. This current appendix nevertheless very briefly expands on pension funds (that is, the intertemporal trade in savings – section 3A-2) and the secondary markets of shares and bonds (that is, re-substitution trade – section 3A-3). The introductory first section makes a systematic distinction between the finance-capital market and the financial market at large.

3A-1 *The finance-capital market*

The main text of Chapter 3 dealt with, what I now call, the *finance-capital market*, that is, the market for the finance of production enterprises. It was indicated that there is a tendency for capital owners to substitute, in part, for the bank-provided finance capital (3§6). It is contingent whether this substitution takes place via the direct intermediation of banks (the banks bringing the parties together) or via other credit brokers or via a public or private issue of 'finance capital titles' (shares, bonds and other loans).

On the demand side of the *finance-capital* market we have only enterprises. On its supply side we have:

1. Banks. All of the following (2–4) may substitute *ex post* for the pre-validating bank finance (see 3§6).
2. 'Other financial institutions', that is, other savings channelling institutions: pension funds, insurance companies, other financiers' companies (i.e. portfolio 'investment' companies, including hedge funds). Next to banks, especially the pension funds are a major vehicle for channelling savings by labour (3§3).
3. 'Private financiers', i.e. individual capital owners operating on this market (including rich wage earners).
4. Enterprises (especially large corporations) as financiers of other enterprises. This category is today especially important amongst the enterprises quoted at the top of the equity market (i.e. shares market). (Because of such finance, the adding up of the assets of all enterprises would involve double counting).

I make a systematic distinction between the 'finance-capital market' (the main text of Chapter 3 together with the current appendix) and the 'financial market' at large. The latter includes the 'finance-capital market' together with the contingent market for loans to labour and to capital owners (briefly treated in

Appendix B). All of the institutions listed above may also operate on the financial market at large.[51] These distinctions are a matter of perspective. For the financier, the several variants of the finance of enterprises, households (or governments) may be just a matter of degree of security in face of expected (uncertain) revenues. However, the starting point of our exposition in Chapter 3 is *not* the individual financier (portfolio 'investor'), but rather the investment of enterprises in face of the accumulation of capital (cf. 3§1), which requires finance. The distinction between the finance-capital market and the financial market is relevant for this perspective.

3A-2 *Pension funds: intertemporal trade – premiums, pension and degree of recollected surplus-value for labour*

The income distribution between capital and labour (surplus-value and wages), as well as the distribution of surplus-value into interest, retained profit and dividend, is called the primary distribution of income. From these we may have a derived intertemporal redistribution of income. Pension funds are one of the main vehicles dealing in this derived redistribution. They collect premiums today (such as out of wages), and with these they purchase financial paper or other assets. From the revenues (or perhaps in part from their liquidation) they redistribute pension benefits. Indirectly labourers so intertemporally recollect some share of the surplus-value that they produced – basically the rate of revenue (such as interest) on their premium. (Thus, merely as a very rough indication, if the premium is 2% of the wage and the average revenue (e.g. the real rate of interest) is 3%, then the recollected surplus-value is 0.06% of the wage – neglecting compound interest. At compounded interest – and depending on the pension scheme – the recollection of SV is, averaged over the wage earning premium years, most often under 1% of the yearly wage).

3A-3 *Re-substitution trade in financial paper*

Section 3§8 introduced the distinction between dealings on the 'primary' shares and bonds markets and dealings on the 'secondary' shares and bonds markets. The current section expands on this distinction. I will mainly refer to the shares market. The same applies most often to the bonds market: only the differences will be indicated.

---

51 Anticipating Chapter 8, public finance is also part of the financial market.

Substitution for the banks' RPVF: the primary market's flow of shares

The primary flow of shares is the *net addition to the stock* of shares. The primary flow of shares concerns the issuance of new shares by enterprises. In the light of 3§6 the purchase of newly issued shares is merely an ex post substitution for the banks' remaining pre-validating finance (RPVF) out of the capital owners' savings. (The enterprises' buying back their own shares is in effect the reverse).[52]

The purchase of new shares can stem from: savings by capital owners (out of their dividends or interest); savings by labour (out of their wages); or, in each case, non-bank financial institutions that collect these savings (see the more detailed list in 3A-1); incidentally, banks may also substitute between *their* RPVF, thereby substituting loans for shares or bonds.

Re-substitution for the banks' RPVF: the secondary market's trade in the stock of shares

The trade in the stock of shares effectuates the spread of risk and uncertainty for shareholders (referred to in 3§5). However, it also opens up the possibility for liquidation of the share's value. That is, for an individual shareholder. It is important to note that macroeconomically there can be no exit from the stock of shares (the exceptions being the enterprises' buy back of shares, or the final liquidation of an enterprise). For most types of bonds this is different as these are usually time-limited loans (e.g. 10 or 30 years). Microeconomic (individual) liquidation is always a matter of re-substitution between an existing shareholder that exits value (acquiring a current account addition) and a novice shareholder that enters value (current account deduction). That is, the novice in this respect: the novice shareholder might own other shares already. Note that even if this novice shareholder buys existing shares out of dividends that the novice received, this is still a re-substitution (a deduction from the current account of the novice from dividends, and a current account addition for the liquidating seller of shares).

52 For the enterprise this action is either one of a reshuffling of their liabilities, or one of (relative) disinvestment resulting in a positive current account balance with the bank, the latter being transferred to shareholders.

Appendix 3B. Contingent lending by banks to labour and to capital owners

Next to the validation of production, the main text of Chapter 3 focuses on the finance of enterprises and especially the key role of banks in this finance. However, banks not only (pre-)finance enterprises. As a corollary to the main text, this appendix briefly expands on banks' lending to labour and to capital owners. Although such lending is contingent (it is not necessary to the existence of the capitalist system), it nevertheless seems logically inherent to the systemic necessities treated so far.

3B-1 *The lending power of banks: money dealing and interest paid by banks*

Banks not only create money (2D4, 3D2); they also deal in their own creation. In order to improve their lending power, banks are out to keep their existing clients and to attract clients from competing banks. In other words, they are out to collect money created by competitor banks, and to prevent their 'own' account money being collected, via account transfers, by competitor banks.

The main mechanism is that of offering clients an interest. This tends to be accomplished via interest on time accounts, or 'savings accounts' (and perhaps current accounts). Note that this may improve the lending power of an individual bank, but not that of the banking system as a whole.[53]

The lending power of an individual bank may also increase via the sale of bank-issued bonds or via the issuance of new shares.[54] Whether in this case the lending power of the banking system as a whole increases will depend solely on whether these additional bonds (or shares) operate on the margin of rules set by the Clearing Bank (ClB) regarding liabilities' reserve ratios, perhaps in face of the ClB's standards regarding the composition of the assets (2§9–2§10).

3B-1-a Amplification. Level of the rate of interest offered

In order to consolidate their liabilities, the offering of interest by banks to their clients seems necessary (for common current accounts this may also take the form of non-charging for bookkeeping services, i.e. transfers). However, the

53 This can easily be seen when the banks are analytically integrated.

54 Note that the issuance of bank bonds (or also additional share capital) in effect directly decreases the amount of money in circulation (current account money is substituted for the bank bond). For enterprise-issued bonds this is so indirectly, that is, in case the enterprise uses the bond proceeds to cancel a loan with the bank.

level of the interest paid is highly dependent on the competitive or collusive structure of the banking constellation.

3B-2 *Generalisation of the form of money lending*

The interest bearing 'money-creating lending' by banks for and to enterprises is a systemic necessity. It is also a (potentially) profitable activity for banks. Because this is profitable, banks tend to generalise the *form of money lending* vis-à-vis any social actor. In particular they may lend money to labourers and to capital owners. They so create money in a reciprocal credit relationship similar to the money creation for enterprises (2§8). Although the generalised form of lending is contingent, the generalisation seems inherent to the *form* of lending to enterprises.[55]

3B-3 *Lending to labour*

1 Loans for durable commodities and other consumer loans

For lending to labourers the collateral will be some asset that they own (such as a house or another durable consumer good) or an expected future income stream (wages). This lending facilitates the enterprises' sale of relatively expensive and durable commodities.[56] More important for enterprises is that consumer loans affect the net profit of enterprises, as such loans are an *ex ante substitution* for the pre-validating finance requirement for the enterprises' payment of wages. This is so because in terms of credit, enterprises receive 'for free' revenues from consumption that they otherwise would have had to pre-finance upon wages payment. Hence enterprises pay less interest to the banks (instead labourers pay interest). *Circuit 3.18* illustrates this. Thus, whereas the saving by labour is a 'nuisance' for enterprises (3§3), non-saving and consumer credit is a pleasure.

This *ex ante* substitution is also a main distinction between loans to capital owners and loans to labour. Whereas loans to labour do affect the finance capital requirement of enterprises (decrease), loans to capital owners have no such effect.

---

55 Even so, the Clearing Bank (or at a later stage of the exposition the state or the Central Bank) might put limits on such lending.

56 It may also facilitate the 'saleability' of labour-capacity in case (higher) formal education is financed by loans.

CIRCUIT 3.18 *Enterprises' saving on PVF for wages due to consumer credit: case of zero saving out of wages*

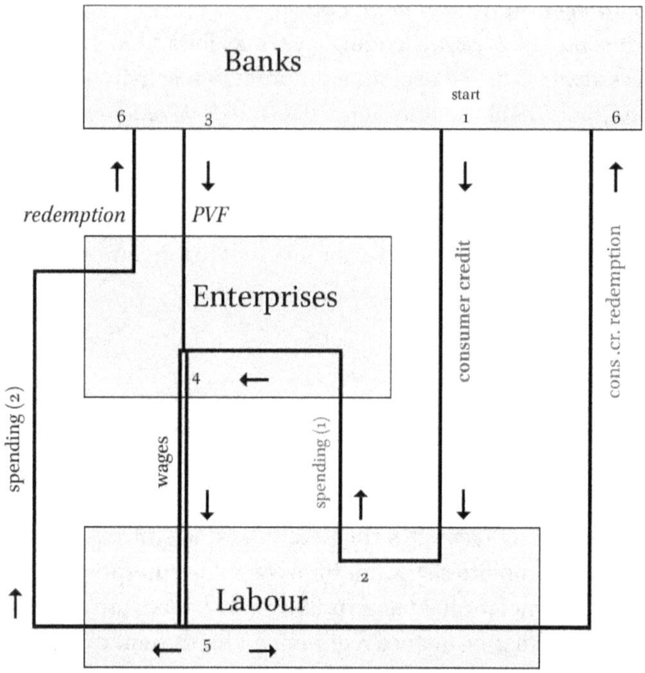

Note: For simplicity and transparency it is assumed that the consumer credit (stream 1) is equivalently redeemed (stream 6). In fact stream 1 might (temporarily) be larger than stream 6. (For the latter case see Chapter 5, Appendix A).

2 *Interest as a share in surplus-value or as a share in wages*

Macroeconomically, the interest paid by labour on loans may or may not outweigh the interest received by labour (3B-1). Any macro or micro net interest from labour is paid out of *wages* income. This is analogous to the interest on finance capital being paid out of the enterprises' net income, that is, out of *surplus-value* (3§4).

Although this is analogous, it is nevertheless conceptually different and so systemically different. The interest that enterprises pay to banks is a share in the surplus-value produced by labour. Should it be the case that labourers are macroeconomic or microeconomic net recipients of interest paid by the bank, then they indirectly reclaim a slice of the surplus-value.[57] (Whether this is the case is an empirical matter).

57 The following merely serves as an indication. Suppose that for labourers the macroeco-

3B-4 *Lending to capital owners: finance doubling*

Individual capital owners, or institutions in which they participate (3A-1), may want to increase their ex post financing potential (on primary or secondary financial markets – 3§8) by borrowing from banks on the basis of, most often, financial paper collateral. Especially for bank loans regarding secondary markets (existing financial paper), this means that, in *sum*, the lending power of banks is allocated away from enterprises.

It was indicated that, because the lending of money to enterprises against an interest is a (potentially) profitable activity, banks may apply the form of money lending vis-à-vis any social actor (3A-2). Remarkably this may also include the lending by banks to capital owners. Banks may grant loans to these potential ex post financiers on the basis of financial paper (shares, bonds) as collateral security. (Explication 3B–4a shows the possible leverage mechanism of such loans in cases of so-called 'margin buying').

By itself this leverage is a mere consequence of the constellation in which banks do grant loans on the basis of financial paper. That by itself is not remarkable: we may have analogous leverage mechanisms for loans to enterprises. What is remarkable about it is that (to the extent that banks are contingently allowed by the Clearing Bank to open up this constellation) we have a *doubling of the credit system*. Consider *Sheet 3.19*.

SHEET 3.19 *Finance doubling*

balance sheet enterprises			**balance sheet capital owners**		
assets (material)	*liabilities*		*assets (financial)*	*liabilities*	
assets →	1. bank loans (60%)				
assets →	2. bonds (20%)	–	2. bonds →	2. bank loans	(*the doubling*)
assets →	3. shares (20%)	–	3. shares →	3. bank loans	(*the doubling*)

Recall that banks necessarily provide pre-validating finance to enterprises (the left panel of *Sheet 3.19*). The collateral securities for these loans are the assets of

nomic interest bearing net loans to banks were 5% of wages at a real-interest rate of 2%, then, neglecting compounded interest, they would reclaim 0.1% of the wage in surplus-value.

the enterprises ('material' means of production). Ultimately banks might perhaps be willing to grant loans of up to, say, 60% of the total material assets (the number does not matter).

However, there is a balance sheet liabilities side to the remaining value (say, 40%) of these assets (bonds and shares).[58] The *finance doubling* occurs when not only the enterprises call on the bank for credit, but also the non-bank holders of the enterprises' bonds and shares. This is indeed credit on the basis of financial paper (entries 2 and 3 at the right hand panel of *Sheet 3.19*). Because of the lending on the basis of *financial* assets (and especially so with margin buying) there may be a self-reinforcing inflationary boosting of especially the shares market. (Suppose the bank is willing to grant loans to the enterprise up to 60% of the assets of the enterprise, and at a rate of 80% to bond and shareholders. Then, integrated, the bank – or different banks – in fact grant loans up to 92% of the underlying material assets of the enterprise).

3B–4a Explication: The leverage of margin buying

'Margin buying' is the exemplary pattern for bank loans to dealers in financial paper (individual dealers and portfolio financiers companies). Suppose the dealer owns, e.g. *€10,000* in shares, which is offered as collateral security to the bank for lending money.

- the bank lends, e.g., on a margin of 80%: €8,000
- for which the dealer buys additional shares, and then borrows anew on a 80% margin: €6,400
- and again: €5,120
- and again: €4,096
- et cetera: ....
- In total (on top of the initial €10,000) *€40,000*

(At a 70% margin the leverage is factor 2.3; at a 90% margin the leverage factor is 9).

This boosts a booming stock market in a self-reinforcing way (rising prices, rising credit, rising prices). This also works the other way around: with falling prices there is enforced selling when the margin ceiling is reached. (The same pattern may be applied to portfolio dealings in commodities and real estate).

This margin buying also applies for hedge funds. For the latter this is also an instrument to exert (temporary) power over a corporation (given that for quoted shares often only a small minority of the shareholders appears in share-

58 If the bank is the first, agreed creditor in case of a failure, then the bank may not care much about the composition of these liabilities.

holders' meetings). The fund may so impose its will on the corporation for short-term purposes, and next jump on to another corporation.

3B–4b Amplification. The doubling of finance and the (in)dependency of non-bank finance and saving

Recall from 3§9 that macroeconomically *investment is independent of saving* in the sense that saving is no condition for investment. (Rather, saving dampens investment, both in terms of expenditure and in terms of credit limits set by the bank.) In 3§8 it was posited that *non-bank finance* (purchase of financial paper) *is not independent of saving*, in the sense that 'a' prior saving is a condition for it. We can now see the reason for the qualification of 'a' prior saving. Because of the doubling of finance, and so the granting of credit on the basis of financial paper, even this finance may require merely 'some' prior saving (its degree depending on the leverage that banks allow for).

Appendix 3C. Rent as a contingent share in the production enterprises' surplus-value

Lease as a particular way of finance

This appendix presents the concept of rent. For its treatment I introduce the term 'production enterprises', that is, enterprises producing surplus-value through the production of commodities (including commodified services). Generally rent is the price for the use of something, for a period of time stipulated by contract (instead of the price for the purchase of something). In the history of economic theory, and especially Classical Political Economy, rent has predominantly been associated with the ownership and lease of land.[59]|[60] For

59 Adam Smith (1776) posits: 'The whole of what is annually either collected or produced by the labour of every society, or what comes to the same thing, the whole price of it, is in this manner originally distributed among some of its different members. *Wages, profit, and rent, are the three original sources of all revenue* as well as of all exchangeable value. All other revenue is ultimately derived from someone or other of these.' (Book I, Ch. 6, para. 17, emphasis added).

Karl Marx (*Capital III*) posits: 'The value freshly added in a year by freshly added labour – and so also the part of the annual product in which this value is expressed ... can ... be divided into three ... parts ... *three different forms of revenue*, ... one part ... accruing to the owner of labour-power, one part to the owner of capital and a third part to the owner of landed property.' (Ch. 51, para. 1, emphasis added – next he expands on the relations of production behind this distribution).

60 See, for example, Campbell (2002b) for an appreciation of Marx's theory of rent.

many, the rent of land is something of a sacrosanct category and I agree that the private ownership of the earth is a core issue (1§1). Nevertheless, for production enterprises, 'land' is merely a capital asset serving the production of surplus-value, like any other capital asset. I will treat it as such in this appendix. I consider the *actual* payment of rent.[61] I will conclude that lease is a particular way of finance and that rent is not a distinct final income category. Instead it is taken account of as the profit of enterprises. More specifically: *any net rent that production enterprises pay originates from surplus-value.*

3C-1 *Rent as a contingent share in the production enterprises' surplus-value*

1 The 'pure concepts' presented so far

In the main text of Chapter 3, the concepts of 'enterprises' and 'capital owners' were mostly treated as pure categories. That is, enterprises (now called production enterprises) only engage in production (whence K is production capital) and capital owners only own financial paper (mainly shares and bonds). 'Banks' were presented purely as money-creating financiers, as against 'banking entities' that may produce various services, the latter constituting part of production enterprises (3§1). Appendix 3A introduced 'financial enterprises'. Pure financial enterprises own only financial paper (shares, bonds, direct placements), that is, next to their premises. In the current appendix, banks have been included in the financial enterprises. This is summarised in *Figure 3.20*, rows 1a–c. Recall that, so far, internal profit is equal to surplus-value after the payment of interest (3§1, *Figure 3.2b*).

2 Hybrid enterprises and hybrid capital owners

So far we considered the *purchase and sale* of commodities and of financial paper. This appendix introduces the *lease* of commodities and, with it, the category of rent. Along with it 'hybrid entities' are introduced (production enterprises, capital owners, financial enterprises) that combine various activities of the pure entities, as well as the renting out of assets. Note, however, that all of this hybridity is *contingent.*

61 I have no intention to impute rent where no rent is paid – see below on the SNA.

3 *The concept of rent as a way of finance (user) and profit opportunity (owner)*

I consider rent as the price for the lease of *means of production*, including land and buildings (this pertains to enterprises) or for the lease of *durable consumer goods*, including dwellings (this pertains to households, foremost labour households). For the user (lessee) of means of production or durable consumer goods, the decision to lease instead of purchase is a matter of *finance* (and sometimes a matter of speculation, that I will neglect in this appendix). For the owner (lessor), renting out is a matter of profit opportunity.

Thus, for example, for a low-paid worker it may not be possible to finance the ownership of a dwelling, though out of wages it might finance its lease. A starting enterprise may be able to get finance for the running production process, though not for all the means of production, whereby it leases the latter. A mature enterprise may see new investment opportunities, for which it is prepared to give up ownership in part of its means of production – so leasing these.

4 *The merging of rent income into the profit of enterprises*

Surplus-value is produced within production enterprises, and production enterprises only. Hypothetically, all means of production could be leased by one set of production enterprises (in which the surplus-value is produced) and leased from a second set of enterprises that owns the means of production without producing. The rent that the latter secure is a share in surplus-value (like interest as a share in surplus-value).

Actually, *regarding means of production* it is immaterial whether or not production enterprises lease means of production from other (hybrid or non-producing) enterprises. If they do, the users (lessees) pay rent out of their surplus-value; the owners (lessors) receive rent which for them (after the deduction of costs of maintenance) results in their profit. Thus the latter profit derives from the surplus-value produced in the lessee's (user's) enterprise. (This is summarised in *Figure 3.20*, rows 2a–2b).

Regarding *durable consumer goods*, the rent for their lease is paid out of wages (or if capital owners lease, out of their capital income; in what follows I will neglect this). The owners of the durable consumer goods (lessors) receive rent, which for them (after the deduction of costs of maintenance) results in their profit. (See *Figure 3.20*, row 2c).

FIGURE 3.20 *Original and final income from rent: non-rent case (rows 1); renting out of means of production (MP) and durable consumer goods (DCG) by specialising lease enterprises (rows 2); renting out means of production by hybrid enterprises (rows 3). (sv is an abbreviation for surplus-value)*

	ownership of assets			ultimate origin final income ⁎	transfers	penultimate origin final income	transfers	penultimate origin final income †	transfers †	final income category
	means of production	financial paper	assets rented out *							
(1)	(2)	(3)	(4)	(5)	(6)	(7)	(8)	(9)	(10)	(11)
1. pure categories: finance to enterprises only (main text Chapter 3) ‡										
a. pure production enterprises	x			surplus-value	interest paid	internal profit	dividend paid			retained profit
b. pure financial enterprises		x			interest received		dividend rec.	(sv derived) profit	dividend paid	retained profit
c. pure capital owners		x			interest received		dividend rec.		dividend rec.	int. & div.
1d. Macroeconomic sum				***sum = total sv***	***sum = 0***		***sum = 0***		***sum = 0***	***sum = total sv***
2. enterprises specialising in lease only (rows 3b and 3c) – ***introductory for rows 3***										
a. production enterprises				surplus-value	interest paid; rent paid (= 3b)	internal profit				
b. enterprises leasing out MP			MP		rent received (= 3a)			(sv derived) profit	dividend paid	retained profit
c. ent. leasing out DCG (to labour)			DCG	wages	rent received			(wages der.) profit	dividend paid	retained profit
3. hybrid categories ‡										
a. hybrid production enterprises	own use			surplus-value	interest and rent paid					
		x			interest received		div. rec. (internal a)	(sv derived) profit	dividend paid (column 8, row b)§	retained profit
			MP		rent received					
			DCG	wages	rent received			(wages der.) profit		
b. hybrid financial enterprises.ʃ and hybrid capital owners/enterprises.⁑ [*all non-production enterpr.*]		x			interest received		dividend rec.	(sv and wages derived) profit	dividend paid (to capital owners)	retained profit
			MP		rent received					
			DCG	wages	rent received					
3c. Semi-macroeconomic sum				***sum = total sv + rent from wages***	***sum = rent received from wages*** *(sum interest = 0; sum rent MP = 0)*		***sum = total dividend received from prod-ent.***	*sum is as next column*	***sum = total sv + rent from wages (neglecting interest paid or received by labour)***	

* Means of production (MP) and durable consumer goods, including dwellings (DCG). Lease of DCG to capital owners is neglected.
⁎ Surplus-value in this column is the surplus-value produced in (hybrid) production enterprises.
† Neglecting interest paid (accounting for it would require extra columns).
‡ Each owns only one type of assets.
ʃ This may also include (in fact non-financial) enterprises specialising in leasing (such as real estate companies without financial assets).
⁑ Because capital owners now own MP assets, these function (for that part) as enterprise, whence their penultimate income category is profit (column 9).
§ Doing this properly would require two extra columns.

5 *The income of hybrid enterprises – a more detailed presentation*

Rows 3 of *Figure 3.20* present a more detailed conceptualisation of the treatment of rent for hybrid entities (mentioned in subsection 2 above). Below I expand on each of the three hybrid categories.

A. Hybrid production enterprises. The category of hybrid production enterprises owns means of production for its own use and has its labour producing surplus-value. However, groups of enterprises within this category also deal in financial paper, and also rent out means of production to other enterprises. For this part the latter share in the surplus-value produced elsewhere. (*Figure 3.20*, row 3, top three sub-rows). Another group within this category leases out durable consumer goods (DCG) to workers (mainly). (*Figure 3.20*, row 3, bottom sub-row).

Overall, however, all surplus-value is produced within or among these hybrid production enterprises.

B. Hybrid financial enterprises. Hybrid financial enterprises deal not only in financial paper (as the pure financial enterprises do), but also in the lease of means of production (MP) and of DCG. (See *Figure 3.20*, row 3b).

C. Hybrid capital owners functioning as enterprises. Enterprises own the means of production (1§1). Capital owners thus far owned financial paper (shares and bonds – 3§5), thereby in part financing ex post the enterprises' ownership of the means of production (3§6). Now 'hybrid capital owners' are introduced. These may also own means of production (MP) that they rent out to production enterprises. They may also own and lease out DCG. Consistency requires that such MP-owners are treated as (non-producing) enterprises – and often such ownership is actually converted into corporate form. As a result these capital owners can be treated in the same way as the 'hybrid financial enterprises'. (See *Figure 3.20*, row 3b). However, any final distribution of income in the form of dividends ends up with capital owners (row 3b, column 10).

In conclusion. Any rent that enterprises pay (and particularly also any rent that hybrid production enterprises pay) is a share in their surplus-value. (See *Figure 3.20*, row 3c).

6 *Capital, investment and durable consumer goods – the SNA treatment*

Capital is a form of wealth. However, this does not mean that any wealth is 'capital'. Capital is a form of wealth geared to production, with the purpose of selling that production so as to make a profit (this makes the mainstream economics denotation of labour capacity as 'human capital' a rather ideological one). Investment is an addition to the capital stock ($I = \Delta K$).

Therefore, 'durable consumer goods' (DCG) are indeed what the term indicates; these are consumer goods and the expenditure on these is 'consumption'. Having said this, it must be observed that the classification under DCG is rather arbitrary. For example, many households use their cutlery for over 50 years. Nevertheless, cutlery and similar items are in the statistics usually not considered as DCG.

On the other hand, in the SNA (the *System of National Accounts* – the official international standard for national accounting and national account statistics – UN 2009), the purchase of dwellings is not treated as the purchase of a DCG at all. Instead it is treated as an investment! In order to accommodate for a lurking inconsistency about their own (SNA) treatment of 'investment', the owner-occupied dwellings of households are treated as an artificial branch of enterprises! (Around the year 2015, this statistical ruse includes, depending on the country, 50–70% of the labour households as part of capital-owning enterprises).

The SNA's counterpart to this artificial treatment of households is that an artificial rent income is *imputed* to these households. (The argument is that this treatment makes the macroeconomic income indifferent to who owns dwellings. This is true – if the imputation were reliable; however, these households do not have this income, just as they do not derive an income from their cutlery or from all kinds of DCGs that they might lease but do not lease. Thus, even this artificial treatment is not a consistent one).[62|63]

In the conceptualisation of *Figure 3.20* I restrict the focus to actually paid rent. Then, as a counterpart, the purchase of an owner-occupied dwelling would be an act of consumption even if its use were spread out over many years (like cutlery).

The SNA treatment has the effect that the actual macroeconomic income is upgraded. That apart, macroeconomically the rent payments and receipts between the total of enterprises (non-financial and financial) cancels out. The remaining rent payments from wage earners to enterprises are indeed expenditures out of wages.

---

62 To be sure, many heterodox economists have resisted, and do resist, this SNA treatment.

63 Piketty notes that: 'durable goods (not included in official wealth accounts) generally account for between 30% and 50% of national income, and that this level seems to be relatively stable: during the period 1970–2010 as well as on the long the run, from the 18th to the 21st century' (2014 [2013], pp. 179–80 and technical appendix p. 30).

List of figures of chapter 3

3§7. The foundation of banks and enterprises

Appendix 3B. Contingent lending by banks to labour and to capital owners

Appendix 3C. Rent as a contingent share in the production enterprises' surplus-value

CHAPTER 4

Market interaction and stratified production

Competition, cartel formation and monopolisation

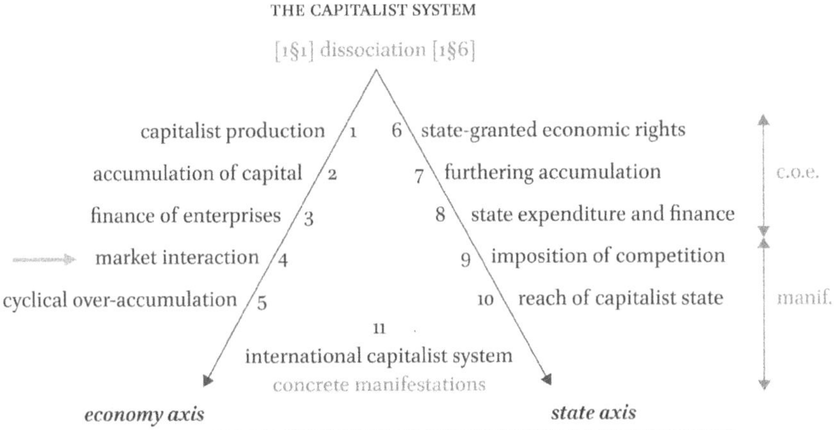

Note: 'c.o.e.' abbreviates conditions of existence and 'manif.' manifestations.

Contents

DOI:10.1163/9789004392809_006

Introduction

Chapters 1–3 presented the necessary conditions of existence of the capitalist economy (with the state yet bracketed). Chapters 4 and 5 (the last two chapters of Part One) present no further conditions of existence, but rather concrete manifestations of the earlier exposition (see also the pyramid figure at the opening of the chapter).

Manifestations have three main characteristics. First, they are implications of the necessary moments – implications that most often have a 'tendency' character. Second, manifestations are the culmination of the synthetic exposition – building on that of the grounding moments. Third, whereas those grounding moments reveal the reproductive strength of the capitalist system, the implications of the simultaneous interaction of these grounding moments are also expressed in concrete manifestations that thus reveal *not only* reproductive strength but also reproductive vulnerability.

Chapter 4 introduces the market interaction between enterprises into the exposition. Even though the exposition of Chapters 1–3 was prompted by the commodification and the transactions that are necessary to overcome the initial bifurcation between households and private units of production (1D1), the term 'market' has hardly been mentioned up to this point. This has been due to the method of exposition, which starts by seeking the connection between phenomena in the elements that unite them into a totality, that is, the totality of the capitalist system, and so far the capitalist economy.

Until now the exposition treated the totality of the capitalist economy in a way that combined a macroeconomic emphasis with the actions of the 'average capitalist enterprise'. Broadly the focus was thus on, first, the interconnection between enterprises and labour, and second, the interconnection between enterprises and banks. Now, in that light, the exposition in the current chapter focuses on the interconnecting interaction *between* enterprises.

In this chapter the market interaction between enterprises is not presented from the perspective of an individual enterprise (the starting point of much of orthodox economics), but rather from the perspective of the constellation of enterprises in one sector (branch) of production. The central concept throughout the chapter is the 'stratification of enterprises' in a sector (introduced in Division 1). As we will see, this concept is related to the technique of production adopted.

Analytically the form of market interaction between enterprises may be classified along a continuum of rivalrous competition on the one end, and – via cartel formation – monopolisation on the other. The position on that continuum

SCHEME 4.1 *Market interaction and the stratified structure of production: competition cartel formation, oligopolisation and monopolisation (outline Chapter 4)*

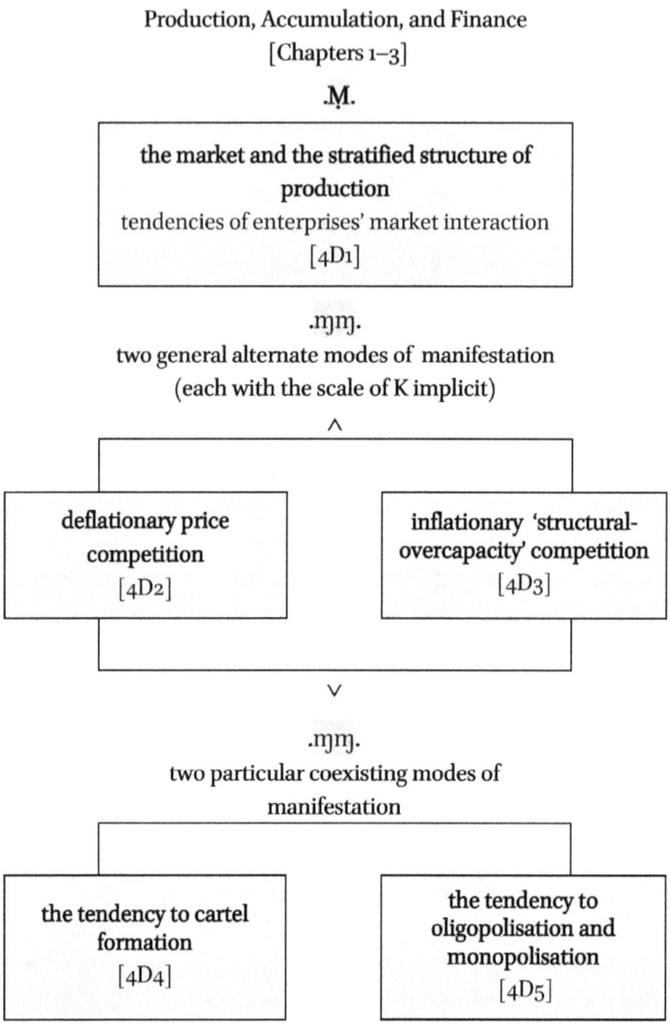

Legend
.Ṃ. concrete manifestation
.ŋɱ. mode of manifestation

would then seem to be contingent and each such position might be analytically modelled (this is the main approach in orthodox economics).

In the exposition of this chapter, the forms of market interaction – competition, cartels, oligopoly and monopolisation – are presented as being predicated on the stratified structure of production in particular sectors. This structure is again predicated on the accumulation of capital as conditioned by technical change. (Divisions 2–5.)

In comparison with the competitive interaction (Divisions 2–3), relatively little space is devoted to cartel formation, oligopolisation and monopolisation (Divisions 4–5). This is not because the latter are of minor importance. On the contrary. It is rather that their exposition is less complicated than that of competition – noting here already that the latter is not presented from the perspective of equilibrium, nor of 'perfect competition'.

The two divisions on competition are associated with price deflationary (4D2) and, alternatively, price inflationary (4D3) constellations. It will be seen in the latter division that 'deflation' or 'inflation' are not purely monetary phenomena; rather these result from the 'real' interaction of enterprises, *together with* their monetary *accommodation* by banks. (Again, monetary matters are not a negligible 'veil', but of key importance).

The chapter starts with an exposition of 'market interaction' in general (independent of its particular forms). Here we will see in particular how this interaction is grounded in the structure of production (Division 1).

Scheme 4.1 outlines the systematic of the present chapter.

Division 1. The market and the stratified structure of production

Tendencies of enterprises' market interaction

This division presents the previous exposition's (Chapters 1–3) general manifestation in the 'market interaction' of enterprises – independent of its particular *modes* of manifestation presented in the rest of the chapter. As indicated in the Introduction, like the following divisions it provides no conditions of existence of the earlier exposition.

4§1 *Market interaction*

Enterprises are first of all interconnected as units that have *the same aim*, that is, the production of surplus-value as measured by the rate of integral profit (1§13–1§14), along with production on an increasing scale (2D1). This is the primary determinant of the enterprises' similarity. However, enterprises may also be similar insofar as they are engaged in the production of a similar physical product and in similar transactions, through which they are part of 'a market'.

In going for the same aim enterprises may, in principle, engender competition, cartels or monopolisation. These are three forms of what will be called the '*market interaction*' of enterprises. In this first division, I present this market interaction in general – applying to each of these three forms. Market interaction (as competition, cartels or monopolisation) is the enterprises' processes of trade through which they, directly or indirectly, *force the determinants of the capitalist system upon one another and upon themselves*.[1]

Whereas enterprises have their capital necessarily invested in particular sectors of production, and so operate in particular markets, they are nevertheless merely *units of one and the same thing – capital – that strive between, or with, each other for one and the same thing: capital accumulation*. In this respect production enterprises are no different from banks or entities engaged in non-banking financial or property businesses, or combinations of these.[2] For the market perspective of this chapter, therefore, these sectors and their enterprises are treated alike.[3]

For the purposes of this chapter, the current division's exposition of market interaction will be restricted to its three main moments: first, inter-market rates of integral profit (4§2); second, intra-market prices (4§3); and a third moment, 'stratified production', which is a consequence of these first two moments (4§4).

4§1-a Explication. Effective demand and supply

This chapter presents the *enterprises*' market interaction. Macroeconomic effective demand, and more specifically its effect on the validation of surplus-value, was presented in 3D5. How this demand is allotted to specific microeconomic sectors of production cannot be determined theoretically. We can say no

1 In terms of our exposition, these are the necessary determinants presented in Chapters 1–3. The last sentence paraphrases Marx, regarding competition, in his *Grundrisse* (1973a {ms 1857–58}, p. 651): 'Competition merely *expresses* as real, posits as an external necessity, that which lies within the nature of capital; competition is nothing more than the way in which the many capitals force the inherent determinants of capital upon one another and upon themselves.' Thus, what Marx writes about 'competition', I generalise to 'interaction' (including competition).

2 This is so even if, as we have seen (3§1 and Figure 3.2b), 'banks as pure financiers' are non-production enterprises that do not produce surplus-value and are, for the growth of their finance capital, parasitically dependent on the production of surplus-value in production enterprises.

3 For current purposes, the terms 'market' and 'sector' are used interchangeably. However, the term sector is usually more appropriate in reference to production (as in 'sector of production').

more about it than that enterprises will try to attract demand via the design of their products and via (broadly) advertisement, which below is treated as part of the production costs. Given that, the effective demand for sector-products is taken as given, at least for the horizon of the investments in fixed means of production.

4§1-b Addendum. 'Competition' in economics dictionaries and textbooks

Although this division is about market interaction in general, it seems useful to say something about the term 'competition' now rather than later. Mainstream economics does not seem to have a general name for what I call 'market interaction' (or it should be 'market behaviour'). It tends to take cartels and monopolisation, including forms of collusion, as a 'deviation' from 'competition'. Nevertheless, no textbook of economics that I have seen provides a succinct definition of 'competition'.

However, in a paper specifically devoted to the matter, Saviotti and Krafft (2004, p. 2) write:

> 'we have come today to a rather consensual definition of competition … Competition is taken to mean that range of actions aimed at ensuring the realization of the choices of a given firm while restraining at the same time the sphere of actions of its rivals. Competition is a process of rivalry between firms which takes the form of contests within existing markets (intra-industry competition), and the form of potential entry into new areas (inter-industry competition). Competition includes rivalry in terms of price, but also in terms of altered or improved techniques of production or products …'

4§2 *Inter-market interaction: the tendency to equalisation of average inter-sector rates of integral profit*

> The dominance of monetary valorisation over the technical labour-process (1D5, 1§11) entails that enterprises are *indifferent* to the particular output produced, an indifference that we have seen to be expressed in the measure of the rate of integral profit, omega (1D5, 1§13).

Because integral profit is the internalised external driving force of enterprises, capital valorised and validated in one sector tends to flow to another one when its owner expects a higher rate of integral profit from that operation. This flow will affect supply. Because a change in supply will have, ceteris paribus, an inverse effect on prices and profits – the inter-market interaction thereby establishes a *tendency to equalisation of average inter-sector* (*i.e. inter-market*) *rates of integral profit* (TERP). (This is indeed a *tendency*. In 4D5 we will see how it is counteracted by tendencies to oligopolisation and monopolisation). We will see in 4§4 why the qualification of 'average' inter-sector rates of profit is significant.

4§2-a Explication. Status of tendencies

Much of the current division runs in terms of tendencies. See 2§12-a for the status of tendencies. Recall that a tendency is the generation of a particular *form* of an entity *or* the particular *quantitative expression* of an entity, this generation being predicated on certain forces or compulsions. In 4§2 this 'entity' is a rate of profit. A tendency may be *counteracted* by other tendencies, or by other lower level complexities. (A standard example from physics is the (tendency) law of gravity. Because that tendency law is counteracted by other tendencies we may, for example, feel fairly safe to sleep or work on the 7th floor of a building). See the General Appendix A§14 for a more elaborative account of tendencies.

4§2-b Amplification. Equalisation of rates of profit via 'restructuring of capital'

The process of effectuation of the tendency to equalisation of average inter-sector rates of profit (TERP, 4§2) is a gradual one. It is concretised as a 'restructuring of capital' (ROC), which encompasses two major phases. The first one involves the *liquidation* of existing plants or divisions of an enterprise – either by selling them and/or by the non-replacement of depreciated means of production. The second phase is that of a gradual investment in a new sector of production, or, far more likely, that of taking over an enterprise (or a division of it) in a new sector, whence we have *conglomerate take-overs*, followed by investment in the new sector of production.[4] The two phases may also be combined in processes of *conglomerate merging* of enterprises, together with a shift in investment from one to another part of the conglomerate. This type of restructuring of capital, that is, inter-sector 'TERP-associated ROC', is one that takes place rather continuously even if unevenly.

This 'restructuring of capital' is one of two modes of ROC. In Chapter 5 (5§8–5§9) a second mode will be presented, which is connected with the business cycle.

4 The term 'conglomerate' refers to enterprises having vested interests in more than one sector.

4§3 *Intra-market interaction: the tendency to uniform prices*

For the concept of a market to make sense, we must analytically start from a considerable degree of similarity between the commodities traded – so making up a market (see Explanation 4§3-a). Given the similarity of the physical outputs – including services – of a collection of enterprises (4§1), intra-market interaction is generally determined as price setting in reaction to that interaction. Starting off from any prevailing modal price in a market, there are analytically and practically two positions.

The *first* position is that of *selling above* the modal price. However, enterprises are compelled to *continuously* (rather than accidentally) realise the value produced. Therefore, even if in some period an enterprise were to accidentally be in a position to sell above the modal market price, such sales would tend to be declined, as it would have the effect of repelling buyers in a subsequent period.

The *second* position is that of *selling below or at* the (current) modal price. decline Because selling below the modal price would affect profits negatively, the individual enterprise has no interest in doing this, unless it is currently producing at overcapacity. In the absence of overcapacity then, prices will tend to stabilise at the existing level. *In the case of overcapacity*, and at a given effective demand, it does make sense to decrease the price.[5] This implies that other enterprises will be burdened with overcapacity. The price then tends to establish at the uniform level at which the overcapacity is (pro rata the enterprises' capacity) evenly distributed.

Market interaction, therefore, establishes a *tendency towards uniform prices in a market* (TUP). (See also the one but last footnote on product differentiation.)

inter-market interaction *tendency to equalisation of average inter-sector rates of integral profit* [TERP; 4§2]	intra-market interaction *tendency to uniform prices* [TUP; 4§3]

↓

structure of production:
stratification of enterprises [4§4]

5 When an enterprise produces at overcapacity, the profitability of a price decrease will depend on its effect on demand (the price 'elasticity').

4§3-a Explication. Intra-market interaction and product differentiation
The main text stated that for the concept of a market to make sense, we must analytically start from a considerable degree of similarity between the commodities traded – thereby establishing a market. For both the actors and the economist studying markets, a 'market' is ultimately a relative matter – depending on the particular courses of action or the problem at hand. Some product differentiation is often a factor in *intra*-market interaction. At some grade of differentiation it is useful to consider a market as partitioned or split off (and conversely, two markets as integrated). Theoretically and practically, we then have the inter-market determinant of the TERP (4§2). However, to the extent that product differentiation is increasingly the main focus, we either lose the concept of a market, or each individual enterprise must be considered as a monopolist. I think that in both analytical and practical terms, the latter approach is not a fruitful one.

4§4 *Stratification of enterprises and plants*

1 Interaction as reinforcing technical change

The articulation of the two main tendencies of market interaction (TERP and TUP, 4§2–4§3) means that the rate of integral profit of any enterprise comes to depend on its production process for any output: the reduction of the costs of production (given the input prices) and increase in the value-productivity of labour. These are determined by the valoro-technique of production adopted, together with the management of the power of labour as engendering increase in the productivity of labour (2§3). (Having stressed the dual character of techniques, from now on I will simply use the term 'technique' instead of valoro-technique.) The interaction of enterprises therefore reinforces and reproduces more concretely the compulsion to the accumulation of capital in new techniques of production (2§3–2§4).

In the remainder of this section, and in most of this chapter, I build on the similarity of the products sold on a market (4§3; 4§3-a). Hence the focus for techniques is on the *process* (as in 'process competition') rather than on the *product* (as in 'product competition'). This is the most transparent case for the interconnection of production and the market; product innovation is just a more complicated case, including market strategic considerations, which might in principle be incorporated in the framework below.

2 *Stratification of plants*

Stratification of enterprises refers to sectors of production being composed of not technically uniform, but rather technically heterogeneous enterprises, as explained below. Because, concretely, the technique refers to a 'plant', and because large enterprises tend to be composed of several divisions and 'plants' each with – at least internally – separated accounts, I will refer to this plant level of the enterprise.[6]

The investment of capital in new plants incorporating new techniques of production tends to be a discrete 'lumpy' process.[7] In any case, the enterprise that successfully initiates a new technique of production secures a rate of profit above that for the existing enterprises (plants) in the sector. The consequent *threat of price competition* by the initiating enterprise, and the necessity for continuous valorisation, might seemingly compel the other enterprises to follow suit.[8] However, because each enterprise is burdened with the fixed costs of its already accumulated capital, it will only scrap old plants when a new technique offers net profits ('net' that is, taking into account the costs of scrapping old plants) greater than the profits on its existing plant.

In other words, the preservation of *capital* already accumulated may prevent immediate moves towards investment in new-technique and maximum rate of profit *plants*.[9] Scrapping of plants is only enforced when prices no longer cover prime costs.[10] Before that, the scrapping of plants in favour of investment in new ones is determined by, first, the difference in rates of profit on the investment in an already existing plant, and on that in a new plant (inclusive of the capital foregone because of scrapping); and second, by the availability of finance.[11]

---

6 I will restrict myself to this one term 'plant'. For financial or commercial enterprises, 'plant' refers to the establishments or branches of such enterprises, i.e. those with at least internally separated accounts.

7 Next to these lumpy investments there may be, additionally, more continuous investments. Note that in the small business sector and in parts of the services sector, the (lumpy) 'plant' aspect of investment is only moderately dominant or sometimes even negligible. (To the extent that this is, contingently, *inherent* to a sector of production, this applies to the configuration set out in 4D4.)

8 This is the mainstream neoclassical equilibrium idea.

9 I am drawn into this way of presentation by the conventional neoclassical static equilibrium analysis of this matter, wherein the rate of profit is identified with the 'physical' plant-rate of profit. Note also that, in this chapter, interaction, and later on competition, should not be conceived of as neoclassical 'perfect'. Salter (1960) has shown that in the case of neoclassical perfect competition, capital would always immediately move to the new-technique plant.

10 'Prime costs' are the costs exclusive of those of fixed means of production.

11 This implies that a maximum rate of profit can only be gained by fully amortised plants. The conceptualisation here and in the remainder of this section differs from neoclassical vintage models (discussed in 4§4-b).

Since, therefore, plants embodying new technology will in general not be immediately adopted by all enterprises, each sector of production tends to be composed of a *stratification of plants* dated according to technique, cost of production, value-productivity of labour and a resulting *stratification of rates of integral profit* (see *Figure 4.2*).[12] The difference in these aspects between the top and the bottom of the stratification is called the *range* of the stratification. Later we will see that the degree of this range depends on the speed of technical change (4§13).

Recall my claim in the first sentence of this subsection. I do not claim that enterprises in all markets are so technically heterogeneous for the concept of stratification to make sense. However, I do claim that it applies for the economy on average. In the remainder of this chapter, I merely focus on the sectors that are clearly stratified.

4§4-a Explication. Stratification and scrapping of plants

The concept of stratification implies that at each point in time, enterprises within the same sector are physically non-identical (this may go without saying for non-economists; however, economists educated within the standard models of neoclassical economics are trained to see physical identity as the starting point for analysis). The focuses for the non-identity are the characteristics indicated at the end of 4§4: technique; costs; value-productivity of labour; and rate of integral profit. The reason for this non-identity is that enterprises will introduce new techniques of production only when these are expected to result in a higher rate of profit in comparison with capital accumulated in existing plants. However, preservation of *capital* already accumulated may prevent immediate moves towards investment in new-technique and maximum rate of profit *plants*. Therefore capital tends to be stratified according to technique, cost of production, value-productivity of labour and resulting rates of profit (4§4), as visualised in *Figure 4.2*. The oldest plant within a sector is indicated by the number 1, while the most recently invested plant is indicated by the number n.

---

12 If rates of profit are calculated over the lifetime of an asset, and if there were such a thing as perfect foresight, then calculated rates of profit might be equal. However, this does not affect the argument (see also 4§6 on devalorisation). The exposition in this chapter highlights that the state of the economy conceptualised is generally not one of equilibrium, nor is it one of 'perfect competition'.

FIGURE 4.2 *Stratification of plants*

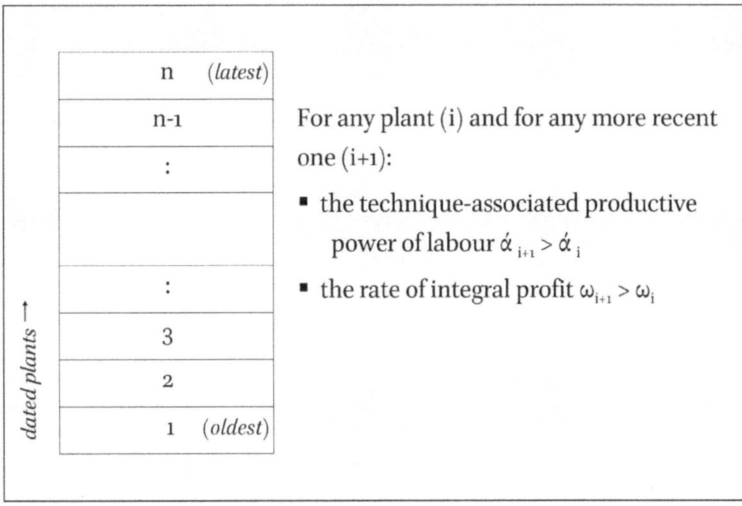

Recall from 1§14 the equations for the integral rate of profit (ω) and for production (X), which are now applied to the microeconomic plant level (suffix i). All variables in the four equations below refer to time (t) – time subscript omitted to avoid cumbersome notation.

$\omega_i = \Pi_i / K_i = [m_i L^{\acute{\alpha}\ddot{\imath}}_i - (wL)_i] / K_i$ (4.1) cf. 1.3 and 1.6

Recall also that ά denotes the technique-associated productive power of labour, and ï the intensity of labour. Whereas in Chapter 2 the primary focus was on the latter, the primary focus in the current chapter will be on ά. Although the current chapter does not exclude variations in intensity, it may be helpful for the reader to assume ï to be constant throughout the chapter.

For each plant we have running material costs (μK_i) and a depreciation of fixed means of production (δK_i). Thus we have for the plant output (X_i):

$X_i = \delta K_i + \mu K_i + wL_i + \Pi_i$ (4.2) cf. 1.2

Then any scrapping of plants is only *enforced* when their returns (pq_i) outrun their 'prime costs' ($\mu K_i + wL_i$), i.e.:

$pq_i \leq \mu K_i + wL_i$ (returns ≤ 'prime costs') (4.3)

Thus treating the costs of the fixed means of production as a complete loss, the plant(s) at the bottom of the stratification may ultimately keep on producing until this point.

However, rather than the complete loss case, we may suppose the scrap-value of a plant, or its liquidation value, to be LV_i. Suppose that there are no obstacles of finance, technique, etc., so that any one plant at the bottom could in principle be lifted to the top ('n', hence K_n), then the simple decision criterion would be:

$$\Pi_n /(K_n - LV_i) > [pq_i - (\mu K_i + wL_i)]/LV_i \quad (4.4)$$

To the extent that LV_i is 'small', then – even if in 4.4 the LHS > RHS[13] – it may be profitable to keep the bottom plant going along with an investment at the top by the same enterprise. Equation (4.4) presents the simple idea. A more sophisticated comparison would go in terms of the discounted profit flow of each alternative.

(In most markets, there is some degree of product differentiation. We could make this part of the stratification, whence there may be price differences that are reflected in the divergent rates of profit. However, for simplification this is neglected here.)

Figure 4.2 is the general basis for the entirety of this chapter. The following divisions set out specifications.

4§4-b Addendum. Stratification and vintage models

Conventional neoclassical general equilibrium theories assume 'small' *homogeneous* plants, or firms, engaged in atomistic competition. It is hard to understand what would then keep competition going. Indeed, that conception of competition is highly ambiguous. As each unit is a perfect copy of every other, no more than comparative static states (differing from each other only to the extent that *exogenous* variables differ) can be described (see Blaug 2001). Such a conception may be traced back to the lack of differentiation between homogeneous capital as value and the heterogeneous embodiment of capital in a technical sense (that is, in our terminology, the internally bifurcated form of capitalist production).

However, neoclassical 'vintage models' are less simplified (see Solow 1970, ch. 3; the seminal references are: Johansen 1959; Salter 1960; Kaldor and Mirrlees 1962; Solow, Tobin, von Weizäcker and Yeari 1966; and Cass and Stiglitz 1969). One main difference from the concept of stratification as presented in 4§4 is that in the neoclassical conception, the obsolescence of plants is determined by the real wage (wage costs exceeding the average labour-productivity on a plant), rather than by the addition of plants to the stratification, introducing new cost-reducing techniques of production, and the resulting price decrease and/or overcapacity (see 4§6).

The notion of the extra profits gained by the enterprise (plant) at the top of the stratification is closely related to Schumpeter's notion of temporary monopoly profits accruing to the first enterprise to innovate, which are gradually eroded as the innovation diffuses through the industry and even the economy (see, e.g., Schumpeter 2003 [1943]).

---

13 LHS: left hand side; RHS: right hand side.

4§4-c Addendum. Earlier work on stratification

I first set out the concept and a fairly simple model of stratification in Reuten and Williams 1989 (Chapters 4–5) and in Reuten 1991. At that time I used the concept and model particularly in the context of a theory of the business cycle and a particular type of technical development (a type characterised by an increasing capital-labour ratio), even if I already noted then that the scope of the model is wider than that context. A similar notion was adopted by Brenner (1998, e.g., p. 24 ff.). I have now explicitly generalised the model to characterise market interaction in general (4§4) competition (4D2 and 4D3), cartels (4D4), and oligopolistic and monopolising interaction (4D5).

4§4-d Addendum. Stratification, capital-labour ratios and the tendential equalisation of average inter-sector rates of integral profit – a note on marxian political economy

A concept of a stratified structure of production within sectors is implicit in Marx's notion of the development of the technique-associated 'productive power of labour' as giving rise to intra-sector divergent 'potencies of labour' (my L^{α}_{i}).[14] Especially to the extent that new techniques would entail an increasing capital-labour ratio (K/L), an increasing L^{α}_{i} along with it is a precondition for the introduction of such a technique. Regarding a comparison between sectors, it may be remarked that inter-sector capital-labour ratios usually diverge, which has largely to do with a limited diffusion of techniques between sectors. This implies that, along with it, the average productive power of labour (L^{α}) for each sector also diverges. All this implies that given some average intensity of labour ($L^{\ddot{\imath}}$), we have the variables as set out in *Table 4.3*.

TABLE 4.3 *Stratification related intra- and inter-sector variables*

	Within sectors	Between sectors
technology and technique	diffusion	limited diffusion
K/L ratios	divergent*	divergent
productive powers of labour (L^{α})	divergent*	divergent
rates of exploitation ($e = \Pi/wL$)	divergent*	divergent
rates of integral profit ($\omega_t = \Pi_t / K_{t'}$)	divergent*	tendential uniform

* Pending the diffusion.

14 *Capital I*, chapter 12 – chapter 10 of the German edition.

Especially the diverging between-sector rates of exploitation have been a much-contested issue within marxian political economy.[15] All this is amplified in Reuten 2017.

4§5 *Instrumentality of the form of market interaction*

For enterprises, the form of market interaction (competition, cartels, monopolisation) is merely *instrumental* to their production and accumulation of capital. This does not mean that any individual enterprise has the choice of adopting any instrument such as competition or cartel formation. As indicated (4§1), in their market interaction, enterprises force the determinants of the capitalist system upon one another and upon themselves. Whilst any enterprise is a constituent of this enforcement, one or another form of market interaction may nevertheless be imposed on the enterprises. In internalising that form, or in complying with it, they impose that particular interaction on themselves and on the others.[16] This means that we have distinct market constellations in which one particular form (competition, cartels, monopolisation) is dominant.

Even so, this does not imply that the impetus that might give rise to another form disappears altogether. Rather, in the mutual counteraction of the respective forces that gives rise to each of the forms, one force comes to manifestly dominate within a particular constellation. The other ones become subordinate or latent. We will see later on that the pace of process innovation (technical change) or of product innovation is one of the main forces that determine these constellations.

Divisions 2–3 present competitive constellations, Division 4 cartels, and Division 5 oligopolisation and monopolisation.

Division 2. Deflationary price competition

This division presents the first general mode of manifestation of the enterprises' market interaction. There are two main modes (or forms) of rivalrous interaction of enterprises (that is, forms of competition), each one based on the sector's enterprises' resignation to a rotating price-leader. The first general mode of 'deflationary price competition' is presented in the current division. The second general mode will be presented in the next division.

---

15 It is the main issue that is associated with the so-called 'transformation problem'.

16 In this case, that form of interaction constitutes a configuration in connection with the forces, 'the determinants of the capitalist system', developed earlier (Chapters 1–3). The distinction between compliance and internalisation was set out in 2§7-b.

4§6 *Stratified price competition: devalorisation via a decreasing 'unit monetary value of labour'* (*m*)

1 Preliminary remarks

We have seen that sectors of production tend to be composed of a stratification of plants (4§4). This is the basis for market interaction in general. I start the exposition with 'stratified price competition' (though note that I do not assume neoclassical equilibrium or so-called 'perfect' competition typified by homogeneous small-sized firms). We have also seen that in the absence of overcapacity, market prices will tend to stabilise at the existing level, whereas in the case of overcapacity it does make sense to initiate price decrease (4§3). At near to full capacity utilisation, price competition fades away.[17] Hence effective price competition is conditioned by overcapacity.[18]

Reading the exposition below might be facilitated if the reader briefly reviews the terminology of 1§14 (especially that around equations 1.3–1.8) – see, alternatively, the list of equations at the end of the book.

2 Stratified price competition

With competition, enterprises will try to eliminate competitors, or at least to make them fall behind. In a constellation of general price competition, the *initiator* of competitive action tends to combine:

- a technical advance (such that it might reduce prices);
- the creation of *potential* overcapacity in a market by investing in a new plant;
- actual price decrease (so as to effectively put behind or eliminate competitors).

It thus acts as price-leader – a function that might rotate between enterprises – setting the price at a level that maximises its profits. Given the technical advance and the production capacity of the price-leader, the other enterprises will tend to resign to the price-leadership. Explication 4§6-a sets this out in detail in reference to the stratification framework initiated in 4§4. Here I present the main thread.

So the initiator (i.e. the innovator) introduces a new technique. For its competitors, nothing changes in their techniques and the associated production power of labour (α, more precisely $\acute{\alpha}$). Nevertheless, due to the market price decrease, the latter are in effect confronted with a *devalorisation* (a decreased

17 It might be argued that the threat of entry from relatively low rate of profit sectors (4§2) might induce price decrease. However, in the absence of any form of cartels (4D4), no enterprise has an interest in pre-empting this.

18 Cf. Clarke 1994, pp. 281–3.

valorisation – on valorisation see 1§10).[19] Its benchmark is the valorisation of the same capitals (enterprise, plant) in the previous period. This devalorisation is due to the actual monetary value of labour (mL^{α}) for any single capital lagging behind that in the previous period. This applies not on the unchanged L^{α}, but on a decrease in the 'm' (the unit monetary value of labour – 1§14, heading 6). For the initiator, on the other hand, the comparative rate of surplus-value increases, because of the relatively greater value-productivity of the labour employed in the plant added to the stratification (its α moves ahead of that of competitors). Thus, denoting the initiator by (n+1) and the previous price-leader by (n), $mL^{\alpha}_{(n+1)} > mL^{\alpha}_{(n)}$, for any 'm'. In fact (n+1)'s price decrease, means that 'm' decreases for the whole sector, making this itself good via its higher α, such that its integral rate of profit (ω) is higher than that of (n) – and all competitors. The initiator's strategic consideration is that it introduces this new technique at the point when its price-decreasing action still secures a higher rate of profit for itself. The effect is that for all the competitors, the rate of integral profit decreases in comparison with the previous period (see further 4§6-a).

Next to this devalorisation, and to the extent that plants from the bottom of the stratification are eliminated prior to their full amortisation, there is also an annihilation of previously accumulated capital.

I call this articulation of production and competition through time 'stratified price competition'.[20]

3 *Summing up*

So far, in sum, we have a tendency to equalisation of average inter-sector rates of profit (4§2), which, together with the tendency to uniform prices in a market (4§3), gives rise to an intra-sector stratification of plants with corresponding stratified rates of integral profit (4§4). Stratified price competition, the addition to the stratification of new technique embodying plants, gives rise to price decrease and so devalorisation for the previous stratification and thus to a decline in the rate of profit for that previous stratification.[21]

19 Devalorisation refers to the value-added, and should be distinguished from *depreciation*, i.e. the (calculated) normal returns for the wear and tear of means of production (δK).

20 It might also be called 'stratified dynamic price competition' (cf. Schumpeter 2003 [1943], pp. 103–4), who coined the term 'dynamic competition', in face of the taking into account of sequences of production periods.

21 Note that a rigorous product innovation may have the same result: scrapping of 'bottom' plants and of devalorisation.

4§6-a Explication. Stratified price competition

This explication sets out some analytical details on which 4§6 is based. It builds on the framework introduced in 4§4-a. Most of the formulations of the second half of 4§6 have been integrated in this explication.

Capital invested in a new plant (n+1) and added to the stratification operates with up-to-date techniques of production – those with minimal unit costs of production and maximal value-productivity of labour (4§4). If (n+1) were to undertake no further action (hypothetically), this investment would increase the total production capacity of the sector. The new investment is supposed to be one that potentially fully results in overcapacity of the stratification; this is the most transparent case – see *Figure 4.4*. (In a more complicated picture, we could account for degrees of extra capacity in relation to economic growth and effective demand. Macroeconomic demand effects of investment and scrapping will be presented in Chapter 5. Another simplification is that the overcapacity created by n+1 is assumed to be proportionally distributed over all plants).

In case of the currently presented (4D2) form of competitive interaction of enterprises, (n+1) anticipates the potential overcapacity (*Figure 4.4*) by price reduction. As a result, the plants at the bottom of the stratification that no longer cover prime costs will have to be scrapped (cf. 4§4 and 4§4-a). We may suppose that the enterprise that added the new plant is the one to initiate the price competition, i.e. an effective price decrease. Hence this enterprise acts as price-leader – a leadership that might be rotating. Thus when plant (n+1) is added to the stratification (1,…,n), and when h plants are scrapped, the previous stratification (1,…,n) becomes (1+h,…,n,n+1). (See *Figure 4.5*.)

(Note that the general employment effect depends on:

1. The scale of n+1, in comparison with the scales of the scrapped plants h;
2. The capital-labour ratios (K/L) of n+1 in comparison with h.

Chapter 5 presents the macroeconomic effect.)

Due to the price decrease, the revenue of the remaining part of the previous stratification (1+h,…,n) decreases, whereas the revenue of the new stratification (1+h,…,n,n+1) typically increases with the average rate of growth (to keep the analysis concise, it is assumed that the share of the sector in the total economy remains constant).[22] I call the decrease in revenue of the capitals in the previous stratification *devalorisation* (decreased valorisation). Its benchmark is

22 In case of (macroeconomic or sector) recession, the revenue may remain constant or decrease (see Chapter 5). Generally, one sector may, of course, grow above average.

the valorisation of the same capitals in the previous period. The devalorisation is due to the actual monetary value of labour (mL^{α}) for any one capital (enterprise, plant) lagging behind that in the previous period.[23] Thus, because their investments, costs and production processes are unaffected, whilst revenue decreases (they have to share with n+1), the rate of integral profit of the capitals accumulated in the remaining part of the previous stratification (1+h,…,n) decreases.[24]

FIGURE 4.4 *Stratification of plants after plant addition: hypothetical constellation prior to market interaction*

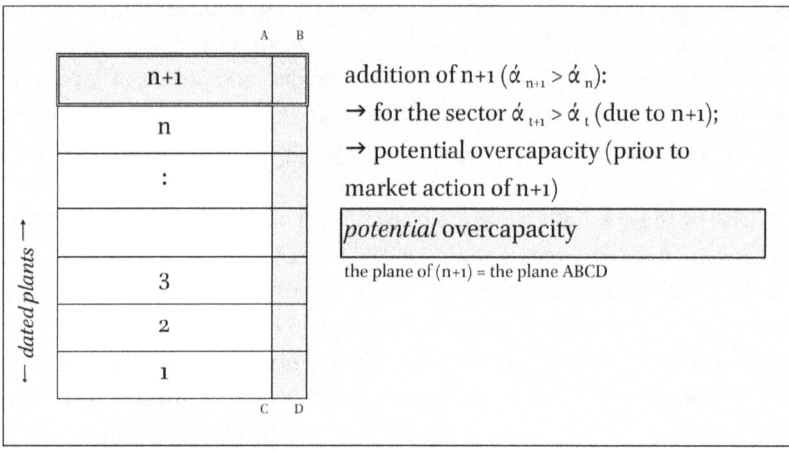

23 It might be argued that to the extent that devalorisation is foreseen at the point of investment, it is incorporated in calculating the 'marginal efficiency of capital'. But even if there were perfect foresight in this, the argument is unaffected. It cannot prevent devalorisation. Even with devalorisation, the net profits over the lifetime of the asset may still be positive and 'optimal'.

24 At the new price, the rate of profit of the capital invested in the new plant (n+1) will **tend** to be above the average rate of profit of the capitals making up the previous stratification (1,…,n) at the previous price; or also above the rate of profit of the plant (n) that was previously at the top of the stratification. In any case, since the new plant (n+1) operates at lower costs and higher productivity than the previous plant (n), the rate of profit of the new plant capital at the new price is above both that of the nth and the average rate of profit.

FIGURE 4.5 *Stratification of plants after plant addition: actual constellation after price decrease, devalorisation and scrapping*

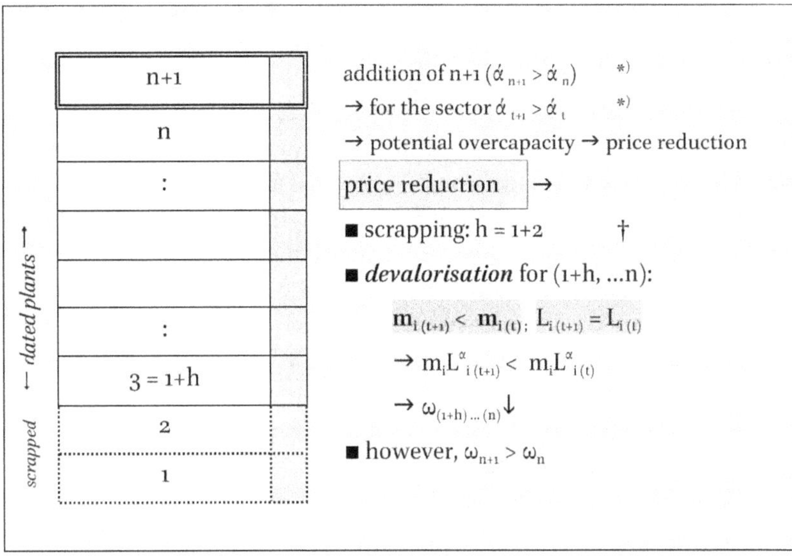

* Identical to Figure 4.4

† Scrapping of two plants instead of one assumes that plants grow in size (in case of equally sized plants (1)-(n+1), only plant (1) would be scrapped)

In other words, because of the relatively greater actual monetary-value-productivity of the labour employed in the plant added to the stratification (n+1), its comparative rate of surplus-value increases, whilst the actual monetary value of the labour in the (1+h,…,n) plants decreases (typically by a decrease in output prices). Therefore, not only is the 'unit monetary value of labour' (1§14, heading 6), $\mathbf{m}_i$, stratified increasingly from (1,…,i,…,n), but it also tends to decrease (devalorisation) for all i when the stratification is extended.[25]

In sum, stratified price competition is a form of accumulation of capital along with the driving out, from the bottom of the stratification, of plants belonging to competitors. To the extent that these plants are driven out prior to their full amortisation, there is an annihilation of previously accumulated capital.

25 If there were some collaboration between the enterprises then we might have the sequence price decrease, scrapping, price increase. However, in a pure competitive constellation, there is no mechanism to bring this about. Moreover, price increase is predicated on the definitive scrapping. Especially enterprises that operate several plants may keep latently the non-used plant – at least for some time.

(Quite apart from the stratification introduced here, this is analogous to Schumpeter's 'creative destruction' (2003 [1943], ch. 7). Incidentally, Marx (1981 [1894], p. 265) cast this in terms of his famous phrase of 'neue Kombinationen' (new combinations) that inspired Schumpeter (1934 [1911].))

4§7 *Devalorisation accounted on devalued capital*

(At this point this section seems a detail. Its relevance will become clear in the next division.) The previous section (4§6) posited a decline in the rate of integral profit (ω) for the previous stratification (h, … n). This is based on the convention of *historical (dated) accounting*. Alternatively, enterprises (when they, through competition, have become aware of the stratification change) may immediately apply the alternative convention of *current cost accounting* (or present value or replacement value accounting).[26] They then apply a *devaluation of capital* proportional to the difference between the historical value of their assets as compared with the assets purchase price of the innovator's technique. Hence via this pure balance sheet operation, their decreased profits due to devalorisation are accounted on the now *devalued capital*. This second convention is most often the practice today. Its dubbed 'advantage' is that the implied losses are not revealed in a permanent decline of the rate of profit, but rather in an immediate capital loss.[27]

Thus, depending on the accounting practice, devalorisation may be manifested either directly in a declined rate of profit or in an annihilation of capital accumulated. The net effect (the cash flow effect, i.e. the sum of depreciation allowances and profits) is the same.

4§8 *Derived price decrease and derived devaluation of capital*

Generalised price competition gives rise to *generalised price decrease*. This implies that even if for specific sectors no new profit-increasing techniques are available, these are still affected by the technical change and price competition of other sectors.

This is so for the following reason. Consider an enterprise – currently producing at the bottom of the stratification of a sector A – which moves without

---

26 As Polak (1940, pp. 15–16) indicates, this accounting method was originally set out by Kovero in 1912 and by Schmidt in 1921.

27 We have for the integral rate of profit of any plant i:

$$\omega_t = \Pi_t \,/\, K_{t'} = [(mL^{\alpha})_t - (wL)_t] \,/\, K_{t'} \qquad \text{(1.6) plant version}$$

When because of devalorisation 'm' decreases, the rate of profit decreases. The balance sheet operation referred to results in a devaluation of K, such that ω remains about constant.

innovating to the top (n′) by merely duplicating the technique of the top plant (n). It buys the new plant and equipment inputs from a (composite) sector B in which there was technical change and price decrease along with it. Therefore the fixed capital outlay of the new plant (n′) in sector A which it buys from B is nevertheless lower than that of A's (n) – because (n′) can buy the identical plant at lower prices than (n) did – whence (n′) is in a position to decrease the sector A output price. Thus the competitive process and price decrease in sector A is predicated on technical change and competition elsewhere (B).

Again we have a devalorisation for the previous stratification (of A), in this case one that I call *derived devalorisation*. Again, depending on the accounting convention, the implied rate of profit decrease may alternatively be expressed as a *derived devaluation of capital.*

In sum, (primary) devalorisation/devaluation stems from changes in the labour process, induced by new technical change within the sector under consideration. Derived devalorisation/devaluation comes about by a mere price decrease due to process changes and price decreases in *other* sectors. However, this derived price decrease equally tends to multiply through the economy, thus developing into (further) *general price deflation.*

4§8-a Explication. Physical reproduction and reproduction of capital

From a one-sided physical (use-value) approach, it might seem that the derived devaluation of capital does not affect the reproduction. Indeed, physical reproduction (that is, the number of units of output of a plant) need not be affected by the input price decrease because new means of production can be bought at the lower price. But this does not take away the fact that the accumulation of capital (or the valorisation potential) has decreased. This becomes obvious when a plant is wholly financed by loans: then the amortisation reserves may be sufficient to buy a new plant, but not to cancel the loans.

4§8-b Explication. Quality (or product) competition

So far the exposition of competition has been mainly phrased in terms of price competition. Along with it we have product (or quality) innovation and competition. For the (primary) devalorisation (and devaluation of capital), the distinction is not relevant because product competition has the same effect. This also applies for the derived devalorisation (or devaluation) with respect to producer goods since their quality increase has a cost of production decreasing effect.

4§8-c Explication. Small business sector and services sector

Even if stratified competition is on average less prominent in sectors that are product-inherently supplied by small businesses and in much of the services sector, the latter are nevertheless affected by generalised deflation and particularly derived devalorisation/devaluation of capital.

4§9 *Generalised price competition and the pace of technical change: price deflation and the tendency to stagnation*

It was indicated in Chapter 2 that profit augmentation is limited by the possible increase in the intensity of labour, and that this limit is overcome by the investment of capital in technology and the application of technical change (2§2). Even if this is a high level determinant of the capitalist system, *the pace* of technical change is contingent. However, when this change is triggered such that its combination with price competition generally precludes the full amortisation of (modal) capital investments – as revealed in continuous devaluation of capital – and when this multiplies through the economy in the form of price deflation, then it develops into a system-destructive or at least paralysing force.

Insufficient amortisation implies that the general accumulation of capital is in some degree annihilated. Then the uncertainty about this annihilation (or the expectation of annihilation) tends to dampen investment. This is first revealed in a dampening of the pre-validating finance (PVF) requested by enterprises and provided by banks (3§2). Thus the production of surplus-value dampens and so the part of surplus-value in the form of interest that accrues to banks dampens.

Further, and more specifically, for the PVF that *is* being provided, general price deflation implies that the redemption of the PVF is impeded.[28] Note that an actual non-redemption in this case – we may call this the 'deflationary PVF gap' – is quite different from a non-redemption of the PVF due to savings (named RPVF in 3§6). In the latter case, savers may substitute for the non-redemption. In case of a deflationary PVF gap, there are no potential substituents, i.e. no potential non-bank financiers (for this gap). For those gaps there is a permanent increase in borrowing from banks. Ultimately this may outrun the securities that the enterprises can provide to the banks.

---

28 Although this is generally so, it is most obvious for the case in which the PVF is used for the purchase of fixed means of production. The depreciation (δK) returns in many tranches, with each subsequent tranche being smaller than the earlier one because of the devaluation of capital.

Thus the result is not only a decrease in the quantity of bank finance (PVF), but also an increase in its risk and uncertainty. Any likely risk premium that banks will put on the going interest rate will further dampen the investment.

As to the (other) remaining part of the PVF (i.e. the RPVF apart from the gap), that is, the part for which there are potential financiers in the form of bonds, general price deflation puts these potential financiers in a position of relative power. The point is that they can *wait* with substituting for the RPVF provided by banks – so improving their bargaining position – because with generalised price deflation the purchasing power of their credits with banks increases anyway. In other words, general price deflation empowers potential ex post financiers with the means of 'striking'. This tends (ceteris paribus) to put an upward pressure on the 'real' rate of interest. (An actual strike increases the banks' risk, whence banks will increase the rate of interest.)[29]

General price deflation brings on two subsidiary problems for enterprises. One is that normally wages tend to be sticky downwards (this may be different in crises and recessions; however, we are considering a structural constellation). A second, though temporary, problem is that the prospect of price decrease may have the effect of postponement of purchases of consumer durables as well as purchases of means of production in the branches with a relatively slower rate of technical change (e.g. services).

In conclusion, the *combination* of generalised speedy technical change (or a fast increasing pace of technical change) *and* generalised price deflation tends to generate stagnation. However, next to the deflationary constellation presented in the current division, an inflationary constellation (4D3) is also an implicit system possibility. Yet – recalling that Part One yet abstracts from (or brackets) the state and its economic policy – there are no economy-inherent forces that turn a deflationary constellation into an inflationary one. Further, there are no economy-inherent forces to get out of stagnation.[30]

4§9-a Amplification. The paradox of 'beneficial technical change' and 'beneficial competition' in combination

Both technical change and competition are often conceived of as beneficial features of the capitalist system (not least of all in ideological discourses; discourses in which, moreover, technical change is indiscriminately called 'tech-

29 Further, an increasing rate of interest means that shares (as compared with bonds) become inferior to financiers; this aggravates an inferiority of shares due to devaluation of capital.

30 In the systematic of this book, wars are contingent.

nical progress'). However, it appears that prolonged fast technical change in combination with price competition does not fit the system.

4§9-b Addendum. The tendency of the rate of profit to fall in marxian political economy

Within one main strand of marxian political economy, an important theorem regards the 'tendency of the rate of profit to fall'.[31|32] Recalling that the exposition still has the state bracketed, a corollary of the main text of Division 2 is that the positing of such a tendency makes sense for a deflationary constellation with a generalised high pace of technical change. However, as we will see in the next division, that constellation cannot be generalised as a unique or dominant one for capitalism. That again does not imply that there could be no declining profit rate in the constellation that I present in Division 3. Generally, from my own perspective, the development of the profit rate is especially relevant as an indicator for the accumulation of capital.

Basu and Manolakos (2010; 2012), using data from Duménil and Lévy, show the long run secular movement of the rate of profit for the USA as reproduced in *Graph 4.6*.[33]

Note that *Graph 4.6* inevitably shows the result of both structural and cyclical movements (the latter are presented in Chapter 5) as well as contingencies.

In reference to the dotted line that Basu and Manolakos plot (a Lowess trend), it is relevant that according to data for the USA from Piketty (2014, technical appendix), the period 1870–1913 is on average deflationary (-0.7%) and the period thereafter inflationary (for that period he provides for intervals of 20 to 37 years, average inflation rates of 2.2% to 5.6% – ending with 2.2% for the period 1990–2012). However, from Piketty's source (Piketty and Zucman 2013) it can be seen that the period 1921–33 is on average highly deflationary (-3.5%).

31 Roberts (2012) is a concise 13 pages paper with empirical findings (1963–2008 for the G7) and references to other empirical findings. It shows a sharply declining profit rate for 1963–1975, half of which recovers between 1975–1988, with next, until 2008, again a gradually bending down to the early 1970s level. https://thenextrecession.files.wordpress.com/2012/09/a-world-rate-of-profit.pdf.

32 Regarding Marx's work I think that there is hardly a basis for this theorem in Marx's *Capital* if we neglect Engels' additions to that text – this is shown in Reuten 2004c. Nevertheless, there is a basis for it in Marx's manuscripts of before 1864 – as shown in Reuten and Thomas 2011. However, such a (non-)basis in Marx's work is irrelevant for the (in-)appropriateness of the research findings of current marxian political economy.

33 I am grateful to the authors for putting the graph at my disposal.

Those two periods have been shaded in the graph. This shading merely puts the focus on *one* determinant – one that is focused on in Divisions 2 and 3 – among many others (see Chapter 5).

GRAPH 4.6 *Long waves in the rate of profit:* USA *1870–2007*

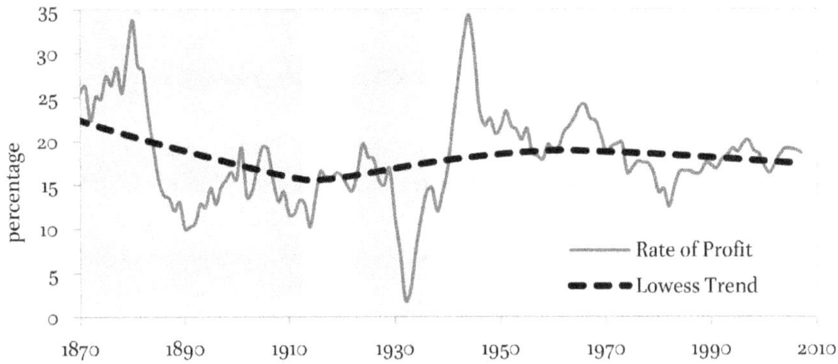

SOURCE: BASU AND MANOLAKOS (2010, P. 45), ON THE BASIS OF DATA FROM DUMÉNIL AND LÉVY (SHADING ADDED).

Division 3. Inflationary 'structural overcapacity competition'

This division presents the second general mode of manifestation of the enterprises market interaction. It is a competitive mode alternative to the one presented in Division 2. The current division does not set out how the economy goes from a deflationary to an inflationary constellation, because there are no economy-*immanent* forces to reach such a transition.[34]

Deflationary price competition is not difficult to understand – in mainstream economics, it is the prototype of competition. Understanding the mechanisms of inflationary competition is far more difficult.

4§10 *Overcapacity competition: introduction*

'Inflationary structural overcapacity competition' is a form of competition in which competitors are not eliminated by way of price decreases, but rather by burdening them with overcapacity. Overcapacity generally implies that, given the fixed cost (including especially those of fixed means of production

34 The state's efforts to prevent generalised price deflation are presented in 9§5 (and briefly anticipating that in 7§8).

and overheads), unit cost increases in comparison with full capacity production. Production at overcapacity thereby results in decreasing revenue, whence marginal producers at the bottom of the stratification are forced out. Further details are presented in 4§12.

Alternative names are 'structural excess capacity' or 'structural underutilisation of capacity'.[35] It is to be emphasised that *structural* overcapacity is not the effect of market demand, but rather an overcapacity at any given demand. It is an overcapacity for market strategic reasons, at least so for the price-leader in a sector.

The constellation of prolonged fast technical change together with price competition, as presented in Division 2, is almost *incompatible* with the capitalist system. (By 'almost incompatible' I mean that the constellation engenders a tendency to stagnation.) The main reason is the primary and the derived devaluation of capital, set out in 4D2 (4§6, 4§8). We have seen that this implies a degree of annihilation of the general accumulation of capital, and that this tends to dampen investment. We saw also that this affects not only production enterprises but also banks. For the latter it not only affects the quantity of their credit provision (PVF), but also their risk and uncertainty.

For these reasons, banks and production enterprises have a common interest in evading general price deflation. Although there is this common interest, there are no economy-immanent forces to bring it about (coordinated action would either presuppose the state, or a grand cartel via 'joint meetings' and decision making of captains of industry and banks, to which all others would have to comply).

The presentation below presupposes the existence of an inflationary constellation, in whatever way it is reached. There are two major conditions of existence for this constellation. The first one is presented in 4§11 and the second in 4§12.

35 The OECD glossary of statistical terms states: 'Excess capacity refers to a situation where a firm is producing at a lower scale of output than it has been designed for'. It adds: 'Excess capacity is a characteristic of natural monopoly or monopolistic competition'. Note that the current division broadens this considerably. It also adds: 'Firms may also choose to maintain excess capacity as a part of a deliberate strategy to deter or prevent entry of new firms'. This somewhat approaches the issue as presented in the current division, even if the focus will not be primarily on entrants but rather on squeezing out current producers. https://stats.oecd.org/glossary/detail.asp?ID=3209.

4§11 *The monetary condition of an inflationary constellation: banks'* PVF *and the 'unit monetary value of labour'* (*m*)

One major condition for a constellation of *generalised price inflation* is the willingness of banks to accommodate that constellation via their credits to enterprises (PVF) as affecting the money in circulation. More specifically this has the effect of an increasing 'unit monetary value of labour' (m).

This accommodation has three further general effects. (Below any comparisons with a deflationary constellation are indented.)

> In comparison with a deflationary constellation, banks now *in effect* accommodate a 'socialisation of private losses'. That is, they in effect socialise private losses that would be due to the devaluation of capital induced by technical change in the absence of price inflation.[36] Relative to a deflationary constellation, price inflation results in an increased profit of enterprises and banks.[37]

First, its counterpart is a loss of purchasing power for social actors with non-equity financial assets (including 'small savers') and of actors with fixed incomes or with incomes that are (in part) adapted to inflation with a time-lag.

> Note that even a constellation of zero inflation makes quite a difference in comparison with some deflation, because it takes away the derived devaluation of capital (4§8).[38]

Second, inflation generates an actual *derived revaluation of capital* – the counterpart of the derived devaluation of capital presented in 4§8. This revaluation is expressed in the balance sheets of enterprises as capital 'reserves' (part of the equity).

Third, inflation puts employers (enterprises, including banking entities) in an advantageous bargaining position.

> At a given, bargained, nominal wage, price decreases implied by labour productivity increase would automatically compensate labourers for the productivity increase.

36 The concept of socialisation of losses is set out in De Brunhoff (1978 [1976]) and derives initially (to my knowledge) from De Brunhoff and Cartelier (1974), though for each not in the context of devaluation of capital and competition. However, Aglietta (1979 [1976], pp. 313–15 and 365–70) theorises inflation in terms of 'anticipated obsolescence', which the current chapter connects to the structure of production (stratification).

37 For banks this is a matter of quantity and quality of the finance provided (as indicated above). Note that credits can be made 'inflation proof' for banks by flexible interest rates or by interest rate indexation.

38 In case of zero inflation there may still have been an accommodated socialisation of losses.

In case of inflation, workers will have to re-bargain for the productivity compensation or even for a mere maintenance of the purchasing power of the initial wage. (In the case of partial or full compensation, these compensations tend to come about with a time-lag.)

4§12 *Stratified structural overcapacity competition*

Recall from the beginning of 4§10 that overcapacity competition involves the burdening of competitors with overcapacity, whence their unit costs increase in comparison with full capacity production. The second main condition of inflationary overcapacity competition (next to the one presented in 4§11) is generalised '*structural* overcapacity'. It prevents a, continuously lurking, shift into a deflationary constellation. I present this constellation in three steps, starting with 'simple overcapacity'.

1 Simple overcapacity: merely transitional overcapacity

Similar to the constellation of price competition (4D2), stratified overcapacity competition is initiated by a (rotating) price-leader that has added a new plant to the stratification, which embodies a technical advance over its competitors. Again, this plant addition increases the (potential) total production capacity of the stratification. Now, however, the price-leader aims to squeeze out competitors from the bottom of the stratification *not* by price decrease as affecting their revenue, but rather by burdening them with overcapacity as affecting their revenue (their unit costs increase in comparison with full capacity production, because they continue to be burdened with the fixed cost, including especially those of fixed means of production and overheads). Thus the price-leader creates actual overcapacity in the sector (equivalent to the size of its own plant). Along with it, the aim is to increase the price, or to keep it at least constant. In order to keep the exposition concise, I present the analytical case of marginal inflation, that is, constant prices. Thus the price-leader sets a price equal to that of the previous period.

See 4§6-a, Figure 4.4 (plant addition). Now, however, read in that figure for 'potential overcapacity', '*actual* overcapacity'. *Figure 4.7* shows that situation with the bottom plants next having been scrapped (note that these plants were already operating marginally or near to it). This scrapping may not occur immediately, as at a constant output price these plants might be kept going for some time at merely a coverage of their prime costs (4§4, penultimate paragraph).[39]

[*continued*]

39 Their aim is to move to the top of the stratification (or near to it by merely copying the (n) or (n+1) technique), as this increases their rate of integral profit. This is actualised in case there is no financial bottleneck.

FIGURE 4.7 *Stratification of plants with simple overcapacity (non-stable in case of marginal inflation)*

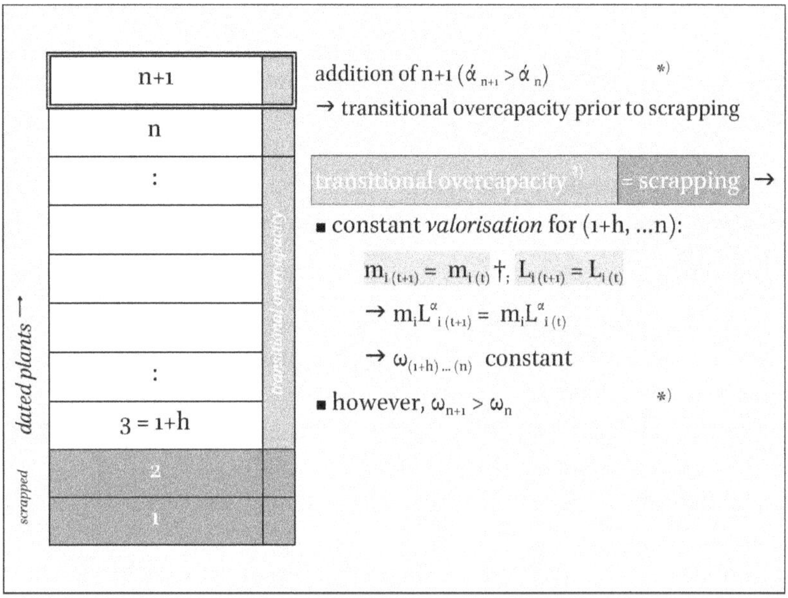

* Analogous to Figure 4.5 (deflationary price competition).
⁑ Disappears after scrapping of bottom plants
† The equality applies for the analytical case of a constant price; in fact we have $m_{i\,(t+1)} \geq m_{i\,(t)}$

4§12 *Continued*

2 *Structural overcapacity*

The following is relevant for marginal or low rates of price inflation and not so much for 'moderately high' rates (see Amplification 4§12-b).[40]

So far an inflationary overcapacity-competition seems feasible on the basis of a constellation of a mere transitional 'simple overcapacity' as outlined above. However, considering *Figure 4.7* it appears that such a constellation may not be stable (especially not on the edge of inflation – marginal inflation – that we are discussing; it might be more stable at higher levels of inflation). The point is that rotating price-leaders require an instrument to effectively respond to competitors that might contest their price-leadership via price decrease. This

40 Theoretically, it cannot be pinpointed what the relevant borderline is between 'low' and 'moderately high' rates. Perhaps the borderline is at around a rate of 4% price inflation.

instrument is a *structural* overcapacity. That is, overcapacity beyond the transitional overcapacity. When the price-leader (n+1) has a structural overcapacity, it is in the position to immediately respond to contesters (such competitors know that a, further, price decrease by the price-leader will immediately take away a large part of their market share). Because the price-leader must have a structural overcapacity, it will keep on having this overcapacity when in the course of time it moves down the stratification (its top position having been taken over by a new price-leader). Therefore, once an inflationary constellation is vested, all plants will tend to operate at a structural overcapacity. (See *Figure 4.8.*)[41]

3 *Stratified overcapacity competition via 'transitional extra overcapacity' beyond 'structural overcapacity'*

With competition, enterprises will try to eliminate competitors, or at least to make them fall behind. In a constellation of structural-overcapacity competition, the *initiator* of competitive action tends to combine:

- production at structural overcapacity (like all the competitors – see heading 2 above);
- a technical advance (such that it might effectively reduce the price in case a contestation of its price-leadership would make price reduction necessary – see heading 2 above);
- the creation of *transitory extra* overcapacity, such that it might take over the market share of competitors down the stratification (this extra overcapacity is equal to the potential production of the plant that was added, net of its structural overcapacity); after the bottom plant(s) is (are) scrapped, all of the extra overcapacity disappears. (See *Figure 4.9*, which is further expanded on below.)

It so acts as price-leader – a function that might rotate between enterprises – setting the price at a level that maximises its profits. Given the technical advance and the structural overcapacity of the price-leader, the other enterprises will tend to resign to the price-leadership.

With generalised price inflation 'm' (interpreted as the price or price index of NDP) changes roughly in the same direction and the same pace as the prices of means of production. As indicated above, to keep the presentation transparent and concise, I present the case of marginal inflation, that is, constant

41 Depending on the particular sector and its technique of production, the size of a plant may be somewhat flexible. In that case plants *down* the stratification, which speculate that there will be no longer price competition, might downsize their plant. This does not apply to the upper plants.

prices and a constant 'unit monetary value of labour' (m). (This is empirically relevant – see Explication 4§12-b.) Thus the price-leader sets a price equal to that of the previous period. I denote the initiator/price-leader and its plant added to the stratification by (n+1). We may assume that the expected effect of this investment, especially on its integral profit and rate of integral profit (ω), has been taken into account prior to the investment in the top plant.

As a result of the transitory extra capacity (n+1), and given the demand for this sector's output, the revenues for all plants in the previous stratification initially decrease (devalorisation), tantamount to this overcapacity. (See *Figure 4.9*.) As a result the plants (1…h) at the bottom of the stratification produce at marginal or zero profit, and will be scrapped.[42] The result is that the *extra* capacity (not the structural overcapacity) is undone.

The total result (that is, pending the exposition of Chapter 5) is that for the remaining plants of the previous stratification (1+h … n), the conditions are similar to that of the previous production period. This includes equal (rates of) integral profit. In comparison with the constellation of price competition this is due to the inflationary 'socialisation of private losses' (4§11). Note that from the perspective of enterprises, the structural overcapacity is in fact a 'desired overcapacity' (a term that will frequently be used in Chapter 5).

I end this section with two remarks. First, as with the deflationary constellation, the pace of technical change is important. Speeded up technical change and investment in new plants may mean insufficient amortisation of the plants at the bottom of the stratification, whereby for these the accumulation of capital is in some degree annihilated (with effect on the environment, including the climate and natural resources – cf. 4§12-a). Independently of these effects on the bottom of the stratification, the question as to whether there is also a macroeconomic annihilation of capital accumulated depends on the combination of the speed of technical change and the inflationary 'derived revaluation of capital' referred to in 4§11.

Secondly, as with the deflationary constellation, the general employment effect of the inflationary constellation depends on: the scale of n+1, in comparison with the scales of the scrapped plants h; together with the capital-labour ratios (K/L) of n+1 in comparison with h. (Chapter 5 presents the macroeconomic effect.)

42 I neglect that, for strategic reasons, these bottom plants might be kept going for some time, producing at prime costs. In that case the end result would be reached in a subsequent production period.

FIGURE 4.8 *Stratification of plants with structural overcapacity*

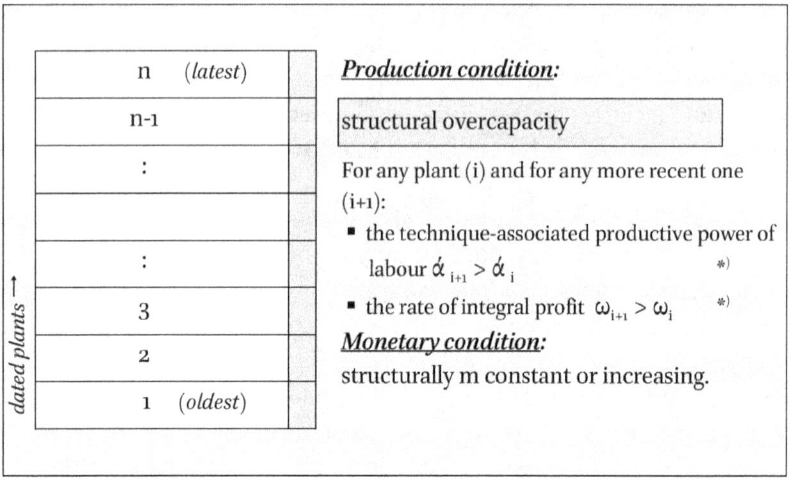

* Analogous to Figure 4.5 (deflationary price competition), though now with structural overcapacity

4§12-a Amplification. Continuous overcapacity and 'efficiency'

The term 'efficiency' is never a neutral one, and should always be specified as to the efficiency criterion. From the point of view of the climate, environment and natural resources, continuous overcapacity is not efficient. From the point of view of the generation of surplus-value for and the accumulation of capital of enterprises, it is efficient.

4§12-b Amplification. Merely transitory versus transitory-cum-structural overcapacity: the degree of inflation and the measurement of overcapacity

The measurement of overcapacity in a sector is not an easy matter, as such measurement is dependent on questionnaires among enterprises that for market-strategic reasons may not be keen to disclose the relevant information. Recall that the main section made a distinction between transitional 'simple overcapacity' and 'structural overcapacity'. It was indicated that the former tends to be unstable in the case of marginal or low rates of price inflation, and that it tends to be more stable at higher rates of inflation. This means that we can expect *structural overcapacity* to occur at especially 'low' rates of price inflation (perhaps a range of rates from 0 to 4%?) and a merely *transitional overcapacity* at higher rates (below called the upper range). In the latter case, enterprises might not mention this, even if they are upfront in questionnaires.

FIGURE 4.9 *Stratification with structural overcapacity: marginal inflation $\Delta m = 0$*

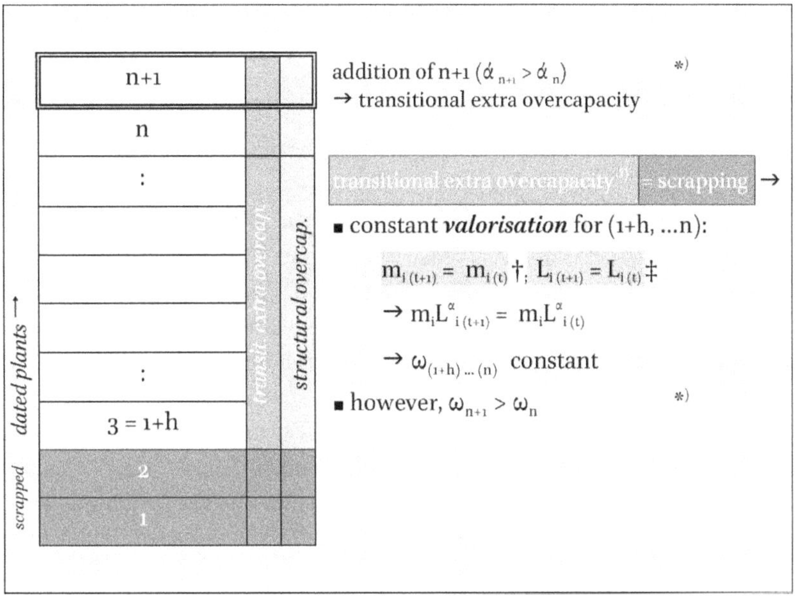

* Analogous to Figure 4.5 (deflationary price competition), though now with structural overcapacity.

** Disappears after scrapping of bottom plants.

† The equality applies to the analytical case of a constant price; in fact we have $m_{i\,(t+1)} \geq m_{i\,(t)}$.

‡ This full row indicates the main difference between the inflationary and the deflationary constellation (cf. Figure 4.5 for the latter).

The point about the upper range is that within it there could be recurrently some degree of price competition within some sectors (contesting the price-leadership) without falling into *generalised* deflation. Should it tend to more structured price wars, then the price-leader will build up structural overcapacity (like in the lower inflation range).

4§12-c Addendum. Kalecki and kaleckians on overcapacity

Kalecki suggested that there is on average a structural overcapacity: 'Even on the average the degree of utilization [of equipment] throughout the business cycle will be substantially below the maximum reached during the boom' (1971 [1943[1]], p. 137, see also his 2003 [1954], pp. 129–31). Ever since, there has been a controversy about this matter among heterodox economists. (See Lavoie 2014, ch. 6, who provides a thorough review of this controversy.) Its context is mainly the business cycle, and in this context that is an important matter (see also Chapter 5).

However, the current 4D3 does not (directly) intervene in that debate. My concern has been to understand the constellation of inflationary competition. It is rather in that context that structural overcapacity seems plausible, especially at marginal or moderate rates of price inflation.

Division 4. The tendency to cartel formation

This division presents a third, and particular, mode of manifestation of the enterprises' market interaction. Please refer to the outline of Scheme 4.1 about the systematic of the current chapter. The previous two divisions presented two alternative (and perhaps alternate) general constellations of competition. Divisions 4 and 5 present two particular modes of manifestation that coexist with *each* of the earlier general modes of manifestation (those of Divisions 2 and 3). Within each of these modes of manifestation, enterprises seek – in some way and to some degree – to overcome the rivalry associated with the competitive constellations. For Divisions 4 and 5 in particular, the reader is reminded once again that the state, and regulation by the state, has not yet entered into the exposition.

4§13 *The tendency to cartel formation: stagnant innovation*

Cartel formation may contingently occur in various circumstances. I emphasise that in this section I *restrict myself to* its impetus as related to the stratified structure of production and to innovation.

1 Range of the stratification of production

The frequency of the innovation in a sector of production (be it process or product innovation) determines the *'range' of the stratification* – the range being the difference in the value-productivity of labour between the top and the bottom of the stratification (that is, the number of layers; several enterprises/plants may operate at the same layer – see *Figure 4.10*). In sectors where *innovation is stagnant*, the range of the stratification narrows down. This implies that it will be more difficult, and in the end impossible, for the top plant to induce the scrapping of bottom plants.

2 *Stagnant innovation and the tendency to cartel formation*

The more or the longer innovation slackens, the more time the bottom and medium plants will have to more or less copy the technique or the product of the top plant. Competition then approaches *stagnant competition* (somewhat similar to neoclassical static competition). Stagnant innovation and stagnant competition clear the ground for cartel formation.[43] The object of a cartel is most often the fixing of prices.[44]

3 *Cartel types as related to the number of enterprises*

In stagnant sectors cartels, as based on firm agreements between enterprises, tend to be restricted to such sectors with a moderate number of enterprises supplying the commodity at hand. The reason is that agreements are difficult to maintain when a large number of enterprises operates in a sector.[45]

When the number of enterprises in a stagnant sector is relatively abundant, cartels tend to be implicit ones, taking the form of a tacit price-leadership.

Although cartels maintain profits higher than in the absence of the cartel, 'too' high profits might evoke entry into the sector. However, entry into a technically stagnant sector is hardly attractive for entrants.

4§13-a Explication. The range and density of the stratification of production

It has been implicit so far that a stratification of production is not only characterised by some *range* (the number of layers), but also some *density* (the number of plants at the same level) – see *Figure 4.10*. However, plant addition to the top of the stratification (n+1) tends to be accomplished by a single innovator. Later on other enterprises may move to the top by more or less copying the technique of the innovator.

43 As indicated, this division is restricted to cartel formation related to the stratified structure of production and to innovation. Cartels also have advantages to enterprises with dynamic innovation.

44 'The most common practices employed by cartels in maintaining and enforcing their industry's monopoly position include the fixing of prices, the allocation of sales quotas or exclusive sales territories and productive activities among members, the guarantee of minimum profit to each member, and agreements on the conditions of sale, rebates, discounts, and terms.' (Editors Encyclopaedia Brtittanica, 'Cartels'.) https://www.britannica.com/topic/cartel – accessed 17 September 2016.

45 See also Ivaldi, Jullien, Rey, Seabright and Tirole (2003, p. 32) and Europe Economics (2001). The latter research institute mentions few firms, stable market conditions, and 'mature market with low innovation and low uncertainty' as conditions for collusion (p. 120; cf. pp. 27, 71–2 and 79).

FIGURE 4.10 *Stratification of production: range and density at each point in time*

n_1	n_2	...	n_j	...	n_m
$n\text{-}1_1$	$n\text{-}1_2$	...	$n\text{-}1_j$	...	$n\text{-}1_m$
:	:		:		:
i_1	i_2	...	i_j	...	i_m
:	:		:		:
2_1	2_2	...	2_j	...	2_m
1_1	1_2	...	1_j	...	1_m

range (vertical)

density (horizontal)

4§13-b Amplification. Agreements regarding tenders and market sharing

Independently of the make-up of the stratification of production, there is also a tendency to collaboration in case of recurrent tenders for big projects (ranging from construction to ICT). In this case the enterprises provide each other with information about their offer (all but one make a fake offer), so as to reach market sharing. This market sharing is generally more likely when a market is oligopolistic.

4§13-c Addendum. Adam Smith on cartel formation: conspiracy

The phenomenon of cartels of enterprise is as old as the early emergence of capitalism. In 1776, Adam Smith wrote: 'People of the same trade seldom meet together, even for merriment and diversion, but the conversation ends in a conspiracy against the public, or in some contrivance to raise prices' (Book I, Ch. 10, section 82).[46]

Division 5. The tendency to oligopolisation and monopolisation

This division presents a fourth, and particular, mode of manifestation of the enterprises' market interaction. Like Division 4 it is particular in that it coex-

46 He continues: 'It is impossible indeed to prevent such meetings, by any law which either could be executed, or would be consistent with liberty and justice. But though the law cannot hinder people of the same trade from sometimes assembling together, it ought to do nothing to facilitate such assemblies; much less to render them necessary' (cf. Book I, Ch. 8, sections 12–13 on 'combinations' not to raise wages).

ists with either a deflationary or an inflationary constellation. Although this is a brief division (one section), the content is far-reaching in its effects. The tendency outlined in this division is presented purely from the perspective of the capitalist economy. (See Chapter 9 about the involvement of the state.)

4§14 *The tendency to centralisation of capital*

1 *Centralisation of capital*

The particular market interaction is a mere instrument for the profit-making of enterprises (4§5). This equally applies to the two competition extinguishing forms of market interaction, one of which is the *merging* of fellow enterprises within a sector, that is, the vesting of some degree of *centralisation of capital.* The other is the *take-over* form of centralisation. The ultimate form of centralisation of capital is that of vesting oligopolies and next a monopoly in a market.[47]

2 *Oligopolistic sectors: capital-labour ratio and scale*

Although mergers and take-overs are a general phenomenon, there is a tendency to centralisation of capital particularly in sectors with, first, a relatively high capital-labour ratio (K/L), and secondly, when extra surplus-value can be gained from a large *scale* (K).[48] This applies to a large variety of sectors, ranging from the production of energy, agricultural seeds, means of transport (cars, trains, aeroplanes), industrial intermediates (steel, aluminium), means of communication, pharmaceuticals, to banking and insurance. The larger the scale grows, the more the entrance to the sector is precluded (and if there is entrance, this tends to be from the part of conglomerating oligopolies).[49]

3 *Stratification of oligopolistic sectors*

As with the general constellations of competition (4D2 and 4D3), one enterprise tends to act as price-leader (tacit or agreed). In this case, however, the effective range of the stratification tends to be such that each oligopolistic enterprise operates at all levels of the stratification, which, in comparison with (full) competitive sectors, may be a relatively small ranged one. To the extent

---

47 More precisely, this is the *penultimate* form of centralisation of capital. The ultimate shape of centralisation is the centralisation of all capital in one inter-sector monopoly.

48 This is a particular case of increasing returns to scale.

49 For example, an oligopolistic pharmaceutical enterprise may, by way of a merging conglomeration, enter the oligopolistic agricultural seeds sector (the case of Bayer initiated in 2016).

that oligopolistic enterprises have an about even production and market power (spread over their plants), they tend to evade price competition and to restrict to capacity competition.[50]

4 *Monopolisation*

To the extent that, within an oligopolistic sector, a further centralisation via mergers or take-overs creates a new unevenness in power within that sector, this may temporarily reinforce the rivalry for the vesting of a price-leadership and next reinforce mergers of competing oligopolies. In this way the centralisation of capital tends to develop into a self-reinforcing process: centralising actions within a sector tend to evoke centralising actions by other enterprises so as to counteract the shift in the balance of power. When the result of such a series of mergers is a duopoly with uneven production and market power, then their merging into a monopoly tends to be the final outcome.[51]

5 *Profit criterion*

From the perspective of the enterprise, the 'centralisation of capital', and hence the limitation or exclusion of competition, is in line with the (from their perspective) 'rational' optimal profit-seeking. All along the criterion for these (and other) enterprises is the rate of integral profit (1§13). The form of oligopoly and monopoly seems frightening for many. However, more threatening to the capitalist system is that it openly puts the 'why' of the criterion on the agenda.

6 *Counteraction of the tendency to average inter-sector equalisation of profit rates*

For all these constellations it holds that – as long as sectors of production are unevenly populated by oligopolies (and monopolies) – the joint market power within a sector results in prices above competitive prices (4D2, 4D3), which affects the costs for other sectors, and ultimately the prices of consumer goods. This unevenness, together with the entrance impediments referred to, counteracts the tendency to average inter-sector equalisation of rates of profit (4§2).

50 It is often argued that oligopolies 'compete' in terms of product differentiation. This argument is fine as far as it goes. Either such differentiation is negligible in terms of the oligopolies constituting a market; or it is effective whence we in fact have a constellation of monopolies in single markets. (Cf. 4§3-a on intra-market interaction and product differentiation.)

51 Recall again that the state is still bracketed at this stage. To the extent that the state prevents monopolisation, a powerful oligopolistic enterprise may allow a weaker one to continue operating.

4§14-a Amplification. Centralisation of capital and the monetary value of labour

Recall from 1§14 that the valorising exertion of labour is measured as value-added: mL^{α}, with the surplus-value being measured as $mL^{\alpha} - wL$. This applies both macro- and microeconomically.

To the extent that centralisation of capital is technique related – that is, along with relatively high capital to labour ratios (K/L) and large scale (K) – the productive power of labour (L^{α}) increases concomitantly. However, when on top of the technique related centralisation, centralised enterprises (oligopolies or monopolies) also gain extra profits from market power, these profits do not stem from labours' productive power (L^{α}), but rather from the unit monetary value of labour (m).[52] Empirically the two (L^{α} and m) are not distinguishable (we can measure just value-added, mL^{α}, and regarding surplus-value the latter minus wages). More precisely, they are directly indistinguishable. *Indirectly*, the two can be distinguished via average inter-sector equalisation of rates of integral profit. That is, when in a sector the average rate of integral profit is structurally above the total economy's rate of integral profit, we can *infer* that this stems from between-sectors differing market power positions as reflected in a between-sectors diverging unit monetary value of labour (m).

That we can measure this only indirectly is a shortcoming, even if similar ones also apply to many accepted theories in the social and natural sciences.

A similar indirect measurement relates to cartels (4§13). However, without additional information about the structure of sectors, this would mean that cartel formation and centralisation power are difficult to separate.

Summary and conclusions

Rather than presenting conditions of existence of the earlier exposition (Chapters 1–3), this chapter has set out the concrete manifestation of the earlier exposition in the market interaction between enterprises.

Division 1 set out how the interaction of enterprises gives rise to the inter-market tendency to equalisation of average inter-market rates of integral profit, and the intra-market tendency to uniform prices (4§2–4§3). The articulation of these tendencies implies that the rate of integral profit of any one enterprise comes to depend on its production. To the extent that the structure of

52 I stick to the term 'unit monetary value of *labour*' because without labour's production, there would be no production at all (1§14) and hence also no gains from market power.

production is dynamic, as measured by the degree of technical change or other innovation, enterprises in a market – particularly their plants – tend to be stratified as to the production power of labour and concomitant rates of integral profit (4§4).

On the basis of this framework of the stratification of enterprises, Divisions 2–5 presented four main *forms* of the market interaction between enterprises.

Division 2 set out, what was called, 'deflationary *price competition*'. Depending on the degree of process and product innovation, price competition tends to result in a combined accumulation and devaluation of capital (4§6–4§7). Generalised price competition gives rise to deflationary generalised price decrease. Price decreases then affect not only the sector at hand, but also the input prices of other sectors and again their stratification, whence we have a derived devaluation of capital (4§8). It was indicated how the *combination* of generalised fast technical change (or a fast increasing technical change) and generalised price deflation tends to generate stagnation. There are no *economy-*inherent forces to get out of such stagnation (4§9).

Division 3 presented the alternative competitive constellation of 'inflationary *structural overcapacity competition*'. In terms of effects, the main distinction with the deflationary constellation is that it leaves undone not only price decreases in the sector at hand, but also its multiplication throughout the economy via input prices (i.e. the derived devaluation of capital). It was indicated that within this constellation (pending the exposition of Chapter 5), enterprises may over time maintain their integral rate of profit. However, depending on the pace of technical change, this may go along with insufficient amortisation (hence a degree of annihilation of previously accumulated capital) for enterprises successively operating at the bottom of the stratification – with effect on the environment including natural resources (4§12).

It was also indicated in this division that the just mentioned maintenance of the rate of integral profit is (in comparison with deflationary price competition) the effect of 'inflationary socialisation of losses' due to the banks' accommodation of inflation. The counterpart of the comparative profits deriving from it are in a loss of purchasing power for social actors with non-equity financial assets (including 'small savers'), for actors with fixed incomes or with incomes that are (in part) adapted to inflation with a time-lag, the latter including workers who will have to re-bargain for the productivity compensation or even for a mere maintenance of the purchasing power of the initial wage (4§11).

Divisions 4 and 5 presented two particular constellations that coexist with *each* of the earlier general constellations. Within each of these constellations, enterprises seek to, in some way and to some extent, overcome the rivalry that is associated with the competitive constellations.

Whereas Divisions 2–3 presented the enterprises' interaction in dynamic sectors and their markets – that is, the sectors in which innovation is flourishing – Division 4 turned to sectors and their markets that are stagnant in terms of innovation. In such sectors, competition fades away and clears the ground for cartel formation of enterprises.

Division 5 presented a final form of market interaction: the centralisation of capital via mergers and take-overs giving rise to oligopolisation and monopolisation. Such centralisation is particularly prevalent in sectors producing at relatively high capital-labour ratios together with a large scale of capital. Centralising actions within a sector tend to evoke centralising actions by other enterprises, whence centralisation is a self-reinforcing process. The final form of centralisation is the vesting of a monopoly in a market. Centralisation (as long as it is unevenly distributed over sectors) counteracts the tendency to equalisation of inter-market rates of integral profit (4§2). The joint market power within a sector concomitant with this centralisation results in prices above competitive prices (4D2, 4D3), which affects the costs for other sectors, and ultimately the prices of consumer goods.

List of figures chapter 4

4§12. Stratified structural overcapacity competition

4§13. The tendency to cartel formation: stagnant innovation

CHAPTER 5

The cyclical over-accumulation and destruction of capital

Business cycles

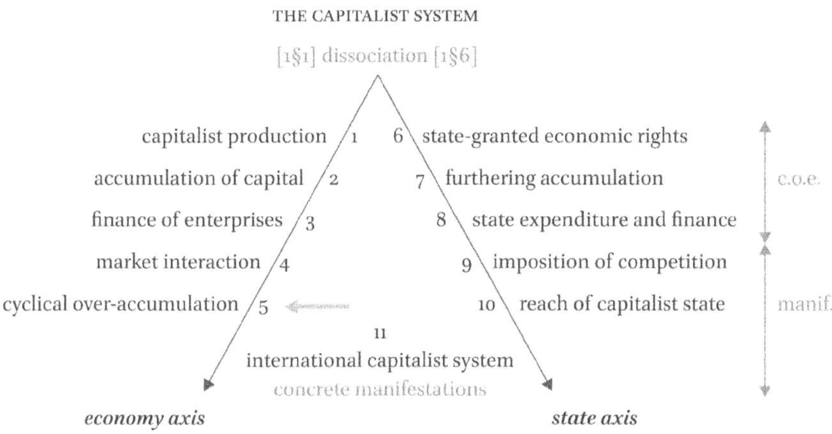

Note: 'c.o.e.' abbreviates conditions of existence and 'manif.' manifestations.

Contents

DOI:10.1163/9789004392809_007

Introduction

This chapter reaches the most concrete level of the exposition of the capitalist economy in this book. Chapters 1–3 presented the necessary conditions of existence of the capitalist economy – with the state yet being bracketed. Chapter 4 presented the concrete manifestation of the earlier exposition in the market interaction between enterprises as predicated on the stratified structure of production. Like that chapter the current one presents no conditions of existence of the capitalist economy. Rather it presents the concrete manifestation of all of the previous exposition (Chapters 1–4) in the diachronic cyclical movement of capital.

The alternation of economic expansion and contraction – commonly referred to as 'the business cycle' – is an empirical phenomenon that mainstream economists have sought to explain by an alternation of merely contingent 'exogenous shocks'. This chapter shows that the production and accumulation of capital in the form of its cyclical movement derives from the capitalist system's *immanent* forces.

In brief it will be set out how cyclically recurrent barriers to a continuous accumulation of capital develop in the second half of the economic upswing. These are next violently resolved in the recession. Whereas system-immanent forces engender the accumulation of capital, the same forces generate over-accumulation of capital in the form of excessive overcapacity. This is a constellation that cannot be simply corrected and that leads to reactions that are perverse to the accumulation of capital. In presenting this constellation I build on the financial determinants of accumulation (PVF and RPVF) and the macroeconomic determinants of the realisation of surplus-value (including the obstacle of savings). Their concretisation will be assembled by the stratified structure of production, which is now lifted to a macroeconomic level. (Division 2.)

The exposition in this chapter synthesises many of the threads of the earlier exposition at this concrete level. However, as economic reality is inevitable always actual in some phase of this movement (one phase of the business cycle), its exposition is also a *concrete* synthesis of the earlier exposition.

In preparation for the main exposition in this chapter, Division 1 presents a number of concretising concepts. The cyclical movement of capital itself is presented in Division 2 (see *Scheme 5.1*).

SCHEME 5.1 *The cyclical over-accumulation and destruction of capital (outline Chapter 5)*

Production, Accumulation, Finance and Stratification
[Chapters 1–4]

.mȩ.

The internal profit of enterprises
surplus-value net of its distribution to external financiers
[5D1]

.M̦.

The cyclical over-accumulation and destruction of capital
[5D2]

Appendix 5A. On the particular structural background of the 2008 crisis
Appendix 5B. Stratified production and Marx's unfinished theory of the cyclical movement of capital

Legend
.mȩ. concretising mode of existence
.M̦. concrete manifestation

Division 1. The internal profit of enterprises: surplus-value net of its distribution to external financiers

Preparatory concretising concepts for 5D2

This division is a conceptually *preparatory* one for the outline of the cyclical movement of capital in Division 2. The investment of enterprises will be seen to be a main determinant of the cyclical movement of capital (Division 2). One main factor that determines investment decisions is the 'internal profit' of enterprises – that is, the surplus-value after a share of it has been distributed to external financiers. The current division expands on this internal profit in the perspective of the earlier exposition – especially that of finance. Along with it (and building on 3D5) this division expands on the determinants of macroeconomic expenditure that result in the internal profit of enterprises.

This division starts by considering the *rate* of profit (5§1), moving to the mass of profit in the later sections.

Unless otherwise indicated, all equations in this division refer to the period (t).

5§1 *The rate of integral profit and the rate of internal profit*

This section presents the interconnection between the finance of production enterprises (Chapter 3) and their rate of profit. This is relevant for the enterprises' investment decisions as presented in 5§5.

1 The rate of integral profit (the rate of surplus-value on capital)

The production of capital being predicated on the monetary-value dimension and the commodification of labour-capacity (1D2 and 1D3), 1§13–1§14 presented the *rate of integral profit* on capital (ω) as the core measure of the production of capital.

$$\omega = \frac{\Pi}{K} = \frac{mL^{\alpha} - wL}{K} \tag{1.6}$$

Much of its dynamic determinants were concretised in 2D2 and its synthesis in 2§6 (see also Figure 2.5). Prior to the exposition of money expansion (2D4) and of the finance of enterprises (Chapter 3), the latter determinants were only implicit in the rate of integral profit on capital (ω). This rate indeed applies to the totality: it is independent of how production capital is financed and independent of what part of surplus-value accrues to financiers including banks (Chapter 3).

2 *The rate of internal profit of production enterprises*

I now make explicit this earlier concretisation (Chapters 2–3) regarding the profit rate that will be called the 'rate of internal profit' of enterprises, which is their profit rate after the distribution of surplus-value to external financiers (banks, bondholders and holders of other loans). External finance and the calculation of profit over the internal (own) capital of enterprises affects the numerator and the denominator of (1.6).

- Let the share of 'external' finance (banks plus other financiers) in capital be ε (epsilon). Hence the internal finance capital is (1- ε)K.
- Let *i* be the average rate of interest (the weighted average of the rates paid to banks and to other external financiers). Then the interest paid by production enterprises is *i*εK. This is the part of surplus-value that production enterprises share with external financiers.

Thus we have for the 'internal profit', R (first introduced in 3§1; cf. Figure 3.2b):

$$R = \Pi - i\varepsilon K \tag{5.1}$$

That is, surplus-value minus its share distributed to external financiers.[1]

The rate of internal profit on the internal capital is called ρ (rho):

1 Recall that 'banking entities' generate surplus-value for their service of bookkeeping, and that these, for their part, are considered as production enterprises. However, their branch

$$\rho = \frac{R}{K - \varepsilon K} = \frac{mL^{\alpha} - wL - i\varepsilon K}{K - \varepsilon K} \qquad (5.2; \text{cf. } 1.6)$$

Dividing (5.2) by K we have:

$$\rho = \frac{[mL^{\alpha} - wL]/K - [i\varepsilon]}{1 - \varepsilon} = \frac{\omega - i\varepsilon}{1 - \varepsilon} \qquad [\text{implication}] \quad (5.3)$$

- As long as $i < \rho$ (or $i\varepsilon < \omega$), external finance acts as an amplifier on ρ. Conversely $i > \rho$ pulls down ρ.

Thus ε is a finance factor and ρ takes account of this finance.[2]

We can interpret each of the equations presented above both microeconomically (then the subscript 'i' is used) and macroeconomically (properly: a semi-macroeconomic two sector account – one sector for production enterprises and the other for external financiers as including banks).

A corollary of this subsection is that 'the tendency to equalisation of average inter-sector rates of *integral* profit' (4§2) takes the form of 'the tendency to equalisation of average inter-sector rates of *internal* profit'.

In sum, the internal capital measure ρ is the 'concentration' of the determinants that were developed so far. Nevertheless, the rate of integral profit ω remains relevant for the total economy's *production capital*, and for the production capital of any one enterprise. The share of $i\varepsilon K$ is 'merely' an important distributional component.

5§2 *The realisation of surplus-value (Π), and the internal profit (R) as a distributional result*

1 Validation of surplus-value produced

3D5 (3§10) presented the macroeconomic validation (realisation) of surplus-value.

$$\Pi_t \triangleleft = [I + Ck + (Cw–W)]_t \qquad (3.10)$$

and

$$\Pi_t \triangleleft = [I + Ck - Sw]_t \qquad (3.12)$$

---

of 'banks' regards purely their finance, for which these share in surplus-value (their part of $i\varepsilon K$) – 3§1.

2 Mainstream business accounting uses the term 'net profit after taxes'. Let us call this Rat ('at' for after taxes). Then it has for what is called the 'return on equity' (ROE): ROE = Rat / (K–εK). This is a consistent measure (ρ_{at}). It also adopts what is called the 'return on assets' (ROA): ROA = Rat / K. This of course measures what it does. Note though that the numerator (Rat) is dependent on how the enterprise is financed, whereas the denominator (K) is independent of the way of finance. Our $\omega = \Pi/K$ has each of the numerator and denominator independent of the finance. More significant is that in the conventional measures it is rather implicit that each of the internal profit (R) and interest (εK) descend from surplus-value.

(See http://thismatter.com/money/stocks/valuation/profitability-ratios.htm for a brief outline of the ROE and ROA definitions.)

(Ck denotes the consumption expenditure by capital owners, both the external and the internal financiers – the latter being the (quasi) shareholders. Sw denotes the saving out of wages.)[3] Recall the essential sequence of 'production of surplus-value' as predicated on the pre-validating finance by banks, of 'validation of surplus-value produced' and of the 'distribution of surplus-value' (3§10).

2 *The internal profit as a result of production, validation and distribution*

Substituting (3.10) in (5.1) we have, ex post, that is, after the distribution of $i\varepsilon K$, the result of the internal profit:

$$R_t = [I + Ck - Sw]_t - i\varepsilon K_t \qquad \text{[validation–distribution mix]} \quad (5.4)$$

Hence, in contradistinction to (3.10) and (3.12), (5.4) is not a pure validation equation. Substituting (5.4) into (5.2) we have, after the validation of surplus-value, for the rate of internal profit:

$$\rho = \frac{R}{K - \varepsilon K} = \frac{I + Ck - Sw - i\varepsilon K}{K - \varepsilon K} \qquad \text{[validation–distribution mix]} \quad (5.5)$$

The following sections of the current division expand on the determination of equation (5.4): consumption and saving (5§3), external finance and the rate of interest (5§4) and investment (5§5).

5§3 *Determinants of saving by labour and consumption by capital owners*

This section briefly expands on the determination of Ck and Sw in equation (5.4). (The same applies for equation 3.12). Consumption and saving by labour and capital owners were introduced in 3§10. Here I briefly expand on these in connection with the phases of the business cycle broadly considered (the particularities of these phases are presented in 5D2).

1 *Saving by labour*

We have by definition that $Sw \equiv s_w(wL)$. However, the savings ratio s_w out of the wages income wL is not constant. When wages rise, the savings ratio tends to increase (and vice versa). The unemployed will dis-save as long as they can, and further survive on the savings of relatives and friends or perhaps saved funds of labour unions. Thus in all these cases the (cyclical) variation of unemployment tends to go along with a variation in savings.

3 In 3§2 it was indicated that the term 'dividends' is considered to include the 'quasi dividends' that flow from non-incorporated enterprises to their owners.

2 *Consumption and saving by capital owners*

The income of capital owners varies over the phases of the business cycle. Regarding (quasi) shareholders: when profits (R) rise, more dividends tend to be distributed (and vice versa). Regarding external financiers: when banks and other financiers perceive an increase in risk and uncertainty, the rate of interest tends to increase (and vice versa). Therefore the income of capital owners varies over the business cycle. Nevertheless they tend to hold on to an autonomous constant standard of living and so expenditure (Ck). When their income exceeds their expenditure, they save, and when it falls short, they dis-save.[4] Therefore their *expenditure* functions as an automatic stabiliser.

Thus, generally, in a recession the savings ratios tend to decline and in an upturn they tend to rise. (In 5D2 this is set out more specifically for the various phases of the cycle.)

5§4 *External finance: the PVF, the RPVF and the rate of interest*

This section amplifies on the determination of *i*εK in equation (5.4).

1 *Variations of the PVF and RPVF*

Recall from Chapter 3 the concept of the 'pre-validating finance' by banks (PVF). An increase in economic growth requires an increasing PVF (and vice versa). To the extent that there are savings by labour and by capital owners, and a fortiori when these increase, production enterprises are unable to redeem the PVF whence we have a 'remaining PVF', abbreviated as RPVF (see the summary in Figure 3.14 of 3§6-c). The ΔRPVF varies with the PVF alongside the savings that are themselves dependent on the phase of the business cycle (5§3 and amplified in 5D2).

2 *The RPVF and the rate of interest*

This subsection introduces some simplifications that serve to reduce the complication of the exposition of the business cycle in the next division.

Figure 3.14 also summarises the point that non-bank financiers may ex post substitute for the RPVF. In 5D2 I will hardly emphasise this, and merely take

---

4 Behind this is in fact a Kalecki consumption function (Kalecki 1971 [1933], p. 1), which is similar to a Keynes one applied to capital owners separately. Kalecki has: $C_k=B_0+\lambda P$ (where B_0 is an autonomous component and P stands for profits). He remarks 'where λ is a small constant'. In what follows I neglect this 'small' profit-dependent component. Thus, as already indicated in 3§10, even if the capital owners' level of consumption is autonomous, some *ex post* level of savings (Sk) from the dividends and interest distributed (PD) results: PD ≡ Ck + Sk.

In case capital owners borrow from banks, this is (macroeconomically) not for consumption, but rather for their primary or secondary finance activities (Appendix 3A, §3A-2).

changes in the RPVF *as an approximation for the external finance cost of enterprises* (analogous to a change in $i\varepsilon K$ – 5§1). Hence in 5D2 the issuance of new shares is neglected (this means in effect that this issuance is taken as constant). Then we have as an *approximation:* ΔRPVF ≈ $\Delta\varepsilon K$. To the extent that an increase in the external finance ratio ε implies a risk for external financiers, they will require a risk premium on the rate of interest (and vice versa). Then a Δi moves along with a ΔRPVF (hence we have for a $\Delta i\varepsilon K$, a quantity effect $\Delta\varepsilon K$ combined with a price effect Δi in the same direction).

5§5 *Determinants of investment*

This section outlines the determinants of investment (I), the remaining component of profits equation (5.4).

1 Investment: preliminary conceptualisation

K being the total capital accumulated, investment is the addition to it:

$\Delta K_t = I_t$ [neglecting devaluation by scrapping beyond obsolescence] (5.6)

$\Delta K^*_t = I_t - scrap_t$ [including scrapping beyond obsolescence][5] (5.6a)

Relative to consumption the determinants of investment are rather complex, and in outcome investment is far more volatile than consumption. Investment is mainly determined by two factors (each of which being the concentration of many determinants): the rate of internal profit (ρ) in the previous period; and the rate of undesired overcapacity (ø) in the previous period.

$I_t = f(\rho_{t-1}; ø_{t-1})$

[I being positively related with ρ and negatively with ø] (5.7)[6]

2 *Investment and the rate of internal profit* (ρ)

Next to the rate of integral profit (ω) the rate of internal profit (ρ) is the 'concentration' of the determinants that were developed so far in this book. This concentration is also transmitted into the determination of investment. I especially refer to all the factors determining the process of production of capital (1D5), including its management (2§2), and its conditions in the expansion of labour capacity (2D3), money expansion (2D4), finance (3D2, 3D3), the production validating macroeconomic expenditure (3D4), as well as the constellation

---

5 Equilibrium models do with (5.6). Equation (5.6a) makes explicit why accumulation of capital cannot be reduced to investment.

6 This equation deviates somewhat from equation (3.8) in 3§10. First, the PVF condition is now implicit in ρ via $i\varepsilon K$. Second, the factor of desired production (X^d) in (3.8) (posited prior to the introduction of stratification in Ch. 4) is now specified via the overcapacity factor ø, as amplified below.

of the stratification of enterprises (4D1, 4D3). Thus the rate of internal profit is the capitalist system's key immanent measure for the movement of capital and so investment.[7]

I reemphasise that in this book's exposition – on this issue inspired by Kalecki – profits do not determine investment in the sense of financing investment – contrary to mainstream economics – but that investment is, via the validation of surplus-value produced (3§10), a main determinant of profit ('main', that is, next to $i\varepsilon K$). Nevertheless this profit as a *result* determines the rate of profit (ρ) as a *result*, which as a success indicator co-determines the investment in the next period. Thus the combination of equations 3.10 and 5.7, or 5.4 and 5.7 (including their time indices) is essential.

Note that, *given the determination of* ρ (equation 5.2), *the finance of investment is taken account of via the rate of interest* (i). The assertion behind it is that enterprises can always get credit from banks even if perhaps at a rate of interest that they consider exorbitant, as a result of which they might decline.

3 *Investment and the rate of undesired overcapacity* (ø)

The rate of technical (over)capacity measures the current production in reference to the qua cost optimal production at the current capital assets (K).[8] I make a distinction between desired overcapacity (o) and undesired overcapacity (ø). Individual enterprises may want to hold on to some degree of overcapacity (o), first, because they expect an increase in effective demand in the near future, and second, for market strategic reasons (regarding the market share or competitive price reactions).[9] The rate of undesired overcapacity (ø) measures the overcapacity beyond its desired rate.[10] From now on 'desired overcapacity'

---

7 The following point is *not* relevant for the business cycle but rather for the structural movement of the capitalist system. Even if the rate of internal profit is a key determinant of investment, 'the' rate of internal profit provides no *absolute* benchmark, as the appropriateness of the going average or modal rate of internal profit is customary and related to the broad stage of structural development. Relevant for the business cycle is the rate of internal profit in the going epoch, which stretches over a multiple of cycles.

8 This (over)capacity applies for plant and equipment as well as for the part of the labour capacity that cannot (or not easily) be varied. Any overproduction is considered to be a temporary factor to which enterprises can adapt fairly quickly in most sectors.

9 We saw in 4D3 that enterprises may produce at overcapacity either of their own free will for strategic reasons (the price-leader), or because the market circumstances enforce them to do so (those that are enforced to comply with the price-leader).

10 Any overcapacity has a negative effect on the current rate of profit via, mainly, the denominator K. For the desired overcapacity this negative effect is expected to be compensated in the future.

will be indicated as such. For brevity 'overcapacity' always stands for '*undesired overcapacity*' (ø).

We will see in 5D2 that this overcapacity (ø) is a crucial determinant for the course of the cyclical movement of the production and accumulation of capital. More precisely it bounds the investment as determined by the rate of internal profit. Even if at some juncture enterprises would consider the rate of internal profit (ρ) 'high' or high enough to undertake profitable additional investment, it makes no sense to further increase the capacity when there is overcapacity, that is, beyond its desired rate. Note that the desired overcapacity also indicates the degree of the enterprises' 'optimism' about the future.[11]

5§5-a Addendum: Steindl on investment

Capacity and undesired overcapacity as a determinant of investment can also be found in Steindl (1976 [1952]). Steindl also has what he calls 'a factor of indebtedness' as affecting profits (cf. equation 5.5 above, and my approximation of ΔRPVF ≈ ΔεK in 5§4). On Steindl see also Hein (2015), esp. sections 3–4, and the references he provides.

5§6 *A condensed macroeconomic sequence*

This section takes some of the previous threads together in terms of an utterly condensed economic sequence. It is difficult to present a macro process sequentially, because we in fact have microeconomic and macroeconomic circuits in which everything is a simultaneous movement. Nevertheless (a change in the level of) economic activity starts inevitably with production.

(0) A *state* of the economy *results* in a rate of internal profit (ρ) at some rate of overcapacity (ø) – the latter might be zero. This result determines the next *state* and the sequences thereof. (See *Figure 5.2*, column 1.)

(1) The result determines the intended level of the new ***production*** – mL^{α} being its core. The level of change is determined by PVF mediated *investment* for which the realised ρ and ø are decisive. (*Figure 5.2*, column 2.)

(2a) Labour generates production (α) whereas its wages are output realising (sales of producers of consumer goods). Investment is capacity generating (production) as well as output realising (sales of the producers of means of production).

11 The distinction between the desired and the undesired overcapacity thus includes the factor that Keynes (1936) called 'animal spirits' (instincts of the enterprises' management about the future).

(2b) The expenditures by enterprises and capital owners (their investment and consumption) minus the savings by labour *realise profits* (via the realisation of surplus-value). (*Figure 5.2*, column 3.)

(3) This *results* in a rate of internal profit (ρ) at some rate of overcapacity (ø), which determines the next *state* and the sequences thereof (analogous to (0) above). (*Figure 5.2*, column 4.)

FIGURE 5.2 *Condensed macroeconomic sequence of production and profit determination*

	(1)		(2)		(3)		(4)	
	t-1		**t**		**t**		**t**	
	Result state		**Production**		**Validation & distribution**		**Result state**	
→	ρ at degree of ø	→	I	→	$\Pi \Leftarrow = I + Ck - Sw$ $R = \Pi - i\varepsilon K$	→	ρ at degree of ø	→
	$\rho = R/(1\text{-}\varepsilon)K$		· I → ΔK → K_t (at desired overcapacity o)		· I is determined and Ck is stable		$\rho = R/(1\text{-}\varepsilon)K$	
Finance			· level of new production via banks' PVF		· Sw and Sk: determination of new external finance factor ε (RPVF)[12] [Sw, Sk and ε are variables]			
remarks			· level of new production: $X^P = [(\delta+\mu)K + mL^{\alpha}]^P$ · R^P(planned) = $(mL^{\alpha})^P - wL - i\varepsilon K$[13] [all the items in these two expressions are variables]		· validation: ø may deviate from the desired overcapacity on which investment was based; · ø may in part take the form of Δ inventories			

5§6-a Addendum: Theories of the business cycle

Until the 1960s the business cycle was hardly theorised by mainstream neoclassical economists, presumably because it was hard to fit within their equilibrium framework. By that time Friedman and his collaborators took up the matter, followed by Lucas towards the end of the 1970s. Prior to it, business cycles had been mainly studied and theorised by the non-mainstream heterodox strands in economics/political economy, Marx being the first business cycle theorist (see Appendix 5B). As indicated in the General Introduction, it is generally beyond the scope of this book to review the literature (references are mainly restricted to tributes and acknowledgements). For a series of brief overviews regarding strands of business cycle theories, I refer to articles in *An Encyclopedia of Macroeconomics* (editors Snowdon and Vane 2002) and the literature discussed in those. Mainstream strands: Monetarist approach (Hammond 2002); New Classical approach (Snowdon and Vane 2002b); Political Business Cycle approach (Frey and Benz 2002); Real Business Cycle approach (Ryan 2002). Heterodox strands: Austrian approach (Garrison 2002); Keynesian approach (Trigg 2002); Marxian approach (Reuten 2002b).

5§6-b Amplification. Empirical business cycle indicator USA 1950–2015

As preliminary to the next division, *Graph 5.3* shows the change of GDP and the recession periods in the USA from the second half of the twentieth century onwards.

GRAPH 5.3 *Change of GDP and recessions in the USA 1950–2015*

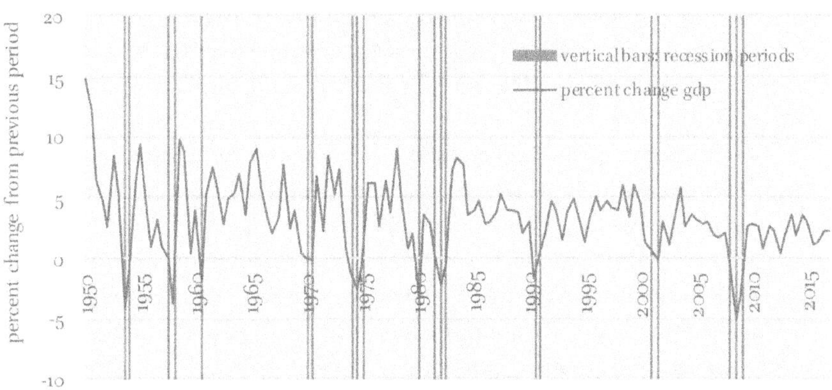

Line: Real GDP, % change from preceding period, semi-annual, seasonally adjusted annual rate. Vertical bars: NBER based recession indicators from the period following the peak through the trough, semi-annual.

DATA SOURCE: FRED economic data (Federal Reserve Bank of St. Louis)[12]

12 https://fred.stlouisfed.org/. GDP updated 21 December 2017; NBER index updated 3 January 2018 (each accessed 11 January 2018).

Division 2. The cyclical over-accumulation and destruction of capital
Business cycles

With this division we reach the most concrete level of the exposition of the capitalist economy in this book. Although the movement of capital is necessarily cyclical in some way, this should be understood as a necessary up and down movement, a movement of accelerating expansion and next a stagnation and contraction. In that sense the cycles of movement are regular. This regularity does not apply to the *length* of cycles (the time between the top of one cycle and the top of the next) or the *amplitude* of cycles (the difference between the accumulation level at the top of a cycle and its trough). In the last sense this Division 2 definitely reaches contingency. In the first sense, however, the cyclical movement of capital is a concrete synthesis of *all* the necessary moments that were presented so far. The fact that the particular exposition in this division will not *explicitly* touch on each one of the moments presented in Chapters 1–4 is a matter of self-imposed restriction in terms of space (i.e. text). Division 1 prepared the floor for the moments on which this synthesis will explicitly touch.

Those readers who are accustomed to accounts of the business cycle just in terms of models should be warned that the current division – as a 'moment' – rather presents the framework for a model.

5§7 *The phase-wise stratified cyclical movement of capital: preliminaries*
The determinants of the capitalist economy that were presented so far seem to sustain the continuous accumulation of capital via expanding production (Chapters 1–4). In fact, as we will see in 5§8, these determinants sustain this accumulation so much that they recurrently generate an over-accumulation of capital that leads – for a considerable time at least – to apparently system perverse dis-sustaining reactions. We will see that the 'logic' of accumulation so turns in its opposite of destruction of capital along with the expulsion of labour, that is, of the generator of surplus-value. The euphemism for it is economic 'contraction'. Then, for the reproduction of the capitalist system, there should be system-immanent forces that lead from this contraction to renewed expansion (presented in 5§9). Together these are called the cyclical movement of capital.

Section 5§6 presented a condensed macroeconomic sequence of the production, finance and accumulation of capital. In the following sections, the cyclical movement of capital is presented as one where such sequences *move phase-wise in the same direction*: expansionary or contracting. *Figure 5.4* shows a stylised curvature of this cyclical movement, ordered in six phases that I will clarify in the next two sections.

FIGURE 5.4 *Stylised shape of one business cycle (growth of production in 6 phases)*

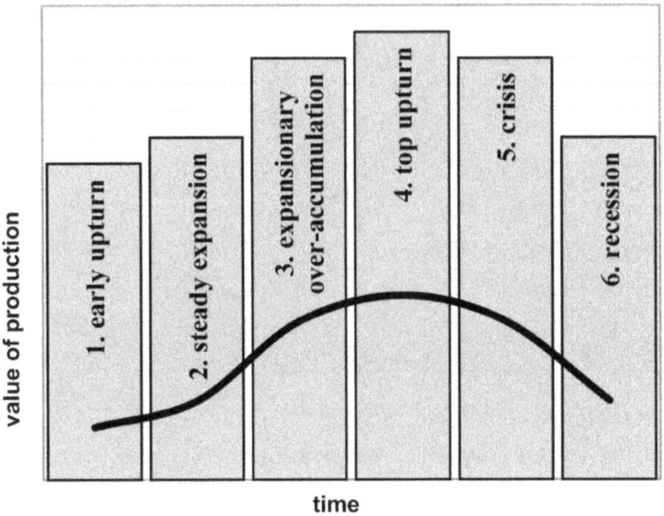

Note: Although the duration of each phase has been put to unity, the duration of the phases varies considerably in practice. Amplitudes (the value difference between trough and top) also vary considerably between cycles.

One major systematising framework for the exposition of the cyclical movement will be the stratification of capital (Chapter 4). On the one hand, the stratification will now be considered in macroeconomic perspective. On the other hand, it will be disentangled as the phase-wise form of the movement of capital. In adopting this framework the focus is on the competitive dynamic sectors of the economy within a constellation of marginal inflation (cf. 4D3). However, because the current exposition integrates all stratifications into one macroeconomic stratification, the stagnant sectors (cf. 4D4) are part of it.

Following on from Chapter 4, *Figure 5.5* below could be interpreted as the movement through time of one random microeconomic sector (with plant addition at the top and scrapping at the bottom). However, in the remainder of the current division it is interpreted as a macroeconomic constellation. In what follows the regular scrapping (below the fat line at the bottom) will be neglected.

FIGURE 5.5 *Phase-wise macroeconomic stratification of capital*

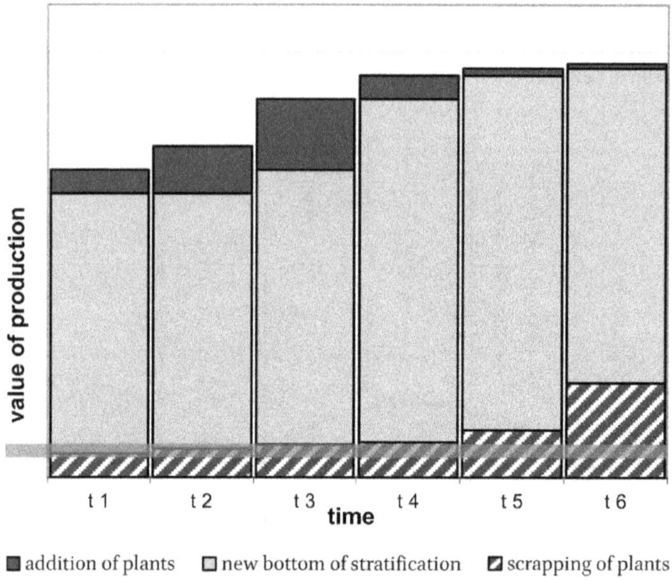

5§8 *Cyclical movement (1): from expansion to stagnation*

(In reading the text below the reader may want to consult the summaries in *Figures 5.6 and 5.7* (on pp. 262–63). Expanding on the latter figure, all cyclical phases are outlined in some more detail in Explication 5§9-b, to which the reader may turn selectively as required. Note that especially *Figure 5.7* is to serve those readers that require an overview of the details.)

A The early and the steady expansion (phases 1 and 2)

In the first two phases of the expansion (the early upturn and the steady expansion) we have a negligible overcapacity and along with it an internal profit rate determined, increasing investment (5§5).[13] The result is rising profits (R) and a rise in the rate of internal profit (ρ). After the hesitating early upturn phase (phase 1), actors perceive the second phase as one of 'back to normality', which generates a climate of optimism. Indeed, considering all the phases of the cycle, this second phase of steady expansion is one of modal ('normal') circumstances (see the list in the second column of *Figure 5.7*).

13 In 5§9 we will see how the early expansion starts from an increased rate of profit as an outcome of the recession (i.e. the previous phase).

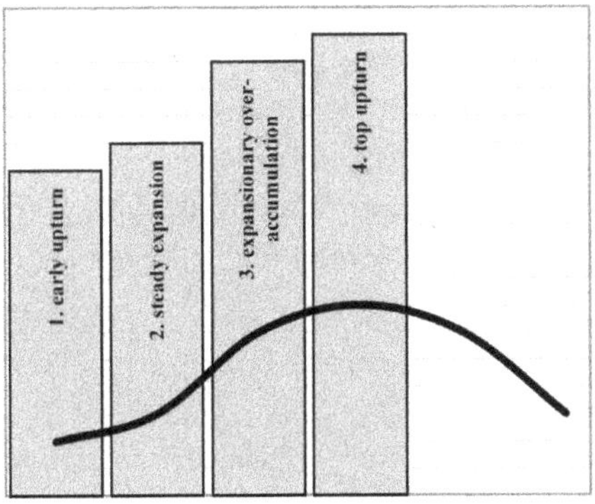

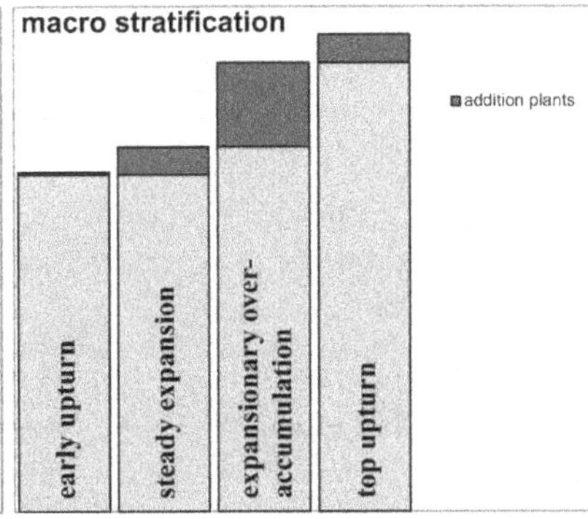

B *Expansionary over-accumulation (phase 3)*

The main conditions for the crisis and downturn are laid in the third phase of the expansion. Actors generally perceive this phase as one of prosperity, which regarding incomes and employment it indeed is. Recall from 5§2 that

$$\rho = \frac{R}{K - \varepsilon K} = \frac{[I + Ck - Sw] - i\varepsilon K}{K - \varepsilon K} \tag{5.5}$$

1. The rising profits (R) and profit rate (ρ) and the slim overcapacity in the previous phase engender a generalised euphoric investment. Enterprises are keen not to miss the opportunities. Overall the sector stratifications get extended boosts. By itself this generates another investment-determined boost in profits (R). However, the (inherently uncoordinated) broad increase in investment – and hence capital accumulated (K) – also generates vast overcapacity (ø). Taking these two issues in isolation, we have, regarding the rate of internal profit (ρ), the profits increase effect from investment expenditure, dominating over the capital increase effect, whence ρ increases.

2. However, the profits (R) are mitigated by increased savings (hence pressure on effective demand). Because the expansion goes along with increased employment as well as increased wages, the savings from the part of labour rise (Sw – recall that this is mediated by an increasing savings ratio s_w). Recall that the consumption expenditure by capital owners is roughly constant (nevertheless their savings, Sk, which increase due to an increased distribution of profits, affect the RPVF – point 3 below).

3. The profits (R) are further mitigated due to finance. Because of the expansion, not only is the pre-validating finance by banks (PVF) boosted, but, more important, the increased savings mean that a larger part of it cannot be redeemed (ΔRPVF). Thus we have an increasing $\Delta\text{RPVF} \approx \Delta\varepsilon K$. Because of the increasing risk, the rate of interest increases (i). This means (cf. 5§4) that the leverage effect of external finance is pressed down (and perhaps already starts becoming negative).

The net effect (1–3) on profits and the rate of internal profit (ρ) is an empirical matter. Say that, in comparison with the previous phase, ρ is roughly constant. Perhaps it declines or increases. For the further course of the cyclical movement this is not particular important, as we will see below.

Generally this third phase turns the steady accumulation of phase 2 into over-accumulation of capital (nevertheless this fits the 'logic' of accumulation – 2D1).[14]

C *The top of expansion and turning point (phase 4)*

Most important for the next phase – the top phase of the expansion – is the overcapacity that has been built up.[15] Given the determinants of investment (the rate of internal profit and undesired overcapacity) the enterprises weigh these factors. Faced with undesired overcapacity they perceive that extra investment makes no sense (5§5).[16] Hence enterprises will generally cut back on investment (some investment may still go on, first, because of investment plans in the pipeline, and second, because of a number of enterprises remaining optimistic). This decrease in investment implies that the investment expenditure effect on profits now dominates negatively, whence the rate of internal profit definitively declines, and sharply so. Note that whereas the *growth* of the PVF and RPVF decline because of the declined investment, the risk for banks is still increasing whence the interest rate further dampens the profits (R).

Because the growth of production goes on (though at a slackened rate) employment increases and hence there is a further upward pressure on the wage rate, with the same effects as indicated above (B-2) for savings – now further reinforced.

On the basis of the composition of forces it is not evident what action enterprises should take. For small and medium-sized enterprises there is no easy way out. For large to very large enterprises, however, this tends to be differ-

14 The over-accumulation of capital is measured, ex post, by the rate of undesired overcapacity (ø); see further Explication 5§9-b.

15 Overcapacity is openly observable in cases such as real estate ('for rent'). The previous construction of buildings boosted employment and profits. Similar phenomena occur, less openly observable, behind the gates of production enterprises – less openly, that is, until plants are closed down.

16 This is so except when an individual enterprise could make a great innovative leap (4D3) – great, that is, on top of the advances already implemented in the previous phase on a broad scale.

ent.[17] Their size and the fact that these are often composed of several plants put them in a position to undertake a cost-cutting restructuring (reorganisation) of their enterprise. Along with it they will, selectively, slow-down their replacement investment as well as their hiring of labour-capacity (hence *for those* enterprises/plants we have a slow to negative rate of growth for each). Although from their perspective this makes sense, the macroeconomic effect of these actions takes off the remaining growth and puts an end to the general expansion.

A note on the duration of phases
I end this section with a note on the calendar time of the various phases. The duration of *each* of the phases is an empirical matter. The duration of a phase might, for example, be half a year, but also three years or longer. Empirically it appears that the length of a complete cycle takes between 6 and (rarely) 12 years. This matter is relevant for the characterisations of each phase (see also *Figure 5.7*). For example, should the phase of over-accumulation (the third phase) be an extended one with perhaps a gradually developing over-accumulation and overcapacity, then the rate of profit (ρ) will tend to move to declining during that phase, perhaps halfway or towards the end.

5§8-a Explication. Summary of the phases of the cyclical movement of capital

Figure 5.6 outlines a simple summary of the phases of the movement of capital (taking together the four expansion phases and the two contraction phases). *Figure 5.7* is a more detailed summary. At this point only the expansion is relevant (the reader can turn to the contraction part after reading the next section).

17 The relative importance of 'large' enterprises is contingent on a particular economy. Just as an example, for the Netherlands in 2010 'large enterprises' (above 100 workers) made up almost 1% of the total number of enterprises with just over 60% of the total employment. (Amongst these the 'very large enterprises' (> 500 workers) made up 0.2% of the number of enterprises with 44% of the total employment.) (Source: Netherlands Central Bureau of Statistics, '*Statline*', accessed 12 March 2012.)

FIGURE 5.6 *Simple summary of the cyclical movement: expansion and contraction*

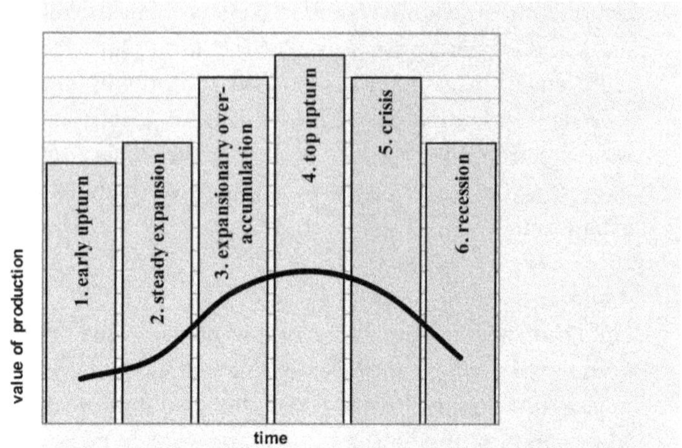

	EXPANSION (ph. 1–4)	CONTRACTION (ph. 5–6)
Production and Investment		
Investment (ΔK)	from ↑ via ↑↑ to ↓	↓
Production and employment	↑	↓
Wage rate	↑	↓
Unemployment rate (u)*	↓	↑
Finance		
PVF from banks	↑	↓
savings effect on RPVF	Sw↑; Sk↑ (each increasingly)	Sw↓; Sk↓
resulting RPVF and εK	↑	↓
resulting *i*εK	↑	↓
Expenditure		
Expenditure (I + Ck – Sw)	I↑; Ck const.; Sw↑	I↓; Ck const.; Sw↓
Total expenditure	↑	↓
Capital and capacity		
Overcapacity (ø)	from negligible to ↑↑	capital destruction (to ø=0)
Capital (K)	↑	↓
Results		
Profit (R = [I + Ck – Sw] – *i*εK)	↑ (expenditure dominates)†	↓ (expenditure dominates)
rate of profit (ρ = R / K – εK)	from ↑ to ↓	from ↓ to ↑ (K effects dominate)

* Ceteris paribus the labour population growth.

† Profit declines at top of expansion.

FIGURE 5.7 *Stylised summary of the cyclical movement of capital: core macroeconomic variables (amplified in 5§9-b)*

early upturn	steady expansion	over-accumulation	top upturn	crisis	recession
hesitating growth	steady growth	accelerating growth	decreasing growth	sudden zero growth	zero to neg. growth
I↑; K↑ → L↑, Y↑ [hesitating]	I↑; K↑ → L↑, Y↑ [steady]	I↑; K↑ → L↑, Y↑ [accelerating]	I↓; K↑ → L↑, Y↑ [damping]	I↓; K↓ → L↓, Y↓ [fast]	Iconst; K↓→L↓,Y↓ [rickety]
recall from 5§5 that investment (I above) is determined by ρ and ø in the previous phase (see below)					
u const. w const., α↑, e↑	u↓ (steady) w↑, α↑, e↑	u↓ (accelerating) w↑, α↕, e↕	u↓ (damping) w↑, α↕, e↕	u↑ (hesitating) w↓, α↑, e↑	u↑ (fast accelerating) w↓, α↑, e↑
***stylised** movement of 'macro' stratification* the surface of the stratification indexes the capital accumulated and the production in each phase					
		(I overshooting)	Σn+5	Σn+5	Σn+5
		Σn+4 plant addition	*running I plans & remaining optimism*		
thin addition plants	Σn+1 addition plants				
ø ≈ const.	ø ≈ const.	ø↑↑	ø↑	ø↓	ø↓
I effect: R↑	I effect: R↑	I effect: R↑↑	I effect: R↓↓	I effect: R↓	I effect: R const.
Sk and Sw ≈ const.	Sk↑; Sw ≈ const.	Sk↑; Sw↑	Sk↓; Sw↑	Sk ≈ const.; Sw↓.	Sk ≈ const.; Sw↓
Sw effect: R≈const.	Sw effect: R≈const.	Sw effect: R↓	Sw effect: R↓	Sw effect: R≈const.	Sw effect: R↑
RPVF ≈ const.	RPVF↑ modest	RPVF↑↑ steep	RPVF↑ modest	RPVF↓ modest	RPVF↓ strongly
RPVF-lever: positive	RPVF-lever: positive	RPVF-lever: down	RPVF-lever: down	RPVF-lever: negative	RPVF-lever: to pos.
K↑; R'>K'	K↑; R'>K'	K↑; R'≈ K'?	K↑; R'<K'	K↓; R'≈ K'<0	K↓; R'>K'<0
ρ↑ modest	ρ↑	ρ↑ or ≈ const.?	ρ↓ heavy	ρ ≈ const.	ρ↑
					scrapping plants physical and devalue-ating destruction
Σ2	Σ2	Σ2	Σ2	Σh+1	
Σ1	Σ1	Σ1	Σ1	Σh	

- Remarks drawn in the stratification apply to the average of the full range of stratification.
- **Changes (↑↓ > <) or non-changes (constant) are in reference to the previous phase.**
- x' = rate of growth of x.
- The summation sign Σ sums the micro sector stratifications (Chapter 4) to the macro level.
- The figure does not show continuous obsolescence and the replacement investment for it (Chapter 4).
- The figure does not show that in the crisis and recession a moderate (replacement) investment goes on.
- The figure abstracts from any 'normal' bad management failures over the cycle.

α	productive power of labour	ø	overcapacity, undesired (rate)	Sk	savings: capital owners
e	rate of surplus-value (Π /wL)	PVF	pre-validating finance	Sw	savings: wages
I	investment	RPVF	remaining PVF	u	unemployment rate
K	capital (assets)	R	internal profit	w	wage rate
L	labour employed	ρ	rate of internal profit	Y	macroeconomic income

5§9 *Cyclical movement (2): from stagnation to contraction and renewed expansion*

The interconnection of all the determinants of the capitalist system means that it can cope very well with economic growth – and hitherto most of the time indeed generates growth. However, the system can hardly cope with declining growth, and even less with shrinking activity (negative growth or decline). For these cases the system-immanent reactions are rather perverse, over-reactive and problem-aggravating.

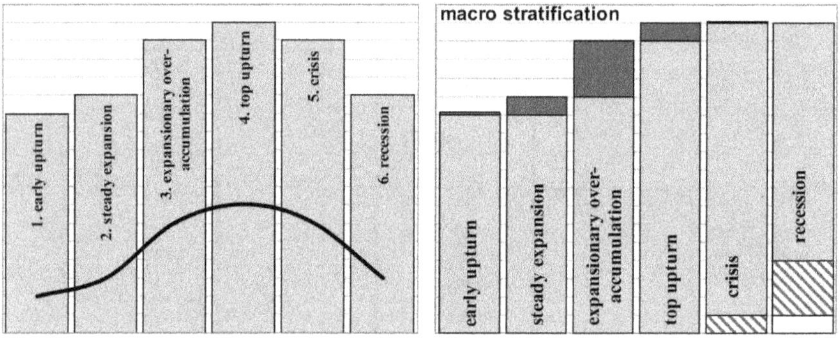

A *Economic crisis, or early recession (phase 5)*

A-1 Spiralling down

We saw in 5§8 that at the top of the upturn, the reaction to a declining rate of profit by, initially, large enterprises, is a restructuring and alongside this a selective slowing down of investment increase and cuts in their hiring of labour-capacity. This gives rise to a general, effective demand generated, negative spiral in employment, investment and profits. Once this negative spiral is underway it is hard to stop. Once the economy moves into a (early) recession, lack of investment is not the sole problem; there is also a lack of effective demand in general. Further, although the PVF declines, the required interest on the RPVF built up earlier turns into a deleverage and so further squeezes internal profits.

In this phase the large enterprises continue their restructuring course of action from phase 4, and also close down plants. Small and medium-sized enterprises that already operated at a loss go bankrupt. The others do their utmost to cut on costs. Because of the physical destruction and/or devaluation of capital along with it (K↓), the rate of profit may not further decline on top of the earlier sharp downfall.

How long this phase lasts, and how deep it cuts, much depends on the suddenness and length of the preceding top of expansion phase. A brief and sudden top phase tends to bring forth a steep crisis (or early recession).

A-2 Crisis and failure of banks

The early recession phase may but need not be associated with a banking crisis, including failure of banks. When accompanied by a banking crisis, then this phase cuts deep and tends to be of extended duration. The term 'crisis' is most appropriate for the combination of an 'early recession' and a banking crisis.[18] We know from Chapters 2 and 3 that banks are essential to the capitalist system. Therefore the term crisis for the combination is appropriate, as a banking crisis is not only a crisis for banks, but indeed a crisis of the system.

B *Recession (phase 6)*

In the recession phase the spiralling down (A-1 above) goes on. At the same time, however, this phase prepares the conditions for a new take-off. The remainder of this section primarily focuses on these conditions (B-1 to B-6) that result, as we will see, in a restoration of the rate of profit (ρ).

B-1 Restructuring of capital: annihilation of capital accumulated

The main characteristic of the recession is 'restructuring of capital' much reinforced from its moderate start in the previous phase. In brief this involves reinforced internal reorganisations, bankruptcies, take-overs and mergers – for the latter two we so have a cyclical centralisation of capital (in contradistinction to a structural centralisation – 4D5). With it, and on top of the bankruptcies, the least efficient plants are closed down. Together these undo most of the overcapacity built up in the expansion phase.[19] In sum we so have a violent cyclical destruction and so cyclical devaluation of capital. Hence part of the capital produced and accumulated in the previous phases of the cycle is annihilated ($K'<0$). Thus the apparently insurmountable problems that came to expression at the end of the expansion (5§8) are 'resolved' by in part annihilating the expansion.

However, with it, the applied natural resources are destroyed – those that are accounted for in the MVD as well as those that are not (1§14, heading 2). This so affects the, at least eventual, system requirement for a symbiotic metabolism of human beings with nature (1§9). More directly grinding, the destruction of

18 Before 1940, about one third of the cyclical tops ended with some form of banking crisis. The more scarce banking crises afterwards are related to state regulation (see Chapter 10).

19 'Most' of the overcapacity is done away with. Large corporations with sufficient reserves can often survive with overcapacity, perhaps assisted by banks.

productive activity and productive capacity destroys employment of labour. The resultant misery is concentrated in those expelled into unemployment. Predominantly these, and their children, are sacrificed for the process of 'creation and destruction'. (Even if along this Sisyphean process the average real income per head may increase, the heads are not equal and especially the unemployed are 'hors catégorie' in this respect.)

The following factors are the 'by-products' of this restructuring assisting a new expansion.

B-2 Survival on savings and a declining RPVF

Due to the restructuring of capital, workers are laid off. Thus whereas many enterprises and financiers lose part of their capital (even if the corporate form of the enterprise mitigates risks – 2§12 and 3§5), many workers lose their means of subsistence. Often workers can, for some time at least, survive by drawing on previous savings (their own, that of relatives and friends, or of means collected by labour unions, for example). These dis-savings press down the RPVF. This also applies for capital owners who, with decreased or zero profits distributed, maintain their standard of living from their previous savings. From the part of the employed workers, savings are further pressed down due to wage decreases that result from the generalised unemployment.

B-3 Losses of banks along with rebuilding the structure of finance capital

Due to restructuring of capital, and especially bankruptcies, banks too have to take finance capital losses.[20] On the other hand, these also rebuild the structure of their balance sheet as presumably dubious assets disappear from the assets side.

Further, starting from the top of the upturn and continuing throughout the recession, banks take a breath from a too spurious increase of the PVF, and especially of the RPVF, in the phase of over-accumulation.[21] This breath also rebuilds the structure of their balance sheet.

---

20 Even if banks may have reserves from risk premiums built up in the expansion, this still shortens their balance sheet.

21 Jakab and Kumhof observe that 'especially during the boom periods of financial cycles when all banks simultaneously decide to lend more, [this] is [the result of] their own assessment of the implications of new lending for their profitability and solvency.' However, 'an individual bank that considers whether to deviate significantly from the behaviour of its competitors' is faced with the dilemma of 'increased credit risk when lending too fast to marginal borrowers' and of a diminution of its clients when 'too many of them are lost to competitors' (2015, p. 5).

B-4 Compliance of labour: disciplining by the recession

Along with the restructuring of capital, the rate of internal profit for the remaining enterprises is further pushed up because the unemployment affects the *compliance*, and so the power of labour in production – that is, of those that remain employed. Recall from 2D2 and 3D6 that the compliance of labour is in fact a major open end (under-determined). The restructuring of capital is a chief disciplining factor.

The result of the restructuring of capital (B-1 to B-4) is that the rate of internal profit for the remaining enterprises increases. By itself this is no sufficient impetus for extra investment, as long as there is no extra effective demand forthcoming, or at least an expectation of it.

B-5 Cyclical 'hoarding' and implementation of techniques

Because, through the restructuring of capital, the least efficient plants are scrapped, we have a reduction in the range of the stratification.[22] With it, we saw, the structural overcapacity that was built up during the expansion is cut away.

Generally any successful new plant investment requires either extra demand (which is not the case in the recession) or a degree of productivity *difference* between the top and the bottom of the stratification. This difference should be such that the general overcapacity that emerges through that investment enforces the scrapping of plants down the stratification – so relieving the general overcapacity. Conversely the general range reduction through the restructuring has reduced this opportunity of productivity difference.

However, along the recession, when new plant investment does not come forth, research and development goes on but new technology is not implemented in new techniques.[23] We so have a 'hoarding' of new techniques. When such a hoarding has been built up it pays at some point to invest in new techniques, with the intention that bottom plants are scrapped (this is the intention; however, in case a *generalised* renewed *investment* generates sufficient macroeconomic growth, this scrapping might not be forthcoming – see phase 1, and its fragility alluded to in 5§9-b). Hence, overall, we have a cyclical (de)concentration in the implementation of new technology.

22 See Figure 4.9 on the range of the stratification.

23 Even in severe recessions, enterprises tend to keep at least the core of their R&D workers because the rebuilding of a R&D department takes enormous effort and time. (The main text puts primary emphasis on process innovation; however, the same applies for product innovation.)

Note that, as for all of the above, this is a macroeconomic account. In a recession, some sectors may keep on investing even if at a lower scale, whence for these the hoarding also is a mitigated one.

B-6 Renewed bank credit

Because of the factors B-1 to B-4, banks are inclined to accommodate the investment projects B-5.

C Early expansion (phase 1)

To the extent that the 'dishoarding' of techniques macroeconomically synchronises (and along with the factors B-1 to B-4) there arises a moderate though general boost of investment (without, initially at least, required scrapping). This provides the take-off to a new expansion (the early upturn phase, as presented in the previous section).[24]

5§9-a Addendum. Marx and Schumpeter on cyclical movement and 'neue Kombinationen'

Marx presents his exposition of the cyclical movement of capital in *Capital I*, Part Seven, and in *Capital III*, Part Three (Marx 1976 [1867], and 1981 [1894]). Schumpeter credits him not only for being the first business cycle theoretician, but also for detecting the phenomenon: 'We find practically all the elements that ever entered into any serious analysis of business cycles, and on the whole very little error. Moreover, it must not be forgotten that the mere perception of the existence of cyclical movements was a great achievement at the time' (2003 [1943], pp. 40–1).

The exposition of 5§9 builds on Marx's major insight that in the recession the rate of profit is restored via destruction and devaluation of capital. However, Marx also posits that the competitive struggle in the recession impels the introduction of new methods of production. He cast this in terms of his famous phrase of 'neue Kombinationen' (new combinations) that inspired Schumpeter (1934 [1911]).[25] In Marx's text it is not very clear as to whether these 'neue Kombinationen' start being applied in the recession or (mainly) in the upturn. Anyway, for Schumpeter this happens in the early upturn – to which I agree.

24 Compare Schumpeter who, in contradistinction to the current theory, provides no mechanism for the impetus to the upswing (see 5§9-a).

25 Marx 1972 [1894], p. 265: '... Anwendung neuer Maschinen, neuer verbesserter Arbeitsmethoden, neuer Kombinationen'. The English edition (Fernbach translation) uses the phrase 'new forms of combination' (1981 [1894], p. 363).

However, neither Marx nor Schumpeter offer any account of why inventions are produced during the slump and implemented in the upturn. The argument above about 'hoarding' and 'dishoarding' of techniques is that innovations are produced all along, but that – on average – their implementation in the slump would not pay because the restructuring and centralisation of capital produces a decrease in the range of stratification, whence the dynamic competition between enterprises remains only latent (hoarding of innovations) until sufficient productivity difference between the (potential) top and the bottom of the stratification has been built up.

5§9-b Explication: Phases of the business cycle – a macroeconomic account

This explanation sets out the course of the business cycle in mainly macroeconomic terms. *Figure 5.7* serves as a synopsis for it. Although this explication adds details to the outline of the main sections 5§8 and 5§9, the purpose is far from being exhaustive. It is meant to be in line with all of this book's purpose of setting out the main interconnections of the capitalist system. Now, however (as was already the case in Chapter 4), contingency creeps in increasingly.

I classified the cycle into six phases. This number is somewhat arbitrary (other accounts may adopt more or fewer phases).

Below I adopt the term CG sector (the sum of the consumer goods producing industries) and MP sector (the sum of the means of production producing industries, including the intermediate production), first introduced in 3§2-a.[26] Unless otherwise indicated the terms change/increase/decrease refer to comparison with the previous phase.

For all of the phases described below, it may be useful, as before, to keep in mind the equations for internal profit and the rate of internal profit.

$$\rho = \frac{R}{K - \varepsilon K} = \frac{I + Ck - Sw - i\varepsilon K}{K - \varepsilon K} \qquad (5.5)$$

26 The MP producing industries encompass far more than is measured by 'investment', as these include all of the 'intermediate' production. Very roughly today the intermediate production (of MP) is equivalent to the total of GDP, thus total gross production being twice GDP. (This varies depending on the structure of an economy; the number can be read off from the statistical input-output tables of a particular economy.)

1 *Early upturn (or recovery)*

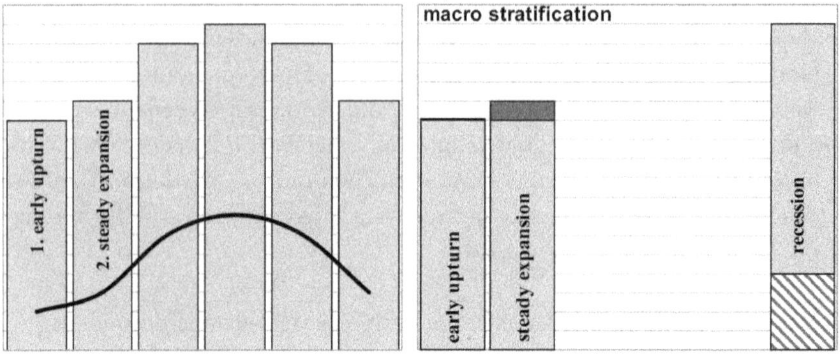

This first phase is inherently the most fragile one. (In so-called 'double dips', the fragility of the early upturn is such that we have a fall back into recession.)

- In the early upturn we have a moderate: I↑ and L↑, and hence Y↑. The lead for the increase in production is taken by the MP sector that initially increases the production of replacement investment, which next has a multiplier effect in net investment. The investment, as well as the production for it, embodies new techniques.
- The demand for additional replacement investment, and next the I, L and Y increasing production of it, is triggered by a combination of three factors, which is the result of the recession, whence their explanation must be postponed (see phase 6 and 5§9). Here I just mention these: (a) a restoration of the rate of profit due to a devaluating 'restructuring' of capital (through which inefficient plants/enterprises have been scrapped or eliminated) and through which the remaining plants can produce at near to full capacity; (b) for survived enterprises a further restoration of the rate of profit due to declined wages together with increased compliance; (c) 'hoarding' of techniques (dishoarded in the current early upturn). All these factors result in a rise in labour productivity.
- The restoration of the rate of profit provides confidence for banks to accommodate investment via additional PVF. The recession factors just mentioned are (further) effectuated in the early upturn. We also have a rise in productivity for plants that 'hoarded' labour-capacity.[27]

27 'Labour hoarding' (in fact labour-capacity hoarding) refers to the reluctance of enterprises to lay off in the recession the specialist echelon of their workers that may be difficult to replace by other workers in an expected upturn. Thus during the recession these are in part idle at a perhaps full wage.

- Although the PVF rises, the RPFV tends to be constant in comparison with its strong decline in the previous phase: the slim savings by capital owners (due to thin distribution of profits) and by the employed (due to decreased wages) more or less outweigh the dissaving by, or for, the unemployed.
- The previous strong decline in RPVF, together with the decreased risk in face of the previous restructuring of capital, mean that the rate of interest is at a low ebb, whence the RPVF leverage effect (for the existing *i*εK) is positive.
- The merely moderate increase in investment means that there is hardly any overcapacity.
- In sum, profit (R) rises – mainly due to the investment effect – and its rate of increase is larger than the rate of increase of capital accumulated (R'>K') whence the rate of internal profit (ρ) rises.

Early upturn

finance	*general*	*determinants* RPVF *and expenditure*	*results*		
PVF↑; RPVF ≈ const. RPVF lever: pos.	I↑, K↑; L↑;Y↑ hesitating growth I' > K'	Sk and Sw ≈ const.	ø ≈ const.	R'>K'	R↑; ρ↑ hesitating

x' = rate of growth of x

2 *Steady expansion*

Based on the increased rate of profit and the cuts of overcapacity we have in this phase a steady growth of macroeconomic investment, employment and income. Generally there is a restored confidence and optimism about the future. For the management of enterprises, the previous crisis and recession gradually moves to the back of their minds. On the other hand, much of labour is still distressed with unemployment even if its rate decreases.

Through investment there is a net addition of plants along with a moderate increase in capacity, which takes it near to the desired capacity. Whereas the PVF increases along with the employment and investment, there is also a modest increase in the RPVF because of a gradual modest increase in savings on the part of capital owners. The interest rate is still near to its low ebb, whence the RPVF leverage effect is positive. The sum of profits (R) rises steadily due to the investment effect. Its rate of increase is larger than the rate of increase of capital accumulated (R'>K') whence the rate of internal profit (ρ) rises.

Steady expansion

finance	*general*	*determinants* RPVF *and expenditure*	*results*		
PVF↑ RPVF↑: modest RPVF lever: pos.	I↑, K↑; L↑;Y↑ steady growth I′ > K′	Sk↑ Sw ≈ const.	ø approaching desired rate	R′>K′	R↑; ρ↑ hesitating

3 *Expansionary over-accumulation*

This is the phase of a generally violently increasing accumulation and growth. Investment fiercely accelerates based on the previous phase's increased rate of profit and the narrow overcapacity. Enterprises hate to miss the opportunities. The CG sector (consumer goods) swings and reinforces the MP sector's growth. Considering the investment effect on profits taken in isolation, the growth in profits accelerates (R = I + Ck – Sw – *i*εK). Investment considered in isolation would also positively affect the rate of internal profit (ρ), because the rate of growth of investment (and hence profits) is larger than the rate of growth of accumulation (I′> K′). However, each of these effects is mitigated by the savings effect by itself (Sw) via expenditure, and by saving effects (Sk and Sw) on the RPVF and hence on *i*εK.

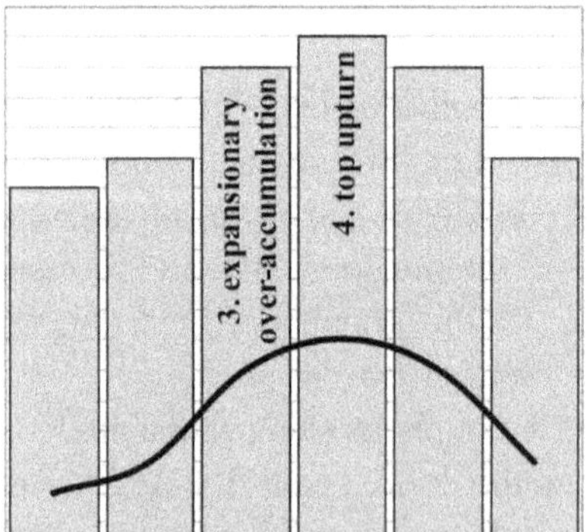

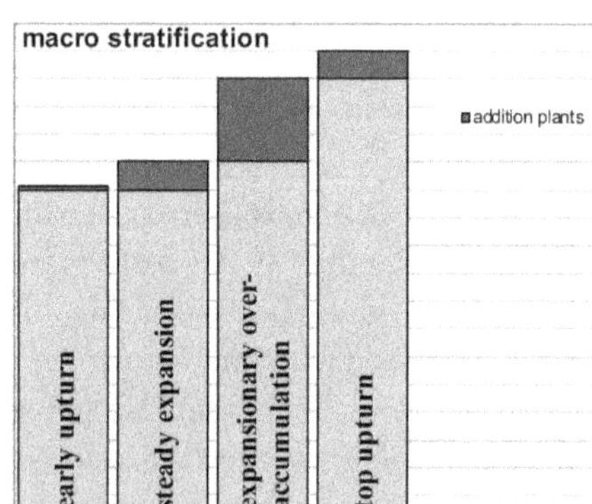

First, the acceleration in investment goes along with both an increase in employment and an increase in the wage rate (together wL). The extra saving from it (Sw) directly mitigates the profits (R). Second, the growth in both investment and wages is conditioned on an increasing PVF from banks. This will go along with a disproportionate rise in the RPVF because of extra saving by capital owners (Sk) from increased distributed profits, and because the extra savings out of wages, as mentioned (Sw). This rise in RPVF affects the external finance ($i\varepsilon K$) in volume (εK) as well as in price (i) because of the extra risk premiums required by banks and other financiers. The RPVF lever on the rate of profit moves down, or is perhaps becoming negative (this depends on the concrete situation and may be different for specific cycles).

As indicated in the main text, the net effect of these factors on the rate of internal profit is an empirical matter. Decisive for the next phase is that the (inherently uncoordinated) broad increase in investment also generates vast overcapacity.

Expansionary over-accumulation

finance	*general*	*determinants* RPVF *and expenditure*	*results*		
PVF↑ RPVF↑: heavy RPVF lever: ↓	I↑ violent; K↑; L↑;Y↑ increasing growth I′ > K′	Sk↑; Sw↑	ø↑ steep	R′≈ K′?	R↑ ρ ≈ constant?

The macroeconomic rate of overcapacity (ø) is a measure for the macroeconomic over-accumulation. The current phase was characterised as 'expansionary over-accumulation'. In fact, actors (as well as the economist-spectator) usually perceive the over-accumulation only towards the end of this phase or perhaps halfway. However, even if enterprises might perhaps have some earlier inkling that their investment could be excessive, they will most often be reluctant to leave the floor to competitors. All the enterprises that withdraw miss out against those that do not, especially if the latter are few. Cyclical over-accumulation of capital is at the edge of being the necessary form of accumulation. Grand cartels, sector monopolies forming inter-sector cartels or in the end one grand monopoly might perhaps prevent it.

4 *The top of expansion and turning point*

Even if at the end of the previous phase the rate of internal profit would have been increasing instead of damping or stagnant, investment falls back because of overcapacity. Even at a comparatively high rate of profit, it makes no sense to invest when this increases the overcapacity still further (5§5, heading 2).

Macroeconomically there may still be a moderate investment because of running investment plans and investment orders, and also because some enterprises remain optimistic about sales and the rate of profit. Given that individual investments are most often complementary to others, once the plans are definite and investment purchase orders have been placed, investments are rather fixed for (t) and (t+1) or even longer.[28]

The fall back in investment is the decisive characteristic of this phase, and the one that makes the business cycle turn downward. Because investment expenditure decreases sharply, profits (R) go down sharply in comparison with the previous phase. At the same time, because L keeps increasing (though mitigated), wages keep increasing (non-mitigated). Hence saving out of wages (Sw) increases, which also negatively affects the validation of surplus-value and hence profit.

Whereas the PVF decreases in comparison with the previous phase (it increases due to the increased wage sum, but decreases more due to the decreased investment), the RPVF nevertheless increases modestly due to the Sw increase, which is counteracted by a decrease of Sk because of a decrease in profits distributed. This volume effect of external finance, along with the increased risk of it, makes the interest rate rise so that the leverage effect of external finance goes further down.

As a result, profits and the rate of internal profit decline sharply (cf. equation 5.5). Once the seriousness of the constellation is apprehended (perhaps in the second half of this phase), it is not evident what actions the smaller echelons of enterprises should take in reaction to this. Large to very large enterprises, by contrast, are in a position *to start* undertaking cost-cutting reorganisations. As indicated in 5§8 they will tend to, selectively, slow-down their replacement investment as well as their hiring of labour-capacity (hence we have for those enterprises/plants a slow to negative rate of growth for each). The macroeconomic multiplier effect of these actions takes off the remaining growth and puts an end to the general expansion.

28 In this context Kalecki (1971 [1933], pp. 2–4) distinguishes between 'investment orders', 'production of investment goods' and 'deliveries of finished equipment' (see also the discussion by López and Assous 2010, pp. 29–30).

Top of expansion and turning point					
finance	*general*	*determinants* RPVF *and expenditure*	*results*		
PVF↓ RPVF↑ (modest) RPVF lever ↓	I↓; K↑; L↑; Y↑ (slow-down of growth) I′ < K′	Sk↓; Sw↑	ø↑	R′< K′	R↓; ρ↓

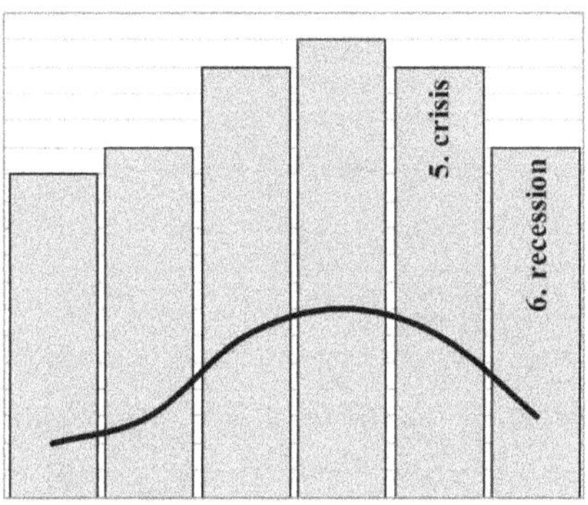

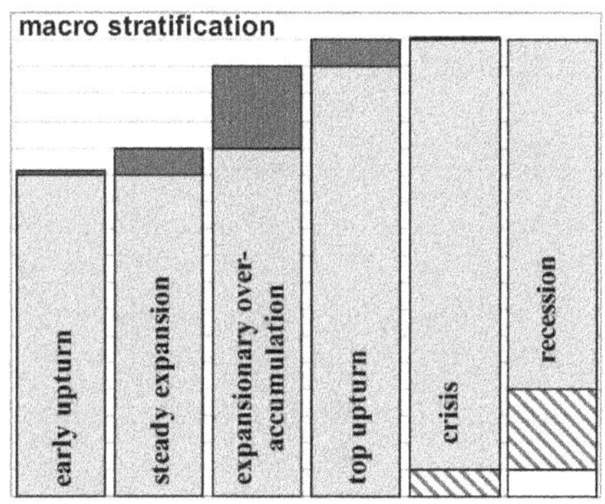

5 *Crisis (early recession)*

I will not repeat here the main outline of this phase, which was, for the current purposes, sufficiently described in the main text of 5§9 (introduction and under subsection A). Here I briefly expand on the spiralling down process of this and the next phase, as well as on some details for the current phase regarding the macroeconomic profit (R) and profit rate (ρ).

The downfall in investment of the previous phase first hits the sales of the MP producing sector, and so the rise in unemployment starts here. The effect is a decline in consumption, which affects the sales of the CG producing sector whence it cuts back production, and lays off labour. This re-affects its own sales. In response this sector will cut back on replacement investment, so re-affecting the means of production producing sector. And so forth. This is the spiral down process that was alluded to in the introduction of 5§8, and the reason for the statement that the capitalist system is not suited to cope with declining and shrinking economic activity. (As indicated this applies for the crisis phase and especially also for the recession discussed in the next subsection under phase 6.)

In the current early recession we have the first bankruptcies of small enterprises. Next to it the reorganisations started by the middle and large enterprises in the previous phase now mature into the scrapping of plants down the stratification. This implies that we have a decrease in the capital accumulated (K) and hence also a decrease in overcapacity. Because K declines, and although the macroeconomic profit (R) decreases, the rate of internal profit tends to be roughly constant – that is, in comparison with the sharp decline in the previous phase 4. The net decline in profit stems from, first, the investment expenditure effect (negative), second, a modest positive effect from decreased saving out of wages, and third, an increase in the interest on the RPVF. Although the RPVF volume modestly decreases, the sharp decline in ρ from the previous phase, which now endures at that low ebb, means that debt extensions require a risk-motivated higher interest rate.

Crisis (early recession)

finance	*general*	*determinants* RPVF *and expenditure*	*results*		
PVF↓ RPVF↓: modest RPVF lever: negative	I↓; K↓; L↓;Y↓ fast decreases $I'=0$; $K'<0$	Sk ≈ const.; Sw↓	ø ↓	$R' \approx K' < 0$	R↓; ρ ≈ const.

6 *Recession*

In effect, as we will see below, the recession prepares the conditions for a renewed accumulation of capital (in the early upturn of phase 1). In the recession phase we have a continuation of the *restructuring of capital* (ROC), initiated by large enterprises at the end of the upturn. Now we have a generalised and enforced ROC as well as centralisation of capital. The enforcement is due to a growing number of enterprises being at the edge of bankruptcy and that for others the rate of internal profit is at a low ebb or negative (phases 4–5).

ROC: intra-enterprise reorganisation and inter-enterprise centralisation of capital. Generally the duration and the intensity of the ROC (and hence the duration and intensity of this phase) depend on the intensity of the over-accumulation of phase 3. There are many possible forms of ROC. These include the reshuffling of the departments of an enterprise but also the closing down of plants or perhaps particular departments of plants. However, this ROC may also be combined with inter-enterprise reorganisations. In that case it is combined with the selling and buying of plants between enterprises or with take-overs or with mergers (followed each time by, then, intra-enterprise reorganisation). This inter-enterprise reorganisation is called '*centralisation of capital*'. This term (stemming from Marx) is appropriate as the governance of enterprises moves from local in degree to central in degree.[29]

Actual bankruptcies, as well as the closing down of plants, means that we have in part a destruction of what was built up in the previous upturn of the cycle. Much of the previous labour employment growth is extinguished into unemployment. From the point of view of enterprises we have, along with the physical counterpart, a *destruction of capital*, an annihilation of previous accumulation (hence K↓).[30] In terms of the stratification of capital we have an enforced *shortening of the range of stratification* as the least efficient plants get scrapped (cf. Figure 4.9 on the range of the stratification).

Further effects of ROC. Along with these pure capital effects, the concomitantly increasing unemployment gives rise to wage rate decreases. This implies not only a vast decline in saving from the employed, but also dissaving from the part of those unemployed who had built up savings previously (or, in case these are lacking, from relatives, for example). Along with it the RPVF declines, which pushes the profits for the remaining enterprises. This profit push somewhat compensates for the primary negative effect on profit, which stems from investment approaching nil (a continuation from the previous phase).

At the same time unemployment, or the threat of it, also enforces a 'disciplining' and compliance of labour during production (2§5, Figure 2.4), which in effect increases the productivity of labour.

These effects on capital and labour together constitute the 'curing' effect of the recession. In sum, so far, the vast destruction/devaluation of capital from the ROC means that even if profits are at a very low level, the rate of internal profit increases for the remaining enterprises.

This increase is reinforced by the following finance factors. First, because of the decreased saving (from the part of labour, and from the part of capital owners as a continuation from phase 4 onwards), the running PVF – for wages – is near to fully redeemed by enterprises. Second, the restructuring bankruptcies imply that banks, and other external financiers, have to write off their loans, whence the RPVF decreases. Third, the balance sheets of the production enter-

29 In mainstream economics this is called 'concentration'. (Marx also uses the term concentration, but rather for the growth of enterprises – big enterprise, i.e. local growth. See Marx, *Capital I*, Ch. 25; German edition Ch. 23).

30 Regarding ROC, and up to this point of the text, I take inspiration from the work of Fine and Harris (esp. 1979, pp. 83–7) and Weeks (1981, pp. 208–13).

prises have been cleaned up, whence for the existing RPVF the risk of banks is moderated. These factors, together with their favourable effect on the rate of profit, mean that banks are increasingly prepared to charge a lower rate of interest on debt extensions (just the opposite of the previous two phases). This means that the leverage effect now starts becoming positive.

Recession

finance	*general*	*determinants* RPVF *and expenditure*	*results*		
PVF↓ RPVF↓: strongly RPVF lever: towards positive	I const. (0); K↓; L↓; Y↓ all rickety I′= 0; K′< 0	Sk ≈ const.; Sw↓	ø ↓	R′>K′< 0	R ≈ const.; ρ↑

The curing in the recession provides a *precondition* for recovery and renewed accumulation of capital. However, it is not evident at all what might take off renewed investment at an overall declining production and income (Y↓). Its key lies in range of the stratification of capital and the (dis)hoarding of new techniques as explained in 5§9, heading D.

5§9-a Addendum. An immanent appreciation

Generally this book presents an immanent critique of the capitalist system, that is, from its own norms. It so leaves any further appreciation to the reader. From its own norms (in brief, the monetary-value dimension and the rate of profit as criterion for economic activity, which engenders the motive for accumulation of capital for the sake of accumulation of capital), the cyclical movement of the accumulation of capital is at least paradoxical. The accumulation of capital recurrently results in a great deal of annihilation of that accumulation. This is so continuously (the continuous scrapping as presented in Chapter 4) but especially cyclically. Individual enterprises and capital owners always hope to escape the dance. However, only few corporations survive a long series of cycles. In jointly over-accumulating capital (phase 3), enterprises do no more than applying the 'logic' of the system that they so reinforce.

On an individual level, capital owners take a risk of their own free will (the big ones can spread that risk) and may win or lose. Workers, however, do not take a risk of their own free will: lacking command over means of production and access to sufficient bank loans, they are forced to sell their labour-capacity and get 'employed' (used) under penalty of starvation. That is immanent to the system. Being used along with wage increases and again wage decreases is one thing. However, it is also immanent to the system that the uppermost dark side of its cyclical movement gets concentrated within one particular echelon: those that are laid off to be unemployed.

Further, it is questionable – to say the least – as to how long the cyclical over-accumulation and destruction of capital is physically sustainable in terms of the climate and natural resources. The monetary-value dimension and the rate of profit merely measure what they do measure and thus what is subsumed under these measures.

Summary and conclusions

This chapter has set out the concrete manifestation of the earlier exposition in the cyclical movement of capital. We have seen how the production and accumulation of capital concretely takes the form of this cyclical movement. Its exposition synthesised many of the treads of the earlier exposition (Chapters 1–4) at this concrete level. However, as economic reality is inevitable always actual in some phase of this movement (one phase of the business cycle), its exposition is also a *concrete* synthesis of the earlier exposition.

Division 5D1 presented concretising connections from the earlier chapters to the current one, especially that of the macroeconomic 'internal profit' of enterprises and the 'rate of internal profit', each of which accounts for the external finance of enterprises and its (de)leverage effect. Investment being the main locomotive for the cyclical movement, the rate of internal profit as bounded by the rate of overcapacity were presented as the core macroeconomic determinants of investment decisions. The final section of this division presented a condensed macroeconomic sequence of production predicated on bank finance, of validation by expenditure, of distribution of surplus-value to external financiers and of the resulting rate of internal profit.

Division 5D2 set out how phase-wise series of these sequences cyclically develop from phases of expansion (5§8) into phases of crisis and contraction (5§9). In this cyclical movement, the capitalist systems' *immanent* expansive forces generate over-accumulation of capital (5§8).[31] In the crisis and recession,

31 This is an almost necessary process. 'Almost': in 5§9-b, at the end of the account for phase 3, it was indicated that grand cartels and monopolies (in fact a privately planned capitalist economy) might possibly outstrip this necessity.

this is violently cured by destruction of capital that prepares the conditions for a renewed expansion and again contraction (5§9). That is, inwardly bifurcated productive activity is cyclically destroyed. With it the applied natural resources are destroyed – those that are accounted for in the monetary-value dimension (MVD) as well as those that are not. Along with the destruction of productive activity and productive capacity, employment of labour is destroyed. The misery is condensed in those who are expelled into unemployment. Predominantly these, and their children, are sacrificed for the process of 'creation and destruction'. Even if during this Sisyphean process the *average* real income per head may increase, the heads are not equal and the unemployed in particular are 'hors catégorie' in this respect.

Chapter 5 in the perspective of Chapters 1–4

The MVD determined bifurcated production (Chapter 1) enforces accumulation of capital (Chapter 2) as conditioned by bank finance and next the (in part) ex post substitution for it (Chapter 3). Because the competitive dynamic interaction between enterprises is ultimately battled out in production, and because enterprises are out to optimally preserve their capital accumulated, the structure of production tends to be stratified according to the value-productivity of labour and rates of profit (4D1). This structure, therefore, is a main focus for the exposition of the cyclical movement of capital. As indicated, the rate of internal profit is the core determinant of investment decisions and the cyclical movement (as bounded by the rate of overcapacity). Like its twin of the 'rate of integral profit' (with surplus-value at its base, first posited in 1§13, cf. 5§1) – it is the concentration of the determinants that were developed so far (Part One), as it is in the everyday practice of enterprises. It is the reflection of the concrete internally bifurcated process of production of capital; that is, labour's production of capital through the production of surplus-value ($\Pi = mL^{\alpha} - wL$) for the owners of capital – the productive power of labour (α) being the prime mover (1§14). The point is indeed that practically abstract entities (i.e. abstractions in practice, 1§4, 1§4-b) – that is, monetary value and the rate of profit – determine the capitalist world as it concretely appears in our experience as including the economic high and low tides.

Whereas labour is the prime mover of the production of value and capital, capital itself is the prime mover of its cyclical course of accumulation and again the partial annihilation of this accumulation – labour is passively confronted with the ups and downs of employment and unemployment.

Banks are a top-level institutional determinant of the capitalist system (money as presented in 1§4 was concretised as bank-issued money in 2D4). Banks are the only originator of the external finance of enterprises (as well as of their internal finance). The bank-provided PVF is a continuous capitalist necessity (2D4, 3D2). To the extent that there are savings – the big financial nuisance for enterprises – there is a non-redeemed part of the PVF (the ΔRPVF equal to the ΔεK), which needs to be substituted for, in part, by other external financiers. The degree of saving so affects the required degree of external finance. This is reflected in the rate of interest. Its variation over the cycle determines whether external finance acts as a (de)leverage on the rate of internal profit.

On average, saving out of wages negatively affects the validation of surplus-value (3§10), and so the resulting profit (5§1). Because the savings ratio out of wages varies over the phases of the cycle, this affects the resulting profit phase-wise (negatively in the second half of the expansion and positively in the recession). Savings out of wages are – directly or indirectly – a last resort for the unemployed. From the point of view of labour, the cyclical movement of capital develops behind their backs. Producing capital for the owners of capital is immanent to the capitalist economy (1D5, 5§8). We have now seen that along with the recessive annihilation of their product, labourers are hit by the scourge of unemployment – all potentially, many actually. This is equally immanent to the capitalist economy (5§9). From the sweat of one's brow to redundancy and pauperism.

Appendix 5A. On the particular structural background of the 2008 crisis[32]

Introduction and synopsis

No cycle, including its crisis, is identical to the previous one. Chapter 5 indicated their general pattern. However, the 2008 crisis and its aftermath is no cyclical phenomenon. The 2008 financial-economic crisis in especially the EU and the USA results from a *structural* change that developed from the early 1980s onwards (see below). The *extended* recession period following it combines, first, the aftermath of this structural change, and second, the restructuring of capital that is characteristic of a 'normal' recession.

This structural change combines two main issues. First, a considerable shift in the macroeconomic distribution of income between capital-labour in favour of capital income (which 'normally' would have a negative effect on consumption expenditure). Second, a shift in the structure as well as the size of bank

32 This appendix is based on an article that appeared in *Science and Society* (Reuten 2011). The current version is more refined and also corrects some mistakes (for which I apologise).

credits, the latter involving vastly increased credits to consumers/wage earners. The latter so maintained or even increased their consumption (counteracting the wage effect).

Within this period of structural change (i.e. from the early 1980s to 2008), we had the 'normal' cyclical alternation, though with modifications regarding the destination of the PVF, and of the sources of savings and the RPVF.

Below this structural change is phrased in terms of a 'postponement of stagnation'. While the policies of banks played the core role in postponing the stagnation, the roots of the crisis are located at a deeper level. The implication is that the economic problems are much more difficult to overcome than the usual analyses suggest.

I hesitated over whether I should include this Appendix at this point or rather at the end of Chapter 10. The point is that the empirical figures below are – evidently – predicated on the existence of the state (even if rather implicitly) as well as on policies concerning, for example, unemployment payments (presented in Part Two). I finally decided to include it here, first, because the subject intimately relates to the finance of capital (Chapter 3) and especially the course of the cyclical movement of capital (Chapter 5), and second, because the structural changes referred to mainly developed independently of state policy – or rather because the state (in fact many states) mainly refrained from legislation on this matter (i.e. the structural causes including the role of banks).

5A-1 *The general constellation*

This appendix considers the era of so-called 'neoliberalism' (from about 1980) until the year 2010 and in comparison with the two decades prior to it (1960–80). *Graph 5.8* shows graphs for various variables as a share in the GDP of the USA and the EU-15 countries.[33]

Investment. Of the variables shown, investment is the best measure for the cyclical movement. However, because the graphs show its share in GDP, the cyclical volatility of investment is flattened out (as for all these variables).[34] From 1980 onwards the average investment share was roughly constant in the |EU-15 and declined in the USA.

33 The EU-15 are the 15 countries that made up the European Union until 2004 (statistically this is a useful group because much of the relevant data for these countries often go back to 1960).

34 GDP shares show changes of one variable relative to the change of another. One advantage of measurement in GDP-shares is that we need not correct for price inflation.

GRAPH 5.8 *Macroeconomic income and expenditure shares in GDP: EU-15 and USA 1960–2010*

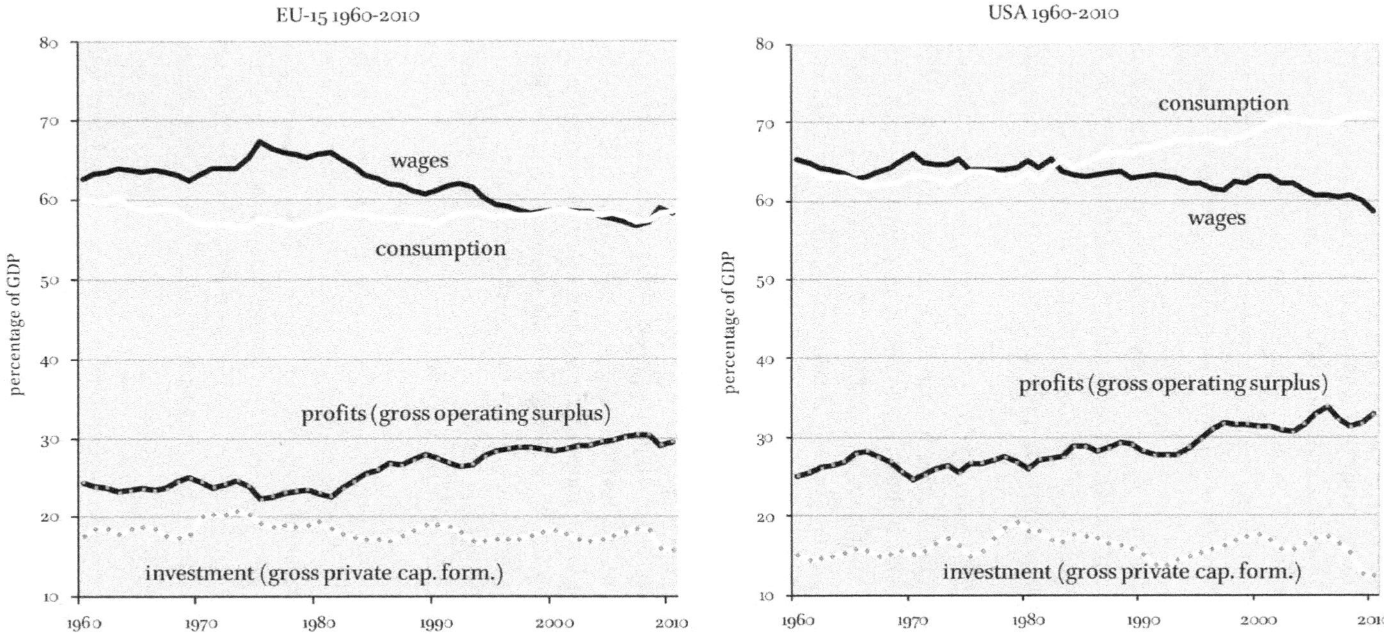

DATA SOURCE: EU, Economic and Financial Affairs, Economic databases an indicators, AMECO database, accessed 1 May 2011 http://ec.europa.eu/economy_finance/db_indicators/ameco/index_en.htm. The EU profit share 1960–90 is in ECU and excludes Luxembourg and East Germany; the EU profit share for 1960–69 excludes Belgium, Denmark, Ireland, Spain, France, Italy, Netherlands (data not available). Investment is gross investment of enterprises and the capital income is the gross operating surplus (including net interest). Capital income and wages have been adjusted for wages assigned to independent producers.

Wages. From about 1980 the wages share decreases considerably in the USA and vastly in the EU-15 countries. This structural change relates to developments in the *labour market* and the *production* aspects of income determination.[35] In brief, the enduring vast unemployment following on from the severe 1981–82 recession shifted the balance of power between enterprises and labour, such that wage increases could continuously be held below labour productivity increases.

Consumption. Remarkably the wages share decrease is not reflected in a consumption share decrease. The latter slightly increased in the EU-15, and vastly in the USA. For the reasons set out in 5§2 I take it that the Ck-share (from capital income) is roughly constant. The next section expands on the consumption by wage earners (Cw).

Surplus-value. The share of the operating surplus shown in the graphs is merely a very rough indicator for the share of surplus-value in GDP (this is due to the way in which the National Accounts are constructed – see 3§10-b; Chapter 3, App. 3C, §3C-1 under point 6, and in 8§6-e).

Recall (from 3§10 or 5§2) the following equations for the realisation of surplus-value.

$$\Pi \triangleleft = I + Ck + (Cw - W) \qquad (3.10)$$

$$\Pi \triangleleft = I + Ck - Sw \qquad (3.12)$$

- For the EU-15 we had a vast decrease in the W-share (from 1980 in total about 10 percent), with the Cw-share roughly constant, which accounts for a great deal of the rise in the Π-share.
- For the USA we had a more moderated W-share decrease together with a vastly increasing Cw-share (a gap moving to 10% in 2008). Together these equally account for a great deal of the rise in the Π-share.
- This is the broad picture – I abstract from the effects of changes in state expenditure and from those of the foreign sector.

5A-2 *From declining savings out of wages to 'colonisation of the future'*

Refer to Chapter 3 for *Circuits 3.9 and 3.18* that are here reproduced, with in the last circuit an extra column added at its outer right ('or colonising postponement'). Regarding *Circuit 3.9* recall that saving out of wages (as well as those out of capital income distributed) account for an increase in the debt of enterprises (the ΔRPVF).[36] To the extent that saving out of wages decreases (spending

35 There are four determinants for the distribution of income: (1) the labour market; (2) production; (3) price setting; (4) expenditure. (This fourfold determination has been forcefully stressed by Bellofiore – e.g. 1999, pp. 64–5.)

36 Recall also that *ex post* the initial finance by banks (the PVF), capital owners or wage

CIRCUIT 3.9 *(reduced). Pre-validating finance* (PVF) *by banks for wages: case of savings out of wages*

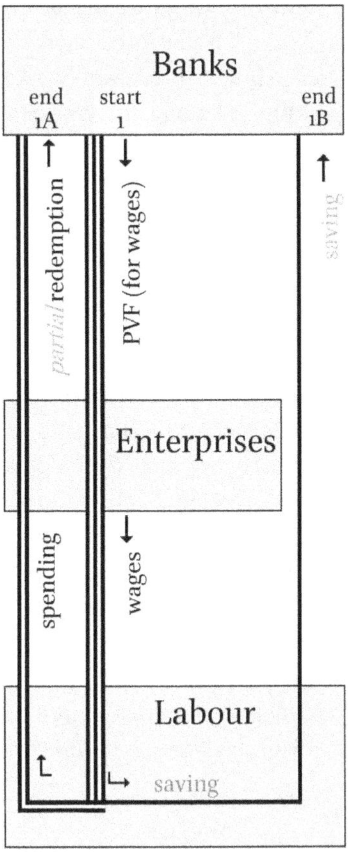

CIRCUIT 3.18 *Enterprises' saving on* PVF *for wages due to consumer credit: case of zero saving out of wages (outer right column added)*

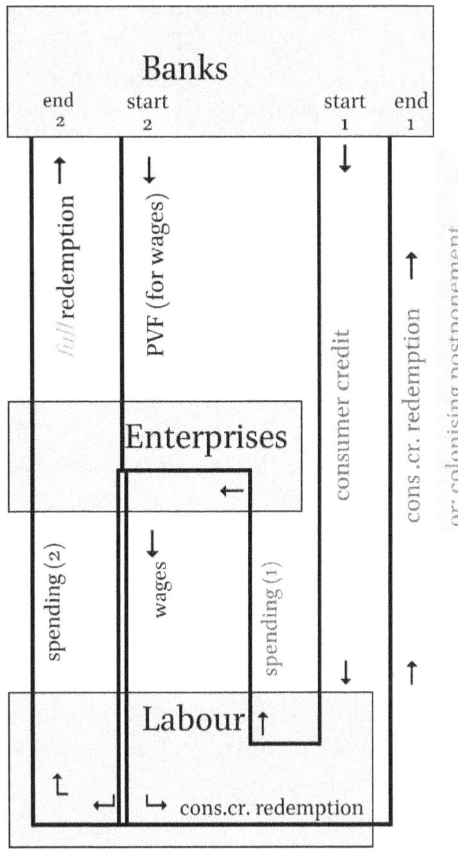

consequently increases), this source of the debt of enterprises decreases. Declining saving out of wages therefore affects the distribution of surplus-value

---

earners might substitute for the enterprises' stock of debt with banks, for example, by buying bonds from enterprises (either directly or indirectly, for instance, via pension funds). Pending such a substitution, the triadic credit-debt relationship between banks, enterprises and labour is normally favourable for banks in terms of interest margins.

between banks and production enterprises, in favour of the latter.[37] This is a partial effect (see the end of this section).

The further step is the movement of consumption *beyond* wages (see *Circuit 3.18*). This divergence was financed by direct consumption credit and by indirect consumption credit via mortgages – the latter in face of (expected) increasing collateral value. For the first time in history we saw consumption being financed on a massive scale by banks and next, in securitised form, substituted for by wealthy financiers, mostly via hedge funds. In this way, workers 'compensated' what they had lost on the wage front. All along, this prevented aggregate demand stagnation, even if this was not the motive.

However, loans require interest and must, at some point, be redeemed. Hence the banks – as well as other financiers via the banks – made claims on future wages of labourers. Lysandrou (2009) aptly called this the 'colonisation of the future'. Because this implies less future spending, the effect was a postponement of stagnation.

Note that *Circuit 3.18* shows the simple case of an immediate redemption of consumer credit out of wages. This is the case of the pure substitution of consumer credit for PVF. In actual fact this redemption was – and remains – postponed, resulting in a *stock of debt* owed to banks by workers: the colonisation of the future.

I indicated that declining saving out of wages affects the distribution of surplus-value between banks and production enterprises, in favour of the latter. This is a partial effect because the surplus-value distributed to capital owners vastly increased (compare the shares in GDP of investment and the operating surplus). Given the capital owners' stable consumption, this accounts for a structural savings increase, and hence an increased RPVF from their part (compare 3§6 and Circuit 3.13). The effect on the RPFV of the two saving categories might well balance out.

5A-3 *Conjunction of interests*

Due to a conjunction of interests, all the elements for this postponement of stagnation seemed to fit, that is, until about 2007.[38]

37 Where other financiers partially substituted for the stock of debt (i.e. an ex post substitution for the non-redeemed part of the PVF), it is of course these financiers that receive a smaller share of surplus-value.

38 I am not arguing that the grand process of financing the divergence between wages and consumption was a concerted action. I merely indicate that there was a temporary, contingent fit so that no interest group had a motive for behaving differently.

First, the direct beneficiaries were *enterprises*. After the initial and continuing wages moderation – that of wages growth lagging behind labour productivity increases – enterprises saw a decrease in the proportion of saving out of wages and hence, through higher spending, a decrease in the *stock of debt* owed to banks (*Circuit 3.9*). Presumably, though, this was roughly balanced out by increased saving from the part of capital owners. On top of this, once banks provided workers-consumers with consumer credit that was spent with enterprises, there was – for an amount equal to the amount of consumer credit – an *ex ante* substitution for PVF. Thus consumers took on a part of the credit that banks 'normally' would have provided to enterprises (*Circuit 3.18*).[39] On the other hand, due to the increased distribution of surplus-value to non-bank financiers, the PVF for those must increase. In sum, enterprises pay lower wages, without being punished in terms of lower consumption expenditures.

Second, supposing that the PVF effect as well as RPVF effects cancel out (first, above) *banks* won in interest from labour (their share in wages). Further, for those mortgages that banks resold via securitisation, they received commissions.[40]

Third, the banks' securitisation of the mortgages provided an outlet for *wealthy financiers* that cried out for portfolio-investment opportunities. Thus in the relatively short period from 2000 to 2007, the securities issuance of banks in the USA and Europe quadrupled from US$400 to nearly US$1600 billion.[41]

The behaviour of banks resulted in the postponement of stagnation and a vastly increased share of surplus-value (operating surplus) in GDP. However, along with the mortgage-driven housing market bubble that the postponement evoked, it also laid the minefield of risky assets. Once this process of postponement of stagnation was well under way, there were no sensible institutions to prevent its continuation: neither central banks nor other supervising authorities, nor governments. States had declared the 'independence' of central banks, while central banks – as intertwined with commercial banks via personal ties – declared 'self-regulation' for commercial banks. Commercial bankers may not have sat at the Basel assemblies, but they were important consultants for its

39 Note that if consumer credit is provided by the enterprises themselves – or specialised branches thereof – the enterprises would require a PVF for that credit. Hence this case ultimately reduces to a sub-case of that of Sheet 3.10.

40 In a report from the Basel Committee on Banking Supervision it is calculated that over the 15 years preceding the crisis (1993–2007), banks secured an (after tax) average rate of profit of 14.8% on their own capital. See 'An assessment of the long-term economic impact of stronger capital and liquidity requirements', BIS, August 2010, p. 48. http://www.financialstabilityboard.org/publications/r_100818a.pdf.

41 This is amplified upon by Lysandrou 2009.

weak 'framework' and weaker performance. (In this respect all this is not alien to the constellation of private 'Clearing Banks' as presented in Chapter 2 and onwards in Part One.)

5A-4 *Course of the 2008 crisis and its crisis-ridden aftermath*

The course of the crisis itself is not particularly difficult to follow, and it has been detailed at great length in the literature. Because most banks were weak on the assets side of their balance sheet, they had reason to distrust other banks in that respect. Once one or several main banks got into actual trouble – i.e. insurmountable debts to other banks – the distrust domino-ed around the world, affecting the USA and the EU most directly. Ultimately even the banking system as a system of money transfer (payments) nearly collapsed: banks did not want to receive payments from other distrusted banks as this puts the one bank in risky debt with the other. States ultimately had to step in, nationalising or semi-nationalising major banks, so as to at least preserve the payments system.

In sum, enterprises and banks had no choice but to accept reduced profits. The portfolio investors who had bought the securitised loans were the least affected group because banks had generally provided off-balance sheet guarantees. The biggest misery was imposed on the increasing numbers of the unemployed, with still-employed workers in a close second spot, facing wage cuts and ultimately lower living standards through cuts of state-provided transfers.

5A-5 *Problem of stagnation not resolved*

(Conclusions below apply to the state of affairs when I completed this book.)

The financial and economic crisis is the expression of the *reaction* to the substantial shifts in the distribution of income beginning around the early 1980s. However, the 2008 crisis and its aftermath have not resolved the problem of potential stagnation. On the contrary:

- *If banks do not face more effective regulation* than what has so far been proposed (when I completed this book), the banking system risks renewed collapse. A new round of massive state assistance, apart from being politically less likely, would once again encroach on the financial means of states. On the other hand, *if banks are going to be effectively regulated*, then the postponement of stagnation will come to an end: relative consumption will substantially decline as consumer credit stagnates and plays a lesser role in financing consumption.
- Besides this, we have the colonisation of the future labour incomes: income claims that will also result in a relative decline of consumption.

- With a relative decline in consumption, the investment of enterprises will also slacken.[42]

In sum, the economies of the USA and the EU are likely to enter a period of stagnation.

5A-6 *Modification of the 'normal' course of the business cycle*

As remarked in the introduction to this appendix, along with the period of structural change (i.e. from the early 1980s to 2008) we had the 'normal' cyclical alternation, though with modifications. These regard the destination of the PVF (shifting from enterprises towards labour), the sources of savings (shifting from wages towards capital owners) and the diverse effect of these on the ΔRPVF (even if the sum of the ΔRPVF may not have been much affected).

Regarding the outline of the cycle presented in Chapter 5, it should first of all be recalled that the outline refers to a constellation with the state bracketed. As we will see in Chapter 10 (10D1), this has a main effect on the cycle's *amplitude* to the extent that the state impacts as an (automatic) stabiliser. In face of unemployment benefits it also affects the degree of savings decrease by labour in the crisis and recession.

That said, refer to the stylised summary of *Figure 5.7*. Generally, the structural change referred to flattens the cyclical changes in Sw. On the other hand, because of the structurally increased distributed capital income, the Sk effects are reinforced. These savings differences also affect their impact on the RPVF. These do not seem to have major effects on the directions of the change in the core determinants of investment, that is, the rate of internal profit (ρ) and the rate of overcapacity (ø).

Given that the income of capital owners is rather functionless (whilst their consumption acts as an automatic stabiliser, their savings are not only non-necessary but also make the RPVF increasing), a restoring re-shift in the distribution of income could prevent stagnation.[43] However, in case of an effect-

---

42 An additional and vast 'deepening investment' might in principle keep up investments but there seems to be no market incentive for these to come about at just the right time, in large enough amounts. An obvious field for such investments might be that of non-conventional energy. A 'market' incentive for that might be a heavy taxation on conventional energy. The problem with such a solution is that this would *further* depress consumption in the following two decades – and hence non-deepening investment. Such a programme would have to be combined with an intensification of the measures discussed in the next section.

43 The first part of this sentence is reminiscent of one of Keynes's judgements: 'I see therefore, the rentier aspect of capitalism as a transitional phase which will disappear when it has done its work. … [T]he euthanasia of the rentier, the functionless investor [presum-

ive stagnation via consumption decrease, much depends on its pace. A fast decrease would tend to take the economy into depression. At a slow decrease, such that at least an on average poor rate of macroeconomic growth is maintained, cyclical movements would tend to be imposed on that poor rate of growth.

Appendix 5B. Stratified production and Marx's unfinished theory of the cycle

As indicated in Addendum 5§9-a, Marx presents his exposition of the cyclical movement of capital in *Capital I*, Part Seven and in *Capital III*, Part Three.[44] Although I have taken much inspiration from Marx's treatment of the matter, his exposition is quite different from the one presented in Chapter 5, mainly because he systematically introduces finance only after the cyclical movement – as specified below.

Marx's *first* treatment (*Capital I*) – as he is very much aware – is based purely on the production and accumulation of capital, without having systematically presented at that point: the (any) rate of profit; the expenditure side of the economy; banking and finance.

When Marx reaches his *second* treatment (*Capital III*) he has developed the rate of integral profit (surplus-value based), though he has still bracketed expenditure, banking and finance.[45] Thus in Marx's systematic he would have to return to the business cycle after his treatment of banking and finance (the second half of the current *Capital III*). Alas, however, he did not reach this in his lifetime. Therefore Marx's theory of the cyclical movement of capital is an incomplete one.

Even so, insight is to be gained from an abstract treatment such as Marx's that we have. I briefly expand on Marx's second treatment. (In comparison with Chapter 5 all effects of external finance (the RPVF and *iε*K) and of saving in relation to expenditures are thus bracketed.) Marx focuses on surplus-value, the rate of integral profit, accumulation and technical development.

---

ably he means financier or portfolio investor], will be nothing sudden, merely a gradual but prolonged continuance ... and will need no revolution' (Keynes 1936, p. 376).

44 Marx 1976 [1867] and 1981 [1894].

45 This is so in his last manuscript on the matter. Presumably he planned to include the expenditures side that he had developed largely after that manuscript in his manuscript for the last part of Volume II of *Capital*.

Marx's view on technical development is that this of a K/wL rising type. Then, assuming that the rate of surplus-value (Π/wL) is more or less constant in the upturn, he has for the upturn:

$$\omega = \frac{\Pi}{K} = \frac{\Pi/wL}{K/wL} \quad \frac{\text{(roughly constant in upturn)}}{\text{(rising in upturn)}}$$

As a result the rate of integral profit (ω) declines in the upturn. Then, what I called 'restructuring of capital' in the downturn (destruction and devaluation of capital) restores the rate of profit, whence – as Marx expresses it – 'we go round the whole circle once again', a vicious circle (*'Zirkel vicieux'*).[46] This rate of profit curing effect of the recession reveals Marx's tremendously impressive insight of the matter (one that also impressed Schumpeter, as indicated in 5§9-a).[47]

Some critics of Marx have questioned this presentation on the grounds that micro foundations are lacking for it. In their view, capitalists would not generally introduce rate of profit decreasing techniques of production.[48] I have indicated (Reuten 1991) that from the perspective of a stratified structure of production, it is quite feasible that new techniques have a rate of profit decreasing effect for a sector or the economy at large.[49] I should now add that this is especially the case in a constellation of price competition. (Compare 4D2 where the price-leader introduces a new technique – perhaps a K/wL rising one – whence for the totality of the stratification the rate of profit declines.) From this perspective the critic alluded to can be refuted.

However, further scrutiny of Marx's theory indicates that it is quite compatible with a more general theory of over-accumulation of capital, one of either a K/wL increasing or a K/wL decreasing type of technical change (as I remarked in my 1991 paper). This more general theory has been presented in Chapter 5, including the main complexities of finance and expenditures (via savings), which affect the distinct movement of the various phases of the cycle.

---

46 Marx 1993 [ms. 1864–65], p. 329; cf. the somewhat deviating formulations for *'Zirkel vicieux'* in Marx 1964 [1894 ed. Engels], p. 265 and 1981 [1894 ed. Engels, English translation], p. 364.

47 In studying the cycle Marx gradually developed this view. Along with it he put increasing emphasis on the rate of profit restoring character of the recession. See Reuten and Thomas 2011, and Thomas and Reuten 2013. Note also that in Engels's edition of Marx's manuscript for *Capital III*, there are significant changes (by Engels) that deemphasise the restorative role of the recession (Reuten 2004c; this article also provides a commented general outline of the three chapters constituting Marx's theory of the cycle in *Capital III*).

48 See the references in Reuten 1991.

49 Cf. Reuten and Williams 1989, Chapter 4.

List of figures chapter 5

PART 2

The capitalist state

Introduction to part two: the capitalist state

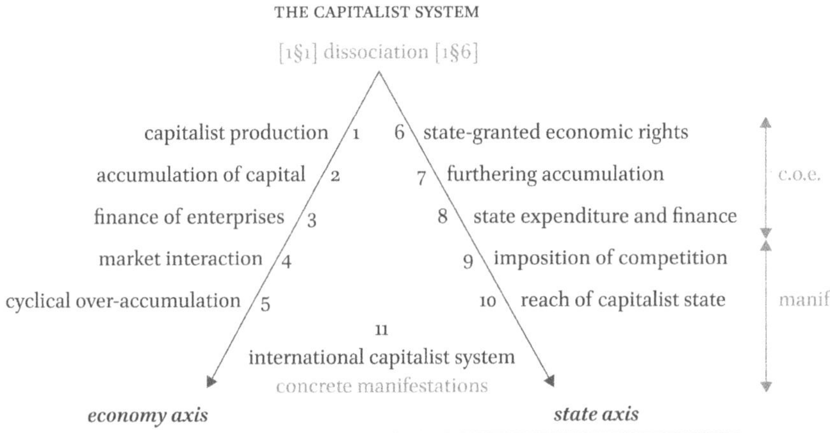

Note: 'c.o.e.' abbreviates conditions of existence and 'manif.' concrete manifestations.

Part Two of this book presents the state and economic policy (Chapters 6–10) vis-à-vis the capitalist economy (Chapters 1–5). Part One sought to ground the capitalist economy 'within itself'. In Part Two, we will see why and how these grounds are insufficient. Early on in Chapter 6 it is shown that the capitalist economy's existence necessarily requires the capitalist state (6D2 will clarify why the term 'capitalist' state is used at all). The exposition will then be confronted with a twofold task. It must show how the state's doing and not doing can provide sufficient grounds for the economy's existence. However, along with it, the conditions for the existence of the state itself must be presented. Recall from the General Introduction the following schematic outline.

The starting point of Chapter 6 is similar to that of Chapter 1: the dissociated bifurcation between households and privately owned enterprises. Inasmuch as Chapters 1–3 next sought its economy-immanent conditions of existence, Chapters 6–8 will seek sufficient conditions of existence for the economy as well as for the state itself. A similar analogy applies to the last two chapters of this Part: Chapters 9–10 will present the concrete manifestations of the state vis-à-vis the economy.

The order of the book is evidently as it is: from Chapters 1–11. This is in line with one object of the book – as indicated in the General Introduction – which is that Part One endeavours to show to what extent the capitalist economy might be thought to conceivably stand on itself. In line with this, the systematic exposition runs from Chapters 1–5 and again Chapters 6–10.

 DOI:10.1163/9789004392809_008

However, the book also sets out a complementary systematic, which runs zigzag from Chapter 1 to the juxtaposed 6, and from Chapter 2 to the juxtaposed 7, and so forth. In principle the book might be read in that order. This last systematic mainly determines the dividing lines between the chapters of Part Two.

As before, the exposition is a systematic one, not a historical one. Therefore the abstract existence of the capitalist state is presumed. Systematically this presumption refers indeed to an abstract existence, that is, as long as its conditions of existence have not yet been presented.

Finally, when I use the term 'state' this includes, when relevant, the central state of a federation or of a union of states.

CHAPTER 6

State-granted capitalist economic rights

The capitalist state in general

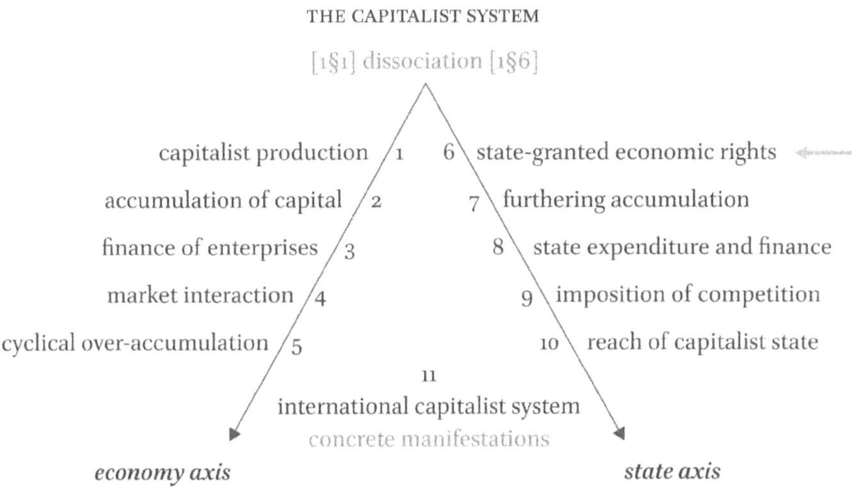

Contents

Introduction

The exposition started in Chapter 1 with the concept of 'dissociated bifurcation of households and privately owned units of productions'. The rest of that chapter – and Chapters 2–3 – presented the capitalist way of 'sublating' the outward bifurcation (that is, stages of partially resolving the bifurcation without the bifurcation itself being undone – 1§1, heading 4). The outcome – Chapters 1 through 5 – is a constellation that often appears problematical (presumably also from the point of view of enterprises and owners of financial titles), though one that apparently may have seemed a systematic reproducible whole.

However, it will be shown in Division 2 in general terms (see its introduction below) – and more concretely throughout the chapters to come – that the capitalist economy cannot exist without the capitalist state. Thus the *grounding* of the starting point so far is an insufficient one, whence the exposition must be extended – throughout Part One extension in case of such insufficiency has always been the dialectical procedure.

As the starting point of the total exposition (Parts One and Two) is *the capitalist economy* and its dissociated bifurcation, the systematic exposition of the capitalist state starts in Division 1 again with the capitalist economy's bifurcation. This is all the more opportune, because in hindsight, as we will see, key 'insufficiencies' that cannot be resolved within the capitalist economy are already prevalent at the very early stages of the capitalist way of sublating the bifurcation.

For these systematic reasons the starting points of 1D1 and 6D1 coincide, although the presentation in Division 1 of the current chapter will be an abbreviated one.

Division 2 introduces the state into the exposition. In Part One it was all along implicit that the actors (enterprises and households) have the *freedom* to act as outlined. Implicitly they *claimed to be entitled* to act as outlined and that these claims (for example, claims to entitlement of property) are respected by the other actors. Division 2 sets out that the institutions of the capitalist economy by themselves cannot guarantee the actualisation of such claims, whence an extraordinary institution, the state, is required to grant these claims in the form of *rights*.

Division 3 presents a first set of major abstract-general conditions of existence of the state, especially regarding the form of the state's operation. The first one of these is that the state must gain legitimation for its (non-)actions. Further conditions ground this first one.

Division 4 presents a categorisation of the required capitalist economic rights: legal rights to property and to the employment of labour. At the level

SCHEME 6.1 *Systematic of state-granted capitalist economic rights – the capitalist state in general (outline Chapter 6)*

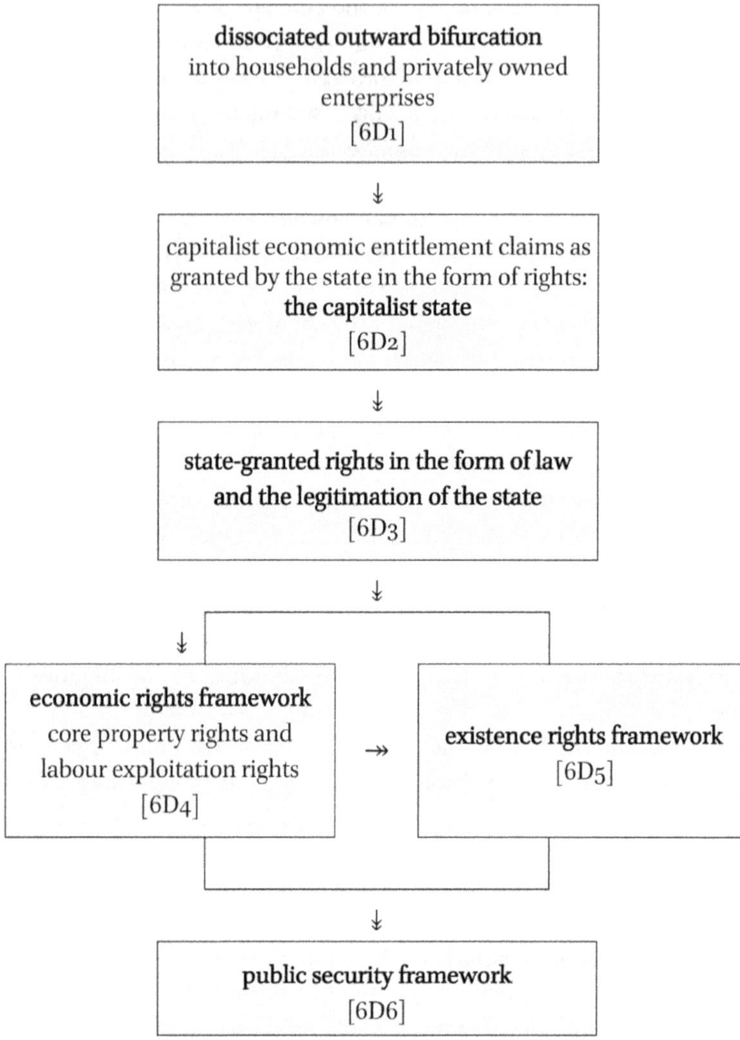

Legend

↡ grounded in (conditioned by) downward moment

↠ grounded in juxtaposed moment

of the state these constitute the primary condition of existence for the exposition in Chapter 1.

As economic rights are futile without legal rights to existence, Division 5 presents a categorisation of the latter.

Granted legal rights (6D3) are empty without their upholding. The final Division 6 presents the upholding of these rights in 'public security', which includes, among others, the police and public prosecution.

It should be kept in mind that – in line with the systematic-dialectical method as outlined in the General Introduction – this chapter is about actual right and law only to the extent that rights are necessary (an absolute condition) for the continued existence of a capitalist economy – now the capitalist system (including the state). On top of these, there are many rights that are morally or culturally important, but that are nevertheless *contingent* from the point of view of the reproduction of the capitalist economy. Throughout this book, as indicated, such contingencies are ignored.

Scheme 6.1 outlines the systematic of the moments presented in this chapter.

Division 1. Dissociation – outward bifurcation into households and privately owned enterprises

As the starting point of the total exposition (capitalist economy and state) is the capitalist economy, the systematic exposition of the capitalist state starts with the capitalist economy's dissociated outward bifurcation (here briefly summarised). Thus this division is systematically analogous to 1D1. See also the Chapter Introduction.

6§1 *Dissociated outward bifurcation into households and privately owned enterprises*

The capitalist economy (and the capitalist system generally) is characterised by the dissociated outward bifurcation between households and privately owned enterprises, the latter being private owners of *appropriated earth* and of *means of production*. Generally, enterprises are not owned by the labourers that carry out the production (see 1§1-e, or the Glossary, for the term 'general'). Hence capitalist society is characterised by an extended outward bifurcation into, on the one hand, the *owners of private enterprises*, and, on the other, the – generally non-overlapping – *labourers carrying out the production*. Along with these private property relations, the enterprise appropriates the product produced by labour – in whatever way, and for what, and to what extent, labour receives a 'compensation' for its production.

Apparently this constellation is dissociative, even if we know that in reality the bifurcated poles are bridged. The object of the exposition is to comprehend the range of this apparent dissociation, to comprehend the extent of its actual resolution, and to set out the necessary *conditions of existence* (or grounds) of the starting point above.

6§1-a Explication. The twofold grounding of the starting point

Because the starting point of the total exposition (capitalist economy and state) is the capitalist economy, the grounding of the starting point (1D1) is systematically a twofold one – alluded to in the Introduction. *Scheme 6.2* visualises this twofoldness.

SCHEME 6.2 *The twofold grounding of the starting point*

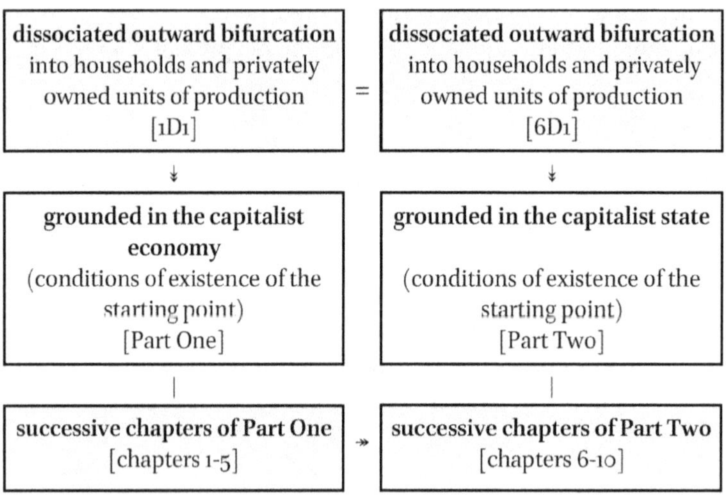

Legend
= similar
↡ grounding in downward moments
↠ grounding in juxtaposed moments

Division 2. Capitalist economic entitlement claims as granted by the state in the form of rights: the capitalist state

In this book's systematic- rather than historical-dialectical exposition, the *existence* of the state is presumed (General Introduction, C§3). Pending the exposition, this is methodologically yet an abstract existence. This division sets out why and when the state in a capitalist system is to be characterised as a 'capitalist state'.

6§2 *Capitalist economic entitlement claims*

In the exposition of the capitalist economy, it was *implicit* that dissociation and its grounding requires the private enterprises and the households to have the *freedom* to act as set out in Chapter 1 and later chapters. Freedom, however, is utterly abstract. These freedoms are therefore posited as specific *claims of being entitled* to act as set out. The core of these are:

- first, claims of entitlement to private property in the earth;
- second, claims of entitlement to private property in means of production other than for production by the claimant;
- third, claims of entitlement to employ labour as combined with the appropriation of the surplus-value produced by that labour.

Together I call these in brief the 'capitalist core economic entitlement claims' (concretised in 6D4).

6§2-a Explication. Freedom and compulsion

The private enterprises and the households require the *freedom* to act as set out in Part One. However, the freedoms that are necessary for capitalism also result in a structure of compulsion. We have seen that the capitalist economy is structurally determined by the monetary-value dimension and the forces deriving from it.

Predicated on the dissociative bifurcation (1D1), economic actors are enforced to trade in order to survive (consumer goods, inputs, outputs).

To the extent that workers own no means of production, they are forced to sell their labour-capacity to any enterprise (1§6). Hence their freedom is restricted to selling it to company *i* or *j* – they are materially not free to sell at all, because they have no alternative. To the extent that workers command restricted monetary reserves, they are, moreover, forced to sell their labour-capacity immediately (affecting their bargaining position). Further, depending on the growth patterns (2D2) or the cyclical state of the economy (5D2), the freedom to sell labour-capacity may even be void altogether (unemployment).

Finally, a large number of restrictions and forces operate on any enterprise. For example, their position in the stratification of enterprises (4§4) may enforce them to acquire extra finance capital; or, the cyclical restructuring of capital may mean that enterprises lose property and/or are enforced to merge or be taken over (5§9).

It follows that whereas the existence of the capitalist economy requires economic actors to have economic freedoms, the same capitalist economy negates freedom in force, compulsion and restriction. There is no general freedom, but rather an asymmetric freedom, or, conversely, asymmetric compulsion.

It may be argued that any association into which persons enter at least constrains freedom (for some marriage might be an example). Nevertheless, if one engages freely and consciously in association, its constraints are not compulsive. However, the institutions of the capitalist economy are not based on a freely willed social contract – even when perhaps a majority would consent to these institutions.

6§2-b Amplification. Interconnection of the three claims to entitlement

Of the three core claims set out in 6§2, claim 3 is the key one. The ownership of means of production (claim 2) is a precondition for any production; however, claim 3 (appropriation of the surplus-value produced by the labour *employed*) requires not merely some ownership in means of production, but rather such ownership corresponding to the amount of labour employed.[1] (Self-employed workers or worker cooperatives would not require this extra claim, because they have no employees, and hence require no such means of production.)

Of the first two claims, the first is the most far-reaching one. Much of the earth functions as means of production (hence this is, more specifically, included under claim 2). Given that the earth cannot be expanded (like production can be expanded) it is in fact a monopoly claim for the category of owners of land and other natural resources. (This would not be so if, for example, land were rented from the collective world population in some institutionalised form.)[2]

6§3 *The claim of entitlement to existence*

Economic entitlement claims (6§2) are futile without a claim of entitlement to existence. Thus the former are necessarily grounded in the latter. (When actors are not free from violence regarding their person, the exercise of their economic claims is barren.)

1 Adam Smith writes: 'The value which the workmen add to the materials, therefore, resolves itself in this case into two parts, of which the one pays their wages, the other the profits of their employer (…). In this state of things, the whole produce of labour does not always belong to the labourer. He must in most cases share it with the owner of the stock which employs him' (Smith 1776, Book I, Ch. 6, paragraph 5).

2 During feudal times in much of Europe, as well as in many other cultures, there was at least the idea that land is a God-derived collective property (governed by stewards). See, for example, Locke 1689, Second Treatise, Chapter V.

6§4 *The capitalist state: capitalist economic entitlement claims in the form of granted rights*

The claims to the capitalist core economic entitlements and to existence entitlement are necessary to the capitalist economy (6§2, 6§3). However, within the economy there is no institution guaranteeing these claimed entitlements. Within the economy, dominated by the monetary-value dimension, commodification and the criterion of the rate of integral profit (1§13), these claims can be no more than moral strivings – perhaps conflicting ones – in face of the structure and forces of that economy (Part One). So we have a fundamental continuity impediment: the actualisation of these claimed entitlements is necessary and impossible within the economy.[3] Hence the capitalist economy cannot stand on its own.

The state is an institutional constellation granting (constructing) these claims in the form of *rights*. It demarcates these granted rights and it upholds them. In doing so, the state grounds the *actual mode of existence* of the capitalist economy.

To the extent that the state actualises particularly the capitalist economic entitlement claims (listed in 6§2) as granted rights, the state is identified as *the capitalist state.*

6§4-a Explication. The state, agents of the state and moral norms of the latter

Throughout Part Two, I use the term state, or capitalist state, denoting the state as institution. As much as possible I avoid notions of 'agents of the state', or 'state actors'. This implies that the reference is mainly to the state in its *effect* as laid down in legislation and other regulation, rather than to processes leading to that effect, including the motives of agents of the state. Therefore I also avoid using the term 'government', which often has a connotation of a group of people staffing the state. Emphasising the state as institution in reference to its effects also implies that I am not concerned with the moral or ethical norms of agents of the state. I am not denying that state officials might be intrinsically motivated by these norms. I am also not denying that they might not.[4]

---

3 See Addendum 1§1 j on the term 'continuity impediment' versus 'contradiction'

4 The same applies for perhaps self centred economic drives. Thus the exposition is the reverse of much of the 'public choice' approaches of the state.

6§4-b Explication. State and nation: the systematic order of the exposition

'The state' is usually associated with a national context. Nationality and geography will be introduced only in Part Three (Chapter 11). In terms of nationality and geography, the current level of the exposition is to be associated with one capitalist country operating in isolation, or alternatively with world universality without national borders.

6§4-c Explication. Rights presented in this chapter

The rights presented in this chapter are restricted to rights that are necessary for the existence of the capitalist economy. Many rights that have been enacted, for example, those of free speech or assembly, are contingent to the existence of the capitalist economy (which does not qualify these as 'unimportant').

6§4-d Addendum. 'Society' vis-à-vis the capitalist economy

In this book the term 'society' is used only in 1D0 (sociation), in 1D1 (dissociation) and in the current division. Quite apart from the introduction of the state in the current chapter and its further concretisation in the following chapters, I thus far presented a reduced account of capitalist *society* – that is, the capitalist economy (Chapters 1–5). The point is that I do not intend to present concrete society in its entirety. The aim is to present the necessary conditions of existence of the capitalist *economy*; indeed the state is a major condition for it.

Gender, racial and sexual diversity, the arts, religion, sports and so on, all comprise key elements of social life hitherto. However, in terms of the existence of the capitalist economy, these social elements are contingent. However, this again does not imply that these are not *affected* by the monetary-value dimension. We know all too well that they are.

On the other hand, such social elements may well *assist or support* the reproduction of the capitalist system. (Marx, for example, once called religion the opium of the people. Later, Max Weber argued that Protestantism, especially Calvinism, propelled the capitalist ethos.) Many cultural and political constellations are compatible with capitalism – e.g. liberalism, conservatism, religious fundamentalism, corporatism or fascism. All this is not the object of the current investigation.

6§4-e Addendum. The state: systematic exposition and history

As always, considerations of *systematic* order are different from considerations of historical order.

Regarding history Hirsch (2005) argues that 'the state' emerges with the emergence of capitalism, and that it is wrong to 'naturalise' the state by extending its history. Historically feudal domains were the unity of a governing entity and an entity including exploitative social-economic power (only in hindsight might these perhaps be discerned as an entity that includes an 'economy'). Historically the capitalist economy *bifurcated away from* the feudal domain (in my terminology), and became a power in itself – initially in opposition to the feudal domain. The feudality as a governing entity then collaborated with the capitalists because it had to. Historically the feudal entity, including (in hindsight) a governing branch, was gradually transformed into a capitalist state – as mediated by the mercantile state (see the qualifications by Hirsch 2005).

By implication it is hard to imagine how a capitalist economy could ever have emerged without a feudal polity *de facto* sustaining that emerging economy. The 'thought experiments' about the 'state of nature' by British classical political philosophy from Hobbes (1651) to Smith (1776) concluded that 'civil society' has no existence without the state – that is, unless we allow for a 'war of all against all', as Hobbes phrased it. Smith (1776) writes: 'Where there is no property ... civil government is not so necessary.' And: 'Civil government, so far as it is instituted for the security of property, is in reality instituted for the defence of the rich against the poor, or of those who have some property against those who have none at all.'[5]

The current systematic exposition bypasses the collaboration, etc. and presents a, so to speak, 'fresh' state (devoid of feudal remnants and so on). The existing state is exposed insofar as it is necessary for the capitalist economy.

Division 3. Granted rights in the form of law and the legitimation of the state

In this division the state is grounded in five conditions of existence regarding the form of the state's operation. These are listed in *Scheme 6.3*. The reader should be warned that at this point (this division) this is a grounding in fairly abstract-general terms. The key concept of 'legitimation' of the state, will only gradually gain content in the current and in the next chapter.

---

5 *Wealth of Nations*, Book V, Ch. I, paras 45 and 55.

SCHEME 6.3 *The initial conditions of existence of the state: the form of its operation*

The State
[6§4]
↓
legitimation in compliance
[6§5]
↓
(action posited in terms of)
the putative general interest
[6§6]
↓
putative impartiality
(versus separation-in-unity)
[6§7]
↓
the positing of granted rights in the form of law
[6§8]
↓
arbitration and sanctioning
[6§9]

6§5 *Legitimation in compliance*

The capitalist state as an institutional constellation positing particular entitlement claims in the form of granted rights (6§4). The first condition of existence of the state is that it is *legitimated* in the compliance of a vast majority of the actors. The state must continuously *seek* this legitimation – outlined in general terms in the remainder of this division.

6§5-a Explication. Seeking legitimation: general theoretical position regarding the capitalist state

In very broad terms the exposition in this chapter, and that of legitimation in particular, is not a *normative* one (a main strand being 'social contract theory') but rather a *descriptive* one (on the distinction see Peter 2016, section 1).

This amplification briefly outlines the general theoretical position that underlies the exposition in this chapter in contrast with 'social contract theory' from which I distance myself. Much of political philosophy and political theory is in some way based on a 'social contract theory'. The early formulation goes back to Hobbes, Locke and Rousseau, in works published between 1651 and 1762.[6] In brief: Given opposing interests and continuous conflicts among the people, the institution of the state (in feudal times a 'sovereign') is conceived of as the result of a 'social contract' between 'the' people. In the social contract view they 'will' and submit to the authority of the state (or a sovereign) in order to mitigate or overcome conflict.

The position in this chapter (and ones that follow) is, first of all, that there cannot be a 'pre-state' capitalist constellation from which such a contract and 'general willed' state could be seen to emerge. The feudal economy and the feudal governing entity *gradually* transformed into a capitalist economy and state (see 6§4-e). However, amid this process, and continually within full-fledged capitalism (that is, including capitalist production), it is the *state* that has *to seek* its legitimation (and hence the legitimation of the capitalist system). Thus this position is rather the reverse of a social contract theory. The state's seeking legitimation will be made explicit, albeit still in abstract-general terms, in the following sections. It will be further expanded in Chapter 7.

6§5-b Amplification. Legitimation and authoritarian regimes

The upshot of 6§5 is that compliance, at least, is necessary. At this level, however, compliance is abstract-general, thus any particularisation is premature – that is, there may be various ways to gain compliance. The abstract-general level of the exposition demands refraining from linking legitimation and compliance to a contemporary constellation of the reader's preference – perhaps some form of political democracy. As history has shown, the capitalist system is compatible with democracy (including abuses in the shape of fraudulent elections and/or presidents elected by only a minority of the actual voters) as much as with corporatism and fascism. In all cases the point is merely that, for example, the majority or minority presidency or the fascist leader has *to gain the compliance of the majority of the people*. Even a non-elected dictator has to seek (and obtain) the compliance of the majority of actors. That is, ultimately: in periods of transition, compliance may be weak.

6§6 *The state and the putative general interest*

The state's legitimation in the compliance of the actors (6§5) is ultimately grounded in the gaining of that compliance by positing its actions in terms of the putative *general interest*.[7] At this point of exposition these actions regard the positing of certain claims in the form of granted rights (6§4). 'In the name

6 For an overview, see Friend (n.d.) [accessed 2016].

7 The adjective 'putative' in the phrase 'putative general interest' is to be taken to mean that

of' the general interest, the state seeks legitimation to uphold (its definition of) these granted rights. Conversely it posits the rights as being in the general interest. (That is, of what it conceives as the general interest.) This framing of these rights being in the general interest is particularly precarious when granted rights conflict, so that the state must prioritise the one right over the other. Conflicts of interest are again resolved in terms of the putative general interest.

Whereas 'general interest' is inherently abstract, it is *in actual practice*, and recurrently so, offered by the state as the legitimising basis for its (non-)actions. Nevertheless, by any new (non-)action the state further concretises its implicit concept of the general interest, which is again defended in reference to the general interest, and so on.

Even if and when the state's reference to the general interest is abstract, this general interest is ultimately the *de facto* continual existence of the capitalist system (ultimately the granting and upholding of the three core economic entitlement claims in the form of granted rights – 6§2 and 6§4). This 'de facto' is falsifiable, and it would be falsified if the state no longer granted these claims as rights.

6§6-a Explication. Legitimation and implicit actions of the state

So far, the actions of the state merely regard the positing of certain claims (6§2–§6§3) in the form of granted rights. Other actions of the state are still implicit. In the remainder of this chapter and in the next, these actions will be further extended. Legitimation in terms of the putative general interest also applies to these extended actions, albeit implicitly.

6§6-b Explication. The undefined general interest

In the context of legislation (properly introduced in 6§8), the state's reference to the general interest is circumventing and circular. This is what it is. No definition of it is provided by the state (even if we can infer that implicitly it is ultimately defined by the continual existence of the capitalist system). The state may posit such a reference in general preambles. However, when it comes to the defence of laws or law proposals in actual practice, such reference is also the last straw when there are insufficient arguments for particular legislation.[8]

---

the state proposes its actions to be in what the state itself considers to be the general interest. In this way the state in fact *defines* its actions to be in the general interest. Other actors may have different views about what the general interest would be.

8 This has also been my own experience when I was a member of the senate in the parliament of the Netherlands (2007–15). I can point to numerous legislative debates where 'the general interest' was indeed presented as a last straw.

6§7 *The state's self-imposition as impartial institution; versus the state as constituting vis-à-vis the capitalist economy a 'separation-in-unity' within the capitalist system*

The state's recurrent reference to the 'general interest' for its seeking of legitimation (6§6) requires that it (putatively) positions itself *above and outside* the opposing particular economic interests. Thus a condition of existence of the legitimation in terms of the general interest is that the state imposes itself (putatively) as an *impartial extraordinary social institution*, unlike all other social institutions.[9]

In this sense the state is an institution separate from the economy. However, given that the state *de facto* grants the core economic claims in the form of rights (6§6), it constitutes vis-à-vis the capitalist economy a ***separation-in-unity*** within the capitalist system.

Possible and potential conflicts between entitlement claims, as well as between rights granted by the state, are not overcome by this separation-in-unity; rather, such conflicts are *settled* by the state as extraordinary social institution, in some mode of (perhaps still conflicting) existence.[10]

6§7-a Explication. The state's 'separation-in-unity' within the capitalist system: the *de facto* objective of the state

The term 'separation-in-unity' (*s-i-u*) was first introduced in 2§11 in the context of the separation between enterprises and banks, which was posited as an *s-i-u*. The term was expanded on in 2§11-a (see alternatively the Glossary). Like an outward bifurcation, an *s-i-u* is a main institutional separation. The key difference is that, in contradistinction to an outward bifurcation, the institutions, or bodies, or component parts, of an *s-i-u* are '(*ultimately*) *each driven by the same objective, which articulates their unity*'.

In the context of the main text of 6§7 the previous sentence requires specification. The state is considered vis-à-vis the capitalist economy, the latter being institutionally bifurcated (recall that this is the meaning of 'outward' bifurcation). The poles of that bifurcation are driven by different objectives. Together these constitute the *capitalist economy as entity*, which is not a unity

9 'Impartial' is always a tricky concept as it is inevitably based on impartiality premises. If the continual existence of the capitalist system is the premise, then the state may indeed posit itself as impartial.

10 Note that the exposition is still at the level of abstract-generality. At more concrete levels of the exposition, the state's positioning of itself above the opposing interests may require that it bounces back to the economy hyper-conflicting issues, either directly or in the form of a relegation to bodies such as a Central Bank or a Competition Authority (cf. Chapters 7 and 9).

but rather a dissociated bifurcated entity. The main text (6§7) posited: 'given that the state *de facto* grants the core economic claims in the form of rights (6§6) it constitutes vis-à-vis the capitalist economy a *separation-in-unity* within the capitalist system'. Ultimately, given the state-granted rights, the *de facto* objective of the state is the *reproduction* of the capitalist system – whence it (pro temps the granting of those rights) is identified as the *capitalist* state (6§4). In that sense it constitutes a separation-in-unity within the capitalist system.

A recurrent theme in this chapter and ones to follow is that the state has to seek legitimation for this position. In seeking this legitimation – as we will see in especially Chapter 7 – the state is required to take account of several conflicting interests, including those that are articulated by the different objectives of the bifurcated poles referred to above.

In reference to explication 6§4-a (on state agents, or state actors and their motivations) it should be emphasised that the state as entity has no 'subjective' objectives. Objectives of the state are identified by the *effects* of the operation of the state as laid down in legislation and other regulation, and by the state's upholding of that legislation.

6§8 *The positing of granted rights in the form of law – taking position: legal rights as political rights*

The positing of the state's actions in terms of the general interest (6§6) and its separation-in-unity (6§7) is grounded in the positing of granted rights in *the form of law*. Thus the state posits rights granted in the form of *legal rights*. The form of law explicitly posits that these rights apply equally to all. Herewith the state (putatively) establishes its extraordinary impartial status.

The positing of the state's actions (so far regarding these granted rights) in the form of law requires a precise and often complicated demarcation and specification of these, also in face of the practicable upholding of these. This implies that the state must take a stance on the specific content of rights. Especially when rights are actually or potentially in conflict (6§7), this stance of the state articulates its position as a political position – even if framed in terms of the general interest. In this way legal rights appear as political rights.

6§8-a Explication. Stages of the exposition and the 'construction' of rights

Note the three stages of the exposition: from (1) entitlements claimed (6§2–6§3); via (2) these claims as posited in the form granted rights (6§4); to (3) these granted rights in the form of law (6§8). As posited in the last form these are further concretised in 6D4–6D6.

Granted rights in the form of law may also be called 'legal rules that construct the entitlement'. Morris (1993, p. 823) remarks: 'Entitlements must be constructed so that they do more than simply "give legal force" to certain interests. They must also specify the extent and type of legal force that a given interest has in any particular context and in relation to any other particular entitlement.'

6§8-b Explication. Codified and non-codified law
The state may define right by way of codified law or other law-creating acts, such as judgments or verdicts. In what follows my implicit reference will be the 'code law systems'. However, the exposition equally applies to 'common law systems' even though this might often require some reformulation.

6§8-c Amplification. 'Natural rights' versus state-granted rights
In political philosophy and political theory, there is a longstanding tradition of conceiving rights as 'natural rights' or at least as rights that exist independently of the state (e.g. Gavison 2003). I take distance from this tradition because there is no criterion to demarcate one 'pre-state right' from another.[11] In 6§2–6§3, therefore, I used the term entitlement *claims*. With respect to 'property' the former position (rights existing independently of the state) has been called 'full liberal ownership', and the latter position (rights are granted by the state) 'bundle theory' (see the overview by Breakey n.d.; see also Azevedo 2010). In the latter tradition, authors often use the term 'rule' instead of right. (See, for example, Morris 1993; the same applies for Calabresi and Melamed on whose work she builds.)

6§9 *Arbitration and sanctioning*

The state posits granted rights in the form of law (6§8). However, in order for legal rights not to be empty, in the sense that actors could neglect the law, the state must maintain these legal rights. Thus the grounding of legal right requires the state to be the *arbiter* and *sanctioner* of deviation from the law.

(At this point of the exposition, the public prosecution of such deviation is implicit – it is amplified in 6§18. At this point of the exposition, arbitration is part of the state's administrative body. In 7D6 the judiciary is presented as a separate body of the state.)

11 In Reuten and Williams 1989, we took, in my current view, insufficient distance from this tradition, by merely distinguishing between right and legal right.

Division 4. The capitalist economic rights framework

In this division, and all following ones in the book, 'framework' is a shorthand for 'legislative framework'. This division presents a brief categorisation of necessary legal rights to property and to the employment of labour. At the level of the state, these constitute the primary condition of existence for the exposition in Chapter 1. Together these are called the economic rights framework. 'Framework', here and in the next divisions, merely denotes that I present a very general categorisation instead of detailed specifications (in the end those that one finds, depending on the framework, in the hundreds or thousands of pages of the legislative codes).

6§10 *Necessary categories of the legal right to property*

This section merely lists the categories that necessarily make up the legal property rights framework. More detail is not required for this chapter's purposes. The legal right to property is concretised in civil law and in criminal law. Although all the rights listed below are necessary, none is necessarily a full right.

Regarding property, the focus of the exposition in 6§2 and 6§4, and by implication in 6D3, was on 'claims of entitlement'/'granted rights'/'legal rights' to (1) private property in the earth and (2) private property in means of production other than for production by the claimant. For capitalism these are the core granted property rights, comprising part of the wider category of granted property rights in general. However, to the extent that the state draws no distinction between these two and property right in general, the following connects to property right in general, on the understanding that the earlier two property rights are the essential ones, and that other property rights are subordinate, even if the latter can be necessary corollaries of the former.[12]

- *The legal right to property* (*both for natural persons and corporations*)

The legal right to property is ruled by the convention that *possession* is a sufficient title for *ownership* (whereas the actor challenging that ownership has to prove its own title).[13] Several forms of expropriation, such as theft, are classified as criminal and hence so prosecuted and penalised as concretised in criminal law. However, some forms of expropriation can be legal (cf. 7§2).

---

12 Herewith I make explicit that a systematic exposition need not stick to the categories and the specific generalisations of the object of the exposition. 'Re-categorisation' is often at the heart of scientific investigation and exposition.

13 A more detailed account of this matter would have to treat the question of what may count as property and what may not (e.g. intellectual rights).

- *The legal right to free usage of property*

Ownership is ruled by the legal right to the free usage of property as long as this does not hinder the property of others. This legal right to free usage may conflict with legal rights to existence whence this property right is a restricted one (6§14 below).

- *The legal right to the fruits from property*

Free usage of property might seem to include the legal right to the fruits from property. We will see in 7§1 and 7§18 that these rights are not analogous and that the latter is not a full legal right. Quite apart from the caveat in the last sentence, it is essential to capitalist legal right that surplus-value (see also 6§11 below) is *defined* as a fruit from the property in the earth and other means of production, rather than as the fruit from labour (for the latter view see again the quotations from Smith (1776) and Keynes (1936) in 1§14-b).

- *The legal right to transfer property by agreement*

The permanent transfer of property or the temporary transfer of property (hiring, lending, renting, leasing) is ruled by the right to free contract or agreement (including that of marriage). In face of the shaky basis of possession for ownership (see the legal right to property), substantial property (especially real estate and dwellings) is ruled by law about its registry, its transfer agreements and its conveyance.

- *The legal right to incorporate*

A special form of the right to transfer property is the right to incorporate (cf. 2D6).

Even this brief listing, together with some main restrictions to the full exercise of these rights, may make it clear that the legal formulation of property rights is a complicated matter. Nowadays their legal codes and sub-ordinary regulations take up thousands of pages.

6§10-a Explication. Contingent property right: legal succession of property

The succession of property is a particular form of transfer of property right as concretised in civil succession law.[14] The reason for not incorporating this in the main text of 6§10 is that it is contingent. Schumpeter (2003 [1943]) makes a big point about succession as a cornerstone for the survival of capitalism – whence, in our terminology, it would seem to be necessary for the capitalist system. He might have had a point for a mainly non-corporate organisation of the business structure where enterprises in case of single ownership would die (or perhaps go into public ownership) with the death of the owner. However,

14 Succession to family members seems a feudal remnant.

because there is no escape from ownership of the corporation (unless it goes bankrupt), the corporation does not die with the death of one or more of its current shareholders.

Note also that between capitalist countries today, succession tax rates are highly divergent.

6§10-b Amplification. Limited liability of owners of corporations

The restriction on the free usage or property of 'not hindering the property (and person) of others' implies that property owners are liable in this respect vis-à-vis other property owners. In case of corporate property, the corporation is liable whereas the liability of the owners of the corporation (i.e. the shareholders) is limited to their finance capital contribution. This limited liability is a remarkable aspect of corporate law and hence of capitalist property right (cf. 2D6 that expands on merely the 'economic' aspect of this). In the absence of corporate limited liability, enterprises might still engage in joint ventures with unlimited liability.

6§11 *The legal right to employ labour as combined with the employer's legal right to appropriate the surplus-value produced by that labour*

Labour law makes no distinction between trade in labour-capacity and labour (1§6). In this section, therefore, the distinction is bracketed. The enterprise's legal right to trade and employ labour as combined with its legal right to appropriate the product and particularly the surplus-value produced by that labour is essential to the capitalist system.

- *Trade and appropriation: property in persons*

Market trade of commodities is based on the premise that the actor selling a commodity is its legal owner, the ownership being transferred by the trade contract. With commodity trade in the form of lease (also called renting), the owner (lessor) transfers *the use* of a commodity to a contracting party (the lessee), for a time and other conditions a stipulated by contract.

The legal right to the market trade of labour derives from the notion that human beings (in this case workers) are tradable in some form, which is indeed the case in a capitalist economy (as well as, more broadly, in systems of slavery). Market trade of labour is based on the remarkable premise that a person (the worker) is the owner of its own person. (This notion seems to have originated with Richard Overton, 1646, and was, more influentially, phrased by John Locke, 1689, who wrote: 'every man has a *property* in his own *person*'.)[15] Only on the

15 Overton writes in *An Arrow against all Tyrants*: 'To every individual in nature is given an

basis of this premise can some entity (land, horses, persons) be traded in either the form of ownership transfer, or the form of use transfer.

Only on the basis of this premise could – in the case of a labour lease contract – the enterprise command the fruits of the use of the commodity, that is, appropriate the product, including the surplus-value produced by labour – labour's 'compensation' being the wage (a form of rent).

If a person (the worker) would indeed have the property in its own person, then, on the basis of property and contract law, the *ownership* could in principle be transferred. However, labour law does not allow for this (or sometimes is not explicit about it).[16] This seems to imply either that labour has a very limited property in its person, or that the premise of ownership in persons does not hold – whence the lease of labour and the appropriation consequences are shaky.

However, the fundamental point is the capitalist commodification of human beings (1§6), in the case of labour – a commodification that the state grants as a legal right. It could be argued that this is still better than systems of slavery or of feudal appropriations (such as the enforced labour on the land of the lord). Nevertheless 'it could be worse' is not a firm legal basis.

- *Free trade and enforced trade*

A second premise of labour contract law is that the labour contract is a free, non-enforced, one. This was, in a somewhat different context, already alluded to (1§6 and 6§2-a). Workers are free to choose which employer is going to appropriate the surplus-value that they produce. In this sense the appropriation is based on a free contract. However, to the extent that workers lack property in the earth and other means of production, they are forced to engage in an employment contract with some enterprise. In this sense the appropriation is not based on a free contract but on an enforced one. In each sense, nevertheless, the appropriation is a legalised appropriation.

---

individual property by nature not to be invaded or usurped by any. For everyone, as he is himself, so he has a self propertiety, else he could not be himself; ...' (quoted by Ishay 2008, p. 92). Locke (1689) writes the phrase quoted in the main text, in the context of a discussion of the God-given commons. That Locke himself (in the last sentence below) derives an apparently radical conclusion from this thesis – for labour, not for the commons – is another matter. He writes: 'Though the earth, and all inferior creatures, be common to all men, yet every man has a *property* in his own *person:* this no body has any right to but himself. The *labour* of his body, and the *work* of his hands, we may say, are properly his.' (*Two Treatises of Government*, Book II, Chapter 5, §27).

16 In the latter case, the assumption is presumably that people do not engage in the stupidity of selling, knowing that the worker's ownership of the selling price will be transferred to the purchaser along with the purchase of the person.

Finally, we will see in 6§15 that the unlimited exercise of the legal right to employ labour may conflict with the right to existence (initiated in 6§3). Thus although this right is essential and necessary to the capitalist system, we will see that is must be a restricted right.

6§11-a Explication. Employment of labour versus exploitation of labour
I have hesitated over whether, instead of the term employment of labour, I should use the term exploitation of labour (as Marx and most marxian political economist do). Exploitation of labour is an analytical term, which has nothing to do with heavy or not so heavy exploitation (that is measured by the rate of surplus-value). Because in the common language of the past decades 'exploitation' has come to mean 'undue employment' (which would be 'heavy exploitation') I have decided against the term exploitation because that is not the general issue. The general issue is that enterprises appropriate the surplus-value produced by labour ('heavily' or less 'heavily').

I will nevertheless sometimes use the term 'exploitation' if there is no risk of the confusion just mentioned, or when the context requires it. For example, the phrase 'the legal right to employment' *tout court* might be interpreted as a workers' right instead of a right of enterprises. (In Chapters 6–7 employment of labour by the state is implicit – it will be made explicit in Chapter 8.)

6§12 *The general interest and 'objective class' interests*
Economic legislation, and especially the state's giving legal force to entitlement claims, is inherently about opposing and conflicting interests.[17] Throughout this book, the objective is to set out the moments that condition the reproduction of the capitalist system. When the state casts its arguments for particular legislation 'ultimately' in terms of the 'general interest' (6§6), this regards ultimately the reproduction of the capitalist system. However, for the assessment of the position of the state, it is opportune to see what are the particular 'capital' or 'labour' interests served by the state's legislation and other regulation. For this purpose I will henceforth use a shorthand indication that is based on a very broad distinction into two 'categories' – or '*objective* classes': the 'capitalist and managerial class' (CMC) and the subordinated working class (SWC). *Together* these share the general drawbacks of capitalism (in short, the one-dimensionality of monetary value, 1§4). *Particularly* these two categories derive different (dis)advantages from the capitalist system in terms of their *decision-making power* and of their *shares of income and wealth*. In line with 2§15-a these classes are defined as follows:

17 Cf. Morris 1993, p. 823.

- SWC. Subordinated workers are defined as workers who have no decision-making power (in the USA between 1930 and 2010 this category included between 73% and 90% of the relevant population). Their average income is considerably lower than the average CMC income. (2§15-a, *Graph 2.14.*)
- CMC. *Capitalists* have direct or indirect decision-making power. The size of their non-labour income is such that they are not forced to engage in an employment contract – that is, to be employed themselves (although typically they do engage in such employment contracts). *Managers* have decision-making power and benefit from 'super-wages'.[18]

These are called 'objective classes' in terms of these two measures of decision-making power and of income only, and in contradistinction to any notion of 'subjective class', that is, of class-consciousness.

Division 5. The rights to existence framework

After briefly introducing rights in relation to the direct safety of the body of persons, this division focuses on various protections of the person that in some way restrict full property rights. These are consumer and environmental protections, as well as labour protection during the production process.

6§13 *Legal rights to existence*

Legal *economic* rights (6D3) must necessarily be grounded in state-granted rights to *existence* (6§3 and 6§4), and next be posited in the form of *legal* rights (the current division). Hence the state must demarcate, define and so concretise these rights. This concerns, first of all, the respect of the body of the person and hence the forbearance of direct violence regarding the person. More concrete existence rights, and especially those existence rights in demarcation of economic rights, are presented in the following sections of this division.

6§14 *Protection of the consumer and the environment: restrictions on commodity production*

Respect for the existence of the person regards not only direct bodily violence but also violation of the person's safety and health regarding food and the environment (including the climate). Granting these as rights in general seems

18 As indicated in 2§15-a: In the USA between 1930 and 2010 the *average* income of the total managerial class was between 3–4 times higher than the SWC total average. The average income of the capitalist class was between 9–29 times higher than the SWC average. (Cf. Mohun 2016.)

persuasive and simple qua principle. However, when it comes to formulating these rights in the form of law, potential conflict centres on their degree and hence content. What is more, much of the regulation in this field is difficult to enact precisely and hence tends to be extensive and complicated.

- *Consumer protection*

The monetary-value dimension of production determines that the physical quality of output is no intrinsic motif for production, but rather its by-product (1§11). This indifference towards the physical output is a potential threat to the consumers' safety and health conditions (1§11-a).

- *Environmental protection*

Even more than with consumer protection, the scope for protection of the environment is elastic. And even more so than the former, environmental protection can be postponed (even if not without damage). Another key difference is that whereas the transaction of a consumer good passes the market (1§4), free nature inherently does not: it has no monetary value (1§14, heading 2). The other main difference is that neglecting consumer protection may affect a human generation, whereas neglecting environmental protection may affect many, or all, future generations.

- *Conflicts of right: restrictions on commodity production*

Next to the inherent conflict regarding the demarcation of the degree and content of these rights to protection, these protections put restrictions on the production of commodities, and so conflict with, and must restrict, rights to property (6§10).

For both consumer and environmental protection it applies that whereas this protection is necessary as a 'moment' (that is, there must be this protection), the degree and specific content of such protection is contingent and a source of potential conflict. Facing this (potential) conflict, much of the specific content of these protections tends to be delegated to semi-independent regulative authorities and the prosecution to semi-independent inspectorates (see further 6§16).

6§15 *Labour protection regarding labour time and occupational safety and health: restrictions on the production process*

Next to consumer and environmental protections (6§14), the legal right to existence (6§13) is concretised in labour protection.

This protection concerns the regulation of labour time (especially the maximum labour time per day and per week) as well as the regulation of occupational safety and health. Labour protection in general is rather persuasive as it is directly about existence issues. However, the potential conflict about such regulation centres again not so much on their principle but rather on their degree and hence content. Whereas the regulation of labour time is fairly easy to enact precisely, the regulation of occupational safety is not, and tends to be complicated.

Labour protection puts restrictions on the design of the production process, which conflicts with the legal right to free usage of property (6§10) and the legal right to employ labour (6§11). As with consumer and environmental protections, labour protection is necessary as a moment (there must be protection) whereas the actual content is contingent and a source of continuous potential conflict. Again the specific content of the regulation tends to be delegated to semi-independent regulative authorities and the prosecution to semi-independent inspectorates (see 6§16).

6§15-a Explication. Labour time and the minimum wage

For the regulation of labour time it is pre-posited that the permitted maximum labour time is sufficient to gain a 'living wage' or at least a subsistence wage. So far there are no guarantees for this, other than via the compliance of labour (2§7). The (a) minimum wage is presented in 7§10.

6§16 *Delegation of the specific regulation and of the supervision of its execution: purification from conflict*

The upholding of the rights to existence insofar as these require restrictions on commodity production and the production process (protection of the consumer, of the environment and of labour), conflict with capitalist economic rights (6§14–6§15). This clash of rights threatens the legitimation of the state. In attempting to moderate problems, the state tends to enact these protections/restrictions in general terms, and to delegate specific regulation to particular putatively (semi-)independent regulation authorities, and the prosecution to particular putatively (semi-)independent inspectorates.

In this way the state 'purifies' its core administrative body from conflict (to some extent). Nevertheless, the state is ultimately responsible for the actions that it delegates. However, in the case of disasters or heavy conflict, the state can dismiss and replace the board of the authority or of the inspectorate, thereby evading or mitigating any heavy effects on its own legitimation.

6§16-a Amplification. Purification from conflict through delegation

The delegation referred to in the main text is the first occasion of an institutional 'purification' of the state, that is, purification from potential conflict in order to protect its legitimation. Throughout Chapters 7 and 9, similar as well as other forms of purification will recurrently be introduced into the exposition.

Division 6. The public security framework

This division presents the framework of 'public security' (6§18). The first section (6§17) is introductory and applies to (most) public security as well as to rights in general.

6§17 *'Rights' (allowance rights) and 'positive rights'*

Generally a *right* held by one person imposes on other persons the *duty* to respect that right.[19] (In accordance with judicial discourses, when I use the term 'person' this term includes reference to non-natural persons such as business companies and corporations.) Concerning rights a distinction is made between 'allowance rights' and 'positive rights'. So far, when I used the term 'right' I implicitly meant what I will now term 'allowance right'.

An ***allowance right*** held by a person – e.g. the allowance right to property of means of production – entails the *duty* on all other persons to respect that right. That is, the duty of *non-interference, non-obstruction or non-action*. Thus a full allowance right to property entails that *once* a person possesses property, the possession ought not be obstructed and, more specifically, the possessor ought not be expropriated. Similarly, a full allowance right to existence imposes the duty on other persons to not interfere with or obstruct this right, e.g. by violence. (In much of the literature, allowance rights are called 'negative rights', in reference to the duty side of the this type of right – see Addendum 6§17-a.)

A ***positive right*** entails duties that go much further: requiring 'positive action'. (Positive rights require a specification as to whether the duty of positive action falls on all other persons, or on a specific category, or perhaps on the state or some other institution.) A positive right to property, for example, to the earth, might more specifically entail that everybody is granted the right to possess some portion or perhaps an equal proportion of the earth; it might impose the duty on others to transfer their disproportionate share in the earth to the other right holders. Similarly a positive right to existence, for example, specified as the positive right to decent work, or the positive right to a decent living (all to be specified further), imposes the duty on others of sharing the available decent work or to share other means of decent living. Again, the required duty might fall on the state or some other institution.

Returning to allowance rights: a restriction of rights to allowance rights implies the negation of symmetric positive distributions (of property, work, existence, etc.). In other words, the restriction implies *formal equality* for

19 See, e.g., Morris 1993, p. 828.

economic actors regarding duties of the non-obstruction of rights (property, existence), whilst there may be *material inequality* regarding the distribution of property or means to existence.

In capitalism, legal property rights are generally restricted to being legal property *allowance* rights. For existence rights there are several varieties (see further 7D5). Note that the drawing line between allowance and positive rights is not an exact one. Take the case of consumer protection. From one perspective this imposes the 'abstinence' duty on enterprises to *not* obstruct the security of consumers (allowance right). From another perspective it imposes the 'positive' duty (regarding positive right) of producing secure food and other commodities.

Having made this distinction, the term 'right' will henceforth denote allowance right. Other rights will be specified as 'positive right'. The distinction will become especially relevant in Chapter 7.

6§17-a Addendum. Rights (allowance rights or negative rights) and positive rights

Allowance rights (negative rights) are a common, or perhaps the most common, category of rights in a capitalist system. I have refrained from using the term 'negative right' because when I did so in earlier drafts of the book, which were shared with mainly economics students, the latter felt uneasy about the term, questioning especially what is particularly 'negative' about the maintenance of such a right. Because this book provides an immanent critique of the capitalist system, I would not want my terminology to resemble an external criticism, with which the term 'negative right' might be associated. (Alternative terms for 'allowance right' would be 'tolerance right', 'permit right' or 'non-obstruction right'.)

The distinction between negative rights (allowance rights) and positive rights derives from Isaiah Berlin (1958) who made a distinction between negative and positive freedom (see Andre and Velasquez 1990, for an introduction in two pages).

6§18 *The public security framework: upholding of the legal economic and existence rights and of the institution of the state*

- *Public security components*

The state's upholding of both the legal right to property (6D4) and the legal right to existence (6D5) requires a public police and public prosecution, the public police being entitled to use violence.

The upholding of each of the legal rights to property and existence also requires the protection against fire, open water and other elements.

These together – public police and prosecution and the protection against 'elements' – are called 'public security'. They have in common that – for various reasons – their provision cannot, or cannot adequately, be sold on the market. Hence they must be collectively provided by or via the state – even if some of the execution might be outsourced, perhaps via procurement and licences.

Public security, or specific components thereof, can be granted in the form of a provision (weak claim) or in the form of a 'positive right' (strong claim) – see 6§18-a.

- *The state's legalised violence and its limits*

As institutionalised in the public police, the state *grants to itself* the monopolistic right to the use of violence and next institutionalises this right in legal form.[20] This legalised violence is the state's *extreme though limited* legal resource for the protection of the rights that it grants and legalises. It is also the *extreme though limited* legal resource for the protection of the institution of the state itself (6§4).

The state can use this violence against a limited number of actors that deviate from the law. This amount of deviating actors is limited because the state's violent powers are inherently materially restricted – in the end because the means for violence must be materially produced and because there must be a sufficient number of reliable police forces to operate these means.[21] Ultimately, and predominantly, therefore the state must seek legitimation for its actions and non-actions not just in a majority compliance, but in the compliance of a vast majority of social actors (6§5).[22]

6§18-a Explication. Positive right to public security

Note thus that the maintenance of legal rights to property and existence (rights to non-interference) must be translated into *positive rights* to protection (rights to interference) by the police, fire brigades, and so forth. If, for example, the

---

20 The state, Weber noted, 'claims the *monopoly of the legitimate use of physical force* within a given territory. … The state is considered the sole source of the "right" to use violence' (1999 [1919], p. 1). However, there are (degrees of) exceptions to this monopoly, for example, in the USA on the basis of its citizens' right to bear arms.

21 I realise very well that the restrictions to which I refer, and the state's searching the limits of these restrictions, have historically and contemporarily resulted in an enormous amount of blood.

22 It cannot be pinpointed what, in this context, constitutes a 'vast majority'. It is likely more than 75% rather than less. Approaching this from the other side, that is, violent action by state subjects, even such rebellion by 10% of the people seems insurmountable. And even that is a very high number within a 'normal' police force, as measured by OECD averages, and even when the active military is included.

protection of property or person by the police were a positive right (instead of a provision), it is the specific definition of the protection that determines the meaning of the right. Generally the state tends to prefer to formulate its legislation for various elements of public security in terms of 'provisions' rather than rights, because this reduces the effectivity of possible liability claims in case of damage.

Summary and conclusions

This chapter returned to the expositional level of Chapter 1. It started with the capitalist economy's dissociated outward bifurcation between households and privately owned enterprises – now predicated on not only the presumed abstract existence of the capitalist economy, but also presumed abstract existence of the state. (Division 1.)

In the exposition of the capitalist economy it was implicit that actors have the freedom (concretised as entitlement claims) to act as set out in Part One. The core of these are: first, claims of entitlement to private property in the earth; second, claims of entitlement to private property of means of production other than for production by the claimant; third, claims of entitlement to employ labour as combined with the appropriation of the surplus-value produced by that labour; fourth, claims of entitlement to existence.

However, within the economy there are no institutions guaranteeing these claimed entitlements, whence the capitalist economy cannot stand on its own. When the state grants particularly *these* claims in the form of rights, the state is identified as a capitalist state. The state demarcates these granted rights and it upholds them. (Division 2.)

The existence of the state is grounded in five conditions of existence regarding the form of its operation: (1) its legitimation in the compliance of the actors; (2) in gaining that compliance by positing its actions in terms of the putative general interest; (3) the latter requires that it putatively positions itself above and outside the opposing particular economic interests, hence as extraordinary social institution – as a separation-in-unity; (4) this again requires that it posits right in the form of law, equally applying to all, which, however, implies that it must take a stance on the content of right; (5) the form of law requires that the state maintains law by arbitration and sanctioning. (Division 3.)

The 'economic rights framework' is the *first moment* of the state's positing right as legal right. It comprises various necessary 'property rights', and the legal right to employ labour as combined with the employer's legal right to appropriate the surplus-value produced by that labour. (Division 4.)

Economic rights are futile without the right to existence. Hence the former rights are grounded in the latter – the *second moment* of the state's positing right as legal right. Much of the demarcation of the rights to existence in the form of law (consumer and environmental protections and labour protection) conflicts with economic rights. Hence potential conflicts at the level of the economy are transferred to the level of the state. The state attempts to mitigate their effect on its legitimation by delegating the regulation of the specific content of these protections to be delegated to (putatively) semi-independent regulative authorities and the prosecution to (putatively) semi-independent inspectorates. (Division 5.)

The state's upholding of the legal right to property and the legal right to existence is grounded in the state's provision of public security – police, public prosecution and protection against fire and water (Division 6).

This completes the exposition of the capitalist state at the expositional level analogous to that of Chapter 1.

The first main conclusion is that the existence of the capitalist economy can only insufficiently be grounded within the capitalist economy itself. In light of that insufficiency, 'economic freedom' cannot be grounded within the economy.

The second main conclusion is that the state, by granting the 'economic rights' that it does grant, is indeed identified as a 'capitalist state'. Therewith these rights are indeed political rights. However, that adjective is in a way empty, as all actual rights are political rights. We will see in Chapter 7 that the legitimation of the state requires more than 'merely' the granting and upholding of these economic rights (as we have already seen for elementary existence rights).

∵

Note: The reader who would generally skip the Appendices in this book, but who is going to take cognisance of the empirical Amplifications (in the next chapters), is advised to read at least the first section (6A-1) of the following Appendix.

Appendix 6A. Empirical data in chapters 7–10: the OECD-21 average

In the systematic exposition of this book, the starting point of 'dissociated outward bifurcation' in 1§1 and 6§1 set out an abstract-general characterisation of the capitalist system. The concrete meaning of full-fledged 'capitalism' is determined by the starting point's increasingly concrete conditions of existence and their manifestations as exhibited in Chapters 1–10. Throughout the rest of Part Two (Chapters 7–10) I will, especially for various categories of state expenditure and taxation, refer to historical data of the *average* of 21 OECD countries during the period 1870–2015 as explained below.

6A-1 *Empirical reference to 'capitalism' as exemplified by the OECD-21 'strongest version'*

Empirically, the 34 countries that made up the OECD (Organisation for Economic Development and Co-operation) in 2015 are main *examples* of full-fledged capitalist countries. However, not all of those countries can be characterised as capitalist throughout the period 1870–2015. This applies especially for most of the countries that became OECD members after 1990. For historical data I therefore restrict myself to the countries that were OECD members in 1990, though omitting Iceland, Luxembourg and Turkey, because for these countries pre-1960 data are always missing and many data afterwards. This leaves 21 countries. I henceforth use the term '**OECD-21**' for: Australia, Austria, Belgium, Canada, Denmark, Finland, France, Greece, Germany, Ireland, Italy, Japan, Netherlands, New Zealand, Norway, Portugal, Spain, Sweden, Switzerland, United Kingdom (of Great Brittan and Northern Ireland), United States of America.[23|24]

The countries of the OECD-21 are indeed merely examples of capitalist countries, though a specific selection of those, in that on a world scale these are characterised by a relatively high GDP per capita, and many of these built that on a colonial and imperialist history. On the other hand, I consider that a critical exposition of 'the' capitalist system should focus on its hitherto *economically strongest version*, in whatever way that was historically reached. (Personally I have moral views about that history and thus on the appreciation of that 'strength'. These views, however, are irrelevant to the exposition of the reproduction of the capitalist system in its strongest version.)

We will see in Chapter 7 that for the average of the OECD-21, state expenditure increased from about 11% of GDP in 1870 to about 45% in 2015, with the main expenditure component of social security transfers increasing in the

23 In 2015, the share of these 21 countries of the world population was 13%, whereas their share of world GDP was 56% (source: World Bank, database World Development Indicators – update 17 Nov. 2016).

24 In 2015, the 13 other OECD countries were: Iceland, Luxembourg, Turkey – as mentioned (from the year 1961); Czech Republic, Hungary, South Korea, Mexico, Poland (from the years 1994–96); Chile, Estonia, Israel, Slovak Republic, Slovenia (from the year 2010).

same period from about 0% of GDP to 25%. In face of the legitimation in the compliance of the vast majority of the actors (that is necessary for the capitalist system), I will submit that there is a tendency for a similar future development of state expenditure for the more recent and the currently weaker capitalist countries (Chapter 11).

I emphasise that all quantitative references to the OECD-21 form *no part of the systematic exposition*, and these are therefore relegated to Amplifications of the systematic sections. The systematic sections refer to all capitalist countries characterised by the starting point's 'dissociated outward bifurcation', however old or young these are in this respect, and whatever their stage of development in terms of, for example, state expenditure and GDP per capita. To be sure, all of Part One applied to all of these countries.

6A-2 *Empirical references to the* arithmetic average *of the OECD-21*

As with Part One, Part Two is concerned with full-fledged capitalism in general, not individual countries. When in Amplifications I refer to the average of merely the OECD-21, this is for the pragmatic reason of lack of the relevant and reasonably standardised data of the average of all capitalist countries in a long-run perspective (1870–2015).

I refer to the OECD-21 averages except for a number of cases when averages are not available or when averages make no sense (in that case I may refer to an individual country). More specifically, the reference is always to the *unweighted* average or *arithmetic average* (which is the same as the 'arithmetic mean'). The reason for this is that I am not concerned with the possible economic impact of one country on another. My concern is the average OECD country's political economic constellation. Then it does not matter if a country is big or small. In each case it has to uphold a full legislative framework and in each case its state has to gain legitimation for that framework. Therefore, as a matter of principle I have to measure in terms of arithmetic averages (without weighing for the size of an economy).[25]

6A-3 *Data sources for the OECD-21*

When it has the data available I always use the OECD database. Mostly this is the case for data from after 1990 and sometimes for data from after 1960 or 1970. Incidentally I use specialised databases, such as from UNESCO.

---

25 Note that this is rather common in this field. See, e.g., Tanzi and Schuknecht 2000, Castles 2006 and Tanzi 2011. The OECD database often also calculates unweighted averages for its 'OECD Total'.

For the years for which the OECD has no data available, I mainly rely on three sources: Tanzi and Schuknecht (2000); Castles (2006); and Tanzi (2011). For the years prior to 1960, decomposed state expenditure data on a common base are scarce, and the further we go back, the number of countries for which there are data on a common base is also restricted. For all years (1870–2015) I have used the maximum amount of information that my sources provide for the OECD-21.

Finally, the common statistics in the field of 'state expenditure' most often adopt the term 'total government' or 'general government' for the sum of 'federal government' (when relevant), state government and local governments. For graphs and tables I adopt the latter convention of 'general government'.

List of figures chapter 6

CHAPTER 7

Furthering the conditions for the accumulation of capital

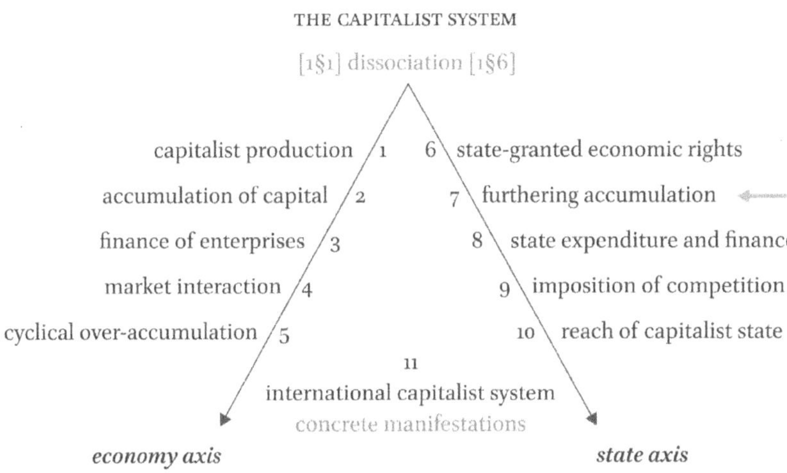

Contents

 | DOI:10.1163/9789004392809_010

Introduction

The exposition in Chapter 6 showed that the capitalist economy cannot exist by itself and that its reproduction necessarily requires the state to grant core economic entitlement claims in the form of legal rights. This chapter starts by setting out that the *material* grounding of the state and its actions requires it to collect means from the economy in the form of taxation. Hence taxation overrides property right. Thus we have the paradox that the state's upholding of property right must intrude property right.

The 'action radius of the state' is that which it can do given the constraint of feasible taxation. The latter is determined by the prevailing condition of the accumulation of capital. The capitalist state's necessary action in face of feasible taxation determines (the degree of) its furthering the conditions for the accumulation of capital. The main body of this chapter consists of the exposition of these conditions. First, monetary conditions (Division 2). Secondly, conditions regarding the quantity and quality of the supply of labour-capacity (Division 3). Thirdly, conditions regarding the economy's infrastructure (Division 4). Especially the concretisation of the second and third conditions require extra state expenditure and hence taxation. However, the feasibility of taxation concerns not so much its absolute amount, but rather the feasibility of tax rates.

A (potentially) quantitatively important category of state expenditure concerns social security provisions. These, and their requirement in face of the legitimation of the state, are presented in Division 5.

Whereas action of the state on all these terrains is necessary, we will see throughout this chapter that the degree is the crucial point. This opens up continuous sources of conflict, which may threaten the legitimation of the state. The last two divisions show how potential conflicts in respect of this legitimation require two major separations within the body of the state. As a result the state exists institutionally within three bodies. The core one is the Administrative, with next to it the bodies of the Judiciary (Division 6) and the Deliberative (Division 7). The latter's seeking of compliance, and ultimately its actual generation of compliance, is an indispensable condition for the existence of the state, and hence for the capitalist system.

Throughout this chapter I never use the term 'state intervention'. I consider that term to be highly ideological to the extent that it is based on the presumption that the capitalist economy could possibly stand on itself. Instead, the capitalist economy and state constitute a necessary unity, be it institutionally distinct as a 'separation-in-unity'.

The current chapter presents the first conditions of existence of the exposition in Chapter 6. At the same time it is the sequel to the exposition in

SCHEME 7.1 *The conditions furthering the accumulation of capital (outline Chapter 7)*

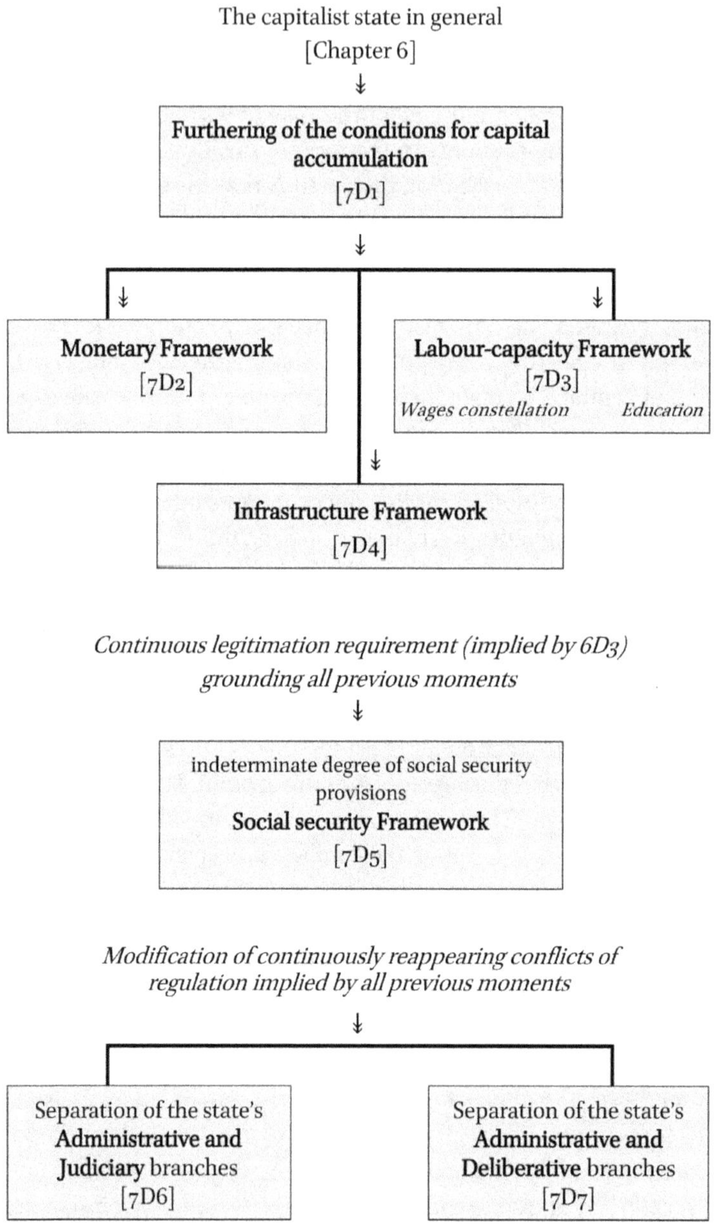

Legend

↓ grounded in (conditioned by)

Chapter 2, setting out the latter's conditions of existence, especially regarding the accumulation of capital and its moments of the expansion of money and of labour-capacity (Divisions 2 and 3 of the current chapter).

The main moments presented in this chapter are summarised in *Scheme 7.1*.

Division 1. The state's action radius as predicated on its furthering of the conditions for the accumulation of capital

General terminological note: I use the term *regulation* for the entirety of laws and of the 'delegated regulation'. When I explicitly refer to the latter I always use the adjective 'delegated'. When I refer to 'regulation', this refers, as said, to the entirety. (See further 10§2.)

7§1 *The material existence of the state: taxation and the state's action radius*

The state's action of the legislation and upholding of right (6D4–6D6) necessarily requires its material reproduction. For that material reproduction the state is dependent upon the economy. The form of separation (6§6) requires, at least in principle, that the state itself does not engage in profit-generating processes of production out of which it might finance its action. Therefore the state is compelled to appropriate means from the economy by taxation. Thus taxation grounds the action radius of the state.

7§1-a Explication. The state and profit-generating processes

The main text refers to an abstaining 'in principle'. In fact, for the average of the OECD-21 countries in the early twenty-first century, about 2% of the total labour force is employed in state enterprises. To be sure: the proceeds from it far from cover the total state expenditure (around the same time on average about 45% of GDP).

7§2 *The fundamental conflict of taxation; the tax base and the tax rate*

The state's material reproduction via taxation (7§1) implies that its maintenance of right requires the overriding of property right through taxation. Hence taxation is fundamentally conflicting. This fundamental conflict cannot be overcome, even if it can be moderated. (I systematically bracket this fundamental conflict until the last division of this chapter – 7D7.)

Quite apart from the fundamental character of this conflict, the *degree* of conflict is determined by the tax base or the tax bases (that on which taxes are levied) and the rate of taxation. The *tax base* is the value amount of the income or property that can in principle be taxed. Thus if the state requires an amount of x in taxes, the macroeconomic tax base (for example, the amount of surplus-value) determines the *tax rate* (t%) that generates x.

7§2-a Explication. Taxation in general

The previous sections – and all of this chapter – posit taxation in general. Chapter 8 presents the various forms of taxation (such as particularly on property, income or expenditures) as well as their effect on profits in face of the accumulation of capital.

7§3 *The potential action radius of the state, the tax base and the state's furthering of the conditions for the accumulation of capital*

The 'action radius of the state' is that which it can do given the constraint of feasible taxation. So far, this action radius is demarcated merely by what was presented in Chapter 6. Thus the state's action radius is grounded in feasible taxation (7§1), which is determined by the 'tax base' and a concomitant 'tax rate' (7§2). The tax base (e.g. that of surplus-value) is again grounded in a constellation of the accumulation of capital (Chapter 2). Thus a prevailing constellation of accumulation would constrain the action radius of the state – one that may not be sufficient for its necessary action. Given the constraint of *feasible* taxation, the capitalist state's necessary action requires it *to further the conditions for the accumulation of capital.* Hence the latter is inherent to the constellation of the capitalist state (methodologically this characteristic again grounds the state's existence – summarised in *Scheme 7.2*).

Whereas this furthering is qualitatively an important determination of the state, the continuously crucial point is its quantitative *degree* in face of feasible tax rates.

Thus the state must seek to further the conditions for the accumulation of capital and along with it the conditions for economic growth.[1] Hence these conditions are instrumental for taxation, the maintenance of the legal rights that the state grants, and the legitimation of the state. Nevertheless economic growth, together with accumulation of capital, tends to be defended in terms of

1 Recall from 2§3 that 'accumulation of capital' or 'economic growth' is a matter of perspective. The state can alternate between these perspectives. The perspective of the accumulation of capital will be popular in discourses between the state and enterprises; the perspective of economic growth can be more appropriate for the formulation of policy in terms of 'the general interest', not excluding though that accumulation of capital is appropriately phrased in terms of 'the general interest'. (This is also a matter of the contingent ideological climate.)

the *'general interest'*.[2] This way the state at least *presents* this as an independent objective even if the tax base might be its primary concern. It does not really matter in what order the state itself presents this in actual practice. Whatever the order, the state must seek legitimation in the compliance of actors not only for its granting and upholding of legal rights (6§5–6§6), but also, concurrently, for its furthering the conditions for economic growth.

As a consequence the monetary-value dimension (1D2) is a constitutive element of the considerations of the state. This applies inherently for taxation and economic growth. Regarding legal rights we have as effect that their specific concretisation in legislation is formulated not only within a qualitative legal discourse, but also – especially in the 'explanatory memorandums' of legislation – in terms of costs and benefits, that is, in terms of the discourse of the quantitative monetary-value dimension.

The next divisions present the three main levers for the state's maintenance and improvement of the conditions for economic growth, that is, those regarding money and banking (7D2), labour-capacity (7D3), and the economic infrastructure (7D4).

SCHEME 7.2 *The grounding of the state's action radius in its furthering of the conditions for the accumulation of capital (systematic of 7D1)*

institution and action of the state [Ch. 6]

||

action radius of the state [7§1]

⤈

taxation [7§1]

||

tax base and concomitant **tax rate** [7§2]

⤈

accumulation of capital (Ch. 2) ↠ furthering its conditions:
furthering the conditions of economic growth [7§3]

Legend
⤈ grounded in
|| implicit in the previous moment

2 Recall from 6§6 that 'the general interest' is inevitably 'the putative general interest': the state

7§3-a Explication. Simplification by assuming surplus-value to be the unique tax base

The main text of 7§3 provides the conceptual grounding for what the state does in actual practice: economic policy; as well as for what it frames as one of the main objectives of economic policy: the stimulation of economic growth. That section also provides the grounds of what mainstream economic theory casually calls the reparation of (potential) 'market failures' – set out in Divisions 2–4.

The main text is perhaps more transparent when, as a provisional simplification, it is assumed that all taxes are levied on surplus-value – prior to any distribution of surplus-value. (In Chapter 8, other taxes, in part substituting for this tax, will be introduced.) This implies that surplus-value is the unique tax base. The tax base constrains the action radius of the state – so far, that which is presented in Chapter 6. In the hypothetical case of zero surplus-value, the action radius would be zero (this would entail an impossibility theorem, to the extent that capitalism cannot exist without the state). This implies that the state for its action radius, and possible extensions of it, must be concerned with the tax base and its growth. More generally, therefore, the state must seek to further the conditions for the accumulation of capital and along with it the conditions for economic growth. Note that given a certain action radius, an increasing tax base – for now increasing surplus-value – may alleviate the tax *rate* and hence the degree of conflict referred to in 7§2 (and the other way around for a decreasing tax base).

7§3-b Amplification. A very rough proxy for the long-run development of the tax base

Graph 7.3 shows the average real-GDP per capita growth rate for up to 21 current OECD countries from 1870–2010 (arithmetic average; see Appendix 6A on the OECD-21 and arithmetic averages). This should serve as a very *rough proxy for the development of the average tax base*. For that purpose, and for this group of countries, during especially the nineteenth-century period, only these data are available. We will see later on (8D2) that until about 1913 state tax receipts were quite below 10% of GDP for the average of the same group of countries; then after a considerable rise between 1913 and 1920, taxes rose continuously after 1937. The top panel of *Graph 7.3* (growth rate per year) shows that prior to 1945 the GDP per capita growth rate developed more erratically than there-

proposes its actions to be in what the state itself considers to be the general interest. Other actors may have different views about what the general interest would be.

after. The bottom graph shows decade averages. The bold suggestion is that the state's furthering of the conditions of economic growth emerged gradually – flattening off after about 1980. This is empirically substantiated for the OECD-21 in Amplifications of the rest of this chapter.

It should be emphasised that because business cycles are not synchronous between countries, *Graph 7.3* does not picture the business cycle, as this averages picture has severely flattened these. (I return to the business cycle in Chapter 10.)

GRAPH 7.3 *Real-GDP per capita 1870–2010, growth rate per year (top graph) and average per decade (bottom graph); average of 20–21 current OECD countries in 2011 US$*

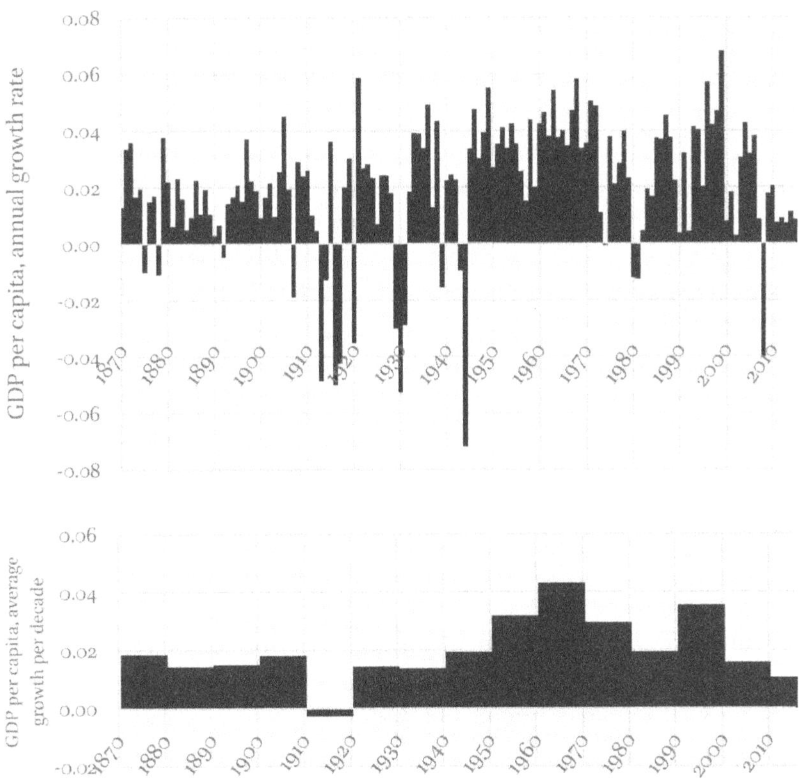

DATA SOURCE: Maddison Project Database, version 2018 by Jutta Bolt, Robert Inklaar, Herman de Jong and Jan Luiten van Zanden. See Appendix 7A, under 7§3-b, for more information on the data

Division 2. The monetary framework

From taxation to monetary regulation furthering accumulation of capital

This division presents the first of the three main levers for the state's furthering of the conditions for economic growth (next to 7D3 and 7D4). The current division is also the sequel to 2D4 on the expansion of money as grounding the accumulation of capital.

7§4 *Imposition of the monetary standard of the Central Bank*

The material existence of the state requires it to appropriate means from the economy (7§1). It is in keeping with the monetary-value dimension of the capitalist economy that the state enacts taxation of economic actors in monetary form, rather than in the form of specific useful objects or services.

Recall from Chapter 2 that the extent of the domain of operation of the money created by banks is an important determinant for the collaboration of banks under the umbrella of a dominant bank which adopts the role of Clearing Bank, grounded in monetary rules set by that Clearing Bank (2§9). Recall also that there may be several such Clearing Banks.

This collaboration between banks, or rather the extension of the collaboration, is reinforced by the state. The state will likely have relations with a dominant bank (i.e. a Clearing Bank). On the one hand, the state will require that taxation be paid in terms of the monetary standard of its Clearing Bank. On the other hand, the state will require that its payments be unconditionally accepted by economic subjects. Hence the state imposes payment in terms of the monetary standard of 'its' Clearing Bank. Herewith all banks are required to adopt the monetary standard of the state's Clearing Bank, now the *Central Bank*.

All the determinants concerning the Clearing Bank and its connection to commercial banks as presented in 2D4, apply to the Central Bank. Because the state is a client of the Central Bank, the latter may provide money-creating loans to the state (similar to the Clearing Bank providing such loans to its clients). The Central Bank tends to abstain from competition with common banks regarding all actors apart from the state (in which case the state is its only non-bank client).

7§4-a Amplification. Legal tender

In 7§4 I have avoided using the term 'legal tender'. This term may refer to the *type of payment* that is protected by law, which is what 7§4 refers to. However, even in the second decade of the twenty-first century, the term often also refers to a type of money itself, especially notes issued by the Central Bank. This is confusing, because the US Treasury, for example, does not expect actors to pay taxes in dollar *notes* (not even 'ultimately').

7§4-b Explication. No monopoly of money creation for the Central Bank

The last sentence of 7§4 re-establishes that the current exposition is at the same level as that of Chapter 2. In 2D4 when the Clearing Bank was 'merely' presented as the bankers' bank, capitalist money (1D2) was concretised as bank-created money. Now (7§4) this is 'stamped' by the state as legally enforced capitalist money.

Regarding *money creation* the current division introduces *nothing new, other than* that one Clearing Bank is now stamped as Central Bank. This *merely* implies that its monetary standard (a standard such as 'dollar') acquires a monopoly status. It does *not* imply that the Central Bank has the monopoly of creating money, even if it may have the monopoly of issuing *its* banknotes (i.e. its own bank notes). On the contrary, ordinary banks do the vast majority of the money creation, and they may also issue their own 'notes', for example, in the form of cheques. (In non-crisis times, ordinary banks do virtually all of the money creation.)

7§5 ***Money and its grounding in monetary legislation***

The state's imposition of the monetary standard of 'its' bank (7§4) implies that it takes *responsibility* for the actions of the Central Bank (CB).

This, primarily, determines the concrete grounding of money in *monetary legislation*. It is necessary because the state (Chapter 6), and hence taxation in monetary form, is necessary to the existence of the capitalist economy.

Secondly, monetary legislation is further determined by the state's requirement of furthering the conditions for economic growth, and hence the accumulation of capital (7§3).

Monetary legislation includes: first, rules regarding the status of the CB; second, rules regarding the authorisation for financial enterprises to operate as bank; third, a general framework for the rights and duties of banks regarding their client debtors and creditors; fourth, a general framework for the supervision of banks. (See the next three sections.)

7§5-a Explication. Supervision and banking licence

Regulation regarding the authorisation, or licence, for financial enterprises to operate as bank, as well as the general framework for the supervision of banks (7§5), may not be very different from the concern of the Clearing Bank (ClB) regarding a standard for securities and liability rules (2§9; 2§9-b). (Recall that these may include conditions on the banks' degree of solvency, on various reserve ratios, on maturity matches, on the interest rates (margins) charged, as well as enforced loans of banks with the ClB.) The main difference now (7§5) is that the ordinary banks that do not comply can be fined or may ultimately lose their banking licence.

7§6 *Conflicts of monetary regulation*

Although monetary legislation is necessary (7§5), the degree of its detail is contingent. This degree of detail determines the executive room for manoeuvre for, on the one hand, the state itself and, on the other, the CB.

This possible room for manoeuvre regards, for example, the placement of state loans or bonds with the CB. Monetary legislation might also be (non-)specific about the monetary accommodation of the development of the general price level (cf. 4D3) and of monetary stabilisation regarding the business cycle (cf. 5D2). Such (non-)legislation includes the level of the rate of interest (either as a target or as a (semi-)instrument).

This room for manoeuvre also regards the tightness of standards for securities and liability rules (generally the composition of the banks' balance sheet – 2§9-b), as well as the intensity of the supervision of banks. The degree of tightness poses the main dilemma of the state's monetary policy: tight prudential regulation affects the banks' accommodation of economic growth negatively; loose regulation increases the risk of bank crises.

In any case – be it via legislation or via executive room for manoeuvre – the state necessarily has to make legislative and/or executive choices (in the latter case, the priority, interpretation, and specification of regulation). These choices affect the distribution of income directly (prices, interest) as well as, indirectly, investment and unemployment. This implies that the state has *to take a side* in the (potential) conflicts between labour, enterprises and financiers. Hence – as with restrictions on the production process in face of labour protection (6§16) – the state's reference to the 'general interest' (6§6) and its self-imposed (putative) impartiality (6§7) may erode, so distorting the ground for its legitimation (6§5).

7§7 *Delegation of the specific regulation, of the supervision of its execution, and of monetary policy to the Central Bank: purification from conflict*

For its monetary regulation the state has to make regulative choices that may distort its legitimation (7§6). Therefore the state tends to enact a general framework for the objectives and tasks of the Central Bank as including its supervision of the other banks. Next it tends to delegate the specific regulation, the execution of its supervision as well as monetary policy to the putatively (semi-)independent Central Bank (see 7§7-a). Through this delegation (and analogous to the earlier delegation – 6§16), the state purifies its core administrative body from conflict (to some extent). Nevertheless the state is *ultimately* responsible for the actions that it delegates.[3] However, in case of disasters or heavy conflict, the state can dismiss and replace the board of the CB, so evading heavy effect on its own legitimation.[4]

Scheme 7.4 summarises the sequence of the grounding moments presented so far in the current division.

SCHEME 7.4 *From taxation to conflicts of monetary regulation and conflict delegation (systematic of 7D2, 7§4–7§7)*

Taxation
(7D1)

↓

Imposition of the monetary standard of 'the' Central Bank
(7§4)

↓

Monetary legislation
(7§5)

||

conflicts of execution monetary regulation
(executive choices; take a side in the conflicts between labour, enterprises and financiers)
(7§6)

↓

conflict dealing delegated to the Central Bank
(7§7)

---

3 Both the delegation and the ultimate responsibility of the state are revealed in the following citation. In 2013 the Minister of Finance of the Netherlands, Dijsselbloem, stated to the country's Senate: '... The Netherlands decided to actualise its monetary policy by delegating it to the European level. The state ultimately determines the "monetary constellation". In the theoretical case in which the euro area would cease to exist, the Netherlands would have to decide again in what way it would want to reshape its monetary policy.' [*'Zoals uit bovenstaande blijkt heeft Nederland er voor gekozen om haar monetaire beleid vorm te geven door deze te delegeren naar het Europese niveau. De Staat is dus uiteindelijk bepalend voor de "monetaire constellatie". In het theoretische geval dat het eurogebied zou ophouden te bestaan ontstaat er voor Nederland een nieuwe situatie en zal zij opnieuw moeten kiezen op welke manier zij het monetaire beleid vorm zal willen geven.'*] (Ministry of Finance of the Netherlands 2013, p. 15).

4 It might make this more difficult when the appointment term is fixed for a number of years, without constraints.

7§7-a Explication. The delegation to the 'technocratic' CB and the inevitable ultimate responsibility of the state.

The delegation of tasks to the CB does not mean that CB policies are cast 'more' in 'the' general interest than in the absence of such delegation. Delegation is merely a means to protect the main body of the state from conflict. This goes against the mainstream assumption that a Central Bank is more independent than (the rest of) the state. This presumes, by the way, that the state is not independent (vis-à-vis the capitalist economy, the state is indeed a capitalist state, but I doubt that this is the quarrel). Thus, those who are sometimes called CB 'technocrats' have to formulate the content of *their* view on the (monetary) general interest. However, these technocrats are no more disconnected from interests (particularly those of banks – perhaps large banks) than other actors. Yes, they like to be labelled as 'independent'.

Because the state in fact delegates the conflict dealing to the CB (regarding especially the distribution of income and wealth – 7§6), it is not only in the interest of the CB but *foremost in the interest of the state* to 'advertise' the CB as being an 'independent' institution.

However, this delegation goes as far as its goes. It works on an everyday basis along with moderate conflicts and along with perhaps moderate failures of the CB. Big failures regarding especially the CB's supervision of (big) banks will again be bounced back to the state (see 7§9).

7§8 *The objective of reaching creeping inflation*

Reaching creeping inflation (euphemistically called 'price stability') is a necessary condition for the accumulation of capital (cf. 4D3). The state tends to encode this objective and to delegate its execution to the Central Bank. Creeping inflation should prevent the economic stagnation associated with the combination of generalised price competition and speeded up technical change (4§9). Because price competition is the impetus for the objective of creeping inflation, this matter will be treated in Chapter 9 on 'the imposition of competition'.

A side effect of the stagnation-prevention impetus to creeping inflation is that workers get one step (one year) behind in wage-bargaining, as price-inflation compensation is most often provided afterwards. I write that this is a side effect, but it may well be a co-objective of creeping inflation.

7§9 *Banking crises and the movement to 'too big to fail' banks*

Over-optimism of enterprises as accommodated by the banks' over-crediting make the banking constellation vulnerable to the failure of banks, and even to failures on a large scale, leading to a crisis of the banking constellation (2§10;

2§10-b). Banking crises and the associated recessions (Graph 2.11 in 2§10-b) have severely damaging effects on the capitalist economy. Nevertheless, in the history of the capitalist system until recently, these have not threatened the reproduction of the system. However, the 2008–12 crisis, followed by the 'great recession' aftermath, did pose such threat.[5] One important factor contributing to it was the gigantic concentration of bank capital and the centralisation of banks from the 1980s.[6] This led to 'big' banks (so big, as we will see in Chapter 9, that these are organisationally too complex to supervise in micro terms) and to so-called 'too big to fail' banks. Failure of such big banks tends to trigger a domino of failures of other banks, up to the collapse of the banking constellation – and therewith tending to the collapse of the capitalist system as a whole. This implies that the CB and/or the state is/are enforced to save the banks that are too big to fail.

Some commentators take the view that for the saving of such banks the Central Bank could 'print' money. But given the principles of double bookkeeping, this is not the case. The CB can lend money, and when it lends money against bad loans this should be reflected in the CB's equity. Then there are only two possibilities: the state makes up for the equity deficit of the CB, or the state settles the finance capital of the big bad banks (via finance capital 'injections' in some form or another, including via the form of take-over). In both these cases, the state is effectively the lender of last resort (not the presumed 'independent' CB). Directly or indirectly, this means that the state is 'tax levier of last resort'. Indeed, economic actors pay the price for it. To be sure, they pay not only the price of saving the banks, but also the price of the recessive or depressive effects of a banking crisis.

The allowance or non-allowance of the concentration and centralisation in the banking sector is ultimately a matter of regulation and supervision, and of the willingness of the state to put constraints on the mode of competition and

---

5 At the point of a threatening collapse, the state officials are constrained not to communicate this publicly, because that would have a self-reinforcing effect. Because of the severe threat of a collapse around 2008–12, a number of members of parliament were informed (as I was, when at the time I was a member of the senate of the Netherlands, as one of its financial spokespersons) though under the clause of strict confidentiality. Luyendijk writes in *The Guardian*: 'Herman van Rompuy waited until 2014 to acknowledge in an interview that he had seen the system come within "a few millimetres of total implosion".' In 2008, Van Rompuy was the prime minister of Belgium, and in 2009–14 the full-time president of the EU council of heads of government. https://www.theguardian.com/business/2015/sep/30/how-the-banks-ignored-lessons-of-crash.

6 By 2005, the assets of the three largest banks as a percentage of the assets of all banks reached 74% for the OECD-21 countries on average (see Appendix 9A, Graph 9.3).

the mode of capital accumulation. Moreover, 'too big to fail' may apply not only to banks, but also to other key sectors (those on which a vast majority of actors is dependent whilst there is no ready substitute) such as the energy sector and the communications sector (currently ICT). Therefore this matter will be treated in Chapter 9 on 'the imposition of competition'.

Division 3. The labour-capacity framework

Accumulation-furthering regulation

This division presents the second of the three main levers for the state's furthering of the conditions for economic growth (next to 7D2 and 7D4). The current division is also the sequel to 2D2 on the expansion of labour-capacity.

7§10 ***Minimum wage: the reproduction of the current labour population***

The state's maintenance of capitalist legal right, and generally its action radius, requires that it furthers the conditions for economic growth and hence the accumulation of capital (7§3). For these and all of its (non-)actions, the state must continuously seek legitimation in the compliance of social actors, particularly in that of, very broadly, the '*objective* classes' of the 'capitalist and managerial class' (CMC) and the subordinated working class (SWC) (6§12).

A wage below at least a subsistence wage would result in labour shortage and impair the reproduction of the labour population.[7] Whereas this is self-destructive for enterprises, there are nevertheless insufficient forces within the economy preventing such self-destruction in at least the medium term (7§10-a below).

The state's furthering of the conditions for the accumulation of capital therefore requires it to impose a legal minimum wage, being at least a subsistence wage (7§10-b).[8] At the same time a legal minimum wage infringes on capitalist economic rights, especially the *extent* of the employers' legal right to employ labour-capacity (6§11).

7 Malnutrition – as well as bad hygienic circumstances that tend to accompany it – affects first of all children and their death rates and hence the potential labour population within a time span of some 10 to 15 years.

8 When there are general *social security* provisions for the structurally unemployed (see 7D5), these may contingently be the effective benchmark for non-imposed minimum wages (in this case employers have to pay a wage at least equivalent to the level of these transfers – as was the case, e.g., in Germany until 2014).

A substantial legal minimum wage is in the interest of the SWC (as always, within the confines of the capitalist system). Although in the perception of individual CMC actors it might go against their interests, it is nevertheless in their common interest, given the requirement of the reproduction of the labour population. For competitive reasons, an important general consideration for enterprises is that any minimum wage restrictions/constraints apply equally to all.

Regarding the potential conflict about this (amplified in 7§11 below), the delicate point is the *level* of the minimum wage. It might vary from minimum subsistence to one beyond some definition of a poverty line or a 'living wage' (each of these always includes a socio-cultural component – 7§10-b).

7§10-a Amplification. The labour population in the absence of a legal minimum wage

Recall that all of the exposition in this book is about the full-fledged capitalist system in general, independently of the contingencies of its particular historical stages (General Introduction). Mere subsistence wages were prevalent throughout the nineteenth century in the current 'strong' capitalist OECD countries (see Appendix 6A on these countries) and throughout the twentieth century in many other capitalist countries.

When there is unemployment (hence labour abundance), competition will tend to press down wages. This would affect the reproduction of the current labour population in case the wage is pressed down below the subsistence wage. That reproduction effect is not immediately actual. Rather, as indicated in the last but one footnote, malnutrition – as well as bad hygienic circumstances that tend to accompany it – affects first of all children and their death rates and hence the potential labour population within a time span of some 10 to 15 years. Co-depending on several macroeconomic conditions, the death rate process would ultimately give rise to labour shortage and a rise of wages to perhaps above the subsistence wage, which would have again a lagged effect on the death rates and so the labour population growth. (Cf. the labour populations theories of Classical Political Economy.) Although there are so 'equilibrating' forces, their long time span tends to produce stagnation rather than flourishing economic growth: ceteris paribus the labour population growth being the constraint. (It is remarkable that this matter plays no part in the conventional neoclassical economics on the labour market and the minimum wage in particular.)

7§10-b Amplification. Subsistence wage and legal minimum wage
It is not obvious how a subsistence wage should be defined. Ultimately measures for it might be devised on the basis of interregional comparisons of death rates. In any case it includes a socio-cultural component, whence a definition by exclusively nutritional components is insufficient. Quite apart from these socio-cultural components, the subsistence wage should also include a component for the raising of children and for sickness. Similar difficulties apply for definitions of the poverty line (e.g. CBS/SCP 2013) or of 'decency' – a term adopted in Human Rights covenants and in ILO covenants (Biermans 2012).

Whereas these problems of definition are relevant for deliberations about a legal minimum wage (see also 7§11), the point of the main text (7§10) is that the state is required to set some legal minimum wage, whatever it is (with the caveat set out in the last footnote).

7§11 *Delegation to minimum wage commissions or councils*

A legal minimum wage infringes on the capitalist economic right to freely employ labour-capacity – the delicate point being especially the level of the minimum wage (7§10).

The potential social conflict about it threatens the legitimation of the state. Therefore the state tends to delegate the determination of the level of the minimum wage to minimum wage commissions or minimum wage councils. This is again an effort to purify the core administrative body of the state from conflict (cf. the purifying delegations presented in 6§15 and 7§7).

7§12 *Temporary unemployment benefits*

- *cyclical (temporary) unemployment benefits*

The accumulation of capital develops cyclically (Chapter 5). To the extent that cyclical unemployment would result in a deprived – hence unfit or even aborted – echelon of labour reserve, enterprises would be deprived of a fresh valorisation potential in the upturn of the cycle.[9] Therefore the state's objective of furthering the conditions for economic growth and hence the accumulation of capital (7§3) requires it to impose regulation on cyclical unemployment benefits. As the emergence of the downturn of the cycle is difficult to define, these benefits tend to be extended to lay-offs in general for a limited duration.[10] It

9 (Cyclical) unemployment is a statistical uncertainty, and hence it cannot be insured; when it can, it is usually at high costs and for limited levels and duration.

10 Given that the downturn period of 'normal' cycles (those not particularly associated with banking crises) is some two years – the duration of these benefits would roughly extend to such a period.

is contingent whether these benefits are paid out of taxation or – perhaps in part – specifically out of contributions by enterprises.

- *sickness benefits*

A similar argument applies for average 'normal' sickness of workers.[11] Enterprises have no interest in immediately sacking these workers, or in their deprivation during a somewhat extended period of sickness. Therefore state regulation of sickness benefits is in the interest of enterprises (as well as of the workers), so providing equal conditions of capital accumulation. The level of these benefits is contingent. The same applies for their way of finance – in this case, however, the finance tends to be imposed on enterprises. (In terms of costs for enterprises this comes down to an extended minimum wage.)

For each of these benefits it applies that these are in the interest of the SWC as well as the CMC. Again their level is the main source of conflict. Given the resolution of a minimum wage level (7§11), the level of the benefits above tends to be set at some percentage of the minimum wage.

7§13 *Labour population growth*

Population policy might seem to be generally contingent. However, in face of the state's objective of furthering the conditions for economic growth and hence the accumulation of capital (7§3), population policy is a requirement in case of a foreseen structural labour scarcity. (Note that whereas 7§10 is about the reproduction of the current labour population, the section at hand is about long run labour population growth.)

Given some current population growth – and given some state of technical development – that population growth, and hence the labour population growth, ultimately operates as a limit on the accumulation of capital (cf. 2D2, especially the interconnections summarised in 2§6 and Figure 2.5). Recall that 2§4 posited labour population growth as a contingency. In terms of the method adopted in this book, this is still an open end.[12]

Given the population growth and the labour participation (see below), the available labour-capacity is determined by:

- *the length of the working day (or week)*

In case of structural labour scarcity, the state might relax the existing regulation on the length of the working day or week (6§14). This, however, is highly conflicting.

---

11 Average 'normal' sickness is distinguished from enduring disability to work (for the latter see 7D5).

12 Recall the conclusion from 2§4, heading 1: 'It is a problem for capitalist enterprises that the reserve of labour is rather indeterminate and thus hard to control.'

The available labour-capacity is also determined by:

- *occupational health and safety*

Equally conflicting would be for the state to relax the occupational health and safety regulation (6§14).

Given the status of the former two regulations, the available labour-capacity is next determined by:

- *labour participation*

The labour participation is the net effect of: first, the division of work within the household; second, the duration of formal education; and third, the retirement age. (1) The first of these is the most complicated as, in the case of families, it is largely a matter of, on the one hand, socio-economic culture and, on the other, the (non-)enforcement of multiple earning in face of the level of a single wage. Anyway, the state might stimulate multiple earning by, for example, tax reductions for the second earner. (2) A reduction in the duration of education conflicts with the enhancement of the labour-capacity required by enterprises (see below, 7§14). (3) The contingency of a (perhaps enforced) retirement age has not been introduced (see 7D5). Should there contingently be old age/pension transfers, then the age of eligibility can be extended.

Given the status of the former three regulations, the available labour-capacity is finally determined by:

- *population growth*

Population growth is the net result of birth and death ratios. Regarding death ratios the state could adopt a wide arsenal of regulation ranging from traffic speed limits (cheap) to a public health service (expensive). The factors operating on birth ratios are more complicated. Nevertheless the state can use the instrument of child benefits to enhance population growth (perhaps by – increasing – benefits beyond the second child). In this case the requirement is for temporary stages of child benefits, as long as the population growth requires to be enhanced.

7§13-a Amplification. Importation of labour-capacity

Up to Chapter 11 the exposition is about a single isolated economy and state, or alternatively a borderless world economy and state. In case of a multitude of nations and states, labour scarcity regions might import labour-capacity from labour-abundant regions.

7§13-b Amplification. State expenditure for the regulation presented in 7§10–7§13

All legislation and other regulation require state expenditure on legislation and supervision, as well as on authorities and commissions to which the state delegates tasks. In comparison with all other state expenditure this is a minor part (see Chapter 10). Apart from that, the regulation of the minimum wage level (7§10) does not require state expenditure (except for the state's own employment). However, temporary unemployment benefits may go along with state expenditure. The same goes for child benefits (7§13). Empirical information on the latter two is provided in 7D5, Graphs 7.9 and 7.10.

7§14 *Public education*

The state is required to further the conditions for economic growth (7§3). One means for this is the enhancement of the quality of the labour-capacity needed by enterprises. The state may further this by way of public education (synonymous with state education), or more generally by state-funded education. There are several (contingent) ways of organising this (see 7§14-b).

Up to this point, the exposition was restricted to state expenditure on legislation, on the maintenance of legal right, and on the quantity of the labour-capacity. State-funded education introduces a qualitatively new moment into the exposition, both in terms of the type of state expenditure (the quality of the labour-capacity), and in terms of the amount of state expenditure (see 7§14-d). Whereas state-funded education furthers the conditions for the accumulation of capital (as contingent on the stage of technical development) a trade-off between its costs and benefits is difficult to determine even in terms of exclusively monetary objectives.

Public education is in the interest of enterprises and the CMC, whilst it is certainly also in the interest of the SWC. (On the classes of CMC and SWC see 7§10 and 6§12.)

7§14-a Explication. Necessity of public education and of all the moments of 7D3 and 7D4

Public education by itself is not necessary to the 'phantom' of a capitalist economy that might be supposed to stand on itself (even if without public education, profits and the rate of accumulation of capital would slacken). It is, however, necessary to the capitalist system to the extent that the furthering of the conditions for economic growth is a necessary objective for the capitalist state (7§3). However, the dodgy question is not about the necessity, but rather about the degree. The latter is inevitably a matter of opposing interests, choices and conflict resolution in practice. A similar remark applies to all the moments of 7D3 and 7D4.

7§14-b Amplification. Reason for state-funded education and the contingent main ways of organising it

Were all formal education left completely to the market, then the education would tend to be restricted to high income earning families. The resulting under-education of the majority of the workers would limit the possible implementation of new techniques of production. On the job education and training of general skills that can be used in any other job secure rents for enterprises that abstain from providing this general education and training. Therefore it is in the interest of enterprises that education is provided, or at least funded, collectively.[13]

The specific way of doing this is contingent. One possibility is that all formal education is provided by profit-driven private institutions (i.e. enterprises), with the state subsidising the pupils and students via grants. The efficiency of such a system is doubtful. Another possibility is that the state funds the educational institutions, requiring these institutions to provide the education for free.

All this tends to be combined with regulation of compulsory education up to some age. The age of compulsory education is contingently related to the state of technical development. It is also contingent whether, and to what degree, the state funds higher education beyond the compulsory age.

Equally contingent is whether, on top of the free education, the state provides subsidies, grants or loans for livelihood during the education. Should the state not provide means for livelihood during especially the duration of the compulsory education, then the average equivalent is required to be part of either the minimum wage (6§7) or there should be – more directly – child benefits to cover this.

Note that – as always – the argument here and in the main text is not about morals, and in this case about any emancipatory aspects of free education. The 'enhancement of the labour-capacity required by enterprises' (7§14) does not univocally imply that the corresponding education is emancipatory (see also 2§7 about compliance with the objectives of the enterprise).

---

13 Ultra-free market proponents question this. In an article in the *American Economic Review*, Blankenau, Simpson and Tomljanovich (2007) suggest that 'the inability of some studies to find a robust relationship between public education spending and growth may reflect a failure to properly account for the method of finance'.

7§14-c Amplification. Development of the years of average formal schooling, and indicators of the current distribution of schooling: case of the OECD-21

(See Appendix 6A on the mere illustrative status of the OECD-21 data, here and in the rest of this chapter.) *Graph 7.5* shows data of the development of the average number of years of formal schooling (not particularly public schooling). For the average of 21 current OECD countries, we see an almost linear increase in the number of years of formal schooling from 1870–1950, followed by an accelerated increase from 1950–80. After 1980 the increase somewhat flattens off. For the distribution we see a sharp decline in the skewedness from 1870–1920 and a considerable decline after 1930. (The Gini measure for the distribution is on the scale of 0–100: the number 0 indicating complete evenness of the distribution, and the number 100 maximal skewedness – all education devoted to one person.)

GRAPH 7.5 *Years of formal schooling and distribution of schooling 1870–2010; average of 21 current OECD countries*[14]

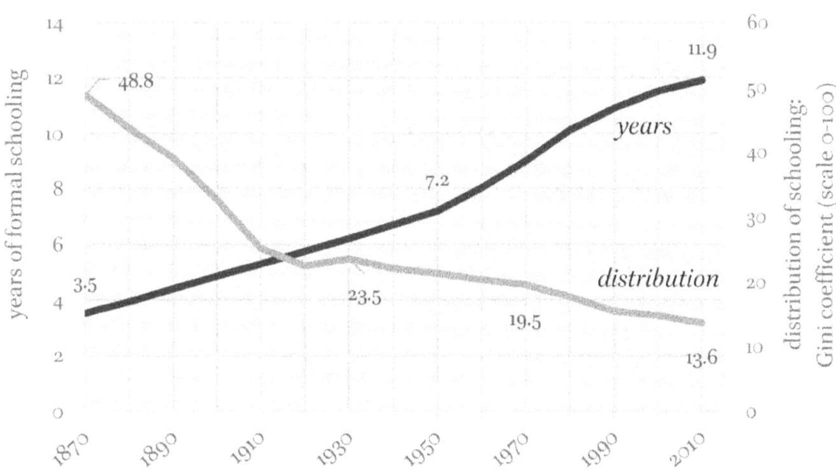

DATA SOURCE: Clio Infra (accessed 27 February 2016). See Appendix 7A, under '7§14-c', for more information on the data

7§14-d Amplification. State expenditure on education: case of the OECD-21.

Graph 7.6 shows data on state expenditure as a percentage of GDP from 1870–2014, for the average of up to 21 current OECD countries. There are some gaps in

14 These are the 'OECD-21' (see Appendix 6A).

these data (these are interpolated), but, as far as I know, we have no more especially for the period prior to 1960 (see Appendix 7A, under '7§14-d'.) Note that '*general government*' is a (statistical) category denoting all levels of government (the central plus the various levels of the local ones).

GRAPH 7.6 *State expenditure (general government) on education, 1870–2014, in % of GDP; average of up to 21 current OECD countries*

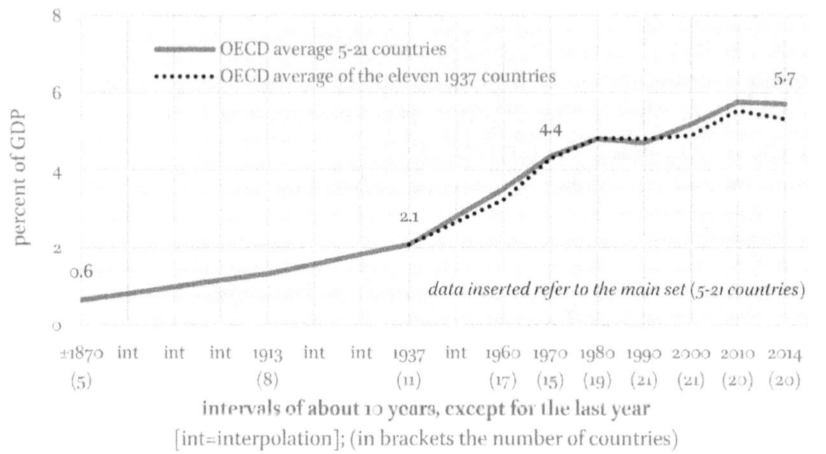

DATA SOURCES: 1870–1960 (Tanzi and Schuknecht 2000, Table II.5); 1970–2014 (UNESCO institute for statistics, May 2017 release, accessed 27 December 2017). See Appendix 7A, under '7§14-d', for more information on the data

It can be seen from *Graph 7.6* that already in 1870 there was, on average, a considerable state expenditure on education of 0.6% of GDP, moving to 2.1% in 1937. After a quite steep increase between 1937 and 1970 (to 4.4%), the degree of increase flattens off in the decades thereafter.

7§14-e Amplification. Impact of varying number of countries in historical datasets

In order to show the possible impact of the scarce number of data for earlier years in terms of number of counties, most of my figures show graphs for separate series of countries – in the main text or in the statistical appendix of a chapter. See, for example, the two series in *Graph 7.6*. There we see that the data for the 11 countries of 1937 approximate the 17 of 1960 and the 21 afterwards, so that it may be concluded that the 1937 figure is probably a reliable proxy for the total.

Division 4. The infrastructural framework
Accumulation-furthering regulation

This division presents the third of the three main levers for the state's furthering of the conditions for economic growth (next to 7D2 and 7D3).

7§15 *Infrastructure*

• ***Infrastructural networks***

There is a category of (potential) economic activities – called infrastructural – that substantially does or would raise the macroeconomic productivity of labour and so does or would raise macroeconomic surplus-value (integral profit), but that nevertheless either cannot microeconomically be profitably produced by enterprises, or, if it could, would generate a monopoly.[15] Most often these concern very costly *networks*. That is, networks for the transport of commodities and of waste, including critical nodes for the former. More specifically, networks for the transport of vehicles (for people and commodities), for commodities (the latter including communication/information, energy) and for waste (including sewers).

• ***State engagement in infrastructural networks***

To the extent that these productivity raising infrastructural activities are not undertaken by enterprises without generating a monopoly, the state's objective of furthering the conditions for economic growth and hence the accumulation of capital (7§3) requires it to engage in these.

In addition, though more controversial than the former, the state might engage in infrastructural activities that are, or could be, undertaken by private enterprises, when these can be produced at a lower cost collectively than competitively. Nevertheless such engagement is in line with the objective of increasing the macroeconomic tax base.

The state's engagement in the provision of networks can be undertaken in various ways. Networks may be produced, maintained and owned by the state. Alternatively these are owned by the state though via procurement produced and maintained by enterprises. In some cases another possibility might be to temporarily license the provision to enterprises perhaps via procurement. Apart from this last possibility, state engagement in infrastructural activity considerably raises the state expenditures and the *amount* of taxation (as with

15 The non-profitability might be merely contingently the case. Technical development might change the tables such that a formerly non-profitable activity may become profitable. Apart from that, Chapter 9 sets out why the state tends to put restrictions on monopolisation.

education), though – in face of the effect on productivity, costs and growth – not necessarily the tax *rates*.

- ***Infrastructural supply (plant)***

In many cases the supply of the commodities transported via infrastructural networks has itself a so-called infrastructural character tending to (regional) monopoly or oligopoly (for example, water resources, mass energy generation, communication, train connection). When in addition there are no ready (regional) substitutes for these, the state cannot allow the possible bankruptcy of the supplying enterprises – that is, without jeopardising the reproduction of the (regional) economy. Because 'too big to fail' implies private profits combined with social losses, this may be a reason for state ownership of the infrastructural supply.

7§15-a Amplification. State expenditure on infrastructure, 1870 to current: case of the OECD-21

For the OECD countries, internationally more or less homogenous data for state expenditure on infrastructure are only available from 1995. However, for state gross investment expenditure (general government) long run data are available. Therefore I use a major fraction (57.5%) of the latter as an approximation for the infrastructure expenditure. In Appendix 7A (under 7§15-a) I provide an underpinning of this proxy, by relating it to the after 1995 infrastructure data.

In this perspective *Graph 7.7* shows data on state expenditure (general government) on gross investment for the average of up to 21 current OECD countries, from 1870 to 2015. Judging from the data available, it can be seen that from 1870 (investment at about 2% of GDP) there is a steady increase until 1970. In the six decades thereafter the average for investment decreases quite substantially, reaching in 2015 a GDP share of just below that of 1920.

Thus the expenditure on infrastructure (as approximated by 57.5% of gross investment) moved from 1.2% in 1870 to a top of 3.2% in 1970, and then gradually decreased to a GDP share of 1.9% in 2015. One cause of the decrease is the substitution of state ownership for private ownership via licenses as indicated in the main text of 7§15.

GRAPH 7.7 *State expenditure (general government) on gross investment, 1870–2015, average of up to 21 current OECD countries*

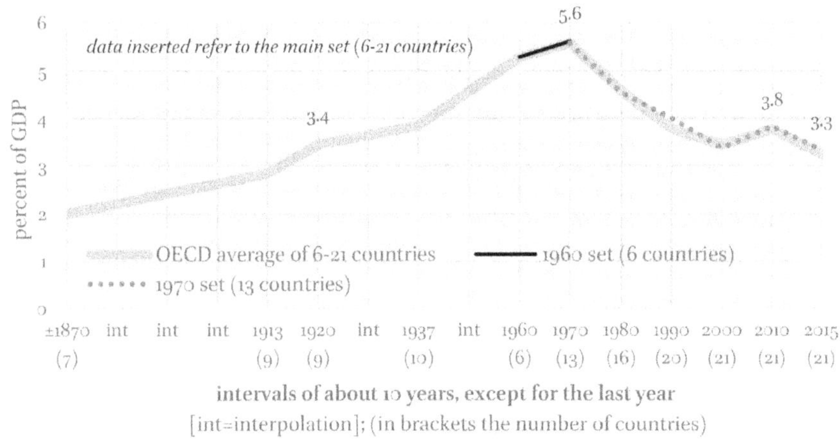

DATA SOURCES: 1870–1937 (Tanzi and Schuknecht 2000); 1960–2015 (OECD Economic Outlook database 2017–2, June, accessed 27 December 2017). See Appendix 7A, under '7§15-a', for more information on the data

7§16 *Fundamental technology research*

Fundamental technology research (in contradistinction to technique and applied technique development) is unlikely to be carried out by enterprises on a considerable scale. Nevertheless fundamental technology research is indispensable for applied research and technique development. Given the state's objective of furthering the conditions for economic growth and hence the accumulation of capital (7§3), the finance by the state of this fundamental research is perhaps not absolutely necessary, but it is (at least today) *de facto* considerable. The dodgy question for the state is how much and on the basis of what criterion (there does not seem to be such a criterion).

7§16-a Amplification. The state's fundamental technology research

In a study that focuses on research and development (R&D) after WWII, Mazzucato (2011)[16] indicates that for the year 2008 in the USA, business companies accounted for 67% of total R&D expenditure. However, regarding the *basic* R&D this was 18%, the rest was undertaken by the Federal government (57%), universities and colleges (15%) and other non-profit institutions (11%). (See Figures 3 and 4 in Mazzucato 2011, pp. 51–2.) She shows that the state is 'a lead-

16 See also Mazzucato 2013.

ing agent in achieving the type of innovative breakthroughs that allow companies, and economies, to grow' (p. 18). It has been 'the state not the private sector that has kick-started and developed the engine of growth, because of its willingness to take risk in areas where the private sector has been too risk-averse' (p. 23). More specifically she shows that the technological revolutions of the computer industry, the Internet, the pharma-biotech industry, nanotech industry and many more are the result of the '*leading* role of the state' (p. 20; and pp. 76ff.).[17] (In the terminology of Chapters 1–2, I call the fundamental research 'technology research' and the research regarding the application of technology 'technique research'.)

Division 5. The social security framework

The indeterminate degree of social security transfers in face of the required compliance of subordinated labour

The legitimation of the state in the compliance of the vast majority of actors (6D3, 6§5), grounds the state-granted economic rights (6D2) at an abstract-general level. Inherent to the latter, this legitimation in compliance is systematically a high-level determinant for all of the more concrete conditions of existence presented in the later exposition. (In this there is an analogue with the monetary-value dimension – 1D2.) More concretely, the legitimating compliance is engendered in the compliance of categories of actors that have a particular (non-)interest in the existence and outcomes of the capitalist system (recall the reference to the two very broad objective classes of the capitalist and managerial class (CMC) and the subordinated working class (SWC) in 6§12).

In this perspective the current division – which focuses on the compliance of the SWC – grounds 6D3, as well as all the later conditions of existence presented so far (see Scheme 7.1).

Recall that in 6§17 a distinction was made between 'allowance rights/provisions' and 'positive rights/provisions'. In terms of the broad category of 'existence rights', and especially '*positive existence rights/provisions*', the current division is a continuation from three moments presented in 7D3 (those of the minimum wage, temporary unemployment benefits and child benefits). These

17 Because I will not return to this matter in Chapter 11 – when I introduce multiple nations and multiple states – it may be noted that specific states may specialise in particular branches of fundamental research. The R&D workers, especially those of the large enterprises carrying out applied research and development, must be equipped to absorb the fundamental research wherever it is located (see WRR 2013a and 2013b).

latter, however, serve primarily the labour-capacity requirements – the 'positive rights/provision' being a corollary. However, the moments presented in the current division are 'self-standing' in face of the legitimation referred to.

7§17 *Legitimation: compliance-dependent social security transfers*

1 *Seeking legitimation in the compliance of the vast majority*

For its actions and non-actions the state inevitably has to seek and gain legitimation in the compliance of not just a majority but the vast majority of actors (6§5; 6§18). Given that the subordinated working class constitutes the vast majority, the state must necessarily seek their compliance.[18] This may require, first, minimum wages that are substantially higher than subsistence wages (7§10) and, second, compensation for actors out of work as well as for expenditures that should be covered by a 'decent' wage but are not.

Such compensations regard these actors' 'existence security', or, as it is commonly called (perhaps less heavily laden), 'social security'. These are necessary.[19] However, their *level* is contingent in the sense that compliance is dependent on a contingent degree of conflict or perhaps resistance in case of non-materialisation of sufficient compensations.

In face of this 'level-contingency', this section outlines a social security framework: first, the main prevailing categories of social security, and secondly, the legal forms in which these can be provided. For 'compensation' I adopt the common term 'transfer'.

2 *Categories of social security transfers*

There are six categories of social security transfers, which can be divided into two groups.

A. Out of work transfers, specifically regarding:

- Unemployment in general – that is, transfers for structural unemployment, next to the temporary unemployment benefits presented in 7§12.
- Incapacity (disability) – that is, incapacity during the regular working life.
- Old-age disability or exemption to work (pensions).

---

18 From research by Mohun (2016) for the USA 1918–2012, it can be inferred that during this period on average, the subordinated working class made up 82% of the total. (See also 2§15-a.)

19 Even in the period 1880–1920 there were some of these, the state expenditure amounting from 0.4 to 0.9% of GDP (average of available data of current OECD countries) – see further 7§17-a. In this early period, poor relief by especially religious institutions was dominant.

B. Expenditures related transfers, specifically regarding:

- Health (cure & care) – these can be transfers, but can also be provided in kind;
- Child related in general – next to transfers required in case of foreseen scarcity of the labour population (7§13).[20]
- Housing – these are housing market dependent, and in fact dependent on whether the minimum wage, or the transfers under A, are sufficient to rent a house.

3 *Legal forms of social security transfers*

A. Protection of the poor

Social security transfers can be granted in the form of *provisions* for the poor. This requires determination of 'the' poverty line. For some ideological stances such provisions clash with their 'free market' principle that there should be no such thing as a 'free income' – an income not deriving from *either work or property*. The state can take such a stance into account, but ultimately it has to seek and gain the 'vast majority' compliance.

B. Generalised social security transfers

The sting seems somewhat taken out of these ideological complaints when the transfers above (apart from housing) are granted to all (the poor and the rich). Such a constellation has also been defended on the basis of the argument that it increases the general public support for these.[21] Quite apart from ideological and supportive arguments, generalised social security prevents stigmatisation of the poor. However, the general effect is also (as with a so-called basic income) the pumping around of large sums of money, increasing state expenditure and taxation (directly or in the form of so-called social insurance contributions).

Within each of these two legal forms (the poor or generalised) there are again two legal forms for these: the form of legal rights and the form of legal provisions. In practice their main difference is that legal provisions are easier to cut back than legal rights once the latter's level has been determined.

The right-hand side column of *Figure 7.8* provides a summary of the previous two subsections. Amplification 7§17-a provides empirical information on social security expenditures.

---

20 Child benefits can also be defended on the basis of equity arguments: everybody is free not to have children; those who have children are rewarded (bought off) for providing the future generation.

21 For example, in the Netherlands.

4 *Social security transfers and surplus-value*

The legitimation of the state – as based on vast majority compliance – requires social security transfers. Because the legitimation of the state is a *sine qua non* for the existence of the capitalist system, these transfers are an indirect condition for the accumulation of capital.

FIGURE 7.8 *Legal forms of regulation of production and of existence security*

<table>
<tr><th>Regulation of production</th><th>Regulation of existence security</th><th></th></tr>
<tr><td>o form of legal allowance rights</td><td>o form of legal positive rights</td><td></td></tr>
<tr><td>level: compliance dependent</td><td>level: at least subsistence; further compliance dependent</td><td></td></tr>
<tr><td rowspan="2">• consumer protection [6§14]
• environment protection [6§14]
• labour protection (safety, time, health) [6§15]</td><td>(regulation labour-capacity market)
• minimum wage [7§10]</td><td></td></tr>
<tr><td>(regulation labour-capacity market)
• temporary unemployment benefits [7§12]
• temporary sickness benefits [7§12]</td><td rowspan="4">social security transfers (in OECD definition)*</td></tr>
<tr><td rowspan="3"></td><td>o form of protection of the poor; OR
o form of general regulation.
AND
o form of provisions for existence; OR
o form of legal positive rights to existence.</td></tr>
<tr><td>level for all: compliance dependent</td></tr>
<tr><td>• child related transfers [7§13]†‡
• health (cure & care): transfers or provisions in kind
• structural-unemployment transfers
• old-age transfers
• incapacity (disability) transfers
• housing transfers (or provisions in kind)</td></tr>
</table>

† Anyway required in case of foreseen scarcity of labour population (7§13).
‡ In *Graph 7.9* these are covered under 'family'.
* The exposition in Chapter 7 makes a systematic distinction between labour-capacity related transfers (top of figure) and pure compliance related transfers. In the OECD categories this distinction is not made.

In effect, some of the appropriated surplus-value that flows to the capitalist and managerial classes CMC is merely handed back to pay for, mainly, the categories of health, old age and incapacity transfers (*Graphs 7.9* and *7.10*). 'Some': a considerable part of these transfers are paid out of gross wages – in the form of social security contributions (see also Chapter 8, 8§9). Further, because of the (intertemporal) redistributive effects of social security from high to low incomes, savings tend to mitigate, which affects the validation of surplus-value positively (Chapter 3, esp. 3§3 and 3§1, and further Chapter 8).

7§17-a Amplification. State expenditure on social security: case of the OECD-21

This amplification presents two graphs of data of state expenditure on social security: a detailed one for the period 1980–2010, and an aggregate one for the period 1880–2015.

For the 'OECD-21' detailed internationally consistent data for social security expenditure are only available from 1980 (detailed, that is, along the categories distinguished in the main text of 7§17). These are shown in *Graph 7.9*, along with the average rate of unemployment in that period.

GRAPH 7.9 *State expenditure (general government) on specific categories of social security transfers 1980–2010, in % of GDP; averages of 19–21 OECD countries*

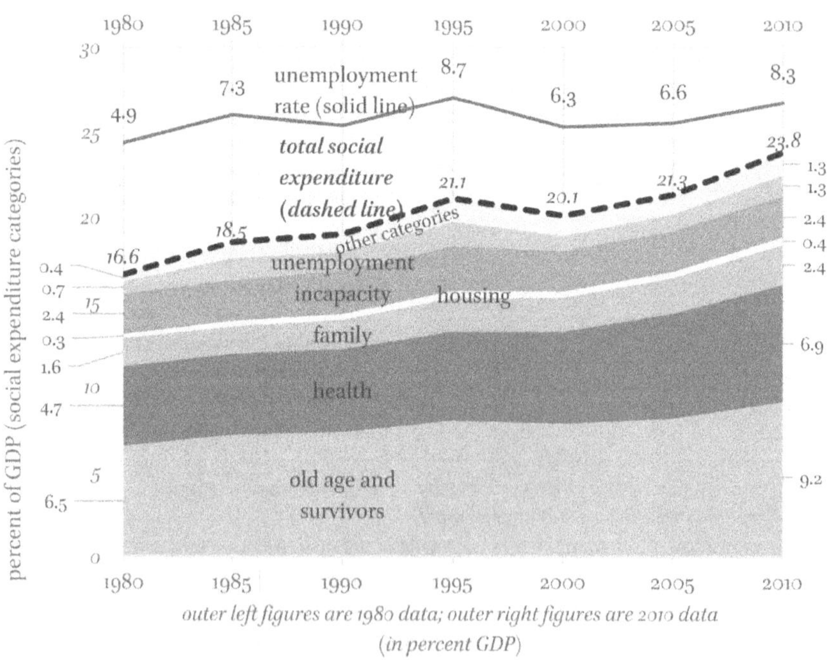

DATA SOURCES: Area charts: OECD, database 'Social Expenditure; Aggregated data (SOCX)'. Unemployment rate: OECD database. (All downloaded in December 2017.) See Appendix 7A under 7§17-a for data details

It can be seen that in this period there are upward trends in the three categories at the bottom of the graph – some of the categories at the top of the graph are in part related to the unemployment rate.

Graph 7.10 shows aggregate data for state expenditure on social security from 1880 for the current OECD-21. It can be seen that after a moderate increase from 1880 to 1930 (data for 1940 and 1950 are lacking), there is a rather steep increase until 1990 – the increase bending off afterwards. (It can also be seen that the trend is not very sensitive for the 17 or 21 countries in the data set.)[22]

GRAPH 7.10 *State expenditure (general government) on social security 1880–2015, average of up to 21 current OECD countries*

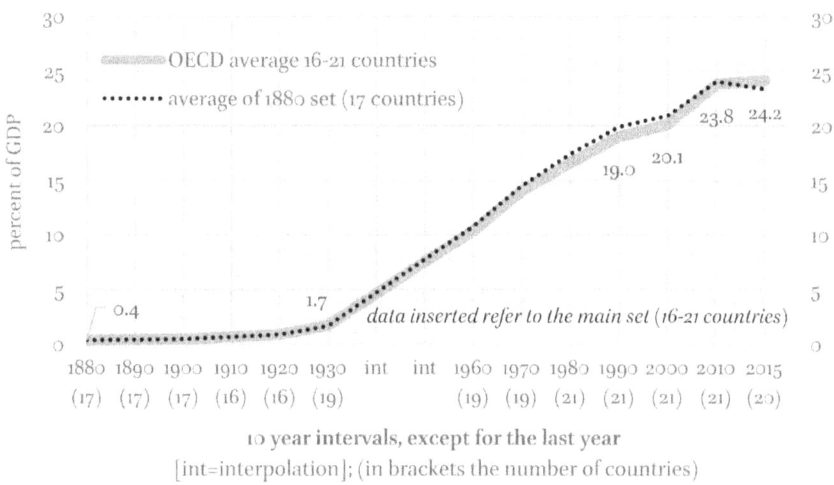

DATA SOURCES: 1880–1970 (Tanzi 2011, Table 1.2); 1980–2014 (OECD, dataset Social Expenditure – Aggregated data, extracted 27 December 2017)[23]

Total state expenditure (all categories) will be systematically introduced in Chapter 8. Anticipating that, *Graph 7.11* already puts social expenditure in the perspective of the total. It can be seen that from 1920 (and for the data available) social security expenditure developed steadier than total state expenditure.

22 The OECD has also collected data on 'mandatory private social expenditure' (available for 9–15 countries of the OECD-21). This expenditure, although in quantity moderate, increased gradually from on average 0.7% of GDP in 1980 to 1.0% in 2011. On these mandatory private expenditures, see Adema, Fron and Ladaique 2011.

23 OECD data available at: http://stats.oecd.org/index.aspx?DatasetCode=SOCX_AGG.

GRAPH 7.11 *Social security expenditure and total state expenditure (general government) 1870–2015 in % of* GDP*; averages of up to 21 current* OECD *countries*

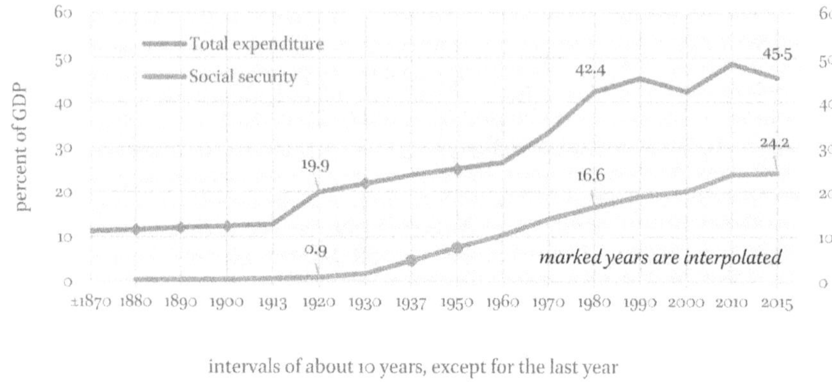

DATA SOURCES: (1) Social security: see Graph 7.10. (2) Total expenditure: 1870–1937 (Tanzi and Schuknecht 2000); 1960–1980 (Castles 2006); from 1990 onwards (OECD Economic Outlook database November 2017, details are provided in Chapter 8: Graph 8.2 and Appendix 8A)

7§17-b Amplification. (In-)decent outcomes

Recall that the exposition, in all of Part Two, is primarily one in terms of *effects* of the state, rather than the motives of agents of the state (6§4-a). It might be argued that even if social security expenditure grounds the state's legitimation, the effect – gradually from 1930 onwards – is an increasing 'decency'. This is correct. ('Decency' is a term used in the 'human rights' discourse, and I am aware that this is a moral or perhaps an ethical term.) However, such an observation and judgement might equally be formulated as a decreasing 'indecency', in which case the perspective on the total is different, namely one of indecency. This is relevant because, as argued in the previous sections of Chapters 6 and 7, the state *de facto* keeps the capitalist system going.

7§17-c Amplification. Aggregate demand effect

Although it is not the impetus for social transfers, we will see in Chapter 10 that these transfers have the important side effect of mitigating the amplitude of the business cycle (to be sure, the latter cannot be read off from *Graph 7.11* as it shows shares in GDP, not fluctuations in GDP).

Division 6. Separation of the state's administrative and judiciary branches

Divisions 6 and 7 present the legitimation of the state from a perspective very different from that of Division 5. Both 7D6 and 7D7 apply to the continuously reappearing conflicts of the *content* of legislation and other regulation, that is, the content of the seven regulative frameworks presented so far: capitalist economic rights (6D4), allowance rights to existence (6D5), public security (6D6), money and banking (7D2), labour-capacity (7D3), infrastructure (7D4), and social security (7D5).

We will see in the following two divisions that the state seeks to mitigate the resulting conflicts, by *institutional* separations within the body of the state. The current division presents the separated off judiciary – separated from the main administrative body of the state.

7§18 *Arbitration and sanctioning – legitimising assignment to a separated off Judiciary, as a separation-in-unity with the main body of the state*

It was indicated in Chapter 6 that the grounding of legal right requires the state to be the *arbiter* and *sanctioner* of deviations from the law (6§9).

Arbitration often entails an interpretation and/or a concretisation of the law. This interpretation or concretisation may not be similar to the understanding of the law by the prosecuted actor. The sanctioning in this case conflicts with the actor's sense of justice.

This is even further at issue for the state's arbitration and sanctioning in case of conflicting rights. Conflicts are especially delicate when the sources of property are in dispute.

In all cases of conflict and senses of injustice, the state's reference to the (putative) general interest (6§6) and its (putative) impartiality (6§7) tend to erode. Thus the necessary grounding of legal right at hand (i.e. arbitration and sanctioning) may erode the legitimation of the state (6§5).

Therefore, in order to mitigate these erosive effects, the arbitration and the sanctioning of deviations from the law, tends to be assigned to a particular separate institution of the state: *the judiciary*. In this way the main body of the state – that is, its administrative branch (the latter being the unity of the legislative and the executive branches) – 'purifies' itself from conflict. Note that this assignment entails a higher degree of purification than, the alternative of, delegation (see 7§18-a).

Inevitably, however, even if the judiciary is so split off from the administrative branch of the state, it is nevertheless a branch of the state as a 'separation-in-unity' *within* the state. (See *Scheme 7.17*.) This, it being a branch of the state, is also how it is experienced by most actors.

SCHEME 7.12 *Arbitration and sanctioning as assigned to the separate Judiciary: separation-in-unity with the state's main body*

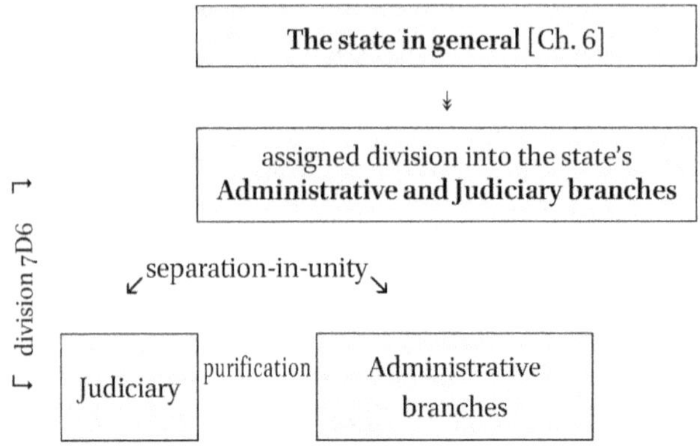

Legend
↡ grounding

7§18-a Explication. Degrees of purification: assignment versus delegation

A distinction is made between the *assignment* and the *delegation* of state functions to separate bodies. Assignment regards a separation of activities within the state (separation-in-unity) without there being a subordination – in principle at least. With delegation (6§15, 7§7, 7§11) there is a relationship of subordination – *ultimately* the state remains responsible for what it delegates, though at distance and most often in a complicated manner. In terms of types of law: an assignment tends to be enacted at the level of the constitution, whereas a delegation tends to be enacted at the level of an ordinary law.

Although both assignment and delegation serve to protect the main body of the state from legitimation-eroding conflicts, their difference in terms of (non-)subordination implies different degrees of purification (a higher degree in case of assignment).

7§18-b Amplification. Purification from conflict versus 'separation of powers'

The exposition of the judiciary in 7§18 is one *from the point of view of the state* and its concern to gain legitimating compliance (6§5) by (putatively) positing itself above and outside the opposing particular interests (6§7). The judiciary is separated off *because* arbitration and sanctioning by the state itself might have a negative effect on the compliance.

This exposition is very different from arguments about this separation in terms of separation of powers (as in Montesquieu's *Trias Politica*) – the latter being an argument from the point of view of the non-state actors ('subjects'). Whereas the purification seems necessary, a separation of powers may merely contribute to a moral ideal (one that I would not want to underrate).

However, in each case (purification and separation of powers) the separation requires a contingent institutionalisation that itself may not be unproblematic. Think for example of the appointment of judges by some institution of the state (e.g. by the presidency or a minister of justice or parliament), which muddles the separation.[24] Further (and perhaps related), in everyday life many actors do have the feeling that the judiciary is an extension of the state. That feeling by itself seems correct – in any case it is covered by the term 'separation-in-unity'.

As indicated, the argument in 7§18 is one from the *point of view of the state* – so as to protect its legitimation – rather than a *normative* one from the point of view non-state actors. This is in line with all of the exposition in this book, which abstains from normative arguments and from morals (6§4-a). Having indicated this, it may be noted that for the rest of the exposition not much hinges on it. In each case the relevant actual effect is the separation-in-unity between the state's Administrative and Judiciary branches.

Division 7. Separation of the state's administrative and deliberative branches

This division presents the 'Deliberative'. (I could have used the term 'parliament' if, today at least, this would not have the direct connotation of being a legislative, a function that I do not exclude, but that I would want to keep hanging for the time being.) The Deliberative is a second (and last) legitimating body within the state. As with the Judiciary, the Deliberative purifies the main body of the state from conflict, and again it constitutes a separation-

24 I am prepared to take small or large scale dismissals of part of the Judiciary as contingent aberrations. Take the case of Turkey in 2016, this country being a developed capitalist nation that forms part of the OECD from 1961. To be sure: within the systematic exposition of this book this is contingent because it is generally not necessary to the reproduction of the capitalist system.

in-unity with the latter. Again this separation tends to have the character of an assignment (rather than delegation). The legitimation reasons for the Judiciary's separation off are rather straightforward, and it is most often also clear what is being assigned. In the case of the Deliberative the legitimation reasons are less straightforward, and the same applies for what is being assigned. This makes that the current separation requires more space than that of the judiciary.

The first few sections of this division (7§19–7§22) present the four main areas of conflict for the action of the capitalist state that are explicit or implicit in the previous exposition. These conflicts seem insurmountable for the legitimation, and hence the existence, of the state as *institutionalised* in the exposition so far (6D3 and 7D6). The last section presents the separation within the body of the state referred to above, one that should overcome this problem of legitimation (7§23).

7§19 *Taxation and the overriding of property right*

> The material existence of the state requires it to appropriate means from the economy by taxation. Taxation so grounds the state's maintenance of legal right, including legal property rights. At the same time, taxation overrides property right (7§2).

Thus it appears that legal full property right – in the earth, means of production and appropriated surplus-value – is impossible: enacting property right requires the restriction of property right. Hence we have a modified reappearance of the impossibility of the actualisation of these claimed property entitlements within the economy (6§4), now at the level of the state. Whilst these claimants may will the state to grant their claims in the form of legal rights, the latter's activities are nevertheless experienced as an externally imposed power, conflicting with their claims. For these claimants, stamped as right holders, this is revealed in a continuously reappearing conflict of 'willing' and 'not willing' the state. (Enlightened property owners may see that full property right is indeed an impossibility.)

7§20 *Conflicts of the form of taxation*

Given that taxation inevitably impairs on property rights (7§19), any concretisation of taxation – that is, regarding various tax bases and the design of tax rates – is further conflicting in that it unavoidably requires the state to take a stance concerning the distribution of income and wealth. This applies to sales taxes and value-added taxes as well as taxes on income and wealth (amplified upon in Chapter 8). For example, there is no obvious reason why a flat tax on income, wealth or succession (on either one or all) should be more impartial than regressive or progressive taxes, or whether the one or the other should be more beneficial to the functioning of the economy.[25]

In taking such a stance about the distribution of income and wealth, the state must inevitably introduce considerations and criteria other than those of 'the' market. Thus, considering the capitalist system – not merely the capitalist economy – the criterion of the monetary-value-form, in particular the profit form, is insufficient. This is so even if ideologues may rightly or wrongly argue that the one form of taxation is *less* market *disturbing* than the other.

The state's unavoidable stance on the distribution of income and wealth is yet another source of conflict (next to those presented in the previous two sections) that threatens the legitimation of the state.

7§21 *The worrying or reassuring state's share in the economy*

The capitalist state's concern of its action radius requires it to further the conditions for the accumulation of capital. Therewith it increases the tax base, whence the tax rate can decrease (7§3).

However, along with it, state expenditure and the amount of taxation increases (7D2–7D4).[26] Indirectly, and in part directly, this is also the case for social security transfers (7D5). Thus directly or indirectly the state commands a larger share of the economy, in comparison with the *hypothetical* case in which the state would or could abstain from these expenditures and taxation. (Hypothetically, because the capitalist economy and state cannot exist without the seven regulative frameworks. None of these can be dispensed with. For the last five – presented in the current chapter – it is merely their quantitative size, or intensity, that is at issue.) Even so, the necessary impact of the state is conflicting among economic actors, in that some perceive it as worrying, whereas for others it is reassuring.

This is even more so for cases when the state's furthering of the conditions for the accumulation of capital, would (along with an increasing tax base) still require increasing tax rates. Then, taking the case of profit taxes, the result might still be that profits increase (7§21-a provides a simple example). The problem for the state is that enterprises tend to isolate the tax (rate) increase as the doing of the state, whilst perceiving the profit increase as their own doing.

---

25 The ongoing controversy about this – from early classical political economy onwards – reveals that there are no *obvious* reasons for one or the other taxation.

26 Structurally this is in fact not the case for the monetary policy (including surveillance) delegated to the Central Bank, as the latter tends to make profits that are usually distributed to the state.

7§21-a Explication. An example of the case of increasing profits along with an increasing tax rate

If ¤100 profits (the tax base) are taxed at 20%, the tax is ¤20, with net profits ¤80. If because of a near to costless furthering of the accumulation-conditions, profits increase to ¤105, the same tax of ¤20 may be collected at a tax rate of 19%. This is the pure case of such a tax alleviation. Now suppose that for a furthering of the conditions an extra tax of ¤3 is required (e.g. for infrastructure). Then, if again profits increase to ¤105, a tax rate of 22% would generate ¤23 taxes (instead of ¤20% before), with net profits ¤82 (instead of ¤80 before). Hence, in comparison with the initial situation (¤100 profits), net profits have increased even if the tax rate increased. With some adaptation of the example it can be shown that profits may increase along with an increasing share of taxes in GDP.

7§22 ***General conflicts of legal right and of legitimation in compliance***

The capitalist economy cannot exist without the core economic entitlement claims being granted by the state in the form of legal rights (6§2–6§4, 6§8). The legitimation of the state is grounded in the compliance of actors to submit to the state for granting these legal rights (6§5), as again, ultimately, grounded in the state's definition of the general interest (6§6). It is further grounded in the state's upholding of the granted rights by public security (6§18) and by the arbitration and sanctioning of deviation from the law, as assigned to the judiciary (7§18).

In terms of the state's (non-)regulation as serving the interests of actors, a large part of this regulation, or their level, is experienced in opposite ways by objective classes of actors. Nevertheless the state must somehow seek actor's compliance for what it does, and at the prevailing level so.

• First, workers must comply with: (1) the enterprises' legal right of their being employed (at the prevailing wage, benchmarked by the prevailing legal minimum wage (7§10), and at the prevailing degree of labour protection (6§15)) whilst the surplus-value that they produce is appropriated by the enterprise; (2) the prevailing content of their (other) rights to existence and of their property (6§14–6§15; 6§10); (3) the prevailing public education (7§14); (4) the prevailing level of social security provisions (7§17).

• Second, owners of enterprises (including owners of financial titles) must comply with: (1) the state's enacting of their employment rights (1 above); (2) the prevailing maintenance of their rights to existence and property; (3) more specifically concerning the latter, the restriction of their property rights via taxation (7§2) in face of the state's furthering of the conditions of the accumulation of capital (7D2–7D4).

The effective benefits from regulation for objective classes of actors tend to be opposite or unevenly distributed in terms of subordination and of the distribution of income and wealth. Therefore the constellation of these legal rights and provisions tends to be gravely conflicting, whence the state's ability to present that constellation as being in (its definition of) the general interest is not obvious.

7§23 *Conflict modification – legitimising assignment to a separated off Deliberative, as a separation-in-unity with the main body of the state*

The conflicts set out in this division (7§19–7§22) threaten the state's legitimation in the compliance of actors. Nevertheless the state's legitimation is a *sine qua non* for the very existence and reproduction of the capitalist system.

Then the point is not so much whether the state's definition of the general interest 'is' but rather whether it is perceived by the actors as in keeping with the variety of interests, or as proportional to the diversity of interests. In this perspective the opposing interests, and conflicts thereof, require a *form of presenting the state's particular legislative choices* as a *perceived* settlement of conflict in the general interest – thus conditioned, the choices are presented as *being* in the general interest.

This settlement of conflict is grounded in an institutional separation within the state between, on the one hand, the core Administrative Branch and, on the other hand, the legitimising Deliberative. This is an assigned separation within the total body of the state, whence it is a separation-in-unity (analogous to the separation-in-unity of the Administrative and the Judiciary – 7D6).

- The *Deliberative* indeed deliberates over legislative choices and over the state's (non-)actions generally, and so seeks or establishes the compliance of the people for these.

  Its particular form is contingent. For example an appointed assembly, a representative assembly of property owners, an assembly of delegates of corporations, a delegated voting of a parliament, a (delegated) voting of a parliament by constituency, or a constitutional democratic representative parliament might all gain the required compliance.

However, given one of these forms, the question of *what* is being assigned to the deliberative is an open one. (It is not only an open one, in practise many actors do not know what has been assigned – 'them' it is all the same dance.)

> The character of the assignment is contingent. The Deliberative might merely 'have a say' and so advice the Administrative. Alternatively it might (in all fields, or merely in particular ones) have final vote, or, together with the Administrative, have a final co-vote on legislative choices.

However, ultimately there must be a particular form and a particular assignment that does adequately gain the compliance.

• The *Administrative body* manages – at least – the execution of the law. It is contingent whether it has the final vote or a final co-vote on legislative choices.

In line with the assignment above, it is contingent if the final legislative vote is allotted to either the Administrative, or to the Deliberative, or to a combination of these two.

It is also contingent if the draw up of proposed legislation is allotted to either the Administrative or to a combination of the latter and the Deliberative.

• Hence the *legislative organ* may contingently consist of the Administrative, or the Deliberative, or of a combination of the two.

Within these contingencies the necessity is that some form of the Deliberative generates the legitimation of the state in the compliance of the vast majority of the people. A condition for it is that at least the influential actors must sufficiently feel to be represented by the legitimising apparatus. It is also necessary that it shields the Administrative *core* of the state, as much as possible, from conflicts arising from legislation, from (non-)action in general and from taxation in particular.

Hence through this separation-in-unity, the core of the state is *purified* from conflict, so that it can execute, in the name of the general interest, the granted core economic entitlement claims in the form of law; and execute the furthering of the conditions for economic growth and so for the accumulation of capital. Thus the Deliberative is the political arena of conflict and so a mode for recurrent conflict settlement. Hence it is a *mode of existence* of conflict.

7§23-a Amplification. Common suffrage: average of OECD-21

All the current OECD-21 countries practice forms of representative democracy – the character of the assignment differs. A common and equal suffrage for all ethnicities (also called universal suffrage) regarding the election of parliaments was, on average for these countries, introduced in 1940. Discriminating for ethnicities, a suffrage for men was on average introduced in 1894, and in 1930 also for women.[27] (Before that time there were restrictions regarding, mainly,

27 The averages are calculated from an anonymous source, and I do not know how reliable it is. https://en.wikipedia.org/wiki/Universal_suffrage#Dates_by_country (accessed October 2017).

a minimum income or property.) Regarding the removal of ethnical suffrage discrimination there is quite some variation between individual countries, ranging from Norway (1821) and Ireland (1829) to the USA (1965) and Spain (1977).[28]

7§23-b Amplification. Purification from conflict versus 'separation of powers'

Again, as for the Judiciary (7§18-b), the exposition in 7§23 is one *from the point of view of the state* and its concern to gain legitimating compliance. Thus it is not one from the perspective of non-state actors, such as in 'separation of powers' approaches, or the, democratically more fundamental, approaches for which political democracy is an aspiration in itself. Again, these two are moral ideals (and once again I remark that I would not want to underrate such ideals). And again (Judiciary and Deliberative) a degree of separation of powers is an effect of the purification from conflict.

Given that the exposition in 7§23 is one from the perspective of the state, the exposition may further be characterised as a *variant* of 'democratic instrumentalism' (see Peter 2016, section 4) to the extent that democratic deliberation and decisions are *a means for legitimation*. However, I add the caveat that I draw not a single normative position from it (as is the case with quite some democratic instrumentalists – see Peter's outline).

7§23-c Explication. Purification from conflict by way of assignment or delegation

In the course of Chapters 6 and 7 we saw a series of 'purifications' – either in the form of assigned separations-in-unity, or in the form of delegated separations (see 7§18-a on the difference between the two). These have in common that conflicts are encapsulated. Nevertheless that does not away with the conflicts. These separations are summarised in *Scheme 7.13*.

28 For the 25 other countries listed, common and equal suffrage for all ethnicities was on average introduced in 1950.

SCHEME 7.13 *Summary of the state's purifications from conflict for its administrative core – assigned division and delegation (Chapters 6–7)*

Capitalist State in General

||

threat of infringing legitimation by arbitration of conflicting right claims
·×·
assigned division into the Administrative and the Judiciary †
[6D3]

threat of infringing legitimation by legislating conflicting interests
·×·
assigned division into the Administrative and the Deliberative †
[7D6]

↙separation-in-unity↘ ↙separation-in-unity↘

legitimising **Judiciary** [7D6]

purification from conflict

Administrative [core]
- legislative and executive, or
- co-legislative and executive,
- or executive

purification from conflict

legitimising **Deliberative** ‡ [7D7]

||

threat of infringing legitimation by the execution of legislation regarding conflicting interests
[7D2; 6D5]

delegation of monetary regulation, supervision and monetary policy ⁑ ↙

delegation of regulation and supervision about production and the minimum wage ⁑ ↘

Central Bank [7§7]

purification from conflict

purification from conflict

Inspectorates and Councils [6§16; 7§11]

† The extent of the assigned division (the degree of authority) being demarcated by law.
‡ It may have (co-)legislative powers (then the powers of the Administrative vary with it).
⁑ The degree of delegation being demarcated by law.

Legend
·×· continuity impediment
|| implicit herein

Summary and conclusions

The capitalist state grants core economic entitlement claims in the form of law, and maintains these (Chapter 6). The state's existence requires taxation, whence it is compelled to override property right in the name of its definition of the (putative) general interest. Because the (potential) action radius of the state is determined by the tax base, it must seek to increase that base – so as to reach feasible tax rates – by furthering the conditions for the accumulation of capital and along with it the conditions for economic growth. (Division 1.)

Divisions 2–4 outlined the concretisation of this condition of existence of the state. In terms of the general systematic of the exposition, the first two of these divisions (the monetary framework and the labour-capacity framework) are also the sequel to Chapter 2's grounding of the accumulation of capital in the expansion of money and the expansion of labour-capacity.

The state's taxation and expenditure requires that it impose the monetary standard of 'its' Clearing Bank, whence all banks are required to adopt the monetary standard of the state's Clearing Bank, now the Central Bank (CB). This imposition implies that the state takes a responsibility for the actions of the CB, as concretised in the state's monetary legislation. Limiting banking to licensees, the major concern of this framework is to bind banks to sound security and liability rules ('prudential regulation'), the ultimate penalty for deviation from those rules being the withdrawal of the licence. A second major concern is achieving 'price stability' (in fact 'creeping inflation' – amplified in 9D2). The state can try to influence the interest rate, but it has virtually no means to control the quantity of money and credit. It is the commercial banks that predominantly undertake the money creation, and hence accommodate the accumulation of capital and economic growth. This poses the main dilemma of the state's monetary policy: tight prudential regulation affects the banks' accommodation of economic growth. This is also the main dilemma regarding the fairly recent phenomenon of the monetary system trembling banks that are 'too big to fail' and moreover organisationally too complex to supervise micro-wise (amplified in 9D2).

Monetary legislation and its execution require choices that affect not only economic growth in general, but more specifically also the distribution of income, investment and unemployment. This implies that the state has to take sides in the (potential) conflicts between labour, enterprises and financiers. As this may erode the ground of the state's legitimation, it tends to delegate the regulative concretisation and execution of monetary policy – including the regulation and supervision of banks – to the Central Bank. By this delegation the state purifies itself from conflict. Nevertheless, as with all delegation, the state is ultimately responsible for the actions that it delegates. The latter is highlighted in times of those banking crises that are so severe that their resolution is beyond the means of the CB, whence the state has to step in as 'tax levier of last resort' – eroding the legitimation of the state. (Division 2.)

The state's furthering of the conditions for the accumulation of capital requires it to promote a sufficient labour-capacity in terms of both quantity and quality. The quantitative aspect is concretised in regulation of minimum wages, of temporary unemployment benefits and of (number scaled) temporary child benefits. The qualitative aspect is concretised in state-funded public education.[29] In face of the conflicting character of especially minimum wages, the state tends to delegate its execution to minimum wage commissions or councils. This is again an effort to purify the core administrative body of the state from conflict. (Division 3.)

An important component of the state's furthering of the conditions for the accumulation of capital is also its engagement in infrastructural networks, as well as, depending on the specific market constellation, in the infrastructural supply itself. A final component is fundamental technology research. (Division 4.)

For its actions and non-actions the state inevitably has to seek and gain legitimation in the compliance of the vast majority of actors. Given that the subordinated working class constitutes the vast majority, it must especially also seek their compliance. This is concretised in various social security provisions, their level being dependent on contingent degrees of (potential) conflict.[30] Because the legitimation of the state is a *sine qua non* for the existence of the capitalist system, these transfers are an indirect condition for the accumulation of capital. (Division 5.)

This completes the exposition of the seven main legislative frameworks: those of legal economic rights (6D4), legal existence rights (6D5), public security (6D6), money and banking (7D2), labour-capacity (7D3), infrastructure (7D4), and social security (7D5).

The so far outlined action of the state that is necessary for the reproduction of the capitalist system is experienced by large groups of actors as conflicting with their interests. Firstly, the state's requirement of taxation implies that legal full property right – in the earth, means of production and appropriated

29 For the case of the average of the OECD-21, state expenditure on public education grew from under 1% of GDP in 1870 to nearly 6% around 2015 (Graph 7.6).

30 For the case of the average of the OECD-21, state expenditure on social security provisions was negligible until 1920 and grew thereafter to about 25% of GDP around 2015 (Graph 7.10).

surplus-value – is impossible: enacting property right requires the restriction of property right. Secondly, given this restriction, any concretisation of taxation (regarding various tax bases and design of tax rates) is further conflicting in that it unavoidably requires the state to take a stance concerning the distribution of income and wealth. This is generally and continuously the case. It is highlighted in times of severe banking crises, when the state as 'tax levier of last resort' saves banks, and so redistributes general means to one particular sector. Thirdly, the state's necessary action – including its furthering of the conditions for the accumulation of capital, and its provision of social security provisions – implies that the state commands a considerable share of the economy. This impact of the state is conflicting among economic actors, in that some perceive it as disquieting, whereas for others it is reassuring. Fourthly, and generally, in terms of the state's actions serving the interests of actors, a large part of these actions are experienced in opposite ways by the objective classes of actors.

All these conflicts threaten the state's legitimation. Nevertheless the legitimation of the state is an absolute requirement for the very existence and reproduction of the capitalist system.

The settlement of these conflicts is grounded in two major institutional 'assigning separations' within the state, between, on the one hand, the core Administrative body and, on the other, the bodies of a legitimising Judiciary and a legitimising Deliberative.

With the necessary arbitration and sanctioning of deviations from the law (6§9), the state gets involved with conflicting claims to right, so eroding both its reference to the general interest and its self-imposition as an extraordinary impartial institution. This is resolved by assigning the arbitration and sanctioning to a separated off judiciary, whence the state's core is purified from the conflicts concerned. (Division 6.)

The Deliberative is the necessary political arena of conflict and so a mode for recurrent conflict settlement. Through this separation, the core of the state is equally purified from conflict, so that it can execute the granting of the core economic entitlement claims in the form of law, and execute the frameworks of furthering the conditions for economic growth and thus for the accumulation of capital. (Division 7.)

Appendix 7A. data and data sources of the graphs in chapter 7

General note: For all years (1870 to current) I have used the maximum amount of information that my sources provide for the OECD-21 countries. Qualifications of this are provided throughout this Appendix. (See Appendix 6A on the 'OECD-21', on OECD-21 averages as 'arithmetic average' and on my main sources.)

[Re **7§3-b**] Data information on ***Graph 7.3.*** *Real-GDP per capita 1850–2010, growth rate per year (top graph) and average per decade (bottom graph); average of 20–21 current OECD countries in 2011 US$.*
The data originate from those collected by Maddison, and which, after his death, continued in the so-called Maddison Project. The data used are those from the 2018 revision.[31] Of its two main datasets I used the real-GDP per capita *CGDPpc* one. (In fact for the average of the OECD-21 countries the differences with the alternative dataset of *RGDPNApc* are not very big.) Continuous data for Ireland are available only from 1921.

[Re **7§14-c**] Data information on ***Graph 7.5.*** *Years of formal schooling and distribution of schooling 1870–2010, average of 21 current OECD countries.*
The data are from Clio Infra. https://www.clio-infra.eu/ (accessed 27 February 2016). The graph of the number of years is of 21 countries throughout. That for the distribution is of 13 countries for 1870–80, 17 for 1890, 18 for 1900, 20 for 1910–20 and 21 for 1930 and after. The Clio Infra website also provides information about the method of calculation of the Gini-coefficients.

[Re **7§14-d**] Data information on ***Graph 7.6.*** *Education expenditure, general government 1870–2014, average of up to 21 current OECD countries.*
Data sources 1870–1960 (Tanzi and Schuknecht 2000); 1970–current (UNESCO institute for statistics, dataset education)

Tanzi and Schuknecht (2000, Table II.5) provide data of 5 current OECD countries in 1870, 8 in 1913, 11 in 1937 and 17 in 1960.

The UNESCO data are from their May 2017 release.[32] There are some gaps in even these recent UNESCO data (from 1970), which I have accommodated by taking for each country the decade year or the nearest year available (in the same way as the OECD often does for its series). This results in the following number of country data for each decade year and for 2014:

---

31 https://www.rug.nl/ggdc/historicaldevelopment/maddison/releases/maddison-project-database-2018, update 11 January 2018. See also Bolt, Inklaar, de Jong and Luiten van Zanden 2018.

32 UNESCO, dataset education (financial resources/government expenditure on education), http://data.uis.unesco.org/OECDStat_Metadata/ShowMetadata.ashx?Dataset=EDULIT_DS&ShowOnWeb=true&Lang=en (accessed 27 December 2017).

1970	1980	1990	2000	2010	2014
15	19	21	21	20	20

[Re 7§15-a] Data information on ***Graph** 7.7. State expenditure (general government) on gross investment, 1870–2015, average of up to 21 current OECD countries.* For the OECD countries, internationally more or less homogenous data for state expenditure on infrastructure are only available from 1995. Therefore, as indicated in 7§15, I use a major fraction (57.5%) of the state gross investment expenditure (general government) as an indicator for this category. Below I provide an underpinning of this proxy. All figures below are averages of up to 21 OECD countries.[33]

Transport is the main component of infrastructural state expenditure. Between 1995 and 2013 this expenditure stood fairly stable at an average of 1.36% of GDP.[34] (Part of COFOG category 4.5.) Expenditure on ***communication*** (COFOG 4.6) was between 1995 and 2013 negligible (though there may be state ownership in communication corporations). Other infrastructural expenditures are classified under the COFOG category 5. These are mainly expenditures on ***waste and waste water facilities.*** The 1995–2013 average expenditure is 0.67% of GDP. The sum of these is 2.0% of GDP.

State gross investment (general government) stood between 1995 and 2013 at an average of 3.5% of GDP (OECD-21). The 0.575 fraction of this is 2.0% of GDP.[35]

In Chapter 10, when I use data for recent decades, the remaining 42.5% of the gross investment is allotted to the other expenditure categories, including

33 In what follows I make use of the OECD 'COFOG' data (Classification of the Functions of Government). In this classification government expenditures are categorised in ten 'functions' ('first digit'), and further down – below called 'digit level'.

34 This figure is decomposed as 'investment in transport infrastructure' at 0.9% (data for 21 countries) and maintenance at 0.5% (data for 15–18 countries). Averages of the 'OECD-21' as calculated on basis of data from the OECD International transport forum http://stats.oecd.org/OECDStat_Metadata/ShowMetadata.ashx?Dataset=ITF_INV-MTN_DATA&ShowOnWeb=true&Lang=en (→December 2015). (These expenditures are part of COFOG category 4.5. The source just quoted has more data. Moreover, the COFOG 4 digit 2 level is organised by sector rather than specifically infrastructural.)

35 Note that the infrastructure indicator regards indeed an average for the OECD-21. In the USA, for example, an above average part of the *federal* government gross investment has a military destination.

mainly the military, health and education (as well as what in that chapter will be called 'hard core' expenditure).

Graph 7.7-a shows the deviation of the investment indicator from the 1995–2013 expenditures on infrastructure.

GRAPH 7.7-A *Infrastructural state expenditure and the infrastructure indicator of state gross investment, 1995–2013, averages of up to 21 OECD countries*

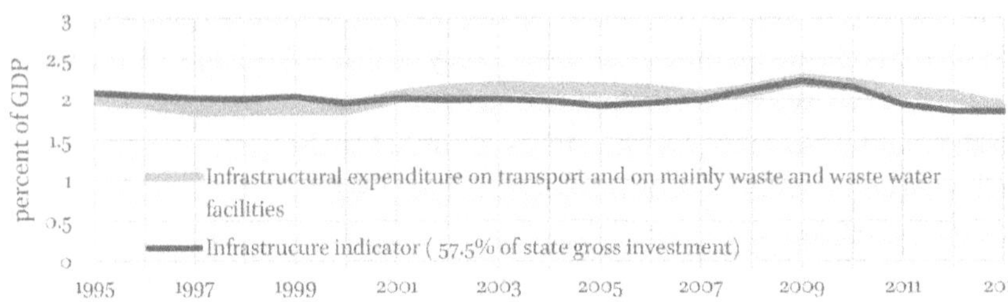

DATA SOURCES: Infrastructural expenditure on transport, OECD International transport forum (see the last but one footnote); waste and waste water facilities, OECD dataset National Accounts at a Glance 2015, General government expenditure by function, environment protection (COFOG 5);[36] state gross investment, see Graph 7.7 (main text)

[Re 7§15-a] Further data information on ***Graph*** *7.7. Gross investment expenditure, general government 1870–2015, average of up to 21 current OECD countries.*

Data sources. 1870–1937 (Tanzi and Schuknecht 2000, Table II.13); 1960–current (OECD Economic Outlook database, November 2017 (Government fixed capital formation, value, appropriation account, divided by GDP, value, market prices)). [Denmark and New Zealand 1970=1971; Germany 1990=1991.]

For reasons of consistency with later years I have started using the Economic Outlook (new) series from as early as possible, which is 1960. For this last year, however, only 6 data are available (Finland, France, Italy, Japan, Sweden, USA), with an average of 5.3% GDP. However, as Graph 7.7 shows there is a considerable fit between 6 country and 13 country averages in 1970; that graph also shows that there is not very much deviation between the averages for 13 countries (from 1970) and for 21 countries (from 2000).

36 http://stats.oecd.org/index.aspx?DatasetCode=NAAG_2015_NOV15 (extracted 24 Dec 2015).

[Re 7§17-a] *Graph 7.9. State expenditure (general government) on specific categories of social security transfers 1980–2010, in % of GDP; averages of 19–21 OECD countries.*

Data sources. Area charts (OECD, database 'Social Expenditure; Aggregated data [SOCX]').[37] Unemployment rate (dataset OECD, Economic Outlook, November 2017).[38]

For most categories these social expenditure data are available of 19–21 countries – 2013 being the last reported year. The unemployment data are available of 18–21 countries (Germany 1990=1992).

[Re 7§17-a]

TABLE 7.9-A *Specification of social security expenditure 1980–2010 in % of GDP; averages of 19–21 OECD countries*

	Percent of GDP (except last row)				**Percent linear change**			
expenditure categories	1980	1990	2000	2010	1980-90	1990-00	2000-10	1980-2010
old age and survivors	6.5	7.4	7.9	9.2	13%	7%	17%	40%
health	4.7	4.9	5.4	6.9	4%	11%	27%	47%
family	1.6	1.7	2.0	2.4	5%	14%	19%	43%
housing	0.3	0.3	0.4	0.4	31%	10%	14%	64%
incapacity	2.4	2.5	2.4	2.4	7%	-6%	3%	3%
unemployment	0.7	1.2	0.9	1.3	58%	-18%	33%	74%
all social security	16.6	19.0	20.1	23.8	14%	6%	18%	44%
total state expenditure	42.4	45.4	42.4	48.6	7%	-6%	15%	15%
rate of unemployment	*4.9*	*6.4*	*6.3*	*8.3*	*30%*	*-1%*	*32%*	*69%*

DATA SOURCE: see Graph 7.9

37 http://stats.oecd.org/index.aspx?DatasetCode=SOCXAGG (extracted 27 Dec 2017).
38 http://stats.oecd.org/index.aspx?DatasetCode=EO102_INTERNET (extracted 27 Dec 2017).

It can be seen from *Table 7.9-a* that from 1980–2010 the sum of social security expenditure increased considerably more than total state expenditure. However, incapacity transfers and especially unemployment transfers lagged behind from 1990–2010, and more so than the movement in the rate of unemployment.

List of figures chapter 7

CHAPTER 8

State expenditure and its finance

Effects on macroeconomic surplus-value and on the distribution of income and wealth

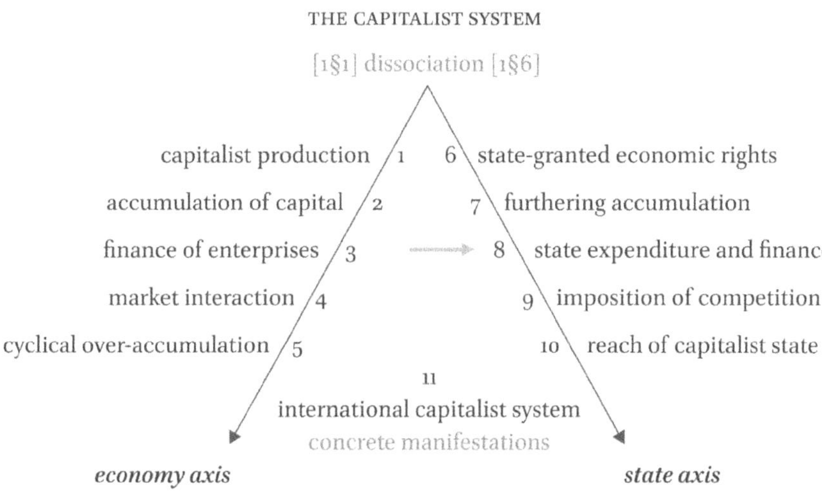

Contents

Introduction

Chapters 6–7 set out why, and in what respect, the capitalist economy cannot possibly exist without the state. Those chapters focused on the necessary content of the state's activities. Chapter 8 focuses on those activities in terms of monetary expenditures of the state and of their finance, outlining in particular their effect on the profits of enterprises.

In economic terms the state 'produces' its activities, requiring wage labour (civil servants) as well as inputs from enterprises. The concomitant expenditures are a category distinct from the expenditures related to transfers, such as those on social security. (Division 1.)

Division 2 presents a general outline of the finance of the production- and transfers-related expenditures by way of taxation and other forms of finance.

The following two divisions present the effect of state expenditure on the macroeconomic surplus-value of enterprises (Division 3) and of taxation on their after-tax surplus-value (Division 4). Along with it the so-called 'tax burden' for enterprises will be presented in a different light from how it is usually perceived.

Taxation being necessary, the state can and must choose between several forms of taxation and combinations thereof. This implies that in terms of the methodological pair of necessity and contingency, *necessity* in this respect (finance, taxation) takes on a *contingent form.* This form is determined by the state's furthering of the conditions for the accumulation of capital as articulated with its legitimation requirements. The particular forms of taxation result in a particular distribution of income (skewed) and in a particular distribution of wealth (even more skewed). (Division 5.)

Division 1 (state production) and Division 2 (finance of the state) provide conditions of existence for the exposition of Chapters 6–7. All the other divisions have the status of concretising implications of these earlier chapters and divisions. *Scheme 8.1* presents the chapter outline.

In amplifications to sections of this chapter, the reader finds empirical illustrations in reference to averages of 21 current OECD countries, extending where possible to 1870. The reader is referred to Appendix 6A for the status of these illustrations and especially the point that the OECD-21 average is meant to represent capitalism in its strongest version in terms of the reproduction of the capitalist system.[1]

1 Generally I repeat that cognisance of the Amplifications and Addenda is not required for the understanding of the further text (main sections and Explications).

SCHEME 8.1 *State expenditure and its finance (outline Chapter 8)*

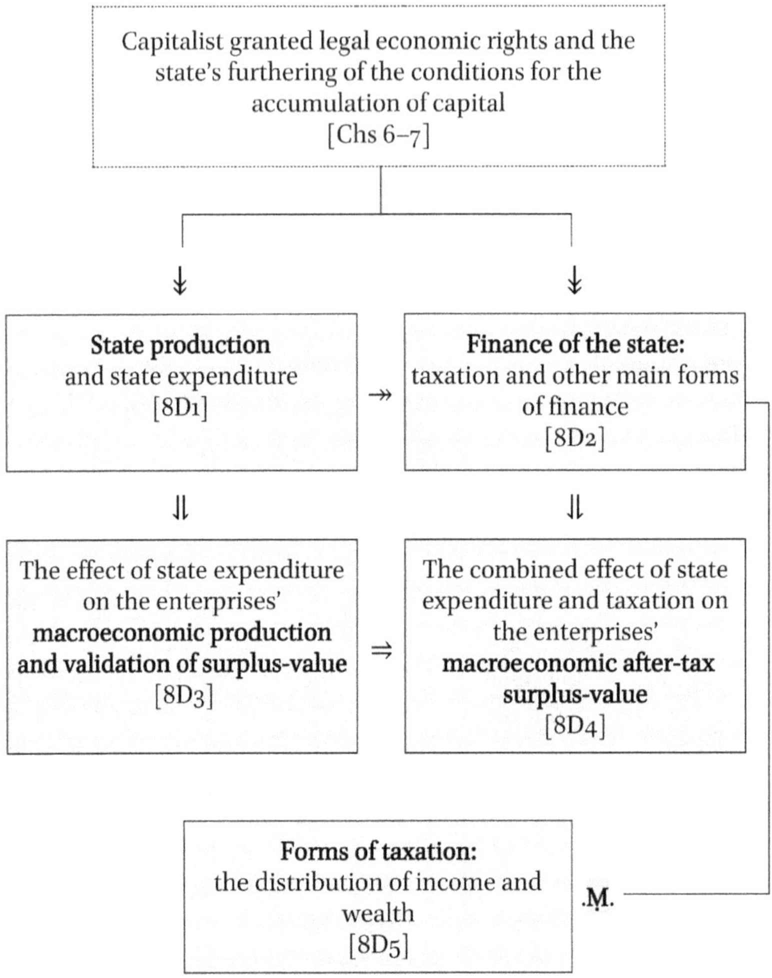

Legend

↡ and ↠ grounded in

⥥ bottom moment derives from top moment

⥤ right moment derives from left moment

.M. manifestation of earlier moment (see introduction to 8D5).

Division 1. State production and state expenditure

This division grounds the previous exposition of the state in its 'production'. In Chapters 6–7 the primary focus was on the *content* of the state's legislative frameworks. The information in Amplifications of Chapter 7 on expenditures on these frameworks was in fact presented as an aside. The following two divisions focus on the state as being also an economic actor. In the current division the perspective is that of 'state production' and of 'state expenditure' in general.

8§1 *Production in monetary terms by state-employed labour ('civil servants')*

Chapters 6–7 presented the capitalist state's granting of economic and existence claims in the form of legal rights (6D2–6D3) and their concretisation (6D4–6D6), its frameworks furthering of the conditions for the accumulation of capital (7D2–7D4) and its compliance-dependent social security provisions (7D5). In brief this is the content of the seven legislative frameworks presented in these chapters.

Economically the state 'produces' the content of the seven frameworks, this production being a condition of existence (ground) for these frameworks. For this production the state employs wage labour (wages sum Wg). For it, the state also purchases inputs from enterprises, both floating inputs (such as paper, transport and cleaning) and replacement investment (together Fg). (Net investment is presented in 8§2.) In monetary terms the product of the state's labour is a set of collective goods and services (G^{COL}):

$$G^{COL} = Fg + Wg \qquad \text{[convention of the state]} \quad (8.1)$$

(I denote state monetary entities by the symbol G or g, for government, so avoiding any confusion with the symbol S for savings.)

The state tends to have its labour (also called 'civil servants') produce these frameworks on a pure costs basis. Thus, in contradistinction to enterprises, the state tends to make no profits, whence wages are the sole component of its value-added (Yg).

$$Yg = Wg \qquad \text{[convention of the state]} \quad (8.2)$$

The reason for this is largely that it cannot sell to individuals most of its activities (e.g. legislation and public security), which so are collectively provided or distributed for free. Even if the state generally does not sell its production, it nevertheless partakes in the capitalist economy's monetary-value dimension and it so calculates its activities in monetary terms from their costs perspective.[2]

2 This is different from commensuration and from ideal pre-commensuration of the output of commodities (1§4 and 1§10).

Given some quantitative level of G^{COL} (*defined* by Fg and Wg), the relative division between the purchases Fg and the Wg depend on the state's contingent preferences and ideological stance. (For example, when the state itself no longer undertakes road construction, but instead moves to purchasing roads from private enterprises, Fg increases and Wg declines. However, if the state labour and the private labour is equally productive then – for the same lot of roads – state expenditure must increase because enterprises require profit.)

Equation (8.1) regards the *production* of the state, not the expenditures on various *transfers* that do not relate to its own production – a main transfer category being that of social security transfers (see 8§2).

8§1-a Addendum. The (non-)surplus-value producing character of the labour of civil servants

In the state's accounts the value of G^{COL} is defined by the values of Fg and Wg! There is no reason to assume that civil servants are less (or more) exploited than privately employed labourers in *physical* terms, even if we have no proper measure to account for it. Assuming that state labour is equally productive as the labour employed by enterprises, it is likely that it contains a surplus component, whence 'the value' of G^{COL} would be underrated in the *System of National Accounts*. Even if the labour product of civil servants were to (implicitly) contain a surplus component (i.e. the difference between the wage and the net product of, e.g., legislation or policing), this surplus is in fact distributed for free over production enterprises, financial enterprises and households (collective goods and services).[3]

Another matter is the appropriation of the (macro)economic surplus-value. Abstracting from any public ownership of capitalist enterprises (selling their output via the market) there is no surplus-value other than that appropriated by enterprises (including that which enterprises distribute to financiers). Thus any state production of a surplus (if there were such a thing) is expressed in the surplus-value of enterprises.

Relevant in this respect is the particular implicit allocation of state services, amongst others, over particular branches of enterprises. Regarding infrastructural works, for example, some branches benefit more directly than others from these being distributed for free. However, the matter of this non-market allocation seems independent of a particular theory of value. Generally we can only

3 This assumes that generally there is no direct link (in the sense of prices being a direct link) between particular taxes and particular state services. In this sense the latter are distributed for free.

say something about it in very rough, imprecise, terms of *implicit subsidies* even if in some cases some aspects of the allocation can be market mimicked (think of port dues).

8§2 *The state's action in terms of state expenditure*

The production by the state (8§1) is conditioned by its monetary expenditure on wages and floating inputs from enterprises. The state's production also requires expenditure on investment input from enterprises. Thus we have the following *production related* expenditure:

- wages of civil servants (Wg);
- floating inputs from enterprises (Fg);
- investment inputs from enterprises (Ig).[4]

Other expenditures – not state-production related – include various transfers:

- Legitimating social security transfers (Zg) – as indicated in 7D5, their level depends on compliance requirements;
- Interest payments on the state debt [Qg]. These are monetary flows from the state to its creditors, i.e. its financiers such as banks and capital owners.
- Subsidies to enterprises, to households and to cultural institutions. I call these transfers 'amenities' (Ag). These contingent subsidies are neglected in this chapter (briefly amplified on in 10§13).

Hence we have the following sum of state expenditure (G* and G):

$$G^* = (Wg + Fg) + Ig + (Qg + Zg) + Ag \qquad \text{[accounting definition]} \quad (8.3Ag)$$

For the purposes of this chapter we have (Ag neglected):

$$G = (Wg + Fg) + Ig + (Qg + Zg) \qquad \text{[definition]} \quad (8.3)$$

8§2-a Amplification. The trend in total state expenditure of the OECD-21 from 1870–2015

Graph 8.2 shows total state expenditure as a percentage of GDP from 1870 to the present for the average of the current 'OECD-21' (see Appendix 6A on the OECD-21). These include the amenities in equation (8.3Ag) – about 7% of GDP in 2015 (see 10§13 – Ag being the sum of 'general amenities' and 'subsidies and other direct assistance for enterprises').

---

4 Contingently some enterprises might be state owned, whilst operating on the market. This does not affect the categories of expenditures. In that case any distributed profits flow to the state in the form of dividends. Contingently the state might also undertake a variety works such as the construction of roads or parks or the collection of garbage by its own staff. In this case the state's expenditures on wages (Wg) and on investment (Ig) are higher and those on floating inputs from enterprises (Fg) lower (though these works will always require the purchase of commodities from the private sector). This is a main reason why this chapter focuses on the total state expenditure (G).

State expenditure as a percentage of GDP more than doubled between 1870 and 1937 (from 11 to 24% of GDP) and then again nearly doubled between 1937 and 1990 (to 45% of GDP). It then decreases (to 42%) until the outbreak of the financial crisis in 2007–08. The fastest increase occurs between 1913 and 1920, followed by the period 1960–80.[5]

Generally, data for all of the OECD-21 prior to 1960 are scarce. Therefore – as mentioned in 7§14-e – in order to show the possible impact of the scarce number of data for earlier years, most of my long run graphs show series for separate numbers of countries.

Note for *Graph 8.2* (and for other similar graphs to come) that the measure of GDP share blends out variations in GDP itself. This is especially relevant for the severe recessions of the 1930s, of the early 1980s and of 2008 to about 2013. In this respect note also that cycles do not run synchronous internationally.

GRAPH 8.2 *Total state expenditure (general government) 1870–2015, in % GDP; average of 10 to 21 current OECD countries*

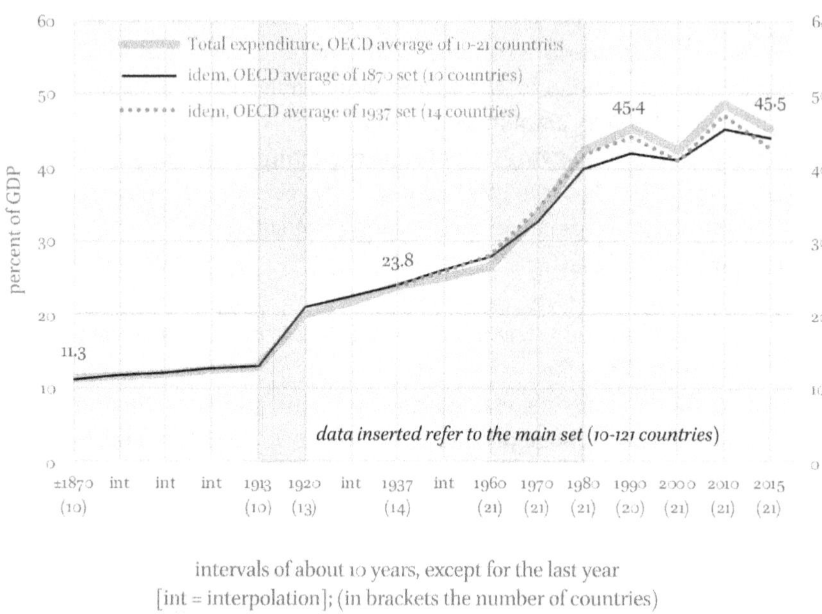

DATA SOURCES: 1870–1937 (Tanzi and Schuknecht 2000); 1960–80 (Castles 2006); from 1990 onwards (OECD dataset Economic Outlook, November 2017; extracted 28 December 2017). For details see Appendix 8.A under 8§2-a

5 Although World War I expenditures play a role in the period 1913–20, there has been, on average, no cut back between 1920–37 and after until about 1995.

8§3 *State production in terms of quantity of employment: state employment*

Because the state produces no surplus-value – or does not account for it (8§1) – gross or net value-added provides no adequate measure for state production in comparison with private production. For that comparison the share of state employment in total employment is a more adequate measure.

8§3-a Amplification. State employment in the OECD-21

Graph 8.3 shows the share of state employment in total employment for an average of the OECD-21 between 1870 and 2015. The data that are used exclude military employment and employment in state-owned enterprises because of the contingency of these categories.[6] We see that this share of state employment in total employment – after a steep increase between 1937 and 1980 – stabilised after 1980 at about 19% of total employment. The graph shows this state employment in comparison with the state expenditure of *Graph 8.3* (note thus their different bases of total employment and GDP).

8§3-b Amplification. Outsourcing of state functions

In 10D3 the major components of the bending in state expenditure will be shown. Here I briefly consider *a quantitatively minor*, though ideologically important, component, which is the state's (states') outsourcing of part of its (their) 'functions', including outsourcing in the form of licences. Minor, because education and social security expenditures are the largest components. This outsourcing has often been defended in terms of cost efficiency (private enterprises would produce cheaper). Examples range from road and rail construction and public transport to maintenance of public parks and monuments. This implies a moderation of state employment, but not necessarily a more than proportional expenditure moderation.[7]

---

6 In the early years of the twenty-first century, the employment in state-owned enterprises amounted, for the OECD-21 on average, to around 2% of the economy's total employment (see OECD, *Government at a Glance 2013*).

7 The two main factors that account for this are the procurement costs and the profits that private enterprises require. Regarding these expenditures a key question is whether any possible production efficiency gain would outweigh the profits and the procurement cost. However, supposed gains may not be the primary motive for outsourcing. A primary motive might be a factional ideological principle that what private enterprises might do should not be undertaken by the state. Again, such a principle may affect the size of state production, though not necessarily the proportional or more than proportional size of state expenditure and taxation.

GRAPH 8.3 *State employment as percentage of total employment*[8] *in comparison with state expenditure (each general government); averages of up to 21 current* OECD *countries, 1870–2015*

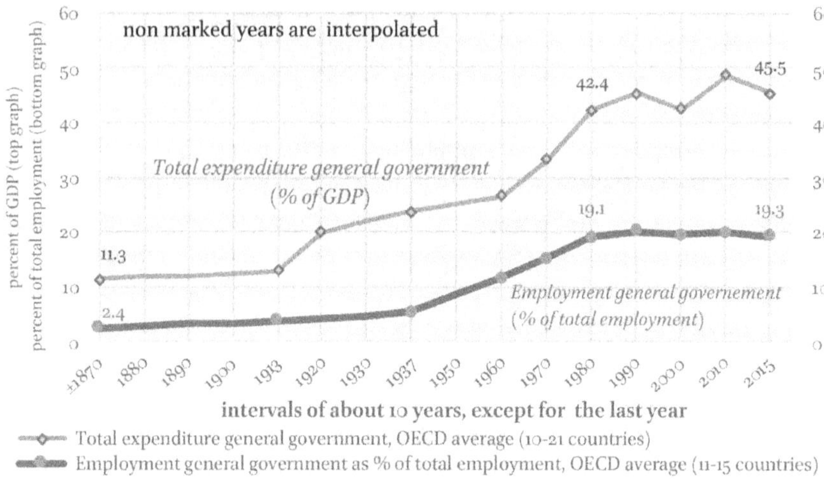

DATA SOURCES: for top line see Graph 8.2; for bottom line: 1870, 1913, 1937 (Tanzi and Schuknecht 2000); 1960 (OECD 1999); 1970–2015 (OECD dataset Economic Outlook, November 2017; extracted 28 December 2017). For further details on the bottom one, see Appendix 8.A under 8§3

Division 2. The finance of the state: taxation and other main forms of finance

As in the previous division the current division focuses on the state as being also an economic actor. This division grounds the previous two chapters, and particularly also the moment of state production and expenditure (8D1), in the finance of the state.

8§4 *Taxation and other main forms of finance of the state*

We have seen that taxation is necessary for the existence of the capitalist state and hence of the capitalist system (7D1). Whereas taxation so is a necessary form of finance of the state, its required amount can *contingently* be moderated by other forms of finance. A particular category amongst these is that of 'social security contributions' (see further 8§9). Contingently, taxation can also

8 Employment general government (excluding military employment and employment by public corporations) as a percentage of total employment (persons, civilian).

be moderated by state borrowing (see further 8§4-a). Then we have for the 'current finance of expenditure' (CFg):

$$CFg = T + SSC + OR + B \quad \text{[accounting definition]} \quad (8.4)$$

where T is the sum of taxes, SSC social security contributions, OR other receipts and B is the net current borrowing flow. B is negative in case of a fiscal surplus. In all cases we have:

$$CFg = G \quad \text{[accounting definition]} \quad (8.5)$$

where G denotes state expenditure. CFg and G are net categories. This means that if the state itself pays any taxes (which are recollected by the state's treasury), these would be deducted from each side of the 'gross budget' to reach the net budget. Similarly, the current borrowing flow B is net, meaning that in case the state at the same time (year) borrows and lends, these are netted.

8§4-a Amplification. The contingent forms of finance other than taxation and social security contributions

Division 5 expands on the finance of social security transfers, including social security contributions (8§9) and on the various forms of taxation (8§10). The current amplification sums up the forms of finance other than taxation and SSC. All of these other forms are contingent.

- *Borrowing*

In order to finance its expenditures – and especially in order to finance temporary extra expenditures as well as investment expenditures – the state may borrow from banks, from other financial institutions, from enterprises with temporary surplus funds and from rich individuals. This can be short-term borrowing through the issuance of treasury bills, or also medium- to long-term borrowing through the issuance of bonds.

Recall that any new borrowing of money (that is, any macroeconomic increase in the sum of money borrowed) must derive from money creation by banks and so originates with banks (2§8, 3§2). The state may also borrow from the Central Bank concomitantly on which the latter creates money (7§4).

Although in practice both 'temporary' extra expenditures and investment expenditures can be flexibly defined, the general idea is that the costs of these expenditures are recovered from future tax amounts without raising tax rates now.

This borrowing itself might approach a quasi-form of taxation to the extent that the rate of inflation increases, or increases above its expected rate.[9]

9 Inflation indexed rates of interest may prevent this implicit quasi-taxation.

- *Enforced lending*

Borrowing by the state other than for the finance of temporary extra expenditures as well as investment expenditures (see above) can be considered as a postponement of taxation. However, when the state manages to issue perpetual bonds (consols) taxation is postponed indefinitely.[10] Enforced perpetual lending at a (near to) zero rate of interest approaches taxation.

- *Royalties on licences*

In principle, royalties on licences could be extended for any (commercial) activity. The broader its base, the more it approaches a quasi-taxation.

- *Sale of state services, often in the form of dues*
- *Dividends on state-owned enterprises*
- *Rent on state-owned property including land*

The degree to which these latter three might contingently substitute for taxation depends on the state's economic constellation in this respect.

- *Fines*

In 7§2 I introduced the fundamental conflict of taxation, in that it overrides property rights. Some of the other finance categories mentioned may also be conflicting. This applies especially to state-owned enterprises when these are considered to compete with private enterprises. This may be different when state-owned enterprises are restricted *either* to specific sectors (such as banking or power provision) *or* enterprises with (potential) extreme market power (e.g. monopolies).

In any case within capitalism it is not plausible that the state might finance its expenditure without any taxation, and empirically this has not been the case.

8§4-b Amplification. The trend in taxes and other state receipts in the OECD-21, 1870–2015

Graph 8.4 shows the trend in total state receipts from 1870 to 2015 (current OECD-21 average) as a percentage of GDP.

The average of the total state receipts quadrupled between 1870 and 2015 (from nearly 11 to 43% of GDP). The fastest increase occurs between 1913 and 1920 (12% to 19%), and from 1937 to 1970 (18% to 35%). After 1970 the rates of increase gradually fade off. For the early decades data are available only for 7–8 countries. However, it can be seen from the thin solid line in the graph that the data for the 8 countries of 1870 roughly approximate those of the up to 21 coun-

10 For a brief description of British consols see http://en.wikipedia.org/wiki/Consol_(bond). On enforced temporary lending see a 2012 proposal by the German DWI: http://www.diw.de/documents/publikationen/73/diw_01.c.405701.de/12-28-1.pdf; for an abstract in English see http://www.diw.de/sixcms/detail.php?id=diw_01.c.405712.de.

tries afterwards. From 1965 more specific data are available for tax and social security receipt (the two dotted lines). We see that the growth of these bends off after 2000.

GRAPH 8.4 *State receipts (general government) 1870–2015, in % GDP: (a) total current receipts; (b) tax and social security receipts; (c) tax receipts. Averages of 8–21 current OECD countries*

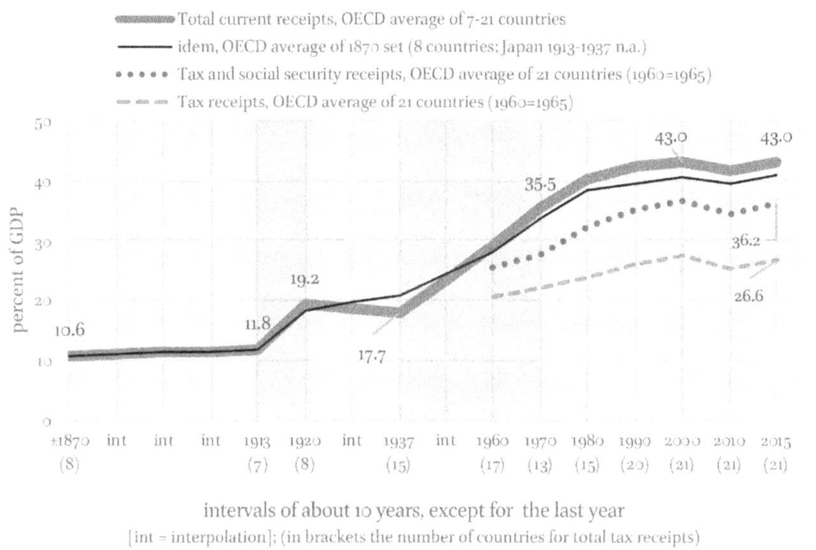

DATA SOURCES: 1870–1960 (Tanzi & Schuknecht 2000); 1960–2015 (OECD data base). For details see Appendix 8.A under 8§4-b

Given that social security *expenditures* were 10.4% of GDP in 1960 and 1.7% in 1930 (Chapter 7, Graph 7.10), it is likely that around 1930 the sum of 'tax and social security receipts' (the middle dotted line in *Graph 8.4*) nearly coincided with 'tax receipts' (the bottom dotted line).

'Total receipts' includes tax and social security receipts (together the main part) and (chiefly) state receipts from state enterprises (dividends) and from concessions, as well as from retributions, dues and fines (see 8§4-a).

Graph 8.5 combines Graph 8.2 and Graph 8.4. Hence this graph also shows the budget deficits. (Note that, depending on the rate of growth of GDP, the state's fiscal deficit may but need not result in gross debt increases as a percentage of GDP.) Note again that because these graphs are in terms of GDP shares, cyclical movement is not shown. Moreover, these would anyway be levelled out due to the OECD-21 average and the international non-synchronisation of cycles. Within one country the tax receipts as a percentage of GDP tend to rise in upswings and decrease in downswings. Nevertheless, OECD-wide heavy recessions or depressions do show up to some extent in *Graph 8.5* in the difference between expenditure and receipts. See the (decade) years 1937 and 2010, and to a lesser extent the 1980s.

GRAPH 8.5 *Total state expenditure and total current receipts (general government) 1870–2015, in % GDP; averages of up to 21 current OECD countries*

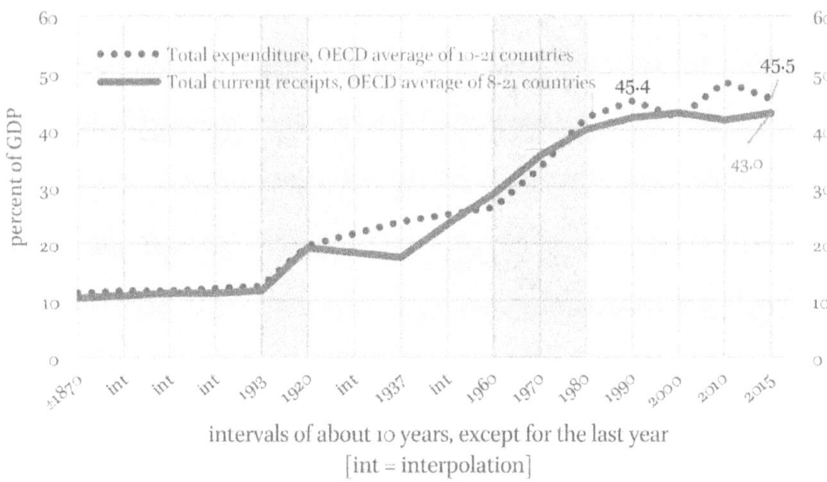

DATA SOURCES: see Graph 8.2 and Graph 8.4

Division 3. The effect of state expenditure on the enterprises' macroeconomic production and validation of surplus-value

After the exposition of state expenditure and finance in general (8D1–8D2), both of the following two divisions present their implications for the enterprise's production and validation of surplus-value (the current division) and for the after-tax surplus-value (8D4). See Scheme 8.1. The current division is the sequel to Chapter 3's 3D5, 'The validation of macroeconomic surplus-value by macroeconomic expenditure'.

8§5 *State expenditure and production of enterprises*

- *Recapitulation of state expenditure*

Recall from 8§2 the following definition of state expenditure (G):

$$G = (Wg + Fg) + Ig + (Qg + Zg) \qquad (8.3)$$

See the left hand side of *Table 8.6* for the recapitulation of the categories.

- *Production of enterprises*

For their production, enterprises anticipate the validation of production by the expenditure of economic actors (3§10; see also Chapter 5, Figure 5.2). With the introduction of the state into the systematic exposition, this also applies for the expenditure by or via the state.

TABLE 8.6 *Expenditure and current finance account of the state*

Expenditure		Finance	
wages (civil servants)	Wg	taxes	T
floating inputs (from enterprises)	Fg	social security contributions	SSC
net investment (fixed inputs from enterprises)	Ig	other receipts	OR
interest on state debt (net payments)	Qg		
social security transfers	Zg		
other expenditure: amenities†	Ag	net current borrowing flow	B
Sum of expenditure	**G***	*Sum of current finance*	**CFg**

† Neglected in the current chapter. G = G*– Ag.

8§5-a Explication. Direct and indirect monetary flows from the state to enterprises

Merely for analytical purposes I record that *in the absence of savings*, all of the expenditures of the state (in whatever way these are financed) end up as sales of enterprises, and so generate income of enterprises. *Circuit 8.7* visualises this.

8§6 *State expenditure and validation of macroeconomic surplus-value*

This section shows the effect of state expenditure on the macroeconomic validation of the surplus-value produced in enterprises. For the latter the integrated production and primary income account of enterprises and banks are considered – that is before taxes – recalling that part of the enterprises' surplus-value is distributed to banks. (Amplification 8§6-b outlines a formally more complete presentation of the current section. Instead of going through the rest of 8§6, the reader might immediately turn to 8§6-b.)

CIRCUIT 8.7 *Destination of state expenditure: purchases from enterprises at zero savings*

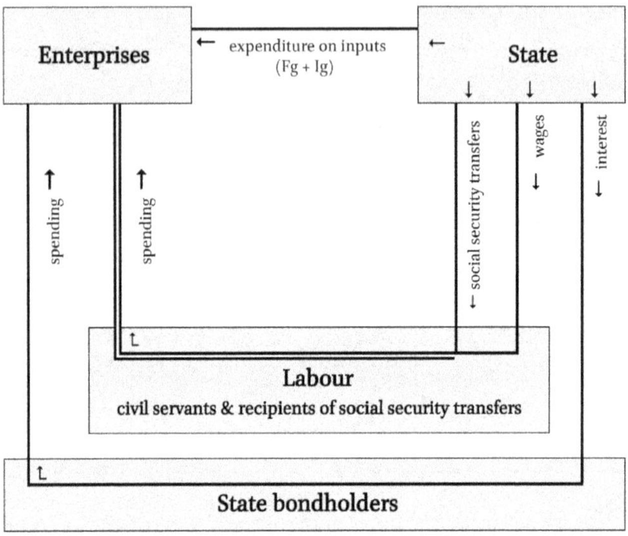

- *Recapitulation from Chapter 3*

It was shown in Chapter 3 (3§10) that given the production of surplus-value (Π^P), the macroeconomic validation of surplus-value (Π) is determined, on the one hand, by the investment of enterprises (I) and the consumption expenditure of capital owners (Ck), and, on the other hand, by the (dis)saving by labour, that is, the quantitative difference between their consumption and their wages (Cw–W).[11] With the introduction of the state and state expenditure, the notation of Chapter 3's enterprises sector is amended by adding extensions 'e' (amplified in 8§6-b.) In this amended notation we had:

$$\Pi \blacktriangleleft = [Ie + Ck] + [Cwe - We] \qquad (3.10^*)^{12}$$

$$\Pi \blacktriangleleft = [Ie + Ck] - Swe \qquad (3.12^*)$$

11 Borrowing by labour (which is contingent) is another determinant (Appendix 3B, section 3B-3).

12 Henceforth an asterisk indicates the changed notation of an earlier equation. Recall that $\blacktriangleleft$ means that the determination is from the right hand side to the left hand side.

Thus the validation of surplus-value is positively determined by the net expenditure of enterprises and capital owners (Ie+Ck) and negatively by the saving of the labour employed by enterprises (Swe).

- *Expenditure with enterprises by and via the state*

We had for state expenditure (8§5):

$$G = \{Fg + Ig\} + \{Wg + Qg + Zg\} \qquad (8.3)$$

The expenditure on floating inputs (Fg) – the latter inclusive of replacement investment – and on net investment (Ig) directly accrue to the enterprises sector. For the other three categories this is indirectly so via the consumption – and depending on the degree of savings – out of these incomes of wages (Wg), interest (Qg) and social security transfers (Zg). For the consumption (Cxx) and savings (Sxx) we have:

$$Cwg = Wg - Swg \qquad \text{[definition]} \quad (8.6)$$

$$Cqg = Qg - Sqg \qquad \text{[definition]} \quad (8.7)$$

$$Czg = Zg - Szg \qquad \text{[definition]} \quad (8.8)$$

These three savings categories together, I call the 'state-mediated savings' (Smg)

$$Smg = Swg + Sqg + Szg \qquad \text{[definition]} \quad (8.9)$$

Focusing on the total of state expenditure (G), it can then be shown (cf. 8§6-b) that

$$\mathit{\Pi} \triangleleft = [(\mathit{Ie} + \mathit{Ck}) - \mathit{Swe}] + G - [Swg + Sqg + Szg] \qquad (8.10)$$

or

$$\mathit{\Pi} \triangleleft = [(\mathit{Ie} + \mathit{Ck}) - \mathit{Swe}] + G - Smg \qquad (8.11)$$

Here the term in square brackets is *analogous* but quantitatively not the same as equation (3.12*). This is so because with the state expenditure (minus Smg) the *production* of enterprises increases. With it at least the investment also increases. To account for the distinction in comparison with Chapter 3 (and all of Part One), the terms [(*Ie* + *Ck*) – *Swe*] and *Π* are written in italics. (This applies for the rest of the current chapter.)

All of the expenditures and savings in 810 and 8.11 are themselves independent of surplus-value (*Π*) and in that sense autonomous quantities (see 5§3 and 5§5 on the autonomy of Ie and Ck).

In sum, all of the state expenditure (G) has a positive effect on the surplus-value produced and validated (*Π*), whereas any saving out of the transfers (Smg) moderates the positive effect. See also *Circuit 8.8*. (When, in 8D4, I present the effect of taxation on the after-tax surplus-value, the (dis)savings by the state itself will also be accounted for.)

CIRCUIT 8.8 *Destination of state expenditure: purchases and saving*

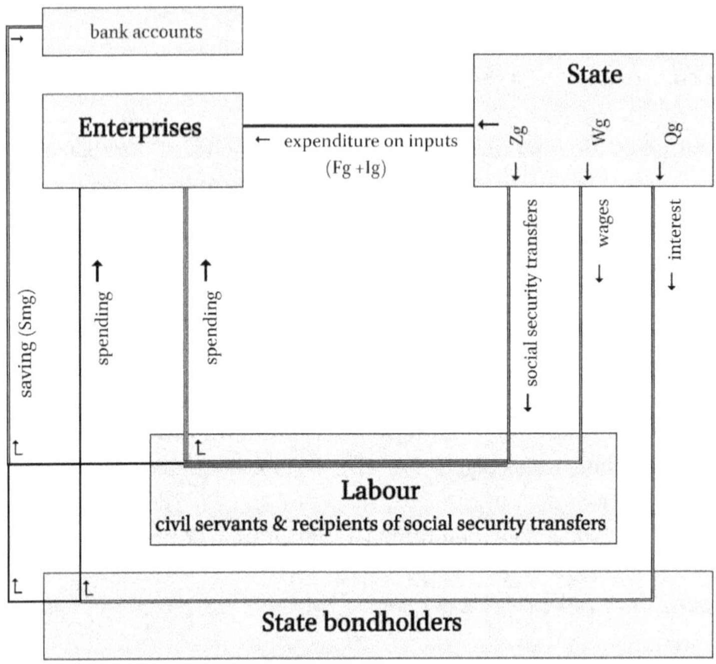

8§6-a Explication. A methodological comment on the production, the validation and the distribution of surplus-value

Onwards from the introduction of capitalist production (1D5), a distinction was made between the *production* of surplus-value and the *distribution* of surplus-value. At first this distinction was only implicit (1D5), but in the course of Chapter 2 and especially Chapter 3 (3D1–3D3) it became explicit, and gradually more detailed (see Figure 3.2b).

With the state's appearance within the exposition (6D2) the activities of the state became *explicit*. In 8D1 these activities were, economically, conceptualised as production by the state's civil servants. For that production, the state requires inputs from enterprises, and so expends with enterprises. This also is what is made *explicit* (made explicit, because the capitalist economy can have no existence without the state). In *that* sense the introduction of the state into the exposition does not give rise to extra production by enterprises. Nevertheless it is the case that an impetus to *extra* expenditure by the state does give rise to extra production of enterprises – and hence (ceteris paribus) of production of extra surplus-value.

Only in the next division (8D5), which expands on taxation, will it become explicit that, via the taxation of enterprises, the distribution of surplus-value is also affected.

8§6-b Amplification. The effect of state expenditure on the (before tax) macroeconomic validation of surplus-value – a formal derivation

Here the *macroeconomic* validation of production through expenditure is considered and therewith the generation of primary income: surplus-value and wages. Only after that is the secondary distribution of income considered: especially the distribution of surplus-value as including taxation (the latter in 8D4). Two distinct macroeconomic sectors are treated: the enterprises sector (the integration of enterprises and the non-lending and borrowing part of banks) with symbol 'e', and the state sector (with symbol 'g').

Equation numbers refer to those of the main sections (equations 8.1–8.11). Equations added in this amplification are numbered 8.6b.1, 8.6b.2, etc. (6b refers to the current amplification, and the last digit to the equation added).

1 *Reconceptualisation of the domain: some minor changes in notation*

With the incorporation of the state into the systematic exposition, we have *formally* a domain extension. In order to keep the formal presentation transparent and concise, I redefine the notation of 3§10, now introducing extensions 'e' for the enterprises sector and extensions 'g' for the state (g for government) – see *Table 8.9*. I could have introduced this notation in Chapter 3, but I did not want to anticipate Chapter 8 too much.

TABLE 8.9 *Notation for the formal domains of Chapters 3 and 8*

	Enterprises sector		**Formal domain**	
	notation 3§10	**notation Ch. 8**	**extension Ch. 8**	
value-added (net)	Y	*Ye*	*Y*	= *Ye* + Yg
investment (net)	I	*Ie*	I	= *Ie* + Ig
wages (sum)	W	*We*	W	= *We* + Wg
consumption out of wages	Cw	*Cwe*	Cw	= *Cwe* + Cwg
saving out of wages	Sw	*Swe*	Sw	= *Swe* + Swg

Because the state produces no surplus-value and capital, I keep for the consumption by capital owners: Ck = Ck. Because surplus-value is produced only in enterprises (Π ≡ Πe) I keep Π, but write this in italics (*Π*), so as to make explicit that, as we will see, the introduction of the state *formally* implies an expansion of surplus-value. Along with it the other Chapter 3 components are put in italics (*Table 8.9*, column 4).

Above and below all the time indices are omitted (implicitly these are all 't'). In this new notation I recapitulate two main equations from Chapter 3:

$$\Pi \sphericalangle = \text{Ie} + \text{Ck} + (\text{Cwe}-\text{We}) \qquad (3.10^*)$$

$$\Pi \sphericalangle = \text{Ie} + \text{Ck} - \text{Swe} \qquad (3.12^*)$$

(Henceforth an asterisk indicates the changed notation of an earlier equation.)

2 *A macroeconomic two-sector approach for the enterprises and state sectors*

I adopt a macroeconomic two-sector approach in which the enterprises sector and the state are not being integrated (hence a separate, though interconnected, Ye and Yg).

$$Y = Ye + \text{Yg} \qquad (8.6\text{b}.1)$$

(where *Y* in italics is total net value-added when the state is explicit).

2a *The state (and state-mediated) sector*

$$\text{Yg} = \text{Wg} \qquad (8.2)$$

We have for state expenditure (8§2):[13]

$$\text{G} = \{\text{Fg} + \text{Ig}\} + \{\text{Wg} + \text{Qg} + \text{Zg}\} \qquad (8.3)$$

The expenditure on floating inputs inclusive replacement investment (Fg) and net investment (Ig) directly accrues to the enterprises sector. For the other three categories this is indirectly so via consumption, and depending on the degree of savings out of these incomes of wages (Wg), interest (Qg), and social security transfers (Zg). For the consumption (Cxx) and savings (Sxx) we have:

$$\text{Cwg} = \text{Wg} - \text{Swg} \qquad (8.6)$$

$$\text{Cqg} = \text{Qg} - \text{Sqg} \qquad (8.7)$$

$$\text{Czg} = \text{Zg} - \text{Szg} \qquad (8.8)$$

These three savings categories together I call the 'state-mediated savings' (Smg)

$$\text{Smg} = \text{Swg} + \text{Sqg} + \text{Szg} \qquad (8.9)$$

2b *The enterprises sector*

From the side of the realised net production of the enterprises sector we have the value-added of:

$$Ye \sphericalangle = [mL^{\alpha}] \qquad (1.8^*)$$

---

13 Here the pure case is considered in which the state does not own enterprises that sell. If it does, then these are subsumed under enterprises, the state receiving dividends.

where m is the realisation constraint resulting in the unit monetary value of labour.

$$Ye = We + \Pi \qquad (3.5^{*})$$

$$\Pi = \text{Ye} - We \qquad (3.5^{*\prime})$$

From the side of expenditure we have the following three equations.

For the final expenditure of the non-state sector with the enterprises sector (Ee):

$$Ee = Ie + Ck + Cwe \qquad (3.6^{\prime *} \text{ and } 3.9^{*})$$

For the direct and indirect spending of the state sector with the enterprises sector (Eg):

$$\text{Eg} = [\text{Ig} + \text{Fg}] + [(\text{Cwg} + \text{Cqg} + \text{Czg})] \qquad (8.6\text{b}.2)$$

Taking the last two equations together we have the determination of:

$$Ye \sphericalangle = Ee + \text{Eg} \qquad (8.6\text{b}.3)$$

The macroeconomic surplus-value is the sum of these expenditures minus the wages of the enterprises sector:

$$\Pi \sphericalangle = (Ee + \text{Eg}) - We \qquad (8.6\text{b}.4)$$

Substituting (3.6′*) and (8.6b.2), into (8.6b.4) we have:

$$\Pi \sphericalangle = [(Ie + Ck) + (Cwe - We)] + [\text{Ig} + \text{Fg}] + [(\text{Cwg} + \text{Cqg} + \text{Czg})] \qquad (8.6\text{b}.5)$$

where the shaded part is analogous to equation (3.10*) above.

Substituting 8.6, 8.7. and 8.8 we get:

$$\Pi \sphericalangle = [(Ie + Ck) + (Cwe - We)] + [\text{Ig} + \text{Fg} + \text{Wg} + \text{Qg} + \text{Zg}] - [\text{Swg} + \text{Sqg} + \text{Szg}] \qquad (8.6\text{b}.6)$$

Here the second term on the right hand side is the state expenditure (equation 8.3 above). When substituting this we get:

$$\Pi \sphericalangle = [(Ie + Ck) + (Cwe - We)] + \text{G} - [\text{Swg} + \text{Sqg} + \text{Szg}] \qquad (8.10)$$

or

$$\Pi \sphericalangle = [(Ie + Ck) - Swe] + \text{G} - \text{Smg} \qquad (8.11)$$

These expenditures and savings are themselves independent of surplus-value (Π) and in that sense autonomous quantities (see 5§3 and 5§5 on the autonomy of Ie and Ck).

Thus the validation of surplus-value (Π) depends positively on the final expenditure by the enterprises sector and by capital owners ($Ie+Ck$) as well as on the state expenditure (G), and negatively on the saving out of enterprises wages (Swe) and out of the state-mediated saving (Smg).

This is most transparent for the case in which there would be no savings (that is, for $Cwe=We$ and Smg=0, whence we would have $\Pi^{*} = Ie + Ck + \text{G}$). Paraphrasing Kalecki, we then have: capitalists earn what they spend and what the state directly and indirectly spends.

Recall that enterprises cannot determine the validation of their surplus-value (3§10). Given the production of surplus-value – that each individual enterprise can control separately – the macro validation of surplus-value (Π) is determined by the expenditure components above (8.6b.5 and the derived 8.11), which the individual enterprises cannot control, even if they can control their own individual investment expenditure.[14]

8§6-c Amplification. From surplus-value to the before tax internal profit of enterprises

Having outlined the validation of surplus-value in 8§6 and 8§6-b, we can now turn to the first stage of the distribution of surplus-value (prior to taxation). This regards the distribution of surplus-value (Π) as interest, whence we move from Π to the internal profit of the enterprises sector (R, now in italics). (At the level of Chapter 3, the internal profit of enterprises was introduced briefly 3§1, cf. Figure 3.2b, and more extended in Chapter 5, 5§1.)

Given the determination of surplus-value validated,

$$\Pi \blacktriangleleft = [(Ie + Ck) - Swe] + \mathrm{G} - \mathrm{Smg} \qquad (8.11)$$

we have for the internal profit of the enterprises sector:

$$R = \Pi - \mathrm{Qe} \qquad \{\text{for net interest payments Qe>0}\} \qquad (8.6c.1)$$

where Qe is the net interest paid by enterprises to their external financiers.[15]

Hence we have for the enterprises' internal profit:

$$R = [(Ie + Ck) - Swe] - [\mathrm{Qe}] + [\mathrm{G} - \mathrm{Smg}] \qquad (8.6c.2)$$

8§6-d Addendum. A comment on the *System of National Accounts* (*SNA 2008*)

The ordering of categories above can be connected to that of the *System of National Accounts 2008* (*SNA 2008*; see UN 2009), which, in general terms, roughly adopts the same order regarding the generation of income versus its distribution. This, however, does not imply that I would agree with all of the SNA's ordering decisions; especially I disagree with almost all of its ordering when this requires an 'imputation' of one economic category to another. (I especially distance myself from the imputation of owner-occupied dwellings to a nominal entrepreneurial branch – from which the owner is a nominal tenant – the branch securing an operating surplus via the imputed rentals (see the very last section of Appendix 3C). I also especially take distance from the way

14 This is a Kaleckian argument.

15 Recall that for the latter we had in equation 5.1 of 5§1 the notation $i\varepsilon$K. This is also adequate at the current point. The notation Qe merely serves to make the reader aware that 'net' interest now may be net of also interest payments to enterprises from the state.

the value-added of banks is accounted for, that is, via the imputation of intermediate uses (bank services) to interest receipts and payments of banks.)[16]

Apart from these imputations my ordering is different from the SNA's in that I consistently treat all taxation (the direct on incomes and the indirect on products) at one and the same level. A rather minor point is that I treat net rather than gross investment (the SNA accounts allow for each one).

Quite a different point is that (at the current general level of exposition) international relations are yet abstracted from. Together this means that – in SNA terminology – I start from macroeconomic production and the realisation of macroeconomic production at the level of 'net value-added' or the 'net domestic product against factor costs', with all international related items put to zero.

Division 4. The combined effect of state expenditure and taxation on the enterprises' macroeconomic after-tax surplus-value

This division presents, first, the combined effect of state expenditure (8D3) and of taxation of enterprises on the latter's after-tax surplus-value (8§7). Next it presents, more specifically, the effect of a fiscal deficit of the state on the enterprises' after-tax surplus-value (8§8).

8§7 *A profits tax: taxation of surplus-value*

- *Finance and pre-finance of state expenditure*

Enterprises usually pay taxes after having realised the surplus-value to pay these. This may seem an obvious statement. Behind it, however, is the perhaps less obvious fact that – depending on savings and other taxes – the state expenditure (G) largely generates the before tax surplus-value equivalent for the enterprises taxes. The state makes the required expenditure and, given the going tax rates, it must await how much tax revenue the two generate (this is how the state makes its budget and carries it out; it may estimate the tax collection, but the outcome is uncertain). Pending this tax collection, the state must (pre-)finance its expenditure via borrowing (directly through banks or indirectly via the issue of short-term bonds or treasury bills).

16 Even if for the *SNA 2008* (UN 2009) the composers may have made a number of arbitrary choices, it seems by and large an impressively consistent and precise whole (of over 600 pages). The sequel representing the accounts in excel (UN 2008a) is a useful leading summary even if that is a summary consisting of many thousands of entries.

- *The effect of a tax on surplus-value*

Total taxes (T) are made up of the 'taxes on surplus-value realised' (Tsv) and all other taxes (To). The latter (To) are specified in 8D5.

$$\text{T} = \text{Tsv} + \text{To} \tag{8.12}$$

The before (*Π*) and the after-tax surplus-value (*Π*at) are related as:

$$\Pi\text{at} = \Pi - \text{Tsv} \tag{8.13}$$

Recall from 8§6 the equation for the realisation of surplus-value (*Π*):

$$\Pi \triangleleft = [(Ie + Ck) - Swe] + \text{G} - \text{Smg} \tag{8.11}$$

(with Swe for the saving out of enterprises wages and Smg for the saving out of the state-mediated spending).

Substituting the last equation into the former we get:

$$\Pi\text{at} = [(Ie + Ck) - Swe] + [\text{G} - \text{Smg} - \text{Tsv}] \tag{8.14}$$

Consider the second term in square brackets [G – Smg – Tsv].

First. The taxes (Tsv) are the costs for enterprises of the state's actualisation in terms of production and expenditure (8D1) of the seven legislative frameworks (Chapters 6–7). Regarding the latter, specifically the state's upholding of the granted legal economic rights for enterprises (Chapter 6).

Secondly, however, these costs (Tsv) go along with benefits in the form of state expenditure on the frameworks, benefits that directly or indirectly expand the output of enterprises (G–Smg), and so their surplus-value.

Given the state and its *actualised* accommodation of the production of surplus-value, the effect of this tax (Tsv) is that part of the pre-tax surplus-value is distributed to the state (see *Figure 8.10*).

Recalling that the savings of the enterprises' labour are the difference between their wages and consumption (Swe = We–Cwe) we can also write (8.14) as

$$\Pi\text{at} = [(Ie + Ck) + Cwe - We] + [\text{G} - \text{Smg} - \text{Tsv}] \tag{8.14'}$$

In sum, therefore, we see that whereas each of the enterprises' wages (We) and taxes (Tsv) are costs for the generation of surplus-value, labour and the state also generate expenditure benefits (Cw and G–Smg).

A corollary of this tax is that 'the tendency to equalisation of average inter-sector rates of integral profit' (4§2) takes the form of 'the tendency to equalisation of average inter-sector *after-tax* rates of integral profit'.

The figure on the next page is a completed version of Figure 3.2b (3§1).

8§7-a Amplification. The effect of a tax on the profit of enterprises

The main text presented the taxation of surplus-value (*Π*). Contingently the state may allow enterprises to deduce interest payments (that is, this distribution of surplus-value) from the surplus-value tax, whence we have in fact a tax on internal profit.

FIGURE 8.10 *The distribution of surplus-value to financiers and to the state*

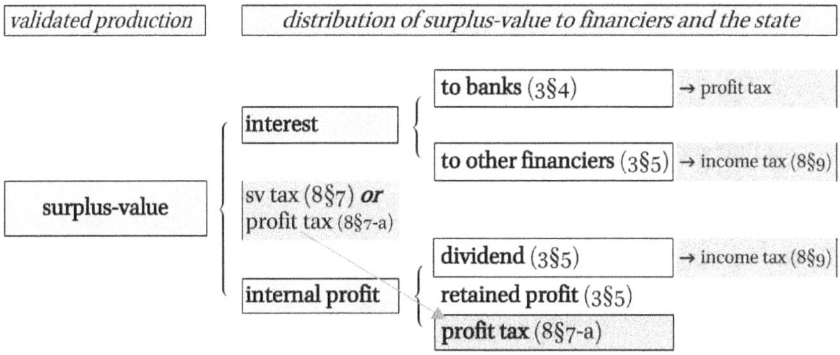

Following on from an earlier amplification on the internal profit of enterprises (8§6-c) the current amplification considers a tax on the internal profit (R), that is, Π after the distribution of interest (thus we now have a smaller tax base). Recall from 8§6-c:

$$R = \Pi - \mathrm{Qe} \quad \{\text{for net interest payments Qe>0}\} \tag{8.6c.1}$$

$$R = [(Ie + Ck) - Swe] - [\mathrm{Qe}] + [\mathrm{G} - \mathrm{Smg}] \tag{8.6c.2}$$

Total taxes (T) are made up of the taxes on the internal profit of enterprises (Tr) and other taxes (To*).

$$\mathrm{T} = \mathrm{Tr} + \mathrm{To}^* \tag{8.7a.1}$$

The after-tax internal profit (Rat) is defined as:

$$Rat = R - \mathrm{Tr} \tag{8.7a.2}$$

Substituting (8.6d.2) into the last equation we have:

$$Rat = [(Ie + Ck) - Swe] - [\mathrm{Qe}] + [(\mathrm{G} - \mathrm{Smg}) - \mathrm{Tr}] \tag{8.7a.3}$$

The last term in square brackets represents the benefits (G–Smg) and costs (Tr) that the enterprises sector derives from the state, for the former's accommodation of the generation of the profits of enterprises.

A corollary of this tax is that 'the tendency to equalisation of average inter-sector rates of internal profit' (5§1) takes the form of 'the tendency to equalisation of average inter-sector *after-tax* rates of internal profit'.

The information provided by equation (8.7a.3) is not much different from that of the last but one in the main text of 8§7:

$$\Pi\mathrm{at} = [(Ie + Ck) - Swe] + [\mathrm{G} - \mathrm{Smg} - \mathrm{Tsv}] \tag{8.14}$$

8§8 *The effect of a fiscal deficit of the state on the after-tax surplus-value*

Although the state's fiscal stance (surplus or deficit) is contingent, the state tends to run structurally a fiscal deficit (See, for example, the earlier Graph 8.5, in 8§4-b, for the OECD-21 between 1870 and 2015. Given the available data it seems that the period of fiscal surpluses between just before 1960 and just after 1970 is exceptional.) It is therefore relevant to consider the effect of a (structural) fiscal deficit, on the after-tax surplus-value of enterprises, which is the subject of the current section. We get to this in subsection (3) below. Subsection (1) serves to simplify the notation. Subsection (2) introduces the concept of saving by the state.

1 *Hybrid taxes*

A fiscal surplus of the state is equivalent to the state's 'saving', and a fiscal deficit to its 'dissaving'. This is not simply the difference between its expenditure (G) and taxes (G), because the state has also other incomes.

Recall from 8§4 the equation for the 'current finance of expenditure' (CFg).

$$CFg = T + SSC + OR + B \qquad (8.4)$$

(T for taxes, SSC for social security contributions, OR for other receipts and B for the net current borrowing flow.)

Recall from 8§7 the equation of taxes (with To for 'other taxes'):

$$T = Tsv + To \qquad (8.12)$$

Substituting (8.12) into (8.4) we have:

$$CFg = Tsv + To + SSC + OR + B \qquad (8.4')$$

In order to simplify the notation below, I introduce the term 'hybrid taxes' (T^H), defined as:

$$T^H = Tsv + To + SSC + OR \qquad (8.15)$$

The last three terms are taken together as 'other hybrid taxes' (T^Ho).

$$T^H = Tsv + T^Ho \qquad (8.16)$$

2 *Saving by the state, or a fiscal deficit as reflected in dissaving*

Substituting (8.12) and (8.15) into (8.4) we have

$$CFg = T^H + B \qquad (8.17)$$

In case of a fiscal surplus, B is negative (thus the state pays off part of its debt).

Recall that the sum of state expenditure (G) equals its current finance.

$$CFg = G \qquad (8.5)$$

The current savings of the state (Sg) are defined as

$$Sg = T^H - G \qquad (8.18)$$

Or: $G - T^H = -Sg$. For a fiscal deficit (thus $G > T^H$ and $B > 0$) the saving Sg is negative (thus we have dissaving by the state).

3 *The effect of a fiscal deficit on the after-tax surplus-value*

In the previous section (8§7) we had for the after-tax surplus-value:

$$\Pi at = [(Ie + Ck) - Swe] + [G - Smg - Tsv] \qquad (8.14)$$

By substituting (8.16) into (8.14) we make explicit both the taxation stance of the state (G–T) and the sum of the 'other hybrid taxes' (T^H), as each determining the after-tax surplus-value of the enterprises sector.

$$\Pi at = [(Ie + Ck) - Swe] + [(G - T^H) - Smg + T^H o] \quad (8.19)$$

Thus to the extent that the state acts such that the appropriators of surplus-value 'share' the total burden of the hybrid taxation with other payers of hybrid taxes ($T^H o$), the after-tax surplus-value is larger – that is, given the other components.

By substituting (8.18) into (8.19), the (dis)savings of the state are made explicit (its fiscal surplus or deficit) as

$$\Pi at = [(Ie + Ck) - Swe] + [- Sg - Smg + T^H o] \quad (8.20)$$

Thus the after-tax surplus-value is *negatively* affected by a *fiscal surplus* (Sg>0).[17] Conversely, a *fiscal deficit* (Sg < 0, hence –Sg > 0) has a positive effect on the after-tax surplus-value.

However, although the statement in the last sentence is formally correct, the total of the state debt – and the interest payments along with it – has a secondary effect on the savings by the state bondholders. (Recall from equation 8.9, in 8§6, that this saving, Sqg, is part of the 'state-mediated savings' Smg.) To the extent that the total state debt would keep increasing (say, as a percentage of GDP) then at some point the savings effect of bondholders (Sqg) is going to outrun the budget deficit effect (Sg).[18] (In considering this, it should be kept in mind that as long as the state's budget deficit as a percentage of GDP, e.g. 2%, is smaller than the rate of growth of GDP, e.g. 2.5%, then the total state debt as a percent of GDP decreases.)

8§8-a Addendum: Kalecki on the state budget deficit and profits

The idea that the budget deficit of the state positively affects profits stems from Kalecki (see, e.g., his 2003 [1954], pp. 48–9), although he does not go into sim-

17 The form of equation (8.20) is in essence no different from the result reached in 3§10 (equation 3.12). This is transparent for the case in which all taxation would be levied on the enterprises sector ($T^H o = 0$). Thus profits are positively determined by the final expenditures of enterprises (Ie) and of capital owners (Ck), and negatively by the savings of all other actors (now including the state). Recall that the exposition in this book takes distance from the orthodox view of investment being a saving (3§9).

18 On the basis of twentieth-century data for the average of the OECD-21 of before and after the early twentieth-century financial crisis on the one hand, and a number of plausible savings assumptions on the other, it can be inferred that this 'outrunning' does not occur for state debts below 100% of GDP. However, this would far from imply that the term [– Sg – Smg + $T^H o$] in equation 8.20 would become negative. For the OECD-21, and at least over the last 50 years, the $T^H o$ has kept increasing from [illegible] of GDP in 1979 to [illegible] in 2015. (Taxes on profits of corporate enterprises in terms of GDP changed from 2.3% in 1970, via 3.7% in 2000, to 2.9% in 2015.)

ilar detail as in the main section. Minsky remarks: 'Ever since the early work of Kalecki it has been known that gross profits equals gross investment plus the government deficit ...'. And: 'Although sustaining and increasing business profits has never been an avowed objective of active fiscal policy – employment or income have been the avowed policy objectives – a major effect of the big deficits that big governments generate when income falls is to sustain profits' (Minsky 1982, pp. 389 and 388).

Division 5. Forms of taxation: the distribution of income and wealth

The previous division presented the effect of taxation on the after-tax surplus-value. In principle the state might levy all the required taxes on surplus-value. Given that the state acts such that enterprises 'share' taxation with households, this final division presents the effect of the particular actual form of taxation on the distribution of the income of households (8§11), and on the distribution of the wealth of households (8§12). These sections are preceded by some categorising outlines (8§9–8§10).

A methodological remark is appropriate at this point. Whereas taxation is necessary, the specific forms of taxation are contingent. Their outcome in the distributions of income and wealth are in fact a 'manifestation' of the capitalist system (presented in Chapters 4–5 and 9–10). However, as these distributions relate qua theme to the current chapter, I have included it here, at the end of this chapter.

8§9 *The finance of social security: taxes and social security contributions*

In 7D5 the framework of legitimating social security provisions (or 'transfers') was presented in general terms. Recall the transfer categories presented in Figure 7.8 and Graph 7.9 (7§17).

Social security provisions are financed in two ways. Mostly one part is financed out of taxation and the other part out of social security contributions (SSC), which are most often in part paid by employers and in part by workers.

SSC-related provisions are considered to have a collective insurance character and to be work-related (e.g. non-structural unemployment, sickness pay, and wage-related pensions). In a way these are not 'pure' social transfers, but rather a collective insurance for which only those who work are eligible, and only those who worked can receive benefits. Regarding wage-related pension benefits in particular, it is to be mentioned that these are either the result of a formal insurance, or have the character of a postponed wage. (Recalling that for the OECD-21, in 2010, pensions constitute about one-third of the social security transfers – see Graph 7.9 – it is indeed dubious whether the wage-related, or premium-related, part of these should be classified as 'social' transfers.)

This is thus different from transfers that are not work related, such as fixed amount (equal for all) state pensions that are financed out of taxation, as well as child and other allowances, social assistance, and state serviced (contributions to) health provisions – all these are most often financed by taxation.

Social security contributions paid by workers are inevitably paid out of their gross wage. However, employers SSC are also part of the gross wage. (This is also how the *System of National Accounts*, SNA 2008 accounts for these.)[19] For the employer these are 'wage costs'.

The distribution of the SSC between employers and workers is contingent on wage bargaining, and in several countries contingent on economic policy decisions. However, to a large extent the outcome is merely an 'optical' matter of take home pay (to the extent that the workers SSC part is larger, the gross wage paid can be larger). What does matter, though, for the distribution of income is any wage bargaining or economic policy decisions that either set an upper threshold for SSC (making the distribution of income more skewed) or that set an upper threshold on the transfers/benefits (making the distribution of income less skewed) – in each case given the total wages sum that employers are willing to pay.

It is contingent (and country dependent) if, and which, social transfers are taxed.

8§9-a Amplification. The finance of social security in the OECD-21: 1970–2015

Graph 8.11 shows how social security in the OECD-21 is financed on average. There is quite some variation among these countries. For example, in Australia and New Zealand 100% is financed out of taxation and in Denmark nearly 100%, whereas in France, Germany, Japan, and the Netherlands over 50% is financed out of SSC (year 2010).

From the point of view of social security contributions (SSC) and for the OECD-21 on average, about one-third of the social security transfers (SST) are in fact a wages component – one that may or may not be taxed – as shown in *Table 8.12*.

19 SNA 2008 (UN 2009), chapter 7B, Compensation of employees, in particular Table 7.4 and the text on pp. 138–9. See also OECD 2013.

GRAPH 8.11 *Finance of social security provisions 1970–2015, shares of social security contributions (SSC) and taxes; averages of OECD-21*

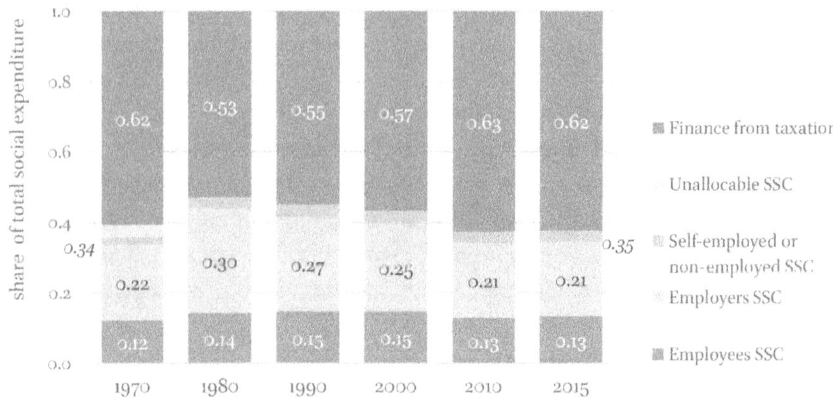

DATA SOURCES: Social security contributions (SSC) (OECD dataset Revenue Statistics – Comparative tables, series 2100, 2200, 2300 and 2400);[20] Social security expenditure (see Graph 7.10)

TABLE 8.12 *Finance of social security, and social security contributions as part of the gross wage*

	Employers	**Workers**	**State**
finance of social security	x% contributions	y% contributions	(1-x-y) out of taxation
component of the 'gross wage' (regarding previous row)†	yes (wage costs)‡	yes	no
taxation of social sec. transfers	n.a.	varies between countries for different transfers	

† This is also how the *System of National Accounts 2008* (SNA 2008) conceptualises this matter (see the previous footnote).

‡ This is also the difference between the concept of 'wages' and 'wage costs'. These contributions are directly paid to the institution administering the social security – hence workers do not receive this in cash, although it is theirs (the same applies most often for the next column).

20 http://stats.oecd.org/OECDStat_Metadata/ShowMetadata.ashx?Dataset=REV&ShowOnWeb=true&Lang=en (last updated August 2017; accessed 28 December 2017).

8§10 *Forms of taxation*

Recall from 8§5's Table 8.6 (and Graph 8.4 in 8§4) the forms of finance of the state. Given that there are limits to contingent borrowing and to other non-tax incomes of the state, taxation is the main and necessary form of finance of the state (8§4). However, the particular form of taxation is contingent. The 'pure' form of taxation would be taxes on the enterprises' property and surplus-value, that is, when taxation would be connected to the initial ground of the state (6§1 and 6§11). In actual practice labour 'shares' in the taxes, regarding both their labour income and their spending. Hence there are four main categories of taxation:[21]

1. *Taxes on profits*
   - taxes on corporate profits (legal corporations);
   - taxes on other profits (non-incorporated firms);
2. *Taxes on property value and property income*
   - property value taxes (taxes on wealth);
   - property income taxes (taxes on distributed interest and on dividends and rent);
   - taxes on the succession of property;
3. *Taxes on labour income and its derivatives*
   - labour income taxes;
   - taxes on social security transfers;[22]
   - taxes on benefits from pension funds (cf. Chapter 3, Appendix 3A-2);
4. *Taxes on products (indirect taxes)*
   - taxes on the value of products (at production, sale or transfer; or at final use); these include the indirect value-added tax (VAT);[23]
   - taxes per unit of goods or services (excise).

In case all these four forms prevail, all classes of actors are subject to levies of the last category and, depending on their roles, they might fall into one or all of the first three categories.

The state can – up to its discretion in face of its legitimation requirement – in principle choose between degrees of these various forms of taxation.

21 Precise definitions can be found in the *SNA 2008* (UN 2009).

22 Among current OECD countries there is quite some diversity as to their taxation. See Adema, Fron and Ladaique 2011.

23 Collected in stages by enterprises; ultimately charged in full to the final purchases.

8§11 *Forms and design of taxation, and their legitimation in compliance to a particular distribution of income*

As with all main state actions, the form and the specific design of taxes must ultimately be legitimated in the compliance of actors. In the end this concerns the compliance to a particular distribution of income and wealth via taxation. The current section focuses on the distribution of income and the next one on the distribution of wealth.

1 *Taxation inevitably takes a stance*

I make a distinction between the forms of taxation (the categories outlined in 8§10) and their design (tax rates and the tax base for these rates). There cannot be 'neutral' taxes or neutral tax rates. More specifically regarding tax rates, flat rates are no more neutral than progressive or regressive ones. Propagating flat rates would seemingly imply a normative judgement regarding the outcome of 'the market' and the resulting distribution of income and wealth before taxation. However – and quite apart from the moral or ethical norm – such a judgement is based on the illusion that '*the* market' could exist at all, and specifically so independently of the state and its expenditure. Independently of judgements about the form and the design of taxes, 'the market' is a phantom to the extent that it has no existence without the rights frameworks and the economic frameworks presented in Chapters 6–7.[24] Moreover, because the state exists, 'markets in a vacuum of non-taxation' do not exist. There can be tax shifts, though no tax shift can be actualised in a vacuum of non-taxation. In sum, any actual form and design of taxation is inevitably based on a normative stance of the state, and only *shifts* in taxation and/or their design can be identified as being redistributive.

2 *Tax rates*

The particular form of taxation being contingent, at least one form must necessarily be implemented. The same applies for their design: there must necessarily be some tax rate (regressive, flat or progressive) that affects the distribution of income or wealth. An important difference between the four main forms of taxation (8§10) concerns their potential for changes in the distribution of income and wealth via progressive, flat or regressive tax rates.

---

24 The so-called 'general equilibrium theory' and the supposed norm of market efficiency is based on this phantom. However, even if we were to bracket this phantom character, that theory is based on non-neutral assumptions. These have been set out by Hahn, for example in his 1981. (This source is relevant because Hahn was an expert working himself in the field of general equilibrium theory.)

• Regarding taxation of products it is difficult or even impossible to build progression into the taxes other than in a rough way, such as a lower rate for common foods.
• For corporate profit taxes progression is possible, for example if the progression would start at a threshold related to the number of labourers employed or via so-called tax brackets. (Nevertheless beyond such brackets the usual corporate taxes are most often a flat percentage.)[25] Another possibility would be to differentiate the rate for retained versus distributed profits.
• The design of a fine-tuned progressive taxation is easiest for a wages tax, and generally for any final income tax of households.

3 *Progressive tax rates: profits and savings*

In terms of the effect of taxes on the profits of enterprises, the exposition in 8D4 implies that a progressive tax on personal income assists integral profits. The more skewed the distribution of this income, the more savings press down profits.[26] Thus progressive personal income taxes support enterprises: their rate of profit and so investment and employment.

This puts on the state's agenda the dilemma as to whether it is primarily concerned with the interests of enterprises or rather with the high-income categories. Essential in this respect is the long-standing ideological supposition that investment would require savings (3§2, 3§3, 3§9). For many this ideology functions as an argument to favour a skewed distribution of income.[27]

4 *Contingency of the redistribution of income and wealth?*

Seemingly the existence of the capitalist system does not pertain to a particular personal distribution of income and wealth. The capitalist system provides plenty of opportunity to purposely build in inequality of income and wealth. On the other hand, it might seem that the capitalist system is compatible with

25 Sometimes small corporations are favoured by a flat lower rate up to some threshold measured for example in amount of profit.

26 This is different for wages income (including that of the management) and current capital income. However, to the extent that the income categories fall under the same 'income taxes' this difference is not effective in practice. Regarding capital income, and to the extent that the consumption out of this income is stable (as, in a Kaleckian vein, has been assumed throughout) saving out of capital income is reflected in the issue of new bonds and shares of enterprises (see 3§6, Circuit 3.13). For this category, however, and to the extent that enterprises issue relatively more bonds than shares, the liabilities position of enterprises is affected.

27 Keynes was very much aware of this, calling 'the rentier' a 'functionless investor' (Keynes 1936, Chapter 24, section II). (He means a functionless financier or 'portfolio investor'.)

an equal distribution of income or 'even' one where the unattractive work (for example, garbage collection – in general the bottom of the current wages ladder) is better paid than the more attractive work.

In fact the interest of the upper income and wealth classes has been served in the past, and is served currently, by the building in of a considerable skewedness in the distribution of income and wealth.[28] However, this skewedness is constrained by the compliance of the majority of the people (2§5, 2§7, 2§7-b, 6§5, 7§17), and particularly also a wages ladder and a disposable income ladder that gains the overall compliance of also the upper-lower and the middle classes (say, the middle 60% of the income distribution – income deciles 3–8). However, whereas this requirement is not contingent, the gaining of this compliance is.

For this gaining of compliance, ideology is a prominent factor: the higher income classes do (not) deserve their income for such and such reasons. The key part of this ideology is the phantom of the market, which in all official statistics is taken as a point of departure, and so as a reference point. When that is taken as the reference point, income is seen to be taken away from the upper classes so as to be redistributed to the lower ones. It is a crucial part of this ideology that the prior production and appropriation of surplus-value is neglected: the market *outcome* of it is the statistical starting point and reference point.

8§11-a Amplification. Examples of distributions of household income in the OECD-21 around 2015

Graph 8.13 shows an example of a deciles distribution of the income of households for various income measures. (In a deciles distribution the population of households is ranked from low to high income, and next divided into ten groups, each of 10% of the population.) 'Market income' (or primary income) is the income before any redistribution. 'Gross income' is the market income after social security transfers. 'Disposable income' is the gross income after direct taxes. These three measure what households actually receive at some point. There is also a fourth measure around, which is 'equivalised disposable income'. For this measure households are standardised as to the number of members in a household; adults have a higher weight than children. If these four measures are compared, it makes a difference which one is the basis for the ranking of the deciles.

The example is of the UK (*Graph 8.13*) – see *Table 8.18* for its OECD-21 income rank.

28 As before, I take class as an objective category – in this case statistical classes of the distribution of income and wealth.

GRAPH 8.13 *Distribution of income: Market, Gross and Equivalised disposable income households by deciles, case of the UK 2015*

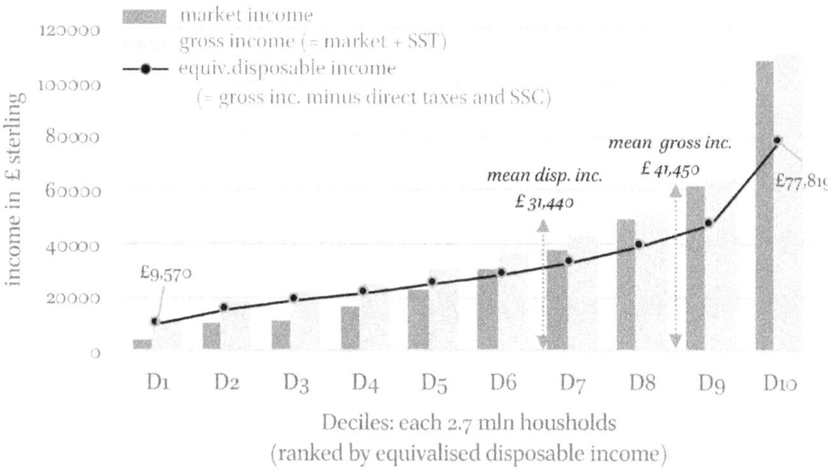

DATA SOURCE: Office for National Statistics (UK), Dataset 'The effects of taxes and benefits on household income' 2015/16, Table 2a (release date 25 April 2017)

TABLE 8.14 *Decile shares in total income of each category: UK 2015 (re. Graph 8.13)*

Shares	D1	D2	D3	D4	D5	D6	D7	D8	D9	D10
market inc.	1%	3%	3%	5%	7%	9%	11%	14%	17%	31%
gross inc.	3%	4%	5%	6%	7%	9%	10%	13%	16%	27%
eq. disp. inc.	3%	5%	6%	7%	8%	9%	10%	12%	15%	25%

DATA SOURCE: As for Graph 8.13

We see in *Graph 8.13* and *Table 8.14* that *on average* the largest redistributive effect results from social security transfers (SST) rather than from taxes. This can be better seen from *Graph 8.15*. This graph shows for an average of up to 20 OECD-21 countries the Gini measure for each income category. The Gini index (or Gini coefficient) is a common measure for the skewedness of a distribution. It adopts a scale of 0 to 1, the number 0 indicating complete evenness of the distribution, and the number 1 maximal skewedness (all income is owned by one unit of the population). This graph shows that social security transfers (SST) are the main factor bringing about a less skewed distribution of income (the difference between the top and the middle bar for the data since 2000). In 2015 it accounted for ¾ of the difference.

GRAPH 8.15 *Distribution of household income (equivalised): Gini indices of (a) market income; (b) income post social security transfers; (c) income post direct taxes; 1985–2015; averages of 4–20 OECD-21 countries*

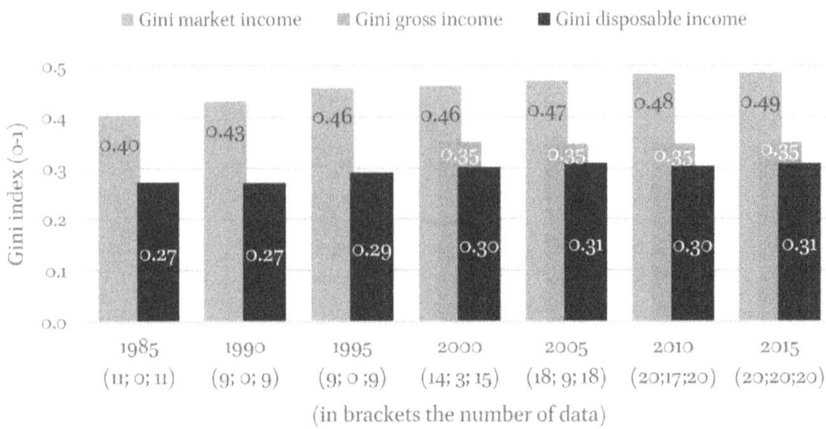

DATA SOURCE: OECD, dataset Income Distribution and Poverty; accessed 8 October 2017.[29] Year as indicated or nearest year available[30]

Graph 8.15 also shows that in the three decades from 1985 to 2015, the Gini for market income increased by 21% and that for disposable income by 13%. This is also the period in which the increase in state expenditure on SST moderated (see 7§17-a, Graph 7.10).

Note that the Gini measure is not very sensitive to the extremes of the distribution. These are more properly measured by, for example, the ratio of the top decile over the bottom decile or of the top quintile (20% groups) over the bottom quintile. Nevertheless, even for the Gini we see in terms of the change in these decades a *redistribution* of income from the broad bottom to the broad top.

The social security transfers in the OECD-21 do not prevent that a considerable part of the households has an income below the poverty line. The poverty line is variously defined. Here I show data for the poverty line that is defined as

29 http://stats.oecd.org/viewhtml.aspx?datasetcode=IDD&lang=en. The following link provides brief OECD definitions of various distributional measures: https://data.oecd.org/inequality/income-inequality.htm.

30 The Gini for gross income before 2000 is only available for one or two countries (data accessed in October 2017). The data used for the graph are those of the income definition 2012 from when it is available for a country (most often the effects of the 2011 versus 2012 definitions are rather small).

half the median household income of the total population. This measure takes account of the degree of access to the goods and services that are regarded as customary in any county in a particular year. (Here the average of the OECD-21.) The poverty rate is defined as the number of households below this line relative to the total population of households. *Graph 8.16* shows this poverty rate before and after transfers and direct taxes – again for equivalised households.

GRAPH 8.16 *Poverty rate before and after transfers and taxes, 1985–2015; averages of 9–21 OECD-21 countries*

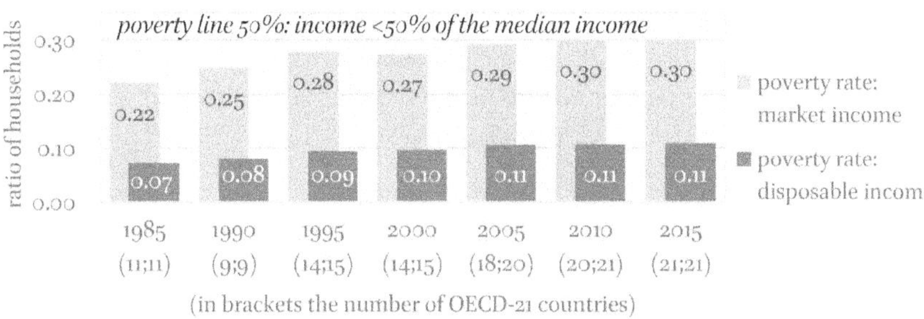

DATA SOURCE: See Graph 8.15. Year as indicated or nearest year available[31]

Graph 8.16 shows that between 1985 and 2015, the before and the post transfers and taxes poverty rates increased by 36% and by 52%.[32] It is certainly relevant that in the OECD-21, 11% of households lived under the poverty line. It is also relevant that without social security provisions this would be 30% of households, which, presumably, would be unsustainable in terms of legitimation.

Table 8.17 shows for three OECD-21 countries the social security transfers (SST) as a percentage of households' gross income. The last column indicates the average for all households, and the other columns indicate the distribution over the household income deciles. These countries are chosen on the basis of the diversity of their OECD-21 skewedness ranking of gross income in 2015 (top, middle and bottom, as shown in *Table 8.18*). For each of these countries

31 The data are those of the income definition 2012 from when it is available for a country.

32 In 2010 the *poverty gap* – that is, the average shortfall from the poverty line – was for the OECD-21 at 30%. In 2010 the median disposable income (equivalised household) for, e.g., Germany was €[illegible],555 per year, with its poverty gap at [illegible]%. Thus the *poverty line* for this country was at €856 per month, and the average poor household disposed over €650 per month. (For the USA this last figure was $920.)

the SST design is quite different. In each case, however, it is the 6th decile that receives about the country's average SST. Thus it is roughly D1–D5 that benefits from average increases in SST (ceteris paribus the design), and vice versa for decreases. I will further comment on this in Chapter 10 (10§12).

TABLE 8.17 *All household share (%) and deciles share (%) of social security transfers in gross income: UK 2015, Netherlands 2014 and Norway 2015*

	D1	D2	D3	D4	D5	D6	D7	D8	D9	D10	All
UK	60%	47%	48%	36%	25%	17%	13%	8%	5%	2%	15%
Netherlands	122%	99%	93%	76%	45%	24%	16%	11%	7%	6%	25%
Norway	53%	42%	34%	27%	22%	19%	16%	13%	11%	6%	18%

DATA SOURCES: UK (as for Graph 8.13); Netherlands (Statistics Netherlands (CBS), Inkomensgroepen; particuliere huishoudens naar diverse kenmerken);[33] Norway (Statistics Norway, Statbank, Income and wealth statistics for households, Composition of total household income and equivalent after-tax income (per cent), by contents, time and equivalent after-tax income).[34] Accessed 21 October 2017

TABLE 8.18 *OECD-21 income rank of the UK, Netherlands and Norway in 2015 (rank 1 is very skewed, rank 20 is skweded)*[35]

	Market income	Gross income	Disposable income
UK	5	3	2
Netherlands	15	11	10
Norway	19	18	19

DATA SOURCE: OECD, Dataset Income distribution and poverty (accessed 8 October 2017)

33 http://statline.cbs.nl/Statweb/publication/?DM=SLNL&PA=71013NED&D1=0-2&D2=a&D3=0-10&D4=0&D5=l&HDR=G4,G1,T&STB=G3,G2&VW=T (data 8 February 2017; accessed 10 October 2017).

34 https://www.ssb.no/statistikkbanken/selectout/pivot.asp?checked=true (accessed 21 October 2017).

35 No 2015 data for Japan.

8§11-b Amplification. The development of the top 5% and the top 10% shares of income between 1910 and 2010 for averages of current OECD-21 countries

The great advantage of data from the OECD is that country data are based on uniform definitions that guide the work of the national statistical bureaus. For long run historical data this is quite different, because data collection from the past cannot be remade. We have what we have, and efforts at uniformity must be made via estimates. Income data of the non-recent past are mostly based on data from taxation authorities, which have been devised not on the basis of theoretical definitions (such as the components of 'gross income'), but rather on the varying legislation of taxation (tax codes) between countries and over time. Thus, for example, the 'tax units' (individual, household and household composites) diverge between countries and over time.

The data used for *Graph 8.19* are based on the painstaking work of many people from different countries that got together to construct the 'World wealth and income database' (best-known amongst the general public is Thomas Piketty, and among economists also Emmanuel Saez and Tony Atkinson). Incidental data on top incomes (and wealth) go back to the early nineteenth century, but more or less continuous series for several countries date from the early twentieth century. (See Roine and Waldenström 2014, pp. 12–22, or Roine and Waldenström 2015, section 2.1, for a brief description of the data and the problems thereof.) In sum, the data used are of an approximation of 'gross income', the tax unit being mostly individuals (personal income). The focus is on top incomes because given the historical tax codes, these are the most reliable (though for top income shares, the income of the total population has to be estimated).

Graph 8.19 shows that each of the top shares moderately decreased until 1950 and next far more steeply from 1950 to 1980. In the following three decades we see a steep increase, reaching in 2010 to above the 1950 levels (considering three-decade periods this steep increase moved faster than the earlier steep decrease).

Very roughly the steep decrease period coincided with the steep increase in SST that was shown in Graph 7.10 (probably, as SST data for 1940 and 1950 are lacking) – the SST increase turning to a moderate one after 1990. Whilst this does not explain all of it, it does seem to explain some of it.

GRAPH 8.19 *Distribution of income: shares of the top 10% and the top 5% in the total personal income, 1910–2010; averages of up to 14 current OECD countries*[36]

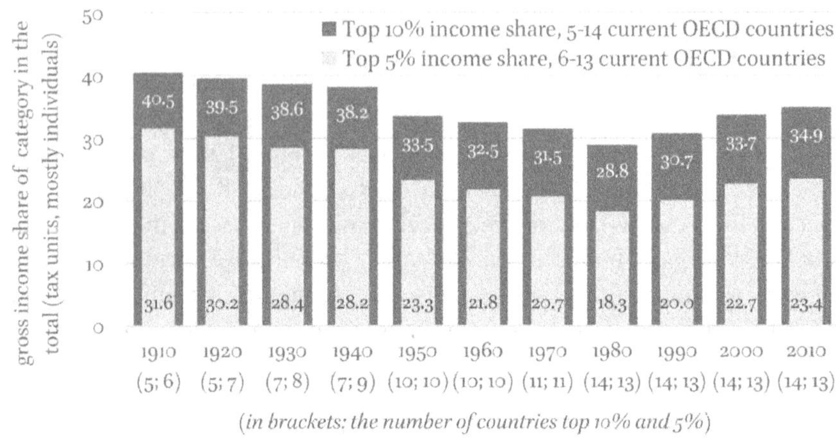

DATA SOURCE: World wealth and income database (decade years or nearest year available)[37]

8§12 *The after-tax resulting distribution of wealth*

- *The distribution of wealth*

The constellation of taxes and their design (8§11) results in a particular distribution of wealth. Given that taxation on wealth is usually accounted as a deduction from current income, the prevailing distribution of wealth is the end result of:

- first, the revaluation or devaluation of previous wealth;
- second, taxation of wealth and current income;
- third, current income saved.

The distribution of wealth tends to be far more skewed than the distribution of income (Amplification 8§12-a).

- *The distinction between capital and wealth, and the distribution of capital*

'Wealth' refers to all durable entities or claims that have a monetary value. 'Capital' is a form of wealth. However, this does not mean that all wealth is 'capital'. Capital is a form of wealth geared to production, with the purpose of selling

36 Australia, Canada, France, Germany, Ireland, Italy, Japan, Netherlands, Norway, Portugal, Spain, Sweden, Switzerland, USA. (There are data available for other countries: Denmark, New Zealand and the UK. However, their base of households differs too much from that of the current group for calculating a consistent average.)

37 http://www.wid.world/ (accessed 20 October 2016).

that production so as to make a profit. Directly this applies to 'active capital' (Figure 3.2a, in 3§1, summarises the distinction between active and passive capital). In one of these active or passive forms of capital, a category of households is the owner of capital (for the non-incorporated enterprises these households are the owner of active capital).

Note that whereas bonds issued by enterprises are a form of passive capital, bonds issued by the state are not capital (from the point of view of the financier this regards merely a matter of degree of risk).

Capital ownership tends to be concentrated at the top of the distribution of wealth – in fact the top 10%.[38] Thus within the wealth skewedness, the distribution of capital is even more skewed (Amplification 8§12-b).

The distribution of wealth is a matter of monetary distribution. If we look at its capital component it is still a monetary distribution, but it is also a distribution of potential or actual economic power.

Unless stated otherwise, 'wealth' in the amplifications of this section refers to 'net wealth', that is, assets minus debts. These amplifications are:

8§12-a. An estimate for the distribution of wealth of the OECD-21 for 2015.
8§12-b. The distribution of wealth and its components: case of the Netherlands 2015.
8§12-c. Top wealth shares of 19 OECD-21 countries around 2014.
8§12-d. The top 5% and top 10% shares of wealth between 1910 and 2010.
8§12-e. Taxation of inheritance of wealth.

8§12-a Amplification. An estimate for the distribution of wealth of the OECD-21 for 2015

Country data about wealth distribution are most often not collected on an internationally standardised basis. Shorrocks, Davies and Lluberas (2015) provide an *estimate* of the global distribution of wealth. In *Graph 8.20* I have used their estimates for the OECD-21 countries. It can be seen that the wealth distribution over deciles is far more skewed than the income distribution over deciles (compare Graph 8.13 in 8§11-a). For example, whereas in 2010 the ratio of the mean to the median disposable income is 1.1, the ratio of the mean to median wealth is 2.6 (2010 and 2015 estimate).

38 The relative concentration increases to the extent that we consider the top 5%, the top 1% and so forth. For the top 10%, 5% and 1% Murtin and Mira d'Ercole show this for 18 OECD counties around 2010 (see Murtin and Mira d'Ercole 2015, Figures 2 and 3).

GRAPH 8.20 *Wealth distribution: shares of deciles and of top 5% and top 1%, estimate for 2015; average of OECD-21*

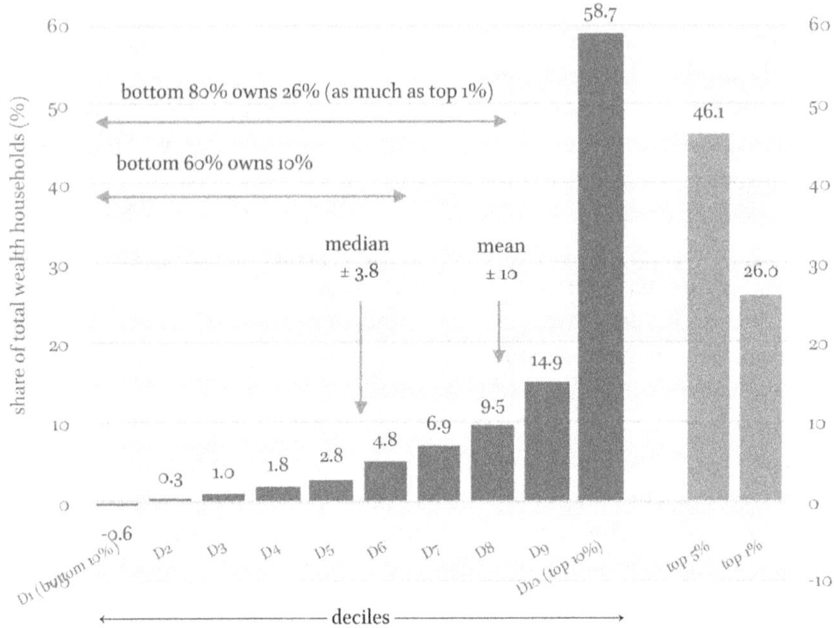

DATA SOURCE: Shorrocks, Davies and Lluberas 2015, p. 149, Table 6–5

The distance between the median and the mean is a simple measure for the skewedness of the (wealth) distribution.

The following amplifications are about the factual distribution of wealth. The next two sentences are on facts about beliefs. According to research on beliefs about the distribution of income and of wealth in the USA, the average interviewee (in 2011) thinks that these distributions are far less skewed than they are in fact.[39] On the other hand, 61% of interviewees (in 2013) believe that the USA economic system favours the wealthy.[40]

8§12-b Amplification. The distribution of gross wealth and its components: case of the Netherlands 2015

This amplification presents the distribution of the main components of gross wealth for the Netherlands in 2015 – assets and debts (see *Graph 8.21*). Of the 19

39 https://www.scientificamerican.com/article/economic-inequality-it-s-far-worse-than-you-think/ (Nickolas Fitz, *Scientific American*, 31 December 2015).

40 http://www.pewresearch.org/fact-tank/2013/12/05/u-s-income-inequality-on-rise-for-decades-is-now-highest-since-1928/ (Drew Desilver, *Facttank*, 5 December 2013).

OECD-21 countries for which the OECD has data available for around 2014, the Netherlands ranks, regarding the wealth share of each of the top 10%, top 5% and top 1%, second in skewedness after the USA.[41]

The general picture of this graph is no different from the previous one. However, its main point is that we now see the degree of concentration of the capital component of wealth at the top of the distribution: in 2015 the top 10% owns 89% of the total capital of households.

GRAPH 8.21 *Deciles distribution of gross wealth and its components: the Netherlands 2015*

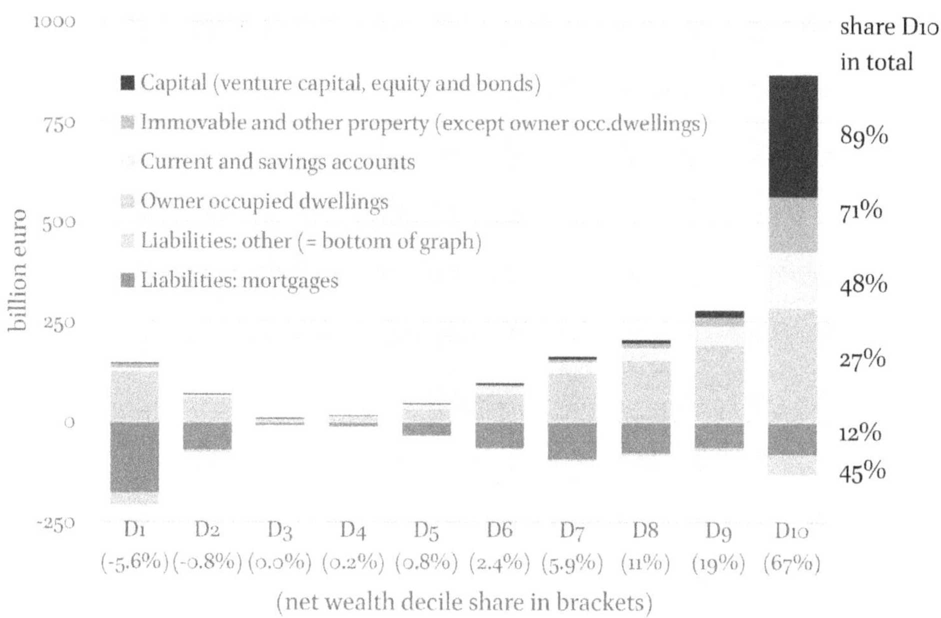

DATA SOURCE: Statistics Netherlands (CBS): 'Vermogen van huishoudens; huishoudenskenmerken, vermogensbestanddelen', 2015 (release date 7 February 2018)[42]

The D10 liabilities reveal, mainly, that the wealthiest class uses debt as an amplifier of wealth (in Chapter 3, Appendix 3B-4, I called this 'finance doubling').

41 OECD dataset Wealth (net wealth) http://stats.oecd.org/index.aspx?DatasetCode=WEALTH (accessed 30 Jan 2018).

42 Accessed 7 February 2018. http://statline.cbs.nl/Statweb/publication/?DM=SLNL&PA=83834NED&D1=1-3&D2=0,51-60&D3=0-14&D4=9&HDR=G3,T&STB=G1,G2&VW=T.

The negative wealth share of the first two deciles reveals an insufficient dwellings coverage of mortgages. Especially for the D1 it also reveals over-crediting to small non-incorporated enterprises.

(In 2015 the total net wealth of households was 160% of GDP; for D10 this was 108%.)

8§12-c Amplification. Top wealth shares of 15 OECD-21 countries around 2010

The OECD remarks on its website that until it issued guidelines for the collection of wealth data in 2013, there was no agreed standard that statistical offices could use for collecting these data.[43] The data that I have used in *Table 8.22* for the top-wealth shares are probably the only ones currently available that have been collected on a uniform base.

Table 8.22 shows, as usual, OECD-21 averages (insofar as they are available). However, as an exception this time I also specify the top and bottom deviations from the average.

TABLE 8.22 *Top wealth shares of 19 OECD-21 countries in or around 2014*†

	Share top 10%	Share top 5%	Share top 1%
average OECD-19	52.4	38.6	18.6‡
top skewed distributions	(with their rank in brackets)		
USA (2013)	78.2(1)	65.9(1)	37.6(1)
Netherlands (2015)	68.3(2)[44]	52.5(2)	27.8(2)
Denmark (2015)	64.0(3)	47.3(3)	23.6(5)
Germany (2014)	59.8(4)	46.3(4)	23.7(4)
Austria (2014)	55.6(5)	43.5(5)	25.5(3)

43 See also Murtin and Mira d'Ercole [OECD] 2015. http://www.oecd.org/std/household-wealth-inequality-across-OECD-countries-OECDSB21.pdf.

44 This figure deviates from that shown in Graph 8.21 (67.1%), which stems from a different release date. For the country comparison only the OECD data are relevant.

TABLE 8.22 *Top wealth shares of 19 OECD-21 countries (cont.)*

	Share top 10%	Share top 5%	Share top 1%
least skewed distributions	(with their rank in brackets)		
Finland (2014)	45.2(15)	31.4(15)	13.3(14)
Italy (2014)	42.8(16)	29.7(17)	11.7(16)
Belgium (2014)	42.5(17)	29.7(16)	12.1(15)
Greece (2014)	42.4(18)	28.8(18)	9.2(18)
Japan (2014)	41.0(19)	27.7(19)	10.8(17)

† OECD-21 minus Sweden and Switzerland (and for the top 1% of wealth also New Zealand). For each of these countries only 1–3 observations are available between 2009 and 2015. The table is based on the data nearest to 2014 (which is the year for which data are most frequently available).

‡ This column regards 18 countries (no data for New Zealand).

DATA SOURCE: OECD Dataset Wealth (net wealth)[45]

Because of their social security constellation, the Netherlands, Germany, and Austria have been classified as 'Rhineland capitalist countries'. It can be seen from *Table 8.22* that such a constellation is far from detrimental to their, in terms of wealth, capitalist upper class.[46]

45 http://stats.oecd.org/index.aspx?DatasetCode=WEALTH (accessed 29 January 2018).
Anticipating the next amplification, the following table compares two OECD data from the second row of Table 8.22 with the figures of amplifications 8§12-a and 8§12-d.

Source	Top shares wealth (%) top 10%	top 1%
OECD data, 18–19 countries [around 2014]	52.4	18.6
Roine and Waldenström (WWID data), 6–7 countries [around 2010]	58.9	21.9
Shorrocks, Davies and Lluberas, *estimate* 21 countries [for 2015]	58.7	26.0

46 See also Bavel and Frankema 2013.

8§12-d Amplification. The top 5% and top 10% shares of wealth between 1910 and 2010

The historical OECD averages that I present in this amplification are based on data collected by Roine and Waldenström (2014). As these authors indicate, 'the empirical literature on wealth inequality is still limited, particularly when it comes to the long run perspective' (p. 40). For various problems of the data I refer to these authors, and for what they did about these when possible (pp. 40–9).[47] However, many of these problems do not just relate to long run historical data.[48]

GRAPH 8.23 *Distribution of wealth: top wealth decile and percentile as share of the total private wealth, 1910–2010; 6–10 current OECD countries*[49]

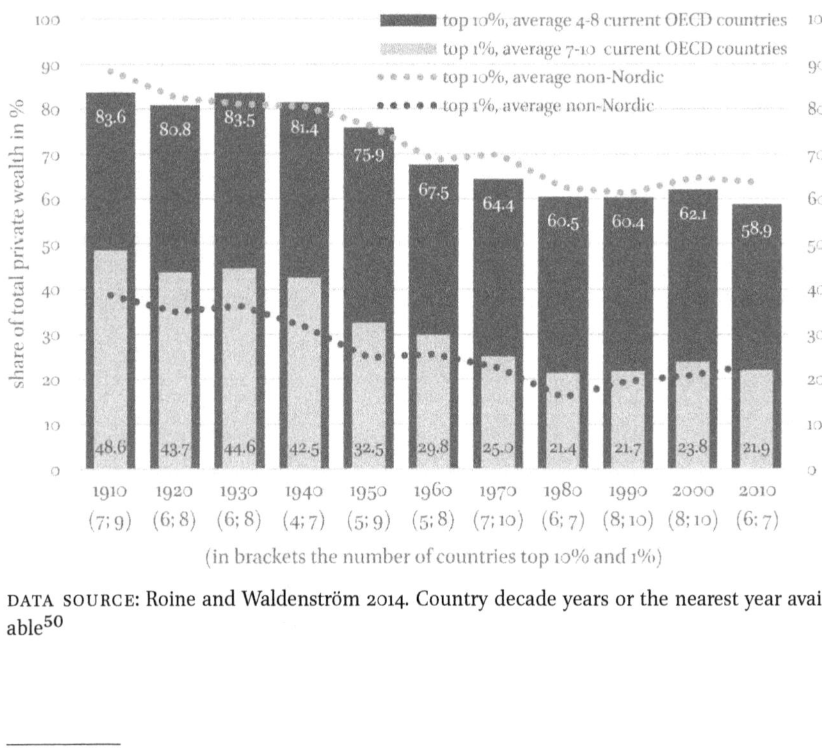

DATA SOURCE: Roine and Waldenström 2014. Country decade years or the nearest year available[50]

---

47 Roine and Waldenström 2015, pp. 40–9. For the sources of the data that the authors collected, see their Table A1, pp. 141–2.

48 For the detection of problems of recent data (such as those collected by the EU), see Salverda 2015, pp. 7–14.

49 Top wealth decile: Denmark, Finland, France, Norway, Sweden, Switzerland, UK, USA. Top wealth percentile, idem plus Australia and the Netherlands. The 'Nordic' countries are Denmark, Finland, Norway and Sweden.

50 http://www.uueconomics.se/danielw/Handbook.htm. The authors closed off their study

Comparing the 2010 data from Roine and Waldenström with those of the OECD nearest to 2010 (see the table in the last but two footnote), it appears that for the data that overlap qua country (5–6), the OECD data are 10% lower for the top 10 and 20% for the top 1 (these are in percent, not percentage points of the shares). Hoping that the deviations are more or less consistent over time, the data from Roine and Waldenström can be used as an indicator of the trend – see *Graph 8.23*.

The Nordic countries (Denmark, Finland, Norway, Sweden) make up 19% of the OECD-21 countries. However, for these wealth data this is 50% (top decile) and 40% (top percentile). Therefore *Graph 8.23* also shows the averages of the non-Nordic countries (dotted lines). Throughout this period the Nordic countries entertained above OECD-21 average social security provisions, but that did not impair their wealthiest classes in comparison with the OECD average.[51]

We see in *Graph 8.23* that around 1910 the wealth share was starkly concentrated at the top. Throughout the period thereafter we see a continuous decrease in this concentration, and relatively more so for the top 1% (1910–2010: a fall of 55%; against a fall of 30% for the top 10%). A substantial part of these shares decreases presumably has to do with the increase in the value of owner-occupied dwellings in the *other* deciles (especially deciles 7–9). Another important factor is taxes. *Graph 8.24* shows how the top wealth share varies (or at least coincides) with total tax receipts (for details about the latter, see the text around Graph 8.4 in 8§4-b). We see especially that with the bending off of the tax receipts from 1980 onwards, the top wealth share more or less stabilises. (Regarding the *shares* of wealth at hand, taxation seems a more important determinant than financial crises – see 2§10-b, Graph 2.11, for their occurrence in this period.)

This again would suggest not only the thesis that the state bought off the legitimation for the capitalist system, but that, in particular, the rich – that is, those who generally have a vested interest in the capitalist system – had to pay a price for it.

in 2014. For reasons of data consistency I have refrained from adding data for 2010 that are now available from other sources.

51 As indicated earlier, the same applies for 'Rhineland' countries such as Germany, the Netherlands and Austria, though for these *from* about 1960 – and for the Netherlands *until* about 2000 when its social security provisions moved below the OECD-21 average.

GRAPH 8.24 *Distribution of wealth: the share of the top wealth decile as connected with total taxes, 1910–2010; averages of 7–8 current OECD countries*

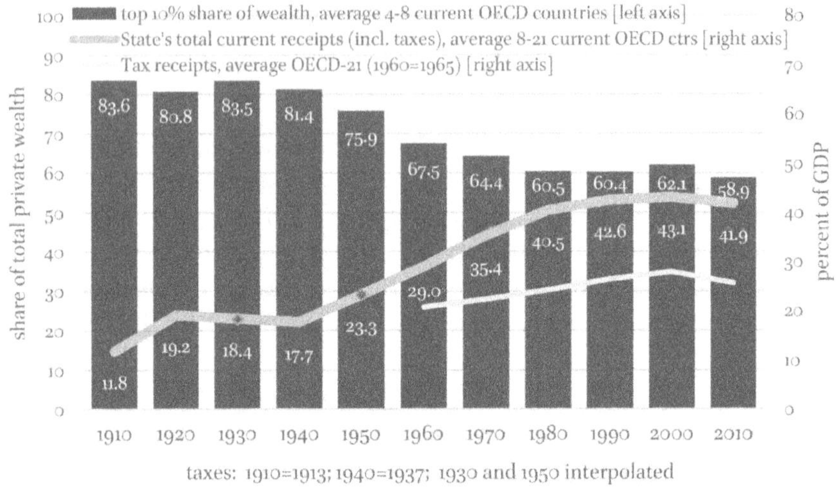

DATA SOURCE: Top wealth share, see Graph 8.23; Taxes and other state receipts, see Graph 8.4

8§12-e Amplification. Taxation of inheritance of wealth

It is often argued that taxation of wealth and of the inheritance of wealth is 'unfair' because taxes have already been levied on income. This argument neglects that the tax burden for the average household consists of two main components, namely direct taxes on income and indirect taxes on income spent. Thus the income spent is taxed twice. The non-spent income, that is, savings, is taxed once. The contra argument is that when savings are spent, the second round (indirect taxes) comes in. However, this contra argument neglects the fact that most of the top of the wealth (the top 10% and above) is never actually spent and is instead bequeathed.

Another contra argument is based on the presumed benevolence of saving as based on the loanable funds theory – this was already dealt with (3§6, 3§6-a, 3§6-d).

Anyway, whereas direct taxes (including those on current wealth) are substantial for the top incomes and wealth layers, inheritance taxes seem moderate in the perspective of indirect tax rates (which are thus *not* levied on savings).

Unfortunately, long run data of effective inheritance tax receipts are lacking for the OECD-21.[52] *Graph 8.25* shows what is available for estate and inheritance

52 Piketty (2014) shows long data for top *statutory* inheritance tax rates (1910–2010 for France,

taxes for the average of the OECD-21: data from 1965 onwards.[53] It can be seen that the receipts from estate and inheritance taxes are not tremendous.

GRAPH 8.25 *State receipts from estate, inheritance and gift taxes in % of GDP, 1965–2015; average of OECD-21*

DATA SOURCE: OECD dataset Revenue Statistics – Comparative tables, series 4300[54]

Summary and conclusions

This chapter's Division 1 (state production) and Division 2 (finance of the state) provided concretising conditions of existence for the exposition of Chapters 6–7. All the other divisions presented concretising implications of these earlier chapters and divisions.

Economically, the state 'produces' the content of the economic rights framework and the frameworks furthering the accumulation of capital as presented in Chapters 6–7. For it, the state employs wage labour (i.e. civil servants) and purchases inputs from enterprises, but it tends to make no profits. Moreover,

---

Germany, UK and the USA). These are not irrelevant, but in the end it is the effective tax rates that count. https://www.quandl.com/data/PIKETTY/TS14_2-Top-inheritance-tax-rate-in-rich-countries-1900-2013 – updated 29 April 2014; accessed 13 September 2017.

53 'An estate tax is applied to an estate before the assets are given to the beneficiaries. In contrast, an inheritance tax applies to assets after they have been inherited by someone. In the case of inheritance tax, each beneficiary may have to pay a different amount, depending on how much is inherited.' (*Investopedia*, January 2016 http://www.investopedia.com/terms/e/estatetax.asp.)

54 http://stats.oecd.org/OECDStat_Metadata/ShowMetadata.ashx?Dataset=REV&ShowOnWeb=true&Lang=en (last updated August 2017; accessed 21 January 2018). Investopedia (source previous footnote) mentions for the USA: 'As of 2016, the Internal Revenue Service (IRS) only requires estates with combined gross assets and prior taxable gifts exceeding $5.45 million to file a federal estate tax return and pay estate taxes.'

it distributes its produce for free as collective goods and services. Next to the state's expenditure on its production, its expenditures include transfers in the form of, mainly, social security and interest. (Division 1.)

Taxation is a necessary, and main, form of finance of the state. Next to this finance, the state may contingently collect social security contributions, and it may contingently collect other receipts (mainly) from royalties, sale of state services, and dividends of state-owned enterprises. Finally, the state may contingently borrow to finance any budget deficit (or lend in case of a surplus). The state's finance, in its particular forms, grounds the state's expenditures and hence the moments prior to it. (Division 2.)

All of the state's expenditures – though apart from the savings out of the state's wages and transfers – end up as expenditures with enterprises, and so also realise a major part of their surplus-value. Increases in state expenditure increase the production and validation of surplus-value – vice versa for expenditure decreases. (Division 3.)

Part of this state-accommodated surplus-value is distributed to the state via taxation of surplus-value (or narrower, taxation of profit). Thus, for enterprises in macroeconomic perspective, the benefits from state expenditure are in part offset by these taxes.

These taxes are the enterprises' costs of the state's granting and upholding their legal core economic rights to property and to the appropriation of surplus-value, as well as of its accommodation of the accumulation of capital (that is, the costs of the seven legislative frameworks as presented in Chapters 6–7). Thus these are the costs for the state's accommodation of the enterprises' appropriation of surplus-value in general – not merely those that stem from extra surplus-value along with extra state expenditure.

In principle, all state expenditure might be financed by taxation of surplus-value. In actual capitalist practice, however, the state acts such that enterprises 'share' the taxation with taxation of the wages income of labour, as well as of taxation of the surplus-value that enterprises distribute to owners of finance capital. From the perspective of labour, it is in fact immaterial where the taxes on surplus-value are levied (either at the point where these are generated within enterprises, or at the point where these are distributed). Thus in sum, the state acts such that enterprises and capital owners 'share' the taxation of surplus-value with the taxation of wages. (Division 4.)

Herewith the grounding of the capitalist state vis-à-vis the capitalist economy is completed.

At this point the exposition moves to the particular *forms* of taxation and their *manifestation* in the distribution of the income of households and in the distribution of the wealth of households. Households as such are, without further specification, not directly identified as workers' or capital owners' households, but rather as households that have some share in the income from wages or from surplus-value (recall 2§15-a's Graph 2.14 about the historical movement of the totals in the USA).

The main forms of taxation include taxes on profits, on property value and property income, on labour income and on products. In principle, the state might choose between these forms or combinations thereof. Some form of taxation being necessary, it is contingent which particular form or forms are actually applied, and to what extent.

Taxation has inevitably non-neutral distributive effects on income and wealth. This applies for the particular form of taxation and also for the design of tax rates (regressive, flat, progressive). More specifically, a flat tax rate is not more neutral than a non-flat one. Any actual form and design of taxation is inevitably based on a normative stance. This leaves unaffected the fact that with a more skewed distribution of income, more savings press down profits. Thus progressive taxes support enterprises: their rate of profit and so investment and employment. This puts on the state's agenda the dilemma as to whether it is primarily concerned with the interests of enterprises or rather with the privileges of the wealthy and high-income categories. The ideological supposition that investment would require saving is of key importance here.

The legitimation of the state in the compliance of the actors – and hence the legitimation of the capitalist system – tends to be shaped in at least some redistribution of income in favour of the lower echelons. However, this redistribution is mainly engendered via social security transfers rather than via effective progressive rates of taxation.

Appendix 8A. Data and data sources of the graphs in chapter 8

[**Re 8§2-a.**] *Graph 8.2. Total state expenditure (general government) 1870–2015, in % GDP; average of 10 to 21 current OECD countries.*

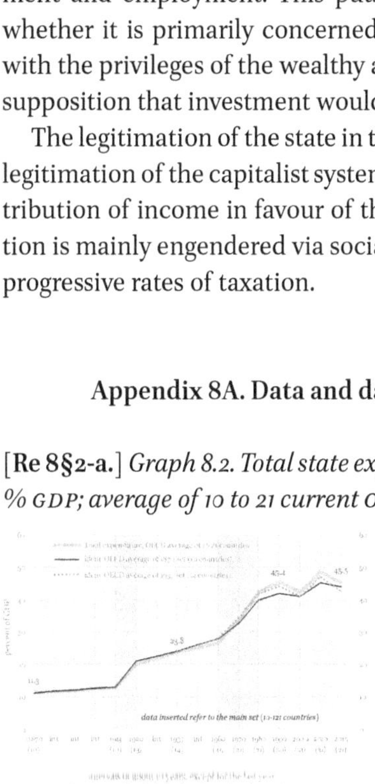

The graph shows the development of the average for: (1) a set of 10 countries for which data are available from 1870 to present (Australia, Austria; France, Germany, Italy, Japan, Norway, Switzerland, UK, US); (2) a set of 14 countries for which data are available from 1937 to present (the former plus Canada, Ireland, New Zealand and Sweden); (3) the OECD-21 from 1960 to present.

Data sources. For 1870–1937 (Tanzi and Schuknecht 2000, Table I.1). I have omitted their data for 'central government' only, as this would disturb the comparison. For 1960–80 (Castles 2006, Table 1). To his data I have added the data for New Zealand, Norway and Switzerland from Tanzi and Schuknecht. For 1990–current (OECD, http://stats.oecd.org/OECDStat_Metadata/ShowMetadata.ashx?Dataset=EO102_INTERNET&ShowOnWeb=true&Lang=en extracted 28 December 2017).

I have considered using data from Cusack and Fuchs 2002, who for the period 1870–1950 collected total expenditure data from various sources (different from Tanzi and Schuknecht's) of 12–17 current OECD countries – more than the number of 10–14 that I have used from Tanzi and Schuknecht. Moreover, they also provide data for the years that I have interpolated. However, the disadvantage of their data (as for the full set that Tanzi and Schuknecht provide) is that these are mixes of General government and Central government data. Therefore I have declined using the Cusack and Fuchs data.[55] *Graph 8.2A* shows the data differences (I have included for all series the 1960 data from Castles), and *Table 8.2B* shows the various numbers of data for each year of the three sets.

GRAPH 8.2A *Total state expenditure 1870–1950 in % GDP for current OECD countries: comparison of data from Tanzi and Schuknecht with data from Cusack and Fuchs*

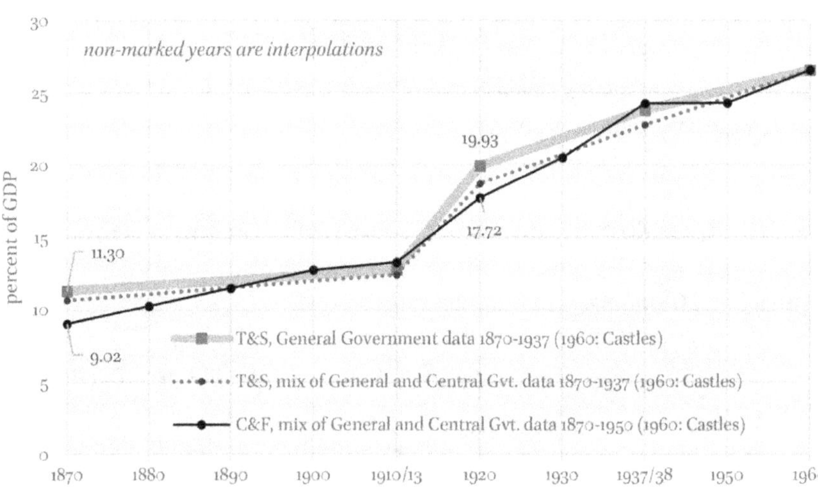

DATA SOURCES: Tanzi and Schuknecht 2000, Table I.1 and Cusack and Fuchs 2002, Table 1 and Appendix

55 For this graph – and the following ones – I have also declined using the database of Jordà-

TABLE 8.2B *Number of expenditure data 1870–1950: Tanzi and Schuknecht (2000) and Cusack and Fuchs (2002)*

	1870	1880	1890	1900	1910/13	1920	1930	1937/38	1950
T&S, General Government	10	..	..	..	10	13	..	14	..
T&S, mix of Gen. and Centr. Gvt.	12	..	..	..	13	17	..	17	..
C&F, mix of Gen. and Centr.Gvt.	12	11	11	11	14	14	14	16	18

DATA SOURCES: SEE *GRAPH 8.2A*

Comparing the T&S set for general government that I have used (row 1) with the C&F set, the main differences are for 1870 and 1920. Because for one and the same country the datum for central government expenditure is smaller than that for general government expenditure, more central government data for one year generally implies that the average is pressed down further. C&F have generally more data for one year; however, it is also the case that for 1870 T&S have (row 1) data of Australia and Switzerland, and for 1920 of Australia and Ireland that C&F do not have. This intensifies the general versus central government diversity for those years.

However, given these differences it is comforting to learn from the C&F data that my decade interpolations seem not to miss up and downs for these intervals.

[**Re 8§3**] *Graph 8.3. State employment as percent of total employment*[56] *in comparison with state expenditure (each general government); averages of up to 21 current OECD countries, 1870–2015.*

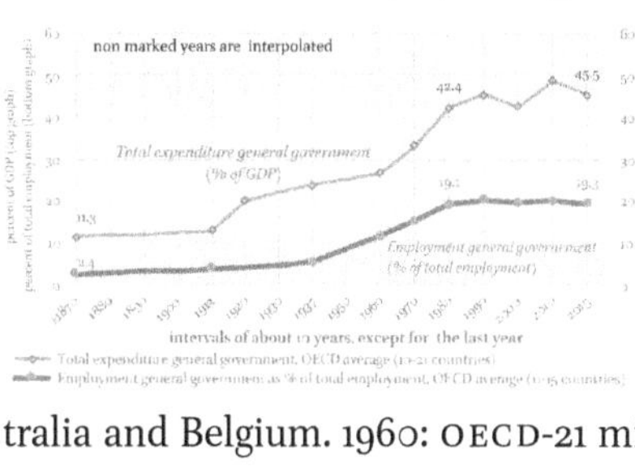

Employment general government, as a percentage of total employment (persons, civilian); average of 11–15 OECD countries 1870–2015. For 1870 and 1913: OECD-21 minus Canada, Denmark, Finland, Greece, New Zealand, Portugal, Spain. 1937: as for 1913, minus Australia and Belgium. 1960: OECD-21 minus Australia, Denmark, France, Greece,

Schularick-Taylor because it only pertains to central government. (Between states there is quite a divergence in what is allotted to the central or the lower government levels.)

56 Employment general government (excluding military employment and employment by public corporations), as a percentage of total employment (persons, civilian).

Ireland, Japan, Norway, Spain. 1970–80: OECD-21 minus Australia, Austria, Germany, Greece, Ireland, New Zealand, Switzerland (Norway 1970=1972; UK 1970=1971. 1990 onwards, as for 1980, plus Ireland).

Data sources: 1870, 1913, 1937 (Tanzi and Schuknecht 2000, Table II.2); 1960 (OECD 1999, Table 2.13), though with Australia omitted (datum includes public enterprises) and with Canada and Italy added from Tanzi and Schuknecht; 1970–current (OECD http://stats.oecd.org/OECDStat_Metadata/ShowMetadata.ashx?Dataset=EO102_INTERNET&ShowOnWeb=true&Lang=en – accessed 28 December 2017).

[**Re 8§4-b**] *Graph 8.4. State receipts (general government) 1870–2015, in % GDP: (a) total current receipts; (b) tax and social security receipts; (c) tax receipts. Averages of 8–21 current OECD countries.*

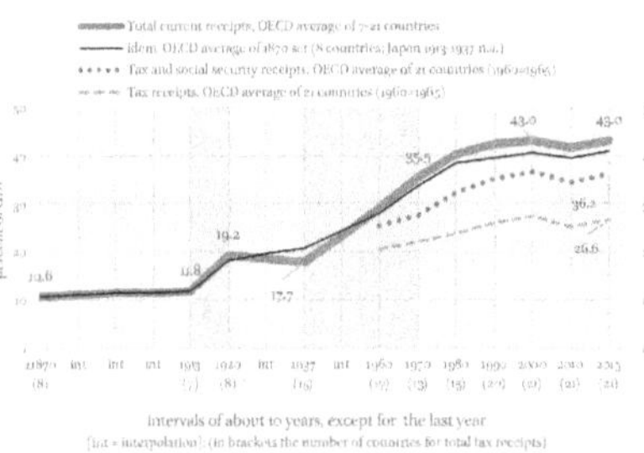

The two top lines show the development of the average *total state receipts* (general government) for two sets of current OECD countries: (1) a set of 8 countries for which 1870 data are available (Australia, France, Ireland, Italy, Japan, Norway, UK, USA); (2) the set of these counties, together with a through time increasing number of countries – though with a gap for Japan in 1920 and in 1937, and for several countries in 1970 and 1980. (As follows: 1920 as for 1870 plus New Zealand minus Japan; 1937 plus Austria, Canada, Germany, Netherlands, Spain, Sweden, Switzerland; 1960 plus Belgium, Finland, Japan, though minus New Zealand; 1970 as for 1960, minus Australia, Germany, Ireland, Sweden – Denmark 1970=1971; 1980, as for 1970 plus Norway and Portugal; 1990 OECD-21 minus Greece – Germany 1990=1991; 2000 onwards, OECD-21.)

The bottom lines show the total tax and social security receipts for the full OECD-21. Note that there are these full data only from 1965. In the bottom graphs 1960=1965.

Data sources. 1870–1960 (Tanzi and Schuknecht 2000, Table III.1). I have omitted their data for 'central government' only, as this would disturb the comparison. Their data for 1960 have been updated for those countries for which the OECD Economic Outlook (2017–2) provides these. Total receipts 1970 onwards: OECD Dataset: Economic Outlook No. 102 – November 2017, General governments current receipts http://stats.oecd.org/index.aspx?DatasetCode=EO102_INTERNET. Tax and social contributions: OECD http://localhost/OECDStat_Metadata/ShowMetadata.ashx?Dataset=REV&ShowOnWeb=true&Lang=en (updated 23 November 2017 – accessed 28 December 2017).

List of figures chapter 8

CHAPTER 9

The imposition of competition

A framework of constraints on the modes of market interaction

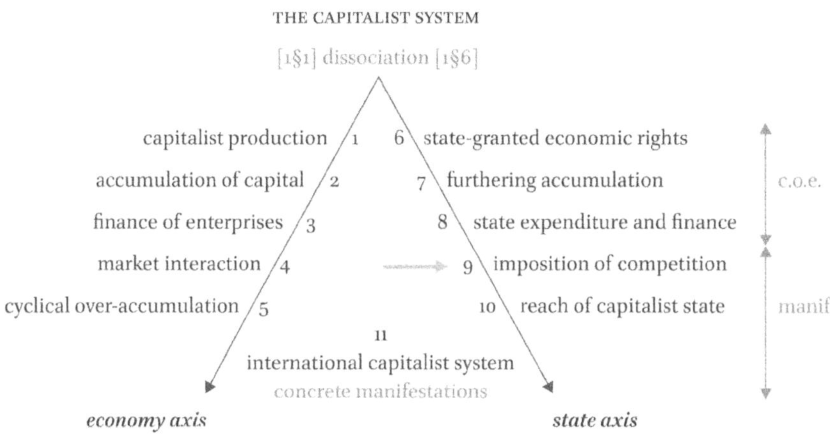

Note: 'c.o.e.' abbreviates conditions of existence and 'manif.' concrete manifestations.

Contents

Introduction

The previous chapter completed the grounding of the capitalist state vis-à-vis the capitalist economy. As with the last two chapters of Part One regarding the economy, Chapters 9–10 present the concrete manifestations of the state. These concrete manifestations are about the reproductive strength of the capitalist system, but also its vulnerabilities (General Appendix on Systematic Dialectics, section A§12).

This chapter presents the state's concrete manifestation in its imposing a framework of constraints on the modes of market interaction of enterprises and banks, and of constraints on the outcomes of that interaction.

Division 1, which is a sequel to Chapter 4, surveys the state's engagement in constraints of market interaction that is 'conventionally' regarded as 'competition policy' as encoded in competition law. It will be seen that the state's rationale for such a legislative framework is rather ambiguous. In the form of 'competition policy' the state imposes on enterprises and banks *its* view about 'proper' competitive interaction.

Division 2 presents two main effects of market interaction on the market constellation, ones that when left unconstrained would generate vulnerabilities for the reproduction of the capitalist system. The first one regards the competitive constellation that would result in (potential) generalised price deflation (4D2) and the state's response to it. This response takes the form of a monetary policy engendering 'creeping inflation'.

The second vulnerability regards a phenomenon that was only thrown into relief with the emergence of the 2008 financial crisis, that is, entities, especially banks, that have grown 'too big to fail'. The state's response to this phenomenon is as yet (at the time of completing this book) insufficient, although the *germ* of an instrument more adequately dealing with it seems in the making. Even if such a (potential) instrument were to exist, its effective implementation would require big entities to break up into several smaller ones. This is highly conflicting as it puts in fact a penalty on the successful accumulation of capital.

The latter point is dealt with in a single section of Division 2. An appendix deals more extensively with its empirical background.

Scheme 9.1 presents the outline of this chapter.

SCHEME 9.1 *The imposition of competition* (*outline Chapter 9*)

Two manifestations of the state as associated with its imposition of the mode of competition

.Ṃ.	.Ṃ.
The imposition of competition a framework of prohibitive regulation of competition (9D1)	**Constraints on the mode of competition and (potential) constraints on the mode of capital accumulation** (9D2)

Appendix 9A. Too big banks: too big to fail and too big for supervisors

Legend
.Ṃ. concrete manifestation

Division 1. The imposition of competition

A framework of prohibitive regulation of the enterprises' market interaction

This division sets out the state's engagement in constraints of market interaction that is 'conventionally' regarded as 'competition policy' as encoded in competition law.

9§1 *The state's manifestation in competition policy: engendering a particular mode of existence of the capitalist system*

The primary aim of enterprises is the production and accumulation of capital (Chapters 1–2). In achieving this, the particular form of market interaction is purely instrumental to enterprises (4§5). Thus competition, cartel formation and centralisation of capital are mere instrumental alternatives. (See *Figure 9.2* for a recapitulation.)

With a framework of 'competition law' the state might be concerned to impose competitive market interaction. Such a framework is not obvious to the extent that non-competitive market behaviour does not interfere with, first, the production and accumulation of capital, and, second, the material existence of the state (7D1). The state's entertainment of a framework of competition law seems rather the manifestation of a particular mode of existence of the capitalist system. Even so, it is a mode that – in a variety of forms – is ubiquitous among capitalist nations.

FIGURE 9.2 *Recapitulation of the forms of market interaction as set out in Chapter 4*

	Forms of interaction	**Degree of rivalry (top: top rivalry)**
rivalry interaction	competition†	1a. deflationary price competition: resignation to rotating price-leadership (4D2) 1b. inflationary 'structural overcapacity competition': resignation to rotating price-leadership (4D3)
non-rivalry interaction‡	cartel formation	2. tacit price-leadership (implicit cartel) (4D4)[1]
		3. cartel (4D4)
rivalry tending to non-rivalry interaction	centralisation of capital	4. oligopolisation (via merger or take-over): tacit or agreed price-leadership (4D5)
annulment of interaction	centralisation of capital	5. monopolisation (via merger or take-over) (4D5)

† 1a and 1b are alternative general constellations. 2–5 in particular sectors coexist with each of the general constellations in other sectors.

‡ This layer (as based on stagnant innovation in a sector, 4§13) is a recurrently evanescent one, next being 'replaced' by new stagnant ones.

9§2 *The imposition of competition: the fairy tale's 'free market' turned into 'unfree free markets'*

We have seen that the capitalist economy cannot stand on itself and requires the state for, so far, seven regulatory frameworks.[2] In fact the capitalist 'free market economy' is a phantom that can only figure in fairy tales of so devised models (cf. 8§11, under 1). On top of these seven frameworks the state might

1 Tacit price-leadership need not involve 'collusion' in a legal sense; nevertheless it is often categorised under 'tacit collusion' (Ivaldi, Jullien, Rey, Seabright and Tirole 2003, see esp. footnote 2).

2 (1) The capitalist economic rights framework (6D4). This was successively grounded in: (2) the

engender a framework of pro-competitive legislation. However, the state's rationale for such a framework is troublesome, because with it the state openly declares that the capitalist economy cannot stand on itself. (A major capitalist state promulgated this as early as 1890 with the USA Sherman Act of that year.)

If 'competition' as generated by the 'free market' were supposed to be inherent to the capitalist economy (the fairy tale that many entertain), then it is rather paradoxical that when the 'free market' is left to itself, this should lead to the evaporation of competition (cartels, and non-rivalry oligopolisation and monopolisation).

If, instead (or therefore), the state uses its voice to teach 'free market' enterprises what competition is or should be, this is paradoxical. In fact the state does teach enterprises, by imposing *its* view of competition on enterprises. Thus in the fairy tale jargon we seem to have unfree free markets.

With the regulation of competition the unity of the capitalist economy and state reaches its most concrete manifestation regarding the functioning of ordinary markets (that is, all markets apart from the labour and money markets).

In practice the field of 'competition law' is not about competition but rather about the prohibition of, so-called, 'anti-competitive conduct' (see amplifications 9§2-b and 9§2-c). This is quite far-reaching, as it limits property rights (6§10) and especially 'free contract' – 'free contract', that is, 'free' cartel agreements (now deemed 'collusion') and 'free' share purchase agreements in case of mergers and take-overs (those that would entail excessive market dominance).

9§2-a Amplification. A twofold fairy tale

Neoclassical general equilibrium theory is a fairy tale within a fairy tale. The first one is that it ignores even the first two frameworks and its consequences. Within that fairy tale it constructs a world of firms none of which has any market power. Rather more immanently, Blaug (2001) indicates that it is rather ironic to denote something that cannot exist (general equilibrium) as 'perfect competition'. He argues how general equilibrium theory entertains an 'end-state' notion of competition in which rivalry has come to a rest, rather than a dynamic notion of competition as a process.

framework of allowance rights to existence (6D5); (3) the public security framework (6D6); (4) the monetary framework (7D2); (5) the labour-capacity framework (7D3); (6) the infrastructural framework (7D4); (7) the legitimating social security framework (7D5).

9§2-b Amplification. 'Free competition' – the EU's objective of a non-defined goal

The European Union is an interesting case for the current matter, first, because it is predominantly an economic and monetary union, and second, because it started building its legislation from scratch. To begin with, it is one of the few state-like constellations that has warranted a free market economy in its 'constitution' (i.e. the Lisbon Treaty, as entered into force in 2009):[3]

> '… the activities of the Member States and the Union shall include … the adoption of an economic policy which is based on the close coordination of Member States' economic policies, on the internal market and on the definition of common objectives, and conducted *in accordance with the principle of an open market economy with free competition.*'
>
> European Union, Treaty on European Union, art. 119, emphasis added[4]

This is quoted from the general part of the Lisbon Treaty. A second part, the 'Treaty on the Functioning of the European Union', contains six brief articles on competition (arts. 101–106 TFEU). It is remarkable – and indicative of the tricky problematic of the matter – that these articles abstain from outlining what constitutes 'free competition' (art. 119 TEU just quoted); instead these describe, in general terms, what it is *not*. Similarly, the European Commission abstains from setting out what free competition or even what competition is (Senate of the Netherlands 2014, p. 3).

Arts. 101–102 TFEU use normative qualifications such as 'restriction or distortion' of competition; 'abuse' of a dominant position; and 'unfair' purchase or selling prices or other trading conditions.

9§2-c Amplification. Prohibitive competition law

The duality of defining 'competition' versus 'non-competition' is expressed succinctly in an OECD 'background paper' by Schwalbe, Maier-Rigaud and Pisarkiewicz:

'The role of competition law is *to assure that effective competition prevails by preventing* the creation or the strengthening of market power or to prohibit the

---

3 The signification of a 'free market economy' already applies for the Maastricht Treaty of 1992.

4 Official Journal C 83, 30.03.2010 or http://www.lisbon-treaty.org/wcm/the-lisbon-treaty.html
Article 3 (3) states: 'The Union shall establish an internal market. It shall work for the sustainable development of Europe based on balanced economic growth and *price stability*, a highly competitive social market economy, aiming at full employment and social progress, and a high level of protection and improvement of the quality of the environment. It shall promote scientific and technological advance.' A brief 'Protocol on the Internal Market and Competition' states: 'the internal market as set out in Article 3 of the Treaty on European Union includes a system *ensuring that competition is not distorted*'. (All emphases added.)

abuse of a position of substantial market power (monopolisation). Competition authorities have to assess the competitive effects of decisions concerning mergers or potential anticompetitive conduct.' (2012, p. 24, emphasis added.)

9§3 *The proclamation of moral economic norms*

Legislation enacts norms. All the legislative frameworks that were presented in Chapters 6–8 are conditions for the capitalist economic rights granted by the state (6D2) including the right to employ labour and to appropriate the surplus-value produced by that labour.

'Competition law' is no such condition. With its terminology such as 'restriction or distortion' of competition; 'abuse' of a dominant position, 'unfair' market practices, and 'anti-competitive conduct' (9§2-b and 9§2-c), the state proclaims moral economic norms. Seemingly this puts on the agenda the question of why the state entertains these particular moral economic norms, whilst seeing apparently no harm in the employment of labour (in the sense of exploitation of labour). However, these are moral norms about market interaction, not about production. Under normal conditions of unemployment (2D2, 7D3) the level of the market wage allows for the production of surplus-value.[5] Moreover – quite consistently – 'market power', 'dominant market power' and 'monopoly power' in itself is not the target of competition policy. The target is rather the 'abuse' of such power (documented later on in 9§6-b). Although this is consistent, it is also ambivalent.

9§4 *Execution of competition regulation as delegated to an 'independent' market authority: purification from conflict*

Regulation of competition is generally highly conflicting as it infringes on free contracts between enterprises (9§2), as well as again in its required elaboration. The state therefore tends to phrase the legislation on competition in fairly general terms, and to delegate its execution – as including the design of specific (discretionary) rules – to an 'independent' market authority (or several market authorities).[6] By way of this delegation, again, the state purifies itself, at least to some extent, from conflicts of right in concrete situations. (This fits into a series of similar purifications as summarised in Scheme 7.13.)

5 Considering as a main example the EU legislation on competition: none of the formulations in its two key articles (TFEU arts. 101 and 102) stands in the way of the exploitation of labour.

6 See 7§7-a on the term 'independent' in the context of delegation (in that section delegation to an 'independent' Central Bank). As with the CB, market authorities like to be labelled as independent. However, as the state delegates conflict dealing, it is foremost in the interest *of the state* to label (in this case) the market authority as being an 'independent' institution.

Conflicts of right are especially opportune for prohibitions, or non-permission, of mergers and take-overs and of monopolies (as conflicting with state-granted rights to property). Furthermore, regarding prohibitions of collusion and tacit or agreed price-leadership, its legal proof is most often difficult (besides, actors may perceive several types of agreement to be fair, if perhaps not legal or on the verge of it). It is equally difficult to define and to prove when a (reshuffling of a) market constellation should result in a too dominant market power of an enterprise or a group of enterprises.[7]

In face of the often considerable financial interests involved, much of the market authority's decisions are disputed before a court and so end up as (deviating) court rulings and hence case law. Again the 'independent' court shields the state from conflict.

Division 2. Constraints on the mode of competition and (potential) constraints on the mode of capital accumulation

This division moves beyond conventional 'competition policy' in the strict sense. It rather regards two key (potential) effects of the market interaction of enterprises and banks, that, when left unconstrained, would generate vulnerabilities for the reproduction of the capitalist system. The first one, in 9§5, is the sequel to 4D2 (on deflationary price competition). The second one regards an open end in 7D2 (too big to fail banks), one that in 9§6 is specified, rather than it being the exposition of a systemic resolution, because it is actually not resolved (at the time when this book was completed).

9§5 *Precluding a deflationary constellation: creeping inflation*

Section 4§9 outlined how the combination of generalised price competition and speeded up technical change tends to generate economic stagnation. It was also indicated that there are no economy-inherent forces that turn a deflationary constellation into an inflationary one.

Because of this major economic-system continuity impediment, the state is forced to prevent this combination. (For reasons of general legitimation, 6§5, and for reasons of furthering the conditions of the accumulation of capital, 7§3. See 4§11 on the advantages of creeping inflation for enterprises and banks.)

As it is practically difficult to impose limits on technical change, the way out is to lay the conditions for 'creeping inflation' – in practice its euphemistic

7 See Schwalbe, Maier-Rigaud and Pisarkiewicz 2012, pp. 21–103 for a review of the problems.

name is 'price stability'. The state tends to delegate to the Central Bank the task of realising this price stability (i.e. creeping inflation).[8]

Even if creeping inflation is a 'target' for the CB (though see 9§5-c), in order to reach this target the CB merely has the instrument of influencing the rate of interest. When despite the efforts of the CB price deflation is nevertheless on the verge, extra state expenditure is more effective than monetary policy.

9§5-a Explication. The systematic position of the creeping inflation objective

The policy of creeping inflation regards competition policy carried out with monetary instruments. That is the reason why it is treated in this chapter. Because of the monetary instrument and because the policy tends to be delegated to the CB, it is usually subsumed under 'monetary policy' (I merely 'nominally' posited it as such in the brief section 7§8).

9§5-b Amplification. A target of creeping inflation at close to 2% – the cases of the EU's ECB and the USA's Fed

The CBs of the USA and of the EU interpret their mandate to seek price stability, by aiming at a rate of inflation of 2% per year (at the time of writing). For each this target is motivated by the avoidance of price deflation.

The ECB writes: 'In the pursuit of price stability, the ECB aims at maintaining inflation rates below, but close to, 2% over the medium term.' The stated reason is: 'It avoids that individual countries in the euro area have to structurally live with too low inflation rates or even deflation.'[9]

The USA's Federal Reserve states: 'The Federal Open Market Committee (FOMC) judges that inflation at the rate of 2 percent ... is most consistent over the longer run with the Federal Reserve's mandate for price stability and maximum employment. ... Having at least a small level of inflation makes it less likely that the economy will experience harmful deflation if economic conditions weaken.'[10]

---

8 Creeping inflation is commonly defined as an inflation below 3% per year. ('Walking inflation' as one of 3–10%, 'galloping inflation' as one of 10–50% and 'hyperinflation' as one exceeding 50% per year.)

9 https://www.ecb.europa.eu/mopo/strategy/pricestab/html/index.en.html (accessed November 2016).

10 https://www.federalreserve.gov/monetarypolicy/files/FOMC_LongerRunGoals_20160126.pdf.

9§5-c Amplification. A price inflation target – from systemic contingency to systemic necessity

Within the history of full capitalism the state's monetary policy stance regarding price inflation or deflation is contingent. However, a policy target of creeping inflation (a term that the state itself evades by calling it 'price stability') is an important case of a contingency's 'becoming necessary' – here that of a particular monetary policy stance (see the General Methodological Appendix A§13, point 5). Such a 'becoming necessary' also applies to regulation regarding banks and other enterprises becoming too big to fail, which is the subject of the next section.

9§6 *The movement to oligopolies as entities being too big to fail and (potential) constraints on the mode of capital accumulation via its capping*

Capital may be so concentrated within a single enterprise that enterprises in key sectors of the economy become too big to fail. (By itself this is a phenomenon that was only thrown into relief with the emergence of the 2008 financial crisis.) Key sectors are those on which a vast majority of actors is dependent whilst there is no ready substitute. This regards primarily the banking sector, the energy sector, and the communications sector (currently ICT).

Potential bankruptcy of main enterprises in such sectors – without the ready possibility of other enterprises in the same sector taking over the production – would severely affect the general conditions for the accumulation of capital. This requires the state to financially assist those potentially bankrupt enterprises. In effect this means that in good times profits are private, whereas in bad times losses are socialised.

In the context of the monetary framework, the exposition in Chapter 7 already alluded to this matter for banks (7§9). However, the threat of too big to fail applies also, at least potentially, for other sectors, such as those mentioned above.

So as to prevent the failure of big entities through the socialisation of losses, these 'big' entities would require to be intensely and effectively regulated and supervised. For banks such regulation and supervision would have to apply to entities that together make up 80–90% of the banking sector (Appendix 9A, section 9A-1). However, at least for the banking sector, and given the complex internal structure of big banks, this is practically unachievable. (See Appendix 9A, section 9A-2. Providing a gist of that section I mention here that in 2014 Andrew Haldane – as chief economist at the Bank of England responsible for the stability of the financial sector as a whole – declared that the balances of the big banks are 'the blackest of black holes'.)

The alternative would be for the state to put a cap on the accumulation of capital in single banks and enterprises – as a general form of regulation. (Such a cap would put absolute limits on the size of banks and enterprises, such that they become small enough to fail.) However, a cap on the accumulation of capital in single banks and enterprises would be highly conflicting, as it would castigate the success in the accumulation of capital, which in fact clashes with the economic rights granted by the state.

Moreover (or therefore), such a cap does not fit the long-standing practice of *market regulation* in which (since the 1890 USA Sherman Act) the focus is on regulation in terms of the aspect of competition in the sense of *market* power (as measured by market shares or more sophisticated alternative tools), rather than economic power in a broader sense, which might include the *absolute* size of enterprises and banks, as measured by the capital accumulated. (Amplification 9§6-b.)

Nevertheless, a cap on the accumulation of capital in single banks and enterprises could – in principle – be endeavoured indirectly, by a regulation that 'discriminates' between 'normal' banks and enterprises, and those that pose a so-called 'systemic risk' (too big to fail). This can take the form of imposing on the 'systemic risk' entities much tighter reserve ratios than for 'normal' entities. To the extent that this would effectively and substantially affect their rate of profit, big entities might choose to break up into smaller entities of their own 'free will'. (See Amplification 9§6-c about the Basel III, 2014, rules that might, still modestly, foreshadow this).[11]

However, whereas a focus on a (tighter) regulation of the liabilities side of balance sheets makes sense, its reliability keeps on depending on the unreliable valuation of the 'black hole' assets side. This is so because too highly valuated assets (an insufficient valuation of their risk) inevitably shows up in too highly evaluated equity, the latter being the 'bookkeeping result' on which the (tighter) reserve ratio applies.

At the same time, modestly tighter reserve ratios for big banks especially pose an enormous dilemma for the state, as – prior to their breaking up – tighter reserve ratios affect the profit and credit capacity of the big banks, and hence the credit-conditions for economic growth.[12] For the state this is not a matter of a simple trade-off between economic growth and the statistical *risk* of another

---

11 When I completed this book such (still modest) regulative norms were agreed within the Basel Committee on Banking Supervision, being only partly implemented in regulation, and not yet effective. (Basel Committee on Banking Supervision 2014.)

12 Bankers are aware of this dilemma for the state, and use it in their lobbying against tighter rules. See the not more than 12 lines in a statement of the European Banking Feder-

overall banking crisis. It is rather a matter of the *uncertainty* about it. Yet modestly tighter reserve ratios for big banks may indeed result in lower structural rates of growth. However, alternative to structurally lower growth rates, the state would have to accept the uncertainty of a (sooner or later) next overall banking crisis that may go along with an output loss of 100% to 500% of GDP (Appendix 9A, section 9A-3).

9§6-a Explication. A cap on the accumulation of capital in single enterprises?

Section 9§6 is in fact the observation of a vulnerability of the capitalist system as associated with the accumulation of capital as concentrated in single banks and enterprises. Putting a cap on this single entity concentration of capital would be alien to the capitalist system as it has existed hitherto. However, it seems necessary for the reproduction of the system.

9§6-b Amplification. Market power in contradistinction to 'big' economic power

The conventional competition policy is concerned with economic power in the sense of relative market power, not with the power of enterprises and banks in terms of their absolute size. For (conventional) competition policy I already referred to Schwalbe, Maier-Rigaud and Pisarkiewicz (2012, pp. 21–103) who provide an overview of the field with ample attention for the legal aspects. They remark (quotes within the following quote are their references to case law):

> 'In EU competition law, a firm is assumed to have a dominant position if it can "... prevent effective competition being maintained on the relevant market by affording it the power to behave to an appreciable extent independently of its competitors, its customers and ultimately of the consumers ..." Under US competition law, a firm is considered to have monopoly power if it has "... the power to control prices and exclude competition." *A dominant position or monopoly power is not per se illegal as a firm could have achieved this position because it was more efficient than its competitors, supplied superior products or outperformed its rivals through some*

ation's complaint about the tightening of the rules: http://www.ebf-fbe.eu/wp-content/uploads/2016/07/EBF_022191-Statement-Basel-banking-reforms.pdf. This regards the proposals under a supplement of Basel-III, and what they misleadingly call Basel IV. In a statement of the CEO of ING (a world top-10 bank in 2007, in 2016 down to a rank of about 25) this is phrased in terms of a specific cash nexus: 'If you want that banks keep on supporting the economy, then they must be able to make a rate of profit of above 10% – if not there will be contraction.' (*Het Financieele Dagblad*, 4 October 2016.)

> *other legitimate means*. Nevertheless dominant firms will tend to have a wider range of instruments to their disposal to abuse market power to exclude competition.'
>
> SCHWALBE, MAIER-RIGAUD and PISARKIEWICZ 2012, pp. 73–4, emphasis added

I quote this in order to emphasise that, at least within competition law, dominant relative market power seems by itself no reason to force enterprises to break up into smaller entities (small enough to fail). Thus the breaking up of banks and enterprises for reason of their absolute size – their being too big to fail – will require a brand new field of legislation, and one that is bound to be highly conflicting.

An enforcement for corporations to break up by itself would be no novelty, if it were for reasons of abuse of market power. There is the famous case of the 1911 breaking up of Standard Oil in the USA into about forty smaller entities. Another famous case is the 1982 breaking up of AT&T, again in the USA, into eight smaller entities. (In 1999–2000 there was an unsuccessful effort to break up Microsoft.)

9§6-c Amplification. The proposals of the Basel Committee on Banking Supervision (2014) as an indirect instrument for putting caps on the accumulation of capital in single entities.[13]

The proposals of the Basel Committee on Banking Supervision (2014) put to some extent, and indirectly, a cap on the accumulation of capital within single banks.[14] The proposals entail a tighter regulation of the 'too big to fail' systemic risk banks in comparison with 'normal' banks. The required tighter reserve ratios for the former, for example (there are more requirements), dampen their potential profit rates, and so also change the competitive relations between the

13 The *Basel Committee on Banking Supervision* of the Bank for International Settlements (BIS) sets rules for the regulation and supervision of banks. Its members are the 13 largest (GDP) OECD-21 countries, plus Argentina, Brazil, China, European Union, Hong Kong SAR, India, Indonesia, Korea, Luxembourg, Mexico, Russia, Saudi Arabia, Singapore, South Africa and Turkey. https://www.bis.org/bcbs/index.htm?m=3%7C14.

In 2011 the 'Basel-III' rules were agreed upon, together with a phase-wise implementation between 2013 and 2019 (https://www.bis.org/bcbs/basel3.htm?m=3%7C14%7C572; the table referred on its first page summarises the key rules). Basel-III replaces the 2004 Basel-II agreement, and reflects the 2008 crisis and its aftermath. In 2014 Basel-III was supplemented by a 'Supervisory framework for measuring and controlling large exposures'.

14 See also the proposed EU implementation in November 2016: http://ec.europa.eu/finance/bank/crisis_management/index_en.htm#161123. The USA was much ahead of this (and in fact of the Basil 2014 proposals). For a summary see, e.g., http://www.shearman.com/~/media/files/newsinsights/publications/2014/06/basel-iii-framework-large-exposures-framework-fia-061614.pdf.

big and the less big banks. Such a precautionary regulative discrimination is unprecedented. Although the proposed tightened regulation of the 'too big to fail' banks seems as yet moderate (it may take another financial crisis before a heavier discrimination is proposed and implemented), it is, when less moderate, an indirect instrument to enforce big banks to break up into smaller entities, as that would positively affect the rate of profit of each smaller entity.

One major hot regulative issue is the 'identification' – by exact regulative rules – of a bank being too big to fail (one posing a 'systemic risk') or of approaching it.

Potentially the Basel instrument for banks could, as modified, in principle be applied to all sectors of the economy, by putting restrictions on the proportion between equity and loans (thus affecting leverage ratios and so the rate of profit on the internal capital). Potentially it could be applied to other key sectors of the economy with too big to fail risks. Connecting it to conventional competition policy in the narrow sense (9D1 and 9§6-b) it could also be applied to enterprises with 'merely' a large market power. However, this would require quite an increase in regulation, as well a change of the scope of competition policy.

As indicated in the main text, putting directly or indirectly a cap on the accumulation of capital in single banks and enterprises would be highly conflicting, as it would put restrictions on being successful in the accumulation of capital. Nevertheless the 'discrimination' as entailed in the regulation agreements of the '2014 Basel III Supplement' seems a cautious first move towards it.

Summary and conclusions

This chapter presents the state's concrete manifestation in its imposing a framework of constraints on the modes of market interaction of enterprises and banks, and of constraints on the outcomes of that interaction. Division 1 sets out the state's engagement in constraints of market interaction that is 'conventionally' regarded as 'competition policy' as encoded in competition law. Division 2 sets out two main effects of market interaction on the market constellation – that is, generalised price deflation and entities that have become 'too big to fail' – ones that when left unconstrained would generate vulnerabilities for the reproduction of the capitalist system.

The state's manifestation in competition policy engenders a particular mode of existence of the capitalist system. This manifestation is paradoxical as, in its prohibition of free contracts of cartel formation and of a category of take-overs and mergers, the state teaches enterprises what 'proper' market interaction is.

With the state's imposition of *its* view on proper market interaction, the unity of the capitalist economy and state reaches its most concrete manifestation regarding the functioning of ordinary markets. Nevertheless this is so conflicting that the state sets out the framework in general terms, delegating its details and execution to 'independent' market authorities. (Division 1.)

So as to prevent a market constellation associated with generalised price deflation (cf. 4D2), the state ordains a monetary policy resulting in creeping inflation (which is labelled by the state as 'price stability'). It tends to delegate its concretisation and execution to the 'independent' central bank. (Division 2, 9§5.)

Whereas the state has engendered an effective monetary instrument for countering price deflation (even if its proportions, euphemistically called 'quantitative easing', may at times be grandiose), this is as yet (when I completed this book) not so for the enormous problem of the 'too big to fail banks', and, potentially, the too big to fail entities in other key sectors. The gradual movement to 'too big to fail' is an effect of market interaction that was only thrown into relief with the emergence of the 2008 financial crisis.

Regarding especially the banking sector, the complex internal structure of big banks has evolved such that effective regulation and supervision is practically unachievable. They have become 'too big to know what is going on', or the balances of the big banks have become 'the blackest of black holes'. Therefore the system vulnerability stemming from 'too big to fail banks' can be countered only by putting a cap on the accumulation of capital such that entities become small enough to fail. However, this would be highly conflicting, as it would castigate the success in the accumulation of capital, which in fact clashes with the economic rights granted by the state.

Nevertheless it seems that the state (via the 2014 supplement to the Basel III agreements) is cautiously preparing the way for it. That is, by a 'discrimination' between big and small banks regarding leverage- and risk-weighted capital ratios. Such a precautionary regulative discrimination is unprecedented. This is not to say that, as yet, the 'discrimination' is heavy enough to compel big banks to break up into smaller entities. What is more, the cautious halfway house will merely press down the profits and the credit capacity of the big banks and so generate structurally lower growth rates – without solving the too big to fail threat. There seems no way out other than intensifying the discrimination, thereby enforcing a 'small enough to fail' constellation, even if its effectuation may 'require' another trembling financial crisis. (Division 2, 9§6.)

Appendix 9A. Too big banks: too big to fail and too big for supervisors

It was stated in 9§6 that putting a cap on the concentration of capital in single banks seems inevitable for the survival of the capitalist system. This statement is based on the incapability of the 'conventional' regulation of the banking sector as revealed in the 2008 banking crisis. The main objective of this appendix is to provide an underpinning of this incapability (section 9A-2). This is preceded by empirical information on the degree of centralisation and concentration of capital within the banking sector, and on the 'systemic risk' characteristics of big banks (section 9A-1). In the last section (9A-3) I provide empirical information on the social costs of the 2008 crisis and on the average bank rate of profit from 1996–2015 in the OECD-21.

9A-1 *Centralisation and concentration of capital within the banking sector, and characteristics of big banks*

1 Centralisation within the banking sector

A large bank failing causes bigger damage than a small one. I first present the common measure for market authorities of the relative size of entities in a market – in this case the banking sector. That is, the degree of centralisation in the banking sector is relevant. (I use the, in my view adequate, marxian term 'centralisation' as introduced in Chapter 4; the mainstream term is 'concentration'. In brief, my term *centralisation refers to the relative size* in comparison with other entities in the same sector; my term *concentration refers to the absolute size* of an entity – measured in absolute money terms, or in percentage of GDP.) *Graph 9.3* shows the average degree of centralisation within the banking sector for the OECD-21, as measured by the assets of the top-5 banks – and of the top-3 banks – over the assets of all banks in an OECD-21 country.

The most important point about *Graph 9.3* is that after 2007 the centralisation has hardly changed (some increase for the top-5 and a slight decrease for the top-3). It can further be seen that on average there is a huge difference between the share of the top-3 banks, and those that rank 4 and 5. Over the last five years shown, a top-3 bank is on average 3.5 times bigger than banks ranged 4–5.

Because we know that the banking sector is a 'large' one within the economy, the data above provide some relevant information for the degree of 'too big to fail' banks. However, this measure does not account for the degree of interconnectedness of banks, and hence not for possible domino effects. Nevertheless, assuming that all banks are equally interconnected, the failure of a large bank has a larger domino effect than the failure of a smaller one.

GRAPH 9.3 *Centralisation in the banking sector: assets of the five and three largest banks, as % of the assets of all banks – average of the OECD-21, 1996–2015*

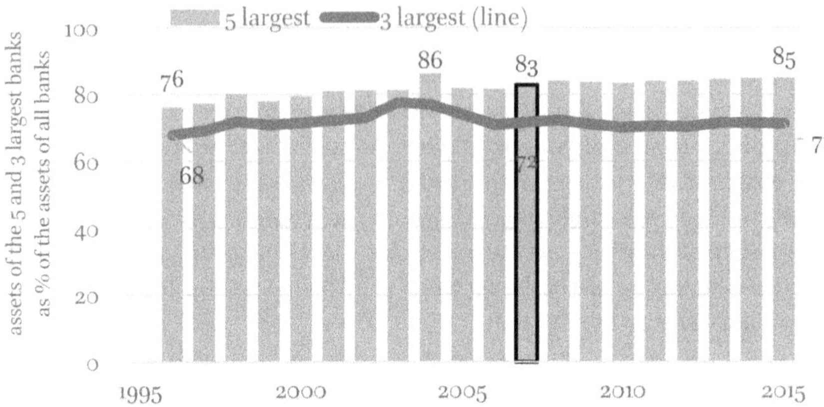

DATA SOURCE: World Bank database *Global Financial Development*, '5-bank asset concentration' and 'Bank concentration' (each updated 16 June 2017)[15]

2 Concentration of capital within the banking sector: money-creating banks

Too big to fail depends especially on the absolute size of banks as an indicator of the costs of saving a failing bank. It could be argued that a bank that is too big to fail must be saved at all costs (in that sense 'too big to save' does not exist, or it should be a terminology to describe a situation of collapse). *Graph 9.4* relates the average asset-size of a country's top-3 bank to its GDP. This measures the maximal *direct* costs of saving a large bank – maximal because when a bank fails, not all of its assets may be foregone and some of these can be sold to other parties. (This is about the direct costs – see section 9A-3 on the indirect costs.)

It can be seen from *Graph 9.4* that the size of a top-3 bank as a proportion of GDP somewhat decreased from 2007 to 2012, moving back to near the 2007 level in 2015. This means that the degree of direct damage that goes along with the saving of a large bank is about the same in those two years.

15 http://databank.worldbank.org/data/reports.aspx?source=global-financial-development. Most years are for 21 countries, some for 16 to 20 countries.

GRAPH 9.4 *Assets of* ***one*** *bank (top-3, or range 4–5) as a proportion of* GDP *– average of the* OECD*-21, 1996–2015*

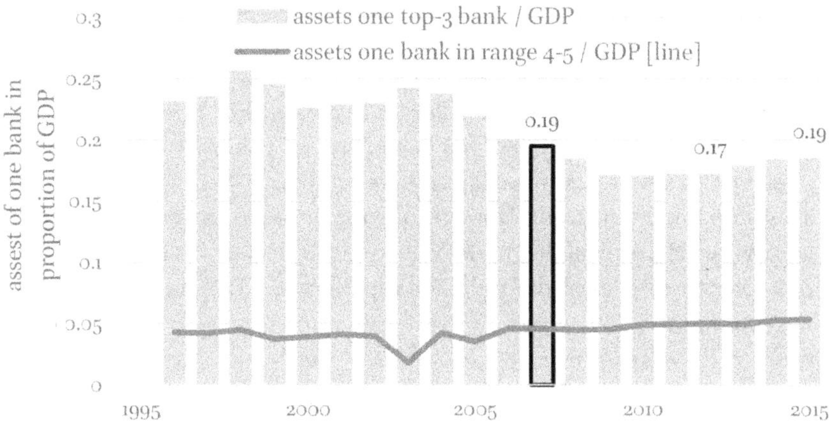

DATA SOURCE: World Bank database *Global Financial Development*, '5-bank asset concentration'; 'Bank concentration'; 'Deposit money banks' assets to GDP' (all updated 16 June 2017)[16]

3 Characteristics of big banks

In an IMF paper, Laeven, Ratnovski and Tong (2014) study the connection between bank size and systemic risk (systemic risk is described as 'the externalities of bank distress onto the rest of the financial system or the real economy' – p. 14). They use a sample of 1,250 banks in 54 countries, among which 137 large banks (11%), the latter being defined as banks with assets of over US$50 billion in 2011. (The sample includes 15 OECD-21 countries.) The banks in the sample are money-creating banks (called 'deposit-taking' banks). The authors find (among other things):

- 'First, large banks today engage disproportionately more in market-based activities.[17]
- Second, large banks hold less capital than small banks, as measured either by risk-weighted capital ratios or a simple leverage ratio.
- Third, large banks have less stable funding than small banks, as measured by the share of deposits in total liabilities.
- [Fourth], large banks are more organizationally complex, as measured by the number of subsidiaries.' (Laeven, Ratnovski and Tong 2014, p. 8.)

16 http://databank.worldbank.org/data/reports.aspx?source=global-financial-development. For the number of countries information see the footnote with the previous graph.

17 That is, they do not (as in traditional banking) restrict to lending and borrowing – I add this because the latter is also a market activity.

- 'This [1–4] suggests that large banks may have a distinct, possibly more fragile, business model.' (Laeven, Ratnovski and Tong 2014, p. 3.)

Focusing on 2007–08 in comparison with 2006 they also find:

- 'Size per se is an independent factor that drives individual bank risk. Large banks are riskier than smaller ones.
- However, among large banks only (over US$50 billion in assets), size per se ceases to be an independent risk factor. Instead, risk is driven by insufficient capital.' (Laeven, Ratnovski and Tong 2014, p. 14.)[18]

This is an important study. However, the big question for researchers and for supervisors is the reliability of the valuation of the assets of banks, and hence of a leverage ratio or of risk-weighted capital ratios. This is the subject of the next section.

9A-2 *Big banks: too big to know what is going on*

It was indicated in 9§6 that putting a cap on the concentration of capital ('bigness') in single banks seems inevitable for the survival of the capitalist system. But why would 'conventional' regulation and supervision of banks not be sufficient? It is insufficient because regulators and supervisors, but also the management and the internal supervisors of banks, lack information of what they are supposed to supervise.

In 2014 Andrew Haldane (as chief economist at the Bank of England responsible for the stability of the financial sector as a whole) declares to *Der Spiegel*: The balances of the big banks are 'the blackest of black holes'.[19] The

---

18 The authors 'proxy systemic risk through an SRISK measure, defined as a bank's contribution to the deterioration of the capitalization of the financial system as a whole during a crisis.' (Laeven, Ratnovski and Tong 2014, pp. 14–15.) Using this measure they find:
- 'Large banks contribute more to systemic risk when they have less capital;
- Large banks contribute more to systemic risk when they have fewer deposits;
- Large banks contribute more to systemic risk when they engage more in market-based activities, as measured by the share of noninterest income in total income or the share of loans in assets;
- The economic effects are substantial, especially for bank capital.' (Laeven, Ratnovski and Tong 2014, p. 17.)
- '... large market-oriented banks may not be more volatile than traditional banks on a stand-alone basis, but they are more likely to fail together, and this creates risks for the financial system and the economy as a whole.' (Laeven, Ratnovski and Tong 2014, p. 18.)

19 Luyendijk 2015, ch. 13 and *The Guardian*: https://www.theguardian.com/business/2015/sep/30/how-the-banks-ignored-lessons-of-crash. Thus, as Luyendijk remarks, a main responsible actor tells us that supervisors have no idea of what the banks have on their books.

blackness in fact *mainly* applies to the (unknown) risks – or rather 'uncertainties' – taken by banks on the assets site of their balance sheet. However, the valuation of the assets is reflected in the value of the equity, which 'blackens' a leverage ratio or risk-weighted capital ratios.

In what I consider an important document on the 2008 financial crisis, Luyendijk (2015) sets out views from inside the banking sector and its supervisors. It is based on over 200 interviews with its actors (many of which also appeared in *The Guardian*). Below I quote from this book in the perspective of the supervisors' lack of information on the 'object matter' of their activity.

In the early twenty-first century at least, supervisors, as well as the management of banks, lost a grip on the *valuation of the assets* of banks, and hence on the total of banks' balance sheets. This valuation is (or is supposed to be) an important focus of the 'prudential' regulation and supervision.[20]

I quoted Haldane's statement that the balances of the big banks are 'the blackest of black holes'. In the same vain, Alistair Darling, in 2007–10 UK minister of finance (Chancellor), wrote in 2011: 'There is much talk about whether [financial] institutions are too big to fail, or even too big to save, but there is another category too: too big to know what's going on.'[21]

An anonymous senior regulator (supervisor) interviewed by Luyendijk states: 'Ultimately, as supervisors, we rely upon *self-declaration*, upon what is presented to us *by a bank's internal management*. But often they don't know what's going on, because banks today are so vast and hugely complex. ... The real threat is not a bank's management hiding things from us: *it's the management not knowing themselves what the risks are*, either because nobody realises it or because some people are keeping it from their bosses.'[22] (Emphasis added.) Apparently affirming this, an anonymous internal accountant (financial reporting) of a mega bank states: 'The question is not only how much risk you are running as a bank. The question is if you even know what you own at any given point.'[23]

An anonymous former head of structured credit at a large bank explains to Luyendijk:

20 In quite some countries the so-called 'prudential' regulation and supervision is institutionally separated from the 'conduct' regulation and supervision, each so with separate authorities and delegations. In that case the CB adopts only the prudential part.

21 In *Back from the Brink: 1000 Days at Number 11* (2011) – cf. Luyendijk 2015, ch. 7. Too big to fail is a phenomenon that gradually developed from the mid-1980s via mergers and takeovers (Luyendijk 2015, ch. 4).

22 Luyendijk 2015, ch. 8 and *The Guardian*: https://www.theguardian.com/commentisfree/joris-luyendijk-banking-blog/2012/jun/25/senior-fsa-regulator.

23 Luyendijk 2015, ch. 7.

> '… most in the bank didn't understand our products. Even the risk and compliance people who were supposed to be our internal checks and balances … We began to realise that we had to teach them how to monitor us. Then there were the people I reported to, who were getting calls from the people they reported to. I learned that the people high up know just enough for the role they're in. "Just enough" is not enough in an emergency. I would be on the phone for hours explaining to people of increasing seniority what we were doing. And I realised, they don't understand, not on a fundamental level.'[24]

If banks themselves are, to an unknown degree, ignorant about the risk-weighted value of their assets, could supervisors improve on this? Luyendijk mentions that about one million people work in the UK's financial sector, against 5,000 for supervisors (0.5%).

I guess that even by a tenfold increase of the latter, 'the blackest of black holes' will not turn grey. Only when we have at least 'grey', sensible regulation of the assets side of banks' balance sheets could come in. However, supervisors supervise on the basis of the existing rules. A former treasurer at a collapsed bank tells Luyendijk: 'Regulation to keep the City in check? Don't hold your breath. No matter what rules you put in place, they'll always find ways around it.'[25] (Many other commentators have observed this. Regulators are not one step ahead, but rather one or more steps behind the financial sector 'innovations'.)

The focus in the last paragraphs has been on the assets side of the bank balance. But, as indicated, the valuation of the assets is reflected in the leverage ratios.

9A-3 *Social costs of an encompassing banking crisis, and the temporary decrease in bank profit rates*

1 Estimates of the costs of the 2008 crisis

Estimates of the losses associated with the 2008 financial crises are quite diverse, depending on what variables are taken into account and on the horizon beyond 2008.

In general terms an EC paper (European Commission 2014, pp. 41–2) refers to a 2010 study by a working group of the Basel Committee on Banking Supervision (BCBS), which reviewed 'the literature estimating output (measured

24 Luyendijk 2015, ch. 7 and *The Guardian*: https://www.theguardian.com/commentisfree/joris-luyendijk-banking-blog/2012/apr/05/former-head-structured-credit-voices-finance.

25 Luyendijk 2015, ch. 12 and *The Guardian*: https://www.theguardian.com/commentisfree/joris-luyendijk-banking-blog/2012/mar/12/former-treasurer-voices-of-finance.

cumulatively in present value terms and as the deviation from trend GDP). Considering only the studies that assume a permanent level change in output, the median is 158%.'

The EC paper also refers to a 2010 paper by Haldane who suggests that 'the output loss resulting from this crisis could amount to anything between 100% to 500% of GDP, depending on assumptions about how permanent the drops in output will be.'

The EC paper itself estimates that 'output losses in the EU may end up as high as 100% of EU GDP, measured cumulatively in present value terms going forward.'

But there is more to take account of than output losses. Laeven and Valencia (2012) also include variables such as fiscal costs, increased public debt, and monetary expansion.[26] However, there are also a variety of other important aspects of the 2008 crisis (and all crises), which are difficult to catch in monetary terms. Not least the effect that unemployment has on the lives of the unemployed and their children.

In a staff paper of the Federal Reserve Bank of Dallas, Atkinson, Luttrell and Rosenblum (2013) tried to incorporate a wider variety of measures to estimate the costs of the 2007 financial crisis for the USA. (Note that in the USA and the UK the crisis started in 2007.) These authors conclude that:

> '40 to 90 percent of one year's output ($6 trillion to $14 trillion, the equivalent of $50,000 to $120,000 for every U.S. household) was foregone due to the 2007–09 recession. We also provide several alternative measures of lost consumption, national trauma, and other negative consequences … This more comprehensive evaluation of factors suggests that what the U.S. gave up as a result of the crisis is likely greater than the value of one year's output.'

They also refer to the legitimation affect (in other terms):

> 'Similarly to reduced opportunity, the financial crisis resulted in a significant loss of trust in government institutions and the capitalist economic system. (…) [T]he officials they entrusted to govern and to impartially regulate the financial services industry offered massive support and preference to a handful of the largest institutions. (…) [F]inancial institutions aggressively pursued profits and growth strategies that benefited management and, to a degree, owner-shareholders and creditors. Subsequent

26 The EC paper does refer to the latter IMF paper. These authors studied the effects of a variety of financial crises from 1980 onwards, but regarding the 2008 crisis, and within their framework, they refrained from estimates beyond the last year of their data (2011).

losses when the boom turned bust were disproportionately borne by taxpayers. Privatized gains, socialized losses …

However, saving the system in itself – especially with extraordinary government assistance provided to a handful of giant financial institutions – reinforced a perception that public support exists primarily for large, interconnected, complex financial entities.'

ATKINSON, LUTTRELL and ROSENBLUM 2013, p. 14

2 The bank rate of profit

How were banks themselves affected by the 2007/08 crisis and its aftermath? *Graph 9.5.* shows the bank rate of profit for the OECD-21 in the lead up to the crisis and afterwards.

GRAPH 9.5 *Bank rate of profit on equity, before and after tax – average of the OECD-21, 1996–2015*

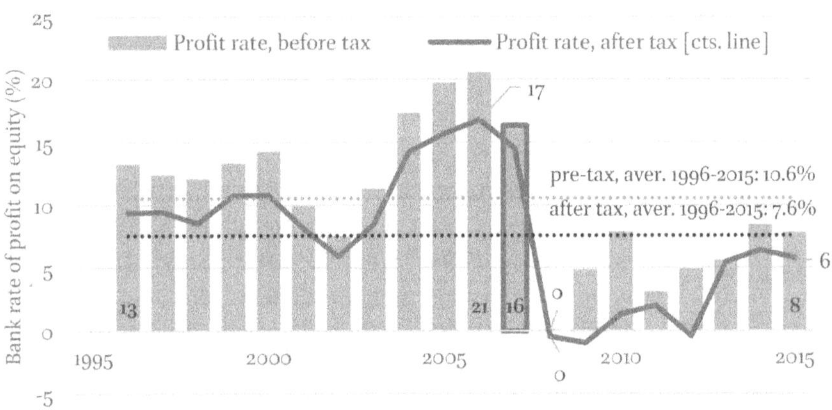

DATA SOURCE: World Bank database *Global Financial Development*, 'Bank return on equity (%, before tax)' and 'Bank return on equity (%, after tax)' (updated 16 June 2017)[27]

Although the effect on the profit rate of the crisis has been enormous, the rates of profit in especially 2004–07 were also enormous. Various authors that have observed banking from the inside (e.g. Luyendijk 2015) conclude on the basis of their sources – as against mainstream textbook economics – that the structure of banking is such that the aim is not the realisation of long-term profits, but rather short-term profits, which has to do with the incentive structure of

27 http://databank.worldbank.org/data/reports.aspx?source=global-financial-development (21 countries throughout).

bonuses and 'shareholder value'. Having said this, it can be seen from *Graph 9.5* that, at least over the period 1996–2015, the average rate of profit has not been too bad. One can only fall deep from a high top – this remark is not helpful when the trough is reached. However, especially large banks did (or could) know, or guess, that they were taking high risks in the pre-2008 years.

The following regards a detail. I suppose that the differences after 2006 between the pre- and after-tax profits have to do with the often very complicated tax rules about the carrying back and the carrying forward of (subsidiaries') losses. (For one part losses of after 2007 are *carried back* to 2007, whence that year shows a small difference between the pre- and after-tax profit rate. The volatile pre- and after-tax differences between 2009 and 2013 are presumably the effect of the *carrying forward* of earlier losses.)

List of figures chapter 9

CHAPTER 10

The reach of the capitalist state

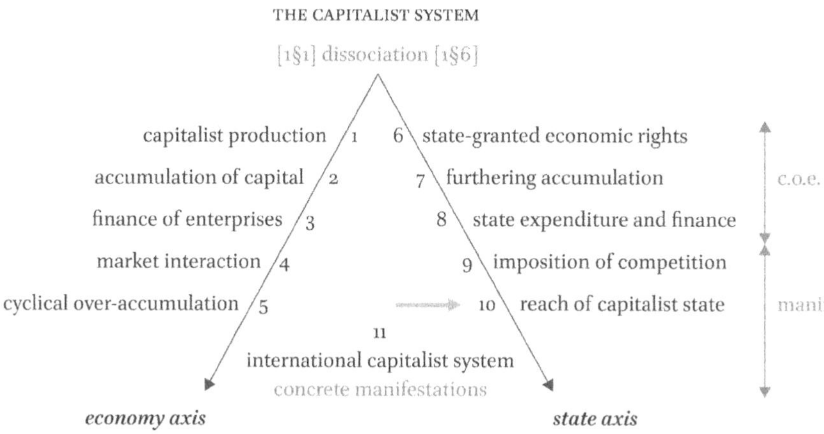

Note: 'c.o.e.' abbreviates conditions of existence and 'manif.' concrete manifestations.

Contents

Introduction

This chapter presents the reach of the capitalist state in three of its concrete manifestations.

The first division – which is the sequel to Chapter 5 – shows how the development of the size of the state in terms of its expenditure modifies the cyclical accumulation of capital. More specifically, a structurally increasing state expenditure decreases the amplitude of the cycles.

Whereas Chapters 6–9 presented the content of the state's regulation, Division 2 presents the manifestation of the state in the character of legislation and other regulation. It will be shown that, for various reasons, not only does the amount of regulation increase over time, but also the dynamic of regulation inevitably results in more complicated as well as more complex regulation.

Division 3 presents a synthetic overview of the state's manifestation in its expenditure. Although all expenditure categories will be briefly reviewed, the main focus in this division will be on social security expenditure and the problematic thereof for the state and hence for the capitalist system.

A brief final division, called 'the vulnerabilities of the capitalist state's reach', takes some threads of Divisions 2 and 3 together. Whereas Chapters 6–8 successively presented the conditions of existence of the state – vis-à-vis the capitalist economy with which it constitutes a separation-in-unity – the final division detects the major vulnerabilities in these conditions of existence. In other words, it detects the potential impediments to the continued reproduction of the capitalist system.

Scheme 10.1 presents the outline of this chapter.

Division 1. The size of state expenditure and its effect on the amplitude of the capitalist economic cycle

This division considers how the state and its expenditure are manifested in the cyclical movement of capital as set out in Chapter 5. As such it is the sequel to that chapter.

10§1 *The size of the state: state expenditure as mitigating economic recessions*

This section briefly outlines the general effect of state expenditure on the cyclical accumulation and over-accumulation of capital (Chapter 5).

[*continued*]

SCHEME 10.1 *The reach of the capitalist state (outline Chapter 10)*

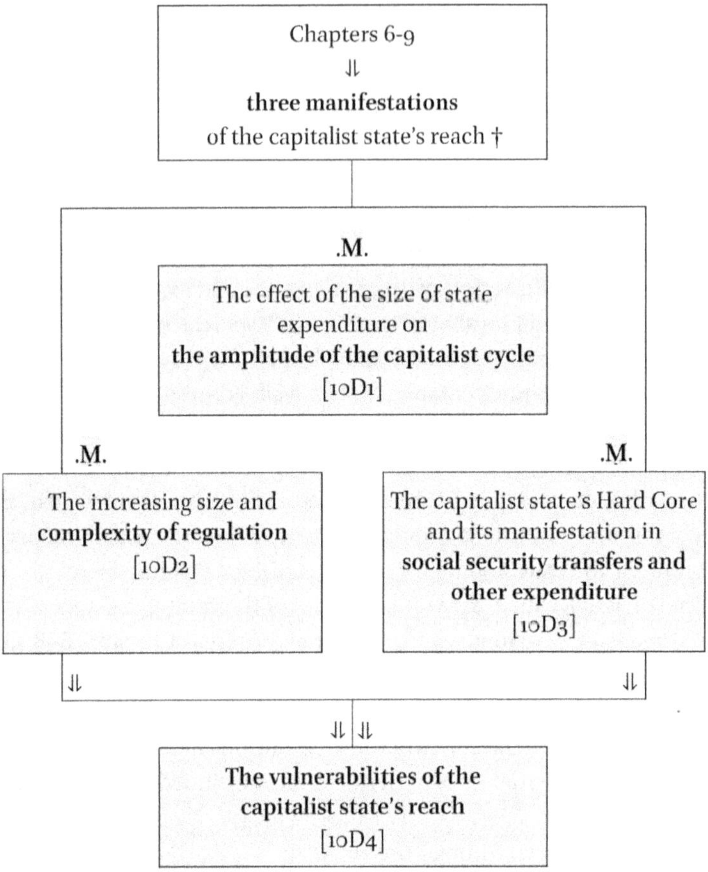

Legend
.M. concrete manifestation
⇃⇂ bottom moment derives from top moments

† The three manifestations regard the first three moments (10D1–10D3). The last moment (10D4) builds on 10D2 and 10D3 in a particular synthetic manner.

10§1 *Continued*

Generally the degree of state expenditure (measured as a percentage of GDP) affects the potential degree of its mitigating the amplitude of the cycle.

'Potential', that is, when the state does not expend pro-cyclically. Thus to the extent that in a recession the state maintains its expenditure, it puts a considerable floor in the general cyclical expenditures (that is, state expenditure together with private investment and the consumption that is independent of social security transfers). Then, to the degree that state expenditure is structurally large in comparison with the private sector, the composition of the potentially non-volatile general expenditure (that of the state) and the potentially volatile expenditures (those of private investment and the transfers-independent consumption) structurally changes in favour of the non-volatile expenditures, so that the general cyclical volatility decreases. In other words, state expenditure acts as an automatic stabiliser. (See further Amplification 10§1-a.) This effect is independent of any discretionary *counter*-cyclical policy (see 10§2).

Given the floor of state expenditure (and provided the state abstains from pro-cyclical policy) the course of the capitalist business cycle is broadly as presented in Chapter 5, though with a moderated amplitude of the cycle. This would be one aspect that positively contributes to the legitimation of the state and so the capitalist system as a whole (that is, amongst the negative and other positive aspects). Actors, however, tend to evaluate the cycle 'within their own times' – that is, given the 'normal' size of the state within their own times.

10§1-a Amplification. Historical changes in the amplitude of the cycle along with changes in state expenditure

In the first two sub-sections of this amplification there is no mention of state expenditure; these two sub-sections are merely on observations about amplitudes.

(*1*) ***The amplitude 1870–1989***. For a sample of 16 current OECD countries,[1] Maddison (1991, pp. 3–4) shows 'that peacetime business cycle history has been much milder since the Second World War than before, and that the 1920–38 period was generally much worse than 1870–1913.' He produces the following average 'amplitude of recessions in aggregate output, 1870–1989: maximum peak–trough fall in GDP or lowest rise (annual data)'.

	1870–1913	1920–38	1950–73	1973–89
amplitude in % of GDP: arithmetic average for 16 current OECD countries	−5.5	−12.1	+0.2	−1.8

1 OECD-21 minus Greece, Ireland, New Zealand, Portugal and Spain.

Maddison mentions that this average for the group is dampened by the fact that individual country cycles are not synchronised.

(2) ***The amplitude 1990–2000.*** In a 2002 OECD working paper, Dalsgaard, Elmeskov and Park observed that for a sample of 13 OECD countries,[2] the amplitude of the business cycle for most of these, when proxied by the average size of output gaps over ten-year periods, declined in the period 1980–2000 in comparison with the decade of the 1970s (Dalsgaard, Elmeskov and Park 2002, p. 7). 'Divergencies of output gaps across OECD countries have diminished since 1960 with a particularly strong tendency since the early 1990s' (Dalsgaard, Elmeskov and Park 2002, p. 23).

In an IMF publication, Kannan, Scott and Terrones (2009) show that from the mid-1980s (and until 2007) there was an even further moderation. (See 10§2-a for their findings concerning financially driven crises.)

As an illustration *Graph 10.2* shows, for a much longer period, the amplitude in growth rates of real-GDP per capita for the USA.[3]

(3) ***Amplitude and size of government expenditure.*** As the thesis that the increasing size of government expenditure mitigates the amplitude of business cycles (main text 10§1) does not quite fit in with most mainstream economic models, this sub-section quotes empirical research in this field. In an OECD working paper empirically assessing government budgets in relation with business cycle amplitudes in the 1990s for 20 OECD countries (OECD-21 minus Switzerland), Van den Noord observes:

> 'The most important factor determining the cyclical sensitivity of the fiscal position is the *size of the general government sector*. For the most part, the larger the share of government expenditure in domestic output, the greater is the sensitivity of the fiscal position to fluctuations in economic activity ... The *tax structure* also has a significant impact on the size of automatic stabilisers: the higher the taxation of cyclically sensitive tax bases, the more the tax take will vary with the business cycle and hence the greater will be the cyclical sensitivity of the fiscal position. The *progressivity* of taxes, the generosity of unemployment benefits and the cyclical sensitivity of various tax bases and unemployment,

2 OECD-21 minus Belgium, Denmark, Finland, Greece, Ireland, Netherlands, Portugal, Switzerland.

3 We also see a considerable decrease in amplitude for Japan and especially France. In some countries, such as the UK and Italy, the decrease is much less pronounced. In Germany, the decrease is also considerable compared with the period 1920–38; for this country, however, the amplitudes in the period 1870–1913 were rather moderate (between +6% and –4%).

GRAPH 10.2 *Growth amplitudes as measured by the growth rate of real-GDP per capita, USA 1870–2015 in 2011 prices (annual data). Panel 1: all years; panel 2: the world wars related years (1914–19 and 1939–49) dropped*

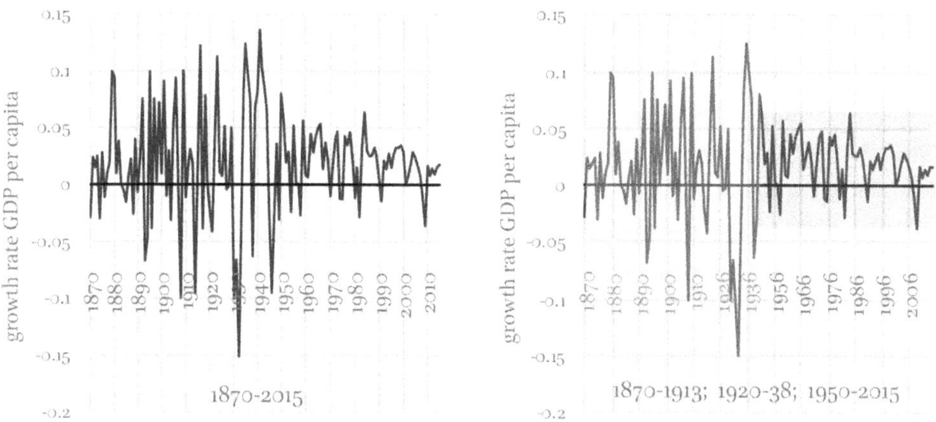

DATA SOURCE: Maddison Project Database, version 2018 by Jutta Bolt, Robert Inklaar, Herman de Jong and Jan Luiten van Zanden[4]

> finally, are other significant factors in determining the cyclical sensitivity of the fiscal position.'
>
> 2000, p. 7, italics in original[5]

Earlier Galí (1994) showed that for a sample of 22 OECD countries (OECD-21 minus New Zealand plus Iceland and Luxembourg), 1960–90, 'both taxes and government purchases seem to be effectively working as "automatic stabilizers".' Economies with 'large governments' 'have experienced milder economic fluctuations than economies with "small governments"' (Galí 1994, pp. 130–1). Galí considered the stabilising effect of the ratio of government purchases over GDP (government expenditure minus wages and transfers).

Fatás and Mihov (2001) consider the total of government expenditure for 20 OECD countries covering the years 1960–97. They find:

> 'a strong negative correlation between government size and output volatility ... This correlation is robust to the inclusion of a large set of controls as well as to alternative methods of detrending and estimation. In

4 https://www.rug.nl/ggdc/historicaldevelopment/maddison/releases/maddison-project-database-2018 (CGDPpc set), update 11 January 2018. See also Bolt, Inklaar, de Jong and Luiten van Zanden 2018.

5 Van den Noord also observes that in some countries governments' "discretionary actions ... have reduced, or even offset, the effect of automatic fiscal stabilisers" (abstract).

> the international sample, a one percentage point increase in government spending relative to GDP reduces output volatility by eight basis points.'
>
> Their abstract

They also observe (in reference to Van den Noord 2000):

> 'Traditionally, the stabilizing role of fiscal policy has been associated to the size and volatility of the budget deficit and not the budget itself. Although, as we have argued before, there is evidence that overall size and responsiveness of fiscal variables are strongly correlated, our results raise the question whether the size of governments is important in itself.'
>
> FATÁS and MIHOV 2001, p. 18

Fatás and Mihov (2002/2003) reach similar results for a sample of 51 countries covering 1960–99.[6] (In the same paper they also study the effect of pro-cyclical policy.)[7] By the year 2008, Andrés, Doménech and Fatás (2008) can refer to the thesis that large governments are associated with less volatile economies as being an empirically well-established 'stylized fact' that has been refined by several recent studies.[8] They confirm the earlier results for 20 OECD countries (OECD-21, minus New Zealand and Switzerland plus Turkey) covering the period 1960–2004. (Much of this paper – as is Fatás and Mihov 2002/2003) as well as other literature in the field since Galí (1994) – is concerned with the question of how this empirical fact could (or cannot) be accounted for in an amended 'real business cycle' model.

I close this sub-section by noting that, generally, international synchronisation of business cycles would, by itself, have an amplitude increasing effect. Dalsgaard et al. (2002) observe: 'international divergencies of cyclical positions have diminished but, outside the euro area, there is little evidence of increased synchronisation of cycles' (their abstract; see also p. 9 and especially note 15). This is different for recessions with financial origins, to which I briefly turn in the next section.

---

6 See esp. working paper version (2002) pp. 15 and 27.

7 They somewhat misleadingly define 'discretionary policy' as 'changes in fiscal policy that do not represent reaction to economic conditions.' They add: 'In theory, it is useful to think about fiscal policy as consisting of three components: (a) automatic stabilizers, (b) discretionary fiscal policy that reacts to the state of the economy, and (c) discretionary policy that is implemented for reasons other than current macroeconomic conditions.' (working paper version pp. 3–4) Regarding the last component (c) they find that the volatility of output induced by [this] discretionary fiscal policy lowers economic growth by 0.6 percentage points for every percentage point increase in volatility, and that 'there is evidence that the increase in volatility is in part due to electoral cycles; nevertheless, we do find that political constraints restrain fiscal policy beyond their impact on the traditional election-year volatility' (abstract).

8 Abstract and working paper version p. 13.

10§2 *State policy in recessions versus depressions*

Given the capitalist state's furthering the accumulation of capital (7§3) and given that the incentives for the accumulation of capital result in cyclically recurrent over-accumulation of capital (5§8), it seems that the state is bound to passively await the cyclical curing of that over-accumulation (5§9).[9] With considerable automatic stabilisers there is, in ordinary recessions, generally no necessity for additional state policy. Keeping state expenditure and state expenditure commitments as well as tax rates unaffected puts a floor into the general macroeconomic expenditure during recessions (10§1).

However, when a recession takes on the character of a depression (a prolonged recession – often triggered by a financial crisis and bank failures and often in combination with price deflation), the mere state expenditure floor may not be a sufficient base for getting to a recovery via restructuring of capital (5§9).[10] Then the reproduction of the capitalist system requires a substantial discretionary state policy. As Keynes (1936) indicated, monetary policy is not likely to be sufficient in a depression, whence the state is required to engage in substantial additional *spending*.[11] (See also Kannan, Scott and Terrones 2009.)

10§2-a Amplification. Frequency of recessions/depressions associated with financial crises, and their severity and duration comparison with non-financial ones

In an empirical IMF study, Kannan et al. conclude that:

> 'recessions associated with financial crises tend to be unusually severe and that recoveries from such recessions are typically slow. Similarly, globally synchronized recessions are often long and deep, and recoveries from these recessions are generally weak. Countercyclical monetary policy can help shorten recessions, but its effectiveness is limited in fin-

---

9 Though see Addendum 10§2-b on indicative planning.

10 In a 2008 IMF working paper, Claessens, Kose and Terrones characterise a depression as 'an extremely severe recession, in which the peak-to-trough decline in output exceeds 10 percent' (2008, p. 15). Kannan et al. (2009, p. 5) also take this view.

The three periods of 1873–96 (esp. for the UK and somewhat briefer for the USA), of 1929 until WWII, and of 2007/08 and after have been identified as depressions (see, e.g., http://www.nytimes.com/2010/06/28/opinion/28krugman.html?_r=0). Note, however, that the state expenditure floor has considerably increased since the second depression.

11 In much of the post-WWII period, Keynes has been looked upon as a business cycle theoretician (this is what at least the Neo-Keynesians made of him). In my view – and apart from its theoretical innovations – his 1936 work makes Keynes primarily a depression economist.

> ancial crises. By contrast, expansionary fiscal policy seems particularly effective in shortening recessions associated with financial crises and in boosting recoveries.' (2009, abstract)

These conclusions are based on evidence from a sample of 21 OECD countries (the OECD-21) for the period 1960–2007, excluding emerging financially originating recessions in their last year (2007). Of the 122 recessions in their sample, 15 are associated with financial crisis (i.e. 12%).[12]

GRAPH 10.3 *Average number of recessions per decade and per country 1870–2008, for a sample of 14 current OECD countries*[13]

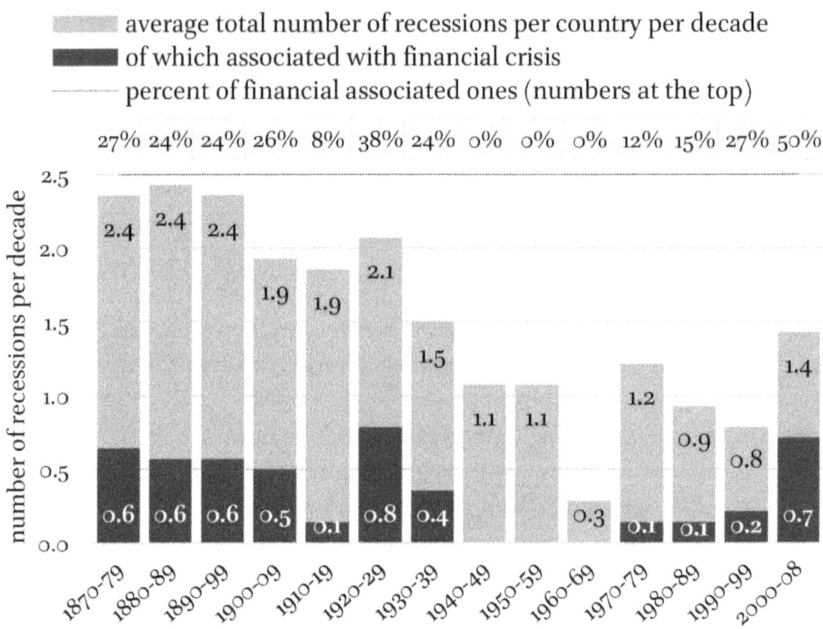

DATA SOURCE: calculated from Jorda, Schularick and Taylor 2012, Table 1

Jorda, Schularick and Taylor (2012) go back to 1870 for a sample of 14 OECD countries.[14] They do take into account the 2007/08 financial crises. For their sample 22% of the recessions/crises in this period are of financial origin. However, doing a calculation from their sample, which restricts to the 1960–

12 Kannan et al. 2009, p. 8. The last financially associated crisis within their sample dates from 1997q2–1999q1 in Japan.

13 See the previous note.

14 The OECD-21 minus Austria, Belgium, Finland, Greece, Ireland, New Zealand, Portugal. (See 7§3-c for the 'OECD-21').

2007 period (and excluding the 2007/08 financial crises as do Kannan et al.) results in 11% of the recessions/crises in this 1960–2007 period being of financial origin. This is not far removed from the 12% of the Kannan et al. data for 21 countries.

In this light – and given that this chapter is confined to broad outlines that go back to early full capitalism – *Graph 10.3* shows decade averages that I have calculated from the sample of Jorda et al.

Noting that *severity* of recessions (10§1) is at least as important as their frequency, it can be seen from *Graph 10.3* that, roughly, there is a downward trend in the average *number* of cycles per decade, and that, especially after 1910, crises from financial origin are an irregular phenomenon.[15]

Kannan et al. (2009, p. 10) indicate – for the period 1960–2007 – that credit growth during the expansions preceding financial crises is higher than during other expansions, and that credit booms have frequently followed financial deregulation.

10§2-b Addendum: French and Japanese indicative planning

Given the cyclically recurrent over-accumulation of capital, which gives rise to recession and destruction of capital, it is not a ludicrous idea for a capitalist state to try to prevent such over-accumulation. Throughout the 1960s and 1970s the French and the Japanese states institutionalised, in various ways, an 'indicative investment planning' (non-binding investment schedules that combine forecasts and planning). On the French variant see, for example, Dalton (1974, pp. 154–60), Bonnaud (1975, pp. 93–110) and Nielsen (2008). On the Japanese variant see, for example, Caves and Uekusa (1976a; 1976b), Trezise and Suzuki (1976) and Nielsen (2008).

Division 2. The increasing size and complexity of regulation

The state's eight regulative frameworks (Chapters 6–7 and 9), as well as the forms and design of taxation (Chapter 8), engender an increasingly complicated, as well as complexity of, regulation. This division is not about the content of regulation and tax legislation; rather it concerns the characteristics that determine their reach. Because this division will introduce a lot of interconnected concepts within few pages, it is probably one of the more difficult ones

15 For graphs of the GDP growth effects of financial crises 1975–2015 see https://knoema.com/xflgvk/40-years-in-financial-crises.

of this book. At the same time it is a key one. In the conclusions to this chapter I will state that the inevitably *increasing* quantity, complication and complexity of regulation within capitalism is one of the latter's core vulnerabilities.

10§3 *Regulation: laws and delegated regulation*

Much of the organisation and terminology of the legislative and regulatory frameworks is country-specific. Generally the 'rules framework' includes 'primary legislation' (laws/acts), which is passed at the highest administrative level, and 'secondary legislation' (other rules), which is passed at lower administrative levels (including field-specific regulatory bodies). The former formally provides the delegation for the latter, and may also withdraw this delegation. Secondary legislation is often more detailed or field specific.

Though in most countries (and all of the OECD-21) there is this distinction, what is allotted to different levels is highly contingent (also within one country).[16] This is a matter of institutional organisation and of the possible speed of change of a rule (speedier for delegated legislation). Further, for actors the level makes no difference: the required compliance is independent of the level.

For the purposes of the current division, therefore, I adopt the following terminology. I use the term *regulation* for the entirety of laws and of the 'delegated regulation'. When I explicitly refer to the latter I always use the adjective 'delegated'. When I refer to 'regulation', as said, this refers to the entirety. I refer to one particular regulation as 'a' regulation or, in case of a set, 'regulations'.

10§3-a Amplification. Execution of delegated regulation: 'orders'

This amplification is not relevant for the further main text, though it is relevant for especially Amplification 10§5-a.

Delegated regulation may be promulgated by executives (such as presidents), governments, ministers or other executive bodies (especially regulatory agencies), always depending on the type of delegation as formulated in the laws (sometimes in the constitutional law). Specific types of delegated regulation go under different names in different countries. In this division I merely use the term '*order*': presidential order, government order (or order in council), ministerial order, field order (the latter referring to the orders of a designated authority within, or under the supervision of, a ministry – also called regulation agencies or authorities).

---

16 Parliaments may in some cases require detailed primary legislation (on which they have more influence); in other cases their concern is to delegate detail.

In what follows I will *not* refer to further various country specific names for these, such as 'regulation' (for the entirety of the delegated regulation), 'statutory instruments', 'codes', 'rules' or 'decrees'.[17]

10§4 *A conceptual outline of the reach of regulation: lack of operational measures*

This section is a preview. Clarifications are set out in the sections to come. *Figure 10.4* provides a conceptual outline of the rest of this division. The following 10§5 starts with the quantity of regulation. (See the section indications at the left hand border of the figure.) Next we move to the degree of complexity of regulation (10§6) and finally to the change of regulation (10§7). Almost all of the concepts outlined concern 'degrees' (of complexity, for example) as indicated at the right hand border of the figure.

The economy-wide ***total quantity*** of regulation is determined by the 'densities' of regulation in regulation fields (e.g. banking, telecommunication or shoe repair); the density being determined by whether a field is covered at all by regulation, and in what degree of intensity (highly or barely regulated; this regards the degree of detail of regulations).

The degree of ***complexity*** of the regulation in a field – and, summed, the total complexity – is determined by the degree of '*complication*' of regulation, and the degree in which the regulations in one field (e.g. regarding competition) are '*interwoven*' with other regulations in that field or adjacent fields (e.g. taxation). Additionally, complexity is also determined by the degree in which economic actors (the subjects of regulation) dynamically *'fuse' fields* of regulation (especially by product and process innovations). Despite the importance of the latter two, I will show that 'complication' is in effect the key concept for the reach of regulation.

The dynamics regarding regulation come together in the factors that drive the continuously *changing regulation*. These drives (unintended loopholes in regulations; and new or re-perceived social-economic problems) tend to increase not only the (initial) density of regulation – by its determinants of coverage and intensity – but especially also the complication of regulation. (See the dotted arrows in *Figure 10.4*.) Despite factional political efforts and wide-ranging actors' demands to roll back regulation, or (in my view rather naïve) demands to at least decrease complication, I will conclude in 10§7 that, for the

[***continued***]

17 For the US case see, e.g., http://dictionary.law.com/Default.aspx?selected=1771 (or http://legal-dictionary.thefreedictionary.com/regulation.)
For the UK see, e.g., https://www3.law.ox.ac.uk/lrsp/overview/legislation.php.

FIGURE 10.4 *Conceptual outline of the reach of regulation*

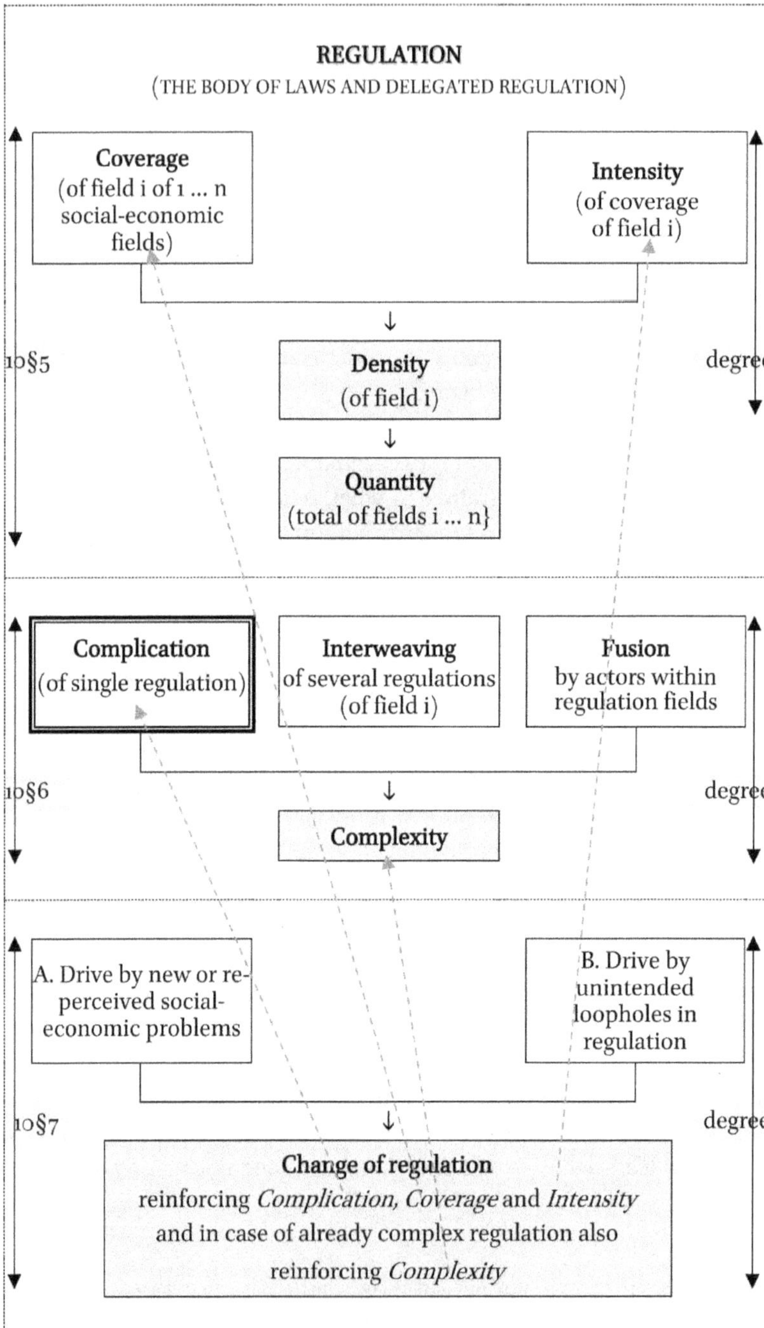

10§4 *Continued*

capitalist system to survive, a continuously increasing complexity of regulation is inevitable.

All along the following exposition we will be confronted with the problem that – apart from the mere quantity of regulation – this research field lacks operational measures for key concepts.

10§5 *Quantity and density of regulation: (too) simple measures*

A fair amount of attention has been given to complaints about the amount of regulation and, along with it, efforts to push the state back.[18] Note, however, that there are also pressures to increase regulation (pulling the state in). Think of various property claims and of tax and non-tax subsidies. In the field of competition policy we have the push and pull pressures on the same terrain. Enterprises seek to push out the state for their own non-rivalrous (anti-competitive) supply activities, though they pull in the state for their own purchasing activities for which they seek competition. The same applies for regulation of the quality of output and production, including for concerns of health and a sustainable environment such as the climate: regulate *them*, not us! However, once regulation is generally deemed inevitable, enterprises want parity. Simultaneous push and pull pressures, and next parity requests, also apply for social security.

More generally, change of the economic structure calls for extension of regulation (for example, the evolution of traffic and of ICT). As 'old' processes and products only gradually die off (if at all), we have an increase in the quantity of regulation. Scrapping of regulation is rare (unless some surviving together with an evolving field is covered by a brand new law).

Mere Quantity. The simple question of how much regulation there is in force in a country is already difficult to answer (see Amplification 10§5-a). However, counting titles of laws and other regulation is not particularly telling because their size is highly divergent, ranging from tens to many thousands of pages for one title (the latter, for example, for the '*Code civil*' in French oriented codes).[19]

---

18 See, for example, the OECD publications on administrative simplification http://www.oecd.org/gov/regulatory-policy/administrative-simplification.htm as well as its series of country studies on regulatory policy http://www.oecd.org/gov/regulatory-policy/by-country.htm and KPMG International (2011). The latter document includes a questionnaire among worldwide top-management on complexity of management in general. Complexity of non-tax regulation ranked highest (71% of respondents) and that of complex tax regulation somewhat lower (57% of respondents). For these managers at least, it seems that the coping with regulation dominates much of their job.

19 See Amplification 10§5-a for numbers of titles of codes around 2010.

Some researchers propose to add up the sections of regulation,[20] but their sizes also highly diverge, especially between country traditions. A better simple measure seems to count pages, though with the qualification that these are layout dependent.[21] Even if the stock of regulation at some initial date were unknown, one could still count the rate of mutation of the quantity of regulation (Amplification 10§5-a provides an example.)

Whatever measure one adopts, the common opinion between researchers in this field is that the quantity of regulation has enormously increased between the end of the nineteenth century, or between halfway through the twentieth century, and the early twenty-first century. The main question is merely whether or not in some periods the speed of increase has slowed down.[22]

Density. As indicated in 10§4, the total quantity of regulation is determined by the *density* of regulation in each field. The latter is again determined by, first, the fields that are *covered* at all by any regulation, and second, by the degree of *intensity* of regulation in those fields, that is, the degree of detail.[23|24] (See the first block of *Figure 10.4*.)

Each of these could *in principle* be counted, the latter (intensity) in a very rough way by the number of pages of regulation, assuming for the time being that – in one country – these are of equal complication (see the next section).

Quantity, impact and measures. Measures of mere quantity of regulation are defective in measuring the impact of regulation because these do not measure the complexity of regulation (see the next section). For the latter, however, adequate operational measures are lacking so that for long run and for between country comparisons we have no more than simple quantity measures.

---

20 For example, de Jong and Herweijer 2004, p. 57.

21 The best simple measure would be a word count (supposing digitalisation), but I have not seen word count based quantifications.

22 Note though that towards the end of the coming into office of a government, the quantity of legislation passed is usually higher than at the beginning (due to legislation preparation effects).

23 For 'field' one can refer to the SNA (System of National Accounts) economic sector division at some digit level. Next there is the general regulation that applies across fields (Chapters 6–7 and 9).

24 Van Gestel and Hertogh (2006, p. 31) and Van Gestel (2011, p. 8 n. 5) adopt the term 'density of regulation' for the combination of Quantity (Coverage and Intensity) and Interweaving. They do not cover Complication and Fusion, and hence not Complexity of regulation.

10§5-a Amplification. Some examples of simple quantifications of the amount of regulation

Even the mere adding up of the titles of all of the regulation in force is painstaking work that is not often undertaken (however, recent mutations are well known).

Limited country-wise information about the total quantity of regulation in force. In terms of estimating the number of USA federal laws in force, Shameema Rahmana, a senior legal research specialist at the USA Library of Congress, writes in 2013: 'trying to tally this number is nearly impossible'.[25]

A 2013 report of the UK Office of the Parliamentary Counsel mentions: 'It is extremely difficult to estimate how much legislation is in force at any one time.' (p. 6; the difficult estimation is not undertaken by the office.)[26]

Graph 10.5 shows some data for the laws in force of the Netherlands. (This is an example; in 2015 the country ranked 17th in terms of world GDP. Whereas that rank does not seem important for the quantity of regulation – any country has to regulate – there can be cultural differences in the degree of delegation – including 'orders'.)

GRAPH 10.5 *Number of laws in force, the Netherlands 1980–2015* (*central government, exclusive delegated and EU regulation*)

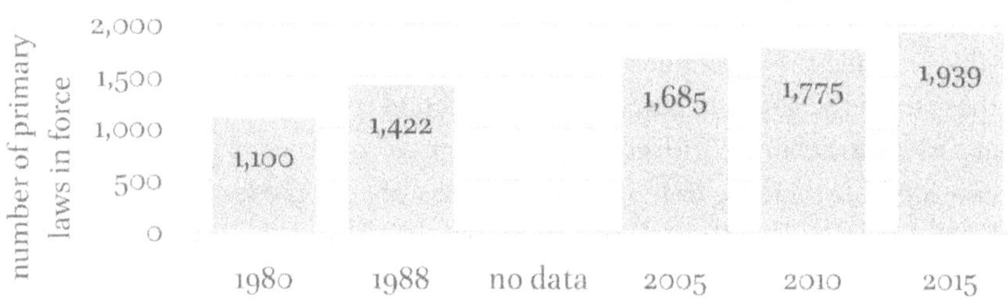

DATA SOURCES: 1980 and 1988 (Overhoff and Molenaar 1991, pp. 5–6);[27] 2005 and 2010 (Government of the Netherlands 2013; 2015; Vester 2017)

---

25 http://blogs.loc.gov/law/2013/03/frequent-reference-question-how-many-federal-laws-are-there/.

Apparently in the USA around 2010, each year some 100 brand new bills are passed into law http://www.kowal.com/?q=How-Many-Federal-Laws-Are-There%3F.

26 On the mutation it states: 'Every year, new legislation and amendments result in over 15,000 (over 30,000 when considering secondary legislation) legislative effects' (p. 7).

27 Quoted in de Jong and Herweijer 2004, p. 19.

Regarding primary laws there is limited historical information (*Graph 10.5*). It can be seen that in the 35-year period 1980–2015, the number of laws in force increased by 76%. Information on delegated central government regulation is even more limited (available only from 2004). In 2015 there were for this country 9,136 central government regulations in force (exclusive regulatory agencies and exclusive EU regulation). These comprised 1,939 laws (21%) and 7,197 orders in council and ministerial orders (79%).[28|29]

I now turn to the EU regulation that is not included in the numbers above.

Quantity of regulation in force: the EU. EU regulation consists of two main categories. One category regards the so-called 'directives'. Because national governments are obliged to implement these directives in their national regulation, these should not be added to the national quantities of laws in force (thus the 'implementations' are included in the numbers of the example of the Netherlands above). All the other EU regulation is not implemented in national regulation, thus this is regulation that is additional to the national ones. This other EU regulation is summarised in *Graph 10.6*. Note that the EU jurisdiction is *mainly* economic and monetary, excluding jurisdiction on especially taxation and social security legislation (though there are exceptions).

The area charts at the bottom of *Graph 10.6* show the quantitative development of the delegated EU regulations newly issued from 1967. These come in two main types. The fist type includes orders with usually a general character (the EU calls these 'Regulations' that I write with a capital R to differentiate these from the genus 'regulations'). The second type includes orders with usually a specific character ('Decisions'). The three bottom charts show that after a considerable increase from 1967–95 (a factor of 8 for the total) – which relates to the EU's establishment – the issue of new regulation slows down afterwards, but nevertheless keeps forthcoming considerably (a number of 1,864 in 2012).

As an indicator for the *stock* of delegated regulation in force, we can use the delegated general regulations ('Regulations') without an expiry date, corrected for repeals – see the columns in *Graph 10.6*. In 2012 their total was 21,792. Their increase from even 1995–2012 amounts to a factor of 9.

28 See Vester 2017.

29 For another example I point to information related to a pages count regarding *newly issued* central government laws and delegated regulation of Finland (excluding regulatory agencies and excluding EU regulation). As such this is not about the stock of the regulation in force. This newly issued regulation increased from 1,000 pages per year in 1920 to just over 2,000 pages in 1985 and to 3,500 pages in 2000 (de Jong and Zijlstra 2009, p. 139; from the Finnish Government 2002).

GRAPH 10.6 *Number of total delegated regulations issued each year, and cumulative total of the delegated general regulations without expiry date; European Union 1967–2012*[30]

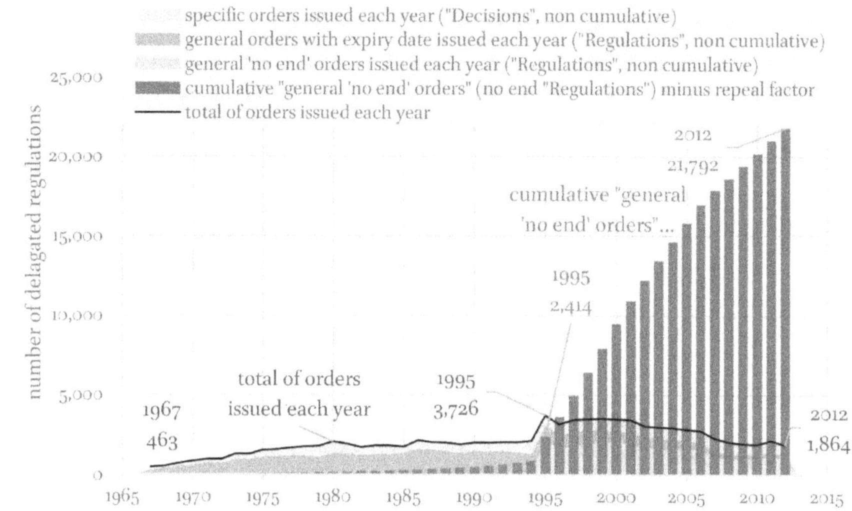

DATA SOURCE: Toshkov 2014[31] and House of Commons [UK] 2010, p. 13[32]

Stock of delegated federal regulation in the USA: number of pages. Even if, as noted above, for the USA the stock of federal laws is apparently unknown, there are data for the stock of the federal 'delegated regulation' that not only go back to 1950, but also provide this information in terms of number of pages (see *Graph 10.7*).

The USA Code of Federal Regulations (CFR) annual edition is 'the codification of the general and permanent rules published in the Federal Register by the departments and agencies of the Federal Government.'[33|34]

30 A restricted forerunner of the EU dates from 1957. The starting date for the Graph below is 1967, the year of the creation of a single Commission and a single Council to serve the then three European Communities (EEC, Euratom, ECSC).

31 http://www.dimiter.eu/Eurlex.html / http://www.dimiter.eu/Data.html [February 2014→19 December 2015].

32 From the repeal of regulation (all regulations) provided by the last source for 1997–2009, an average repeal ratio of 25% can be calculated. To be on the safe side I have applied this ratio to Regulations without expiry date from Toshkof's database. (Their repeal ratio is probably less than the average for all Regulations.)

33 https://www.gpo.gov/fdsys/browse/collectionCfr.action?collectionCode=CFR.

34 The CFR is a stock measure that is to be distinguished from the Federal Register's data on the annual flow of new regulation. Measured in pages this flow increased considerably

GRAPH 10.7 *Development of the quantity of delegated regulation in force at the federal state level in the USA: total number of pages 1950–2015*

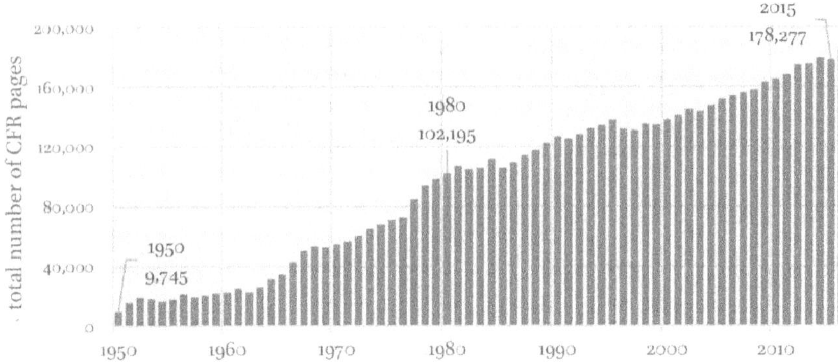

DATA SOURCE: USA Federal Register, Code of Federal Regulations (2017/04)[35]

Graph 10.7 shows that the pages increase of the delegated regulation in force is quite enormous (between 1950 and 2015 there is a factor increase of 18). If the increase were to continue at the same rate, then the number of pages will have increased to one million by 2050. Note, however, that the 178,000 pages of Federal delegated regulation in force in 2015 far from measures the total quantity of regulation for the actors in some US state. In a 2015 OECD report, it is mentioned that of the total number of laws (i.e. federal plus local state), only 1.7% are national, i.e. federal – a number for the similar proportion of the delegated regulation is not provided.[36]

from 1937–70. From 1970–80 the increase accelerated, next dropped until 1985 and then again gradually increased afterwards. However, from the mid 1970's the flow of the *number* of new 'final rules' decreased (with fluctuations) from 7,401 in 1976 to 3,281 in 2017 (the latter numbers reveal that the pages count is relevant). Carey, 2016, provides qualifying comments on these flow measures. For a pages count of the stock (CFR), and especially the long term trend thereof, these qualifications are less relevant (one of his correct points is that the elimination of an existing rule is executed by a new rule; however, in terms of pages this is usually not weighty, and it is likely that such drops occur throughout time).

35 https://www.federalregister.gov/reader-aids/understanding-the-federal-register/federal-register-statistics → Code of federal regulations, Total Pages and Volumes 1936–2016 (xls) → tab CFR volumes (2017/04, accessed 1 February 2018). See also https://www.federalregister.gov/blog/learn/tutorials, Federal Register & CFR Publication Statistics – Aggregated Charts. A similar graph can be found at the website of the Regulatory Studies Center, George Washington University; Regulation statistics http://regulatorystudies.columbian.gwu.edu/reg-stats.

36 OECD 2015a, Annex A. [OECD Regulatory Policy Outlook 2015.]

In conclusion of this amplification. Even the data we have on merely the quantity of regulation is limited. The available information points to considerable increases over time.

10§6 *Complexity of regulation: the combination of complication, interweaving and field fusion*

The degree of 'complexity' of regulation lies in the *combination* of the 'complication' of single laws or orders, and of the 'interweaving' of several laws and their lower level orders. Additional complexity arises through 'field fusion'. (Sub-sections A–C below.)

A *The degree of complication of regulation: the apparent paradox of equity of simple regulation*

Regulation must apply at the same time to actors that are merely engaged in simple (economic) processes and to actors engaged in complicated processes. The degree of complication of regulation is determined by three main components.

- First, the degree of complication *of concepts* and *of language*;
- Second, the degree of complication of the *application* of rules, that is, the requirement of (non-)action of the actors (the does and don'ts);
- Third, the degree of complication of the required *record-keeping and reporting* (for example, for taxation, assets of banks, or compliance with environmental norms).

Each of these three determines the *degree of expertise* that is required for taking cognisance of the regulation that is relevant to an actor, as well as their compliance. Along with it, the degree of complication and of required expertise also determines the degree to which enterprises and other actors have to hire legal experts for the cognisance of and compliance with regulation (as determining the cognisance costs and the compliance costs).[37]

The alternative to complicated regulation is simply formulated as well as broad regulation. A degree of precision is then substituted by more vagueness and ambiguity, contributing to multi-interpretative regulation. This can only be resolved by leaving the filling in of detail and precision to the courts – that is, in case of conflict between actors and regulating authorities over the

37 See also Partlow 2013, pp. 307–8. Where Partlow in this excellent article uses the term complexity I use the term complication. I reserve the term complexity for additional intricacy (see below). Partlow focuses on the legislation and regulation of taxation, from which he also takes his examples.

interpretation of rules. As courts interpret the law and other regulation, the latter's 'simple' formulations become again complicated, so coming full circle. And as long as the regulation is not adapted into complicated formulations there has to be continuous reference to 'case law' (the courts' interpretation). In the meantime, because court procedures, including appeals, most often take an enormous amount of time (quite apart from their being expensive), 'simple' regulation introduces uncertainty into the regulative constellation.[38]

This is the apparent paradox of equity of regulative complication. On the one hand, equity would require that the reading of regulation not be a matter of high judicial expertise, whilst on the other hand, the interpretation of 'simple' regulation always ends up with high judicial expertise before the courts and such expertise for reading the case law.[39]

Note that especially for taxation, the complication of legislation/regulation increases in degree due to taxation 'instrumentalism', that is, the use of taxation not merely for the collection of money, but also for all kinds of incentives and compensations.[40] The result is a wide range of often complicated tax subsidies (tax deductions, also called 'tax expenditures').[41]

B Interweaving of regulation

Interweaving of regulation refers to the interconnection between separate regulations at the same level or at different levels. Almost all laws refer to other laws for (at least) definitions and various specifications. In those other laws there are most often again references to still other laws. (See *Graph 10.8* in Amplification 10§6-a.) The same applies for delegated regulation. The degree of these cross-references determines the degree of interweaving of regulation. As a consequence a new law, or an amendment of a previous one, induces a series of required amendments of other laws and of delegated regulation (hoping that none is missed).

38 Partlow 2013, pp. 314 and 320–1.

39 Perhaps there might be a way of simplifying the concepts and language of regulation by explaining these in more common language within the law or regulation (it would nevertheless have to be unambiguous common language). However, apart from the problem of the interweaving of regulation (the next sub-section), this will lead to a huge extension of the length of regulation, which also does not contribute to equity because length requires perseverance.

40 Such as for proper environmental behaviour, the hiring of disabled workers, technical innovations, mortgage-type dependent interest deductions, pension-type dependent premium deductions, loss carry back deductions. Much of the instrumentalist objectives could be reached by straight subsidies or by straight prohibitions and injunctions.

41 See also Partlow 2013, pp. 316–17.

If one, even very complicated, law were to stand on itself, this would be 'doable'. It is the interweaving of several or a series of complicated laws that multiplies into the *complexity* of the body of laws and their derived regulation. (See the second block of *Figure 10.4*.)

In practice the interweaving can be quite desperate, even for a legal expert, when the understanding of one section of a law requires the consultation of a series of other laws and delegated regulations.[42] In principle at least, this might be overcome by integrating the cross references within each one law. However, its 'price' would be an exponential growth of the quantity of regulation (along with experts each time having to go through lengthy repetitions when they go from one law to the other).

C The fusion of fields of regulation by economic actors

Additional complexity occurs when the field of operation of an actor is a (new) fusion of fields covered by the existing regulation of fields. (See the second block of *Figure 10.4*.) Thus it is the actors who dynamically fuse fields. Field fusion occurs, firstly, along with product and especially production process innovations (including, for example, ICT driven innovations). It occurs, secondly, through the integration of formerly separate functions – such as banks' fusing with insurance functions, or car producers' or real estate companies' integrating shadow banking (the point is not different divisions within an enterprise, i.e. conglomeration, but rather full integration). This is not uncommon within technical and organisational dynamic constellations. For both of these types of field fusion, there may be inconsistent rules from different existing regulation fields. Thus the regulation lags behind such changes, though it may eventually catch up – for the time being.

10§6-a Amplification. Interweaving of regulation, an illustration from the UK

In a report about legislation in the UK by the UK Office of the Parliamentary Counsel, it is indicated that:

42 There are field experts. However, experts of 'the' law and other regulation do not exist. Wilhelmina Thomassen, judge in the Supreme Court of the Netherlands, said in a 2011 interview: No one knows even all the laws and each year 29,000 relevant court decisions are being published (case law relevant) – amongst a total of each year about 1.8 million decisions (in the Netherlands the decisions to population ratio in 2011 was 11%; the 'relevant' decisions to population ratio was 0.2%). http://www.nrc.nl/rechtenbestuur/2011/04/09/niemand-kent-alle-wetten-en-regels/.

> 'new and existing legislation can appear inconsistent. Regulation emanating from different sources sometimes overlaps and commencement can be difficult to follow. Every year, new legislation and amendments result in over 15,000 (over 30,000 when considering secondary legislation) legislative effects. The statute book therefore is an ever-evolving network of complex information that expands organically and is extremely difficult to map.'
>
> UK Office of the Parliamentary Counsel 2013, p. 14

The legislative effects are indeed convoluted by their interweaving ('network'). *Graph 10.8* visualises an example of this interweaving for one single Act (the Companies, Audit, Investigations and Community Enterprise Act 2004).

GRAPH 10.8 *Visualisation of the interweaving of the UK 'Companies, Audit, Investigations and Community Enterprise Act 2004' with other earlier and later Acts*[43]

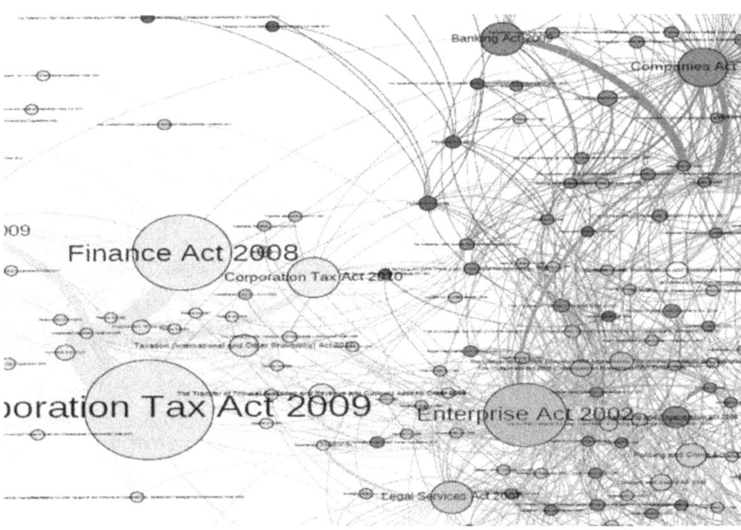

SOURCE: UK OFFICE OF THE PARLIAMENTARY COUNSEL 2013, P. 16

10§7 *Change: the tendency to increasing complexity of regulation*

This section presents change of regulation, starting from some state of regulation (and hence a state of complexity of regulation) at one point in time. There are two very different impulses for a change of regulation. Each of these

---

43 As the Office notes: 'It represents the proportion of the statute book to be taken into consideration when looking at the current in-force state of just that one Act.'

separately engenders an increasing complexity of regulation. However, in combination these reinforce the increase in complexity. (A and B below, and A and B in the third block of *Figure 10.4*.)

A *Increasing complexity as driven by new or re-perceived social-economic problems*

Changes of regulation – as driven by new, or re-perceived, social-economic problems – are an ongoing aspect of regulation. For one part these stem from legitimation problems. For another part these stem from changes in the economic structure and product and process innovations, as well as the fusion referred to at the end of the previous section. These affect the 'coverage' and the 'intensity' of regulation, and so the density and quantity of regulation (see the dotted lines in *Figure 10.4*). The more convoluted the social-economic problems, the more complicated regulations tend to be. (Think of new problems within the financial sector such as those of 'too big to fail', re-perceived problems of the climate and other environmental matters, of new technologies such as those regarding communication and health, and of redesigns of taxation in face of changes in the organisational structure of enterprises.) This results, together with the interweaving, in an increasing complexity of regulation.

B *Increasing complexity as driven by unintended loopholes in regulation*

However, changes of regulation – and especially continuous amendments of existing regulation – are also determined by unintended loopholes in regulation. Their reparation continually increases the complication of single regulations, and in connection with the interweaving of regulations, multiplies into further complexity of regulation.

I define 'loopholes' in laws and/or delegated regulation as rules or stipulations that, unintended by the legislator, permit actors (e.g. enterprises) to achieve goals, or more specifically advantages or benefits, not contemplated by the legislator.[44]

Especially when large financial interests are at stake, enterprises' lawyers – and, for taxation, also accountants – painstakingly search the relevant laws and other regulations for ways to take advantage of gaps and ambiguities. By way of borderline (non-)compliance the rules are then tested, and when regulators accuse actors of abuse, perhaps imposing fines, this is often followed by appeal

44 I do not exclude that there are also ambiguities in laws as a result of lobbying pressures (there are even cases in which specific articles of laws derive from lobbyists). Below, however, the focus is on unintended ambiguities.

procedures before courts. (Note that anticipating all this, regulators themselves also continuously search the law and other regulation for gaps and ambiguities.)

The outcome is a continuous amendment of laws and delegated regulations so as to repair the gaps and ambiguities. 'Because the devices used to take advantage of loopholes are intricate, the amendments addressing loopholes must also be intricate.'[45] This increasing complication – together with the interweaving of increasing complication – results in a tendency to cycles of gaps and ambiguity search, amendments and further complication and complexity.[46]

C *The combined reinforcement of complexity increase*

Whereas increasing complication and complexity stemming from the 'loopholes amendments' (heading B) is a continuous process, any new regulation stemming from new problems (heading A) opens new cycles of loopholes amendments (heading B). The already enormous number of regulations increases (shown in *Graph 10.6* for the EU) and the ditto pages of regulation increase (shown in *Graph 10.7* for the USA) merely measure the quantity increase, not the complication and complexity increase.

In conclusion. Regulation is inevitable for the reproduction of the capitalist system (Chapters 6–9). However, social-economic changes, and especially the dynamic interaction of the complication and interweaving of regulation, means that an increasing complexity of regulation is inevitable. This is reinforced by the enterprises' profit-driven search for gaps and ambiguities in existing regulation, whence much of the increasing complexity is immanent to this profit drive.

---

45 Partlow 2013, p. 316.

46 Complication and complexity are not the object of governments, but inevitable. As an anecdote in this respect I might add that when I served as a senator in the parliament of the Netherlands and when in 2015 a complicated seven-page amendment to the corporate taxation law was proposed (with direct repercussions for four other taxation laws) – requiring an explanatory memorandum of no less than 52 pages – I asked the secretary of state in official written communication if he himself considered this a proposal that would result in a further complexity of the corporate taxation law. His written answer was (in brief) that 'the complexity increase is undeniable' but that, in the cabinet's opinion, 'this complexity increase is just about acceptable' (Government of the Netherlands, Secretary of State for Finance 2015, p. 22). I retorted by asking whether the cabinet ever proposes laws that it considers just not acceptable.

Division 3. The capitalist state's hard core and its manifestation in expenditure as quantitatively dominated by social security transfers

The previous division presented the reach of the capitalist state as manifested in the character of regulation. The current division presents the manifestation of the state in the development of its expenditure. All of the main expenditure categories will be briefly reviewed. However, the focus will be on the development of the quantitatively dominant category of social security expenditures and its interconnection with public education and the communications part of infrastructure – in the division's last section (10§12).

10§8 *The manifestation of the state: the actors' experience of the state's existence*

- *The hard core of the capitalist state*

The existence of the state is manifested in processes of legislation, public security and the upholding of the law. As indicated in 6§2–6§3, the existence of the capitalist economy requires that these processes regard primarily state-granted legal rights of:

(a) claims of entitlement to private property in the earth;
(b) claims of entitlement to private property in means of production other than for production by the claimant;
(c) claims of entitlement to employ labour as combined with the appropriation of the surplus-value produced by that labour;
(d) claims of entitlement to existence (in the sense of 'allowance').

In granting particularly these claims as legal rights, the state is identified as the capitalist state (6§3). In this division this constellation, together with the other moments of the exposition in Chapter 6, will be denoted as the capitalist state's 'hard core' (HC).

- *The hidden hand of the capitalist state*

For many people the economic rights that the state grants (a–c above), and the legislation about them, are not part of their conscious experience. For them 'the state' is an abstract entity. They are aware of the state as persons staffing the coming and going governments, associated with 'them' in the capital city, with 'them' in the municipality's building, and with the police or other authorities rapping people on the knuckles.

At the same time they may feel, or know, that 'the state' consolidates a skewed 'economic' distribution of power, property, income and esteem. In fact they experience the granted legal rights (a)–(d) in the form and at the site of the actually claimed property and employment entitlements, that is, their everyday workplace – if they have paid work. They also experience it in the level of their pay cheque at the end of the week or month – one that, if they are lucky, allows them to live a life above the poverty line, or a comfortable one. Thus in this everyday experience, the hard core of the state is a 'hidden hand'.

- *The experience of the capitalist state in terms of its expenditure*

Most people experience the reach of the state predominantly in its expenditure and the allocation thereof. That is, in the supervision of the safety of production and products (10§9), in public education (10§10), in infrastructure (10§11), in the public goods part of social security (especially health) and in the other components of social security (10§12).

10§8-a Amplification. Notes on the synthetic overview of state expenditure in the OECD-21, 1870–2015, in the amplifications of the current division

The amplifications in this division present a most brief synthetic overview of the components of state expenditure for the average of the current OECD-21 in the period of full-fledged capitalism hitherto (1870–2015). Most of the space will be devoted to the social security expenditure (10§12), which, as we will see, appears as one of the two main 'inevitable vulnerabilities' of the capitalist system (the other one being the increasing complexity of regulation).

The overview in the amplifications is merely one in terms of graphs of the decade development since 1870, the idea is that in each one single decade (e.g. 1920) the state is manifest in its expenditure on the Hard Core (the hidden hand) and in the other, experienced, expenditure. Many of the amplifications of Chapters 7–9 anticipated on the synthesis in the current division. As much as in those amplifications, the current ones refer to an average of the hitherto 'strong' capitalist countries as empirically exemplified in the average of the current OECD-21 countries (see Appendix 6A, section 6A-1).

The overview will – to the extent that empirical statistics are available – follow the order of the eight regulative frameworks presented in Chapters 6–7 and 9. The Hard Core frameworks (Chapter 6) have a special status regarding their necessary intensity. The other frameworks are necessary, whereas their regulative intensity and the degree of expenditure may vary over time. In fact, however, to a large extent these seem to have a ratchet character: substantial expenditure decreases are rare.[47] Capitalism is a dynamic system that may generate

47 Infrastructure is an exception (with a decrease in % of GDP from 3.2% in 1970 to 1.9% in 2015). See 10§11.

outcomes threatening its continued existence, thence requiring new necessary action of the state.

For all of the categories that were presented in the eight regulative frameworks of Chapters 6–7 and 9, empirical statistics are available from 1995. In this division, however, state expenditure is put in the long-term perspective of 1870–2015, for which the detailed data are most often lacking. This implies a reliance on compromises and sometimes rough estimates. These are set out in Appendix 10.A, under 10§8, see especially Table 10.13.

10§9 *The necessary state expenditure on the Hard Core and Inspectorates, and the contingent military and interest expenditure*

The term Hard Core was explained in 10§8. 'Inspectorates' regard those of production (working conditions and the minimum wage), of products, and of the environment.

The military expenditure and interest expenditure of the state are taken as contingent.

10§9-a Amplification. State expenditure on the Hard Core, Inspectorates, and the contingent military and interest expenditure of the OECD-21, 1870–2015

As explained in Appendix 10.A under 10§9-a, for throughout the 1870–2015 period I pragmatically adopt constant expenditure figures for the Hard Core and Inspectorates (3.3% and 0.1% of GDP, as an estimate derived from actual 1995–2015 data). This means that these expenditures absolutely increase (or decrease) with GDP.

Graph 10.9 is the first one of a series of four graphs on the OECD-21 state expenditure in the period 1870–2015. This is an introductory graph, which is not interesting in terms of the constant reference figures for the Hard Core and the Inspectorates (3.3% and 0.1%). The main point of this graph is the incorporation of the two contingent expenditures referred to: military and interest expenditures. It can be seen that these two contribute considerably to the relative decline (in percentage of GDP) of total state expenditure between 1990 and 2000. (A separate graph for military expenditure is included in Appendix 10.A under 10§9. Military expenditure already steadily declines after 1960; sufficient data for 1950 are lacking. The same location provides a separate graph for (the rather volatile) interest expenditure.)

GRAPH 10.9 *Total state expenditure (general government) and expenditure on the Hard Core, as well as on contingent military and interest expenditure, 1870–2015, in % of GDP; averages of up to 21 current OECD countries*†

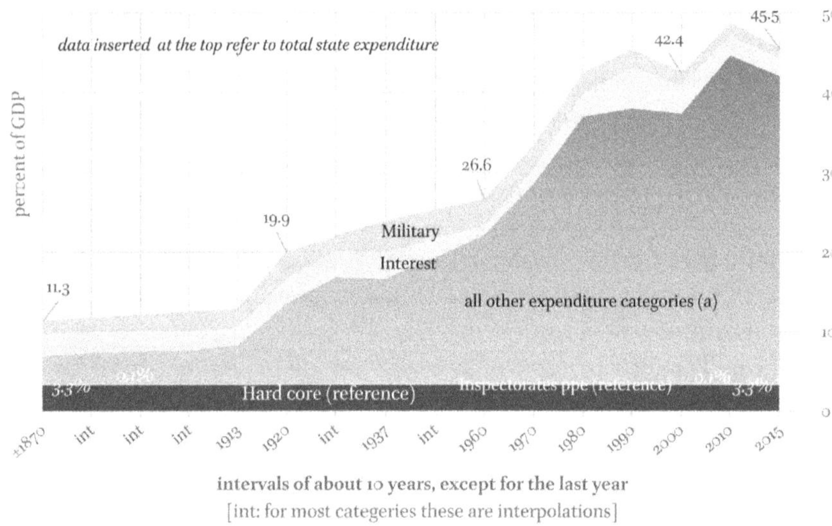

† Inspectorates ppe = Inspectorates of production, of products, and of the environment.
DATA SOURCES: For total expenditure, see Graph 8.2. For military expenditure: 1870–1980 (mainly Sabaté 2013); 1990–2015 (World Bank database, details are in Appendix 10.A under 10§9). For interest expenditure: 1870–1937 (Tanzi and Schuknecht 2000); 1960–current (OECD Economic Outlook database, details are in Appendix 10.A under 10§9)

10§10 *Expenditure on the monetary and labour-capacity frameworks*

The primary conditions furthering the accumulation of capital regard the monetary framework (7D2) and the labour-capacity framework (7D3). Net state expenditure on the monetary framework (supervision of banks and other financial institutions) can be neglected. The main part is carried out by the central bank, which on average makes profits that are distributed as dividends to the state.[48]

The main expenditure on labour-capacity regards public education.

10§10-a Amplification. The labour-capacity expenditure of the OECD-21

The expenditure on this category will be shown later on in *Graph 10.10*. Regarding the labour-capacity framework, the expenditures associated with temporary unemployment and labour population growth (child benefits), will

48 This distribution may not be the case in all countries.

pragmatically be subsumed under the social security transfers. Equally for pragmatic reasons, the expenditure on minimum wage 'inspectorates' (and commissions) has been subsumed under Inspectorates (see Appendix 10.A, Table 10.13).

This leaves the substantial state expenditure on public education and its increase from 1870 to 2015 (see also Graph 7.6). Its content and the degree of expenditure may generally change along with technical change. As shown in Graph 7.5, the average of the total years of education increased between 1870 and 2010 from 3.5 to 12 years.

10§11 *Expenditure on the infrastructural framework*

As with education, state expenditure on infrastructure may generally change along with technical change (cf. 7D4). Think of the introduction of new energy carriers (e.g. electricity), transport (e.g. rail) or communications (telephone, ICT), which require new networks. (These and other technical changes also require extensions and changes of public education for at least the middle and higher levels.) Regarding state expenditure proper, it should be noted that quite some infrastructural provisions may be carried out by state-owned enterprises or by (for that purpose regulated) private enterprises – perhaps via concessions or licenses. In such cases these provisions are not shown in the figures as state expenditures but rather, conversely, as state revenues (dividends, royalties).

10§11-a Infrastructural expenditure of the OECD-21

The last remark in 10§11 is relevant for the interpretation of the relative decline of infrastructural expenditure after 1970. State expenditure on infrastructure is approximated by a factor 0.575 of state gross investment (Graph 7.5 in 7§15 and Graph 7.5-a in Appendix 7.A).

Graph 10.10 shows the state expenditure on education and infrastructure in the total expenditure context.

As measured in percentage of GDP, expenditure on education rose continuously from 0.6% in 1870 to 4.8% in 1980, and after that year somewhat fluctuated, though with still an upward trend (5.7% in 2014). The expenditure on infrastructure moved from 1.2% in 1870 to a top of 3.2% in 1970 and then gradually decreased to a level of 1.9% in 2015.

Regarding the labour productivity increases that can be reached for the production of these two categories *themselves* (that is, apart from their labour productivity effect for other sectors), it is noted that these are quite different (see Amplification 10§11-b on 'Baumol's cost disease').

GRAPH 10.10 *Total state expenditure (general government) and the expenditure on education and infrastructure, 1870–2015, in % of GDP; averages of up to 21 current OECD countries*

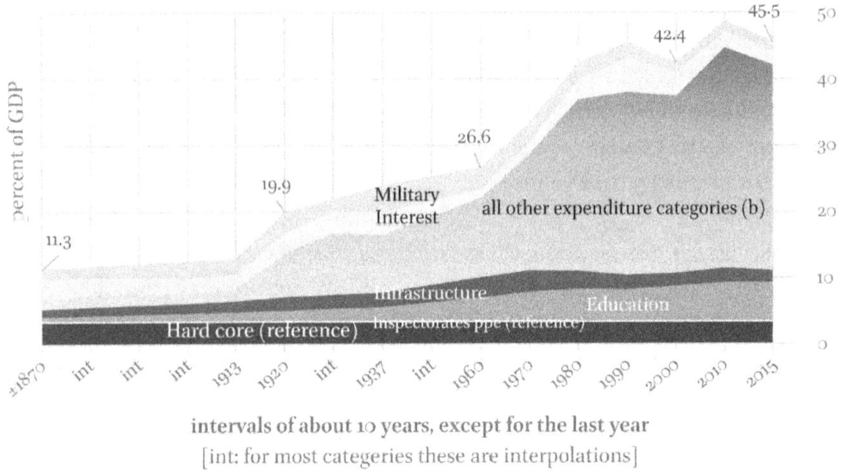

Education 1920 is interpolated and 2015=2014
DATA SOURCES: for education see Graph 7.6; for infrastructure see Graphs 7.7 and 7.7a; for the other categories see Graph 10.9

10§11-b Amplification. Diverging labour productivity changes: 'Baumol's cost disease'

Labour productivity increases that can be reached for the production of infrastructure and for education are quite different. Think of road construction and of a class in economics now and 100 years ago (for the latter the main difference is the use of PowerPoint instead of chalk and a blackboard). Baumol's theorem of 'cost disease' refers to the phenomenon of structurally enduring productivity differences between particular economic sectors. The theorem originated with a paper by Baumol and Bowen (1965), which illustrated differences in labour productivity change with the example of a symphony orchestra whose productivity for performances today is pretty much the same today as in 1870. In various different degrees, similar labour productivity obstacles apply for many state expenditure categories, such as the Hard Core processes, Inspectorates, Education and the care part of the Health sector.

10§12 *Expenditure on social security as connected with the development of the accumulation of capital*

- *Social security transfers*

In the terminology of the current division, the legitimation for the state's 'hard core' may require 'the price' of considerable generalised social security transfers (henceforth SST). The expenditure categories presented so far in this division are in a way straightforward: the bare accumulation of capital requires these. The SST are necessary to the extent that the legitimation of the state requires these, and so have 'become necessary' for the existence of the state and hence the capitalist system.[49]

- *Three discourses of the appreciation of SST*

In the appreciation of the development of the SST there are three discourses. The first one applauds SST from a moral or ethical perspective (assistance to the poor, although generalised SST goes beyond that). The second one complains about the SST's lack of 'market conformity' or 'economic efficiency' (much of the instrumentalist public choice approaches). The third discourse conceives of SST as the failure of a production and market system that is incapable of providing a major part of the population with the opportunities to make a decent and equitable living of their own, including provisions for their old age.

In the state's *argumentation* for a particular degree of SST being in the putative 'general interest' (6§6), it has to take account of each of these discourses. Regarding the reproduction of the capitalist system, however, it is in the end not these discourses that count, but rather the compliance of the vast majority.[50]

The current level of SST is one thing, another is its future level. Each time in the history of full-fledged capitalism it was considered that 'today' we have reached a level of SST that for the future sufficiently safeguards this component of the state's (hence the capitalist system's) legitimation. In hindsight erroneously so. In 1960, 1980 or 2000 there was such a 'today'. Even if erroneous in hindsight, nevertheless SST as a percent of GDP cannot feasibly increase forever. (The end point would be reached when 50% of the aggregate dis-

49 See also the General methodological Appendix, A§13, point 5, on the notion of 'becoming necessary'.

50 I am not arguing that SST is the only component of the state's legitimation. However, it is a predominant one within the complex of legitimation determinants. After 6D3 (when introducing the state's legitimation requirement in general terms in 6§4 and 6§5) I explicitly referred to legitimation in the context of: (1) the introduction of the state's furthering of the conditions for the accumulation of capital and economic growth (7§3 of 7D1); (2) the social security framework (7D5); (3) various institutional assignations and delegations (7D6–7D7); (4) the forms and designs of taxation (8§11 of 8D5); and (5) the framework of competition (9D1–9D2).

posable income of households consists of transferred income. Depending on the exact distribution of this 50%, this would mean that the skewedness in the distribution of disposable income would fade. I mention this only as a brief 'thought experiment' that has little to do with the exposition of the *actual* capitalist system.)

- *Accumulation of capital and the trend in SST*

The state's hard core legislation allows enterprises and their owners to monopolise the property of the earth and other means of production, and to appropriate the surplus-value produced by labour (6D2). One main result is a skewed distribution of income – and, derived from it, of wealth (8D5) – which is extenuated by SST. Along with it, SST is a dominant component of the vast-majority-compliance that the state's existence requires for its legitimation.

In re-distributional terms 'generalised SST' – rather than 'mere' assistance to the poor – tends to positively affect roughly the bottom 50% of the income distribution (Table 8.17).[51]

Trends in the distribution of income and in SST do not stand on their own. Widespread information (knowledge and its communication) about the distribution of income is a key catalyst for SST. This information correlates, on the one hand, with public education – especially also its distribution (cf. Graph 7.5) – and, on the other, with means of communication. These two, again, correlate with the development of the macroeconomic accumulation of capital. Thus, in brief, the capital accumulation requirements of increasing public education and of the communication parts of infrastructure (7§14; 7§15; 10§10; 10§11) engender SST. Thus, even briefer, the state of the accumulation of capital determines the state of SST. This is a major destiny of the capitalist system.

Increasing SST as a percentage of GDP is thus generally driven by the articulation of two factors: on the one hand, the state's vast-majority-legitimation requirement, and, on the other, the degree of widespread information as associated with the accumulation of capital. It is the thus determined information that catalyses the necessity for the state to raise the SST.

Given that SST tends to positively affect roughly the bottom 50% of the income distribution, a raising SST thus primarily contributes to the compliance of the bottom. However, the question is where the burden for the increasing SST is going to fall. (Effectively this question is less urgent to the extent that the average per capita growth rate structurally booms. The deciles mean-income lays

51 I derive this from data about recent years for OECD countries. Perhaps this borderline has gradually moved from a lower one to the current one. For many non-OECD countries the borderline might perhaps (still) lay at 20% to 40%. For countries with (yet) non-generalised SST, assistance to the poor may regard the bottom 20%.

well above the median income.)[52] If the burden of the increasing SST initially is going to fall on the upper-middle classes (income deciles D6–D9), the state risks a fading legitimation in this echelon.[53] If it is going to fall on the upper class (D10), members of this class may wonder about the further rationale of the capitalist system for them.

There seems to be no obvious way to evade this dilemma.

10§12-a Amplification. Social security expenditure of the OECD-21, 1870–2015

Graph 10.11 shows the OECD-21 state expenditure on SST in the context of total state expenditure from 1870–2015.[54] As for similar graphs before, this graph shows a per decade summary of the manifestation of the reach of the state in terms of its expenditure.

GRAPH 10.11 *Total state expenditure (general government) and state expenditure on social security, 1870–2015, in % of GDP; averages of up to 21 current OECD countries*†

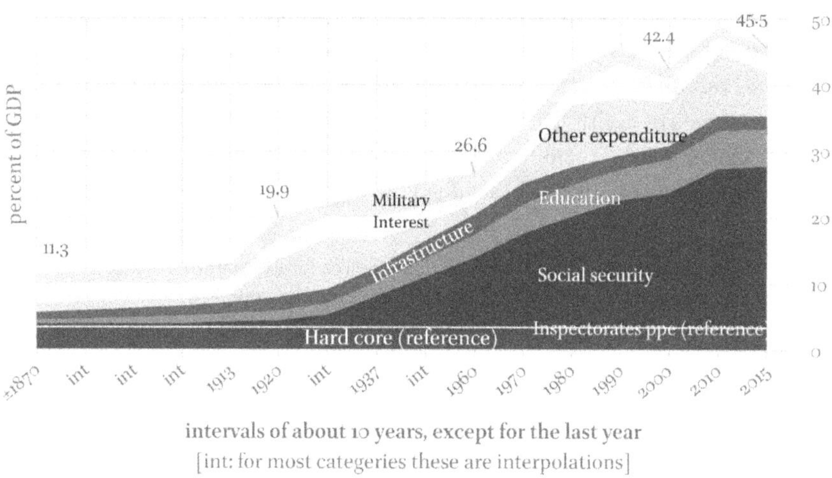

† Social security 1870=1880. SST interpolations are for 1937 and 1950 only
DATA SOURCES: for social security see Graph 7.10; for the other categories see Graph 10.10

52 For OECD-21countries it lays in 2015 around decile 7.

53 See the one but last footnote. At a lower borderline of generalised SST, this may stretch to, for example, D4–D9

54 Including temporary unemployment benefits and child benefits – see Appendix 10.A under 10§12 for details.

Graph 10.11 shows that in 1920 the average of the SST amounted to 1% of GDP, increasing to 24% in 2015. Total state expenditures in this period increased from 20% to 45% of GDP. (See also Graph 7.10, which is somewhat more detailed.) From 1930–90 we see a rather continuous and stable upward trend in SST. After 1990 the increase bends off, but at least until 2015 it kept increasing (very moderately after 2010).[55]

10§13 *'Other state expenditure': contingent expenditure and required expenditure on especially 'too big to fail' banks*

Under 'other state expenditure' I classify the so far (10§9–10§12) not mentioned state expenditures. I subsume these under the following two categories.

- *Subsidies and other direct assistance for enterprises*

Most of these can be considered as contingent. However, the direct assistance also includes assistance related to 'too big to fail banks' which, as an expenditure, is definitely necessary given the phenomenon (cf. 9§6).

- *General amenities*

This is a rather heterogeneous category, which includes mainly expenditure on culture, religion, community, recreation, foreign aid, and research and development of a general character. Much of the last one is necessary (7§16). For the others I refrain from scrutinising their (non-)contingent character, also because their degrees of contingency may evolve over time. (Expenditure on religion, for example, may at certain times and in certain places serve an indispensable function, which at other times fades.)

---

55 Although there are quantitative level differences for different OECD-21 countries, these have, with some fluctuation, all moved in the same direction.

SST of current OECD-21 countries as % of GDP, 1880–2015: SST range

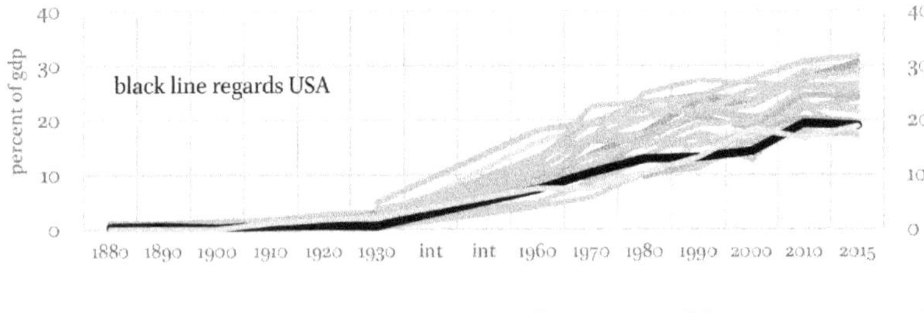

Take the example of the USA. In 1920 its SST was a fraction 0.81 of the OECD-21 average. In 1980 the fraction was 0.77 and in 2015 it was 0.78, which is a rather stable deviation from the average. Thus its SST moved at about the same pace as the OECD-21 average. Including the USA there was a stable increase in nine countries. In eight countries there were slight fluctuations, and in the remaining four there were some heavy fluctuations (Ireland, the Netherlands, New Zealand and Norway).

10§13-a Amplification. Contingent and required 'other expenditure' in the OECD-21, 1995–2015

Graph 10.12 provides the movement of the two main categories of 'other expenditure' mentioned in 10§13.[56] (Graph 10.12-b, in Appendix 10.A, under 10§13, is a more detailed one; Graph 10.12-a provides a subdivision for the 'subsidies and other direct assistance for enterprises'.) Internationally more or less homogeneous data for these expenditures are only available for the years 1995–2015. Their total stood at a relative low around 1960 (in fact 1.6% of GDP – not much above the 1870–1913 levels). In 2015 it had increased to 6.8% of GDP, though with fluctuations in between.

It appears that most of the *fluctuation* in total state expenditure from 1990–2015 can be traced to the 'other direct assistance for enterprises' and to interest expenditure.

GRAPH 10.12 *Total state expenditure (general government) and state expenditure on 'general amenities' and on 'subsidies and other direct assistance for enterprises', 1870–2015, in % of GDP; averages of up to 21 current OECD countries*

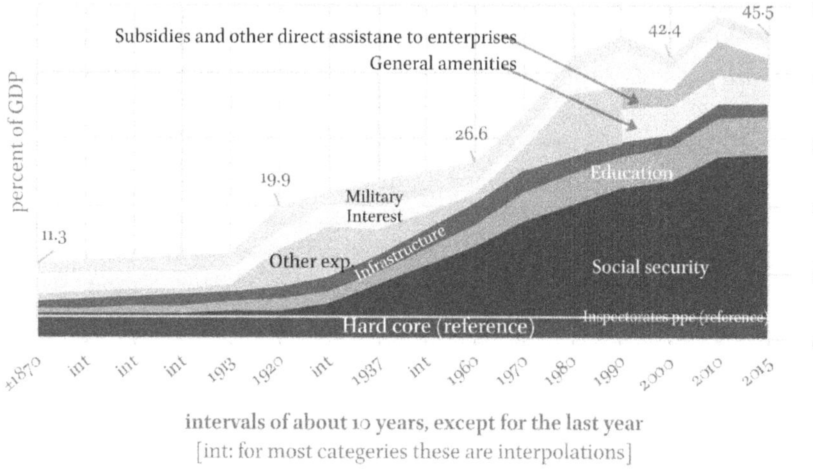

DATA SOURCES: for General amenities and Subsidies and other direct assistance for enterprises: OECD COFOG data (for these two subcategories 1990=1995) – see Appendix 10.A under 10§13 for further details. For the other categories see Graph 10.11

56 The two result from a regrouping the OECD's COFOG categories – for details about this see Appendix 10.A under 10§13.

Division 4. The vulnerabilities of the capitalist state's reach

This is a brief single section division that builds on the threads of the exposition in the previous two divisions. Whereas Chapters 6–8 successively presented the conditions of existence of the state vis-à-vis the capitalist economy, this final division detects the flaws, the loose ends in these conditions of existence. In other words, it detects the potential impediments to the continued reproduction of the capitalist system.

10§14 *Vulnerabilities and impossible necessities*

- ***The vulnerability of increasing complexity of regulation***

As indicated in Division 2, the capitalist system has been and is being sustained not just by regulation, but rather by a continuously increasing amount of complicated as well as complex regulation. There is no evidence that this trend could be countered. This means that each year a 'free market economy' will become further removed from the economics textbook phantom ('phantom' because it never existed anyway).[57]

- ***'Too big to fail': the vulnerability of the banking constellation – countered by capping the accumulation of single capitals?***

The last section of Division 3 coloured a main part of the state's 'other expenditure' with the somewhat anonymous 'other assistance to enterprises'. Behind it lurks, what will be for the future, rather unpredictable state expenditure on 'too big to fail' banks (7§9 and 9§6). Within the history of capitalism this is a new phenomenon, one unprecedented in the proportions of its system-wide consequences. It might seem that the solution – a cap on the size of banks – is rather obvious. However, capping capitalist success – success that, by all prevailing standards, is not illegal – would seem to be alien to the capitalist logic and to the capitalist state's hard core. (Moreover, concretising such a cap in watertight legislation will be complicated.) Regarding banks, the solution – for the time being – is that of tighter, discriminating regulation of the too big to fail banks (those that pose a 'systemic risk') as opposed to the regulation of the not so big banks (see 9§6). In fact this is a (yet moderate) indirect regulative movement towards putting a cap on the size of big banks.[58]

---

57 Recall from 10§5-a that, counting merely the size (numbers of pages), the number of pages of the USA Code of federal regulations stood at 22,877 in 1960 and 178,277 in 2015. Their average rate of growth was 4.9% per year, which was 1.5 times faster than the annual GDP growth. Recall that at the same rate of growth, the number of pages of regulation will have increased to one million in 2050.

58 Although this is what it does, a moderate indirect cap (as in Basel Committee on Banking

- ***Over-accumulation of capital: the unresolved environment restoration***

Protection of the environment (including the climate) is a systematically high-level requirement, albeit an apparently 'elastic' one (6§14). Whereas this is a continuous and structural requirement, its aberrations are cyclically highlighted. Chapter 5 showed the manifestation of the capitalist economy in the cyclical accumulation, over-accumulation and destruction of capital. I focus on this because it is key to the dynamic of the capitalist system: its way to get out of the inevitable economic crises of capitalism. Along with it we have a recurrent destruction of the earth's resources. We also see the despair of recurrent super-unemployment, which, in terms of family lives, extends further than losing income. State expenditure, as we have seen in 10D1, does not annihilate this process, but rather mitigates it, which is a blessing in disguise.

Given the social security transfers (yet especially in the capitalistically developed countries), it would seem that the capitalist system generates a mode of coping with the unemployment side of the cyclical over-accumulation of capital. It has not done similar for its environmental side (at least at the time of writing). However, when a sustainable environment withers away, it is not just that capitalism will also come to an end; so too will humankind.

This is the 'tragedy' of the private property of the earth associated with the structural accumulation and the cyclical over-accumulation of capital. Nevertheless the capitalist system could in principle cope with it at the 'price' of a further increase in the size of complicated and complexity-raising regulation – an unprecedented further increase in such regulation. By now all the even slightly enlightened top management of enterprises knows that the earth is vulnerable. Nevertheless, the motivational structure of profit-seeking, engrained within the capitalist system, leads actors to test and retest the loopholes of the law, seeking what they regard as a better way for enterprises to share the burdens of the tragedy (10§7 of 10D1).[59]

- ***Vast majority legitimation: the vulnerability of increasing social security transfers***

We have seen in 10D3 (10§12) that widespread information (knowledge and its communication) about the distribution of income is a key catalyst for SST.

Supervision, 2014) may not do away with too big to fail banks. It may take another banking crisis before the indirect cap becomes sufficiently tight so as to force the too big banks to partition into smaller entities in face of their rate of profit.

59 It is one thing to make a target agreement (as in the 2015 Paris Agreement on climate change); it is another to carry it out in practice. (A major drawback of the 2015 Paris Agreement is that it includes no instruments through which to enforce the reaching of its targets.)

Increasing SST as a percentage of GDP is driven by a complex of, on the one hand, the state's requirement of a vast-majority-legitimation, and, on the other, the degree of widespread information as associated with the development of the accumulation of capital. The state expenditure on public education that is necessary for the accumulation of capital forms a core element within this complex.

Whereas the thus catalysed increasing SST as a percentage of GDP is necessary for the vast-majority-legitimation of the state (this regards the large bottom of the income distribution), the bearing of its burden (by the large upper part of the distribution) implies that the increases' fading off is equally necessary for the state's vast-majority-legitimation.

- ***Impossible necessities***

Parts One and Two of this book set out an exposition of the conditions of existence of capitalism's 'dissociated outward bifurcation into households and privately owned enterprises'. Throughout this book, so far, I have avoided using the term 'contradiction' (see the last addendum of 1D1). In the current context a contradiction is a constellation that is at the same time necessary and impossible. For two of the four vulnerabilities of the state's reach, presented above, capitalism is moving toward such impossibilities that stand on their own: the increasing size and complexity of regulation and the increasing social security transfers. The other two major vulnerabilities might *perhaps* reduce to a further increasing size and complexity of regulation – especially for the climate and natural resources that would be better for the future of humanity.

10§14-a Explication. Further on the main vulnerabilities

I have not argued that capitalism is at, or near to, the point of collapse. I argue that even if the vulnerabilities of the environment and of too big to fail entities could be mitigated or perhaps resolved, the capitalist system that existed from 1870 to the present is *moving* toward being an impossible constellation.

This is based on the state's legitimation requirement (and because capitalism cannot exist without the capitalist state, this is a system requirement). I have also not posited that a representative democracy is necessary for capitalism (alas). However, I posited that the legitimation of the capitalist state in the vast majority of the population is necessary (7§23). *Ultimately* this requirement is connected with the material limits of the state's legalised violence on a large scale (6§18). (However, I have not argued that such large-scale violence cannot exist for a 'relatively' short period – of perhaps one or even two decades – as history has shown.)

Summary and conclusions

This chapter set out three key manifestations of the state, which together determine its reach.

The first of these manifestations applies to the cyclical movement of capital accumulation (which so is the sequel of Chapter 5). State expenditure mitigates the amplitude of 'regular' economic cycles. The degree of this automatic stabilising effect depends on the structural size of state expenditure in comparison with private expenditure. This is different for the 'irregular' economic downturns triggered by financial crises and bank failures. Then the mere state expenditure floor may not be a sufficient base for getting to a recovery via 'normal' restructuring destruction of capital. Reproduction of the capitalist system then requires substantial discretionary state policy. (Division 1.)

The second manifestation regards the character of the state's regulation of the capitalist economy. The mere quantity of regulation in force increases over time, as driven by new, or re-perceived, social-economic problems. For one part these stem from legitimation problems. For another part these stem from changes in the economic structure and product and process innovations, including process fusions. These affect the 'coverage' and the 'intensity' of regulation, and so the density and quantity of regulation. The more convoluted the social-economic problems, the more complicated regulations tend to be. This results, together with the interweaving of regulations, in an increasing complexity of regulation.

However, changes of regulation are also prominently determined by 'unintended' loopholes in regulation, that is, gaps and ambiguities – as tested by way of profit-driven borderline (non-)compliance. The legislative and other regulative reparation of these loopholes by amendments of the regulation increases the complication of single regulations, and in connection with the interweaving of regulations, multiplies into further complexity of regulation. This results in inevitable continuous cycles of finding loopholes, making amendments, and further complication and complexity. (Division 2.)

The third manifestation regards the expenditure of the state. For many people the hard core of the capitalist state – in brief the property and exploitation rights that it grants and the legislation related to this – is not part of their conscious experience. The majority of employed actors experience the state primarily indirectly via their everyday workplace, whence the state's hard core operates as a 'hidden hand'. For most people the state's reach is instead directly manifested in the materialisation of its expenditure, especially in the supervision of the safety of production and products, in public education, in infrastructure, and in social security provisions, including health provisions.

Among the main expenditure categories of the state, spending on social security transfers (SST) is the quantitatively dominant category and it tends to increase over time. SST is a major factor through which the state gains the vast-majority-legitimation that it requires (that is, legitimation for ultimately the hard core property and exploitation rights that the state grants). However, trends in the SST do not stand independently. Widespread information (knowledge and its communication) about the distribution of income is a key catalyst for SST. This information correlates, on the one hand, with public education and, on the other, with means of communication. These two, again, correlate with the development of the macroeconomic accumulation of capital. Thus the capital accumulation requirements of increasing public education and of the communication parts of infrastructure engender SST.

Whereas the thus catalysed increasing SST as a percentage of GDP is necessary for the vast-majority-legitimation of the state (this regards the large bottom of the income distribution), the bearing of its burden (by the large upper part of the distribution) implies that the increases' fading off is equally necessary for the state's vast-majority-legitimation. (Division 3.)

The final Division 4 draws together some threads of Divisions 2 and 3 under the title of 'the vulnerabilities of the capitalist state's reach'. This division sets out the four main vulnerabilities of the reach of the capitalist state and that, as such, comprise potential impediments to the continued reproduction of the capitalist system. The *first* one is the inevitably increasing amount and complexity of regulation. Thus the so-called 'free market economy' will become unlimitedly further constrained by the steering of the capitalist state. The *second* vulnerability regards the 'too big to fail' entities – especially banks. This vulnerability can perhaps be resolved by rounds of complex regulation, but for the time being this is insecure. The *third* vulnerability relates to the deterioration of the environment. This is in fact the most far-reaching one. But perhaps a recuperation is possible by, again, rounds of complex regulation – rounds that will have to be far more stringent than the regulation in prospect (at the time of writing). The *fourth* vulnerability regards the required state expenditure on social security transfers. Whereas increasing transfers as a percentage of GDP are necessary for the vast-majority-legitimation of the state, the increases' fading off is equally necessary for the state's vast-majority-legitimation.

For the continued reproduction of the capitalist system, the state inevitably has to deal with these vulnerabilities. The second and third vulnerabilities are 'imaginably' resolvable. However, for the first and last ones, the capitalist system is moving toward a constellation of, what I called, 'necessities that are impossible'.

Appendix 10.A. Data and data sources of the graphs in chapter 10

General note: For all years (1870 to 2015) I have used the maximum amount of information that my sources provide for the OECD-21 countries.

Re 10D3 ***Limitations of empirical-statistical expenditure categories, and how these have been accounted for***

For all of the categories that were presented in the eight regulative frameworks of Chapters 6–7 and 9, empirical statistics are available from 1995. In 10D3, however, state expenditure is put in the long-term perspective of 1870–2015, for which the detailed data are most often lacking. This implies a reliance on compromises and sometimes rough estimates. The rough estimates regard especially the Chapter 1 categories. One minor compromise pertains to the labour capacity and social security frameworks. *Table 10.13* summarises how the lack of data for pre-1995 has been accounted for.

TABLE 10.13 *The regulative frameworks and empirical-statistical expenditure categories for Division 3*

Regulative frameworks	Chs. 6–7, 9	10D3		Remarks
Capitalist state's hard core (HC)	6D2		HARD CORE OF THE STATE	
1. Capitalist economic legal rights	6D4	10§9		
2. Legal existence rights (allowance)	6D5	10§9		Divided as: • public security† • inspectorates††
3. Public security	6D6	10§9		
+ executive (all frameworks)	6D3	10§9		‡
+ judiciary (all frameworks)	7D6	10§9		*
+ legislative (all frameworks)	7D7	10§9		*
4. Monetary	7D2	10§10		
5. Labour capacity	7D3	10§10		
• minimum wage	7§10-§11	10§10		inspectorates††
• temp. unemployment	7§12	→ 10§11		subsumed under SST
• lab. population growth	7§13	→ 10§11		subsumed under SST
• public education	7§14	10§10		
6. Infrastructure	7D4	10§11		
7. Social security transfers (SST)	7D5	10§12		

TABLE 10.13 *The regulative frameworks (cont.)*

Regulative frameworks	Chs. 6–7, 9	10D3	Remarks
8. Competition	9D1	10§13	
Regulation and regulative failures		10§13	

† Component of forbearance of direct violence regarding the person: under public security. Components of protection of the consumer (products), of the environment, and of labour during production: under 'inspectorates'.
†† One single figure for all inspectorates.
‡ In 6D3 (prior to the presentation of the legislative and the judiciary in Ch. 7) it is implicit that the state in general encompasses the state as 'executive'.
* Subsumed under hard core (for details see this Appendix 10.A, the text around Graph 10.9-a).

Re 10§9 *State expenditure on the Hard Core: general remarks*

Hard Core expenditure: granted rights to property, employment of labour and appropriation of surplus-value. For an estimate of the Hard Core expenditure 1870–2015, I make pragmatic use of the detailed data that we have for the period 1995–2015 and project these on the full period as a 'reference figure'. For the hard core expenditures (except one category amplified on below) this is 3.3% of GDP. (See below for the details.)

Hard Core expenditure: granted rights of or provisions for allowance existence. Part of this is subsumed under public security and the other part under 'inspectorates' (see Table 10.13). For pragmatic reasons I take the latter together with inspectorates on minimum wages. For these inspectors together I equally use a single reference figure throughout the 1870–2015 period, in this case of 0.1% of GDP.

[Re 10§9] *Expenditures on the hard core, inspectorates, military and interest*

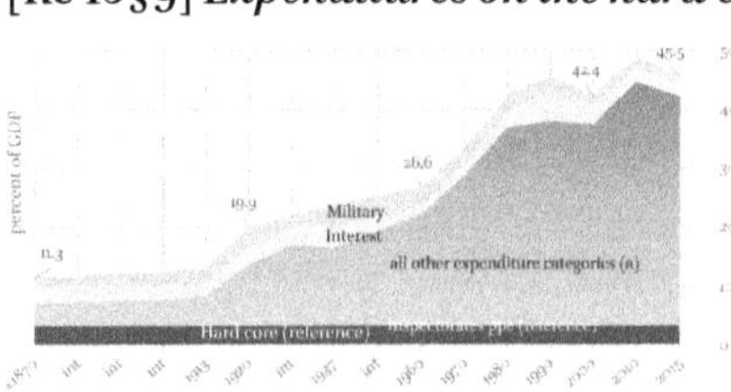

The following two graphs and the surrounding information form the basis for the bottom and top of Graph 10.9 (left).

The reference figures for the Hard Core and for Inspectorates. The reference figure for the Hard Core expenditure is a rough estimate, based on a cautious use of 1995–2015 data for legislative and administrative expenditure as well as for expenditure on public order and security.

General data information: COFOG classification. The data derive from OECD 'COFOG' data (Classification of the Functions of Government). In this classification government expenditures are categorised in ten 'functions' ('first digit'). The first digit information has been used for 'Public security expenditure'. This regards COFOG category 03 (Public order and safety). For a (further) limited number of countries a subdivision is available ('second digit'), which has been used for 'Legislative and executive expenditure'. This regards COFOG category 01.01 ('Executive and legislative organs'). See also the manual COFOG, Eurostat (2011); its Appendix (pp. 155–81) sets out the COFOG structure.

Graph 10.9-a shows for these two categories the data available. For *legislative and administrative expenditure* these regard 9–16 countries, and for public security expenditure 16–19 countries.

GRAPH 10.9-A *Hard core expenditures 1995–2015, averages of 9–19 OECD-21 countries*

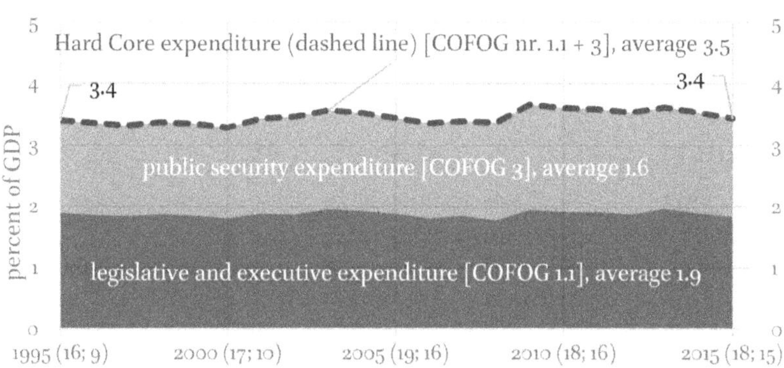

(in brackets the number of countries of the two bottom series)

DATA SOURCE: Public security (OECD dataset, National Accounts at glance – general government, expenditure by function; accessed 25 January 2018);[60] Legislative and executive (OECD dataset, National Accounts, 11. Government expenditure by function (COFOG); accessed 25 January 2018)[61]

60 http://stats.oecd.org/OECDStat_Metadata/ShowMetadata.ashx?Dataset=NAAG&ShowOnWeb=true&Lang=en.

61 http://stats.oecd.org/OECDStat_Metadata/ShowMetadata.ashx?Dataset=SNA_TABLE11&ShowOnWeb=true&Lang=en.

It can be seen from *Graph 10.9-a* that the averages of the data available are hardly fluctuating for these years (taking into account the recession years of the early 2000s and of about 2008–13). The data available (early 2018) are geographically biased to European countries (public security OECD-21 minus Canada and New Zealand, legislative and executive OECD-21 minus Australia, Canada, New Zealand, Switzerland and the USA).

As a rough estimate for the reference figure for the full 1870–2015 period I adopt a Hard Core expenditure of 3.3% of GDP. This means that I classify expenditure above 3.3% as contingent (appearing in my category 'other expenditure' – see this Appendix under 10§13).

The reference figure for inspectorates concerning production processes, products and the environment. In principle these expenditures are classified under COFOG category 4: Economic affairs. However, for this specific category there are no data available. The reference figure of 0.1% of GDP (main text) is a rough estimate based on expenditures for these inspectorates for the Netherlands around 2010. These regard mainly inspectorates for labour safety, of food and consumer safety, of environmental health, of fire prevention and protection from floods, and of construction. As indicated in the main text of 10§10, all these are mainly a matter of expenditure on civil servants' wages. (That main text also indicates why financial supervision is not included in the 0.1% number.)

The upshot is that – as with Hard Core expenditure above 3.3% – I classify expenditure above 0.1% as contingent (appearing in my category 'other expenditure' – see this Appendix under 10§13).

Re 10§9 *Graph 10.9: Military expenditure*

It can be seen from Graph 10.9-b that from 1950 the averages of the different sets of countries converge. In 2015 the military expenditure as a percentage of GDP approaches the 1870 level.

Data for 1870–1937 are mainly from Sabaté (2013), Figures 7–12. Added to these are data for various years from 1900 to 1937 from Tanzi and Schuknecht (2000, Table II.3) concerning Austria, Australia, Belgium, Ireland, Japan and New Zealand.

GRAPH 10.9-B *Military expenditure 1870–2015, average of up to 21 current OECD countries*

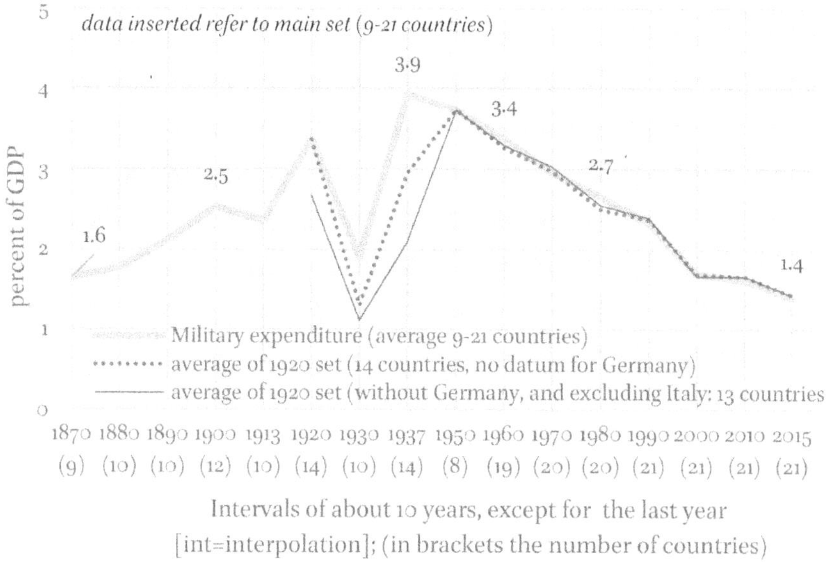

DATA SOURCES: for 1870–1937 (Sabaté 2013 with additions from Tanzi and Schuknecht 2000). For 1960–2015 (World Bank database, World Development Indicators, updated 19 January 2018, extracted 23 January 2018)

Re 10§9 *Graph 10.9: Interest expenditure*

The data from before 1970 are rather scarce. Tanzi and Schuknecht provide data for 7–8 countries for 1870 and 1913, and for 13–16 countries for 1920 and 1937. Some of these data are for central government only (the data for Australia, Canada, UK and USA are for general government).

The OECD data from 1960 are for 'gross government interest payments, value', divided by GDP (Spain 1960=1964; Switzerland 1960=1965; Denmark 1970=1971; Germany 1990=1991). To the OECD data for 1970 and 1980 I have added the data for Australia, Germany, Ireland and the Netherlands from Tanzi and Schuknecht (they provide no data for 1960).

GRAPH 10.9-C *Gross interest expenditure 1870–2015, average of up to 21 current OECD countries*

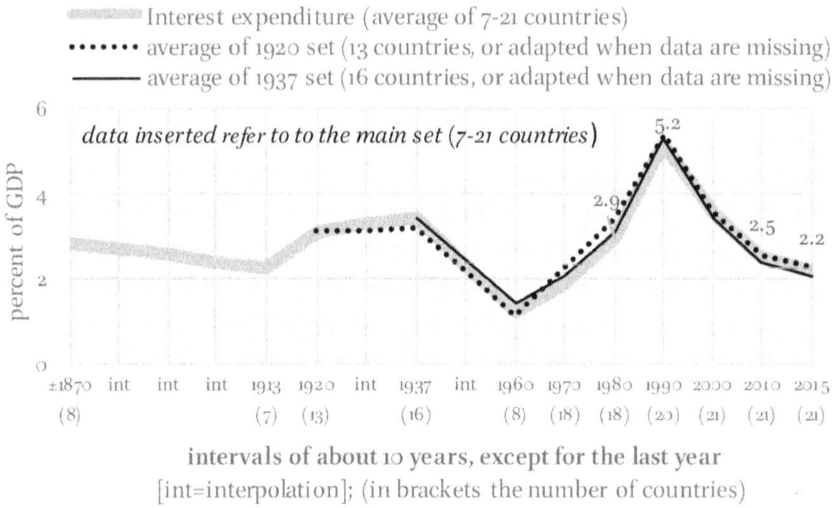

DATA SOURCES: 1870–1937 (Tanzi and Schuknecht 2000); 1960–current (OECD Economic Outlook database, November 2017, extracted 13 January 2018)

Re 10§12 ***Social security transfers 1880–2015***

The available data for this category go back to only 1880, not 1870.

Chapter 7 distinguished between the social security transfers that are necessary as regulation of labour capacity (7§12–7§13), and the 'generalised' transfers that may be necessary for the state's legitimation – and hence for the capitalist system. (See the summarising Figure 7.13.) Unfortunately the statistical data – and especially long-term historical data – are insufficiently applicable to this distinction. In 10§12, therefore, I take the 'temporary unemployment transfers' together with the other social transfers. In 2015 the major transfers regard public pensions, health (cure and care), and transfers to the working-age unemployed (broadly including disablement). However, only from about 1980 does the available statistic (internationally common based) allow for a distinction between these (see Graph 7.9). In *Graph 10.11*, therefore, I show data for the sum of the average 'OECD-defined' state expenditure on social security transfers.

[Re 10§13] *'Other expenditure' 1995–2015*

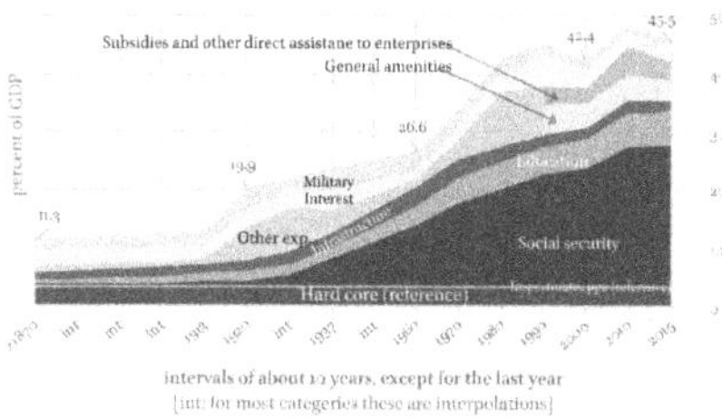

The following information regards *Graph 10.12* here reproduced in reduced form (*Total state expenditure (general government) and state expenditure on 'general amenities' and on 'subsidies and other direct assistance for enterprises', 1870–2015, in % of GDP; averages of up to 21 current OECD countries*). That graph shows, from 1990 (in fact 1995), a subdivision of the category 'other expenditure'.

OECD *total* expenditure data from 1995–2015 are available of 21 countries. OECD expenditure data at COFOG digit 1 level are available of 16–18 countries (and at digit 2 level of 9–16 countries) (COFOG: Classification of the Functions of Government).[62]

Graph 10.12-a shows the statistical difference of the total expenditure of the 21 and the 16–18 countries (top of graph). This graph also shows the average expenditure of the digit 2 level 9–16 'COFOG countries' on *General amenities* and on *Subsidies and other direct assistance for enterprises.*

It can be seen that at the COFOG first digit level, the statistical difference with the total non-COFOG data for 21 countries is for some years rather large. This may also apply for the second digit level (bottom categories). In *Graph 10.12* of the main text I therefore applied from 1990 the *proportions* of the two specifications (shown at the bottom of 10.23-a) to the category of 'other expenditures' of the dataset of 21 countries.[63] See rubric D of *Table 10.14*.

- *The category of 'direct subsidies' within the category of 'subsidies and other direct assistance for enterprises'.* Subsidies to enterprises, and especially in international comparison, are (perhaps surprisingly) a rather unexplored terrain.[64] Internationally comparable data can be traced back to 1960, as shown in *Graph 10.12-b*. Subsidies are defined as transfers to enterprises, including public corporations, and are exclusive of loans and loan guarantees.

---

62 This applies for when I consulted this database in January 2018. The countries for which COFOG data are available at the first digit level are the OECD-21 minus Canada and New Zealand. On top of these, second digit level data are also lacking for Australia, Switzerland and the USA.

63 This includes COFOG category 06, housing and community amenities.

64 In a 2010 OECD paper, Spector writes that the delineations of state aid are 'based on heterogeneous definitions', and that 'the most comprehensive data about state aids are those covering the European Union' and that 'data about non-EU countries are less available and usually lack homogeneity' (Spector 2010, pp. 18–19).

GRAPH 10.12-A *Expenditure on general amenities and on subsidies and other direct assistance for enterprises* (COFOG *data*) *and statistical difference between the* COFOG *and total dataset, 1995–2015, various* OECD-*21 averages*

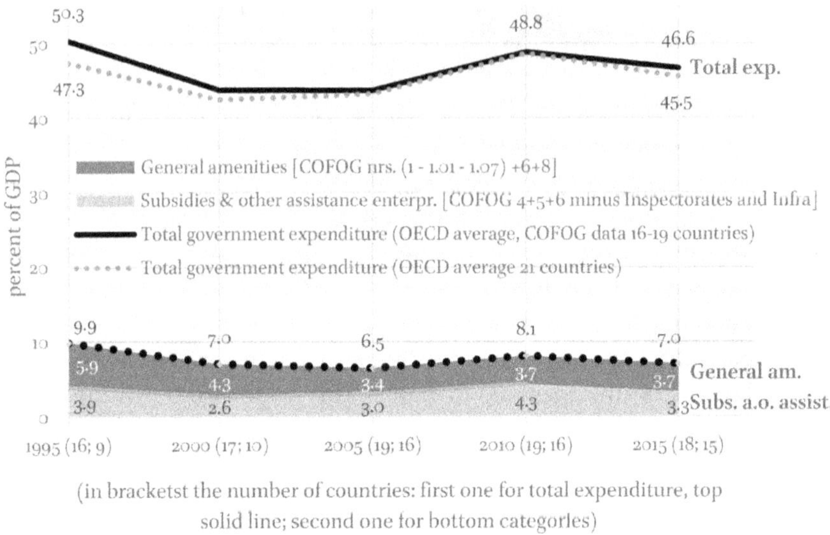

DATA SOURCES: (1) Total expenditure 21 countries, see Graph 8.2; (2) Total expenditure, COFOG data, OECD dataset National accounts at glance – general government, expenditure by function (accessed 25 January 2018);[65] (3) Bottom categories, OECD dataset National Accounts, 11. Government expenditure by function (COFOG) (accessed 25 January 2018)[66] – see Table 10.6 for further specification of my categorisation of the data

Quantitatively this category is not a minor one. At the beginning of the twenty-first century this was more important, in terms of its size, an expenditure category than infrastructure (average OECD-21). It can be seen from *Graph 10.12-b* that in 2010 the average direct expenditure on subsidies was back to the 1960 level in percentage of GDP. It is very difficult to judge to what extent their downturn after 1981 has been substituted indirectly by tax subsidies (tax deductions).[67] In international comparison these tax subsidies (for example, R&D related ones) are an even more unexplored terrain.

65 http://stats.oecd.org/OECDStat_Metadata/ShowMetadata.ashx?Dataset=NAAG&ShowOnWeb=true&Lang=en.

66 http://stats.oecd.org/OECDStat_Metadata/ShowMetadata.ashx?Dataset=SNA_TABLE11&ShowOnWeb=true&Lang=en.

67 From my practice as a senator in the parliament of the Netherlands (2007–15) I know that such deals are made with enterprises' organisations.

GRAPH 10.12-B *State expenditure (general government) on explicit direct subsidies for enterprises, 1960–2010, in % of GDP; average of up to 20 OECD-21 countries*†

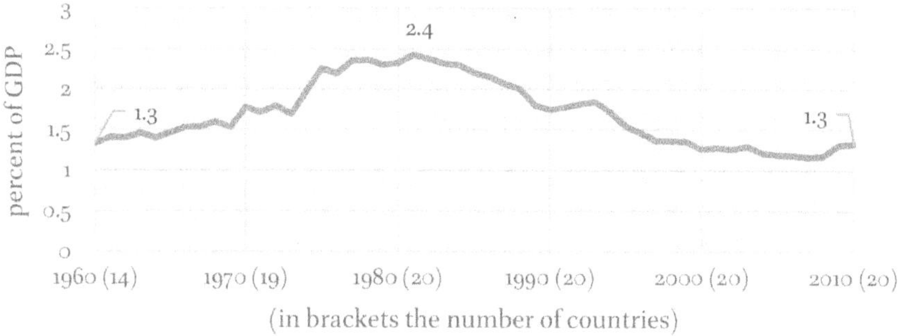

† OECD-21 minus Switzerland. Data source: DICE Database (2013).[68] (Canada and New Zealand 1960=1961; Denmark 1970=1971)

Reconsidering the main *Graph 10.12* it can be seen that from 1960 the category of 'Other expenditure' increases considerably. From *Graph 10.12-b* it can be inferred that the 1960–81 increase in subsidies was a major component of this.

Graph 10.12-c shows for 1995–2015 the expenditure on 'subsidies and other direct assistance for enterprises' together with its share of the direct subsidies.

GRAPH 10.12-C *State expenditure (general government) on subsidies and other direct assistance for enterprises, and on competition policy, 1995–2015, in % of GDP; average of 16–19 OECD-21 countries*

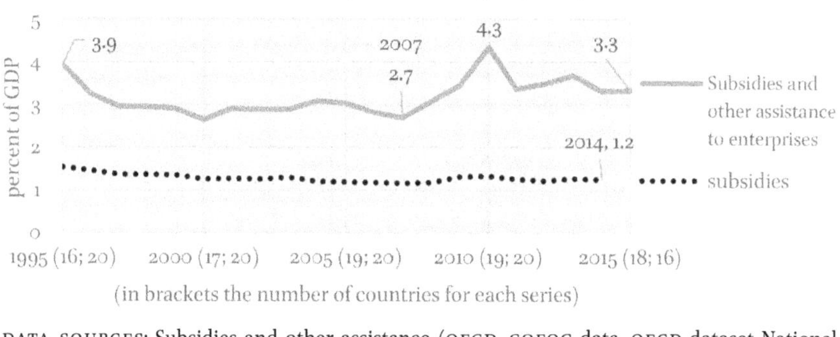

DATA SOURCES: Subsidies and other assistance (OECD, COFOG data, OECD dataset National Accounts at a glance – general government, expenditure by function, accessed 25 January 2018 – category 4, minus expenditure on Infrastructure and on Supervision (inspectorates) of production). Subsidies: see Graph 10.12-b (with projections by DICE for 2012–14)

68 General Government Outlays by Economic Category: Subsidies as a Percentage of GDP, 1960–2014, Ifo Institute, Munich, http://www.cesifo-group.de/DICE/fb/3FRjkpsh8 (accessed 27 January 2018).

'Other direct assistance' includes aid for particular sectors and especially also loans to enterprises. In the three years between 2007 and 2010 this rises by 1.6 points of GDP, which is due to assistance to the financial sector ('too big to fail') and to crisis-related assistance to other sectors.[69] (Note that this state aid far from reflects the total of the social-economic costs of the early twenty-first century financial crisis, which has been estimated at 100% of GDP and over – see Chapter 9, Appendix 9A, section 9A-3.)

Re 10D3 ***Connection between the categories adopted in 10D3 and the COFOG categories***

See *Table 10.14*. The major purpose of this table is to show how the categories adopted in 10D3 are connected to the COFOG categories (table rubrics A–C). Recall from the clarification *General data information: COFOG classification* in this Appendix under 10§9 that the first digit classification of COFOG is one in ten categories.

TABLE 10.14 *Connection between the categories adopted in 10D3 and the COFOG categories (table rubrics A–C); and the proportions of General amenities and Additional amenities for enterprises in the COFOG based 'Other Expenditures' (table rubric D)*

		2015 % GDP example	classification COFOG	Categories Ch. 10†
A	COFOG categories			
1	General public service	6.4	1	
1a	*legislative and executive*‡	*1.8*	*1.1*	
1b	*debt transactions (mainly interest)*‡	*2.3*	*1.7*	
1c	*other public services of COFOG 1 (row 1 minus 1a and 1b)*	*2.2*		
2	Defence	1.3	2	
3	Public security	1.6	3	
4	Economic affairs	4.6	4	
5	Environment protection (infrastructural)	0.7	5	
6	Housing and community amenities	0.5	6	
7	Health	7.0	7	
8	Recreation, culture, religion	1.0	8	

69 Spector indicates that EU data show 'that in spite of a strict control over state aids, their total amount, excluding measures related to the financial crisis, was still €113.4 billion in 2008, or 0.94% of EU GDP. Not taking aid to railways into account, the volume of aid has been halved between 1992 and 2008, from 1% to 0.54%. The inclusion of crisis measures

TABLE 10.14 *Connection between the categories (cont.)*

		2015 % GDP example	classification COFOG	Categories Ch. 10†
9	Education	5.2	9	
10	Social protection	18.3	10	
11	Total expenditure: OECD average, COFOG data 18 countries (2015) (row 1 to 10)	46.6	= 1 to 10	
12	Total expenditure: OECD average 21 countries (2015)	45.5		
13	Statistical difference (row 12–11)	-1.1		
B	Regrouped COFOG categories			
14	Defence (row 2)	1.3	2	Military
15	Debt transactions (mainly interest) (row 1b)	2.3	1.7	Interest
16	Legislative plus public security (row 1a plus 3)	3.4	1.1+3	Hard Core
17	General services, foreign aid, culture, recreation, community (row 1c plus 6 and 8)	3.7	1 – (1.1+1.7) + 6+8	General amenities
18	Infrastructure plus Inspectorates plus subsidies and other assistance to enterprises and competition policy (row 4 plus 5)	5.3	4+5	
19	Education	5.2	9	Education
20	Social security	25.3	7+10	Social security
21	Total expenditure, OECD average COFOG data (row 14 to 20)	46.6	= 1 to 10	
C	Other categories Ch. 10			
22	Inspectorates production, product and environment (reference figure)	0.1		Inspectorates
23	Infrastructure indicator (57.5% gross investment)	1.9		Infrastructure
24	Subsidies and other economic policy amenities for enterprises (row 18 minus 22 and 23)	3.3		Additional amenities for enterprises
25	sum of other categories (row 22 to 24 = row 18)	5.3		

changes the picture dramatically, since they amounted to €212.2 billion, or 1.7% of GDP.' And: 'Aid to agriculture in OECD countries alone amounted to $318 billion in 2002' (Spector 2010, pp. 18–19).

TABLE 10.14 *Connection between the categories (cont.)*

		2015 % GDP example	classification COFOG	Categories Ch. 10†
D	Estimate of General amenities and Subsidies and other economic policy amenities for the total of 20–21 countries (accounting for statistical differences)*			
26	'Other expenditures' (average of 21 countries)	6.8		
27	'Other expenditures' (COFOG average) row 17 plus 24	7.0		
28	Proportion of General amenities in Other expenditures COFOG (row 17 / row 27)	0.53		
29	Proportion of Subsidies etc. in Other expenditures COFOG (row 24 / row 27)	0.47		
30	General amenities: estimate for 21 countries (row 26 * row 28)	3.2		
31	Subsidies a.o. economic policy amenities: estimate for 21 countries (row 26 * row 29)	3.2		

† The 2015 data listed in the third column may slightly deviate from the data provided in various graphs because the former data for 2015 are the average of 19 countries and the latter of 21 countries.

‡ Data for these two COFOG level 2 categories are available for 9–10 countries for 1995–2000 and for 15–16 countries onwards.

* Note that proportions of rows 28–29 (and hence those of rows 30–31) are not constants, but different for each single year (as can be seen from the bottom figures of Graph 10.12-b).

DATA SOURCE RUBRIC A: OECD, Datasets: National Accounts at a glance, and Government expenditure by function (COFOG)[70]

List of figures chapter 10

70 http://stats.oecd.org/. Rows 1a and 1b: Dataset: 11, Government expenditure by function (COFOG), http://stats.oecd.org/index.aspx?DatasetCode=SNA_TABLE11.

10§13. 'Other state expenditure': contingent expenditure and required expenditure on especially 'too big to fail' banks

Appendix 10.A. Data and data sources of the graphs in Chapter 10

PART 3

The international capitalist system

CHAPTER 11

The international capitalist system

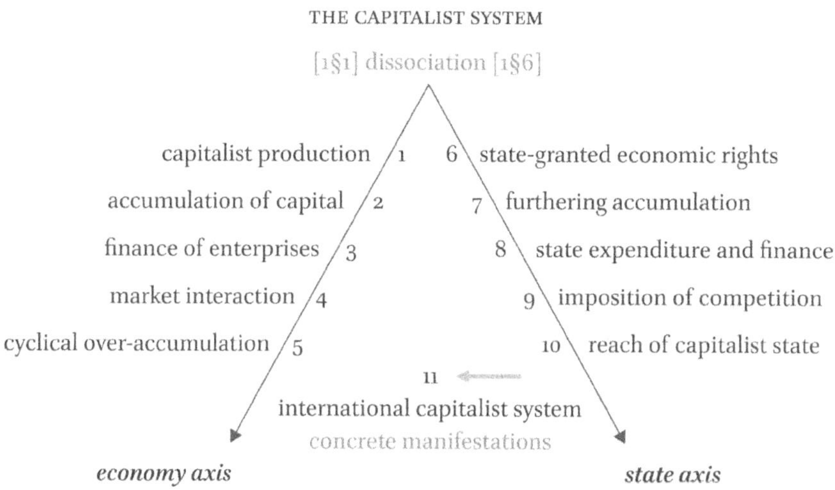

Contents

Introduction to part three and chapter 11

This Part, and chapter, presents the international mode of existence of the capitalist system. As before, this chapter keeps on abstracting from contingencies. Division 1 outlines the chapter's focus and its methodological status. Along with that mode of existence, nations are introduced: national economies and nation-states. The two substantial divisions of this chapter, in terms of content, focus on the two main forms of international economic relations: international trade (Division 2) and the international movement of capital as manifested in the international migration of production (Division 3). We will see that in the character of its effects, international trade is not fundamentally different from intra-national regional sector-wise specialisation of production. However, the consequences of the international migration of production are rather far-reaching.

All of the systematic main sections of Chapters 1–10 apply to any full-fledged capitalist nation. This also applies for the current chapter. It is merely in the non-systematic amplifications of the earlier chapters that I have referred to averages of particularly the OECD-21 between 1870 and 2015, one reason being that only for this country group are such long run data available. In the amplifications of the current chapter data on a world scale and for world country groups will be presented. Their availability is limited, in terms of both the categories that pertain to this chapter and the number of years.

Scheme 11.1 presents the outline of this chapter. The chapter can be relatively brief because it builds on all the earlier chapters in the way as set out in Division 1.

Division 1. The international mode of existence of the capitalist system

11§1 *The exposition of the international capitalist system: programmatic delineations and method*

I begin with a terminological note. As before I always use the term 'state' in reference to a 'central state'.[1] For the purposes of this chapter I define a 'nation' as the geographical territory over which a state (i.e. central state) has jurisdiction.

[*continued*]

1 Some central states result from a union or federation of (what I call) 'subordinate states' in terms of full jurisdiction.

SCHEME 11.1 *The international capitalist system (outline Chapter 11)*

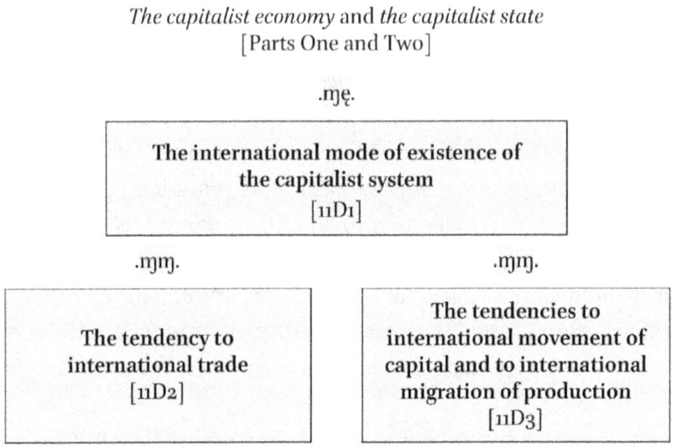

Legend
.mę. concretising mode of existence
.mm. mode of manifestation

11§1 *Continued*

Most often this coincides with a 'country', though a state may have jurisdiction over more than one country. In this chapter I will not use the latter distinction, whence the terms 'nation' and 'country' are used interchangeably.

The exposition in the main systematic sections of Parts One and Two is about each full-fledged capitalist nation. In the exposition of Part Three, nations are 'merely' different regarding:

(1) their geographical location;
(2) the historical point in time at which they became full-fledged capitalist (encompassing capitalist production and the accumulation of capital resulting from it), which implies especially also the adoption of their state's granting of the Hard Core rights and legislative framework as presented in Chapter 6;
(3) the *degree of intensity* of all the other legislative frameworks as presented in Chapters 7–9;
(4) given the population of a country, the degree of the reached accumulation of capital – that degree being co-determined by the legislative 'accumulation of capital frameworks' (7D2–7D4).

Next to these, Part Three merely makes explicit that for reasons of profit capitalist enterprises (or rather one category of capitalist enterprises) seek to expand across national borders. Rather than revisiting all of the exposition of Parts One and Two in this international perspective, my investigative question for Part Three (i.e. the present chapter) is whether, and if so how, the earlier systematicexposition of the conditions for the reproduction of the capitalist system – as well as the conclusions drawn from it – are affected by the capitalist system's international mode of existence. Most of this question will be answered implicitly. That is, I implicitly posit that the earlier exposition is *not* affected by this mode of existence, except for the matters that I do treat in the current chapter.

As it turns out the main exception regards one form of the international movement of capital (this form being the international migration of production), which I treat in 11D3. This also regards one aspect of international trade (11D2) that I nevertheless treat as more encompassing than that one aspect, so as to contrast the international movement of capital with it.

The above regards the programme for the exposition in the current Part (and chapter). I will not go into matters of the international financial constellation that in fact derive from the two forms mentioned. In particular the exposition keeps on abstracting from historical and prevailing contingencies, that is, entities and processes that are not necessary for the reproduction of the capitalist system (Explication 11§1-a). It might be argued that, strictly speaking, there is no outright necessity for international trade and international movement of capital. However, as we will see later on, there are system-inherent tendencies towards it. Implicitly it is posited that such system-inherent tendencies do not apply for the matters that I abstract from (Explication 11§1-a).

In this perspective the current Part (chapter) presents no necessary *conditions of the existence* of the capitalist system (these were completed with Chapters 1–3 and 6–8), but rather a main mode of existence of capitalism as well as manifestations of that mode. However, as we will see, the actualisation of each of the tendencies to international trade and to international movement of capital require as a condition particular state-granted rights.

11§1-a Explication. Abstraction from contingencies

Parts One and Two of this book did not deal with contingencies – not even with all kinds of discrimination regarding gender, ethnicity and religion, and even if these co-determine the concrete existence of the capitalist system. The reason is that capitalism can exist without these. For the current Part the same applies for war, international power politics (hegemonies) and (variants of) colonialism, and for similar phenomena not listed. All the phenomena just mentioned are tremendously important. And all these may be more important for the lives of people than the exploitative character of capitalism. The self-imposed restriction for this book, again, is that capitalism can exist without these, though it should be borne in mind that capitalism has not done away with these.

11§2 *The world's nations and their economic ranking in terms of the per capita income*

Indirectly this chapter will refer to the international trade (11D2) and the international direct investment (11D3) of all the 217 countries of the world. I will not pronounce if, and to what extent, these countries are characterised as full-capitalist (including capitalist production) in the sense of Chapters 1 and 6 – that would require a full study of its own. Because of the organisation's membership criteria, the 34 OECD countries and the 7 non-OECD countries of the European Union are definitively capitalist – but that is very far from an inclusive list.

For pragmatic reasons I will assume that the vast majority of the 217 countries is full capitalist. For pragmatic reasons I will also assume that these have reached in divergent degrees the capitalist maturity of the OECD-21 – with its maturity problems – as set out in Chapter 10.

Recall the diachronic movement of the OECD-21 state expenditure 1870–2015 as presented in Graph 10.12. I propose that contemporary capitalist nations can be variously characterised in terms of not only their accumulation of capital, but also of the intensity of their state's regulative frameworks and expenditure. Roughly we could think of a classification of nations according to the latter as in *Graph 11.2* (replacing the horizontal diachronic axis of Graph 10.12 by a synchronic classification).

[*continued*]

GRAPH 11.2 *Stylised synchronous country classification*

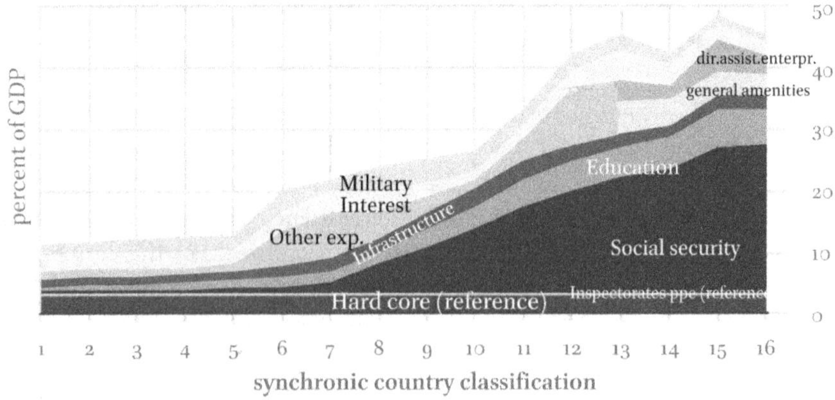

11§2 *Continued*

However, this does not imply that all these capitalist nations go through the same history as the OECD-21. This has to do with the diffusion of technology and techniques of production as well as with distinct mixtures of the intensity of regulative frameworks. Technology, techniques and especially also the state of public education and the communications part of infrastructure are important accelerators that make their histories different. (To be sure, the histories are also different because of historical contingencies such as those of colonialism, imperialism and wars.)

In order to make this chapter manageable as a broad outline, I pragmatically assume that the economic level of a nation can be captured by its GDP per capita in international comparison. I add immediately that (as with the OECD-21's 1920 or 2015 GDP per capita) this tells us nothing at all about the degree of the appropriation of surplus-value or the distribution of income and wealth. A relatively low GDP per capita may go along with a distribution of income that is far more skewed than with a relatively high GDP per capita (recall, for the OECD-21, the development of the top 10% income shares between 1910 and 2010 as shown in Graph 8.23).

For the per capita income of countries I make use of the classification by the World Bank into four income categories of 'High Income', 'Upper Middle Income', 'Lower Middle Income' and 'Low Income'. See Amplification 11§2-a, which defines these categories and shows their shares in the world GDP. See *Table 11.3* for the abbreviations of income country groups that are used throughout this chapter (HIC, UMC, LMC and LIC).

TABLE 11.3 *World Bank definitions of four country income categories from high to low income (2015)*

Income groups	Abbreviation	GNI per capita (2015) income range	
High income	HIC	$12,476	or more
Upper middle income	UMC	$4,036	$12,475
Lower middle income	LMC	$1,026	$4,035
Low income	LIC	$1,025	or less

SOURCE: World Bank, database World Development Indicators (Updated 17 November 2016)

11§2-a Amplification. Ranking of nations into four categories in terms of their per capita income, and the shares of these categories in world GDP

The World Bank classifies countries in terms of their per capita income, as shown in *Table 11.3*. (GNI is the abbreviation for gross national income.)

Table 11.4 makes the link from the OECD-21 to the 'high income' category. This table shows for 2015 that whereas the OECD-21 encompassed 13% of the world population, it acquired 56% of the world GDP. At the other end, 9% of the world population categorised as 'low income' acquired 1% of the world GDP.

TABLE 11.4 *World country income groups: shares of world GDP and average per capita income in 2015*

	Number of countries	Population (in billion)	Share of World population	Share of World GDP	Averages per year in $			
					GNI per capita,†	GDP per capita‡	GDP per capita, PPP*	Index LIC = 1 (GDP cap. PPP)
OECD-21	21	0.9	13%	56%				
Other OECD: high income**	11	0.1	1%	3%				
Non-OECD: high income	46	0.1	1%	2%				
High income (sum row 1–3)	78	1.2	16%	64%	41,366	39,577	44,696	27
Upper middle income	56	2.6	35%	28%	8,186	7,834	15,832	10
Lower middle income	52	2.9	40%	8%	2,035	1,988	6,423	4
Low income	31	0.6	9%	1%	620	616	1,645	1
Total	*217*	*7.3*	*100%*	*100%*				

† Current US$ (Atlas method).
‡ Current US$
* Current international $.
** Mexico and Turkey are UMC countries.

DATA SOURCE: World Bank, database World Development Indicators (Updated 17 November 2016)[2]

2 Accessed 4 December 2016.

Graph 11.5 shows the development of the world GDP shares of the high-, middle- and low-income categories – for as far as World Bank data go back (1960). It can be seen that from 1960–2015 the share of the 78 high-income countries (HIC) decreased from 78% to 64%. Most of this decrease was absorbed by a share increase of the 56 upper-middle income countries (UMC) – and a very minor part by the two lower categories. That seems good for these 78 countries (35% of the world population in 2015). However, as *Graph 11.6* shows, 84% of the UMC share increase was absorbed by the share increase of China from 1995 (an UMC, with 19% of the world population in 2015), which is quite an achievement within two decades.

GRAPH 11.5 *World GDP shares of the high-, middle- and low-income categories: 1960–2015*

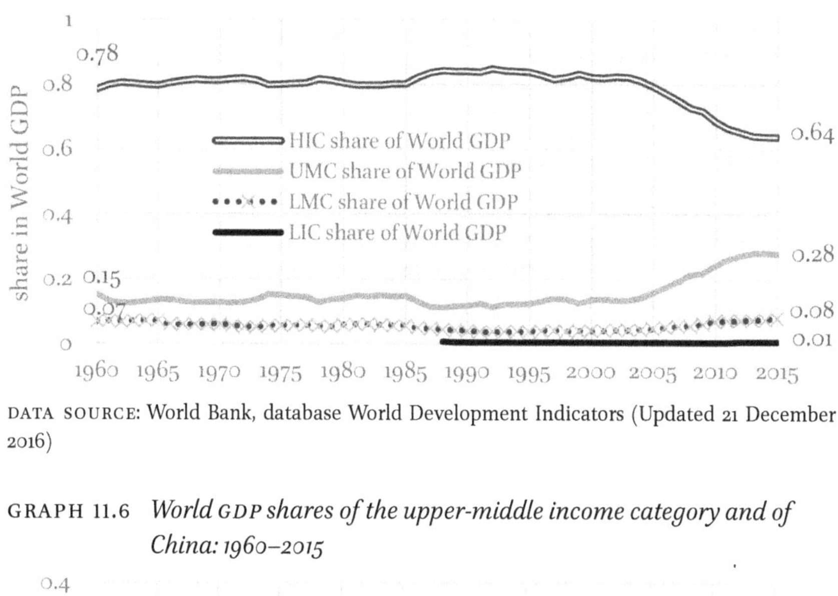

DATA SOURCE: World Bank, database World Development Indicators (Updated 21 December 2016)

GRAPH 11.6 *World GDP shares of the upper-middle income category and of China: 1960–2015*

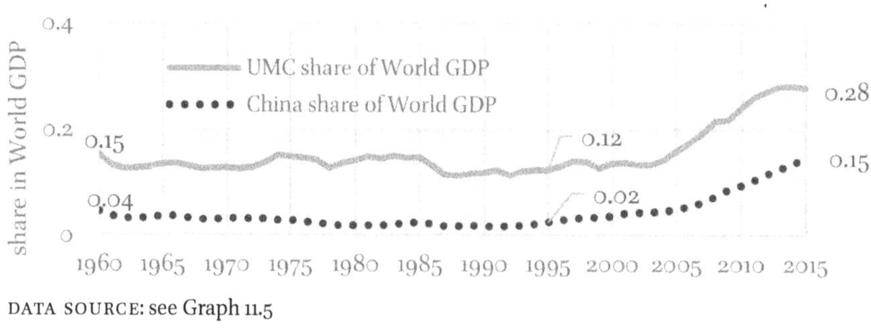

DATA SOURCE: see Graph 11.5

The final *Table 11.7* of this section shows a brief overview of the countries' conditions of most elementary decent life. In comparison with high-income countries, people in low-income countries live shorter (¾) and in much poorer conditions. Many of the measures in this table have improved over the years for which data are available. However, it will not do to tell someone that he should be happy because he received only 10 cane strokes today, in comparison with yesterday's 20. The same applies for any comparison between full-capitalism and prior modes of production.

TABLE 11.7 *Indicators measuring lack of most elementary conditions of life: high-, middle- and low-income countries around 2015*

	Year	HIC	UMC	LMC	LIC
% of world population	*2015*	16	35	40	9
Prevalence of underweight, weight for age (% of children under 5)	*2014*	1.1	2.5	22.4	20.4
Prevalence of undernourishment (% of population)	*2015*		8.2	14.0	26.1
Poverty headcount ratio at $3.10 a day (2011 PPP) (% of population living ≤ this norm)	*2013*	0.9	9.9	46.3	72.0
Life expectancy at birth, total (years)	*2014*	80.6	74.4	67.3	61.3
Physicians (per 1,000 people)[3]	*2011*	2.92	1.99	0.75	0.07
Children out of school (% of primary school age)	*2013*	3.7	4.4	10.2	16.2
Improved water source (% of population without access)	*2015*	0.5	5.0	10.5	34.4
Improved sanitation facilities (% of population without access)	*2015*	0.6	20.0	48.0	71.7
Population living in slums (% of urban population)	*2014*		23.3	32.0	65.2

SOURCE: World Bank, database World Development Indicators (Updated 17 November 2016)

3 Physicians include generalist and specialist medical practitioners.

Division 2. The tendency to international trade

11§3 *The tendency to international trade*

The enterprises' cross-national border sale of output is called export, and the cross-national border purchase of input is called import. In principle the profit-seeking motives of enterprises for interregional-national trade or international trade are not different. They seek expansion at the output side and minimal costs at the input side. It is just the case that enterprises are forced to trade in general, but not necessarily forced to trade internationally.

There are various obstacles to international trade. One is that this trade requires agreement between agents – that is, enterprises and banks – to accept at some exchange rate each other's money (now 'currency'). In principle this is similar to the domain extension set out in 2§9 prior to the introduction of a Clearing Bank and especially prior to the latter's imposing its currency on other (now national) banks. Especially for long-term contracts, international exchange rates imply risks and uncertainties. Another (initial) obstacle for international trade is that enterprises are confronted with different state regulations about products and trade.

A particular impetus for enterprises seeking output expansion internationally relates to their economically optimal technical scale. Depending on the size of a country – thus limits of the 'extent of the market' – this scale may require international expansion. Another (which may but need not be related to the former) is the national market limits to the further concentration of capital within a single enterprise (this is 'concentration' in the sense of absolute size).

11§4 *The state-granted right to export and import*

In principle it is at the discretion of the state to (not) put confines on international trade. It is a matter of a particular state's 'framing' this, whether it encodes non-confines ('freedom') as an extension of enterprises' property rights (that might be repealed), or contrariwise any confines as a restriction of property rights (that might be repealed). The framing matters ideologically, but the effect is the same.

Whereas an actual right to export will usually not be conflicting for a state (contingently there might be strategic reasons to repeal such a right), this is different for imports. For the latter there are, or there may be, conflicting interests between the potential importing enterprise and the nationally operating enterprises (as imports affect their output). The 'framing' referred to matters for the dealing with such conflicts.

11§4-a Amplification. International trade in historical perspective

The following two graphs show the historical development of international trade from 1870 measured in percentage of GDP. *Graph 11.8* shows for world trade a steady increase until the First World War. From 1917–45 protectionist measures caused a considerable decline, the 1917 level being paralleled only in 1974. Afterwards international trade takes further up – with troughs during recessions (severely in 2009).

Trade data decomposed for the four World Bank income classifications (see 11§2-a) are available from 1960, though for the low-income countries only from 1990. Generally the data for the high-income category parallel those for world trade (note that in 2015 their share of world GDP was 64%) – see *Graph 11.9*. The trade of the other categories is much more volatile. That graph shows this for the low-income countries. (An additional graph for these and the other income categories is included in Appendix 11.A under 11§3 – Graph 11.8-a – together with their export–import balances.)

GRAPH 11.8 *Sum of world exports and imports in % of world GDP (divided by two), 1870–2011*

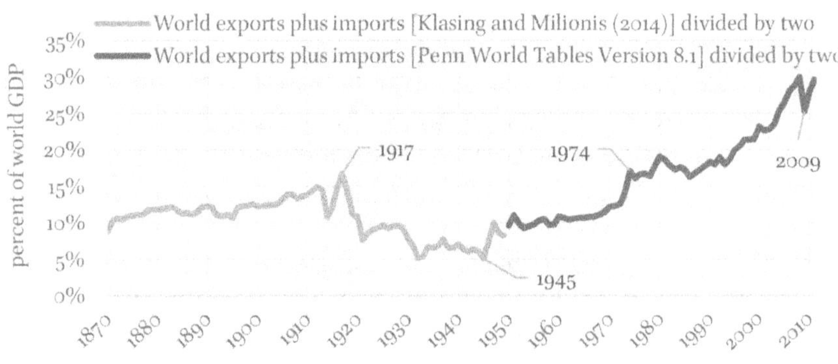

DATA SOURCE: Ortiz-Ospina and Roser 2017 (based on Klasing and Milionis 2014, and Penn World Tables Version 8.1)[4]

4 Retrieved from: https://ourworldindata.org/international-trade (5 November 2017).

GRAPH 11.9 *World exports, HIC and LIC exports, as % of their GDP, 1960–2015*

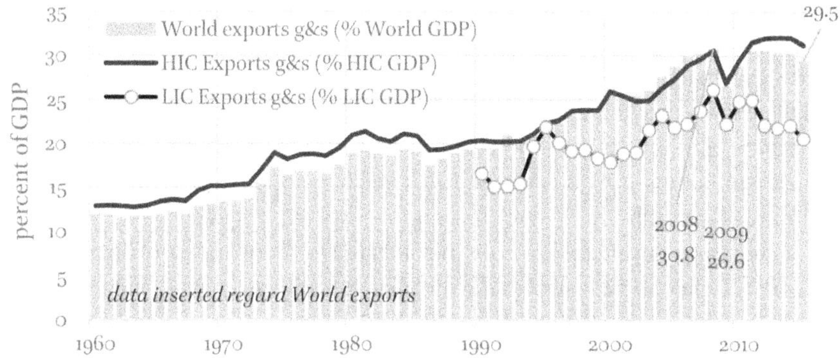

DATA SOURCE: World Bank, World Development Indicators; updated 16 December 2016 (accessed 20 December 2016)

11§5 *The effect of international trade on the sector-structures of production*

One main effect of international trade is a degree of specialisation of production between nations, thus affecting the sector-structures of production.

In principle this is not different from regional specialisation within a nation. During that process regional wage structures will generally be affected, but after a period of adaptation the process does not necessarily affect average regional wages. The same applies for international specialisation.[5] A main difference is that for regions of a nation, workers might – instead of adapting their skills to the new regional production structure – migrate to other national regions. Internationally this is most often excluded (see further 11D3, 11§10-a).

Whereas intra-nation regional specialisation maintains the national production diversity, international trade generates non- or restricted versatile structures of national production. Once a nation has given up sectors of production, it is often very difficult to recuperate these, and if possible at all, this will take much time. This implies that once a nation has 'freely' opted for a non- or restricted versatile structure of production, voluntary ('free') trade turns into enforced trade.

5 To be sure, this chapter does not deviate from the general a-moral discourse of this book in its main systematic sections. Sector-structure changes are often dramatic for the workers concerned.

11§6 *The (uneven) effect of international trade on surplus-value*

International trade is, like any trade, driven by profit motives of enterprises. Mainstream economists since Adam Smith and David Ricardo have argued that international trade is also advantageous for nations, to the extent that they specialise in the production in which they are relatively efficient (exporting those products and importing products that they do not or scarcely produce). This theory of 'comparative advantage' has been questioned on both theoretical and empirical grounds.[6]

One major empirical point is that regarding the world GDP shares of the high-, middle- and low-income countries, hardly any convergence was to be observed from 1960 (the first year for which country income aggregates are available) until about 2005 – that is, when China had joined the international trade scene (and with the exclusion of China that was still the case in 2015). See 11§2-a, Graphs 11.5–11.6.

Nevertheless, international trade is 'advantageous for nations' if this means the enterprises of nations. This is so, because, as argued below, international trade has a positive effect on the ratio of surplus-value to wages ($e = \Pi/wL$).[7] More specifically international trade has the general effect of a relative decrease in the price of the real-wage bundle – that is, given the general rate of inflation.

For what follows it is recalled that the average national real-wage level (now 'national') is determined, in brief, by the interconnection of the productive power of labour, the rate of accumulation of capital, and the rate of unemployment (2§6). Given these determinants and the prevailing sector production structure (11§5) the real-wage is taken as given at each point in time.

International 'free trade' deals are geared at removing trade barriers, especially import duties and import prohibitions (or various substitutes for it). However, at each given production structure – and when some commodity or a close substitute is still produced within a country, enterprises in that country are not forced to import: they will import only when the import price is lower than the national price. Thus when there are national substitutes, imports have a price decreasing effect. This affects the price of the real-wage bundle – either directly for wage goods or indirectly for means of production as inputs for the production of wage goods.

---

6 See, e.g., Went 2002, ch. 2, Samuelson 2004, and Smith 2006, ch. 2, section 4.

7 Section 2§5, equation 2.5. What I set out below is, against the background of 2D2, an international variant of what Marx posited as a tendential increase in 'relative surplus-value' (*Capital I*, Part Four).

The previous paragraph also indicates the constraints for a particular nation of the surplus-value effects. The less versatile a nation's production structure has grown, the more it is forced to import at whatever the world market price is (11§5). This means, or may mean, that the international trade effect on surplus-value is an uneven one for nations.

11§7 *International trade: 'structural national conservation of capital accumulated'*

With both national and international trade we have a, what I call, 'structural national conservation of capital accumulated'. That is, structurally the capital accumulated nationally covers national production and employment (expanded on in Explication 11§7-a).

As we will see in the next division, this is different for the second main lever of the internationalisation of the capitalist system – internationalisation of production. There this conservation no longer holds, making it fundamentally different from international trade.

11§7-a Explication. National structural conservation of capital accumulated

We have seen in Chapter 5 that the capitalist system is characterised by a recurrent cyclical over-accumulation and destruction of capital. 'Structural national conservation of capital accumulated' applies on the capital accumulated over cycles. The point of this structural conservation is that we have a (now national) structural accumulation of capital vis-à-vis a (now national) growth of the labour force, to which the exposition of 2D2 applies.

With international trade this remains to be the case, irrespective of changes in the sector-structure of production (11§5) or in the relative surplus-value (11§6). Changes of these also occur independently of international trade, though perhaps on a smaller or slower scale. When exports and imports of commodities, or commodified services, are roughly in balance, this national conservation of capital is not affected.

This balance is relevant because it indirectly measures national production and national employment. Regarding the period 1960–2015 (for which we have data differentiated for World Bank country income categories), this conservation as measured by the 'external balance on goods and services' in percentage of GDP, occurred on a world scale and for the HIC category within a small margin, though not for the other income categories. *Table 11.10* shows the 1960–2015 average per year for that measure.

TABLE 11.10 *External balance on goods and services in % of GDP; WB income categories, average per year 1960–2015*

Category	External balance goods and services % of GDP	World GDP share	Countries
World	+ 0.1%		217
HIC (high income)	+ 0.1%	64%	78
UMC (upper middle income)	+ 1.1%	28%	56
LMC (lower middle income)	- 2.2%	8%	52
LIC (low income)	- 14.2%[8]	1%	31

DATA SOURCE: World Bank, World Development Indicators, External balance on goods and services (% of GDP), updated 16 December 2016

11§8 *The unsustainability of (international) distance trade*

International trade has been stagnating and staggering for quite a period (Graph 11.8); however, its increase from about 1970 to 2015 was enormous.[9] Along with it goes the transportation of the trade. Their environmental (including climate) costs are not accounted for in the monetary-value dimension (MVD). It is unlikely that this level of international trade (and all the more any further increase) is sustainable in terms of the aggravating environmental damage.[10] However, given the developed international sector-structures of production (11§4), this poses an enormous problem that cannot be resolved in the medium-term, and in some cases not even in the long-term.[11]

8 1990–2015: earlier data are not available.

9 Ortiz-Ospina and Roser (2017) suggest that a considerable amount of this increase was due not to international inter-sector trade (e.g. exportation of manufactures and importation of coffee), but rather to international intra-sector trade (e.g. France both importing and exporting cars to and from Germany).

10 The following data regard greenhouse gas emissions in the European Union. The share of transport in the total of these emissions was 14.9% in 1990. In 2014 this had increased to 23.3% (Eurostat 2016, Figure 3). To be sure, not all of this regards trade. On the subject of international trade specifically, Erickson et al. (2013) quote a study from Peters, Minx, Weber and Edenhofer, reporting 'that the emissions embodied in [internationally] traded goods and services had increased from 4.3 Gt CO2 in 1990, or 20% of global emissions, to 7.8 Gt CO2 in 2008, or 28% of global CO2'. This, on the other hand, does not tell us how much emissions reduction could be gained from international trade reduction.

11 It can be resolved for international intra-sector trade – see the one but last footnote. Considering the long run, the question is to what extent the implementation costs of a *possible*

However, this is not 'merely' an international problem, but also a regional problem within large area nations (Amplification 11§8-a).

11§8-a Amplification. The seven largest countries of the world in terms of land area

The seven largest countries out of 217 are (ranked in order of land area): the Russian Federation, China, the United States of America, Canada, Brazil, Australia and India. The following table shows the sums of their world shares in land, population and GDP.

World shares of the 7 largest countries in land area

land area	population 2015	GDP 2015 (in US$)
42%	46%	50%

This table merely serves as a 'blow-up' for any nation in the world that has specialising regions of production, and hence transportation costs that may not be accounted for in the MVD. Thus transport associated with international trade is a huge problem, but it is in fact a problem of any distance trade and traffic whose costs are not fully accounted for.

Division 3. The tendencies to international movement of capital and to international migration of production

11§9 *The tendency to the international movement of capital*

Enterprises seek to increase their rates of profit by the processes of production and accumulation of capital (1D5, 2D1). These processes are manifest in a number of tendency forces of the enterprises' market interaction. One manifestation takes the form of plant-wise capital movements within a sector of production, or of capital movements between sectors of production (4D1). Another manifestation regards the (conglomerate) centralisation of capital (4D5).

emergence of sufficient emissions reducing transport techniques would be smaller than the implementation costs of reversals of the international sector-structures of production.

Because these are tendency forces in general, these operate – in principle – also internationally in the form of a tendency to the international movement of capital, though under more complicated conditions than nationally (see 11§11 and 11§12).

11§10 *The state-granted right to the international movement of capital*

The international movement of capital (IMC) is conditioned by a two-sided expansion of the enterprises' property rights as granted by the state.

First, in legally granting enterprises or any other agents the right to IMC, the emigrant state expands (fully or limited) the legal right to property (cf. 6§10). Second, in allowing foreign enterprises to immigrate capital, the immigrant state expands the property right (fully or limited) for the immigrant enterprise(s) or other agents.

As with international trade, it is a matter of a particular state's 'framing' these rights, whether it encodes non-confines ('freedom') as an extension of enterprises' property rights (that might be repealed), or contrariwise any confines as a restriction of property rights (that might be repealed). The framing matters ideologically – especially in case of conflicting interests regarding IMC (see 11§13) – but the effect is the same.

11§10-a Amplification. The asymmetric freedom of international movement/migration for capital and labour

Although in most nations labour (any person) is free to emigrate, most nations put severe restrictions on the immigration of labour (persons). Thus in the states' granting of (expanded) claimed rights, enterprises and workers (persons) are again treated asymmetrically. This means indeed that the propagation of economic freedom is partisan and ideological.

This does not imply that immigration of labour is prohibited altogether. It rather depends on the interests of enterprises in face of the available labour capacity – thus the potential migration of labour is used as a reservoir so as to guarantee a degree of unemployment (2§6). (I add that this asymmetry means that there is no free labour market even from the mainstream economics perspective.)

11§10-b Amplification. International movement of capital as measured by 'Foreign Direct Investment' (FDI) and its pattern 1970–2015

The international movement of capital on a considerable world scale is a fairly recent phenomenon, dating from the middle of the 1980s. Prior to this, most states controlled and limited cross-border movement of capital – and many still do, in full or above a threshold.

As a main quantitative indicator for it I adopt the 'Foreign Direct Investment' (FDI). Most of my data on FDI are from the World Bank, which defines FDI as follows.

> 'Foreign direct investment are the net inflows [or outflows] of investment to acquire a lasting management interest (10 percent or more of voting stock) in an enterprise operating in an economy other than that of the investor. It is the sum of equity capital, reinvestment of earnings, other long-term capital, and short-term capital as shown in the balance of payments.' The series show either 'net inflows (new investment inflows less disinvestment) in the reporting economy from foreign investors' or 'net outflows of investment from the reporting economy to the rest of the world'. And: 'FDI data do not give a complete picture of international investment in an economy. Balance of payments data on FDI do not include capital raised locally ... In addition, FDI data omit non-equity cross-border transactions such as intra-unit flows of goods and services.' Finally, the WB uses the 'weighted average' as 'aggregation method'.[12]
>
> Source: WB metadata for the series

Because the WB uses the term 'net' to account for disinvestments, I use the term 'netted' FDI or FDI 'sum' for the inflows minus outflows. All FDI country group averages as presented below are weighted averages as calculated by the World Bank.

World FDI is much dominated by the FDI of the high-income countries (HIC) – their share of world GDP being 64% in 2015. It can be seen from *Graph 11.11* and *Graph 11.12* that world inflows and outflows of FDI beyond 1% of world GDP take off only from the second half of the 1980s, and that the same applies for the FDI of the HIC in terms of their GDP. (Similar graphs for the middle- and low-income countries are shown in Appendix 11.A under 11§10.)

It can also be seen from these graphs that the fluctuations from about 2000 are considerable. One reason is that FDI also reflects international mergers and take-overs – including vast banking mergers and take-overs prior to and after the 2007/08 financial crisis.

12 However, for purposes of characterising 'average capitalist nations', unweighted averages are often preferable (as I did in Part Two). In order not to complicate the graphs below, I have declined to present two measures.

GRAPH 11.11 *FDI inflows and outflows as % of GDP, world average; 1970–2015*

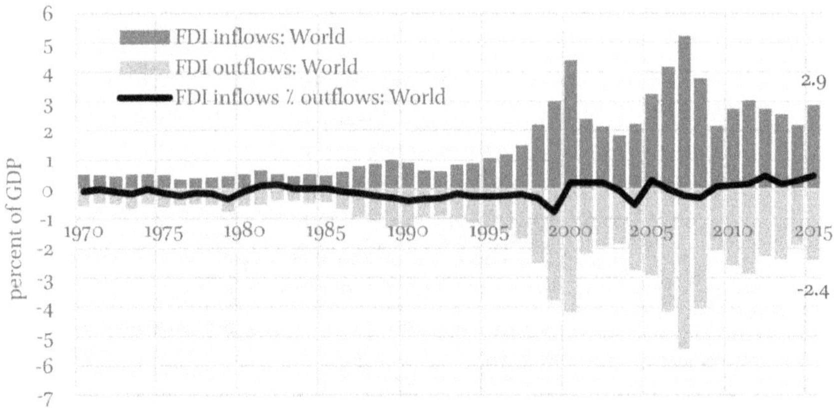

DATA SOURCE: World Bank, database World Development Indicators (updated 21 December 2016; accessed 26 December 2016). Weighted averages

GRAPH 11.12 *FDI inflows and outflows as % of GDP, average of high-income countries; 1970–2015*

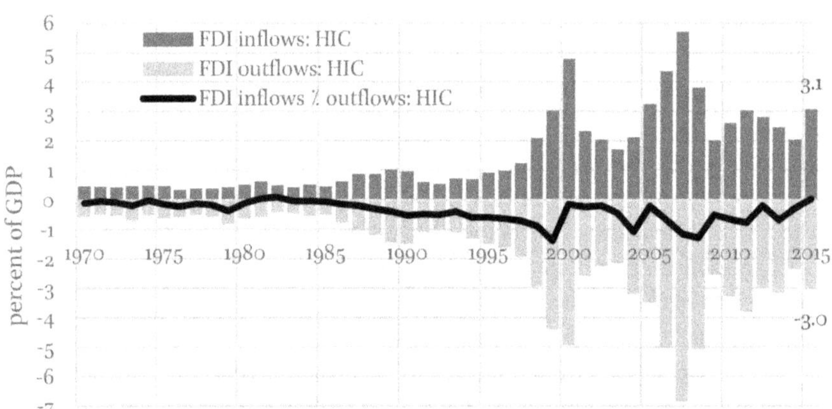

DATA SOURCE: see Graph 11.11

Relevant for this division, however, are foremost the 'netted' FDI inflows and outflows (the black line in *Graphs 11.11* and *11.12*) and especially also those for the middle- and low-income countries.[13] These are shown in *Graph 11.13*. It can be seen that for all of the middle- and low-income country groups, the netted

13 I make a distinction between 'net' and 'netted' as was explained above.

FDI was positive since data are available – though with quite some fluctuation throughout.[14] (For the low-income countries a restricted number of full data are only available from 2005.)

GRAPH 11.13 *Netted FDI inflows and outflows as % of GDP of the country group; averages of the high-income, middle-income and low-income countries (HIC, UMC, LMC, LIC); 1970–2015*

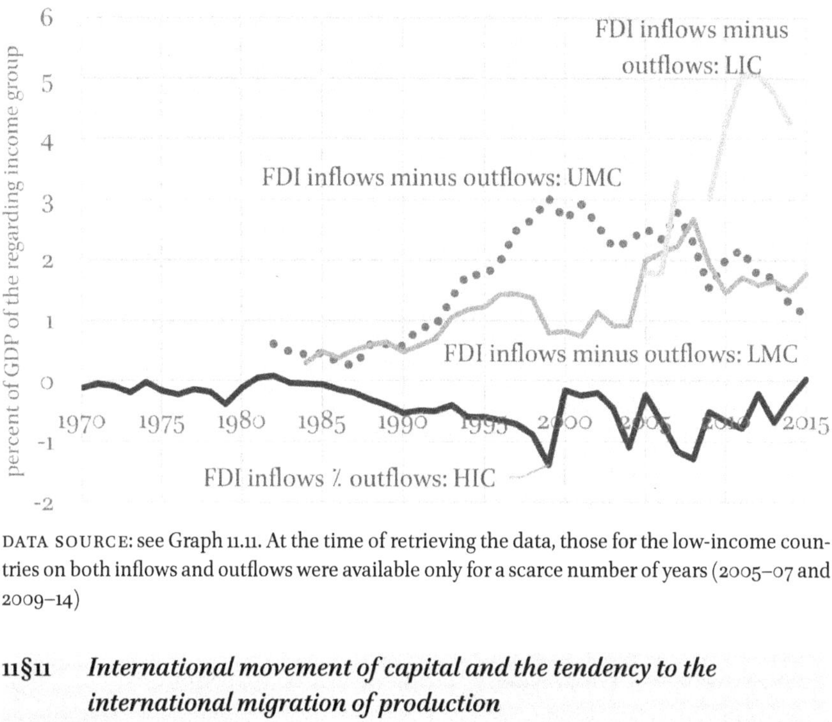

DATA SOURCE: see Graph 11.11. At the time of retrieving the data, those for the low-income countries on both inflows and outflows were available only for a scarce number of years (2005–07 and 2009–14)

11§11 *International movement of capital and the tendency to the international migration of production*

There are two main forms of the international movement of capital (IMC) – summarised in *Table 11.14*.

The first form is the 'international centralisation and concentration of capital', which is associated with 'economic power driven mergers and take-overs'. This form and the drive are no different from the national centralisation of capital (4D5). However, in international form the size of the resulting entities (that is, the concentration of capital) may grow much beyond what would be possible nationally. The resulting entities tend to operate multinationally (as

14 The post-2007 decrease for the upper-middle countries is, to a considerable extent, due to a decrease for China.

multinational corporations) and to bring together assets and finance capital from multinational origin.[15]

Equity transactions are the main process through which this centralisation and concentration of capital is reached.

The second form of IMC involves an 'international migration of production' (IMP).[16] The process through which it is reached is via a gradual 'restructuring of capital' (cf. 4§2-b): the new plant investment in the original country is damped, substituting it by investment in another country.[17] This second form encompasses two variants.

One variant is primarily 'commodity markets driven'. It relates to the geographical distance of selling markets and/or to the supply chain structure as including the related networks. In this case enterprises move (part of) their production to nearby the selling or the supply markets. In this case the international migration of production in effect substitutes for international trade. In principle this variant is not different from intra-national regional relocations of enterprises.

The other variant is primarily 'labour market driven', that is, wage-costs driven. In fact this regards the seeking of relatively abundant labour-capacity markets (as applying on one of the two main conditions for the accumulation of capital – cf. 2D2).

In the remainder of this division the focus will be on the general preconditions for the international migration of production and on its labour-market and wages effects. Although in the two variants distinguished the primary drives are different, each one (also) has similar labour-market effects. It is just that when the labour market is the primary drive, the wages effects are larger than when commodity markets are the primary drive. Further, although the drives may be different, empirically we cannot read off from international migrations of production what the drives are. In the remainder of this division, therefore, I take these variants together as 'international migration of production' in general.

---

15 The UNCTAD World Investment Report 2017 shows in its Annex Tables 24 and 25 a measure of this for a top 200 non-financial enterprises for the year 2016.

16 In the medium- or long-term, a migration of production (relocations from one country to another) might also result from mergers and take-overs. However, these do not start this way.

17 I note that the international 'outsourcing' of production has the effect of a partial migration of production, but it is not a movement of capital. In fact this is a particular form of international trade, and the importation of the goods or services at hand is also measured as international trade.

Another focus in the remainder of this division is on this migration of production from the high-income countries (HIC) to the middle- and low-income countries (UMC, LMC and LIC) and from the middle-income countries (UMC and LMC) to the low-income countries (LIC). (See the details of this country classification in 11§2-a.)

International migration of production only most rarely takes the form of full migration of an enterprise – at least it does not start that way. Instead it is most often carried out by multinational enterprises, taking the form of a partial migration via subsidiary corporations (the initial corporation being the holding company), either via take-overs, or via participations, or via establishing a complete new branch (the latter are called 'greenfield investments').[18]

The generation of each of these forms of the 'international movement of capital' (IMC) has in fact a tendency character (as forces engendering these that may be counteracted).

Each of these forms of IMC is a component of the 'Foreign Direct Investment' (FDI – cf. 11§10-b) – see further 11§11-a.

TABLE 11.14 *The forms of the 'international movement of capital'*

International movement of capital (IMC)		
Forms	**Drives**	**Main process**
(1) international centralisation and concentration of capital	economic power driven mergers and take-overs	financial: equity
(2) international migration of production (IMP)	(a) commodity markets driven (b) labour market driven	restructuring of capital (ROC)

11§11-a Amplification. The forms of the 'international movement of capital' as components of the FDI

Information about the decomposition of FDI as to the type of FDI is limited, and especially so for country groups (at least the WB and UNCTAD databases do not provide these). In an Annex of the UNCTAD *World Investment Report 2017* there is some limited information about the FDI subcategory of Greenfield investments from 2003–16. A greenfield investment is a form of FDI where a parent company builds its operations in a foreign country from the ground up (see also the last footnote). This subcategory is relevant for the 'interna-

18 https://www.investopedia.com/terms/g/greenfield.asp.

tional migration of production'. However, the UNCTAD information regards *announced* greenfield investment projects. In this regard, it remarks: 'The value of announced greenfield projects indicates the capital expenditure planned by the investor at the time of the announcement. Data can differ substantially from the official FDI data as companies can raise capital locally and phase their investments over time, and a project may be cancelled or may not start in the year when it is announced' (p. 39, n. 2). Because limited information is often better than no information, *Table 11.15* brings together the relevant UNCTAD data. Because of the reasons stated in the quotation above I use 2003–16 averages.

Developing economies are roughly all the world economies apart from the World Bank's category of high-income countries (11§2-a). *Table 11.15* shows, as a rough indicator, that greenfield investments are the dominant part of the FDI inflow into developing economies (89% for the indicator).[19]

TABLE 11.15 *Total FDI inflows and announced greenfield FDI inflows; World and developing economies, 2003–16*

Announced greenfield FDI projects = AG-FDI **Developing economies = DE**	**2003–16 average per year in billion US$**	**2003–16 average per year in percent**
total FDI inflow: World	1363	
total FDI inflow: Developing economies	543	
total FDI inflow: ratio DE to world inflow		40%
share of DE in world AG-FDI		60%
AG-FDI: World	811	
AG-FDI: Developing economies	486	
World ratio of AG-FDI to total FDI inflow		60%
DE ratio of AG-FDI to total FDI inflow		89%

DATA SOURCE: UNCTAD 2017, Annex Tables 1 and 19[20]

19 As an aside, I note that in its *World Investment Report 2017* the UNCTAD has a graph (its Figure I.12) headed as 'External sources of finance for developing economies, 2007–2016', in which it includes (next to FDI) a line graph for 'Portfolio investment'. I do not understand how this is a source of finance unless this would solely regard *newly* issued shares, bonds or direct placements.

20 http://unctad.org/en/Pages/DIAE/World%20Investment%20Report/Annex-Tables.aspx.

11§12 *The constellation of an immigrant state as condition for the international migration of production – the perspective of potentially migrating enterprises*

The inward bifurcation of commodities and of the production process (1§7, 1§11) means that enterprises are indifferent to physical-geographic location: all that counts is the criterion of the integral and the internal rate of profit (1§13, 5§1), be it in a national or international context. However, that same criterion implies that enterprises are not indifferent to the particular state that best serves that interest. For multinational enterprises, a national state is an instrumental entity.

A general condition for the actualisation of international migration of production (11§11) is that the state in those nations can gain compliance for defining the interests of capital as being in the putative general interest (6§6). This merely means that migrating enterprises will migrate to capitalist nations. For the more specific conditions of movement, *Figure 11.16* categorises the regulative frameworks of Chapters 6–9 into three broad categories.

FIGURE 11.16 *Division of regulative frameworks into three main categories as relevant for Chapter 11*

Hard Core frameworks (HC-FW)	1. Capitalist economic rights	6D4
	2. Allowance rights to existence	6D5
↓		
	3. Public security	6D6
Capital accumulation frameworks (CA-FW)	4. Monetary	7D2
	5. Labour-capacity (incl. publ. educ.)	7D3
↓	6. Infrastructure	7D4
	8. (mode of) Imposition competition	9D1
Legitimating compliance SWC (LC-FW)*	7. Social security framework	7D5

Legend

↓ grounded in moment below.

* SWC: subordinated working class.

For potentially emigrating enterprises, the immigrant state's Hard Core frameworks and their full upholding are an absolute precondition for the migration. The Capital Accumulation frameworks are also a requirement. However, as a precondition for the immigration of capital their intensity is flexible in face of the wage level difference between the nations of migration. This – and particularly formal education and infrastructure – again varies for different sectors of production and for the particular type of investment (as, for example, requiring different types and degrees of education). A relatively intensive regulation of competition is (merely) important for the suppliers of the immigrant enterprise.

The category of the social security framework is no *direct* consideration for the emigrant enterprises for the following two reasons.

First, this framework is relevant for the legitimation of the state (and hence, as argued in 7D5, for the legitimation of the capitalist economy vis-à-vis which the state constitutes a separation-in-unity – 6§7). However, immigrant enterprises are 'footloose' to the extent that they calculate a relatively brief pay-back period of, say, 3–5 years. That is, they can re-migrate their investment when the legitimation of the state under consideration is actually under threat.

Second, the actual social security framework (and the concomitant transfers) are only indirectly relevant for immigrating enterprises to the extent that these would affect employers' social security contributions and corporate taxes.[21]

The level of the latter (corporate taxes) is a final main determinant of the international migration of production. This regards not so much the statutory tax rates, but rather the effective tax rates – also in face of accounting streams within the international branches of a corporate holding.

In face of the frameworks, and other relevant factors, potentially migrating enterprises calculate the costs and benefits of an international migration of production. Especially because of the comparative frameworks assessment, this is far more complex than for an intra-national migration of production.

11§12-a Amplification. Other determinants

Apart from the conditions indicated in the main text (in brief the intensity of frameworks, wages and taxation), the (non-)migration of enterprises is also determined by *differences* in:

- institutional labour relations (management–labour, labour-unions, local management vis-à-vis international management);

21 The income taxes of the top management are also relevant, but the bulk of these may be anticipated in the gross wage paid.

- local/regional networks of enterprises;
- networks of enterprises and governments (state and local);
- regional markets.

In face of the international movements of production (IMP) between the four grand country categories distinguished by the World Bank (11§2), the following three amplifications expand on the three categories of the state framework that are most relevant for the remainder of this division.

11§12-b Amplification. Formal education

Formal education is a main component of the Capital Accumulation frameworks. In 2015 the formal education differences between high-, middle- and low-income countries were considerable and it seems that these are a major obstacle for widespread IMP to the middle- and low-income countries. Misleadingly the state expenditure on formal education, as shown in *Graph 11.17*, might suggest that the gap is nearly bridged (even the LIC level for 2005 is above that for the OECD-21 in 1960).

GRAPH 11.17 *State expenditure on formal education as % of GDP, 1970–2015; high-, middle- and low-income countries*

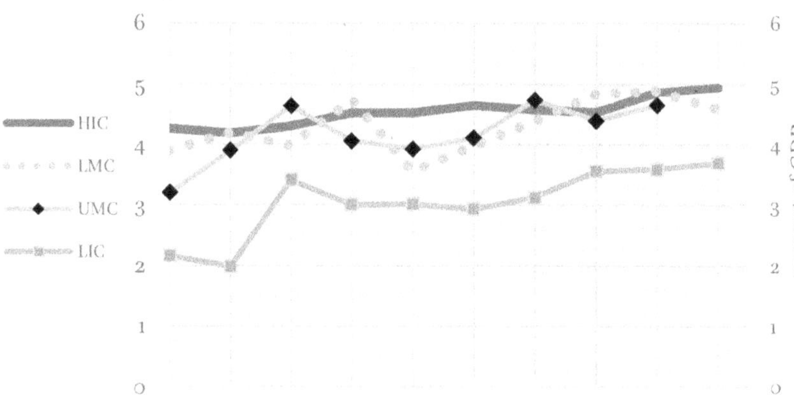

DATA SOURCE: UNESCO database (December 2016 release; accessed 8 December 2016). 1970–2010 nearest year available; 2015 or last year available.[22] (I categorised the UNESCO data for countries according to the World Bank income classification for the year 2015. See Appendix 11.A under 11§12 for more information on the data.)

22 UMC 2015 (sample value 9.5 omitted because of too many not with 2010 coinciding countries). LIC excludes Zimbabwe because of several figures that are difficult to interpret, including the education expenditure of 44% of GDP in 1994.

However, *Graph 11.18* shows that behind the previous flattering figures lurks a distribution of formal education that is more skewed than that of the OECD-21 between 1870 and 1910 (Graph 7.10). Thus it seems that in 2015 the education in many of the middle- and low-income countries is perhaps fitting for an elite top or middle management, but less so for those production floors that require at least moderately skilled labour. On the other hand, in recent decennia the spread of education among the population in those countries increased steeply (as measured by the decrease in their Gini index in *Graph 11.18*).

GRAPH 11.18 *Average years of formal schooling, and spread of education in the total population aged 15 years and older (Gini index); averages of high-, middle- and low-income countries 1950–2010*

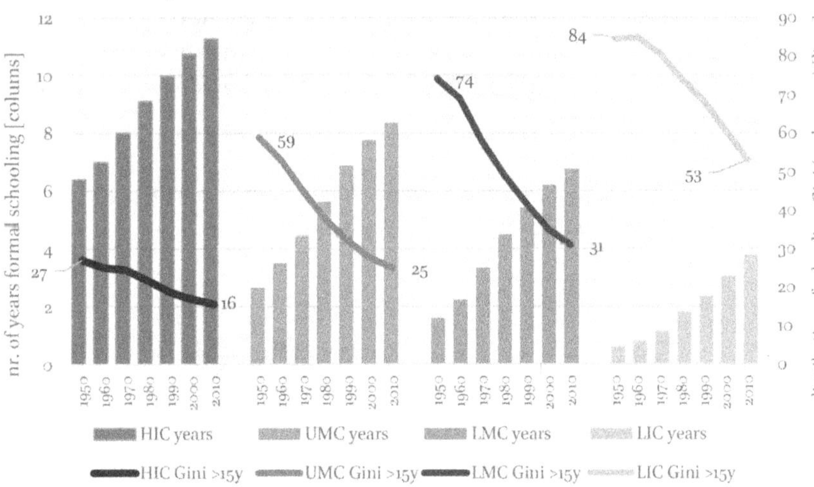

DATA SOURCE: CLIO Infra database (accessed 12 December 2016).[23] The CLIO data for countries were categorised according to the World Bank income classification for the year 2015.[24]

Graph 11.18 shows averages. China, to take a major example, was in 2010 down to a Gini of 14.5 (scale 100–1), that is, below the HIC average (and not far removed from the USA's 13.5). The Russian Federation (15.2 in 2010) and Argentina (15.7) also stand out among the UMCs. Among the LMCs Tajikistan, Cambodia, Moldova, Kenya and Armenia are outstanding (ranging from 9.4 to 15.8 in 2010). Given the actual FDI inflow to middle- and low-income countries, there are apparently niches for these (in face of average wage differences).

23 https://www.clio-infra.eu/datasets/indicators.

24 HIC: 34–39 countries. UMC: 32–38 countries. LMC: 28–34 countries (34 from 1970). LIC: 15–26 countries (25–26 from 1960).

11§12-c Amplification. The communications part of infrastructure

I found no aggregate data for infrastructure (recall from 7§15 that these are also a gap in the long-run OECD-21 data of before 1995). However, there are data on the communications part of infrastructure (and, as we will see in the final section of this chapter, these are very relevant). *Graph 11.19* shows the proportions of the population in the high-, middle- and low-income country groups using the Internet. (Together with formal education this is an important indicator for the degree of widespread information among the population.) In 2015 the middle- and low-income countries indeed move behind the high-income countries, but especially the upper-middle-income countries kept up fast in the decade leading up to 2015.

GRAPH 11.19 *Individuals using the Internet (% of population); averages of high-, middle- and low-income countries, 1990–2015*

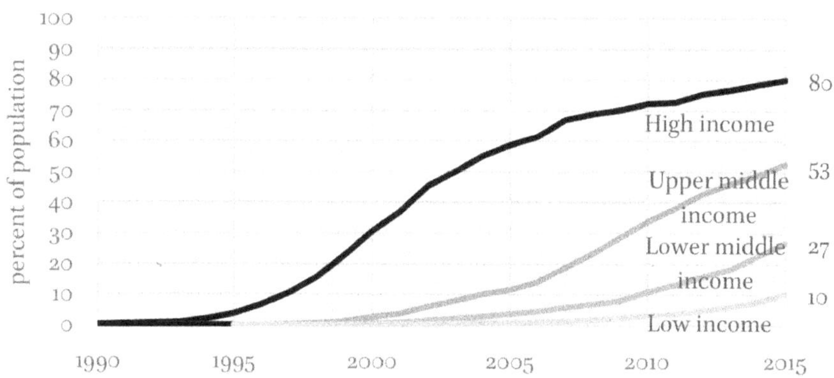

DATA SOURCE: World Bank, database World Development Indicators (last updated 15 November 2017; retrieved 17 November 2017)

11§12-d Amplification. Social security transfers

In 11§15 I will refer to social security expenditure (SSE) in the middle- and low-income countries. There are few standardised data on these. However, the ILO provides data on SSE between 2000 and 2011 for nearly all world countries. To these data I have applied the World Bank country income classification. *Table 11.20* shows the results. It can be seen that in 2000 and 2011 there is quite a gap between the levels of the OECD-21 and other HICs and those of the middle- and low-income countries, but that during this period there has been a very fast increase for the latter (of 24 and 35%).

TABLE 11.20 *State social security expenditure in % of GDP, 2000–11; averages of World Bank country income categories*

Category	Category	Nr†	2000‡	2011‡	Change	Historical OECD-21 comparision
			% GDP			year**
high income	OECD-21	21/21	21.1	24.7	17.5%	2011
high income	HIC*	55/78	15.4	17.4	12.9%	± 1980
upper middle income	UMC	44/56	8.0	9.9	24.4%	± 1955
lower middle income	LMC	46/52	4.7	6.3	35.5%	± 1945
low income	LIC	23/31	3.2	4.4	35.5%	± 1940

† x/x = actual/potential maximum number of countries;
‡ Or nearest year available.
* Including the OECD-21;
** This regards the year around which the OECD-21 reached a similar expenditure (interpolated for 1940 and the semi-decades).
DATA SOURCE: ILO, database Social Protection[25]

11§13 *International migration of production: diversity of conflicting interests*

International migration of production has very diverse, and conflicting, effects within the country of emigration as well as within the country of immigration. This section endeavours to sum these up in a broad manner (precision would require a single country to single country comparison, as well as a host of assumptions).

In any case – and predicated on the unity of capitalist economies and states – the state that permits the IMP must conceive this as either being in the direct interest of the national enterprises and their owners, or indirectly in their interest because of the state's requirement of legitimation in the vast majority of the labour population. I note already that the state's appreciation of this 'either/or' may be different for capital emigrant and capital immigrant nations.[26]

---

25 http://www.socialsecurityextension.org/gimi/gess/ShowSearchIndicators.action (retrieved 1 November 2017). Excluding the ten countries for which only one datum (2000 or 2011) is available. (Country income classification from WB; see Table 11.3.)

26 I also note that China – as a main example of a nation that seems to approach these mat-

Generally there is a positive effect of IMP inflow on the GDP growth and tax receipts of the nation of immigration of production, and a converse effect on the nation of emigration.

The opposite wages effects are the essence of the differences (in the emigrant nation there is a downward wages effect, and in the immigrant nation an upward wages effect). This implies that the workers of the different countries are played out against each other. However, in principle this is not unlike intra-national inter-sector or regional movements of capital. In each case, rates of unemployment and wage rates tend to equalisation (these are tendencies; actual equalisation is an often long-run gradual process).

States are not driven by altruism vis-à-vis other states. The opposite effects on the tax receipts of the nations' states might give rise to the idea that the interests of states are counter-posited. However, reasoning from the point of view of the nation of emigration of production, this would assume that the state is an actor independent of the capitalist economy and the interests of capitalist enterprises. In fact the capitalist state grants enterprises the claimed economic rights (of property in means of production and of exploitation) as set out in Chapter 6. The expansion of granted property rights to international migration of production (11§10) is in line with this. This expansion is not only in the interest of the migrating capital (the holding) but also in the interest of the non-emigrant enterprises (wages are pressed down) – that is, provided that with the remaining taxation the level of the accumulation frameworks can be maintained. The possible downside (and trade-off) is the effect on the state's legitimation in the compliance of labour (see 11§15).

From the same point of view (capitalist economic rights) it is rather the position of the states of immigration of production (capital inflow) that requires further consideration. Those states have to convince the current national enterprises that even if they are confronted with upward wages, they will benefit from the future GDP growth effect, and especially from the amelioration of the 'capital accumulation frameworks' (11§12) made possible by the increasing GDP and the state's taxes. (When wages increase, taxation of wages is facilitated.)

Ultimately, however, the raising of wages somewhat nearer to the world average seems a condition for a stable compliance during production and for the legitimation of states in the compliance of their national working class.[27] (This

ters in a discretionary rather than in a general way – had its netted inflow of FDI peaking to 5.6% of GDP in 1994, which was down to 0.6% in 2015.

27 'World' average is the general formulation. Much of the FDI regards intra HIC flows

is indeed a key important factor in a world that has become engrained by international communication and hence knowledge of world-relative income and wealth levels.)

Figure 11.21 roughly summarises the various conflicting interests (Amplification 11§13-a sets out some qualifications).

FIGURE 11.21 *Diversity of conflicting interests upon global migration of production*

<table>
<tr><td rowspan="2">Positive (+), no (o) or negative (–) effect:
changes</td><td colspan="4">**Migration of production**</td><td rowspan="2"></td></tr>
<tr><td colspan="2">nation of emigration</td><td colspan="2">nation of immigration</td></tr>
<tr><td>***key economy–state effects***</td><td colspan="2"></td><td colspan="2"></td><td></td></tr>
<tr><td>wages</td><td colspan="2">–</td><td colspan="2">+</td><td></td></tr>
<tr><td>tax receipts</td><td colspan="2">–</td><td colspan="2">+</td><td>when dominated by wages-tax effect†</td></tr>
<tr><td>tax associated accumulation of capital frameworks</td><td colspan="2">–</td><td colspan="2">+</td><td></td></tr>
<tr><td>legitimation effect associated with employment and wages</td><td colspan="2">–</td><td colspan="2">+</td><td></td></tr>
<tr><td>***effect on surplus-value***</td><td colspan="2"></td><td colspan="2"></td><td></td></tr>
<tr><td rowspan="2">of migrating enterprises
(subsidiary of holding)</td><td colspan="2">n.a.*</td><td rowspan="2">sum +</td><td>+</td><td>wages effect‡</td></tr>
<tr><td colspan="2">n.a.*</td><td>–</td><td>frameworks effect‡</td></tr>
<tr><td rowspan="4">of non-migrating enterprises (x/x = same sector as migrant / other sector as migrant)</td><td rowspan="4">sum
+ ?</td><td>+</td><td rowspan="4">sum
?</td><td>–</td><td>wages effect</td></tr>
<tr><td>+/o</td><td>–/o</td><td>competition effect</td></tr>
<tr><td>o/–</td><td>o/+</td><td>supply chain effect</td></tr>
<tr><td>–?</td><td>+</td><td>framework effect</td></tr>
</table>

(whence wages are raised towards the HIC average) and, to a lesser extent, intra MIC flows (whence wages are raised towards their averages).

FIGURE 11.21 *Diversity of conflicting interests (cont.)*

effect on growth			
investment	?	+	
consumption (labour)	–	+	
state expenditure	–	+	
GDP	–	+	

† Including indirect taxes
* n.a.: not applicable
‡ See 11§12

11§13-a Explication. Some qualifications regarding the IMP conflicts of interest

Within the confines of the broad outline in this chapter, *Table 11.15* is not very detailed. In general, international *im*migration of production (netted FDI inflow) is GDP expanding, like any investment. There are two main issues that co-determine its effect on the existing enterprises.

First the degree of hidden unemployment and the degree of substitution between self-employment and wage labour. Whereas netted FDI inflow would generally increase the wages sum (wL) and each of the wage rate (w) and the amount of employment (L), their degrees are dependent on the factors just mentioned. The wage rate will increase at least to some extent because the immigrant will compete for the best qualified labour.

A second main factor is whether the FDI is fitted into an existing sector-stratification (Chapter 4) whence it would probably move into its top and directly compete with the existing national enterprises. (By itself this is not spectacular because that is also a normal process in the absence of FDI, though the mechanisms are somewhat different because along with the FDI goes the technical knowledge.) If, on the other hand, the FDI inflow regards a new sector (for this economy), there would not be such direct competition. On the contrary, this would probably be import-substituting and evoke a multiplier of supply chain effects.

Regarding the first factor above it is to be noted that the amount of potential wage labour (the 'extent of the labour market') is dynamically determined by population growth as well as by the competition determined overflow of self-employment to wage labour. So as to provide an idea about the quantities involved *Table 11.22* provides some ILO data that are categorised regionally rather than by country income group.

TABLE 11.22 *Wage-labour as a share of wage-labour plus self-employment; world regions and developed economies 1999–2013*

	1999	2013	Change
Africa	24.6	26.2	6%
Asia	30.7	40.2	31%
Latin America and the Caribbean	59.0	62.8	6%
Middle East	71.9	80.3	12%
Eastern Europe and Central Asia	74.9	78.3	4%
Developed economies	84.1	86.4	3%

DATA SOURCE: ILO, *Global Wage Report 2014/15*, Figure 14[28]

11§14 *International migration of production: rupture of the 'structural national conservation of capital accumulated'*

Recall from 11§7 the 'structural national conservation of capital accumulated' in case of international trade. The international movement of capital along with the international migration of production means that this form of existence of the international capitalist system is fundamentally different from international trade.[29] With this migration the 'structural national conservation of capital accumulated', vis-à-vis the labour population growth within a nation, no longer holds. We have effluxes of capital from where it was produced by labour and appropriated and accumulated by the owners of capital (cf. 1§12). Concomitantly we have equivalent influxes of capital into the immigrant nations. Along with it we have, as indicated (11§13), in the emigrant country a downward pressure and in the immigrant country an upward pressure on wages.

28 http://www.ilo.org/global/research/global-reports/global-wage-report/2014/lang--en /index.htm (excel file data).

29 This also applies for the international capital movement form of international mergers and take-overs (11§11) in case this is going to result in an international migration of production.

11§14-a Amplification. Winners, losers and winners: national 'structural conservation of capital accumulated' versus its international breach

Capital is produced by labour, the surplus-value (integral profit) being appropriated by the owners of the enterprises (1§14, heading 7). Accumulation of capital requires labour and it also requires unemployment. This is a harsh core characteristic of the capitalist system (2D2, in particular 2§6). In a high conjuncture, when unemployment is waning, labour reaps increasing wages. This is so when the national 'structural conservation of capital accumulated' holds, that is, in the absence of international migration of production (IMP). With IMP, however, potentially increasing wages in the country from which capital emigrates are reaped in the country of immigration. Workers in the country of emigration feel that this happens behind their backs. They know that the law (i.e. the rights granted to 'their' capitalist) is such that they cannot effectively claim the surplus-value that they produced. Owners of enterprises will tell them that the international economic constellation enforces emigration of production.

This is the basis of the workers of the different countries being played out against each other. Those politically responsible, or commentators, might argue and judge that this process is morally desirable because in this way international wages levels become closer. The latter is correct. However, such a judgement is a partial one in two respects.

First, within the country of emigration the employment effect hits one particular layer of the labour population, namely those that become unemployed. This would be different if unemployment would be distributed over the total labour population via worktime reduction. (However, as indicated above, accumulation of capital requires unemployment.)

Secondly, the migration of capital is not motivated by this moral judgement (even when the argument and judgement suits enterprises), but rather by profits higher than the current profits. This means that workers in the country of emigration bear its downside, whereas the enterprises and their owners reap extra profit benefits.

11§14-b Amplification. Comparison of international wage rates

Wage rate comparisons for large world country groups are scarce. The ILO provides such data for the years 2000–15 (but even those are restricted as to the number of countries). *Table 11.32* shows these for the full period as well as, in face of the crisis-years, decomposed for three sub-periods.

TABLE 11.23 *Average annual real-wage growth 2000–15; World country groups*†

Country group	Number	% Change: averages per year 2000–15	2000–07	2008–11	2012–15
OECD-21	21/21	0.3	0.5	0.1	0.1
High Income‡	45/78	1.3	2.0	0.4	0.9
Upper Middle Income	33/56	3.8	4.8	3.1	2.2
Lower Middle Income	22/31	4.7	5.2	3.4	4.1

† Non-weighted averages. For the 12 low-income countries included in the ILO data there are too many gaps for a proper averages calculation.
‡ Including the OECD-21.
DATA SOURCE: ILO, *Global Wage Report 2016/17*[30]

It can be seen from the table that for both the total period and all the sub-periods, real-wages grew on average faster the lower the group income.

11§15 *Implications of the tendency to international migration of production for the constellation of capitalist nations*

The tendency to international migration of production has far-reaching consequences for the constellation of capitalist nations.

1 The single nation's balance of forces as determining the nation's reproduction of the capitalist system

Conditioned by state-granted capitalist economic rights, enterprises are ultimately driven by profit and the accumulation of capital, their comparative success being measured by the rate of profit (Chapters 1 and 6). The reproduction of the capitalist system within each single nation is at each historical conjuncture determined by a particular balance of forces. This balance of forces is different in e.g. 1920, 1980 or 2010. These forces are, most briefly:

(a) The monetary-value productivity of labour, together with the labour-market-related determinants of wages, as resulting in the rate of surplus-value (the rate of labour exploitation) and the rate of accumulation of capital (Chapters 1–2).

(b) The state's regulatory frameworks of the accumulation of capital and their articulation with taxation and rates of taxation (Chapter 7).

30 http://www.ilo.org/global/research/global-reports/global-wage-report/2016/lang--en/index.htm ('data from the report').

(c) The legitimation of the state and hence of the capitalist system in face of the structure of market wages (cf. point 1) as articulated with taxation-requiring social security transfers (Chapters 2, 7 and 8).

Very broadly (b) reinforces (a) and the latter again accommodates (c). These three result in after-tax rates of profit and in the after-tax distribution of income and wealth among households (Chapter 8). The degree of widespread information about these (engendered by the degrees of widespread public education and of infra-structural means of communication especially in the form of ICT) again affects the state's legitimation and are a catalyst for increasing social security transfers (10§12; compare Graphs 11.17–11.19).

The resulting single-nation balance of forces stands on itself. However, it is – given the contingent internationally diverging cultures and politico-economic ideologies – co-determined by the degree of widespread information about, in brief, the income and wealth levels and distributions in *other* nations.

2 *The tendency to international migration of production – general remarks*

Even if international trade has, or may have, uneven effects on nations (11§6), it does not fundamentally affect a nation's system-reproductive balance of forces, especially regarding the 'structural national conservation of capital accumulated' (11§7). This is different for the international migration of production (IMP) – 11§14.

Below I will not further stress that a proper state's Hard Core framework is an absolute condition for IMP (11§12).

In what follows I will for convenience keep on using the analytical distinction between high-, middle- and low-income countries; in fact IMP applies across the full continuum of single countries, that is, between each of the high-, middle- and low-income categories, as well as within these.

3 *IMP: the effect on wages, taxes and the accumulation of capital frameworks*

I start from the balance of forces components (1) and (2) of the first sub-section above. Improvements of the state's capital accumulation frameworks are accelerators for the accumulation of capital. The main problem is their take-off. For many middle- and low-income countries the with IMP-associated general growth increase, wages increase and along with it the taxation increase, triggers the take-off (cf. 11§13, Figure 11.21). Once this is on substantial track, the two act as self-reinforcing (yet, further IMP would still step-up the process).

For the countries from which capital emigrates we have contrary effects. Average wages and the concomitant taxes and framework expenditures become gradually under pressure (which need not immediately imply their actual decrease).

This way the tendency to IMP engenders regarding these factors a very gradual process of convergence between high-, middle- and low-income countries.

4 *IMP: legitimation in face of the structure of market wages as articulated with social security transfers*

I now turn to the third component of the system-reproductive balance of forces mentioned in the first sub-section. That is, the legitimation of the state and hence of the capitalist system in face of the structure of market wages as articulated with taxation requiring social security transfers (SST). The more skewed the structure of market wages and of incomes generally, the more are SST required for the vast-majority-legitimation of the state. As indicated, the degree of this requirement is catalysed by the degree of widespread information about these skewed structures. Thus the development of the accumulation frameworks (especially widespread public education and the communication part of infrastructure) affects the SST requirement (cf. Graphs 11.17–11.19 and Table 11.20).

In the context of the international migration of production (IMP) the international convergence of SST will move much behind the very gradual convergence of wages and the accumulation of capital frameworks. Nevertheless, with continued IMP the SST convergence is on the horizon.

For the IMP immigrant nations (especially the middle- and low-income countries) this causes mere moderate problems that may fit a restructured balance of forces for these – coming from a relative low, gradually increasing wages and SST will contribute to the vast-majority-legitimation.[31]

However, this is quite different for the IMP emigrant nations (especially the HICs). For these the wages convergence means the dampening of their increase, and in the end perhaps even their decrease. This by itself affects their vast-majority-legitimation. Along with the downward pressure on wages and the concomitant taxation revenue, the finance of SST squeezes (affecting either the transfers to the broad bottom, or their burden for the broad top of the distribution of income). The question is for how long this will be sustainable for the vast-majority-legitimation of the IMP emigrant countries (see also 10D4, to

31 Nevertheless, the further requirement for SST increases with the difference between the wages of the employed and the resources of those that have no work. Especially the requirement of pension income transfers also increases with increasing life expectancy – see Table 11.7 for the different life expectancies around 2015.

which IMP adds a new dimension). For these countries the balance of forces regarding the reproduction of the capitalist system risks to be moving to disruption.

11§15-a Amplification. Risk of disruption of the system-reproductive balance of forces

We have seen in 10D4 (yet abstracting from the international constellation) that continuously *increasing* SST as a percentage of GDP is for the capitalist system's vast-majority-legitimation requirement a necessity as well as an impossibility (10§12 and 10§14).

International migration of production gradually speeds up for the HICs the capitalist system's SST vulnerability, and adds to this a dampening of wage increases, and perhaps even wage decreases. It seems not unlikely that at least these IMP consequences evoke the repeal of the state-granted right to the emigration of capital (11§10).

Summary and conclusions

The exposition in the main systematic sections of Chapters 1–10 was about each full-fledged capitalist nation. The current chapter made explicit that these nations are different regarding: (1) their geographical location; (2) the historical point in time at which they became full-fledged capitalist as conditioned by their state's granting of capitalist Hard Core rights as concretised in the Hard Core legislative frameworks; (3) the degree of intensity of all the other legislative frameworks; (4) given the population of a country, the degree of the reached accumulation of capital – that degree being co-determined by the legislative 'accumulation of capital frameworks'.[32] This chapter made further explicit that for profit reasons capitalist enterprises seek to expand across national borders.

Given the exposition in Parts One and Two, the current Part (chapter) merely focused on the capitalist system's 'international mode of existence' insofar as it affects the earlier exposition of the conditions for the reproduction of the capitalist system – as well as the conclusions drawn from it. Abstracting from contingencies – as in the earlier exposition – this regards mainly 'the tendency to the international migration of production' (one form of the international

32 The Hard Core frameworks are those of 'granted legal capitalist economic rights', 'granted legal allowance rights to existence', and 'public security' (Ch. 6). The Capital Accumulation frameworks regard the 'monetary', 'labour-capacity' (including formal education) and 'infrastructural' frameworks (Ch. 7).

movement of capital), and one aspect of 'the tendency to international trade'. Throughout the chapter – and especially its Amplifications – these tendencies were presented in reference to the World Bank country income classification of 'High Income', 'Upper Middle Income', 'Lower Middle Income' and 'Low Income'. (Division 1.)

In much of its impetus, *international trade* is not fundamentally different from intra-national regional sector-wise specialisation of production. As a result, it does not affect the 'structural conservation of capital accumulated' vis-à-vis the labour population growth within a nation. However, much of the international trade has uneven effects between nations.

International trade affects the degree of versatility of the national sector-structures of production. This implies that once a nation 'freely' decided to engage in international trade, voluntary ('free') trade turns into enforced trade, together with the concomitant terms of trade. Any intended re-increase of versatility, if possible at all, will take much time; and along with it the establishing of (selective) trade barriers will meet counter measures.

International trade has a positive effect on the world average surplus-value of enterprises because this trade presses down – directly or indirectly – the price of the real-wage bundle. However, the less versatile a nation's production structure has grown, the more it is forced to import at whatever the world market price is. This means, or may mean, that the international trade effect on surplus-value is an internationally uneven one for national enterprises.

Finally, because of the concomitant transport, international trade reinforces environmental damages. Given the developed international sector-structures of production this could be resolved only in a distant future (via rounds of 'general non-trade agreements'). (Division 2.)

The '*international migration of production*' (IMP) is, next to the 'international centralisation and concentration of capital' (ICC), one of the two main forms of the 'international movement of capital'. On a substantial world scale these are fairly recent phenomena. (Until about 1990 the international movement of capital, measured as 'foreign direct investment', stayed within bounds of 1% of world GDP.)

Whereas ICC greatly affects the degree of economic power as concentrated within single enterprises, the latter as a tendency force and its results is not specifically an international phenomenon affecting the reproduction of the capitalist system. This is different for the tendency to international migration of production (IMP).

With actual migration of production, the 'structural national conservation of capital accumulated' vis-à-vis the labour population growth within a nation no longer holds. We have effluxes of capital from where it was produced by labour and appropriated and accumulated by the owners of capital. All the further specificities and effects of IMP in fact result from the rupture of this 'conservation'.

The world's nations can be classified as 'High Income', 'Upper Middle Income', 'Lower Middle Income' and 'Low Income' counties. More specifically these can be pictured as a stratification of nations characterised by the following factors that are most relevant to the IMP perspective: (1) average wages levels; (2) taxation of wages (tax receipts being dependent on the wage levels); (3) levels of the state 'accumulation of capital frameworks' (the state's means for it being tax-dependent); (4) the degree of legitimation of the state and hence of the capitalist system in face of the structure of market wages (cf. factor 1) as articulated with taxation-requiring social security transfers. A country's population's degree of widespread information about the skewedness-structure of wages levels, and of incomes generally, is a catalyst for the required level of social security transfers (SST).

The profit-driven IMP (movements along the stratification) is – given the required Hard Core framework – primarily determined by the (potentially migrating) enterprises' weighing up of factors (1) and (3): wage levels against 'accumulation of capital frameworks'. Actual IMP pushes up the growth of factors (1) through (3) in the country of immigration, and down in the country of emigration. For each of these countries – on a larger scale country groups – the (1) through (3) effects are self-reinforcing. This way the tendency to IMP engenders, regarding these factors, a very gradual process of convergence between high-, middle- and low-income countries.

This gradual convergence also affects factor (4) above. For the IMP immigrant nations (especially the middle- and low-income countries) not only wages but also SST levels tend to be pushed up. This is so because the accumulation frameworks encompass the components of public education and of the communications part of infrastructure (especially ICT); these affect the degree of widespread information in general, and so also the SST-catalysing widespread information about the skewedness-structure of wages and other income levels. This implies that also a gradual convergence of international SST levels is on the (far) horizon. Coming from a relative low, each of the gradual increases in average wages and in SST will contribute to the vast-majority-legitimation in the middle- and low-income countries.

As a tendency the legitimation effects are opposite for IMP emigrant nations (foremost the high-income countries). For these the wages convergence implies the dampening of their increase, and in the end perhaps even their decrease. This by itself affects their vast-majority-legitimation. Along with the downward pressure on wages and the concomitant taxation revenue, the finance of SST squeezes (affecting either the transfers to the broad bottom, or their burden for the broad top of the distribution of income). This means that with further increasing IMP, the vast-majority-legitimation in these countries tends to become increasingly under pressure. (Division 4.)

Conclusions in reference to the main conclusions of Chapter 10

Chapter 10 (10D4) summed up the four main vulnerabilities of the reach of the capitalist state and hence of the reproduction of the capitalist system. Here I briefly return to these in international context – given that Chapter 11 merely focused on the capitalist system's 'international mode of existence' insofar as it affects the earlier exposition.

(1) *The inevitably increasing quantity and complexity of regulation.* For many middle- and low-income countries (MLIC) this may as yet not be acute, but as for the high-income countries (HIC) they will increasingly be confronted with it.

(2) *The insecurities regarding the sufficient regulation of 'too big to fail' entities – especially banks.* Here the same applies as under (1). (Note that in 2015 the MLIC China hosts four of the five largest banks in the world, and 13 of the 50 largest.)

(3) *The insecurities regarding the environment restoration.* The HICs have been the prime movers of the damage. The MLICs can claim that the HICs have to take the lead in a major degree, the MLICs themselves having other priorities. In any case, for the survival of the capitalist system (and humankind in general), a vast restructuring of at least the HIC economies is inevitable (68% of world GDP in 2015). Chapter 11 made explicit that, in face of long distance transport, international trade engendered the snare of decreasing versatile national sector-structures of production and hence of enforced international trade and enforced long distance transport.

(4) *The increase in the level of the social security transfers in percentage of GDP.* It was concluded that whereas increasing social security transfers (SST) as a percentage of GDP is necessary for the vast-majority-legitimation of the state, the increases' fading off is equally necessary for the state's vast-majority-legitimation. The 11D3 outline of the 'tendency to the international migration of production' added to this the tendential downward pressure on HIC average wages, and conversely for MLIC average wages. Given the world nations' uneven GDP per capita levels, the tendency-convergences of average wages and of SST tend to be associated with a process of conversely uneven vast-majority-legitimation. This adds to the future system-reproductive vulnerability of the (yet) HICs. In the (very) long-term, however, the HICs show a mirror to the (yet) MLICs: '*De te fabula narratur*' (of you the tale is told).

Appendix 11.A. Additional detailed graphs and data information

Re 11§4-a *International trade 1960–2015*

Graph 11.8 presented the development of world exports 1960–2015. *Graph 11.8-a* decomposes these for the high-, middle- and low-income countries (including their export–import balances). We see that from 1960 until 2007 the exports of all four country categories fluctuate, though in the same upward direction. Thereafter we see a flattening off or a decline (it is too early to judge whether this marks a structural change).

GRAPH 11.8-A *Exports and External Balance of high-, middle- and low-income countries, as % of their GDP; 1960–2015*

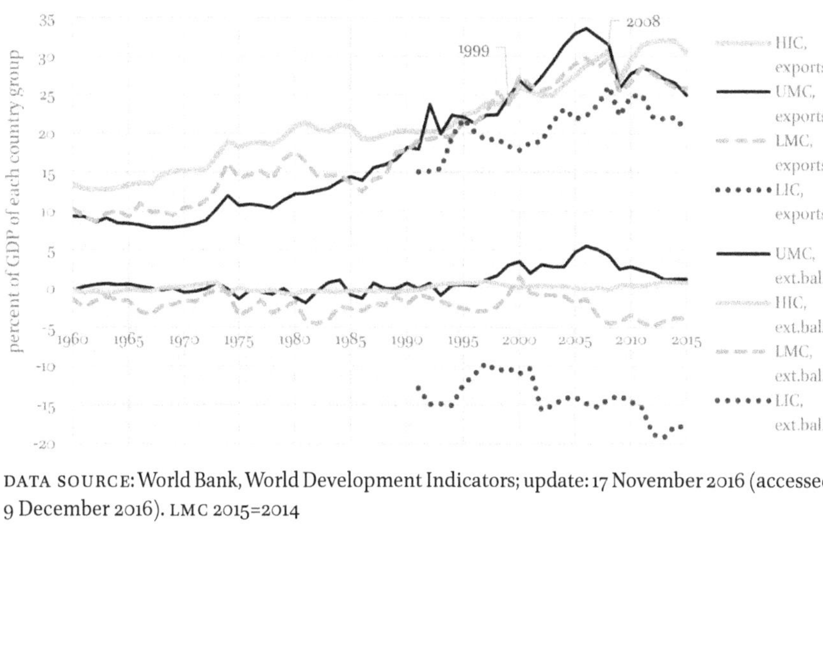

DATA SOURCE: World Bank, World Development Indicators; update: 17 November 2016 (accessed 9 December 2016). LMC 2015=2014

Re 11§10-b ***International movement of capital as measured by 'Foreign Direct Investment' (FDI) and its pattern 1970–2015***

GRAPH 11.12-A *FDI inflows and outflows as % of GDP, average of upper-middle-income countries; 1970–2015*

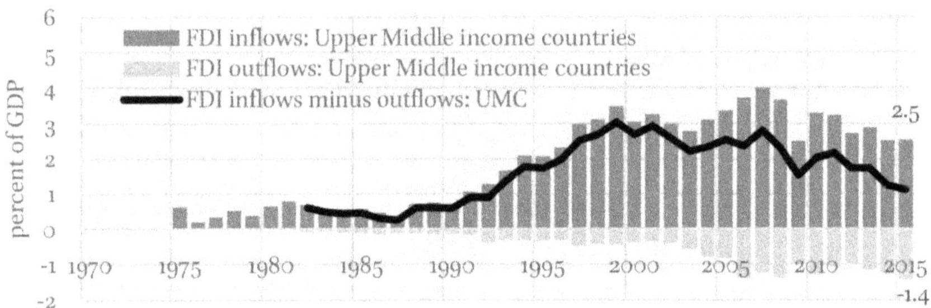

DATA SOURCE: see Graph 11.11

GRAPH 11.12-B *FDI inflows and outflows as % of GDP, average of lower-middle-income countries; 1970–2015*

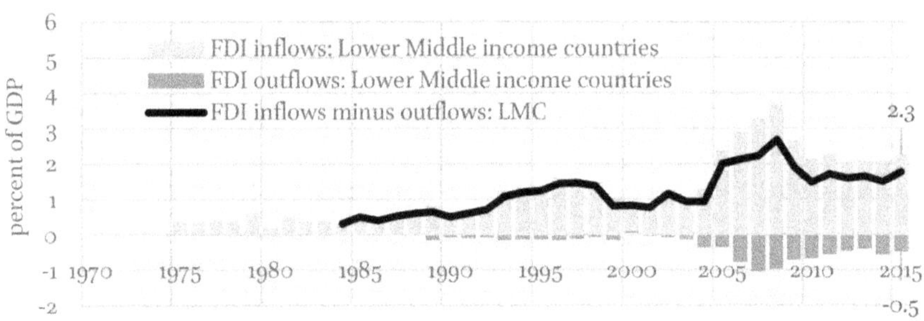

DATA SOURCE: see Graph 11.11

GRAPH 11.12-C *FDI inflows and outflows as % of GDP, average of low-income countries; 1970–2015*

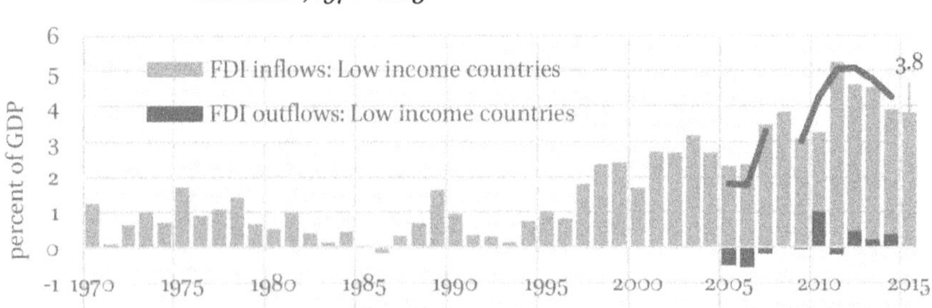

DATA SOURCE: see Graph 11.11

Re 11§12-b ***Expenditure on formal education (Graph 11.17)***
Below are the number of data that are available for each year and country category.

Countries		Number of data for Graph 11.17									
		1970	1975	1980	1985	1990	1995	2000	2005	2010	2015
HIC	78	25	31	35	38	46	49	56	56	58	55
UMC	56	14	14	22	23	28	30	40	41	41	33
LMC	52	19	19	19	16	18	29	41	39	44	31
LIC	31	7	6	12	12	15	12	22	21	27	27

The robustness tests that I did (for example, excluding countries with less than four data) did not fundamentally change the pattern of the graph.

List of figures chapter 11

PART 4

Summary and additions

CHAPTER 12

General summary and conclusions

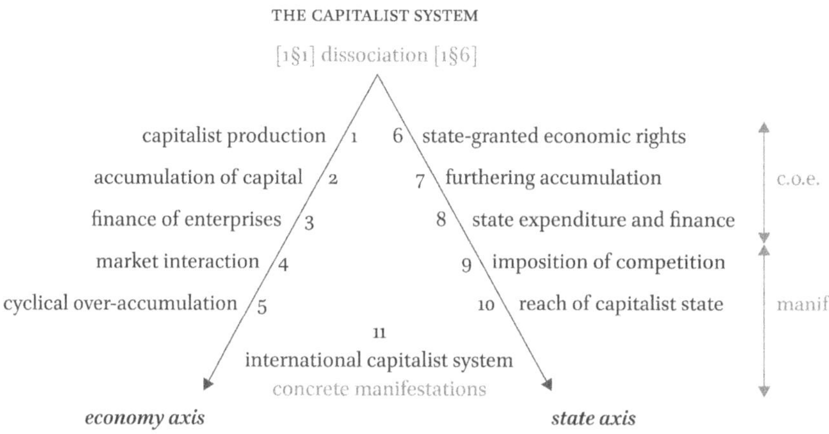

Note: 'c.o.e.' abbreviates conditions of existence and 'manif.' manifestations

Contents

Subject and general aim

This book is about 'full-fledged' capitalism, which emerges when not merely trade but also the production process is dominated by the monetary dimension and profit. The book's aim is to systematically identify the interconnection of the relations, institutions and processes that are necessary for the continued reproduction of the capitalist system – that is, the capitalist economy together with the capitalist state. This results in a synthetic outline of the constellation and functioning of the capitalist system. In short, the aim is to comprehend the capitalist system. Conscious change within and beyond the capitalist system requires its comprehension – in this I am an ardent pupil of Marx. In line with the systematic-dialectical method adopted to achieve this systematic comprehension, the book is therefore restricted to a systematic synthetic *exposition* of the capitalist system. The exposition's systematic entails the abstraction from contingencies.

Part One presents the 'capitalist economy', and Part Two the 'capitalist state'. In Part Three, these are considered in international context. Each of the subsequent chapters of Part One has its sequel in each of the subsequent chapters of Part Two.

In this summary of the book I adopt its rigorous order of the exposition, which is the zigzag one, that is the chapter order of the expositional levels [1;6], [2;7] and so on (General Introduction C§4).

The use of some uncommon terms cannot always be evaded in this summary; for a brief explanation the reader might turn to the Glossary. Some footnotes in this summary are addressed to readers acquainted with Marx's *Capital* and current marxian political economy. These footnotes are starred (*) and can be skipped by other readers.

1 *The starting point: dissociated outward bifurcation (1D1 and 6D1)*[1]

The starting point of the book is the 'dissociated outward bifurcation' (institutional separation) between households and privately owned enterprises. Enterprises claim the entitlement to property in the earth and other means of production. The capitalist state as extraordinary social institution grants these claims in the form of rights (1D1, 6D1, 6D2).[2] The rest of the book sets out how this separation is bridged such that the capitalist system can be a potentially continuous (a 'reproducing') constellation. The main elements

1 The reader who turns to this summary before having read anything else of the book is informed that 1D1 (etc.) refers to Chapter 1, Division 1; 1§1 (etc.) refers to Chapter 1, section 1.

2 The first ground of the state being an extraordinary social institution is presented in 6D3.

of this bridging are called the 'conditions of existence' or the 'grounding moments' of this separation.

2 *Capitalist production and its grounding by the capitalist state (Chapters 1 and 6)*[3]

The poles of the outward bifurcation are apparently bridged via trade relations. However, the inherently multifaceted dimensions of goods and capacities require commensuration in terms of a common denominator.[4*] The latter derives from the everyday market 'trans-abstraction' that ascribes to goods and capacities the super-sensuous dimension of 'value' as mediated by money – money, which itself has no inherent content or value. Entities are made commensurate in terms of this super-sensuous value dimension that we 'know' only through money as its quantifier, a quantifier whose physical form is insignificant. The market interaction thus constitutes goods and capacities as commodities, that is, as dual (or inwardly bifurcated) entities – duality along the multifaceted dimensions of usefulness on the one hand, and the mono-dimension of monetary-value on the other.[5*]

The monetary-value dimension and the commodification of goods and labour-capacity determine the market-interconnection of the poles, the enterprises being driven by monetary profit. The market-interconnection engenders the duality of things and capacities. (1D1–1D4.)

This mono-drive of monetary profit is concretely dominant for what is (not) produced and how it is (not) produced in enterprises. It affects what counts and what does not count. Astonishingly the super-sensuousness of the monetary-value of things and capacities affects their sensuous being, and coming into being. Further: sensuous physical-technical production becomes a mere instrument for valorisation – the production of monetary-value, or value-added. This characterises the general form of the capitalist production process (1D5, sub A).

---

3 The general summary of Chapter 1 below is not much different from the summary at the end of that chapter.

4 * In the current context the main capacity is labour-capacity (the capacity to labour). Here I revert to the term that Marx used until about 1865, instead of his later 'labour-power'. One reason for adopting the term 'labour-capacity' is that, in my view, the term more appropriately covers the concept (i.e. of *potential* activity). Another reason is that I introduce later on the term 'productive power of labour' (a refinement of labour productivity), which I would not want to have confused with 'labour-power'.

5 * When henceforth I use the terms 'value', 'value-added', 'surplus-value' and 'profit' *tout court*, these are without exception in the 'monetary-value dimension'. (The concept and term of so-called 'labour values' form no part of my vocabulary. Incidentally it is worthwhile to remind the reader that Marx never used this term in *Capital*.)

However, this general form lacks a criterion for determining what instrumental guise – what physical commodity and what physical technique – is most efficacious for profit. This requires: first, a common measure for the amount of investments, which is 'capital'; secondly, the grasping of time of investment as 'production time'; and thirdly, a measure for the duration of capital investment in terms of a standard time, which is the calendar year.[6*] The profit – more precisely the surplus-value – gained during a year, over a year's capital investment, that is, the 'rate of integral profit', delivers the criterion.[7*]

Given the enterprises' profit drive, the production must encompass the equivalent of the value-added component of profit. Even if the general form of the capitalist production process is dominated by monetary-value and valorisation, it necessarily also remains a physical-technical process, hence it remains a dual process. Within this duality the main distinction between means of production and *labour-capacity* (L) is that the former are inherently *static* elements, whereas labour-capacity in operation, that is *labour* (L^{α}), is the *active* element. Means of production can merely be operated or not be operated. Labour-capacity operates means of production, and so exerts labour at some productive power (α), including a component of the intensity of labour. At zero intensity (in effect a strike) there is no production, either physical or valorisation. Along with its physical production, labour creates the (as yet potential) value and value-added and so the surplus-value. (More precisely labour creates the value-added mL^{α}, where 'm' is the actual unit monetary-value of labour. Whence we have for the surplus-value $\Pi = mL^{\alpha} - wL$, where Π denotes surplus-value and wL the wages sum.) Thus alpha (α) is the 'parameter' of the productive transformation: the productive power of labour in both of the dual aspects.[8]

Whereas capital constrains the *possible production*, the power of labour (α) determines how much output is actually produced. The implication is that labour – more specifically, the actual productive power of labour – is the unique source of valorisation. Nevertheless this productive power is always based on a going technique of production. Technology and its application in specific techniques is inevitably the result of social labour.[9*]

---

6 * This part of the exposition in Chapter 1 (production time and duration of capital investment) incorporates in a condensed way the problematic of Marx's Part Two of *Capital II*.

7 * Thus the rate of integral profit = (surplus-value)/(capital). I wished that I could have called this (less artificial) 'the rate of surplus-value'. Novice readers would have understood this, but it would have been most confusing for marxian political economists.

8 Labour is not merely in capitalism but also transhistorically the sole determining factor of physical production as indicated in the previous paragraph. However, only when production is dissociated as in full-fledged capitalism is it also the creator of monetary-value-added.

9 * Readers acquainted with marxian political economy (MPE) will see how this diverges from

Labour being the creator of value-added, it is 'compensated' just by the wage, with the enterprise appropriating the surplus-value, that is, the difference between value-added and the wage. Surplus-value is generally the source of the growth of capital. Because labour is the unique source of valorisation and hence of surplus-value, labour essentially produces the equivalent of its own wage as well as that of the growth of capital. Hence labour essentially produces capital. (1D5.)

With labour's production of surplus-value as appropriated by the enterprises, the enterprises' driving force has been given content. It appears to resolve in a major degree the enterprises' dissociated production and so the starting point's dissociated outward bifurcation (so concludes Chapter 1).

However, enterprises can merely *claim* to be entitled to this appropriation of the surplus-value produced by labour. The state grants this claim in the form of a right to this appropriation. I called this 'granted right' together with the granted rights to private property in the earth and other means of production (section 1 above): the core 'capitalist economic rights' granted by the state. This is what constitutes the state as 'capitalist state' (6D2). For doing so the state must seek legitimation in the compliance of the vast majority of actors. The first, yet abstract-general, condition for this legitimation is that the state posits its (non-)action in terms of the (putative) general interest, and that it posits granted rights in the form of legal rights. The state so posits itself as an 'impartial' extraordinary institution *above and outside* the opposing particular economic interests. However, given that the state *de facto* grants the core capitalist economic claims in the form of rights, it constitutes vis-à-vis the capitalist economy a *separation-in-unity* within the capitalist system (6D3).

The concretisation of the seeking of this legitimation is the key continuous theme throughout the exposition of the capitalist state (Chapters 6–10).

---

standard MPE. Firstly, I introduce the rate of integral profit early on in the exposition – *because* it is the major general criterion for capitalist production. Secondly, I take distance from any (remnants of) a homogeneous labour value-productivity approach (whence I have L^{α} and hence – depending on the size of labour's productive power α – diverging rates of surplus-value). Thus I have from beginning to end dimensionally a so-called 'single system' approach (or, in the standard terminology, any 'transformation' in this respect is redundant from Chapter 1 onwards). In fact this is an aside. The substantial point is not only that the productive power of labour is always based on a going technique of production, but also and foremost that technology and its application in specific techniques is inevitably *the result of social labour* (it is not something that capitalists dream up).

Whereas Marx in his 1864/65 draft manuscript for Part Two of *Capital III* posits *in effect* sector-wise diverging rates of surplus-value (that is, after the transformation), I start with diverging rates – not as a matter of *distribution*, but as a matter of labour's *productive* power. (On these and other differences, see the addenda 1§14-c and 1§15-a.)

Analogously, the production and validation of surplus-value (integral profit) is the key continuous theme throughout the exposition of the capitalist economy (Chapters 1–5).

Throughout Part Two of the book, the main systematic clusters of the state's legislation are named 'frameworks' of legislation and other regulation. In terms of conditions of the capitalist economic rights granted (6D2), the three 'proximate' frameworks of legislation are those of, now, legal capitalist economic allowance rights (6D4), of legal allowance rights to existence (6D5), and of public security as including the upholding of the law (6D6). ('Proximate' conditions are – at that and each further point of the exposition – the immediate and most general conditions for that which was posited before. 'Allowance right' refers to the duty of non-obstruction of a right. It does not impose the duty of providing the allowance right holders with the means to exist or with property in the earth and in other means of production, in which case there would be a 'positive right' – 6§17.)

3 *Accumulation of capital and its furthering by the state* (*Chapters 2 and 7*)

The rationale of the enterprises' production for the sake of one-dimensional profit (1D5 above) is to acquire more of the same. This is reached by the investment of profit as accumulated capital (2D1). Within the limits of the intensity of labour and of technical change, there are three major conditions for the continued accumulation of capital.

The first condition: expanding labour-capacity. At each state of technology, the continuous accumulation of capital requires an expanding labour population such that the expanding production is fed. However, the quantitative labour population growth is beyond the control of enterprises. The same applies for its qualitative level: the scope of technical change is limited by the prevailing degree of formal education. At a given growth in labour population, the rate of accumulation of capital is ultimately determined by the rate of unemployment – thus, in face of wage pressures, the accumulation of capital requires unemployment.[10] (2D2.)

Given the labour-capacity available, the management of the enterprise manages what I call the '*enterprise–labour relation*'. This is the employment relation at the point of production through which surplus-value is extracted from labour (cf. 1D5 above), as constrained by, first, the technique of production,

10 Thus we have before us a mode of production that requires not only growth of labour-capacity, but so much growth that there is continuous unemployment.

second, the rate of unemployment, and third (in face of that rate), the management of the compliance of labour during production, as assisted by the managerial devise of a wages ladder that optimises this compliance. (2D3.)

The second condition: expansion of money. The accumulation of capital equally requires an accommodating expansion of money. This could be accomplished by an economy-immanent fragmented banking system, based on a separation-in-unity between enterprises and banks. Banks concretely create quantities of money, based on a reciprocal credit relation with their clients. Banks thus 'pre-validate' the future production of enterprises. (No state – or no state-instituted Central Bank – is required for this creation of credit money. This is what commercial banks do, and what they also predominantly do when there is a Central Bank). Nevertheless, the domain of operation of such banks tends to be limited. Limited also are the means, between these banks, for the enforcement of sound security and liability conventions. (2D4–2D5.)

The third condition: incorporation. Small enterprises can come and go as non-incorporated firms. However, the continuity of the accumulation of capital by medium and large-scale enterprises generally requires their incorporation. Incorporation is driven by perils around succession, by limitation and spread of risk and uncertainty, and by limits regarding the scale of production. The corporate form of the enterprise entails a layered form of its ownership. The shareholders are the owners of the enterprise's equity, which is 'passive capital', and with it the owners of the enterprise. However, the enterprise as corporate body is the owner of the 'active capital', which is administered by the executive management of the corporation. (2D6.)

The last division of Chapter 2 posits the corporate enterprise in the perspective of the exposition's starting point of privately owned enterprises (cf. 1D1 above). Along with the shareholder's objective to limit and to spread its risk and uncertainty, we have a *detached* form of passive capital ownership. The ownership of a particular enterprise is not the capital owner's object, but rather an *instrument* for its passive capital ownership in general. Although for an *individual* enterprise the 'active capital' (assets) and the 'passive capital' (liabilities) are inherently *inseparable*, the detached form of passive capital ownership makes the *accumulation of passive capital* into a separate motive, whence the accumulation of capital (2D1) now appears as a disunited *two-fold accumulation of capital.* Nevertheless *some* enterprise must be the necessary instrument for the detached capital ownership. This way the concrete directly exploitative 'enterprise–labour relation' (2D3 above) is reflected in the actually abstract indirect exploitative relation between the passive capital owner and labour, that is, the actually abstract *'capital–labour relation'.* (2D7.)

The next paragraphs turn to the state's furthering of the accumulation of capital (Chapter 7).

The state's carrying out its 'functions' (Chapter 6) is predicated on its material existence. This requires taxation, whence it is, paradoxically, compelled to override property right in name of its definition of the (putative) general interest. Because the (potential) action radius of the state is determined by the tax base, it must seek to increase that base – so as to reach feasible tax rates – by furthering the conditions for the accumulation of capital and along with it the conditions for economic growth (7D1). The following three legislative and regulative frameworks are geared to this.

Monetary framework. Limiting banking to licensees, the major concern of this framework is to bind banks to sound security and liability rules ('prudential regulation'), the ultimate penalty for deviation from those rules being the withdrawal of the licence. A second major concern is achieving 'price stability' (in fact 'creeping inflation'). The state can try to influence the interest rate, but it has virtually no means to control the quantity of money and credit. It is the commercial banks that predominantly undertake the money creation, and hence accommodate the accumulation of capital and economic growth. This poses the main dilemma of the state's monetary policy: tight prudential regulation affects the banks' accommodation of economic growth. This is also the main dilemma regarding the phenomenon that became manifest in the early twenty-first century: monetary-system-shaking banks that are 'too big to fail' and moreover organisationally too complex to supervise micro-wise. (7D2.)

Labour-capacity framework. Enterprises cannot control the quantity and quality of the labour population (cf. 2D2). The state attempts to regulate the quantity through a minimum wages policy (one sufficient for population growth), through child benefits and through unemployment payments that tide over business cycle recessions. It regulates the quality mainly through public education. (7D3.)

Infrastructural framework. A third condition for the accumulation of capital that 'the capitalist economy' could secure only poorly relates to the infrastructure. (7D4.)

A final key framework is that of *social security transfers* (regarding mainly old age, health and incapacity). This is no direct condition for the accumulation of capital, but rather a condition for the legitimation of the state in the compliance of the vast majority of actors (cf. 6D3 above). Because the legitimation of the state is a sine qua non for the existence of the capitalist system, these transfers are an indirect condition for the accumulation of capital. (7D5.) (The easiest way to illustrate the systemic necessity of these transfers is to anticipate 8D5 where it is shown that without these transfers – in 2010 at least – on average 30% of the population of the 21 most advanced capitalist countries would live below the poverty line.)

Conflicts and conflict modification. This completes the exposition of the seven main legislative frameworks: those of legal economic rights (6D4), legal existence rights (6D5), public security (6D6), money and banking (7D2), labour-capacity (7D3), infrastructure (7D4), and social security (7D5). All these frameworks are necessary for the existence of the capitalist system, as well as conflicting.

A theme running throughout the exposition of the state that I have not emphasised so far is the state's continuous effort *to 'purify' its core administrative body from conflict.* It does so by delegating conflicting regulation and supervision to 'independent' authorities including the Central Bank and a large variety of inspectorates and councils. These bodies like to be called 'independent technocratic'. However, in the face of conflict resolution, it is foremost in the interest of the state to 'advertise' these bodies as being independent.

The settlement of major conflicts is further grounded in two major institutional 'assigning separations' (rather than 'delegations') within the state, between on the one hand the state's core Administrative body, and on the other hand the bodies of a legitimising Judiciary and a legitimising Deliberative.

With the necessary arbitration and sanctioning of deviations from the law (cf. 6D3 and 6D6), the state gets involved with conflicting claims to right that erode both its reference to the general interest and its self-imposition as an extraordinary impartial institution. This is resolved by assigning the arbitration and sanctioning to a separated off judiciary, whence the state purifies itself from the conflicts concerned. (7D6.)

The Deliberative is the necessary political arena of conflict and so a mode for recurrent conflict settlement.[11] Through this assigning separation, the core of the state is equally purified from conflict, so that it can execute the granting of the core economic entitlement claims in the form of law, and execute the frameworks of furthering the conditions for economic growth and so for the accumulation of capital. (7D7.)[12]

---

11 'Deliberative' is a general notion. All of the current OECD-21 countries practice forms of parliamentary representative democracy – the character of the assignation differs. A common and equal suffrage (also called universal suffrage) for the election of parliaments was, on average for these countries, introduced in 1899 for men, and in 1929 also for women.

12 In general the exposition is not about desirability or undesirability, but rather about institutions and processes in their effect, which in these cases is the 'shielding' of the main body of the state.

4 *The finance of enterprises, the expenditure and finance of the state, and their effect on the macroeconomic validation of surplus-value and on the distribution of income and wealth* (*Chapters 3 and 8*)

The first section of Chapter 3 guides the reader through this chapter, distinguishing between 'active capital' (enterprises' assets) and 'passive capital' (the finance of the assets). Along with it surplus-value (the result of production) is qua distribution decomposed into 'internal profit' (the sum of dividends and retained profit) and 'interest' (as distributed to banks and other financiers). (3D1.)[13|14*]

A main requirement for the accumulation of capital and economic growth is that banks 'pre-validate' the future production of enterprises by their creation of credit money (cf. 2D4 above). Through it, banks are also inevitably and *continuously* the initial macroeconomic financiers of enterprises. The banks' 'pre-validating finance' (PVF) of enterprises is not only unconditionally necessary to the capitalist system; it is also fundamentally different from any other type of finance. It is a pure ex-nihilo accounting money operation, which requires no saving – neither prior to the investment that it accommodates, nor after it. Generally, therefore, saving is *not* necessary to the capitalist system. In fact saving is a nuisance for enterprises because it hampers the redemption of their debt with banks. If there would be no saving, the banks' PVF could simply be redeemed out of the proceeds from production. This would then be followed by a new sequence of PVF, production, validation of production and redemption of the PVF and so forth. (3D2.)[15]

In practice enterprises are confronted with ubiquitous savings, which hamper the PVF redemption. These savings may *substitute ex post* for the non-redeemed part of the PVF, whence there are, ex post, types of finance other than the banks' PVF, such as shares and bonds. From a systematic point of view, all other types of finance derive from the bank-provided PVF. All these non-PVF types finance already *accumulated* capital, or ready investments on the basis of the PVF. Therefore, generally, saving does not precede investment; investment is not financed 'out of' saving. Macroeconomically, only the bank-provided PVF finances the *accumulation* of capital. (3D3.)

---

13 See the summary in Figures 3.2a and 3.2b.

14 * From the perspective of marxian political economy, 'rent' seems to be missing here as a separate category (cf. Marx's *Capital III*, Part Six). Appendix 3C sets out why and how any rent that enterprises pay is a share in their surplus-value (as is interest).

15 The exposition in 3D2 and in the following 3D3 is based on the Monetary Circuit theory. The exposition takes distance from the loanable funds view of banking. (See Addenda 3§2-e. and 3§6-a.)

The previous results (3D2 and 3D3) apply to existing enterprises as well as to newly founded ones. Division 3D4 briefly sets out how the foundation of banks themselves also proceeds by a PVF, now to the founders of banks. This division thus provides the systematic (rather than historical) grounds for the starting point's capital accumulated (cf. 1D1 above).[16*]

Whereas macroeconomic investment is independent of saving, the purchase of financial paper (often misleadingly called portfolio 'investment' rather than finance) is not independent of saving. Not only is there no macroeconomic *ex ante* equality of saving and investment, nor is there a macroeconomic *ex post* equality of saving and investment (the positing of such an equality in most of economics is a categorical mistake, confusing expenditure and saving). (3D5.)[17]

The sequential character of the interconnected processes of pre-validation, production, validation and distribution of output and surplus-value is essential to a capitalist economy. The degree of redemption of the pre-validating finance, as well as the validation of surplus-value (integral profit), is conditioned on the macroeconomic effective demand. In line with a Kalecki type of approach it is posited that – at the stage of exposition of Chapter 3 (abstracting from the state and international relations) – the macroeconomic validation of the surplus-value produced is determined by investment (positively), the consumption by capital owners (positively), and the saving by labour (negatively). (3D5.) Taking the state into account, the macroeconomic validation of the surplus-value produced is additionally determined by the total of the state expenditure (positively) and the saving out of the state's wages and transfers (negatively). (8D3.) The distribution of surplus-value (to banks, capital owners and as retained profits) inevitably follows after the validation, whence there is no investment out of a pre-existing surplus-value. This is how the investment–saving dynamic is connected to the investment–surplus-value dynamic. (3D5.)

I now turn to state expenditure and its finance in more detail (Chapter 8).

---

16 * At the end of *Capital*, Volume I, Marx has a famous and interesting chapter on, what he calls, the initial accumulation of capital – describing the historical transition from feudalism to capitalism. That chapter has been interpreted as providing the grounding for his starting point in *Capital*. In my view, however, a systematic exposition should endeavour to provide its grounds systematically rather than historically (allotting the history to an addendum).

17 Thus I posit that macroeconomically we have generally I ≠ S. On this inequality I challenge a broader spectrum than merely the mainstream orthodoxy. The conventional I = S *definition* is ultimately based on the view that the *investment* equivalent of ex post retained profits is a saving rather than an expenditure! (3§9 and 3§-a.)

Economically the state 'produces' the content of the economic rights framework and the frameworks furthering the accumulation of capital as presented in Chapters 6–7. For it, the state employs wage labour (i.e. civil servants) and purchases inputs from enterprises, but it tends to make no profits. Moreover, it distributes its produce for free as collective goods and services. Next to the state's expenditure on its production, its expenditure includes transfers in the form of, mainly, social security and interest. (8D1.)

Taxation is a necessary, and main, form of finance of the state. Next to this finance, the state may contingently collect social security contributions, and it may contingently collect other receipts (mainly) from royalties, sale of state services, and dividends of state-owned enterprises. Finally, the state may contingently borrow to finance any budget deficit (or lend in case of a surplus). The state's finance, in its particular forms, grounds the state's expenditures and hence the moments prior to it. (8D2.)

As already indicated, all of the state's expenditures – though apart from the savings out of the state's wages and transfers – end up as expenditures with enterprises, and so also realise a major part of their surplus-value. Increases of state expenditure increase the production and validation of surplus-value – vice versa for expenditure decreases. (8D3.)

Part of this state-accommodated surplus-value is distributed to the state via taxation of surplus-value (or narrower, taxation of profit). Thus, for enterprises in macroeconomic perspective, the benefits from state expenditure are in part offset by these taxes. These taxes are the enterprises' costs of the state's granting and upholding of their legal core economic rights to property and to employ labour, as well as its accommodation of the accumulation of capital (that is, the costs of the seven legislative frameworks as presented in Chapters 6–7). Thus, these are the costs for the state's accommodation of the enterprises' employment (use) of labour in general – not merely those that stem from extra surplus-value along with extra state expenditure.

In principle all state expenditure might be financed by taxation of surplus-value. From the perspective of labour it is immaterial where the taxes on surplus-value are levied (either at the point where it is generated within enterprises, or at the point where it has been distributed to financiers). In practice the state acts such that enterprises and capital owners 'share' the taxation with taxation of the wages income of labour. (8D4.)

The final division of this chapter is an exposition of the particular forms of taxation in their effect on the distribution of the income and wealth of households. Households as such are, without further specification, not directly identified as workers' or capital owners' households, but rather as households that have some share in the income from wages or from surplus-value.

The main forms of taxation include taxes on profits, on property value and property income, on labour income, and on products. In principle the state might choose between these forms or combinations thereof. Some form of taxation being necessary, it is contingent which particular form or forms are actually applied, and to what extent. Taxation has inevitably non-neutral distributive effects on income and wealth. This applies for the particular form of taxation and also for the design of tax rates (regressive, flat, progressive). More specifically, a flat tax rate is not more neutral than a non-flat one. Any actual form and design of taxation is inevitably based on a normative stance. This has no effect on the fact that with a more skewed households distribution of income, more savings press down profits. Thus progressive taxes support enterprises: their rate of profit and so investment and employment. This puts on the state's agenda the dilemma as to whether it is primarily concerned with the interests of enterprises or rather with the privileges of the high-income categories. The ideological supposition that investment would require saving is of key importance here. (8D5.)

This completes the exposition of the conditions of existence of the capitalist economy and state. From the point of view of the systematic-dialectical method adopted, it is only at this point – that is, when all earlier pre-positions have been grounded endogenously – that we can concretely reflect on the capitalist system in its entirety. In fact the last division (8D5) is literally on the edge of it. The next chapters are an exposition of the capitalist system's concrete manifestations.

5 *The concrete modes of manifestation of the enterprises' market interaction* (*Chapters 4 and 9*)

So far the exposition focused on the extraction of surplus-value from labour as grounded in the state-accommodated enterprise–labour relation and the derived capital–labour relations. Enterprises are first of all interconnected in their unity as entities that go for the same aim, that is, the production of surplus-value as measured by the rate of integral profit. The focus in Chapter 4 is on the manifestation of this unity of enterprises in their rivalry for more surplus-value (4D2–4D3), and next on the manifestation of this unity in tendencies sublating that rivalry through cartel formation, oligopolisation and monopolisation (4D4–4D5). Each of these modes of market interaction is predicated on particular – technical change related – stratified structures of production in particular sectors (4D1).

Regarding the competition apart from the sublating tendencies just mentioned, a distinction is made between 'price competition' (4D2) and 'structural overcapacity competition' (4D3). The *combination* of price competition and generalised fast technical change tends to engender generalised price deflation and stagnation. However, there are no *economy*-inherent forces to get out of such stagnation or to prevent generalised price deflation.

Chapter 9 presents the state's concrete manifestation in its imposing a framework of constraints on the modes of market interaction of enterprises and banks.

The chapter's first division sets out the state's engagement in constraints of market interaction that is 'conventionally' regarded as 'competition policy' as encoded in competition law. This conventional competition policy is paradoxical. In its prohibition of free contracts of cartel formation and of a category of take-overs and mergers (cf. 4D4–4D5), the state teaches enterprises what 'proper' market interaction is. With the state's imposition of *its* view on proper market interaction, the unity of the capitalist economy and state reaches its most concrete manifestation regarding the functioning of ordinary markets. Nevertheless this is so conflicting that the state sets out the framework in general terms, leaving its details and execution to 'independent' market authorities. (9D1.)

The chapter's second division sets out two main effects of market interaction that, when left unconstrained, would generate vulnerabilities for the reproduction of the capitalist system. Firstly, so as to prevent a market constellation associated with generalised price deflation and the concomitant potential stagnation (cf. 4D2), the state ordains a monetary policy resulting in creeping inflation (which the state labels 'price stability'). It tends to delegate its concretisation and execution to the 'independent' Central Bank.[18]

The second vulnerability regards 'too big to fail banks'. The gradual movement to 'too big to fail' is an effect of market interaction that was only thrown into relief with the emergence of the 2008 financial crisis. The complex internal structure of big banks has evolved such that effective regulation and supervision is practically unachievable. Therefore the occurrence of 'too big to fail banks' can be countered only by putting a cap on the accumulation of capital such that entities become small enough to fail. However, this would be highly conflicting, as it would castigate the success in the accumulation of capital, which in fact clashes with the economic rights granted by the state. (9D2.)

18 For systematic reasons this matter – and the following one – is briefly treated in its monetary policy aspect in 7D2, and more extensively in its aspect of 'enterprises market interaction' in 9D2.

6 *The concrete manifestations of the capitalist economy and state (Chapters 5 and 10)*

Chapters 5 and 10 present the most concrete manifestations of the capitalist system reached in this book.

Abstracting from the state, Chapter 5 presents the concrete manifestation of the capitalist economy in the macroeconomic cyclical movement of the accumulation of capital. The actual investment of enterprises is determined by their 'internal profit' and 'rate of internal profit', each of which accounts for the external finance of enterprises and its (de)leverage effect. (Internal profit = surplus-value minus interest distributed to financiers.) Investment being the main locomotive for the cyclical movement, the rate of internal profit as bounded by the rate of overcapacity are presented as the core macroeconomic determinants of investment decisions. These apply on the macroeconomic sequence of: (1) production predicated on bank finance; (2) validation of production by expenditure; (3) distribution of part of the validated surplus-value to external financiers; and (4) the resulting rate of internal profit, as determining (1) and so forth. (5D1.)[19]

Series of these sequences cyclically develop from phases of expansion into phases of crisis and contraction. In this cyclical movement, the capitalist systems' immanent expansive forces generate over-accumulation of capital. In the crisis and recession this is violently cured by destruction of capital that prepares the conditions for a renewed expansion and again contraction. That is, inwardly bifurcated productive activity is cyclically destroyed. With it the applied natural resources are destroyed – those that are accounted for in the monetary-value dimension, as well as those that are not. Along with the destruction of productive activity and productive capacity, employment of labour is destroyed. The misery so gets concentrated with those that are expelled into unemployment. Predominantly these, and their children, are sacrificed for the bifurcated process of 'creation and destruction'. Even if along this Sisyphean process the *average* real-income per head may increase, the heads are not equal and especially the unemployed are 'hors catégorie' in this respect.

Thus whereas labour is the prime mover of the production of value and capital (Chapter 1), capital itself is the prime mover of its cyclical course of

19 Thus (and in reference to footnote 9) throughout Chapters 1–5 surplus-value is the abstract-general as well as the most concrete determinant of production (throughout in single monetary dimension). In other words, workers see all of the surplus-value that they produce being appropriated by 'their' enterprise and its financiers. This is economically relevant. Relatedly it is relevant (although the exposition does not emphasise this) for the capital–labour struggle at the point of production.

accumulation and again the partial annihilation of this accumulation – labour is passively confronted with the ups and downs of employment and unemployment. (5D2.)[20]

Chapter 10 presents three key manifestations of the state, which together determine its reach.

The first manifestation applies on the cyclical movement of capital accumulation. Without affecting the cyclical movement itself, state expenditure mitigates the amplitude of 'regular' economic cycles – the degree of this automatic stabilising effect depends on the structural size of state expenditure in comparison with private expenditure. However, for the 'irregular' economic downturns triggered by financial crisis and bank failures, the mere state expenditure floor and 'normal' restructuring destruction of capital may not be sufficient for a recovery. Recovery then also requires a substantial discretionary state policy. (10D1.)

The second manifestation regards the character of the state's regulation of the capitalist economy. The mere quantity of regulation-in-force increases over time, as driven by new, or re-perceived, social-economic problems. For one part these stem from legitimation problems. For another part these stem from changes in the economic structure and product and process innovations, including process fusions. These affect the 'coverage' and the 'intensity' of regulation, and so the density and quantity of regulation. The more convoluted the social-economic problems, the more complicated regulations tend to be. This results, together with the interweaving of regulations, in an increasing complexity of regulation. However, changes of regulation are prominently also determined by unintended loopholes in regulation, that is, gaps and ambiguities – as tested by way of profit-driven borderline (non-)compliance. The legislative and other regulative reparation of these loopholes by amendments of the regulation increases the complication of single regulations, and in connection with the interweaving of regulations, multiplies into further complexity of regulation. This results in inevitable continuous cycles of loopholes being sought, amendments being made, leading to further complication and complexity. In sum we have a (hardly counteracted) diachronic tendency to not only the quantity of regulation, but also its increasing complication and complexity. (10D2.)

The third manifestation regards the content of state expenditure. For many people the 'hard core' of the capitalist state – in brief the property and exploitation rights that it grants and the legislation about them – is not part of their con-

20 The second part of the Summary and Conclusions of Chapter 5 indicates in more detail how this chapter synthesises Chapters 1–4.

scious experience. The majority of employed actors primarily experience this 'hard core' indirectly via their everyday workplace, whence the state's hard core operates as a 'hidden hand'. For most people the state's reach is rather manifested in the materialisation of its expenditure, especially in the supervision of the safety of production and products, in public education, in infrastructure, and in social security provisions.

Among the main expenditure categories of the state, those on social security transfers (SST) is the quantitatively dominant category and it tends to increase over time. SST is a main factor through which the state gains the vast-majority-legitimation that it requires. However, trends in the SST do not stand on itself. Widespread information (knowledge and its communication) about the distribution of income is a key catalyst for SST. This information correlates, on the one hand, with public education, and, on the other, with means of communication. These two again correlate with the development of the macroeconomic accumulation of capital. Thus the capital accumulation requirements of increasing public education and of the communication parts of infrastructure engender SST.

Whereas the thus catalysed increasing SST as a percentage of GDP is necessary for the vast-majority-legitimation of the state (this regards the large bottom part of the income distribution), the bearing of its burden (by the large upper part of the distribution) implies that the increases' fading off is equally necessary for the state's vast-majority-legitimation. (10D3.)

The final part of the chapter (10D4) reviews the four main vulnerabilities of the reach of the capitalist state and that are so potential impediments to the continued reproduction of the capitalist system. The *first* one is the inevitably increasing amount and complexity of regulation. Thus the so-called 'free market economy' will become unlimitedly further constrained by the capitalist state's necessary steering. The *second* vulnerability regards the 'too big to fail' entities – especially banks. Possibly this vulnerability can be resolved by rounds of complex regulation, but for the time being this is insecure. The *third* vulnerability regards the deterioration of the environment. This is in fact the most momentous one. But perhaps a recuperation is possible by, again, rounds of complex regulation – rounds that will have to be far more stringent than the regulation in prospect (at the time of writing). The *fourth* vulnerability regards the required state expenditure on social security transfers. Whilst increasing transfers as a percentage of GDP is necessary for the vast-majority-legitimation of the state, the increases' fading off is equally necessary for the state's vast-majority-legitimation.

For the continued reproduction of the capitalist system the state inevitably has to deal with these vulnerabilities. The second and third vulnerabilities are 'imaginably' resolvable. However, for the first and last ones the capitalist system is moving to a constellation of, what I call, 'necessities that are impossible'.

7 *The international mode of existence of the capitalist system (Chapter 11)*

The systematic exposition of Chapters 1–10 is about each single full-fledged capitalist nation (country). Part Three of the book (consisting of the single Chapter 11) makes explicit that these nations are different regarding: (1) their geographical location; (2) the historical point in time at which they became full-fledged capitalist – as conditioned by their state's granting of capitalist 'hard core' rights as concretised in the hard core legislative frameworks (cf. Chapter 6); (3) the degree of intensity of their legislative 'accumulation of capital frameworks' (cf. Chapter 7);[21] (4) the degree of intensity of their legislative 'social security framework' (cf. Chapter 7); (5) given the population of a country, the degree of the reached accumulation of capital – that degree being co-determined by the legislative 'accumulation of capital frameworks'. This chapter makes further explicit that capitalist enterprises, for profit reasons, seek to expand across national borders.

The chapter sets out the capitalist system's 'international mode of existence' merely insofar as it affects the earlier exposition of the conditions for the reproduction of the capitalist system (Parts and Two – sections 1–6 above). Abstracting from contingencies – as in the earlier exposition – this regards mainly 'the tendency to the international migration of production' (one form of the international movement of capital), and one aspect of 'the tendency to international trade'. (11D1.)

In much of its impetus *international trade* is no fundamentally different from intra-national regional sector-wise specialisation of production. However, much of the international trade has uneven effects between nations.

International trade affects the degree of versatility of the national sector-structures of production. This implies that once a nation 'freely' decided to engage in international trade, voluntary ('free') trade turns into enforced trade, together with the concomitant terms of trade. Any intended re-increase of versatility, if possible at all, will take much time; and along with it the establishing of (selective) trade barriers will meet counter measures.

---

21 The 'hard core' frameworks are those of 'granted legal capitalist economic rights', 'granted legal allowance rights to existence', and 'public security' (Chapter 6). The 'capital accumulation frameworks' regard the 'monetary', 'labour-capacity' (including formal education) and 'infrastructural' frameworks (Chapter 7).

International trade has a positive effect on the world average surplus-value of enterprises because this trade presses down – directly or indirectly – the price of the real-wage bundle. However, the less versatile a nation's production structure has grown, the more it is forced to import at whatever the world market price is. This means, or may mean, that the international trade effect on surplus-value is an internationally uneven one for national enterprises.

Finally, because of the concomitant transport, international trade reinforces environmental damages. Given the developed international sector-structures of production, this could be resolved only in a distant future (via rounds of 'general non-trade agreements'). (11D2.)

The '*international migration of production*' (IMP) is, next to the 'international centralisation and concentration of capital' (ICC), one of the two main forms of the 'international movement of capital'. On a substantial world scale these are fairly recent phenomena. (Until about 1990 the international movement of capital, measured as 'foreign direct investment', stayed within bounds of 1% of world GDP.)

Whereas ICC greatly affects the degree of economic power as concentrated within single enterprises, the latter as a tendency force and its results is not specifically an international phenomenon affecting the reproduction of the capitalist system. This is different for the tendency to international migration of production (IMP).

The world's nations can be categorised as 'capitalistic mature' and 'capitalistic developing' countries (briefly 'mature' and 'developing' countries).[22] More specifically these can be pictured as a stratification of nations characterised by the following factors that are most relevant in terms of IMP: (1) average wages levels; (2) taxation of wages (tax receipts being dependent on the wage levels); (3) levels of the state 'accumulation of capital frameworks'[23] (the state's means for it being tax-dependent); (4) the degree of legitimation of the state and hence of the capitalist system in face of the structure of market wages (cf. factor 1) as articulated with taxation-requiring social security transfers. The degree of widespread information within a country's populace about the skewedness-structure of wages levels, and of incomes generally, is a catalyst for the required level of social security transfers (SST).[24]

---

22 The main text adopts the World Bank classification into 'high income' countries (for 'mature') and 'upper-middle income', 'lower-middle income' and 'low income' counties (together 'developing').

23 See the first paragraph of the current section.

24 As indicated in section 6 in reference to 10D3.

The profit-driven IMP (movements along the stratification) is – given the required 'hard core' framework – primarily determined by the (potentially migrating) enterprises' weighing up of factors (1) and (3): wage levels against 'accumulation of capital frameworks'. Actual IMP pushes up the growth of factors (1) through (3) in the country of immigration, and down in the country of emigration. For each of these countries – on a larger scale country groups – the (1) through (3) effects are self-reinforcing. This way the tendency to IMP, regarding these factors, engenders a very gradual process of convergence between the 'mature' and 'developing' countries.

This gradual convergence also affects factor (4) above. For the IMP immigrant nations (especially the 'developing' countries) not only wages but also SST levels tend to be pushed up. This is so because the accumulation frameworks encompass the components of public education and of the communications part of infrastructure (especially ICT); these affect the degree of widespread information in general, and so also the SST-catalysing widespread information about the skewedness-structure of wages and other income levels. This implies that also a gradual convergence of international SST levels is on the (far) horizon. Coming from a relative low, each of the gradual increases in average wages and in SST will contribute to the vast-majority-legitimation in the 'developing' countries.

Qua tendency the legitimation effects are opposite for IMP emigrant nations (foremost the 'mature' countries). For these the wages convergence implies the dampening of their increase, and in the end perhaps even their decrease. This by itself affects their vast-majority-legitimation. Along with the downward pressure on wages and the concomitant taxation revenue, the finance of SST squeezes (affecting either the transfers to the broad bottom, or their burden for the broad top of the distribution of income) – see also 10D4, to which IMP adds a new dimension. This means that with further increasing IMP the vast-majority-legitimation in these countries tends to become increasingly under pressure. (11D4.)

8 *General conclusions (Chapter 11 in reference to Chapter 10)*

Chapter 10 (10D4) summed up the four main vulnerabilities of the reach of the capitalist state and hence of the reproduction of the capitalist system. The conclusions of Chapter 11 return to these in international context – given that the latter chapter merely focused on the capitalist system's 'international mode of existence' insofar as it affects the earlier exposition.

(1) *The inevitably increasing quantity and complexity of regulation.* For many 'developing' countries this may not be acute as yet, but as for the 'mature' countries they will increasingly be confronted with it.

(2) *The insecurities regarding the sufficient regulation of 'too big to fail' entities – especially banks.* Here the same applies as under (1).

(3) *The insecurities regarding environment restoration.* The 'mature' countries have been the prime movers of the damage. The 'developing' countries can claim that the 'mature' ones have to take the lead in a major degree, the 'developing' countries themselves having other priorities. In any case, for the survival of the capitalist system (and humankind in general), a vast restructuring of at least the 'mature' economies is inevitable (68% of world GDP in 2015). Chapter 11 makes explicit that, in face of long-distance transport, international trade engenders the snare of decreasing versatile national sector-structures of production and hence of enforced international trade and enforced long-distance transport.

(4) *The increase in the level of the social security transfers in percentage of GDP.* It was concluded that whereas increasing social security transfers (SST) as a percentage of GDP is necessary for the vast-majority-legitimation of the state, the increases' fading off is equally necessary for the state's vast-majority-legitimation. The 11D3 outline of the 'tendency to the international migration of production' adds to this the tendential downward pressure on the 'mature' countries' average wages, and conversely for the 'developing' countries. Given the world nations' uneven GDP per capita levels, the tendency-convergences of average wages and of SST tend to be associated with a process of conversely uneven vast-majority-legitimation. This adds to the future system-reproductive vulnerability of the (yet) 'mature' countries. In the (very) long-run, however, these mirror the (yet) 'developing' ones: '*De te fabula narratur*' (of you the tale is told).

CHAPTER 13

Synopsis of the main moments of *'The unity of the capitalist economy and state'*

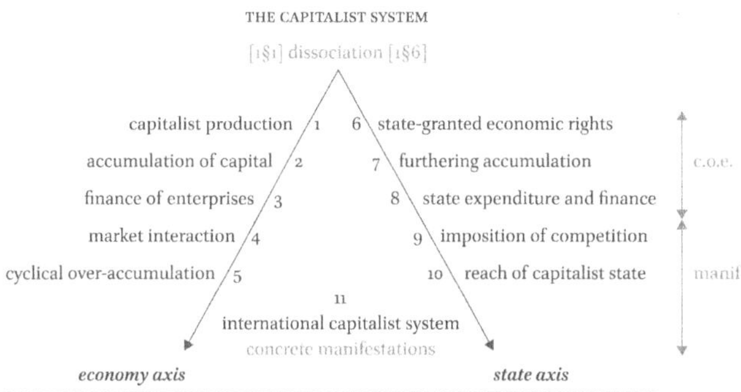

Note: 'c.o.e.' abbreviates conditions of existence and 'manif.' manifestations

This text complements the Summary and Conclusions of the book. It shows how the book's division-wise 'moments' are interconnected. The moments of Chapters 1–3 and 6–7 are necessary conditions of existence for the capitalist system – and qua exposition these ground the starting point (1§1 of 1D1, and 1§6 of 1D6). The moments of Chapters 4–5, 9–10 and 11 are concrete manifestations of the former moments.

SCHEME 13.1 *Synopsis of the main moments of* 'The unity of the capitalist economy and state' (*for explanation of the symbols and abbreviations see the legend on page 600*)

PART ONE	***The Capitalist Economy***	↠ s-i-u	***The Capitalist State***	PART TWO
1. The capitalist mode of production	Dissociated outward bifurcation into households and privately owned enterprises [1D1]	=	Dissociated outward bifurcation into households and privately owned enterprises [6D1]	6. Stare-granted capitalist economic rights
	(idem)	↠	↓ Capitalist economic entitlement claims as granted by the state in the form of rights: the capitalist state [6D2]	
	↓ Monetary value dimension (MVD) [1D2] ⇆ ↓ Commodification (*duality: inward bifurcation*) [1D3]		↓ State-granted rights in the form of law and the legitimation of the state; *legitimation in compliance ↠ putative general interest ↠ putative impartial ↠ form of legal right* [6D3]	
	↓ duality dominated by the MVD; Profit [1D4]	↠	↓ Economic rights framework; *core property and labour exploitation rights* (allowance rights) [6D4] ↠ Existence rights framework; *person: direct and indirect non-violence* (allowance rights) [6D5]	
	↓ The capitalist production process: Labour's productive power and the production and appropriation of surplus-value [1D5]		↓ public security framework [6D6]	
2. The accumulation of capital	↓ Accumulation of capital [2D1]		State's material existence ↓ Taxation ↓ action radius predicated on furthering of the conditions for capital accumulation (*entering of MVD in state considerations*) [7D1]	7. The state's furthering of the conditions for capital accumulation
	↓ Labour-capacity expansion [2D2] / ↓ Money expansion (pre-validation of production) [2D4]	↠	↓ Monetary framework [7D2] / ↓ Labour-capacity framework [7D3] ↓ *Wages* *Education*	
	↓ Managerial labour and the enterprise–labour relation [2D3] ↓ / ↓ s-i-u of banks and enterprises [2D5]		Infrastructure framework [7D4]	
	Incorporation of enterprises (*s-i-u of ownership and management of enterprises*) [2D6]		[*continuous legitimation requirement implied by 6D3*] ↓ Legitimating Social Security framework [7D5]	
	↓ owners of enterprises and owners of passive capital The twofold accumulation of capital *the capital–labour relation* [2D7]		[*modification of continuously reappearing conflict of regulation implied by all previous moments*] ↓ legitimating s-i-u of the state's administrative, judiciary and legitimating branches [7D6 & 7D7]	

3. The finance of the production and accumulation of capital	[*Production & Accumulation of Capital, Chs.1–2*] ↓ Finance of enterprises: finance capital [3D1] ↓ Pre-validating finance by banks (PVF) [3D2] ↓ Ex-post substitution for PVF by capital owners [3D3] ↓ The foundation of banks and enterprises [3D4] ↓ Macroeconomic validation of surplus-value (finance, investment and saving) [3D5]	8D3 grounds (↠) 3D5	[*Regulative Frameworks, Chs.6–7*] ↓ ↓ State production and state expenditure [8D1] ↠ ↓ Finance of the state: taxation and other main forms of finance [8D2] ⥯ Effect of state expenditure on enterprises' production and validation of surplus-value: macroeconomic expenditure [8D3] ⇒ ⥯ The combined effect of state expenditure and taxation on the enterprises' after tax surplus-value [8D4] 8D2 .M. Forms of taxation: the distribution of income and wealth [8D5]	8. State expenditure and its finance
4. Market interaction	[*instrumentality of technical-physical production (1D5) and accumulation of capital and technical change (2D1)*] .M. The market and the stratified structure of production [4D1] .mm. modes of deflationary or inflationary competition [4D2 and 4D3] .mm. tendencies to evaporation of competition [4D4 and 4D5]	moments RHS apply on moments LHS	Manifestations of the state associated with its imposition of the mode of competition .M. The imposition of competition .M. The imposition of competition: a framework of prohibitive regulation (9D1) .M. Constraints on the mode of competition and (potentially) on the mode of capital accumulation (9D2)	9. Imposition of competition
5. Cyclical over-accumulation and destruction capital	[*Chapters 1–4*] ⥯ .me. The profit of enterprises: surplus-value net of its distribution to external financiers [5D1] .M. The cyclical over-accumulation and destruction of capital [5D2]	10D1 affects 5D2 † 10D2 affects all of Part One ‡	[*Chapters 6–9*] ⥯ .M. Effect of the size of state expenditure on the amplitude of the capitalist cycle [10D1] .M. The increasing size and complexity of regulation [10D2] .M. The capitalist state's Hard Core and its manifestation in social security transfers and other expenditure [10D3] ⥯ ⥯ The vulnerabilities of the capitalist state's reach [10D4]	10. The reach of the capitalist state
PART THREE	[*The capitalist economy* and *the capitalist state, Parts One and Two*] .me. The international mode of existence of the capitalist system [11D1] .mm. International trade [11D2]		.mm. International migration of production [11D3]	11. Int. cap. sys.

Legend

		Chs. 1–2, 6–7	Chs. 3, 8	Chs. 5–6, 9–11
↠	grounded in (right moment is condition of existence for left moment)	x	x	
s-i-u	separation-in-unity	x	x	
↡	grounded in (bottom moment is condition of existence for top moment)	x	x	
⇆	dialectical mutuality (moments presuppose each other)	x		
⇃⇂	bottom moment derives from top moment		x	x
⇛	right moment derives from left moment		x	x
.M.	manifestation of the earlier moments		*	x
.mm.	mode of manifestation			x
.me.	mode of existence of the earlier moments			x

Notes

† 10D1 directly affects the degree of the cyclical over-accumulation of capital (5D2).

‡ 10D2 affects the capitalist economy in almost all of its main moments from 1D5 onwards. 10D3 refers to the concrete manifestation of the state's expenditure (see the General Appendix A§12 on 'concrete manifestation').

* Also in the last division of Ch. 8.

CHAPTER 14

An outline of systematic dialectics – General appendix

A systematic-dialectical method for the investigation and exposition of the capitalist system

Contents

Introduction

The General Introduction sketched some elementary principles of the method of Systematic Dialectics (SD) as it is adopted in this book. Other aspects and principles of the method were briefly set out in the Explanations and Addenda of the various chapters when these aspects and principles were first introduced into the systematic exposition. The advantage of this proceeding is the immediate connection of method and content. The disadvantage is that the SD method is explained in fragments. I aim to correct this in the current Appendix, which presents the method in an integrated way. For the elementary parts this means that there is some repetition of the General Introduction and the Explanations or Addenda mentioned above.

'Systematic Dialectics' is the dialectical method pertaining to the study of an object totality characterised by a systematic structure. Authors adopting this method have enough in common that they themselves characterise their method as systematic-dialectical. Having said this, it should be noted that there are often different emphases between authors. Often these pertain to their object totality. My own variant of SD is focused on the capitalist system as including not only the capitalist economy but also the capitalist state. The exposition of such a comprehensive system poses problems of composition that may be less, or differently, articulated for narrower systematic structures (e.g. the capitalist economy). Therefore, when in this Appendix I refer to SD, this refers to SD in general, although especially to the SD adopted in this book.

The text of this Appendix is divided into four divisions. Division 1 provides a synopsis of the method. Division 2 sets out the concepts and principles of research prior to an SD exposition. Division 3 discusses several general principles of an SD exposition. Division 4 is the substantial part of the text, and sets out the principles and method of the systematic-dialectical exposition itself.

Internal references to chapters of the book are as indicated in section E of the General Introduction. Internal references to this Appendix appear as A§1 etc. for sections and as AD1 etc. for divisions. The General Introduction is referred to as GI.

Although the format of this Appendix is different from the main chapters (the Appendix is no part of the systematic exposition), I will include a number of Amplifications and Addenda (below indented) that go into historical details of the method or locate it in the literature. Addenda are for the specialists and may be skipped by the main reader.

SCHEME 14.1 *Division-structure of the text*

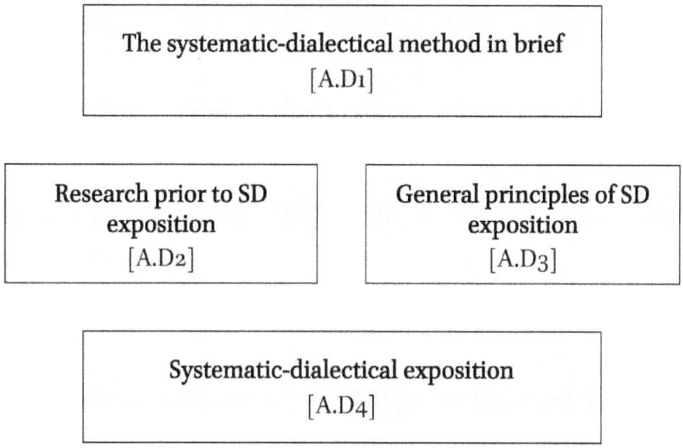

Amplification. Historical roots of the Systematic-Dialectical method (SD)

Generally the SD method springs from a development of, first, Hegel's systematic dialectical method and, second, Marx's appropriation of that method for his critique of the political economy of capitalism as set out in his *Capital*. The interest in *this* influence of Hegel on Marx is fairly recent. Equally recent is the impetus that this has given to the application of this method to current social science. One commentator, Chris Arthur, has called it the turn to a 'new dialectic'.[1] My impression is that most authors engaged in this turn started by discovering the potential power of SD through their renewed SD interpretation of Marx's method in *Capital*. Some of them then took inspiration from this to develop the method for the investigation of current society.[2]

1 Arthur 2002, pp. 1–11.

2 With this is mind the following authors provide, in various aspects, other accounts of the SD method: Eldred 1984, pp. xiv–xxiii [general]; Reuten and Williams 1988, pp. 3–54 [general]; Reuten and Williams 1989, pp. 3–36 [general]; Smith 1990, pp. 3–18 [Hegel], pp. 19–42 [Marx]; Arthur 1993, pp. 63–73 [Hegel–Marx]; Smith 1993, pp. 15–36 [Hegel–Marx]; Arthur 1997 [Marx: Systematic-Dialectical versus Linear Logic]; Arthur 1998, pp. 110–18 [Hegel–Marx]; Reuten 1998, pp. 103–7 [general]; Murray 2000, pp. 36–41 [marxian SD/general]; Reuten 2000, pp. 140–52 [general] (cf. Murray's reply, 2002, pp. 156–67); Murray 2003, esp. 152–8 [general]. For a *general* overview of Hegel's influence on Marx see Murray 1988 and the contributions in Moseley and Smith (eds) 2014.

Division 1. The method of systematic-dialectical exposition in brief

A§1 *Aim and synopsis*

In principle the method of Systematic Dialectics (SD) may apply, with qualifications, to natural and social object realms. For brevity, in this appendix I will refer mainly to the capitalist system, or capitalism, especially as set out in this book, from which I also take examples.

SD has in common with other scientific methods that it seeks to reliably know what can be known. One main distinction from *most* other approaches is the SD claim that the key to the reliability of that knowledge lies in the *interconnection* of all relevant knowledge about some object totality. SD is sceptical of any partial knowledge, including model building, although it does not dismiss this knowledge (see A§3 and A§8). Wider perspectives can show the limits, or the falsity, of partial knowledge. (See the General Introduction, C§1, on the limitations of mainstream methods.)

A second main distinction from *all* other approaches is the method through which the interconnection of the relevant knowledge is found (A§10–A§14). The remainder of this section provides a synopsis of the method (cf. the General Introduction, C§4), which is fleshed out in further divisions.

Figure 14.2 shows the, by now familiar, systematic of the exposition of the capitalist system in this book. For the purposes of this Appendix I adopt the in fact rigorous order of the exposition, which is the zigzag one, that is, the chapter order of the expositional levels [1;6], [2;7], and so on. This is the rigorous one in terms of 'proximate' conditions of existence (GI-C§4 and A§11, point 3).

Its analogue, *Figure 14.3*, was already presented in the General Introduction, but I can now properly introduce the term 'abstract' and its meaning.

The starting point, denoted in the figure by 'α', is an all-encompassing conception of the object totality (i.e. the capitalist system) that abstractly captures the essence of that object totality: 'dissociated bifurcation' (1§1, 1§6). This concept is abstract, because at the point of its introduction it is a non-grounded concept. (On this meaning of the term, all the mainstream economics models – to my knowledge – are, and remain, abstract. The game is played on the basis of assumptions that remain non-grounded.)[3]

The next layers, denoted by β1 … βn, are called 'grounding moments' and these set out the interconnected conditions of existence of the starting point. (Chapters 1–3 after 1§1 and Chapters 6–8 after 1§6.) Each stage of this dialect-

3 Nevertheless, these models can be useful to the extent that the assumptions are realistic.

FIGURE 14.2 *Exposition of the capitalist system as unity of the capitalist economy and state*

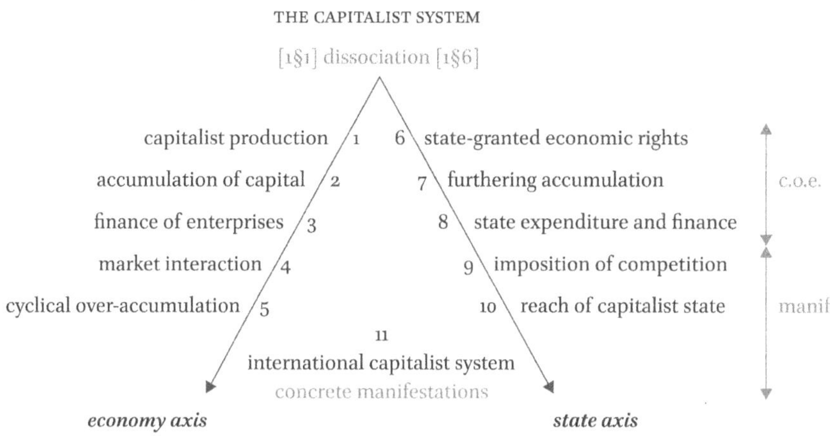

Note: 'c.o.e.' abbreviates conditions of existence and 'manif.' manifestations

FIGURE 14.3 *Systematic investigation and exposition*

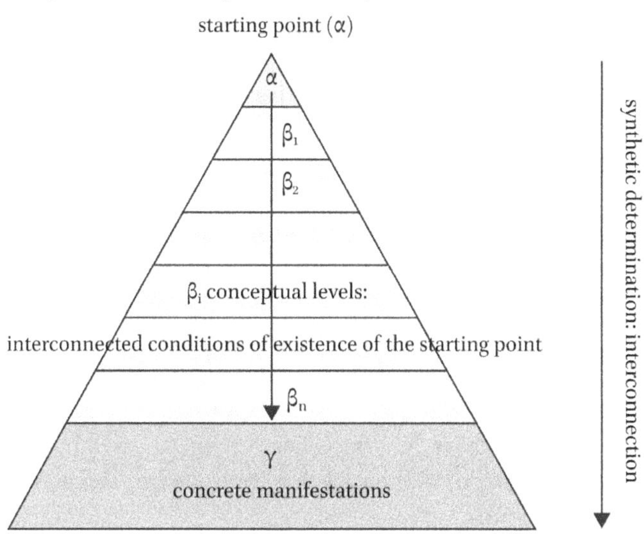

ical exposition increasingly shows *how* the system, initially posited abstractly (α), can exist. The connection of two or more moments has a synthetic character, and the more we move down the pyramid, the more synthesis we reach. Necessary conditions of existence – and again their necessary conditions of existence – are a leading methodological principle. This ensures that we get to the exposition of the *interconnected* totality of the capitalist system. For the same reason it is essential to abstain from assumptions because these would open the way for gaps (A§7 expands on assumptions).

The structure of these conditions (β) culminates in the interconnected synthetic exposition of the 'concrete manifestations' of the system (γ). (Chapters 4–5 and 9–11.) Along the process of the exposition (from starting point to manifestations) we each time extend our grasp of the capitalist system. In the end, this grasp will be appropriate to fully *comprehend* its essential working as appearing in empirical reality. Division 4 sets out these three stages in more detail.

Division 2. Research prior to systematic-dialectical exposition

A§2 *Object totality*

A condition for an SD investigation is that its object realm, in our case capitalism, is inherently systemic, that is, it consists of interacting constituent parts forming an integrated whole. This is an ontological matter. Without wanting to make a divorce between these, an epistemological requirement is that the object realm can also be *exhibited* systematically as a 'totality'. The received SD view, stemming from Hegel, is that an object realm can be exhibited as a totality only when a *unifying* all-encompassing conceptualisation can capture the abstract essence of the totality (α in A§1), such that this can successfully lead to the comprehension of reality (γ).

A§3 *Research prior to SD exposition: analysis versus synthesis*

As indicated in the General Introduction, much of the mainstream science proudly casts its endeavours in terms of 'analysis', whereas systematic dialectics stresses its endeavour in terms of 'synthesis'. Consider the following descriptions (rather than definitions) of the terms analysis and synthesis. *Analysis*: to scrutinise by way of the division of wholes into their elements, or the deconstruction of initial knowledge. *Synthesis*: to connect, assemble, or unite knowledge; the combination of often diverse concepts into a whole by indicating their interconnections.

SD *enquiry* encompasses two phases: *research* prior to the SD exposition, and systematic-dialectical *investigation and exposition*. Only the systematic exposition is reported – this is the material that one finds in a SD text, as in the current book. This A§3 is about the research prior to that exposition.

In principle, the SD method critically appropriates the relevant existing knowledge about an object totality. This is generally considered to be a condition for science in general. In the SD pre-systematic research phase, the *results* of existing analysis and empirical research are critically appropriated.[4] The systematic investigation thus builds on this knowledge (this point will be qualified later). I indicated that one condition for an object realm to be an object totality is that it can be successfully captured by a unifying concept (A§2). Which concept this could or should be is not straightforward – it is the result of an enormous creative research process involving a great deal of trial and error. Within this pre-systematic research phase, the reaching of this unifying concept has the character of a 'preliminary synthesis' – Marx called this 'abstract determination' (abstract constitution).[5]

FIGURE 14.4 *SD enquiry: from pre-systematic research to systematic investigation and exposition*

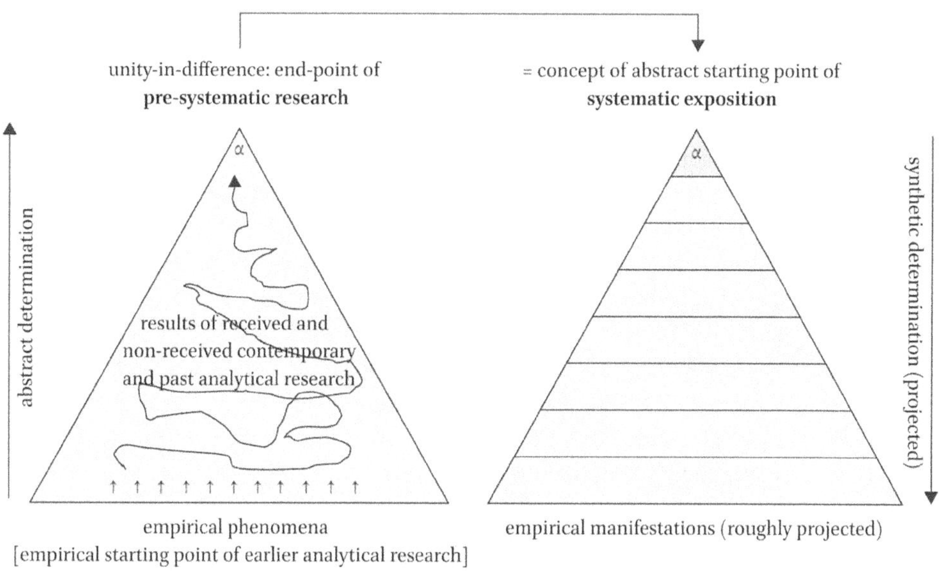

The left pyramid in *Figure 14.4* is a metaphoric image of the past and contemporary research. (Start reading at its bottom, supposing that this past research is

4 Tony Smith (1990, pp. 4–5) calls this the 'stage of appropriation'; Patrick Murray (1988, 2000, 2003) calls it 'phenomenological inquiry'.

5 Marx 1973b [1903^1]{ms1857}, p. 101. 'Determination' is the standard translation for the German 'Bestimmung' (see Inwood 1992, pp. 77–9 on the complexities of the term). 'Delineation' is one of its connotations; instead of determination, 'constitution' might be another approximation. In the current context, one major aspect of this *abstract* determination is the subsumption of phenomena under more general phenomena, as a species under a genus. Note that subsumption does *not* constitute their actual interconnection (see A§11).

based on an assimilation of empirical phenomena.) The bottom of the pyramid represents analytical research and past empirical studies, which developed through the process of making conceptual distinctions between phenomena and of partial analyses, in both everyday cultural history and scientific history.

The 'preliminary synthesis' is the research process of getting to the left pyramid's top α. The convoluted character of the process is indicated by the kinked line. This unity-in-diversity (α) is then the starting point for the SD investigation and exposition, represented by the right pyramid of the figure.

However, there is a distinction but no divorce between these two phases. During the SD investigation (right pyramid) the investigator will often return to this existing knowledge (left pyramid) in order to re-appropriate it in the detailed systematic exposition.

A§3-a Addendum. Pre-systematic research: Hegel versus Marx

We have good reasons to believe that pre-systematic research along these lines was also the path taken by Hegel and Marx, to arrive at the respective starting points of their systematic dialectics.[6]

There is, however, a crucial difference between Hegel and Marx concerning the critical appropriation of existing relevant knowledge at this research stage, which then fed the content of the systematic exposition. The philosopher Hegel drew on the received views of contemporary empirical sciences, for data on the natural and social realms; his task was to gain holistic knowledge from his synthetic systematisation of these received views. He was hesitant about speculating on the fate of knowledge at the research-frontier: 'The owl of Minerva spreads its wings only with the falling of the dusk'.[7]

For Marx this was very different. His study of the then-influential political-economic writings made him sceptical of the received view. Therefore, although he often drew on these writings, he felt compelled to carry out conceptual and empirical *analysis* of his own.[8] In *Capital* this analysis is set out *alongside* and during his systematic exposition. Although this analysis is systematically placed at the appropriate points (by chapter), this gives Marx's systematic-dialectical exposition a very distinctive complexion, particularly since he usually does not clearly distin-

6 See also Smith 1993, p. 18. Marx describes this research in the Introduction to the *Grundrisse*, one of his few methodological writings. (Marx 1973a [1903;1857ms].)

7 End of Preface to the *Philosophy of Right* (Hegel 1967 [1821]).

8 See also Murray (2003, pp. 157, 160) who calls this Marx's phenomenological inquiry, as distinct from his exposition.

guish between his analytical and synthetic texts. This often complicates the detection of the systematic order.[9] (In the current book I solved this problem by relegating any critical analysis to Explications or Amplifications.)

A§3-b Explication. Some provisional analytical definitions for 'social system'

The definition of concepts is central to analysis. An SD exposition does not fix definitions of concepts. Later on we will see why (A§6). Nevertheless, in working up the results of analysis it may provisionally adopt analytical definitions. Merely to provide an idea of the terrain of the social realm within which the object totality of 'the capitalist system' is located, I outline a number of provisional (non-rigorous) analytical general social system definitions. (The mark * indicates that the term is defined later on in this Explication.)

(*a*) ***System.*** A system is an *interconnected composite of structures* and driving forces** such that the system is, in principle, continuous. (Think of an economic structure and a state structure that together constitute a social formation, in our case the capitalist social formation.) The continuous existence of a system always requires *at least* temporary modes for resolving any fundamental conflicts.

(*b*) ***Structure.*** A structure is a static, more or less coherent *set of institutions**. (For examples of institutions, think of: enterprises, trade, markets, taxation, courts, verdicts.) Coherence does not imply that a particular institution by itself, or a set of institutions, is free of conflict or contradiction. Structures have a more or less *determinate* character in that – at the risk of loss of coherence – they cannot be changed at will. However, this does *not* imply that – at that risk – there could not be change.

(*c*) ***Institution.*** An institution is a more or less enduring *pattern of behaviour* that may but need not be established in a formal organisation (e.g. an enterprise or a court). Institutions are an expression of norms (for example, profit making by enterprises or conflict resolution and administration of justice by courts). For the object totality at hand these are primarily *capitalist norms*. Institutions (and/or their norms) may but

9 The insight that the distinct complexion of Marx's text is due to this mixture of analysis and synthesis, I owe to Damsma (2015 and 2019, Ch. 1, Section 3). As with all good ideas, this is obvious in hindsight. For me at least, this at once clarified many of the puzzles of the systematic structure/ordering of *Capital*. Further, Tony Smith's 1990 book has been most important in the detection and delineation of Marx's analytical and synthetic work.

need not be codified in laws or in 'self-regulating' rules. Institutions may endure by way of, firstly, education. That is, education in the narrow sense and in the broad sense of education into discourses (Foucault), including education into the capitalist culture or education into the culture of an organisation. Secondly, institutions may endure by way of social sanctions (generally: approval and disapproval). In the economic domain of enterprises, important direct economic sanctions are profits and losses, which have an indirect counterpart in the status of the management. Stable endurance correlates with the *internalisation* of, in our case, capitalist economic norms. Stable endurance is one important constituent of a structure.

(*d*) ***Driving forces.*** Like institutions, driving forces are the *dynamic ingredients* (*processes*) *of structures*. These are basically institutions (sanctioned patterns) that have gained the character of 'force', 'compulsion' or 'coercion' because of their interconnectedness (coherence) within structures (for example, profit making and accumulation of capital).

Division 3. Systematic-dialectical exposition – general principles

Before I set out the mode of systematic-dialectical exposition in Division 4, this division briefly sets out some general SD principles.

A§4 *Systematic in contrast with historical order*

The relative significance of a contemporary phenomenon does not necessarily pertain to its historical emergence. Although history is important in explaining *how* the existent came into being, it cannot explain why it is 'what it is', nor how the existent is reproduced as an interconnected whole.[10] Therefore the systematic order of SD has nothing whatsoever to do with the historical emergence of institutions and processes. For example, the fact that commodity markets developed before labour markets does not imply that a commodity market is more important than a labour market in terms of the functioning of the capitalist system – both are absolutely necessary. The fact that forms of commodity money (such as gold) evolved long before 'bank account money' does not imply at all that a systematic treatment of money should start with commodity money, or even refer to it.

10 Reuten and Williams 1989, p. 34. See also Smith 1990, pp. 8–9, Arthur 2002, p. 75 and Murray 2003, pp. 152–3.

A§5 *Dialectical 'moments'*

The term 'moment' refers to the constituents of each progression of the SD exposition. Generally, a moment is a composition of concepts that belong together; these concepts are thus posited as immediately connected – for example, 'money expansion' (2D4) or the state's 'monetary framework' (7D2). In other words, a moment is a more or less cohesive institutional make-up, or a more or less cohesive set of entities, that can be analysed in itself (sometimes like a model) but that nevertheless derives its full meaning from the interconnection with other moments, and ultimately from its interconnectedness within the whole exposition.[11] Thus moments derive full meaning through synthesis.

In a text, systematic ordering is inevitably sequential. Nevertheless *ontologically* we always have the simultaneity of all moments.

A§6 *Definition and conceptual progress*

The *definition* of concepts is an inherent part of analysis (A§3), and is useful for that endeavour. To the extent that *conceptual development* is central to the development of science generally, however, the positing of concepts as 'definitive' can hamper this development, even within non-dialectical discourses. Starting from an abstract concept of a totality (α), SD sets out interconnections in a layered movement of setting out, first, the starting point's conditions of existence (β_i) and next its concrete manifestations (γ). Along with this, especially key concepts such as 'money' and 'production' acquire a continuously enriched meaning. Therefore 'the' concept of, for example, money, cannot be meaningfully defined in, say, Chapter 1, as it acquires new meanings (in the exposition of this book) in Chapters 2, 7 and 3. SD therefore eschews fixed definitions. Nevertheless, at each dialectical level, or moment (A§5), it *delineates* concepts 'for the moment'. Even so, in the way this book is written, early concepts and their delineations are claimed to be true, and are (if I made no mistakes) not inconsistent with the later more enriched concepts. Indeed, the early concepts are claimed to be true, but only so abstractly (in the sense of 'encompassing'). Their truth is contained in the newly developed concept.

A§7 *Presumptions and pre-positions (contrary to assumptions)*

This section is almost identical to C§3 of the General Introduction.

SD not only eschews definitions (A§6), it also eschews assumptions. However, the exposition in this book adopts three *'presumptions'*. Firstly, a *cultur-*

11 See also Reuten and Williams 1989, p. 22.

ally determined language (in our case, specifically 'English'). Along with it goes an *episteme*.[12] We can, to a degree, be aware of this, but no scientific endeavour can escape this far-reaching presumption. (Sometimes it is believed that mathematics does. However, mathematics requires at least 'initial translations' from cultural language into mathematics.) Secondly, it is presumed that our object of investigation exists. In our case, that is, capitalist social formations and especially capitalist economies and states. Empirically these are exemplified in OECD countries as well as all other countries with a similar structure, independently of their level of development in terms of GDP per capita and of state expenditure. Thirdly, it is presumed that this object of investigation is systematic (A§2 above). This is a precondition for any scientific study of an object of investigation beyond mere descriptions.

Next to these three presumptions I adopt '*pre-positions*' in Chapters 1–3 and 6–8. I adopt these merely because all the constituent elements of a 'system' cannot be presented at the same time. I use the term 'pre-position' (instead of 'assumption') so as to indicate that these have a temporary status. (In modelling approaches many 'assumptions' have a permanent status.) Thus in the course of the dialectical exposition, I introduce entities that at the stage of their introduction are not, or not fully, 'grounded'. (For example, when I introduce 'money' in Chapter 1, the creation of money by banks in Chapter 2 is pre-posited.) A major difference between systematic-dialectical pre-positions and the assumptions of a standard model-building approach is that systematic-dialectical pre-positions must *always* be grounded within the exposition – an SD exposition is never complete until all determinations relevant for the object realm have been determined *endogenously*, that is, when no pre-positions (or assumptions) are required, and all earlier (temporary) pre-positions have in fact been eliminated. In the main systematic text of this book, I never used assumptions – if I have made no mistakes (in Explications I sometimes used an assumption, merely to simplify an example).

When, in a modelling approach, some assumption is dropped, earlier statements (based on the dropped assumption) may no longer hold. This is different for pre-positions. All the statements formulated at each level (e.g. at the expositional level of Chapter 1 or 2) are claimed to be true, and still to be true when we have reached Chapter 5 or 11.

12 Foucault (in *The Order of Things*) uses the term *épistème* to refer to the 'unconscious' mental arrangements that underpin the production and the *possibility* of the production of scientific knowledge, in a long-term era (think of the Middle Ages versus 'modernity'). An *épistème* is much more far-reaching and inescapable than Kuhn's notion of paradigm.

All the remarks above about pre-positions pertain to the object realm we study here ('capitalism' – A§2). Although capitalism cannot exist in a void, it is hardly opportune to begin a book about the capitalist system by an exposition of natural-scientific entities (if I could).

A§8 *Synthesis and the role of analysis*

SD investigation is the process of enquiry from a systematic starting point (Figure 14.3). This investigation *results* in the *systematic exposition* that one finds in an SD text (such as this book). An SD exposition is *synthetic*.

In A§3, I indicated that SD investigation requires sufficient conceptual and empirical analysis for its synthetic exposition. It selects from this analysis and neglects what is considered deficient. However, if the existing analysis is lacking or poor regarding some moment, then the author of an SD work will need to undertake the appropriate analysis.[13] (In the current book, and if required, I have relegated any such analysis to 'explications' or 'amplifications', so that the systematic exposition proper in the main sections is purely synthetic.)

A§9 *Immanency and immanent critique*

The SD exposition of a social totality is an immanent one. That is, it sets out the system from the perspective of the object totality's principles, norms and standards. This is a principle adopted from Marx. Even if the system is presented *from within itself*, this does not imply the absence of any evaluation or assessment. When the norms and standards are taken to *their* logical conclusions, we may detect possible inconsistencies, which an immanent critique makes explicit. (See the General Introduction, C§6, for some more clarification.)

Division 4. Systematic-dialectical exposition

In this last division I discuss the systematic exposition proper. Strictly, the 'exposition' is the text of an SD work. However, it should be emphasised that alongside the actual writing process, the author is engaging in a complicated SD investigation.

---

13 In A§3-a I noted that Marx was confronted with this exact problem, so that he had to engage in analysis himself. In my 2000 paper on systematic dialectics I neglected the possible requirement for analysis along with the systematic investigation and Guido Starosta (2008) rightly criticised me for this.

A§10 *The systematic starting point*

The pre-systematic research (A§3) leads up to the starting point of an SD exposition. This starting point is an all-encompassing conceptualisation of the object totality. It is abstract in the sense of it being an as yet non-grounded conceptualisation. At the starting point we merely have the appropriation of analysis as an abstract determination (α in *Figure 14.4*). Or, we have 'merely' posited a unity-in-difference. In Hegel's work on society (1967 [1821]) this is 'free will', for Marx (1976 [1867]) 'commodification', and in the current book 'dissociated outward bifurcation' (on the latter two see also 1§1-h, 1§5-b).

At the beginning it is unclear how the starting point can have existence. At the beginning it is, as yet, unproven that the starting moment (α) indeed is the unifying concept of the object totality. This has to be shown in the process of setting out its conditions of existence, along which the starting point appears progressively less abstract. Thus we have a process of progressive concretisation and differentiation (β). As Hegel says, at the beginning 'difference is still sunk in the unity, not yet set forth as different.' Only on completion of the exposition, he continues, will we know that '[t]he truth of the differentiated is its being in unity. And only through this movement is the unity truly concrete'.[14] Once the exposition is complete – and thus when the initial unifying concept is shown to be inherent in the object totality, in its full concreteness (γ) – we will have come full circle, confirming the truth of the abstract starting point.[15] Thus the ultimate test of a starting point is the success of the exposition itself.

A§10-a Addendum. Hegel's Systematic Dialectic

Throughout this division I refer in footnotes to the work of Hegel, and especially his *Encyclopaedia Logic*.[16] However, my own SD is not the same as Hegel's. I rather build on Hegel – the footnotes acknowledge this – in a way that often deviates from him. I especially mention that in my exposition I have no analogue for his 'subjective logic'.[17] Instead I move to 'concrete manifestations' (A§12 below), which in Hegel's terminology would be a further development of his 'actuality'.[18]

---

14 Hegel 1985 [1833], p. 83.

15 Compare Murray 2003, p. 157 and Arthur 1997, p. 31.

16 *Encyclopaedia Logic* (1991 [1817^1; 1830^3]). This book is composed of three main divisions: I. The doctrine of being; II. The doctrine of Essence (also referred to as the Essence Logic); III. The doctrine of the concept (also referred to as the Subjective Logic).

17 See the previous footnote.

18 The last part (C) of the Doctrine of Essence.

In Reuten and Williams 1989 (pp. 26–30), we indicated why an SD of the capitalist system could not reach beyond Hegel's Essence Logic. Tony Smith (1990) made this point in a far more sophisticated manner (unfortunately, at that time we did not know each other and the printing of the books coincided). See also Smith 1993 and 2014. Chris Arthur takes a very different position in his SD project (elements of which are outlined in Arthur 2002, 2011 and 2016). He highlights the dominance of capital within the system (we agree on this) and *therefore* considers Hegel's Subjective Logic to provide an adequate framework for presenting that dominance. Riccardo Bellofiore (2014), without explicitly endorsing Hegel's Subjective Logic, posits that fetishism empowers capital in a way that is similar to it being a Subject in the Hegelian sense.

A§11 *Grounding moments (conditions of existence)*

1 *Exposition of 'how' the system can exist*

Systematic-dialectical 'exposition' refers to the SD mode, or way, of conceptualising an object totality characterised by a systematic structure. The main body of an SD exposition consists in the presentation of the 'conditions of existence' of the starting point. (In this book Chapters 1–3 and 6–8 after the starting point in 1D1 and 6D1.) This way the exposition shows *how* the system can exist. This is the same as showing *how* the starting point – which captures the essence of the system – can exist. In reference to the starting point of 'dissociated outward bifurcation' (1D1 and 6D1), the 'how' regards exposition of how the bifurcation is bridged such that the capitalist system can exist.

2 *Concretisation of the starting point*

Even if the starting point can be phenomenally interpreted and understood, it is abstract to the extent that its conditions of existence have not been set forth (these are either yet pre-posited, or as yet implicit). With the exposition of each condition of existence, the starting point, and hence the existence of the system, is gradually concretised. This is the same as the existence being further grounded. Therefore a condition of existence is, alternatively, indicated by the term *'grounding moment'*.[19] (Metaphorically, and referring to the metaphoric pyramid of *Figures 14.2 and 14.3*, we reach each time *more* concrete ground as

19 The terms 'condition of existence' and 'grounding moment' are used interchangeably. The first term has the advantage of focusing on existence, and is perhaps initially more transparent. The term 'grounding moment' has the advantage of focusing in on the momentary, therefore emphasising its incompleteness.

the dialectic unfolds. The 'foundation' is not in the top, but rather in the movement towards the concrete bottom.)

3 *Systematic order*

The systematic ordering of these conditions/moments is central to the 'art' of SD investigation. At each stage of the exposition it has to be determined what is the necessary *proximate* condition of existence of what was posited earlier on. Beginning from the starting point, an SD exposition must pose its *proximate* grounding moment, that is, the immediate and most general conditions for that what was posited before. To the extent that the proximate grounding moment cannot exist by itself, that moment requires *new* proximate grounding moment(s). This way we have a series of grounding moments.[20] At each point, the dialectical exposition is driven forward by the insufficiency of a posited moment. The grounding moment at a new level (say, Chapter 2) sets out a still (relatively) abstract existence that cannot yet actually exist, which drives the exposition forward as described.[21] This goes on until all conditions of existence have been determined, and so are endogenous to the exposition.

'Insufficiency', above, refers to the cohesive limits of a moment (A§5). Nevertheless there is a truth claim for the conceptualisation of each single moment, one that will not be withdrawn in a later moment. Rather, the truth of earlier moments is contained in later moments (cf. A§6). Thus the more we move down in the metaphorical pyramid, we have 'a concentration of many determinants', as Marx put it.[22]

4 *Systematic interconnection*

Along the process just set out, the exposition posits the interconnection of the grounding moments, and hence the interconnection of the phenomena that necessarily constitute the system. (We reach interconnection because grounding moments are again grounded in further grounding moments.) This is the great merit of the SD method. Each proximate grounding moment posits further interconnections, and therefore further *comprehension* of the system. (We may perhaps 'understand' the starting point and the capitalist system that we had phenomenologically before us. It is through comprehension of the interconnections that we gradually move towards grasping it.)

---

20 This, in my view, is the core of Hegel's Essence Logic (i.e. the Second Part of his Logic) – Hegel 1991 [1817].

21 Cf. Hegel 1991 [1817], §120–§124; 1985 [1833], pp. 81–3.

22 Marx 1973a [1903; 1858ms], p. 101.

In order to guarantee that indeed all the necessary interconnections are posited, it is indispensable that SD abstains from any assumptions. Assumptions would open the way for gaps in the interconnections, hence gaps in the comprehension of the system.

5 *Necessary conditions*

It was indicated above (point 3) that the 'art' of SD investigation consists in the determination of the necessary *proximate* condition of existence of what was posited earlier on. Part of this art is to indeed determine what is a 'necessary' condition, and therefore what aspects of the phenomenological reality are merely contingent (meaning that these phenomena could be either absent or different without changing the essential reproduction of the system).[23] As the necessity–contingency distinction is also relevant for Manifestations (A§12), I amplify on this distinction in A§13.

6 *Necessary forces and enforcements*

The result of the exposition of grounding moments is a structure of interconnected conditions of existence of the starting point. All these have the status of necessary forces and enforcements for the continuity of the capitalist system.[24] Much of this structure is pervaded by two necessary forces that, inevitably, were presented early on in the exposition: those of, first, the *production and appropriation of surplus-value* (1D5) and, second, the *legitimation of the state* (6D3) for upholding the first force in the form of granted rights to production and appropriation of surplus-value.

Other necessary forces and enforcements ground the former two. (For economic agents that, in their self-perception, consider capitalism as the embodiment of freedom, these enforcements must be thought-provoking – cf. 6§2-a.)

7 *Systematic-dialectical synthesis, and the end-point of its first stage*

The SD exposition of systematic interconnection (point 4) is inherently a synthetic exposition (cf. A§3 for the distinction between analysis and synthesis). Analysis aims to gain knowledge through the deconstruction and decomposition of phenomena – or of phenomenological realms – into their elements. SD, as indicated in A§3, uses the results of analysis. However, SD exposition is the opposite (or counterpart) of analysis in that it posits interconnection and hence synthetic knowledge – synthetic comprehension. Nevertheless the SD

23 'Reproduction of the system' refers to its continued existence.

24 Hegel sets out this connection in Division B (subdivision C, on Relationship), of his Essence Logic (1991 [1817], §135–§141).

synthesis may not be the analogous opposite of analysis. Analysis must assume that the phenomena, or phenomenological realms, that it deconstructs relevantly belong together. This assumption may be right, but it may also be wrong.[25] Therefore synthetic conclusions may, qua content, be opposite to analytical conclusions.

The completion of the exposition of the interconnected conditions of existence of the starting point completes the first part of the SD synthesis. With it, all the *grounding* moments have been presented. However, these may not reach the moments that, without requiring further conditions of existence, are nevertheless substantial to the SD synthetic exposition. The next section turns to these.

A§12 *Manifestations: synthetic moments of concrete manifestation*

The final phase of the exposition is that of the 'concrete manifestations' of the capitalist system (Chapters 4–5 and 9–11).

It might have appeared to the reader that in the earlier chapter texts (1–3 and 6–8), I presented manifestations of the capitalist system all along the exposition of the grounding moments (A§12). In a particular way this is the case; however, these could be no more than 'abstract manifestations' (which is a rather contrived terminology). This is so because *prior* to the completions of all the grounding moments (A§12), it is not shown *how* the capitalist system can concretely exist. Hence prior to that point we still have merely multi-interpretable phenomena, rather than the manifestations of the capitalist system that we can concretely comprehend: 'concrete manifestations'.

Therefore all the empirical graphs that I presented at the level of grounding moments could be no more than pre-positions or illustrations. I always relegated these to the non-systematic Amplifications rather than to the systematic main sections.[26]

These concrete manifestations take the exposition further, without (I repeat) introducing any additional conditions of existence. Not being grounding

25 For example, the analysis of unemployment by considering the realm of the employed and unemployed labour may result in the reduction of unemployment to the shortcomings of unemployed individuals. On the other hand, if the analytical starting point would have been the realm of the accumulation of capital, then the analytical conclusion might have been that accumulation requires unemployment, whatever the characteristic of individuals. Generally analysis is more reliable to the extent that its realm is wider, and to the extent that it minimises its assumptions, and to the extent that the assumptions it does use are realistic.

26 In fact I experimented with presenting all that stuff in a very long Chapter 10. I 'fired' this to my students in 2015/16, but that did not work. (I thank them for their polite criticism of it.)

moments, these are nevertheless necessary moments that are the culmination of the synthetic exposition, building on that of the grounding moments. Those grounding moments – posited in their proximate sequence (A§12, point 3) – reveal the reproductive strength of the capitalist system. However, the concrete simultaneous interaction of these grounding moment's forces (A§12, point 6) is also expressed in concrete manifestations that reveal *not only* reproductive strength, but also reproductive vulnerability.[27] I recall in a most condensed way the core of these manifestations.

Whereas enterprises constitute a unity as (in brief) appropriators of the surplus-value produced by labour, they are in their market interaction manifest in their difference. On the one hand, this takes the form of antagonistic competition, but on the other, it takes the form of escaping competition and 'practising unity' through cartels and the centralisation of capital (Chapter 4). Given the economic rights granted by the state, the state's position regarding this practising unity is inevitably ambivalent and paradoxical (Chapter 9). The accumulation of the enterprises' active capital is concretely manifest in its cyclical over-accumulation and partial destruction along with super unemployment (Chapter 5). The state is concretely manifest in its increasing expenditure, not least on social security transfers, and in the increasing size and complexity of regulation (Chapter 10).

The concrete manifestations are a combination of strength and vulnerability. The latter reveal how the walls of the grounding moments (A§12) are perhaps not 'crumbling' (to use Schumpeter's metaphor in his 1943, ch. 12), but nevertheless shaking.

A§13 *Necessity and contingency*

1 *Contingency*

The reach of SD is restricted to the interconnected exposition of phenomena (entities, institutions and processes) that are necessary to the reproduction of the capitalist system (A§11–A§12).[28] Thus it generally abstains from the presentation of contingencies (some qualifications are pointed out later on in this section). The provisional delineation of contingencies as being 'accidentals' is insufficient, as contingencies may have grounds. However, contingencies and

27 Major vulnerabilities are absent from Hegel's systematic dialectic. Smith (e.g. in his 2014) therefore calls Hegel's dialectic a system 'affirming' dialectic.

28 In Reuten and Williams 1989, we endeavoured to present a number of contingencies in the light of necessities. In the present book I refrained from doing this, whilst maintaining the presentation of the type of contingencies set out in the next subsections.

their possible grounds are external to the essential reproduction of the system. Phenomena are contingent when these could be either absent (e.g. gender discrimination or military expenditure and wars) or different (e.g. retail opening hours or bankers' dress codes) without changing the essence, the essential functioning and potential reproduction of the system.[29]

There is in principle 'an endless sea' of contingencies ('it could be this way, or that way') whence it is not opportune to list contingencies and to argue why these have not been dealt with in the exposition. Therefore the implication of the exposition is that everything that is *not* dealt with is contingent. The implication is also that contingencies are 'in principle' changeable within the system.[30]

However, the statements above do not imply that all contingency can be abstained from. This is the subject of the following subsections.

2 *System necessity of moment versus individual contingency*

The moments of the capitalist economy are predicated on capitalist economic forces (A§11, point 6; amplified in A§14). However, even if the moments and these forces are necessary for the totality, a force almost never has such an absolute character with regard to any individual constituent part of that totality. For example, whereas a profitable individual enterprise could deliberately interrupt its capital circuit, cease accumulation and liquidate – in spite of the various constraints that will usually act upon it not to do so – the collective group of enterprises *must necessarily* accumulate in order to reproduce capitalism.

3 *Necessity of moment, contingency of intensity*

All moments of the exposition are necessary; however, their intensity might be contingent. Regarding the capitalist economy this applies first of all for the degree of accumulation of capital. Thus whereas the accumulation of capital is necessary to the system, its expression in a rate of accumulation of three or six percent is contingent, and each structurally positive rate is compatible with the system's reproduction.

---

29 For example, gender discrimination and retail opening hours do have a social and economic impact – huge for gender discrimination; however, these are contingent in the sense that their absence (in case of discrimination) or their variety (in case of discrimination or opening hours) are, in principle, compatible with the capitalist system.

30 Cf. Reuten and Williams 1989, pp. 35–6. Without referring to the methodical necessity-contingency distinction, Smith 1990, pp. 38–40 and 1993, p. 28 casts this in terms of 'fundamental' and 'non-fundamental structures'.

Apart from this main moment of accumulation, the contingency of intensity applies also for other moments of the capitalist economy, especially the degree of incorporation of enterprises (2D6), the degree of the ex post substitution for the pre-validating finance provided by banks (3D3) and the degree of over-accumulation of capital (5D2). The contingency of intensity applies for almost all moments of the capitalist state apart from the Hard Core moments (Chapter 6). In fact, the history of full-fledged capitalism reveals this contingency (10D3). However, this again does not imply that this contingency of intensity is an indeterminate contingency. Quite a few of these have a tendency character, and this category is separately dealt with in the next section (A§14).

4 *Necessity of moment, contingency of form*

Some necessary moments may take on a contingent form (or mode). For example, whereas the moment of taxation is necessary (8D2), the particular form of taxation (i.e. the content of that moment) is contingent (8D5). This nevertheless means that at least one form is necessary, whence the exposition must treat a variety of forms. Another example is the qua moment necessary market interaction of enterprises (4D1). This interaction may take a variety of forms (or modes), amongst which at least one form is necessary (4D2–4D5). Regarding the particularly competitive form of interaction, we have seen that this may take a deflationary or an inflationary form (4D2–4D3).

5 *Becoming necessary*

A particular SD exposition, such as the one in this book, cannot be definitive because the dynamics of the system may evolve in such a way that the content of a particular moment posited may no longer be sufficient. This means that a specific content of a moment (or part of it) posited in this book may at some historical point have *become necessary*. Note that this is due not to an epistemological defect (a defective exposition at the time of its presentation), but rather to new ontological developments. I mention the three cases of this in the current book.

First, the corporate enterprise (2D6). For full-fledged capitalist economies around 1870 the corporate enterprise was prevalent, but it was no dominant necessity. However, given the growth of the enterprises' size within the category of medium and large enterprises, the corporate form for the latter is generally necessary in 2015.[31] Thus the corporate form of the enterprise has *become necessary* for this category.

---

31 This is expressed in both a generalised increasing concentration of capital within enter-

Second, generalised price competition in combination with vast technical change tends to lead to generalised deflation and economic stagnation (4D2). The structural combination of the two may not have been prevalent prior to the 1930s, and not actual in the later decades when the structural overcapacity form of competition was dominant. However, because generalised price competition in combination with speeded up technical change remains lurking, a monetary policy, or an expenditure policy, generating a creeping inflation has *become necessary* (7§8 of 7D2 and 9§5 of 9D2).[32]

Third, banks that are 'too big to fail' are a fairly recent phenomenon, though one with enormous consequences for the reproduction of the capitalist system. Therefore the regulation and finally the prevention of this phenomenon have *become necessary* (7§9 of 7D2 and 9§6 of 9D2).

The protection of the environment might be considered a fourth candidate. That protection is certainly necessary for the reproduction of the capitalist system. However, that protection has been necessary throughout the history of full-fledged capitalism. The fact that many states did not much care about it until around the beginning of the twenty-first century is another matter.

6 *Necessity versus contingency: a matter of content of the exposition*

Phenomena (entities, institutions and processes) are contingent when these could be either absent or different without changing the essential reproduction of the system. The decision to qualify phenomena as either necessary or contingent is a continuous major ingredient of the SD investigation: it is a matter of the *content* of the SD investigation and exposition. I indicated at the end of the first subsection ('contingency') that it is not opportune to list contingencies and to argue why these have not been dealt with in the exposition. Therefore the implication of the exposition is that everything that is *not* dealt with is contingent. Ultimately I must leave it to the reader to show that an instance of what I implicitly consider contingent is in fact a necessity (that is, a necessary condition of existence or a manifestation of forces behind these conditions). If one is found, then it should be included within the systematic of necessary conditions or of necessary manifestations.

---

prises, and a generalised continued centralisation of capital among enterprises, which would be impossible without the corporate form of enterprise (i.e. with limited liability).

32 Cf. Reuten 2003, On 'Becoming Necessary' in an Organic Systematic Dialectic; the case of creeping inflation. The idea of 'becoming necessary' was first developed in this paper (pp. 43–4 and 52–3). In the same book in which that paper appeared, Tony Smith (2003, pp. 26–8) takes a similar view about moments becoming necessary.

A§13-a Addendum. Hegel and Marx on necessity and contingency
The concept of 'necessity' is central to Hegel's Essence Logic.[33] In his lectures, not published by him, Hegel is quoted as saying: 'The sole aim of philosophical enquiry is to eliminate the contingent. Contingency is the same as external necessity, that is, a necessity which originates in causes which are themselves no more than external circumstances.'[34] In his *Encyclopaedia Logic*, Hegel begins the exposition of this issue with the category of 'possibility', in the sense that everything that we perceive is possible (he means 'determinate possibility', not fictional possibility by assumption). Next he introduces the category of 'contingency' (accidental) in order to contrast it with necessity.[35] The point here is that these contingencies (for example, bankers' dress codes) may have grounds (or perhaps must have grounds), though *these* grounds are not a part of, or are not essential to, the object totality at hand. Hegel's third category is that of 'necessity'. Necessities posit the object totality as an interconnected whole (as set out in A§11 above). A 'necessary' moment contains the antecedent moment transcended in itself.[36]

This makes sense as far as it goes. As we have seen above (A§13, subsection 3–4), necessary moments can be of contingent intensity or be expressed in contingent form. 'Normally' this poses no problem in the systematic exposition to the extent that, firstly, this has no consequences for the systematic interconnection of moments, and, secondly, we comprehend these contingent intensities/expressions within a totality, that is, when we have reached the end-point of the exposition.

While Hegel is explicit about necessity and contingency, in his scant methodological writings Marx is not, and we must use the content of his texts to make inferences. These inferences are complicated by the fact that Marx expounded analysis alongside his synthetic exposition, without clearly separating the two (A§3-a). Often his (apparent) analysis does introduce contingency. Even so, considering the general structure of his exposition throughout *Capital* I–III (and considering the preliminary-draft character of especially Parts Four to Seven of *Capital* III), I think that Marx's synthetic exposition mainly addresses necessity. (I cannot substantiate this issue here, as it would require an extensive study).

33 In his *Encyclopaedia Logic* it is the most substantial element of the Essence Logic's last *Division C*: 'Actuality'.
34 Hegel 1984 [1837], p. 28; cf. 1991 [1817], §143–§145.
35 See also Damsma 2015 and 2019, Ch. 1, Section 2, footnote.
36 Hegel 1991 [1817], §142–§149; cf. 1985 [1833], p. 80.

A§14 *Tendencies: dynamic constituents*

Tendencies are important dynamic constituents of an object totality, in our case the capitalist system. A tendency should be distinguished from an empirical 'trend'. A tendency is a process working in a certain direction, such that an entity takes a certain form or a certain quantitative expression. A tendency is always predicated on one or more forces or compulsions. In other words, a tendency sets out the *potential* effect of one or more forces. Therefore an alternative formulation is: A tendency is the generation of a particular form of an entity or the particular quantitative expression of an entity, this generation being predicated on one or more forces or compulsions. For example, the tendency for enterprises to take the corporate *form* (2§12) or the tendency for average inter-sector rates of profit to *equalise* (4§2, 5§1, 8§7, 8§7-a) – predicated on the forces indicated in 2§12 and 4§2.[37]

Tendencies may be *counteracted* by other tendencies, or by other lower-level complexities. For example, the tendency for average inter-sector rates of profit to equalise is counteracted by 'the tendency to centralisation of capital', that is, the tendency to oligopolisation and monopolisation (4§14).

A tendency is a determinant whose *actualisation* might not always predominate in any individual case (for example, enterprises that do not take the corporate form because of their finance structure or for taxation reasons). However, for it to have the status of a tendency (in this book), it must apply to a significant enough number of cases such that, when abstracting from counteracting tendencies, it has a *predominant character for the totality*.

Even if some tendency would not be counteracted, this does not mean that the form or the quantitative expression at hand is actually reached (empirically). A tendency is indeed a process, a generation 'in force', 'in operation'. Thus, taking the rate of profit case, we are never in an 'end-state' of equalised rates of profit (as neoclassical general equilibrium theory would have it);[38] rather we are in a never-ending movement towards equalisation.

Tendencies can be posited at the level of conditions of existence or at the level of manifestations. The most important example of the first (namely conditions) is the tendency to incorporation of enterprises. This regards a strong drive generally, but a necessary one for medium-sized and large enterprises. However, tendencies are most often posited at the level of manifestations.

---

37 The concept of tendency is not found in Hegel's work. Marx does posit tendencies in *Capital*, without, however, elaborating on the meaning of his conception of tendency in this or his other works. In Marx's *Capital* it is often not clear whether his term tendency refers to a force or its expression, or perhaps both (I discuss Marx's use of the term in Reuten 1997).

38 See Blaug 2001 on the notion of 'end-state competition'.

List of figures

Bibliography

Years in square brackets refer to the original edition(s) of a work. When the year of publication of a work considerably deviates from the year(s) of composition the latter is (if known) put in curly brackets.

A General statistical references and sources

Clio Infra: https://www.clio-infra.eu/.

EC/Eurostat, AMECO database: http://ec.europa.eu/economy_finance/db_indicators/ameco/index_en.htm.

Eurostat 2011, *Manual on sources and methods for the compilation of COFOG Statistics; Classification of the Functions of Government* (COFOG), 2011 edition, Luxembourg: Publications Office of the European Union [see Appendix, pp. 155–81 for the COFOG structure] http://ec.europa.eu/eurostat/documents/3859598/5917333/KS-RA-11-013-EN.PDF.

Eurostat 2017 (or later), *Government finance statistics* [entry document for these statistics]: http://ec.europa.eu/eurostat/statistics-explained/index.php/Government_finance_statistics.

Eurostat 2017 (or later), *Government expenditure by function* [COFOG: entry document for these statistics] http://ec.europa.eu/eurostat/statistics-explained/index.php/Government_expenditure_by_function.

ILO, databases http://www.ilo.org/global/statistics-and-databases/lang--en/index.htm.

IMF, datasets http://data.imf.org/?sk=388DFA60-1D26-4ADE-B505-A05A558D9A42.

IMF, World economic outlook data 2017 (or later): http://www.imf.org/external/pubs/ft/weo/2017/02/weodata/download.aspx.

Jordà-Schularick-Taylor, Macrohistory Database http://www.macrohistory.net/data/.

Knoema 2017 (or later), Annual Macro-Economic Database, https://knoema.com/ECAMECODB2017Nov/annual-macro-economic-database-november-2017.

Maddison project database 2018 [data on international comparative economic growth and income levels over the very long run], https://www.rug.nl/ggdc/historicaldevelopment/maddison/releases/maddison-project-database-2018.

OECD Economics Glossary http://www.oecd.org/eco/economicsglossary-glossaireeconomique.htm.

OECD Economic Outlook Data Base Inventory (2017 or later), http://www.oecd.org/000/outlook/Database_Inventory.pdf.

OECD Database Economic Outlook, https://data.oecd.org/searchresults/?hf=20&b=0&r=%2Bf%2Ftype%2Fdatasets&q=Economic+Outlook&l=en&s=score.

OECD National Accounts, http://stats.oecd.org/ → National accounts.

OECD National Accounts at a glance, http://stats.oecd.org/Index.aspx?DataSetCode=NAAG.

OECD Social Expenditure; Aggregated data (SOCX), http://stats.oecd.org/Index.aspx?DataSetCode=SOCX_AGG.

Quandl, Financial and economic databases collection https://www.quandl.com/.

UNESCO, Unesco institute for statistics http://data.uis.unesco.org/.

World Bank databases http://databank.worldbank.org/data/reports.aspx?source=world-development-indicators&l=en.

World wealth and income database http://www.wid.world/.

B All other references

Adema, Willem, Pauline Fron and Maxime Ladaique 2011, 'Is the European welfare state really more expensive?: Indicators on social spending, 1980–2012; and a manual to the OECD Social Expenditure Database (SOCX)', *OECD Social, Employment and Migration Working Papers*, No. 124, OECD Publishing, available at: http://dx.doi.org/10.1787/5kg2d2d4pbf0-en.

Aglietta, Michel 1979 [1976], *A theory of capitalist regulation: The US experience*, translated by David Fernbach, London: NLB.

Alchian, Armen 1950, 'Uncertainty, evolution and the economic theory', *Journal of Political Economy*, 58, 3: 211–21.

Andre, Claire and Manuel Velasquez 1990, 'Rights stuff', *Issues in Ethics*, 3, 1, available at: https://www.scu.edu/ethics/ethics-resources/ethical-decision-making/rights-stuff/.

Andrés, Javier, Rafael Doménech and Antonio Fatás 2008, 'The stabilizing role of government size', *Journal of Economic Dynamics and Control*, 32, 2, working paper version (2007) available at: http://www.bde.es/f/webbde/SES/Secciones/Publicaciones/PublicacionesSeriadas/DocumentosTrabajo/07/Fic/dt0710e.pdf.

Arestis, Philip and Malcolm Sawyer (eds) 2006, *A handbook of alternative monetary economics*, Cheltenham: Edward Elgar.

Argitis, Georgios, Trevor Evans, Jo Michell and Jan Toporowski 2014, 'Finance and crisis: Marxian, institutionalist and circuitist approaches', *Institute for International Political Economy Berlin*, Working Paper No. 45/2014, available at: https://core.ac.uk/download/pdf/39422980.pdf.

Arrow, Kenneth J. and Gerard Debreu 1954, 'The existence of an equilibrium for a competitive economy', *Econometrica*, 22, 3: 265–90.

Arthur, Christopher J. 1993, 'Hegel's *Logic* and Marx's *Capital*', in *Marx's method in 'Capital': A re-examination* (pp. 63–88), edited by Fred Moseley, Atlantic Highlands, NJ: Humanities Press.

Arthur, Christopher J. 1997, 'Against the logical-historical method: dialectical derivation versus linear logic', in *New investigations of Marx's method* (pp. 9–37), edited by Fred Moseley and Martha Campbell, Atlantic Highlands, NJ: Humanities Press. (Revised in Arthur 2002, chapter 2.)

Arthur, Christopher J. 1998, 'The fluidity of capital and the logic of the concept', in *The circulation of capital: Essays on volume II of Marx's 'Capital'* (pp. 95–128), edited by Christopher Arthur and Geert Reuten, London/New York: Macmillan/St.Martin's Press.

Arthur, Christopher J. 2001, 'Value, labour and negativity', *Capital & Class*, 25: 15–39.

Arthur, Christopher J. 2002, *The new dialectic and Marx's 'Capital'*, Leiden: Brill.

Arthur, Christopher J. 2011, 'Towards a systematic dialectic of capital', web paper, available at: https://chrisarthur.net/towards-a-systematic-dialectic-of-capital/.

Arthur, Christopher J. 2016, 'With what must the critique of capital begin?', *Revista Opinião Filosófica*, 7, 1: 64–87, available at: http://periodico.abavaresco.com.br/index.php/opiniaofilosofica/article/view/646/591.

Atkinson, Tyler, David Luttrell and Harvey Rosenblum 2013, 'How bad was it? The costs and consequences of the 2007–09 financial crisis', *Federal Reserve Bank of Dallas, staff paper* No. 20/2013, available at: https://dallasfed.org/assets/documents/research/staff/staff1301.pdf.

Azevedo, Marco de 2010, 'Rights as entitlements and rights as claims', *Veritas*, 55, 1: 164–82, available at: http://revistaseletronicas.pucrs.br/ojs/index.php/veritas/article/viewFile/7327/5292.

Basel Committee on Banking Supervision 2010, *An assessment of the long-term economic impact of stronger capital and liquidity requirements*, Basel: Bank for International Settlements (BIS), available at: http://www.financialstabilityboard.org/publications/r_100818a.pdf.

Basel Committee on Banking Supervision 2014, *Standards Supervisory framework for measuring and controlling large exposures*, Basel: Bank for International Settlements (BIS), available at: https://www.bis.org/publ/bcbs283.pdf.

Basu, Deepankar and Panayiotis T. Manolakos 2010, 'Is there a tendency for the rate of profit to fall? Econometric evidence for the US economy, 1948–2007', University of Massachusetts – Amherst, *Economics Department Working Paper Series*. Paper 99, available at: http://scholarworks.umass.edu/econ_workingpaper/99.

Basu, Deepankar and Panayiotis T. Manolakos 2012, 'Is there a tendency for the rate of profit to fall? Econometric evidence for the US economy, 1948–2007', *Review of Radical Political Economics*, 45, 1: 76–95.

Baumol, William J. and William G. Bowen 1965, 'On the performing arts: The anatomy of their economic problems', *The American Economic Review*, 55, 1/2: 495–502.

Bavel, Bas van and Ewout Frankema 2013, 'Low income inequality, high wealth inequality: the puzzle of the Rhineland welfare states', CGEH *Working Paper Series* no. 50,

Centre for Global Economic History, Universiteit Utrecht, available at: http://www.cgeh.nl/sites/default/files/WorkingPapers/CGEHWP50_vanbavelfrankema.pdf.

Bay, Christian 1979 [1958], *The structure of freedom*, Stanford: Stanford University Press.

Bellofiore, Riccardo 1989, 'A monetary labor theory of value', *Review of Radical Political Economics*, 21, 1–2: 1–26.

Bellofiore, Riccardo 1992, 'Monetary macroeconomics before the general theory: The circuit theory of money in Wicksell, Schumpeter and Keynes', *Social Concept*, 2: 47–89.

Bellofiore, Riccardo 1999, 'The value of labour value: The debate on Marx in Italy: 1968–1976', *Rivista di politica economica*, special issue: *Classical and Marxian Political Economy: A Debate on Claudio Napoleoni's views*, 89, 4–5: 31–69.

Bellofiore, Riccardo 2004, 'Marx and the macro-foundation of microeconomics', in *The constitution of capital: Essays on volume I of Marx's 'Capital'*, edited by Riccardo Bellofiore and Nicola Taylor, Basingstoke: Palgrave Macmillan.

Bellofiore, Riccardo 2005a, 'The monetary aspects of the capitalist process in the marxian system: An investigation from the point of view of the theory of the monetary circuit', in *Marx's Theory of Money – Modern Appraisals* (pp. 124–39), edited by Fred Moseley, London/New York, Palgrave Macmillan.

Bellofiore, Riccardo 2005b, 'Monetary economics after Wicksell: Alternative perspectives within the theory of the monetary circuit', in *The Monetary Theory of Production – Traditions and Perspectives* (pp. 39–51), edited by Giuseppe Fontana and Riccardo Realfonzo, London/New York: Palgrave Macmillan.

Bellofiore, Riccardo 2014, 'Lost in translation: Once again on the Marx–Hegel connection', in *Marx's Capital and Hegel's Logic* (pp. 164–88), edited by Fred Moseley and Tony Smith, Leiden/Boston/Köln: Brill.

Bellofiore, Riccardo and Roberto Fineschi (eds) 2009, *Re-reading Marx – New Perspectives after the Critical Edition*, London/New York: Palgrave Macmillan.

Bellofiore, Riccardo, Guglielmo Forges Davanzati and Riccardo Realfonzo 2000, 'Marx inside the circuit: Discipline device, wage bargaining and unemployment in a sequential monetary economy', *Review of Political Economy*, 12, 4: 403–17.

Bellofiore, Riccardo, Ewa Karwowski and Jan Toporowski (eds) 2013, *The legacy of Rosa Luxemburg, Oskar Lange and Michał Kalecki* (*Essays in honour of Tadeusz Kowalik*, Volume 1), London: Palgrave Macmillan.

Bellofiore, Riccardo, Ewa Karwowski and Jan Toporowski (eds) 2014, *Economic crisis and political economy* (*Essays in honour of Tadeusz Kowalik*, Volume 2), London: Palgrave Macmillan.

Bellofiore, Riccardo and Riccardo Realfonzo 1997, 'Finance and the labor theory of value', *International Journal of Political Economy*, 27, 2: 97–118.

Bellofiore, Riccardo and Riccardo Realfonzo 2003, 'Money as finance and money as universal equivalent: Re-reading Marxian monetary theory', in *Modern theories of money: The nature and role of money in capitalist economies* (pp. 198–218), edited by Sergio Rossi and Louis-Philippe Rochon, Cheltenham: Edward Elgar.

Benhabib, Seyla 1986, *Critique, norm, and utopia*, New York: Columbia University Press.

Berlin, Isaiah 1958, 'Two Concepts of Liberty', in Isaiah Berlin 1969, *Four Essays on Liberty*, Oxford: Oxford University Press, available at: https://www.wiso.uni-hamburg.de/fileadmin/wiso_vwl/johannes/Ankuendigungen/Berlin22_twoconceptsofliberty.pdf.

Biermans, Maarten 2012, *Decency and the market: The ILO's Decent Work Agenda as a moral market boundary*, PhD thesis, University of Amsterdam, Amsterdam School of Economics Research Institute.

Bindseil, Ulrich and Philipp J. König 2013, 'Basil J. Moore's horizontalists and verticalists: An appraisal 25 years later', *Review of Keynesian Economics*, 1, 4: 383–90, available at: http://dx.doi.org/10.4337/roke.2013.04.01.

Blankenau, William F., Nicole B. Simpson and Marc Tomljanovich 2007, 'Public education expenditures, taxation and growth: Linking data to theory', *American Economic Review*, 97, 2: 393–7.

Blaug, Mark 2001, 'Is competition such a good thing? Static efficiency versus dynamic efficiency', *Review of Industrial Organization*, 19, 1: 37–48.

Bolt, Jutta and Jan Luiten van Zanden 2014, 'The Maddison Project: Collaborative research on historical national accounts', *The Economic History Review*, 67, 3: 627–51.

Bolt, Jutta, Robert Inklaar, Herman de Jong and Jan Luiten van Zanden 2018, 'Rebasing "Maddison": New income comparisons and the shape of long-run economic development', available at: https://www.rug.nl/ggdc/historicaldevelopment/maddison/research.

Bonnaud, Jean-Jacques 1975, 'Planning and industry in France', in *Planning, politics and public policy: The British, French and Italian experience*, edited by Jack Hayward and Michael Watson, Cambridge: Cambridge University Press.

Breakey, Hugh (n.d.), 'Property', *Internet encyclopedia of philosophy* (IEP), available at: http://www.iep.utm.edu/prop-con/ (accessed February 2016).

Brenner, Robert 1998, 'Uneven development and the long downturn: The advanced capitalist economies from boom to stagnation, 1950–1998; or, the economics of global turbulence', *New Left Review*, 229 (special issue): 1–265.

Brown, Andrew, Gary Slater and David Spencer 2002, 'Driven to abstraction? Critical realism and the search for the "inner connection" of social phenomena', *Cambridge Journal of Economics*, 26, 6: 773–88.

de Brunhoff, Suzanne 1978 [1976], *The state, capital and economic policy*, translated by M. Sonenscher, London: Pluto Press.

de Brunhoff, Suzanne and Jean Cartelier 1974, 'Une analyse marxiste de l'inflation', *Cronique Sociale de France*, no. 4.

Büge, Max, Matias Egeland, Przemyslaw Kowalski and Monika Sztajerowska 2013, 'State-owned enterprises in the global economy: Reason for concern?', *VOX CEPR's Policy Porta*, available at: http://www.voxeu.org/article/state-owned-enterprises-global-economy-reason-concern.

Campbell, Martha 2002a, 'The credit system', in Campbell and Reuten (eds) 2002, pp. 212–27.

Campbell, Martha 2002b, 'Rent and landed property', in Campbell and Reuten (eds) 2002, pp. 228–45.

Campbell, Martha and Geert Reuten (eds) 2002, *The culmination of capital: Essays on volume III of Marx's 'Capital'*, Basingstoke/New York: Palgrave Macmillan.

Carey, Maeve P. 2016, Counting regulations: An overview of rulemaking, types of federal regulations, and pages in the Federal Register [USA], Congressional Research Service, Report R43056, available at: https://fas.org/sgp/crs/misc/R43056.pdf.

Cass, David and Joseph Stiglitz 1969, 'The implications of alternative saving and expectations hypotheses for choices of technique and patters of growth', *Journal of Political Economy*, 77, 4: 586–627.

Castles, Francis G. 2006, 'The growth of the post-war public expenditure state: Long-term trajectories and recent trends', *TranState working papers*, no. 35, available at: http://hdl.handle.net/10419/24948.

Caves, Richard E. and Masu Uekusa 1976a, 'Industrial organization', in *Asia's New Giant: How the Japanese Economy Works*, edited by Hugh Patrick and Henry Rosovsky, Washington: The Brookings Institution.

Caves, Richard E. and Masu Uekusa 1976b, *Industrial organization in Japan*, Washington: The Brookings Institution.

CBS/SCP 2013, *Armoedesignalement 2013*, The Hague: CBS/SCP, available at: http://www.scp.nl/Publicaties/Alle_publicaties/Publicaties_2013/Armoedesignalement_2013.

Christiansen, Hans / OECD 2011, 'The size and composition of the SOE sector in OECD countries', *OECD Corporate Governance Working Papers, No. 5*, available at: http://observgo.uquebec.ca/observgo/fichiers/60612_ep.pdf.

Claessens, Stijn, M. Ayhan Kose and Marco Terrones, 2008, 'What happens during recessions, crunches, and busts?' *IMF Working Paper 08/274*, Washington: International Monetary Fund, available at: https://www.imf.org/external/pubs/ft/wp/2008/wp08274.pdf.

Clarke, Simon 1994, *Marx's theory of crisis*, London/New York, Macmillan/St. Martin's.

Cusack, Thomas R. and Susanne Fuchs 2002, 'Ideology, institutions, and public spending', Discussion Paper P02–903, Wissenschaftszentrum Berlin für Sozialforschung, Working Group on Institutions, States, and Markets, available at: http://citeseerx.ist.psu.edu/viewdoc/download?doi=10.1.1.333.4763&rep=rep1&type=pdf.

Dalsgaard, Thomas, Jorgen Elmeskov and Cyn-Young Park 2002, 'Ongoing changes in the business cycle: Evidence and causes', *OECD Economics Department Working*

Papers, No. 315, OECD Publishing, available at: http://dx.doi.org/10.1787/480377612415.

Dalton, George 1974, *Economic systems and society: Capitalism and the third world*, Harmondsworth: Penguin.

Damsma, Dirk 2015, *On the articulation of systematic-dialectical methodology and mathematics*, PhD dissertation, University of Amsterdam, Faculty of Economics & Business.

Damsma, Dirk 2019, *How language informs mathematics*, Historical Materialism Book Series, Leiden: Brill [forthcoming].

de Brunhoff, see Brunhoff, de

de Jong, see Jong, de

De Vroey, Michel 1981, 'Value, production, and exchange', in *The value controversy* (pp. 173–201), edited by Ian Steedman, Paul Sweezy et al., London: Verso and NLB.

De Vroey, Michel 1984, 'Inflation: a non-monetarist monetary interpretation', *Cambridge Journal of Economics*, 8, 4: 381–99.

Deleplace, Ghislain and Edward J. Nell (eds) 1996, *Money in motion: The post Keynesian and circulation approaches*, London/New York: Macmillan/St. Martin's Press.

ECB Statute 2012. 'Protocol on the statute of the European System of Central Banks and of the European Central Bank', *Official Journal of the European Union*, 26.10.2012, available at: http://www.ecb.europa.eu/ecb/legal/pdf/c_32620121026en_protocol_4.pdf.

Eldred, Michael 1984, *Critique of competitive freedom and the bourgeois-democratic state: Outline of a form-analytic extension of Marx's uncompleted system*, Copenhagen: Kurasje.

Eldred, Michael, Marnie Hanlon, Lucia Kleiber and Mike Roth 1984 [1982/85[1]], 'Reconstructing value-form analysis' 1–4, *Thesis Eleven*, no. 4, 1982; no. 7, 1983; no. 9, 1984; no. 11, 1985; modified as 'A value-form analytic reconstruction of *Capital*', Appendix (pp. 350–487) to M. Eldred 1984, *Critique of competitive freedom and the bourgeois-democratic state: Outline of a form-analytic extension of Marx's uncompleted system*, Copenhagen: Kurasje.

Ellis, Brian 1968, *Basic concepts of measurement*, Cambridge: Cambridge University Press.

Erickson, Peter, Harro van Asselt, Eric Kemp-Benedict and Michael Lazarus 2013, *International trade and global greenhouse gas emissions: Could shifting the location of production bring GHG benefits?* Stockholm Environment Institute, available at: https://www.sei-international.org/mediamanager/documents/Publications/SEI-ProjectReport-EricksonP-InternationalTradeAndGlobalGreenhouseGasEmissions-2013.pdf.

Europe Economics 2001, 'Study on assessment criteria for distinguishing between competitive and dominant oligopolies in merger control', Final Report for the European Commission Enterprise Directorate General, London: Europe Economics.

European Commission 2014, *Economic Review of the Financial Regulation Agenda*, Commission staff working document SWD (2014) 158 final, available at: http://ec.europa.eu/internal_market/finances/docs/general/20140515-erfra-working-document_en.pdf.

European Union, 'Lisbon Treaty', available at: http://bookshop.europa.eu/uri?target=EUB:NOTICE:FXAC10083:EN and at: http://www.lisbon-treaty.org/wcm/the-lisbon-treaty.html.

Eurostat 2011, see above, rubric *A. General statistical references and sources.*

Eurostat 2016, 'Greenhouse gas emission statistics' (data from June 2016), available at: http://ec.europa.eu/eurostat/statistics-explained/index.php/Greenhouse_gas_emission_statistics.

Fatás, Antonio and Ilian Mihov 2001, 'Government size and automatic stabilizers: International and intranational evidence', *Journal of International Economics*, 55, 1: 3–28. Working paper version available at: http://faculty.insead.edu/ilian-mihov/documents/Journal_Version_Intrafp_2.pdf.

Fatás, Antonio and Ilian Mihov 2002/2003, 'The Case for Restricting Fiscal Policy Discretion', *Centre for Economic Policy Research, Discussion Paper* No. 3277, 2002, available at: http://crei.cat/activities/sc_conferences/14/mihov.pdf; published in *Quarterly Journal of Economics*, November 2003.

Fine, Ben and Laurence Harris 1979, *Rereading Capital*, London: Macmillan.

Florio, Massimo 2014, 'The return of public enterprise', *Centre for Industrial Studies (CSIL), Working Papers 2014–01*, available at: http://www.csilmilano.com/docs/WP2014_01.pdf.

Foley, Duncan K. 1986, *Understanding Capital: Marx's economic theory*, Cambridge, MA: Harvard University Press.

Foley, Duncan K. 2005, 'Marx's theory of money in historical perspective', in *Marx's Theory of Money: Modern Appraisals* (pp. 36–49), edited by Fred Moseley, London/New York: Palgrave Macmillan.

Fontana, Giuseppe and Riccardo Realfonzo (eds) 2005, *The monetary theory of production – Traditions and perspectives*, London/New York: Palgrave Macmillan.

Fontana, Giuseppe and Riccardo Realfonzo (eds) 2005a, 'Introduction: The monetary theory of production', in Fontana and Realfonzo (eds) 2005, pp. 1–19.

Forges Davanzati, Guglielmo 2011, 'Income distribution and crisis in a marxian schema of the monetary circuit', *International Journal of Political Economy*, 40, 3: 33–49.

Freeman, Christopher 1982 [1974], *The economics of industrial innovation*, London: Frances Pinter.

Frey, Bruno S. and Matthias Benz 2002, 'Business cycles: Political business cycle approach', in *An encyclopedia of macroeconomics* (pp. 89–93), edited by Brian Snowdon and Howard R. Vane, Cheltenham: Edward Elgar.

Friedman, Milton 1959, 'Statement on monetary theory and policy', in *Employment, growth and price levels* (Hearings before the Joint Economic Committee, 86th Congress, 1st session, May 25–8, 1959), U.S. Government Printing Office; reprinted in R.J. Ball and P. Doyle (eds) 1969, *Inflation* (pp. 136–45), Harmondsworth: Penguin.

Friedman, Milton 1968, 'Money: quantity theory', in *International encyclopedia of the social sciences* (pp. 432–47), edited by David L. Sills, New York: Macmillan and Free Press; reprinted in A.A. Walters (ed.) 1973, *Money and banking* (pp. 36–66), Harmondsworth: Penguin.

Friend, Céleste (n.d.), 'Social contract theory', *Internet encyclopedia of philosophy* (IEP), available at: http://www.iep.utm.edu/soc-cont/ (accessed February 2016).

Galí, Jordi 1994, 'Government Size and Macroeconomic Stability', *European Economic Review* 3, available at: http://crei.cat/people/gali/pdf_files/gov.%20size%20and%20macro.pdf.

Garrison, Roger W. 2002, 'Business cycles: Austrian approach', in *An encyclopedia of macroeconomics* (pp. 64–8), edited by Brian Snowdon and Howard R. Vane, Cheltenham: Edward Elgar.

Gavison, Ruth 2003, 'On the relationships between civil and political rights, and social and economic rights', in *The globalization of human rights* (pp. 23–55), edited by Jean-Marc Coicaud, Michael W. Doyle and Anne-Marie Gardner, Tokyo/New York/Paris: United Nations University Press.

Gestel, Rob A.J. van (2011), 'Vertrouwen in een lerende wetgever', *RegelMaat*, 26/1, pp. 7–22.

Gestel, Rob A.J. van, and Marc L.M. Hertogh 2006, *Wat is regeldruk? Een verkennende internationale literatuurstudie*, The Hague: WODC (Scientific Research and Documentation, Netherlands Ministry of Justice), available at: http://wodc.nl/onderzoeksdatabase/literatuurstudie-regeldruk.aspx; English summary, *What is regulatory pressure? An exploratory study of the international literature*, available at: http://wodc.nl/images/summary_tcm44-59384.pdf.

Gnos, Claude 2003, 'Circuit theory as an explanation of the complex real world', in *Modern theories of money: The nature and role of money in capitalist economies* (pp. 322–38), edited by Sergio Rossi and Louis-Philippe Rochon, Cheltenham and Northampton: Edward Elgar.

Government of the Netherlands 2013, 'Verzamelbrief Regeldruk', Parliamentary file 29,363 number 224, available at: https://www.eerstekamer.nl/behandeling/20130912/brief_regering_verzamelbrief/document3/f=/vjd2olmm1zyz.pdf.

Government of the Netherlands, Secretary of State for Finance 2015, 'Wijziging van de Wet op de vennootschapsbelasting 1969 en enige andere wetten in verband met de modernisering van de vennootschapsbelastingplicht voor overheidsondernemingen, Memorie van Antwoord', Parliamentary file 34,003 number D, available at: https://www.eerstekamer.nl/behandeling/20150324/memorie_van_antwoord_2/document3/f=/vjshlrhga1zq.pdf.

Graziani, Augusto 1989, 'The theory of the monetary circuit', *Thames Papers in Political Economy*, 1989/1, London, available at: http://www.gre.ac.uk/__data/assets/pdf_file/0009/1147581/TP_PPE_89_1.pdf, also in *Economies et Sociétés*, Série Monnaie et Production (1990), 7: 7–36.

Graziani, Augusto 2003, *The monetary theory of production*, Cambridge: Cambridge University Press.

Hahn, Frank 1981, 'General equilibrium theory', in *The crisis in economic theory* (pp. 123–38), edited by D. Bell and I. Kristol, New York: Basic Books.

Hammond, J. Daniel 2002, 'Business cycles: Monetarist approach', in *An encyclopedia of macroeconomics* (pp. 80–3), edited by Brian Snowdon and Howard R. Vane, Cheltenham: Edward Elgar.

Hammouya, Messaoud 1999, 'Statistics on public sector employment: Methodology, structures and trends', *ILO working paper*, Geneva: International Labour Office, available at: http://www.ilo.org/public/english/bureau/stat/download/wp_pse_e.pdf.

Hausman, Daniel M. 1992, *The inexact and separate science of economics*, Cambridge /New York: Cambridge University Press.

Hegel, Georg Wilhelm Friedrich 1967 [1821[1]], *Grundlinien der Philosophie des Rechts* oder *Naturrecht und Staatswissenschaft im Grundrisse*, edited by E. Moldenhauer and K.M. Michel (1970), Frankfurt a.M.: Suhrkamp Verlag, 1975; English translation T.M. Knox (1942[1]) from the 1821 Hegel edition, with reference to the 1833 and 1854 Gans, the 1902 Bolland and the 1921 Lasson editions, *Hegel's Philosophy of Right*, Oxford: Oxford University Press.

Hegel, Georg Wilhelm Friedrich 1984 [1837[1], 1840[2], 1955[4]], *Vorlesungen über die Philosophie der Geschichte*, edited by J. Hoffmeister (1955), translation (selections) by H.B. Nisbet, *Lectures on the Philosophy of World History, Introduction: Reason in History*, Cambridge: Cambridge University Press.

Hegel, Georg Wilhelm Friedrich 1985 [1833[1], 1840[2], 1940[3]], *Einleitung in die Geschichte der Philosophie* (of 1823, 1825, 1827), edited by J. Hoffmeister (1940), translated by T.M. Knox and A.V. Miller, *Introduction to the Lectures on the History of Philosophy*, Oxford: Clarendon Press.

Hegel, Georg Wilhelm Friedrich 1991 [1817[1], 1830[3]], *Enzyklopädie der Philosophischen Wissenschaften im Grundrisse, I, Die Wissenschaft der Logik*, translation of the third edition by T.F. Geraets, W.A. Suchting and H.S. Harris, *The Encyclopaedia Logic*, Indianapolis/Cambridge: Hackett Publishing Company.

Heilbroner, Robert L. 1986 [1985], *The nature and logic of capitalism*, New York/London: Norton.

Hein, Eckhard 2015, 'Secular stagnation or stagnation policy? Steindl after summers', *Levy Economics Institute*, Working Paper no. 846, available at: http://hdl.handle.net/10419/146974.

Himmelweit, Susan 1984, 'The real dualism of sex and class', *Review of Radical Political Economics*, 16, 1: 167–83.

Hirsch, Joachim 2005, *Materialistische Staatstheorie; Transformationsprozesse des kapitalistischen Staatensystems*, Hamburg: VSA-Verlag.

Hobbes, Thomas 1651, *Leviathan*, available at: http://files.libertyfund.org/files/869/0161_Bk.pdf.

Hollis, Martin 1994, *The philosophy of social science*, Cambridge: Cambridge University Press.

House of Commons [UK] 2010, 'How much legislation comes from Europe?', Research Paper 10/62, October 2010, available at: http://researchbriefings.files.parliament.uk/documents/RP10-62/RP10-62.pdf.

ILO 2014/15, *Global Wage Report 2014/15; Wages and income inequality*, Geneva: International Labour Office, available at: http://www.ilo.org/global/research/global-reports/global-wage-report/2014/lang--en/index.htm.

ILO 2016/17, *Global Wage Report 2016/17; Wage inequality in the workplace*, Geneva: International Labour Office, available at: http://www.ilo.org/global/research/global-reports/global-wage-report/2016/lang--en/index.htm.

Inwood, Michael 1992, *A Hegel dictionary*, Oxford: Blackwell.

Ishay, Micheline 2008, *The history of human rights: From ancient times to the globalized era*, Berkeley: University of California Press.

Ivaldi, Marc, Bruno Jullien, Patrick Rey, Paul Seabright and Jean Tirole 2003, 'The economics of tacit collusion', IDEI, Toulouse; Final Report for DG Competition, European Commission, available at: ec.europa.eu/competition/.../the_economics_of_tacit_collusion_en.pdf.

Jakab, Zoltan and Michael Kumhof 2015, 'Banks are not intermediaries of loanable funds – and why this matters', *Bank of England Working Paper* No. 529, available at: http://z822j1x8tde3wuovlg07ue15.wpengine.netdna-cdn.com/wp-content/uploads/2015/02/wp529.pdf.

Jakubowski, Franz 1976 [1936], *Ideology and Superstructure in Historical Materialism*, translated by Anne Booth, London: Allison & Busby.

Johansen, Leif 1959, 'Substitution versus fixed production coefficients in the theory of economic growth: a synthesis', *Econometrica*, 27, 2: 157–76.

Jong, Edwin P.O. de and Michiel Herweijer 2004, *Alle regels tellen; De ontwikkeling van het aantal wetten, AMvB's en ministeriele regelingen in Nederland*, The Hague: WODC (Scientific Research and Documentation, Netherlands Ministry of Justice), available at: http://wodc.nl/onderzoeksdatabase/toename-van-regelgeving.aspx. (English summary: *Every rule counts; Laws, cabinet regulations and ministerial rules in the Netherlands* http://wodc.nl/images/ob225-summary_tcm44-58541.pdf.)

Jong, Edwin P.O. de and Sjoerd E. Zijlstra 2009, *Wikken, wegen en (toch) wetgeven; Een onderzoek naar de hiërarchie en omvang van wetgeving in vijf Europese landen*, The Hague: WODC (Scientific Research and Documentation, Netherlands Ministry of Justice), available at: http://wodc.nl/onderzoeksdatabase/hierarchie-en-omvang

-van-regelgeving-in-europa.aspx; English summary, *Estimate, weigh and legislate*, available at: http://wodc.nl/images/ob280-summary_tcm44-255500.pdf.

Jorda, Oscar, Moritz Schularick and Alan M. Taylor 2012, 'When credit bites back: Leverage, business cycles, and crises', *Federal Reserve Banks of San Francisco Working paper series* nr. 2011–27, available at: http://www.frbsf.org/publications/economics/papers/2011/wp11-27bk.pdf.

Kaldor, Nicholas 1955/56, 'Alternative theories of distribution', *Review of Economic Studies*, 23, 2: 83–100; reprinted in *Growth Economics* (pp. 81–91), edited by A. Sen, Harmondsworth: Penguin Books.

Kaldor, Nicholas and James Mirrlees 1962, 'A new model of economic growth', *Review of Economic Studies*, 29, 3: 174–92.

Kalecki, Michał 1935, 'A macroeconomic theory of business cycles', *Econometrica*, July: 327–44.

Kalecki, Michał 1942, 'A theory of profits', *The Economic Journal*, 52 (Jun–Sept): 258–67. [Revised as 'The determinants of profits', ch. 3 of Kalecki 1954, next as 'Determinants of profits', ch. 7 of Kalecki 1971.]

Kalecki, Michał 1971 [1933–71], *Selected essays on the dynamics of the capitalist economy 1933–1970*, Cambridge: Cambridge University Press.

Kalecki, Michał 2003 [1954], *Theory of economic dynamics: An essay on cyclical and long-run changes in capitalist economy*, London/New York: Routledge.

Kannan, Prakash, Alasdair Scott and Marco E. Terrones 2009, 'From recession to recovery: How soon and how strong', *World Economic Outlook*, 103–38, available at: https://www.imf.org/external/np/seminars/eng/2012/fincrises/pdf/ch8.pdf.

Keynes, John Maynard 1936, *The general theory of employment, interest and money*, London: Macmillan.

Keynes, John Maynard 1937, 'The general theory of employment', *Quarterly Journal of Economics*, 51, 2: 209–23, reprinted in *Collected Writings, Volume XIII*, pp. 109–23.

Keynes, John Maynard 1973 [1933], 'A monetary theory of production', in *Collected Writings, Volume XIII* (pp. 408–12), *The general theory and after, part I, preparation*, edited by Donald Moggridge, London: Macmillan and Cambridge University Press.

Kowalski, Przemyslaw, Max Büge and Monika Sztajerowska 2013, 'State-owned enterprises: Trade effects and policy implications', OECD Trade Policy Papers, No. 147, OECD Publishing, available at: http://dx.doi.org/10.1787/5k4869ckqk7l-en.

KPMG International 2011, 'Confronting complexity: Research findings and insights', available at: https://www.kpmg.com/Global/en/IssuesAndInsights/ArticlesPublications/Documents/complexity-research-report.pdf.

Kuhn, Thomas S. 1970² [1962¹], *The structure of scientific revolutions*, Chicago: University of Chicago Press.

Laeven, Luc, Lev Ratnovski and Hui Tong 2014, 'Bank size and systemic risk', *IMF Staff Discussion Notes*, 14/4, Washington: International Monetary Fund.

Laeven, Luc and Fabián Valencia 2012, 'Systemic Banking Crises Database: An Update', *IMF Working Paper* WP/12/163 (June), available at: https://www.imf.org/external/pubs/ft/wp/2012/wp12163.pdf; data: https://www.imf.org/external/pubs/ft/wp/2012/Data/wp12163.zip.

Lakatos, Imre 1974 [1970], 'Falsification and the methodology of scientific research programmes', in *Criticism and the growth of knowledge* (pp. 91–196), edited by Imre Lakatos and Alan Musgrave, Cambridge: Cambridge University Press.

Lavoie, Marc 2003, 'A primer on endogenous credit-money', in *Modern theories of money: The nature and role of money in capitalist economies* (pp. 506–43), edited by Sergio Rossi and Louis-Philippe Rochon, Cheltenham and Northampton: Edward Elgar.

Lavoie, Marc 2014, *Post-Keynesian economics, new foundations*, Cheltenham and Northampton: Edward Elgar, available at: http://www.elgaronline.com/view/9781847204837.xml.

Lipietz, Alain 1985 [1983], *The enchanted world: Inflation, credit and the world crisis*, translated by Ian Patterson, London: Verso.

Locke, John (1689[1], 1764[6]), *Two Treatises of Government, Second Treatise, of Civil Government*, available at: http://oll.libertyfund.org/titles/222.

López G., Julio and Michaël Assous 2010, *Michal Kalecki*, Basingstoke: Palgrave–Macmillan, available at: http://digamo.free.fr/kalecki2010.pdf.

Luxemburg, Rosa 1963 [1913], *The accumulation of capital*, translated by Agnes Schwarzschild, London: Routledge and Kegan Paul.

Luyendijk, Joris, 2015, *Swimming with Sharks: My Journey into the World of the Bankers*, London: Guardian Faber Publishing; underlying interviews available at: https://www.theguardian.com/commentisfree/joris-luyendijk-banking-blog.

Lysandrou, Photis 2009, 'Global Inequality and the Global Financial Crisis: The New Transmission Mechanism', *London Metropolitan Business School, Working Paper Series* No. 5., available at: http://www.londonmet.ac.uk/fms/MRSite/acad/lmbs/RESEARCH%20CENTRES/CIBS/Working%20Papers%20new/Lysandrou%20Working%20Paper%20No_%205.pdf.

Maddison, Agnus 1991, 'Business cycles, long waves and cycles of economic development', (abbreviated version of chapter 4 of A. Maddison, *Dynamic Forces in Capitalist Development*, Oxford University Press, 1991), available at: http://www.ggdc.net/MADDISON/ARTICLES/Business_Cycles.pdf.

Maddison, Agnus 2010, 'Background Note on "Historical Statistics"', available at Angus Maddison website: http://www.ggdc.net/MADDISON/Historical_Statistics/BackgroundHistoricalStatistics_03-2010.pdf.

Maddison Project Database 2018, by Jutta Bolt, Robert Inklaar, Herman de Jong and Jan Luiten van Zanden, available at: https://www.rug.nl/ggdc/historicaldevelopment/maddison/releases/maddison-project-database-2018.

Marshall, Alfred 1972 [1890[1], 1920[8]], *Principles of economics*, London: Macmillan, available at: http://files.libertyfund.org/files/1676/Marshall_0197_EBk_v6.0.pdf.

Marx, Karl, *Collected works editions*: (1) *Marx-Engels-Werke* (MEW), Berlin: Dietz Verlag, http://www.mlwerke.de/me/default.htm; (2) *Marx-Engels-Gesamtausgabe* (MEGA), Berlin: De Gruyter, http://mega.bbaw.de/struktur; (3) *Marx Engels Collected Works* (MECW), London: Lawrence & Wishart.

Marx, Karl, *German editions*

Marx, Karl 1953a {ms.1857–58} *Grundrisse der Kritik der politischen Ökonomie (Rohentwurf)*, Berlin: Dietz Verlag.

Marx, Karl 1953b [1903[1]] {ms.1857} 'Einleitung [zur Kritik der politischen Ökonomie]', in Marx 1953a. (First published 1903 in der Zeitschrift *Die Neue Zeit.*)

Marx, Karl 1960 [1852[1]; 1869[2]], 'Der achtzehnte Brumaire des Louis Bonaparte', in *Marx-Engels-Werke*, Band 8, Berlin: Dietz Verlag.

Marx, Karl 1961 [1859], *Zur Kritik der politischen Ökonomie*, in *Marx-Engels-Werke*, Band 13, Berlin: Dietz Verlag.[1]

Marx, Karl 1962 [1867[1]; 1890[4]] {ms.1866–67}, *Das Kapital, Kritik der Politischen Ökonomie; Erster Band, Der Produktionsprozeß des Kapitals*, fourth edition, edited by Friedrich Engels, in *Marx-Engels-Werke*, Band 23, Berlin: Dietz Verlag.

Marx, Karl 1963 [1885[1]; 1893[2]] {ms.1865, 1868–70 and 1877–81}, *Das Kapital, Kritik der Politischen Ökonomie; Zweiter Band, Der Zirkulationsprozeß des Kapitals*, second edition, edited by Friedrich Engels, in *Marx-Engels-Werke*, Band 23, Berlin: Dietz Verlag.[2]

Marx, Karl 1964 [1894] {ms.1864–65}, *Das Kapital, Kritik der Politischen Ökonomie; Dritter Band, Der Gesamtprozeß der kapitalistischen Produktion*, edited by Friedrich Engels, in *Marx-Engels-Werke*, Band 25, Berlin: Dietz Verlag.[3]

Marx, Karl 1993{ms.1864–65}, research manuscript for *Capital III* of 1864–65, in MEGA II/4.2, *Ökonomische Manuskripte 1863–1867, Teil 2: Manuskript 1863/65 zum 3. Buch des "Kapital"*, arranged and edited by Manfred Müller, Jürgen Jungnickel, Barbara Lietz, Christel Sander and Arthur Schnickmann, Berlin: Dietz Verlag.

Marx, Karl, *English editions*

Marx, Karl 1971 [1859], *A Contribution to the Critique of Political Economy*, edited by Maurice Dobb and translated from the German edition by S.W. Ryazanskaya (see Marx 1961), London: Lawrence & Wishart.

Marx, Karl 1973a {ms.1857–58}, *Grundrisse, Foundation of the Critique of Political Economy (Rough Draft)*, translated by Martin Nicolaus from the German edition (see Marx 1953).

1 cf. MEGA II/2.
2 cf. MEGA II/13.
3 cf. MEGA II/15.

Marx, Karl 1973b [1903[1]] {ms.1857}, 'Introduction [to the Critique of Political Economy]', in Marx 1973a. (First publication in German 1903 – see Marx 1953b.)

Marx, Karl 1976 [1867[1]; 1890[4]], *Capital: A Critique of Political Economy. Volume One*, translated by Ben Fowkes from the fourth German edition (see Marx 1962), Harmondsworth: Penguin.

Marx, Karl 1978 [1885[1]; 1893[2]], *Capital: A Critique of Political Economy. Volume Two*, edited by Friedrich Engels, translated by David Fernbach from the second German edition (see Marx 1963), Harmondsworth: Penguin.

Marx, Karl 1979 [1852[1]; 1869[2]], 'The Eighteenth Brumaire of Louis Bonaparte', translated by Clemens Dutt, Rodney Livingstone, Christopher Upward, from the second German edition (see Marx 1960), in *MECW* 11, pp. 99–197.

Marx, Karl 1981 [1894] {ms.1864–65}, *Capital: A Critique of Political Economy. Volume Three*, edited by Friedrich Engels, translated by David Fernbach from the German edition (see Marx 1964), Harmondsworth: Penguin.

Marx, Karl 2015 {ms.1864–65}, research manuscript for *Capital III* of 1864–65 (see Marx 1993), translated from MEGA II/4.2 by Ben Fowkes, *Marx's Economic Manuscript of 1864–1865*, edited and with an introduction by Fred Moseley, Historical Materialism Book Series, Leiden: Brill.

Marx, Karl and Friedrich Engels 1976 [1932[1], 1965/66[2]] {ms.1845/46}, *Die Deutsche Ideologie*, in *Marx-Engels-Werke*, Band 3 (1969). English translation of the second German edition by C. Dutt, W. Lough and C.P. Magill, *The German Ideology*, Marx Engels Collected Works, Vol. 5, pp. 19–539.

Mazzucato, Mariana 2011, *The Entrepreneurial State*, London: Demos, available at: http://www.demos.co.uk/files/Entrepreneurial_State_-_web.pdf.

Mazzucato, Mariana 2013, revised 2015, *The Entrepreneurial State: debunking public vs private sector myths*, London: Anthem (blurb: http://marianamazzucato.com/projects/the-entrepreneurial-state/the-entrepreneurial-state-usa/)

Ministry of Finance of The Netherlands 2013, *Incidentele suppletoire begroting DNB winstafdracht*, written interchange with the Senate, 33.548 D, 8 March 2013, available at: http://www.eerstekamer.nl/behandeling/20130308/nota_naar_aanleiding_van_het_3/document3/f=/vj7qll92qdzz.pdf.

Minsky, Hyman P. 1982, 'Debt deflation processes in today's institutional environment', *Banca Nazionale del Lavoro – Quarterly Review*, 143 (December): 375–95.

Minsky, Hyman P. 2004 [1954], *Induced investment and business cycles*, edited by Dimitri B. Papadimitriou, Cheltenham, Edward Elgar.

Mohun, Simon 2016, 'Class structure and the US personal income distribution, 1918–2012', *Metronomica*, 67, 2: 334–63.

Morris, Madeline 1993, 'The structure of entitlements', *Cornell Law Review*, 78: 822–99, available at: http://scholarship.law.duke.edu/cgi/viewcontent.cgi?article=1373&context=faculty_scholarship.

Moseley, Fred 2005, 'Introduction', in *Marx's theory of money – Modern appraisals* (pp. 1–18), edited by Fred Moseley, London/New York: Palgrave Macmillan.

Moseley, Fred and Tony Smith (eds) 2014, *Marx's Capital and Hegel's Logic*, Leiden: Brill.

Murray, Patrick 1988, *Marx's theory of scientific knowledge*, Atlantic Highlands, NJ: Humanities Press.

Murray, Patrick 2000, 'Marx's "truly social" labour theory of value: Part I, abstract labour in Marxian value theory', *Historical Materialism*, 6: 27–66.

Murray, Patrick 2002, 'Reply to Geert Reuten', *Historical Materialism*, 10, 1: 155–76. [This is a reply to Reuten 2000, which intervened on Murray 2000.]

Murray, Patrick 2003, 'Things fall apart: Historical and systematic dialectics and the critique of political economy', in *New dialectics and political economy* (pp. 150–72), edited by Robert Albritton and John Simoulides, Basingstoke: Palgrave Macmillan.

Murtin, Fabrice and Marco Mira d'Ercole, 2015, 'Household wealth inequality across OECD countries: New OECD evidence', *OECD Statistics Brief*, June 2015, No. 21, available at: http://www.oecd.org/std/household-wealth-inequality-across-OECD-countries-OECDSB21.pdf.

Naples, Michele and Nahid Aslanbeigui 1996, 'What *does* determine the profit rate? The neoclassical theories presented in introductory textbooks', *Cambridge Journal of Economics*, 20, 1: 53–71.

Nauta, Lolle W. 1980[4] [1971[1]], 'Wetenschap en waardevrijheid', in *Argumenten voor een kritische ethiek* (pp. 101–21), edited by L.W. Nauta, Amsterdam: Van Gennep.

Nielsen, Klaus 2008, 'Indicative planning', in *The new Palgrave dictionary of economics*, second edition, edited by Steven N. Durlauf and Lawrence E. Blume, Basingstoke: Palgrave Macmillan. *The new Palgrave dictionary of economics online*, Palgrave Macmillan, accessed 20 September 2014, available at: http://www.dictionaryofeconomics.com/article?id=pde2008_I000060.

Noord, Paul van den 2000, 'The size and role of automatic fiscal stabilizers in the 1990s and beyond', *OECD Working Paper*, ECO/WKP 2000 (3), (DOI 10.1787/816628410134), available at: http://www.oecd-ilibrary.org/docserver/download/5lgsjhvj828s.pdf?expires=1442239523&id=id&accname=guest&checksum=0CB803FF032E8FF36E3DEF59705C6795.

OECD datasets, see references rubric *A. General statistical references and sources.*

OECD 1999, *Historical statistics 1960–1997*, (DOI: 10.1787/hist_stats-1999-en-fr), available at: http://www.keepeek.com/Digital-Asset-Management/oecd/economics/oecd-historical-statistics-1999_hist_stats-1999-en-frpage1.

OECD 2013, 'Compensation of employees', in *National Accounts at a glance 2013*, Paris, OECD Publishing, available at: http://www.oecd-ilibrary.org/economics/national-accounts-at-a-glance-2013_na_glance-2013-en.

OECD 2014, 'The distributional effects of consumption taxes', in *The distributional effects of consumption taxes in OECD countries*, Paris: OECD Publishing, available at: http://

www.oecd-ilibrary.org/taxation/the-distributional-effects-of-consumption-taxes-in-oecd-countries_9789264224520-en.

OECD 2015, *OECD Regulatory Policy Outlook 2015*, Paris: OECD Publishing, available at: http://www.oecd-ilibrary.org/governance/oecd-regulatory-policy-outlook-2015_9789264238770-en.

OECD 2016, *OECD Factbook 2015–2016: Economic, Environmental and Social Statistics*, Paris: OECD Publishing, available at: http://www.oecd-ilibrary.org/economics/oecd-factbook_18147364.

Office for National Statistics [UK] 2015, 'The effects of taxes and benefits on household income, 2013/14 – Reference Tables', available at: http://webarchive.nationalarchives.gov.uk/20160105160709/http://www.ons.gov.uk/ons/rel/household-income/the-effects-of-taxes-and-benefits-on-household-income/historical-data--1977-2013-14/summary--historical-data--1977-2013-14.html.

Ortiz-Ospina, Esteban and Max Roser 2017, 'International Trade', available at: https://ourworldindata.org/international-trade (accessed 5 November 2017).

Overhoff, R.W. and L.J. Molenaar 1991, *De regel beslist; een beschouwing over regelgeving met behulp van beslissingstabellen*, The Hague: Sdu.

Partlow, Jeffrey 2013, 'The necessity of complexity in the tax system', *Wyoming Law Review* 13, 1: 302–34, available at: http://www.uwyo.edu/law/_files/docs/wy%20law%20review/v13%20n1/partlow.pdf

Pastrello, Gabriele 2013, 'Luxemburg as an economist: The unique challenge to Marx among Marxists', in *The legacy of Rosa Luxemburg, Oskar Lange and Michal Kalecki*, Volume 1 (pp. 36–57), edited by Riccardo Bellofiore, Ewa Karwowski and Jan Toporowski, Basingstoke: Palgrave.

Peter, Fabienne 2016, 'Political Legitimacy', *The Stanford Encyclopedia of Philosophy* (Summer 2016 Edition), edited by Edward N. Zalta, available at: http://plato.stanford.edu/archives/sum2016/entries/legitimacy/.

Piketty, Thomas 2014 [2013], *Capital in the 21st century*, Cambridge, MA: Harvard University Press. Data sources and graphs: Technical Appendix, available at: http://piketty.pse.ens.fr/files/capital21c/en/Piketty2014TechnicalAppendix.pdf

Piketty, Thomas and Gabriel Zucman 2013, *Capital is back: Wealth-income ratios in rich countries, 1700–2010*, Paris School of Economics, full document and data series available at: http://piketty.pse.ens.fr/capitalisback.

Plant, Raymond 1977, 'Hegel and political economy', *New Left Review*, 103: 79–93; 104: 103–13.

Polak, Nico J. 1940, 'Goed koopmansgebruik in verband met de winstbepaling', *De Naamloze Vennootschap* 19, 1940/41, reprinted 1965 under the same title, Roermond: Van der Marck.

Reuten, Geert 1988, 'Value as social form', in *Value, social form and the state* (pp. 42–61), edited by Michael Williams, Basingstoke: Macmillan, available at: http://reuten.eu (type year in search box).

Reuten, Geert 1991, 'Accumulation of capital and the foundation of the tendency of the rate of profit to fall', *Cambridge Journal of Economics*, 15, 1: 79–93, available at: http://reuten.eu (type year in search box).

Reuten, Geert 1993, 'The difficult labour of a theory of social value: Metaphors and systematic dialectics at the beginning of Marx's *Capital*', in *Marx's method in Capital: A reexamination* (pp. 89–113), edited by Fred Moseley, Atlantic Highlands, NJ: Humanities Press, available at: http://reuten.eu (type year in search box).

Reuten, Geert 1995, 'Conceptual collapses: A note on value-form theory', *Review of Radical Political Economics*, 27, 3: 104–10, available at: http://reuten.eu (type year in search box).

Reuten, Geert 1996, 'A revision of the neoclassical economics methodology: Appraising Hausman's Mill-twist, Robbins-gist, and Popper-whist', *Journal of Economic Methodology*, 3, 1: 39–67, available at: http://reuten.eu (type year in search box).

Reuten, Geert 1997, 'The notion of tendency in Marx's 1894 law of profit', in *New investigations of Marx's method* (pp. 150–75), edited by Fred Moseley and Martha Campbell, Atlantic Highlands, NJ: Humanities Press, available at: http://reuten.eu (type year in search box).

Reuten, Geert 1998, 'The status of Marx's reproduction schemes: Conventional or dialectical logic?', in *The circulation of capital: Essays on volume II of Marx's 'Capital'* (pp. 187–229), edited by Christopher Arthur and Geert Reuten, Basingstoke: Macmillan, available at: http://reuten.eu (type year in search box).

Reuten, Geert 1999, 'The source versus measure obstacle in value theory', *Rivista di Politica Economica*, 89, 4–5: 87–115, available at: http://reuten.eu (type year in search box).

Reuten, Geert 2000, 'The interconnection of systematic dialectics and historical materialism', *Historical Materialism*, 7, 1: 137–65, available at: http://reuten.eu (type year in search box).

Reuten, Geert 2002b, 'Business cycles: Marxian approach', in *An Encyclopedia of macroeconomics* (pp. 73–80), edited by Brian Snowdon and Howard R. Vane, Cheltenham: Edward Elgar, available at: http://reuten.eu (search year).

Reuten, Geert 2002c, 'The rate of profit cycle and the opposition between managerial and finance capital', in *The culmination of capital: Essays on volume III of Marx's 'Capital'* (pp. 174–211), edited by Martha Campbell and Geert Reuten, Basingstoke: Palgrave Macmillan, available at: http://reuten.eu (type year in search box).

Reuten, Geert 2003a, 'Karl Marx: his work and the major changes in its interpretation', in *The Blackwell companion to the history of economic thought* (pp. 148–66), edited by Warren Samuels, Jeff Biddle and John Davis, Oxford: Blackwell, available at: http://reuten.eu (type year in search box).

Reuten, Geert 2003b, 'On "becoming necessary" in an organic systematic dialectic: The case of creeping inflation', in *New dialectics and political economy* (pp. 42–59), edited by Robert Albritton and John Simoulidis, Basingstoke: Palgrave Macmillan, available at: http://reuten.eu (type year in search box).

Reuten, Geert 2003c, 'Holisme en structuralisme versus individualisme', in *Compendium Wetenschapsleer Economie* (pp. 144–52), edited by Geert Reuten, Amsterdam: Universiteit van Amsterdam, Faculteit der Economische Wetenschappen en Econometrie.

Reuten, Geert 2004a, 'Productive force and the degree of intensity of labour: Marx's concepts and formalizations in the middle part of *Capital I*', in *The constitution of capital: Essays on volume I of Marx's 'Capital'* (pp. 117–45), edited by Riccardo Bellofiore and Nicola Taylor, Basingstoke: Palgrave Macmillan, available at: http://reuten.eu (type year in search box).

Reuten, Geert 2004b, 'The inner mechanism of the accumulation of capital: the acceleration triple; A methodological appraisal of Part Seven of Marx's *Capital I*', in *The constitution of capital: Essays on volume I of Marx's 'Capital'* (pp. 274–98), edited by Riccardo Bellofiore and Nicola Taylor, Basingstoke: Palgrave Macmillan, available at: http://reuten.eu (type year in search box).

Reuten, Geert 2004c, ''Zirkel vicieux' or trend fall? The course of the profit rate in Marx's *Capital III*', *History of Political Economy*, 36, 1: 163–86, available at: http://reuten.eu (type year in search box).

Reuten, Geert 2005, 'Money as constituent of value: The ideal introversive substance and the ideal extroversive form of value in *Capital*', in *Marx's theory of money: Modern appraisals* (pp. 78–92), edited by Fred Moseley. Basingstoke: Palgrave Macmillan, available at: http://reuten.eu (type year in search box).

Reuten, Geert 2011, 'Economic stagnation postponed: Background of the 2008 financial-economic crisis in the EU and the USA', *International Journal of Political Economy*, 40, 4: 50–8, available at: http://reuten.eu (type year in search box).

Reuten, Geert 2014, 'An outline of the systematic-dialectical method: Scientific and political significance', in *Marx's Capital and Hegel's Logic* (pp. 243–68), edited by Fred Moseley and Tony Smith, Leiden: Brill, available at: http://reuten.eu (type year in search box).

Reuten, Geert 2017, 'The productive powers of labour and the redundant transformation to prices of production: A Marx-immanent critique and reconstruction', *Historical Materialism*, 25, 3: 1–33, available at: http://reuten.eu (type year in search box).

Reuten, Geert 2018a, 'Marx's conceptualisation of value in *Capital*', in *The Oxford Handbook of Karl Marx*, edited by Matthew Vidal, Tony Smith, Tomás Rotta, and Paul Prew, Oxford: Oxford University Press, available at: http://reuten.eu (type year in search box).

Reuten, Geert 2018b, 'De Nederlandse vermogensverdeling in internationaal perspectief; een vergelijking met 26 andere OECD-landen' (The distribution of wealth in the

Netherlands: a comparison with 26 other OECD countries), *Tijdschrift voor Politieke Economie* (TPEdigitaal), 12, 2: 1–7; with an English excerpt available at: http://reuten.eu (type year in search box).

Reuten, Geert and Peter Thomas 2011, 'From the "fall of the rate of profit" in the *Grundrisse* to the cyclical development of the profit rate in *Capital*', *Science & Society*, 75, 1: 74–90, available at: http://reuten.eu (type year in search box).

Reuten, Geert and Michael Williams 1989, *Value-form and the state: The tendencies of accumulation and the determination of economic policy in capitalist society*, London/New York: Routledge, Summary and conclusions available at: http://reuten.eu (type year in search box).

Ricardo, David 1981 [1817[1], 1821[3]], *The principles of political economy and taxation*, in *Works and Correspondence of David Ricardo*, Volume I, edited by Piero Sraffa in collaboration with Maurice Dobb, Cambridge: Cambridge University Press, available at: http://oll.libertyfund.org/groups/90.

Roberts, Michael 2012, 'A world rate of profit' (blog, 13 pages), available at: https://thenextrecession.files.wordpress.com/2012/09/a-world-rate-of-profit.pdf.

Robinson, Joan 1953, 'The production function and the theory of capital', *Review of Economic Studies*, 21, 2: 81–106, available at http://theme.univ-paris1.fr/M1/hpe/HPEM1-TD4.pdf.

Rochon, Louis-Philippe and Sergio Rossi (eds) 2003a, *Modern theories of money: The nature and role of money in capitalist economies*, Cheltenham: Edward Elgar.

Rochon, Louis-Philippe and Sergio Rossi (eds) 2003b, 'Introduction', in Rochon and Rossi 2003a (pp. xx–xxxviii).

Roine, Jesper and Daniel Waldenström 2014/15, 'Long run trends in the distribution of income and wealth', *Uppsala Center for Fiscal Studies, Working paper*, 2014: 5 (April), available at: http://ucfs.nek.uu.se/digitalAssets/223/223631_20145_final.pdf; their data are available at: http://www.uueconomics.se/danielw/Handbook.htm. Published in 2015 under the same title in *Handbook of income distribution*, Volume 2 (pp. 469–591), edited by Anthony B. Atkinson and François Bourguignon, Amsterdam: Elsevier.

Rossi, Sergio 2003, 'Money and banking in a monetary theory of production', in *Modern theories of money: The nature and role of money in capitalist economies* (pp. 339–59), edited by Sergio Rossi and Louis-Philippe Rochon, Cheltenham: Edward Elgar.

Ryan, Cillian 2002, 'Business cycles: Real business cycle approach', in *An encyclopedia of macroeconomics* (pp. 93–7), edited by Brian Snowdon and Howard R. Vane, Cheltenham: Edward Elgar.

Sabaté Domingo, Oriol 2013, 'New quantitative estimates on long-term military spending in Spain (1850–2009)', *International Catalan Institute for Peace, Working Paper* No. 2013/6, available at: http://ssrn.com/abstract=2538470 or http://dx.doi.org/10.2139/ssrn.2538470.

Salter, Wilfred E.G. 1960, *Productivity and technical change*, Cambridge: Cambridge University Press.

Salverda, Wiemer 2015, 'EU policy making and growing inequalities', *European Economy Discussion Papers*, 008–2015, European Commission, Directorate-General for Economic and Financial Affairs, available at: http://ec.europa.eu/economy_finance/publications/eedp/pdf/dp008_en.pdf.

Samuelson, Paul A. 2004, 'Where Ricardo and Mill rebut and confirm arguments of mainstream economists supporting globalization', *Journal of Economic Perspectives*, 18, 3: 135–46.

Saviotti, Pier Paolo and Jackie Krafft 2004, 'Towards a generalised definition of competition'; paper presented at DRUID Summer Conference 2004 on Industrial dynamics, innovation and development, Elsinore, Denmark, June 14–16, available at: http://www2.druid.dk/conferences/viewabstract.php?id=2307&cf=16.

Schumpeter, Joseph A. 1934 [1911], *The theory of economic development*, Cambridge, MA: Harvard University Press. (Revised English edition of *Theorie der wirtschaftlichen Entwicklung*, 1911.)

Schumpeter, Joseph A. 2003 [1943[1], 1954[4]], *Capitalism, socialism and democracy*, London/New York: Taylor & Francis e-Library, available at: http://digamo.free.fr/capisoc.pdf.

Schumpeter, Joseph A. 1972 [1954], *History of economic analysis*, edited by Elizabeth B. Schumpeter, London: Allen & Unwin.

Schwalbe, Ulrich, Frank Maier-Rigaud and Anna Pisarkiewicz 2012, 'Background note' (pp. 21–103), in 'OECD, Policy Roundtable *Market definition*', OECD, DAF/COMP(2012)19, available at: http://www.oecd.org/daf/competition/Marketdefinition2012.pdf.

Seccareccia, Mario 2003, 'Pricing, investment and the financing of production within the framework of the monetary circuit: Some preliminary evidence', in *Modern theories of money: The nature and role of money in capitalist economies* (pp. 173–97), edited by Sergio Rossi and Louis-Philippe Rochon, Cheltenham: Edward Elgar.

Senate of The Netherlands 2013, *Incidentele suppletoire begroting DNB winstafdracht*, written interchange with the Minister of Finance, 33.548 C, 7 March 2013, available at: http://www.eerstekamer.nl/behandeling/20130307/verslag/document3/f=/vj7ph535cuys.pdf.

Senate of The Netherlands 2014, *Stroomlijning markttoezicht door de Autoriteit Consument en Markt*, written interchange with the Minister of Economic Affairs, 33.622 E, 21 May 2014, available at: https://www.eerstekamer.nl/behandeling/20140521/nadere memorie van ntwoord/document3/f=/vjjxnogm1qx2.pdf.

Shorrocks, Anthony, James B. Davies and Rodrigo Lluberas 2015, *Global wealth data-*

book 2015, Credit Suisse Research Institute, Zurich, Credit Suisse Group, available at: http://publications.credit-suisse.com/tasks/render/file/index.cfm?fileid=C26E3824-E868-56E0-CCA04D4BB9B9ADD5.

Smith, Adam 1776[1], *An Inquiry into the nature and causes of The Wealth of Nations*, (edited by Edwin Cannan, from the 5th 1791 edition), London: Methuen & Co, available at: http://www.econlib.org/library/Smith/smWNCover.html.

Smith, Tony 1990, *The logic of Marx's Capital: Replies to Hegelian criticisms*, Albany: State University of New York Press.

Smith, Tony 1993, 'Marx's *Capital* and Hegelian dialectical logic', in *Marx's method in Capital: A reexamination* (pp. 15–36), edited by Fred Moseley, Atlantic Highlands, NJ: Humanities Press.

Smith, Tony 2003, 'Systematic and historical dialectics: Towards a Marxian theory of globalization', in *New dialectics and political economy* (pp. 24–41), edited by Robert Albritton and John Simoulidis, Basingstoke: Palgrave Macmillan.

Smith, Tony 2006, *Globalisation: A systematic marxian account*, Leiden: Brill.

Smith, Tony 2014, 'Hegel, Marx and the comprehension of capitalism', in *Marx's Capital and Hegel's Logic* (pp. 17–40), edited by Fred Moseley and Tony Smith, Leiden: Brill.

Smith, Tony 2017, *Beyond liberal egalitarianism: Marx and normative social theory in the twenty-first century*, Leiden: Brill.

Snowdon, Brian and Howard R. Vane (eds) 2002, *An encyclopedia of macroeconomics*, Cheltenham: Edward Elgar.

Snowdon, Brian and Howard R. Vane (eds) 2002a, 'Efficiency Wage Theory', in Snowdon and Vane (eds) 2002, pp. 200–1.

Snowdon, Brian and Howard R. Vane (eds) 2002b, 'Business cycles: New classical approach', in Snowdon and Vane (eds) 2002, pp. 83–9.

Solow, Robert M. 1970, *Growth theory: An exposition*, Oxford: Clarendon Press.

Solow, Robert, James Tobin, Carl C. von Weizäcker and M. Yaari 1966, 'Neoclassical growth with fixed factor proportions', *Review of Economic Studies*, 33, 2: 79–115.

Spector, David 2010, 'Background notes on competition, state aids and subsidies', in OECD, *Competition, State Aids and Subsidies 2010*, DAF/COMP/GF(2010)5 (pp. 17–48), available at: http://www.oecd.org/competition/sectors/48070736.pdf.

Starosta, Guido 2008, 'The commodity-form and the dialectical method: On the structure of Marx's exposition in Chapter 1 of *Capital*', *Science & Society*, 72, 3: 295–318.

Steindl, Josef, 1976 [1952], *Maturity and stagnation in American capitalism*, 1976 edition with a new Introduction by the author, New York and London: Monthly Review Press, available at: http://digamo.free.fr/steindl52.pdf.

Stirk, Peter M.R. 2000, *Critical theory, politics, and society: An introduction*, Oxford: Blackwell.

Tanzi, Vito 2011, *Government versus markets: The changing economic role of the state*, Cambridge: Cambridge University Press.

Tanzi, Vito and Ludger Schuknecht 2000, *Public spending in the 20th century: A global perspective*, Cambridge: Cambridge University Press.

Thomas, Peter and Geert Reuten 2013, 'Crisis and the rate of profit in Marx's laboratory', in *In Marx's laboratory: Critical interpretations of the Grundrisse* (pp. 311–28), edited by Riccardo Bellofiore, Guido Starosta and Peter Thomas, Leiden: Brill.

Toporowski, Jan 2006, 'Methodology and microeconomics in the early work of Hyman P. Minsky', *Levy Economics Institute*, Working Paper 480, available at: http://www.levyinstitute.org/pubs/wp_480.pdf.

Toporowski, Jan 2013, *Michał Kalecki: An intellectual biography, volume 1*, Basingstoke: Palgrave Macmillan.

Toporowski, Jan and Łukasz Mamica (eds) 2015, *Michał Kalecki in the 21st century*, Basingstoke: Palgrave Macmillan.

Toshkov, Dimiter 2014, '55 years of European legislation', online presentation, available at: http://www.dimiter.eu/Eurlex.html; database available at: http://www.dimiter.eu/Data.html.

Trezise, Philip H. and Yukio Suzuki 1976, 'Politics, government, and economic growth in Japan', in *Asia's new giant: How the Japanese economy works* (pp. 753–811), edited by Hugh Patrick and Henry Rosovsky, Washington: The Brookings Institution.

Trigg, Andrew B. 2002, 'Business cycles: Keynesian approach', in *An encyclopedia of macroeconomics* (pp. 68–73), edited by Brian Snowdon and Howard R. Vane, Cheltenham: Edward Elgar.

UK Office of the Parliamentary Counsel, Cabinet Office 2013, 'When laws become too complex: A review into the causes of complex legislation', available at: https://www.gov.uk/government/uploads/system/uploads/attachment_data/file/187015/GoodLaw_report_8April_AP.pdf; web version available at: https://www.gov.uk/government/publications/when-laws-become-too-complex/when-laws-become-too-complex.

UN [United Nations] 2008a, 'The sequence of the SNA 2008 accounts', Excel version of Annex 2 of the 2008 SNA (see UN 2009), available at: http://unstats.un.org/unsd/nationalaccount/docs/SeqAccts.xls.

UN [United Nations] 2008b, United Nations, *International Standard Industrial Classification of All Economic Activities, Rev. 4* (ISIC. Rev. 4), available at: http://unstats.un.org/unsd/cr/registry/isic-4.asp.

UN [United Nations] 2009, United Nations [European Commission, International Monetary Fund, Organisation for Economic Co-operation and Development, United Nations and World Bank], *System of National Accounts 2008* [SNA 2008], available at: http://unstats.un.org/unsd/nationalaccount/sna2008.asp.

UNCTAD 2017, *World Investment Report 2017*, Geneva: United Nations Publication, available at: http://unctad.org/en/PublicationsLibrary/wir2017_en.pdf; statistical annexes available at: http://unctad.org/en/Pages/DIAE/World%20Investment%20Report/Annex-Tables.aspx.

van den Noord, see Noord, van den.

van Gestel, see Gestel, van.

Vester, L.J. 2017, 'De regelgevingsmonitor – ontwikkelingen in het Nederlandse regelingenbestand sinds 2004', in *Slotakkoord*, edited by H.M.B. Breunese, J.R. Groen, W. Peters and W.M. Weeber, The Hague: Ministerie van Binnenlandse Zaken en Koninkrijksrelaties, Directie Constitutionele Zaken en Wetgeving; Ministerie van Veiligheid en Justitie, Directie wetgeving en juridische zaken, available at: https://www.google.nl/url?sa=t&rct=j&q=&esrc=s&source=web&cd=1&ved=0ahUKEwiRnMTlg_bYAhWjD8AKHZdfBa8QFggpMAA&url=https%3A%2F%2Fwww.rijksoverheid.nl%2Fbinaries%2Frijksoverheid%2Fdocumenten%2Fpublicaties%2F2017%2F05%2F01%2Fslotakkoord%2FSlotakkoord.pdf&usg=AOvVaw0u8bkN7sWF5gJRXhA3-FkQ.

Vroey, De, see De Vroey.

Weber, Max 1968 [1920], 'Introduction to Gesammelte Aufsätze zur Religionssoziologie', in Max Weber 1968 [1904[1]], *The Protestant ethic and the spirit of capitalism*, translated by Talcott Parsons, London: Allen & Unwin.

Weber, Max 1999 [1919], 'Politik als Beruf', in *Gesammelte Politische Schriften*, available at: https://www.uwe-holtz.uni-bonn.de/lehrmaterial/weber_politik_als_beruf.pdf; translation 'Politics as a Vocation' (unknown edition), available at: http://anthropos-lab.net/wp/wp-content/uploads/2011/12/Weber-Politics-as-a-Vocation.pdf.

Weeks, John 1981, *Capital and exploitation*, London: Edward Arnold.

Went, Robert 2002, *The enigma of globalization: A journey to a new stage of capitalism*, London: Routledge.

World Bank 2016, 'PovcalNet: an online analysis tool for global poverty monitoring (update 1 Oct. 2016)', available at: http://iresearch.worldbank.org/PovcalNet/home.aspx.

World Bank 2016/n.d., *Financial stability*, website (accessed 2016), available at http://www.worldbank.org/en/publication/gfdr/background/financial-stability.

WRR 2013a, [Wetenschappelijke Raad voor het Regeringsbeleid], *Naar een lerende economie – Investeren in het verdienvermogen van Nederland*, Amsterdam: Amsterdam University Press, available at: https://www.wrr.nl/publicaties/rapporten/2013/11/04/naar-een-lerende-economie.

WRR 2013b, [Scientific council for government policy], 'Synopsis of the WRR report "Towards a learning economy: Investing in the Netherlands' earning capacity"', available at: https://english.wrr.nl/publications/reports/2013/11/04/towards-a-learning-economy.

List of symbols and abbreviations in order of appearance

Symbol or abbreviation	Meaning	Section first use	Remark
Chapter 1			
MVD	monetary value dimension	1§4	
M	money (amount)	1§4-c	
C_i	[in italics] any commodity (other than commodity j) [used in this Explication only]	1§4-c	*used only once*
C_j	[in italics] any commodity (other than commodity i) [used in this Explication only]	1§4-c	*used only once*
CPE	Classical Political Economy	1§5-b	
K	active capital (value in terms of MVD): assets of balance sheet total	1§13	
$K_{t'}$	idem, at beginning of year t	1§13	
K_t	idem, year average	1§13	
Π_t	surplus-value (= integral profit) produced per year	1§13	pi
ω	rate of integral profit (Π_t / $K_{t'}$)	1§13	omega

Symbol or abbreviation	Meaning	Section first use	Remark
L	labour-capacity (amount of in going fte per year, unless specified as per hour)	1§14	
w	wage rate (wage in going fte per year, unless specified as per hour)	1§14	
wL	wages sum	1§14	
δ	fraction of the total assets K, equivalent to the used up fixed assets	1§14	delta
μ	fraction of the total assets K, equivalent to the used up floating means of production (usually a larger sum than the sum that appears on the balance sheet)	1§14	mu
X_t	output of production per year (realised)	1§14	
L^{α}	actual labour (labour-capacity exerted at a power α) [the unique source of valorisation]	1§14	
α	production power of labour (in terms L^{α}) [$L^{\alpha} = L^{ά ϊ}$]	1§14	alpha
ά	technique-associated productive power of labour (in terms $L^{ά}$)	1§14	alpha, with tonos
ϊ	intensity of labour (in terms $L^{ϊ}$)	1§14	iota, with dialytika
m	actual unit monetary value of labour (per year, unless specified as per hour); more specifically: the realisation constraint resulting in the unit monetary value labour	1§14	
mL^{α}	actual monetary value of labour (realised) = net value-added	1§14	
Y^G	gross value-added (macroeconomically this would be GDP)	1§14	
Y	net value-added (macroeconomically this would be NDP)	1§14	
GDP	Gross domestic product	1§14	
NDP	Net domestic product	1§14	
Chapter 2			
Δ	change [see also $\underline{x}$]	2§3	

Symbol or abbreviation	Meaning	Section first use	Remark
å	ratio of capital accumulation out of surplus-value (a variable; amplified in 3§11 and 5D1)	2§3	a, ring
$\underline{x}_t$	rate of growth [of any variable underlined] = $(x_{t-1} - x_t) / (x_{t-1})$	2§4, fn.	
$\underline{x}$	rate of growth [of any variable underlined] = $(x_{t-1} - x_t) / (x_{t-1}) = \Delta x/x$ [time indices omitted]	2§4, fn.	
τ	capital-labour ratio [$\tau = K/L$]	2§4	tau
U	unemployment (number) [reserve of labour-capacity]	2§4	
u	rate of unemployment in % [$u = \{U/(L+U)\} * 100$]	2§4	
e	rate of surplus-value (or profit per labour-year-compensation) [$e = \Pi/wL$]	2§5	
|ï|	limited intensity of labour (physical or compliance limit)	2§5	
$\|\alpha\|$	limited production power of labour (because of limited intensity of labour)	2§5	
$\|x\|$	limited value of a variable (x)	2§5	
ClB	Clearing Bank	2§9	
CB	Central Bank	2§9-a	
Chapter 3			
PVF	pre-validating finance (of enterprises by banks)	3§2	
CG	consumer goods	3§2-b	
MP	means of production	3§2-b	
RPVF	remaining PVF (pre-validating finance of enterprises by banks)	3§6	
Σ	summation	3§6-c	
I	investment by enterprises (net)	3§9	
S	saving	3§9	

Symbol or abbreviation	Meaning	Section first use	Remark
W	wages sum enterprises (W=wL)	3§10	
x^P	planned production value of a variable (x)	3§10	
E	macroeconomic net expenditure	3§10	
C	consumption by households (Ck+Cw)	3§10	
X^d	desired (current) production	3§10	
Ck	consumption by capital owners	3§10	
Cw	consumption by wage earners (enterprises)	3§10	
Sw	saving out of wages (wage earners enterprises)	3§10	
Chapter 4			
TERP	tendency to equalisation of average inter-sector rates of integral profit	4§2	
ROC	restructuring of capital	4§2-b	
TUP	tendency to uniform prices within a sector or market	4§3	
Chapter 5			
ε	share of 'external' finance in capital (banks plus other financiers)	5§1	epsilon
i	[in italics] average rate of interest for enterprises: the weighted average of the rates paid to banks and to other financiers	5§1	
εK	external capital (passive capital furnished by external financiers)	5§1	
$i\varepsilon K$	surplus-value distributed to external financiers	5§1	
R	internal profit (surplus-value after interest payments)	5§1	cf. 3§1, Fig. 3.2b
ρ	rate of internal profit on the internal capital	5§1	rho
s_w	fraction saved out of wages (non-constant)	5§3	
PD	sum of dividends and interest distributed to capital owners	5§3, fn.	

Symbol or abbreviation	Meaning	Section first use	Remark
ø	rate of undesired overcapacity (undesired overcapacity/production capacity)	5§5	o stroke
Chapter 8			
general	*for 'state': symbols G (g), instead of S (s) to avoid confusion with notation for savings*		
Wg	wages sum paid by the state (g for government) = wages of civil servants (before their taxes)	8§1	
Fg	state expenditure on floating inputs, including replacement investment	8§1	
G^{COL}	state expenditure on collective goods and services	8§1	
Yg	net value-added (net product) of the state	8§1	
Ig	investment expenditure by the state (net)	8§2	
Zg	social security transfers	8§2	
Qg	interest payments on the state debt	8§2	
Ag	amenities (sum of subsidies to enterprises, to households and to cultural institutions)	8§2	
G	sum of state expenditure (net)	8§2	
CFg	current finance of state expenditure (net)	8§4	
T	sum of taxes	8§4	
SSC	sum of social security contributions	8§4	
OR	other receipts of the state	8§4	
B	net current borrowing flow of the state (B < 0 in case of a fiscal surplus)	8§4	
Ie	[italics] net investment by enterprises (after the state domain being explicit)	8§6	

Symbol or abbreviation	Meaning	Section first use	Remark
We	[italics] wages sum paid by enterprises (after the state domain being explicit)	8§6	
Cwe	[italics] consumption by enterprises' wage earners (after the state domain being explicit)	8§6	
Cwg	consumption by the state's wage earners	8§6	
Cqg	consumption out of interest paid by the state	8§6	
Czg	consumption out of social security transfers	8§6	
Swg	saving out of wages paid by the state	8§6	
Sqg	saving out of interest paid by the state	8§6	
Szg	saving out of social security transfers	8§6	
Smg	state mediated savings (Swg + Sqg + Szg)	8§6	
Swe	[italics] saving out of wages sum paid by enterprises (after the state domain being explicit)	8§6	
Π	[italics] surplus-value (= integral profit), after the state domain being explicit	8§6	
Y	[italics] net value-added total economy (after the state domain being explicit)	8§6-b	
Ye	net value added enterprises (after the state domain being explicit)	8§6-b	
Ee	final expenditure of the non-state sector with the enterprises sector	8§6-b	
Eg	direct and indirect expenditure of the state sector with the enterprises sector	8§6-b	
R	[italics] internal profit (after the state domain being explicit)	8§6-c	
Qe	net interest paid by enterprises to their external financiers	8§6-c	
Tsv	taxes paid by enterprises, with surplus-value being the tax base	8§7	

Symbol or abbreviation	Meaning	Section first use	Remark
To	all other taxes, next to Tsv (the latter being enterprises' taxes on surplus-value)	8§7	
*Π*at	surplus-value, after taxes on surplus-value (after the state domain being explicit)	8§7	
Tr	taxes on the internal profit (*R*)	8§7-a	
To*	all other taxes, next to Tr (the latter being enterprises' taxes on internal profit)	8§7a	
Rat	internal profit, after taxes on internal profit (after the state domain being explicit)	8§7a	
T^H	'hybrid taxes' (simplifying notation: T^H = Tsv + To + SSC + OR)	8§8	
T^Ho	'other hybrid taxes' (simplifying notation: T^Ho = To + SSC + OR)	8§8	
Sg	current saving of the state (the fiscal surplus T^H– G)	8§8	
Chapter 11			
HIC	high-income country (World Bank definition)	11§2-a	
UMC	upper-middle-income country (World Bank definition)	11§2-a	
LIC	low-income country (World Bank definition)	11§2-a	
LMC	lower-middle-income country (World Bank definition)	11§2-a	
FDI	foreign direct investment	11§10-b	
Throughout			
LHS	left hand side (of an equation)		
RHS	right hand side (of an equation)		
SNA	System of national accounts		
Unusual signs in equations			
∢	right hand side to left hand side determination	1§12	

Symbol or abbreviation	Meaning	Section first use	Remark
∢ =	equality with right to left hand determination	1§12	
Unusual signs in texts			
↓	decrease (e.g. I↓)		
↑	increase (e.g. I↑)		
→	results in / gives rise to		
x −→ y	negatively related effect of x on y	2§4	
x ←− y	negatively related effect of y on x	2§4	
x +→ y	positively related effect of x on y	2§4	
x ←+ y	positively related effect of y on x	2§4	

List of symbols and abbreviations in alphabetical order

Symbol or abbreviation	Meaning	Section first use	Remark
General notation			
$\underline{x}$	rate of growth [of any variable underlined] = $(x_{t\text{-}1} - x_t) / (x_{t\text{-}1}) = \Delta x/x$ [time indices omitted]	2§4, fn	
$\underline{x}_t$	rate of growth [of any variable underlined] = $(x_{t\text{-}1} - x_t) / (x_{t\text{-}1})$	2§4, fn	
$\lvert x \rvert$	limited value of a variable (x)	2§5	
x^P	planned production value of a variable (x)	3§10	
Roman symbols and abbreviations			
å	ratio of capital accumulation out of surplus-value (a variable; amplified in 3§11 and 5D1)	2§3	a, ring
Ag	amenities (sum of subsidies to enterprises, to households and to cultural institutions)	8§2	
B	net current borrowing flow of the state (B < 0 in case of a fiscal surplus)	8§4	
C	consumption by households (Ck+Cw)	3§10	
CB	Central Bank	2§9-a	
CFg	current finance of state expenditure (net)	8§4	
CG	consumer goods	3§2-b	

Symbol or abbreviation	Meaning	Section first use	Remark
C_i	[in italics] any commodity (other than commodity j) [used in this Explication only]	1§4-c	
Cj	[in italics] any commodity (other than commodity i) [used in this Explication only]	1§4-c	
Ck	consumption by capital owners	3§10	
ClB	Clearing Bank	2§9	
CPE	Classical Political Economy	1§5-b	
Cqg	consumption out of interest paid by the state	8§6	
Cw	consumption by wage earners (enterprises)	3§10	
Cwe	[italics] consumption by enterprises' wage earners (after the state domain being explicit)	8§6	
Cwg	consumption by the state's wage earners	8§6	
Czg	consumption out of social security transfers	8§6	
e	rate of surplus-value (or profit per labour-year-compensation) [e = Π/wL]	2§5	
E	macroeconomic net expenditure	3§10	
Ee	final expenditure of the non-state sector with the enterprises sector	8§6-b	
Eg	direct and indirect expenditure of the state sector with the enterprises sector	8§6-b	
FDI	foreign direct investment	11§10-b	
Fg	state expenditure on floating inputs, including replacement investment	8§1	
G	sum of state expenditure (net)	8§2	
G^{COL}	state expenditure on collective goods and services	8§1	
GDP	Gross domestic product	1§14	

Symbol or abbreviation	Meaning	Section first use	Remark
HIC	high-income country (World Bank definition)	11§2-a	
I	investment by enterprises (net)	3§9	
i	[in italics] average rate of interest for enterprises: the weighted average of the rates paid to banks and to other financiers	5§1	
Ie	[italics] net investment by enterprises (after the state domain being explicit)	8§6	
Ig	investment expenditure by the state (net)	8§2	
$i\varepsilon K$	surplus-value distributed to external financiers	5§1	
K	active capital (value in terms of MVD): assets of balance sheet total	1§13	
K_t	idem, year average	1§13	
$K_{t'}$	idem, at beginning of year t	1§13	
L	labour-capacity (amount of in going fte per year, unless specified as per hour)	1§14	
LHS	left hand side (of an equation)		
LIC	low-income country (World Bank definition)	11§2-a	
L^{α}	actual labour (labour-capacity exerted at a power α) [the unique source of valorisation]	1§14	
LMC	lower-middle-income country (World Bank definition)	11§2-a	
M	money (amount)	1§4-c	
m	actual unit monetary value of labour (per year, unless specified as per hour); more specifically: the realisation constraint resulting in the unit monetary value labour	1§14	
mL^{α}	actual monetary value of labour (realised) = net value-added	1§14	
MP	means of production	3§2-b	
MVD	monetary value dimension	1§4	

Symbol or abbreviation	Meaning	Section first use	Remark
NDP	Net domestic product	1§14	
ø	rate of undesired overcapacity (undesired overcapacity/production capacity)	5§5	o stroke
OR	other receipts of the state	8§4	
PD	sum of dividends and interest distributed to capital owners	5§3, fn.	
PVF	pre-validating finance (of enterprises by banks)	3§2	
Qe	net interest paid by enterprises to their external financiers	8§6-c	
Qg	interest payments on the state debt	8§2	
R	internal profit (surplus-value after interest payments)	5§1	cf. 3§1, Fig. 3.2b
R	[italics] internal profit (after the state domain being explicit)	8§6-c	
Rat	internal profit, after taxes on internal profit (after the state domain being explicit)	8§7a	
RHS	right hand side (of an equation)		
ROC	restructuring of capital	4§2-b	
RPVF	remaining PVF (pre-validating finance of enterprises by banks)	3§6	
S	saving	3§9	
Sg	current saving of the state (the fiscal surplus $T^{H} - G$)	8§8	
Smg	state mediated savings (Swg + Sqg + Szg)	8§6	
SNA	System of national accounts		
Sqg	saving out of interest paid by the state	8§6	
SSC	sum of social security contributions	8§4	
Sw	saving out of wages (wage earners enterprises)	3§10	

Symbol or abbreviation	Meaning	Section first use	Remark
s_w	fraction saved out of wages (non-constant)	5§3	
Swe	[italics] saving out of wages sum paid by enterprises (after the state domain being explicit)	8§6	
Swg	saving out of wages paid by the state	8§6	
Szg	saving out of social security transfers	8§6	
T	sum of taxes	8§4	
TERP	tendency to equalisation of average inter-sector rates of integral profit	4§2	
T^H	'hybrid taxes' (simplifying notation: T^H = Tsv + To + SSC + OR)	8§8	
T^Ho	'other hybrid taxes' (simplifying notation: T^Ho = To + SSC + OR)	8§8	
To	all other taxes, next to Tsv (the latter being enterprises' taxes on surplus-value)	8§7	
To*	all other taxes, next to Tr (the latter being enterprises' taxes on internal profit)	8§7a	
Tr	taxes on the internal profit (*R*)	8§7-a	
Tsv	taxes paid by enterprises, with surplus-value being the tax base	8§7	
TUP	tendency to uniform prices within a sector or market	4§3	
U	unemployment (number) [reserve of labour-capacity]	2§4	
u	rate of unemployment in % [u ={U/(L+U)}*100]	2§4	
UMC	upper-middle-income country (World Bank definition)	11§2-a	
w	wage rate (wage in going fte per year, unless specified as per hour)	1§14	
W	wages sum enterprises (W=wL)	3§10	
We	[italics] wages sum paid by enterprises (after the state domain being explicit)	8§6	

Symbol or abbreviation	Meaning	Section first use	Remark
Wg	wages sum paid by the state (g for government) = wages of civil servants (before their taxes)	8§1	
wL	wages sum	1§14	
X^d	desired (current) production	3§10	
X_t	output of production per year (realised)	1§14	
Y	net value-added (macroeconomically this would be NDP)	1§14	
Y	[italics] net value-added total economy (after the state domain being explicit)	8§6-b	
Ye	net value added enterprises (after the state domain being explicit)	8§6-b	
Y^G	gross value-added (macroeconomically this would be GDP)	1§14	
Yg	net value-added (net product) of the state	8§1	
Zg	social security transfers	8§2	
Greek symbols			
α	production power of labour (in terms L^{α}) [$L^{\alpha} = L^{ά ϊ}$]	1§14	alpha
ά	technique-associated productive power of labour (in terms $L^{ά}$)	1§14	alpha, with tonos
|α|	limited production power of labour (because of limited intensity of labour)	2§5	
δ	fraction of the total assets K, equivalent to the used up fixed assets	1§14	delta
Δ	change [see also x̲]	2§3	delta (capital)
ε	share of 'external' finance in capital (banks plus other financiers)	5§1	epsilon
εK	external capital (passive capital furnished by external financiers)	5§1	
ϊ	intensity of labour (in terms $L^{ϊ}$)	1§14	iota, with dialytika

Symbol or abbreviation	Meaning	Section first use	Remark
$\lvert \ddot{\imath} \rvert$	limited intensity of labour (physical or compliance limit)	2§5	
μ	fraction of the total assets K, equivalent to the used up floating means of production (usually a larger sum than the sum that appears on the balance sheet)	1§14	mu
Π_t	surplus-value (= integral profit) produced per year	1§13	pi
Π	[italics] surplus-value (= integral profit), after the state domain being explicit	8§6	
*Π*at	surplus-value, after taxes on surplus-value (after the state domain being explicit)	8§7	
ρ	rate of internal profit on the internal capital	5§1	rho
Σ	summation	3§6-c	sigma
τ	capital-labour ratio [$\tau = K/L$]	2§4	tau
ω	rate of integral profit (Π_t / $\mathbf{K}_{t'}$)	1§13	omega
Unusual signs in equations			
⊲	right hand side to left hand side determination	1§14	
⊲ =	equality with right to left hand determination	1§14	
Unusual signs in texts			
↓	decrease (e.g. I↓)		
↑	increase (e.g. I↑)		
→	results in / gives rise to		
x – → y	negatively related effect of x on y	2§4	
x ← – y	negatively related effect of y on x	2§4	
x +→ y	positively related effect of x on y	2§4	
x ←+ y	positively related effect of y on x	2§4	

List of equations by chapter

Equation	Key equation	Description	Type	Equation number	Section
Chapter 1					
$\omega_t = \Pi_t / K_{t'}$	K	rate of integral profit	accounting convention	1.1	1§13
$X_t \triangleleft = [(\delta+\mu)K + wL + \Pi]_t$	K	output of production realised	accounting convention	1.2	1§14
$L^{\alpha} = L^{\acute{\alpha}\,\ddot{\imath}}$	K	actual labour (labour-capacity exerted at a power α)	definition	1.3	1§14
$X_t \triangleleft = [(\delta+\mu)K + mL^{\alpha}]_t$	K	output of production realised	exposition	1.4	1§14

Equation	Key equation	Description	Type	Equation number	Section
$\Pi_t = mL^{\alpha}_t - wL_t$	K	surplus-value (= integral profit)	exposition	1.5	1§14
$\omega_t = \Pi_t / K_{t'} = [(mL^{\alpha})_t - (wL)_t] / K_{t'}$	K	rate of integral profit	implication	1.6	1§14
$Y^G{}_t \equiv [\delta K + mL^{\alpha}]_t$	K	gross value-added	implication (given concept of Y^G)	1.7	1§14
$Y_t \equiv [mL^{\alpha}]_t$	K	net value-added	implication (given concept of Y)	1.8	1§14
Chapter 2					
$\Delta K = å\Pi$		growth of capital [$0 < å < 1$]	definition	2.1	2§3
$K/L = \tau$		capital to labour ratio	definition		2§4
$\underline{L} = (1/\tau)\, \underline{K}$		growth of labour employed	definition [requirement]	2.2	2§4
$u = f_1(\tau\underline{L}) + f_2(\underline{pop})$		unemployment [$f_1' < 0$; $f_2' > 0$]	definition	2.3	2§4
$\Delta w = f_1(\Delta u) + f_2(\Delta\underline{L})$		change of wage rate [$f_1' < 0$; $f_2' > 0$]	exposition	2.4	2§4
$e_t = \Pi_t / wL_t$		rate of surplus-value	definition	2.5	2§5
$\omega_t = (e_t) / (K_{t'}/wL_t)$		rate of integral profit	implication	2.6	2§5

Equation	Key equation	Description	Type	Equation number	Section
$e_t = f_1(w)_t + f_2(\alpha)_t$		rate of surplus-value [$f_1'<0$; $f_2'>0$]	implication	2.7	2§5
$(\ddot{\imath})_t = (\|\ddot{\imath}\|)_t$		intensity of labour	physical and compliance limit | |	2.8	2§5
$(\alpha)_t = (\|\alpha\|)_t$		production power of labour	implication	2.9	2§5
$\Delta K = \mathring{a}ewL$		growth of capital	implication	2.10	2§6
Chapter 3 (time indices omitted)					
$W = wL$		wages sum	definition	3.1	3§10
$X^P \lessdot = (\delta + \mu)K + m^P L^\alpha$		output, planned production of	exposition (cf. 1.4)	3.2	3§10
$Y^P \lessdot = m^P L^\alpha$		value-added, planned production of	exposition (cf. 1.8)	3.3	3§10
$\Pi^P \lessdot = m^P L^\alpha - W$		surplus-value, planned production of	exposition (cf. 1.5)	3.4	3§10
$Y = \Pi + W$		value-added (enterprises sector)	definition of macro domain	3.5	3§10
$E = I + C$		expenditure (enterprises sector)	definition of macro domain	3.6	3§10
$Y \lessdot = E$		validation of value-added	macro determination	3.7	3§10

Equation	Key equation	Description	Type	Equation number	Section
$Y \blacktriangleleft = I + C$		idem	implication	3.7’	3§10
$I_t \blacktriangleleft = f(\omega_{t-1}; X^d_t; Pvf_t)$		investment	determination	3.8	3§10
$C = Ck + Cw$		consumption, macro	definition	3.9	3§10
$\Pi \blacktriangleleft = I + Ck + (Cw–W)$		validation surplus-value, macro	implication (expositional)	3.10	3§10
$Sw = W – Cw$		saving out of wages	definition	3.11	3§10
$\Pi \blacktriangleleft = I + Ck – Sw$	K	validation surplus-value (by macro expenditure)	implication	3.12	3§10
Chapter 4					
Explication					
$\omega_i = \Pi_i / K_i = [m_i L^{\alpha}_i – (wL)_i] / K_i$		rate of integral profit	implication (cf. 1.3 and 1.6)	4.1	4§4-a
$X_i = \delta K_i – \mu K_i + wL_i + \Pi_i$		output of production realised	accounting convention (cf. 1.2)	4.2	4§4-a
$pq_i \leq \mu K + wL_i$		prime costs (output in terms of price and quantity vectors)	accounting convention	4.3	4§4-a

Equation	Key equation	Description	Type	Equation number	Section
$\Pi_n /(K_n - LV_i) > [pq_i - (\mu K_i + wL_i)]/LV_i$		decision criterion for scrapping	accounting convention	4.4	4§4-a
Chapter 5					
$R = \Pi - i\varepsilon K$	K	internal profit	definition	5.1	5§1
$\rho = R / (K - \varepsilon K) = (mL^{\alpha} - wL - i\varepsilon K) / (K - \varepsilon K)$	K	rate of internal profit on the internal capital	accounting convention (given 5.1)	5.2	5§1
$\rho = (\omega - i\varepsilon) / (1 - \varepsilon)$		rate of internal profit on the internal capital	implication (5.2 divided by K)	5.3	5§1
$R = I + Ck - Sw - i\varepsilon K$		validation of internal profit	implication (3.10 into 5.1)	5.4	5§2
$\rho = (I + Ck - Sw - i\varepsilon K) / (K - \varepsilon K)$	K	rate of internal profit on the internal capital	implication (5.4 into 5.2)	5.5	5§2
$Sw \equiv s_w(wL)$		saving out of wages	definition		5§3
$\Delta K_t = I_t$		growth of capital	definition	5.6	5§5
$\Delta K^*_t = I_t - scrap_t$		growth of capital, net	definition	5.6a	5§5
$I_t = f(\rho_{t-1}; ø_{t-1})$		investment (positively related with ρ and negatively with ø)	determination (see text for distinction from 3.8)	5.7	5§5

Equation	Key equation	Description	Type	Equation number	Section
Chapter 8					
Main sections					
$G^{COL} = Fg + Wg$		state expenditure on collective goods and services	convention of state	8.1	8§1
$Yg = Wg$		net value-added (net product) of the state	convention of state	8.2	8§1
$G^* = (Wg + Fg) + Ig + (Qg + Zg) + Ag$		state expenditure	accounting definition	8.3Ag	8§2
$G = (Wg + Fg) + Ig + (Qg + Zg)$		state expenditure (minus subsidies Ag)	definition	8.3	8§2
$CFg = T + SSC + OR + B$		current finance of state expenditure	accounting definition	8.4	8§4
$CFg = G$		idem	accounting definition	8.5	8§4
$Cwg = Wg - Swg$		consumption by the state's wage earners	definition	8.6	8§6
$Cqg = Qg - Sqg$		consumption out of interest paid by the state	definition	8.7	8§6
$Czg = Zg - Szg$		consumption out of social security transfers	definition	8.8	8§6

Equation	Key equation	Description	Type	Equation number	Section
Smg = Swg + Sqg + Szg		state-mediated savings	definition	8.9	8§6
$\Pi \blacktriangleleft = [(Ie + Ck) - Swc] + G - [Swg + Sqg + Szg]$		[italics] validation surplus-value	exposition	8.10	8§6
$\Pi \blacktriangleleft = [(Ie + Ck) - Swc] + G - Smg$	K	[italics] validation surplus-value	exposition (= 8.10)	8.11	8§6
Amplifications					
$\Pi \blacktriangleleft = \mathrm{Ie} + \mathrm{Ck} + (\mathrm{Cwe}-\mathrm{We})$		validation surplus-value, macro	amended notation	3.10*	8§6-b
$\Pi \blacktriangleleft = \mathrm{Ie} + \mathrm{Ck} - \mathrm{Swe}$		validation surplus-value, macro	amended notation	3.12*	8§6-b
$Y = Ye + \mathrm{Yg}$		[italics] net value-added	definition of macro domain	8.6b.1	8§6-b
$Ye \blacktriangleleft = [mL^{\alpha}]$		[italics] net value-added by enterprises sector	implication of domain extension	1.8*	8§6-b
$Ye = We + \Pi$		[italics] net value-added by enterprises sector	implication of domain extension	3.5*	8§6-b
$\Pi = Ye - We$		[italics] surplus-value	implication of domain extension	3.5*'	8§6-b
$Ee = Ie + Ck + Cwe$		final non-state expenditure with enterprises	implication of domain extension	3.6'* and 3.8*	8§6-b

Equation	Key equation	Description	Type	Equation number	Section
Eg = [Ig + Fg]+[(Cwg + Cqg + Czg)]		direct & indirect state exp. with enterprises	exposition	8.6b.2	8§6-b
Ye ‹ = *Eϵ* + Eg		[italics] total expenditure with enterprises	definition of macro domain	8.6b.3	8§6-b
Π ‹ = (*E*ɜ + Eg) – *We*		[italics] validation surplus-value, macro	implication of domain extension	8.6b.4	8§6-b
Π ‹ = [(*Ie* + *Ck*) + (*Cwe*–*We*)] + [Ig + Fg]+[(Cwg + Cqg + Czg)]			implication (expositional)	8.6b.5	8§6-b
Π ‹ = [(*Ie* + *Ck*) + (*Cwe*–*We*)] + [Ig + Fg + Wg + Qg +Zg] – [Swg + Sqg + Szg]			implication (expositional)	8.6b.6	8§6-b
R = *Π* – Qe		[italics] internal profit	definition	8.6c.1	8§6-c
R = [(*Ie* + *Ck*) – *Swe*] – [Qe] + [G – Smg]		validation of internal profit	implication	8.6c.2	8§6-c
Main section					
T = Tsv + To		total taxes (case of taxation surplus-value)	definition	8.12	8§7
*Π*at = *Π* – Tsv		after tax surplus-value	definition	8.13	8§7

Equation	Key equation	Description	Type	Equation number	Section
$\mathit{\Pi}at = [(Ie + Ck) - Swe] + [G - Smg - Tsv]$	K	idem, decomposed: validation perspective	implication	8.14	8§7
Amplification					
$T = Tr + To^*$		total taxes (case of taxation internal profit)	definition	8.7a.1	8§7-a
$Rat = R - Tr$		after tax internal profit	definition	8.7a.2	8§7-a
$Rat = [(Ie + Ck) - Swe] - [Qe] + [(G - Smg) - Tr]$		idem, decomposed: validation perspective	implication	8.7a.3	8§7-a
Main section					
$CFg = Tsv + To + SSC + OR + B$		current finance of state expenditure (net)	implication (8.12 substituted into 8.4)	8.4	8§8
$T^H = Tsv + To + SSC + OR$		hybrid taxes	definition	8.15	8§8
$T^Ho = T^H - Tsv$		other hybrid taxes	definition	8.16	8§8
$CFg = T^H + B$		current finance of state expenditure	implication	8.17	8§8

Equation	Key equation	Description	Type	Equation number	Section
$Sg = T^H - G$		current savings of the state	definition	8.18	8§8
$\mathit{\Pi}at = [(Ie + Ck) - Swe] + [(G - T^H) - Smg + T^Ho]$		after tax surplus-value: validation perspective	implication	8.19	8§8
$\mathit{\Pi}at = [(Ie + Ck) - Swe] + [- Sg - Smg + T^Ho]$	K	idem	implication	8.20	8§8

Glossary of field-specific terms

- This is a glossary of some of the main terms that are specific to the field of this book. It should assist especially the reading of the first few chapters of Parts One and Two (Chapters 1–2 and 6–7). It also covers most of the field-specific terms used in the 'General Summary and Conclusions'.
- Because the interconnection of concepts is core to this book, it is inevitable that the reader looking up an entry is often referred to other entries.
- Some lemmas start with a brief dictionary definition (in brackets; 'a.o.' is an abbreviation for: 'amongst other' definitions). This is followed by the particular usage of the term in this book in case this (somewhat) deviates from the dictionary definition.
- The sign → means: see the lemma (as indicated after the arrow).
- In the references to sections of the book, 'sub #' refers to a sub-section of the section indicated.
- GI-C§# refers to a section in the General Introduction. A§# refers to a section in the General Appendix, Outline of Systematic Dialectics.

abstract. In this book this term is used in reference to a →'moment' (in brief a 'stage') of the exposition that has not yet been fully →'grounded' (its concrete conditions of existence have not yet been determined). The starting point of the book (1D1 and 6D1) has a special status. It is 'abstract' in the sense above, whereas it is at the same time a (not yet grounded) reference to the essence of the totality. The starting point is therefore referred to as '*abstract-general*'. To the extent that all of Chapters 1 and 6 are starting points in a wider sense, these have also been referred to as 'abstract-general' moments. [A§11.]

abstraction from x (or bracket). This term is sometimes used so as to emphasise that a statement made at that point yet abstracts from x, that is, a →'moment' x (in brief a 'stage') presented later on. This phrase occurs in sentences such as: 'the state yet being abstracted from'. This refers to a stage of the systematic dialectic when some moment (such as the state in the example) is still →'pre-posited' (i.e. not yet presented). Instead of 'abstraction from x' an alternative used is: 'with x bracketed'.

abstraction in practice →'trans-abstraction in practice'.

accumulation of capital. The process of the growth of →'capital'. [2§3 sub 1, 2§6.]

active capital →'capital'.

actor. The term 'actor' or 'social actor' is used in a very general sense of 'activity'. An actor may be an individual (that is, an individual in a particular role, for example that of labourer, entrepreneur, manager) *or* a (corporate) 'person' in the legal sense, hence also an institution such as an enterprise, *or* the agent of a particular institution (e.g. enterprise). [2§7-a.]

allowance rights and positive rights. An allowance right held by a person – e.g. the allowance right to property of means of production – entails the *duty* on all other persons to respect that right ('person' denotes person in the juridical sense, including, for example, a corporation). That is, the duty of *non-interference, non-obstruction or non-action*. Thus a full allowance right to property entails that *once* a person possesses property, the possession ought not be obstructed and, more specifically, the possessor ought not be expropriated. Similarly, a full allowance right to existence imposes the duty on other persons to not interfere with or obstruct this right, e.g. by violence. An 'allowance right' contrasts with a '*positive right*'. The latter entails duties that go much further: requiring 'positive action'. (Positive rights require a specification as to whether the duty of positive action falls on all other persons, or on a specific category, or perhaps on the state or some other institution.) A positive right to property, for example, to the earth, might more specifically entail that everybody is granted the right to possess some portion or perhaps an equal proportion of the earth; it might impose the duty on others to transfer their disproportionate share in the earth to the other right holders. Similarly a positive right to existence, for example, specified as the positive right to decent work, or the positive right to a decent living (all to be specified further), imposes the duty on others of sharing the available decent work or to share other means of decent living. Again, the required duty might fall on the state or some other institution. [6§17.]

articulation (dictionary: the act of joining or the state of being joined). Structured interrelationship/interconnection within the totality of the exposition.

banks versus banking entities. A distinction is made between 'banks' and 'banking entities'. Banks are conceptualised purely as creators of money and as financiers. Any labour that this might require is outsourced to a separate 'production branch' of the banking entity. These production branches are subsumed under the enterprises sector. This means that the (pure) banks are not producers. [3§1, sub 2.]

bifurcation →'outward bifurcation'; →'inward bifurcation'.

bracket →'abstraction from'.

capital. The term capital without adjective refers to 'active capital', that is, the balance sheet assets of a →'production enterprise'. A distinction is made between 'active capital' and 'passive capital' (or passive finance capital). *Active capital* is the ideal →'monetary value' (ideal value or book value) of, first, the enterprise's investment in inputs for production and, second, the running →'valorisation', each measured at one point in time, and reported on the enterprise's balance sheet as assets. The running valorisation is co-materialised in the ideal monetary value of semi-finished products and not yet →'validated' output stocks. [1§13.] '*Passive capital*' (or passive finance capital) is the equivalent of the various liabilities of an enterprise. [2§15; 3§1, summarised in Fig. 3.2a.]

capital as a form of wealth →'wealth'.

capital–labour relation. Shorthand for the *indirect* exploitative relation between →'passive capital ownership' and labour, the counterpart being the directly exploitative →'enterprise–labour relation'. As passive capital grows on the basis of the direct appropriation and next the distribution of surplus-value, passive capital owners are indirectly involved in the exploitative relation. [2§15, sub 3.]

capital accumulation frameworks of the state. This term is a shorthand for the three legislative (or regulative) frameworks of the state that are geared at its furthering of the accumulation of capital, that is: the monetary framework (7D2); the labour-capacity framework (7D3); and the infra-structural framework (7D4). This shorthand term is used in Ch. 11 and in the General Summary and Conclusions. [11§12, summarised in Fig. 11.16.] It is contrasted with the term →'hard core (frameworks) of the state'.

capitalism. The term capitalism refers to 'full-fledged capitalism'. This is a social formation in which the dissociated →'outward bifurcation' (i.e. divide) between households and privately owned enterprises is dominant [1§1; 6§1] and in which the economy (the capitalist economy) and the state (the capitalist state) constitute a unity (→'separation-in-unity'). The following are the further main characteristics of this social formation. *Economic characteristics*: (1) economic entities and processes are expressed and measured in the →'monetary-value dimension' (MVD); (2) labour-capacity predominantly takes the form of wage labour (whence there is a labour market); (3) production (the production process) is equally expressed and measured in the MVD; (4) the production of →'surplus-value' (integral profit) is the driving force of production; (5) the surplus-value is appropriated by the owner(s) of the enterprise [Ch. 1, passim]. *Legal economic rights characteristics*: Owners of enterprises make the following core claims: (1) claims of entitlement to private property in the earth; (2) claims of entitlement to private property in means of production other than for production by the claimant; (3) claims of entitlement to employ labour as combined with the appropriation of the surplus-value produced by that labour. The state grants these claims in the form of legal rights – the granting of these claims makes the state a 'capitalist state'. [6D2.] (Capitalism emerged from about 1800, first in the UK and France [1§0-a].)

capital ownership, passive. Passive capital ownership refers to the ownership of the liabilities of production enterprises. This includes, first, the loans from banks and other external financiers and, second, the internal financiers' equity (the latter for corporations; 'own capital' in case of firms). [2§15 and 3§1.]

capitalist and managerial class (CMC) and subordinated working class (SWC). These are two broad class 'categories', or 'objective classes' that derive different (dis)advantages from the capitalist system in terms of their *decision-making power* and of their *shares of income and wealth*. These are called 'objective classes' in terms of these two measures, and in contradistinction to any notion of 'subjective class', that is, of class-consciousness. SWC: Subordinated workers are defined as workers who have no decision-making power (in the USA between 1930 and 2010 this category covered between 73% and 90% of the relevant population). Their average income is considerably lower than the average CMC income (2§15-a, Graph 2.14). CMC: *Capitalists* have direct or indirect decision-making power. The size of their non-labour income is such that they are not forced to engage in an employment contract – that is, to be employed themselves (although typically they do engage in such employment contracts). *Managers* have decision-making power and benefit from 'super-wages'. [6§12.]

'capitalist economic rights' granted by the state →'capitalist state'.

capitalist state. Private enterprises and their owners claim to be →'entitled' to: first, private property in the earth; second, private property in means of production other than for production by the claimant; third, employment of labour as combined with the appropriation of the surplus-value produced by that labour [6§2]. The capitalist state grants these claims in the form of 'rights' (this is what makes the state a 'capitalist' state) [6§4]. These three together are referred to as the 'capitalist economic rights' granted by the state.

clearing bank (ClB). In this book this term has the specific meaning of a dominant bank that clears interbank debts and credits for other banks. It imposes its standard of money and it imposes a standard for securities and liability rules on the banks for which it clears. It has no legal powers. The ClB is a concept introduced prior to the introduction of the state and a Central Bank, though it may be thought of as foreshadowing a Central Bank. [2§9 and 2§9-d.]

CMC →'capitalist and managerial class'.

commensuration in terms of money →'trans-abstraction in practice'.

compliance (dictionary: the act of conforming, acquiescing, or yielding; a tendency to yield readily to others, especially in a weak and subservient way). Voluntary or involuntary conformation (see further Bay [2§7-b]). Labour's compliance with the requirements of the enterprise during production is one of the main conditions for the existence of a capitalist economy [2§5; 2§7] →'enterprise–labour relation'. Regarding the state, a vast-majority compliance of the actors (a vast majority of all actors) to the state's actions – and at least its granting of the core →'capitalist economic rights' is the main condition for the →'legitimation of the state'.

condition of existence →'ground'.

constellation (dictionary: a.o. a group of objects, etc. related in some way). In this book this term has the meaning of: interconnected organisational units and/or interconnected processes and/or structures (often called configurations). The term may also refer to what in ordinary language is called a 'subsystem' (such as the 'banking system'). Most often the term is used when, for methodological and sometimes for stylistic reasons, I want to avoid the term 'system'. [GI, C§2, fn.]

contingent/contingency. A distinction is made between phenomena that are predicated on →'necessary' moments (Chs. 1–3 and 6–8) or on →'manifestations' (in brief: implications) of those moments (Chs. 4–5, 9–10 and 11). Phenomena (entities, institutions and processes) are *contingent* when these could be either absent or different without changing the necessary moments and their manifested implications. Hence these could be absent or different without changing the essential functioning and potential →'reproduction' of the system under consideration. [A§13, sub 1.] The exposition abstracts from contingent phenomena and their determinants. Nevertheless the *degree of intensity* of the forces engendering necessary moments and their manifestations is often contingent. [A§13, sub 3.]

contradiction. Refers to an entity, institution or process that is *both necessary* to the reproduction (that is, the continued existence) of the subject matter *and impossible* to it. It therefore inevitably requires some kind of →'sublation'. [1§1-j.]

deliberative (dictionary: having the function of deliberating, as a legislative assembly: as deliberative body). The existence of 'a deliberative' is a condition of existence of the →'legitimation of the state'. This deliberative may, but need not, be associated with a parliamentary democracy. The (degree of) legislative power of a deliberative is contingent. [7§23.]

diachronic. A diachronic process refers to one that gains force *through time* (if not counteracted, the same applies for its effect). A synchronic process refers to a process that has force *within each period of time* (if not counteracted, the same applies for its effect). In this book each of these processes refer to the history of full-fledged →'capitalism'.

differentia specifica. Specifics that differentiate a particular configuration (or a particular entity) within a general category of configurations (or a general category of entities).

dissociated outward bifurcation →'outward bifurcation'.

devalorisation. A decrease in →'valorisation'. Devalorisation is due to the actual →'monetary value of labour' (mL^{α}) for any one capital lagging behind that in the previous period. This applies not on the L^{α}, but on a decrease in the 'm' (the →'unit monetary value of labour'). Devalorisation refers to the value-added, and should be distinguished from depreciation, i.e. the (calculated) normal returns for the wear and tear of means of production (δK). [4§6, sub 2.]

enterprise–labour relation. Shorthand for the employment relation through which labour, as determined by its →'productive power', produces the value-added and hence also the surplus-value, the surplus-value being appropriated by the enterprise. In its quantitative aspect (the rate of surplus-value or the degree of exploitation of labour →surplus-value, rate of) this relation is constrained by, first, the technique of production, second, the rate of unemployment and, third (in face of that rate), the management of the compliance of labour during production, as assisted by the managerial device of a wages ladder that optimises this compliance. [2§7.] The 'enterprise–labour relation' is contrasted with the →'capital–labour relation'.

entity (dictionary: something that exists as a distinct, separate, independent, or self-contained unit). 'A something' that has not, or not yet, been (fully) identified conceptually. [1§0, fn.]

entitle/entitlement (dictionary: a.o. to give (a person) the right to do or have something).

epistemology and ontology (dictionary for epistemology: investigation of the origin, nature, methods and limits of human knowledge; dictionary for ontology: study or a theory of the character of being or the kinds of things that have existence.) Much of traditional philosophy makes a (preliminary) distinction between the following fields. *Ontology*: the study of being or existence (what 'is'); *epistemology*: the study of knowledge (what and how we 'know'); *phenomenology*: the study of our experience (how we experience). In line with Hegelian views in this respect, the exposition in this book recognises that whereas we can distinguish these fields, they cannot be divorced.

exposition →'systematic-dialectical exposition'.

finance capital →'capital' (especially 'passive capital' or 'passive finance capital'). [3§1, sub 1; summary Fig. 3.2; 3§2, sub 1; 3§5.]

framework →'legislative framework'.

full-fledged capitalism →'capitalism'.

generally/in general. Something that is predominantly the case. When I use the term 'generally' I explicitly or implicitly refer to contingencies that are compatible with capitalism, whilst if those contingencies were to be generalised, there would no longer be capitalism [1§1-e].

ground. The entity, institution or process that is necessary for the existence of an entity, institution or process posited earlier in the systematic exposition. Thus the ground is a *condition of existence* of a →'moment' presented earlier on. [GI-C§4; A§11.]

See also: 'proximate moments and proximate conditions'.

grounding. The positing of a →'ground'.

hard core of the state | hard core frameworks of the state. These terms are used in Chs. 10–11 and in the 'General Summary and Conclusions'. The term **'hard core of the state'** is shorthand for, in brief, the moments presented in Ch. 6. These are especially the state-granted rights of: (1) claims of entitlement to private property in the earth; (2) claims of entitlement to private property in means of production other than for production by the claimant; (3) claims of entitlement to employ labour as combined with the appropriation of the surplus value produced by that labour; (4) claims of entitlement to existence (in the sense of →'allowance') and the two legislative frameworks in which these four are concretised (6D4 and 6D5); as well as (5) the state's public security framework (6D6). The term '**hard core frameworks of the state**' refers more specifically to the legislative frameworks just mentioned (6D4–6D6). It is contrasted with the term →'capital accumulation frameworks'.

ideal pre-commensuration (dictionary for commensurate: a.o. having the same measure). At the market, commodities are constituted as commodities (→'market transformation of entities'), whence these are commensurated in terms of money, that is, in terms of the money-form of →'monetary value'. 'Ideal pre-commensuration' refers to the anticipation of this process during production, whence the elements of the →'production process' (that is, the stocks and the commodities in process of production) are accounted in terms of monetary value. [1§10.]

integral profit. Identical to →'surplus-value'.

integral profit rate. The year flow of →'surplus-value' validated, calculated over the stock of the capital assets at the beginning of the year (cf. →'validation'). [1§13, sub 3; 1§14, sub 6; 5§1, sub 1.]

internal profit. Internal profit is the 'integral profit' (identical to →'surplus-value') that remains for the enterprise after the distribution of interest to banks and other external financiers. The concept of internal profit is introduced in 3§1 (cf. Fig. 3.2b) and amplified in 5§1 and 5§2. Internal profit includes 'rent' (explained in Appendix 3C). Next to the distribution of interest, another part of the surplus-value (or of the internal profit) is distributed to the state in the form of taxes (8§7 and 8§7-a; cf. Fig. 8.10).

internal profit rate. The year flow of the →'internal profit' validated, calculated over the stock of the capital assets at the beginning of the year. (cf. →'validation'). [5§1, sub 1.]

investment. 'Investment' always means *investment in means of production*. For the purchase of financial paper the terms 'portfolio investment' and 'portfolio investor' are avoided; for the latter, instead, the terms '*finance*' – be it primary or secondary finance – and '*financier*' are used. [3§8; 5§5.]

investment versus saving. For this lemma the state is not relevant. Abstracting from the state, only enterprises invest (→'investment'). This is the enterprises' form of expenditure. As it is an expenditure, it is not a →'saving'. From Adam Smith onwards, mainstream economics posits saving as a precondition for investment – moreover, saving is considered to be a justification for private profits including interest. The mainstream notion of a macroeconomic equality of investment and saving (I=S) can only be defended by way of an utterly strange *definition*, that functions as an *assumption*. This is to *define* the (→'PVF' accommodated) expenditure of investment as saving (!), thus an expenditure is defined as a non-expenditure. More specifically, the investment *expenditure* equivalent of retained profits is *defined* as a saving. This is utterly odd categorially, though it ideologically does the job of providing the alleged justification mentioned. [3§9.]

inward bifurcation (dictionary for bifurcation: to fork or divide into two parts of branches). A particular duality, of which one pole is sensuous and the other super-sensuous. The sensuous pole refers to an entity or process. The super-sensuous pole refers to the →'monetary-value dimension' that in empirical reality is ascribed to the entity or process via a →'trans-abstraction'. This book presents three inward bifurcations: that of the commodity [1§5]; that of commodified labour-capacity [1§6]; and that of the capitalist production process [1§10]. These inward bifurcations implicitly refer to the →'outward bifurcation' for which these inward bifurcations provide major solutions (that is, →'sublations').

labour; labour-capacity. Labour-capacity is the potential capacity to exert 'labour', the latter being a particular manifestation of the former. 'Labour-capacity' is traded at the labour market at a certain →'wage rate'. [1§6; 1§6-c.] 'Labour' is employed within enterprises, the actual labour being exerted at a certain →'productive power', which is a composite of the 'technique-associated productive power of labour' and the 'intensity of labour'. [1§14.] (Marx, and current marxian political economy, uses the term 'labour-power' for the term 'labour-capacity' above [1§6-d].)

legislative framework / regulative framework. The term 'framework' in reference to legislation/regulation denotes that I present a very general categorisation of legislation instead of detailed specifications (in the end those that one finds, depending on the field, in the hundreds or thousands of pages of the legislative codes).

legitimation of the state. There are two main conditions for the legitimation of the state. The first, yet abstract-general, condition is that the state posits its (non-)action in terms of the (putative) general interest [6§6], and that it posits granted rights in the form of legal rights [6§8]. The state so posits itself as an 'impartial' extraordinary institution *above and outside* the opposing particular economic interests. However, given that the state *de facto* grants the core claims to →'capitalist economic rights' indeed in the form of 'rights', it constitutes vis-à-vis the capitalist economy a →*'separation-in-unity'* within the capitalist system [6§7]. The adjective 'putative' in the phrase 'putative general interest' is to be taken as denoting that the state proposes its actions to be in what the state itself considers to be the general interest. Thus, rather than defining what constitutes the 'general interest', the state in fact *defines* its actions to be in the general interest. Other actors may have different views about what the general interest would be. The second main condition for the legitimation of the state is that it must gain a vast-majority →'compliance' for its (non-)actions [6§5]. (The requirement of a 'vast' majority is specified in 6§18 on the state's 'public security framework'.) The state's seeking of this vast-majority compliance, and hence 'legitimation' is a core theme throughout Part Two of the book.

macroeconomic sequence. The interconnected macroeconomic succession of: (1) production predicated on →'pre-validating bank finance', (2) →'validation' of production by expenditure, (3) distribution of part of the validated surplus-value to external financiers, and (4) the resulting →'internal rate of profit', as determining (1) and so forth. [5§6.]

manifestations. In this book 'manifestations' denote the final stage of the →'systematic-dialectical exposition'. Manifestations are presented in the last two chapters of Parts One and Two and in the single chapter of Part Three; that is, at the point when the exposition of the →'necessary' →'moments' (the necessary conditions of existence) of the capitalist system has been completed (Chs. 1–3 and 6–8). Manifestations have three main characteristics. First, they are implications of the necessary moments – implications that have most often a →'tendency' character. Second, manifestations are the culmination of the synthetic exposition – building on that of the grounding moments. Third, whereas those grounding moments reveal the reproductive strength of the capitalist system, the implications of the simultaneous interaction of these grounding moments are expressed in concrete manifestations that reveal *not only* reproductive strength but also reproductive vulnerability. [A§12.]

market transformation of entities. The →'trans-abstraction in practice' at the market, through which entities are constituted as commodities, that is, as dual entities in the aspects of, on the one hand, sensuous →'usefulness', and on the other, non-sensuous →'monetary value'. [1§5.]

metabolism (dictionary: a.o. basic process of organic functioning or operating). [1§9.]

moment (dictionary: a.o. an aspect of a thing; an essential or constituent factor). The term 'moment' refers to the constituents of each progression (stage) of the →'systematic-dialectical exposition'. A moment is a composition of concepts that belong together; these concepts are thus posited as immediately connected, or connected by a mediating concept. In other words, a moment is a more or less cohesive institutional make-up, or a more or less cohesive set of entities, that can be analysed by itself (sometimes like a model) but that nevertheless derives its full meaning from its interconnection with other moments, and ultimately from its interconnectedness within the whole exposition. Thus moments derive full meaning through synthesis. [1§1-d; A§5.]

monetary value. Monetary value is a concretisation and a necessary condition of existence of →'value'. Like value in general it is non-physical and thus super-sensuous, and like value in general it is *ascribed* to entities, without comprising part of the bodily form of those entities. However, monetary value refers to either a past transaction (→'validation') in terms of sensuous money, or to an anticipation of a future transaction in terms of sensuous money. In this perspective (of past and anticipation), current monetary value is always both super-sensuous and ideal in the sense of non-actual – entities in their physical guise are actual. ('Sensuous' money includes pure 'account money' or bookkeeping entries by banks [2§8, sub 2].) Thus 'monetary value' must be distinguished from →'money'. (For example, usually only a minor fraction of enterprises' assets exists in the form of money; all other assets are valued in terms of the super-sensuous monetary value, and moreover of anticipations of this super-sensuous monetary value.) [1§4; 1§10 for the anticipation.]

monetary-value dimension (MVD). The super-sensuous dimension of capitalist economic entities. It is the result of the mundane practice of identifying →'value' with →'monetary value'. [1§4.]

monetary value of labour, actual. The actual monetary-value product of labour (mL^{α}), which is the →'value-added'. [1§14, sub 6.] In 3§10 (sub 2) a distinction is made between this 'actual monetary value of labour' and the prior and during production 'planned' monetary value of labour (that is, prior to the →'validation' (the sale) of the output of production). See also 'unit monetary value of labour, actual (m)'.

money. The unity of *measure* and *medium* of one-dimensional value. Unlike the entities that money measures, money has *no inherent* content (even if some particular form of money may be more adequate than another). Money has *no inherent value*. Money is inherently merely a quantifier of one-dimensional value. [1§4.] Concretely money is created '*ex nihilo*' (out of nothing) by banks, on the basis of a reciprocal credit relationship between the bank and a client. [2§8.]

necessary / necessity (dictionary: being essential, indispensable, or requisite). In this book this term refers to phenomena (entities, institutions, processes) that are required for the existence and reproduction of the capitalist system. A distinction is made between necessary grounding →'moments', that is, moments presenting necessary conditions of existence (Chs. 1–3 and 6–8) and moments presenting implications of those grounds as revealed in their →'manifestations' (Chs. 4–5, 9–10 and 11). Necessity is implicitly or explicitly always counter-posited to →'contingency'. [A§11–A§13, sub 1.]

'OECD-21'. A sample of 21 mature capitalist countries currently organised in the OECD, for which relevant more or less homogenised data go back to 1870. (Australia, Austria, Belgium, Canada, Denmark, Finland, France, Germany, Greece, Ireland, Italy, Japan, Netherlands, New Zealand, Norway, Portugal, Spain, Sweden, Switzerland, UK, USA. In 2015 their share in the world population is 13% and their share in world GDP 56%.) [Appendix 6A.] In Amplifications throughout the book the average of these is used as an empirical 'exemplary' for the capitalist system from 1870–2015. [6A-2 for the notion of 'average' in this context.]

ontology (dictionary: study or a theory of the character of being or the kinds of things that have existence). →'epistemology and ontology'.

outward bifurcation (dictionary for bifurcation: to fork or divide into two parts of branches). A main institutional separation. In this book the only outward bifurcation is that between households and privately owned enterprises [1§1, 1§1-c, 6§1, 6§1-a]. Outwardly bifurcated entities are generally each driven by different objectives. In contradistinction, the different institutional entities of a 'separation-in-unity' are (ultimately) each driven by the same objective (→'separation-in-unity').

passive capital →'capital'.

passive finance capital →'capital'.

passive capital ownership →'capital ownership, passive'.

positive right →'allowance right'.

pre-commensuration →'ideal pre-commensuration'.

pre-position (dictionary: to position in advance or beforehand). [Hegel's German: Voraussetzung ≠ Annahme = assumption.] An entity or constellation that is posited without the grounds of its existence – that is, the conditions of its existence – having yet been (fully) posited. The term 'pre-position' (instead of 'assumption') is used so as to indicate that these have a temporary status. It is claimed that all entities or constellations pre-posited can and will be grounded at a later stage of the exposition, whence at that stage these are no longer pre-positions. Distinguished from →'presumption'. [GI-C§9 and A§7 – these two sections are almost identical.]

presumption (dictionary: something presumed: taken for granted). The exposition in this book adopts three presumptions: (1) language; (2) the existence of the object of enquiry, that is, capitalist economies and states (as empirically exemplified by the current OECD countries as well as all other countries with a similar structure); (3) the object of investigation is systematic – which is a precondition for any scientific study of an object of investigation beyond mere descriptions. Distinguished from →'pre-position'. [GI-C§9 and A§7 – these two sections are almost identical.]

pre-validating finance of production by banks (PVF). The flow of money newly created in a reciprocal relation between bank and enterprise is an *anticipation* of production and realisation of that production in the future. The bank that creates this new money on the basis of a loan performs a *private pre-validation* of production, which is socially validated when the anticipated production is sold – the loan can then be redeemed. [2§10; expanded in 3§2.] Contrasted with the stock of →'remaining pre-validating finance by banks'. Bank provided pre-validating finance (PVF) for enterprises is not only unconditionally necessary to the capitalist system; it is also fundamentally different from any other type of finance. One fundamental aspect is that this PVF is a pure ex nihilo accounting money operation, and another is that it requires no saving, neither prior to the investment that it accommodates, nor after it. Generally, saving is *not* necessary to the capitalist system. [3D2.]

production enterprise. This is a term that at times (when the preciseness of the text requires it) is used in contradistinction to →'banks' and other 'pure' financial enterprises. The latter (non-production enterprises) do not produce surplus-value and are, for the growth of their finance capital, dependent on the production and distribution of surplus-value from production enterprises (in the form of interest and dividend). [2§11; 3§1.]

production process, capitalist. The capitalist production process is a dual process of, on the one hand, a multifaceted physical-technical process, using a →'technique of production' [1§9], and, on the other, a one-dimensional 'monetary valorisation process' (→'valorisation'). As duality the capitalist process is →'inwardly bifurcated' along the two poles indicated above [1§10]. The profit drive of enterprises means that this dual process is dominated by the valorisation process [1§11].

productive power of labour. The productive power of labour goes along with the exertion of labour. Within the agreed amount of labour-time, labour-capacity (L) operates means of production, and so exerts labour at some productive power (L^{α}). The duality of the capitalist →'production process' implies that this productive power is a dual one. First, that of labour's physical working up the plant and equipment to something qualitatively different (the physical gross and net output, for which there are no commensurate measures within and between processes). Second, that of the →'valorising' exertion of labour (measured as →'value-added', mL^{α}). As the poles of this duality are commensurately inseparable, the productive power of labour regards both these aspects. [1§14.] The productive power of labour is the unique source of →'value-added', and hence also of →'surplus-value' (= integral profit). [1§14.] The productive power of labour covers two components (α=($\acute{\alpha}$) ($\ddot{\iota}$)). First, *the technique-associated productive power* ($\acute{\alpha}$), which usually diverges between sectors of production. Technology and techniques are creations by labour. Their commodification implies that these are themselves the result of the productive power of labour (perhaps in sectors different from where these are applied). The second component of labour's productive power is the degree of *intensity of labour* ($\ddot{\iota}$). At zero intensity (in effect a strike) there is no physical production and no production of value. [1§14.] This intensity is inevitably physically limited [2§2].

profit. A distinction is made between '*integral profit*' (= →'surplus-value') and →'*internal profit*' (in brief, surplus-value after the payment of interest to financiers). The term *profit* is used either when this distinction is not relevant, or when this distinction has not yet been introduced. In Chapter 1 (its 1§8–1§11) the term profit refers to the everyday casual meaning of this term: the quantitative difference between the monetary value of the commodity inputs and the commodity outputs. Profit is the monistic driving force of enterprises. Monistic refers to one-dimensional →'monetary value'. The term profit is introduced in 1§8 as a transitional concept, until the introduction of the concept of →'surplus-value' in 1§12.

profit rate →'integral profit rate'; →'internal profit rate'.

proximate moments and proximate conditions (or proximate grounds). The immediate and most general conditions, at that point of the exposition, for that which was posited before. The exposition is not complete before all the conditions of existence of the starting point have been presented endogenously. 'Proximity' determines the *order* of their exposition. [GI-C§4; A§11, sub 3.]

closing or the reorganisation of production plants. Hence part of the capital produced and accumulated in the previous phases of the cycle is annihilated. This may involve intra-enterprise reorganisation and inter-enterprise centralisation of capital. [5§9; 5§9-b sub 6.]

RPVF →'remaining pre-validating finance by banks'.

saving. Non-expenditure of an income flow. Saving is contingent. Whereas the →'pre-validating finance of production by banks' is a precondition for investment, saving is no precondition for investment [3§2]. →'investment versus saving'.

seeming/seemingly (dictionary: external appearance as distinguished from true character; appearing to be true but not being true or certain).

separation-in-unity. A main institutional separation. In contradistinction to an →'outward bifurcation', the different institutional entities, or components, or poles, of a 'separation-in-unity' are (ultimately) each driven by the same objective, which articulates their unity. The core separation-in-unity (s-i-u) presented in this book is that of the capitalist economy and the capitalist state (6§7). Of the four other s-i-u's, two are presented at the end of Chapter 2 and two at the end of Chapter 7. These are the s-i-u of enterprises and banks (2§11); the s-i-u between the shareholders – or more broadly the 'passive capital owners' – and the executive management of the enterprise (2§14); the s-i-u's between the state's administrative and judiciary branches (7§18); and between the state's administrative and deliberative branches (7§23). [2§11-a and 6§7-a.]

sociation. Abstract minimum conditions that any imaginable society must meet, in order for it to be a 'potentially continuous' social whole [1§0].

stratification of enterprises and enterprises' plants: the stratified structure of production. Within most sectors of production, the enterprises (and their plants in case of multi-plant enterprises) are not homogenous. These are rather heterogeneously stratified according to the characteristics indicated at the end of this entry. The enterprise that successfully initiates a new technique of production secures a rate of profit above that of the existing enterprises (plants) in the sector. Because each enterprise is burdened with the fixed costs of its already accumulated capital, it will only scrap old plants when a new technique offers net profits ('net' that is, taking into account the costs of scrapping old plants) greater than the profits on its existing plant. Therefore, plants embodying new techniques will in general not be immediately adopted by all enterprises, whence each sector of production tends to be composed of a *stratification of plants* dated according to technique, cost of production, value-productivity of labour and a resulting *stratification of rates of integral profit.* [4§4.]

sublate/sublation (MW dictionary: to negate or eliminate – as an element in a dialectic process – but preserve as a partial element in a synthesis; see also Inwood 1992, pp. 283–5.) In this book sublation refers foremost to a (partial) supersession/resolution of the shortcomings of the starting point's →'outward bifurcation', without that bifurcation itself being undone. In other words, sublation refers to a derived mode of existence of the starting point's outward bifurcation, a mode that when posited at that stage of the dialectic (without further grounds) may or may not be stable. In this book a sublation has always the character of the (partial) *grounding* of the starting point's outward bifurcation. Grounding is the same as the determination of a (partial) condition of existence of the outward bifurcation. The term is used in Chapters 1 and 6 only. Generally, however, any other grounding of an earlier moment in these and other chapters can be considered as a sublation.

subordinated working class (SWC) →'capitalist and managerial class (CMC) and subordinated working class (SWC)'.

surplus-value; identical to *integral profit*. The component of →'value-added' that is appropriated by enterprises (the other component being wages) – all in monetary dimension. The concept is used either microeconomically or macroeconomically. [1§12.] Surplus-value is independent of the contingent way in which the enterprise is financed. In 3§1, and more detailed in 5§1, surplus-value is decomposed as the sum of *internal profit* (retained and distributed) and *interest*, the latter being the enterprises' external financiers share of the surplus-value.

surplus-value, rate of. A measure for the degree of exploitation of labour as reflected in the capital–labour distribution of income, defined as the capital income share (surplus-value, Π) over the labour income share (wages, wL). [2§5.]

SWC, subordinated working class. →'capitalist and managerial class (CMC) and subordinated working class (SWC)'.

synchronic →'diachronic'.

systematic-dialectical exposition. In this book 'systematic-dialectical exposition' (in brief 'exposition') refers to the systematic presentation of a constellation (the object totality) that is →'ontologically' systematic (in case →'capitalism'). The exposition is about the constellation's constituents (more precisely its →'moments') that are *necessary* for its continued existence (Chs. 1–3 and 6–8) as well as about the latter's implied →'manifestations' (Chs. 4–5, 9–10 and 11). The exposition thus abstracts from →'contingencies'. The core of the exposition lies in the *interconnection* of the constellation's constituents. These constituents (moments) are presented stage-wise (the book's consecutive divisions and sections) as proximate conditions of existence of the constellation (→'proximate moments and proximate conditions'). The focus is indeed on interconnection, rather than on merely the partial analysis of constituents (moments) treated separately. Contrasting 'analysis' with 'synthesis', the systematic-dialectical exposition results in a *synthetic* outline of the constellation and functioning of the capitalist system. [GI, C§4; A§10–A§14.]

technique of production. A qualitatively and quantitatively specific combination of nature, means of production and labour together with a qualitatively specific labour process [1§9]. The particularly capitalist →'production process' means that techniques and the technical production process (rather than being 'pre-given' and neutral) are devised to be geared to →'valorisation'. [1§11.]

tendency. A tendency should be distinguished from an empirical 'trend'. A tendency is the generation of a particular *form* of an entity (e.g. the corporate form of the enterprise) *or* the particular *quantitative expression* of an entity or process (e.g. equalisation of inter-sector rates of profit), this generation being predicated on certain forces or compulsions (see 2§12 or 4§2 for examples). A tendency may be *counteracted* by other tendencies, or by other lower-level complexities (see 4§14 for an example). A tendency is a determinant whose *actualisation* might not always predominate in any individual case. However, for it to have the status of a tendency (in this book), it must apply to a significant enough number of cases such that, when abstracting from counteracting tendencies, it has a predominant character for the totality. [2§12-a and A§14.]

trans-abstraction in practice. Upon the actual market trade, heterogeneous entities are commensurated in terms of money, that is, something that is no part whatsoever of their concrete physical bodily form or concrete constitution. Along with it the alien dimension of →'monetary value' is *ascribed to the entity*, or rather *vested in the entity* – it now *being* a 'commodity'. The 'trans-abstraction in practice' is described in the previous sentence. 'Trans' refers to transcendental (in the sense of a move beyond the ordinary limits of entities); 'abstraction in practice' refers to the fact that this is not a mere mental abstraction (behind the writing desk, so to speak), but one that is executed in the everyday practice of market trade. Indeed we are 'doing' it all the time. [1§4; 1§4-b.]

unit monetary value of labour, actual (m). The component 'm' in the →'monetary-value product of labour' (mL^{α}). Practically 'm' measures the validation, the sale, of the net product of labour [1§14, sub 8]. (See also 3§10, 4§6 and 4§11.)

usefulness (dictionary: being of use or service). The specific characteristics of the physical input and output of enterprises, along multifaceted dimensions. (The terms 'use-value' and 'utility' are avoided because in Marginalist and Neoclassical discourses these terms refer to 'subjective use-value' – which anyway is not applicable as such for the inputs and outputs-supply of enterprises – and in some strands of these also refer to an assumed one-dimensionality.) [1§3-b.]

use-value →'usefulness'.

validation (dictionary: a.o. to make valid). The turning of the output of enterprises into money, that is, the sale of the output [1§10]. Validation may also refer to the realisation of a component of the output, especially surplus-value [3§10].

value. Shorthand for 'abstract general one-dimensional value', which is a homogenous common denominator, which absorbs concrete specificity [1§3 and 1§3-a]. Value is non-physical and thus super-sensuous [1§4]. Money is a necessary condition of existence of value (→'monetary value'). 'Value' is distinct from →'usefulness', 'use-value' and 'utility'. Each of the latter three refers to physical qualities of a good or of a commodity.

value-added. Value-added is the value product of labour (mL$^{\alpha}$) as resulting from the →'productive power of labour'. It is equal to the sum of wages and →'surplus-value', all in monetary dimension. The concept is used either microeconomically or macroeconomically. [1§12; 1§14, sub 8.]

valorisation (translation of the German noun *Verwertung*). The production of ideal →'monetary value'. (See also →'ideal pre-commensuration'.) This monetary value remains 'ideal' until the output of production is actually →'validated'. [1§10 and addendum 1§12-b.]

valoro-technique. A term making explicit that the applied →'techniques of production' are not neutral, but rather geared to *valor*isation and profit making. [2§2-c; 2§4; 2§5.]

wage rate. A sum of money per unit of labour-time – the unit being specified as, for example, one hour or one year, the latter in the going 'full-time equivalent'. More specifically, commodified labour-capacity is bifurcated into 'capacity rented out for a certain amount of time' and 'rent in monetary value for a certain amount of time' the name for the latter being the 'wage for a certain amount of time' or, briefly, the 'wage rate'. [1§6.]

wealth (dictionary: a.o. all things that have a monetary value). Wealth refers to all durable entities or claims that have a monetary value. →'Capital' is a form of wealth. However, this does not mean that any wealth is 'capital'. Capital is a form of wealth geared to production, with the purpose of selling that production so as to make a profit. [8§12; Appendix 3C-1 (sub 6).]

Index of names

GI = General Introduction; A = General Appendix (An Outline of Systematic Dialectics)

Index of subjects

- Lemmas in bold are guiding ones, with many referrals to other lemmas.
- References (section numbers) in bold are the main ones for each lemma, and these are placed first.
- In case a term is explained in the Glossary, the first reference is to the Glossary (abbreviated 'Glos')
- 'GI' refers to the General Introduction. 'A' refers to the General Appendix on systematic dialectics.
- Sub-entries of a lemma may sometimes be in logical rather than alphabetical order.
- In the references to sections of the book, 'sub #' refers to a sub-section of the section indicated.
- fn = footnote of a section.
- When the terms 'economy' or 'economic' are used, these implicitly denote the capitalist economy.
- When the term 'state' is used, this implicitly denotes the capitalist state.

Index of main empirical graphs and tables

Subdivision of the index

I OECD-21 averages

A *State receipts*

B *State expenditure*

• Single expenditure categories: state expenditure (general government), % GDP; average of up to 21 current OECD countries, 1870–2015 (unless otherwise indicated)

II World country group averages (alphabetical) (high, upper-middle, lower-middle and low income)